PROBLEM
SOLVING

A ·N· D

PROGRAM
DESIGN
IN C

PROBLEM SOLVING

A N D

PROGRAM DESIGN IN C

JERI R. HANLY

UNIVERSITY OF WYOMING

ELLIOT B. KOFFMAN

FRANK L. FRIEDMAN

TEMPLE UNIVERSITY

**Addison-Wesley
Publishing Company**

Reading, Massachusetts
Menlo Park, California
New York
Don Mills, Ontario
Wokingham, England
Amsterdam
Bonn • Sydney
Singapore • Tokyo
Madrid • San Juan
Milan • Paris

Lynne Doran Cote Sponsoring Editor
Loren Hilgenhurst Stevens Production Editor
Andrea M. Danese Assistant Editor
Quadrata, Inc. Design, Editorial, and Production Services
Barbara Ames Copy Editor
Lisa Delgado Text Designer
Tech-Graphics Illustrations
Smizer Design Cover Design
Peter M. Blaiwas Cover Art Director
Roy Logan Senior Manufacturing Manager

Library of Congress Cataloging-in-Publication Data
Hanly, Jeri R.
    Problem solving and program design in C / Jeri R. Hanly, Elliot B.
Koffman, Frank L. Friedman.
        p.   cm.
    Includes index.
    ISBN 0-201-57653-8
    1. C (Computer program language)   I. Koffman, Elliot B.
II. Friedman, Frank L.   III. Title.
QA76.73.C15H363   1993
005.13'3--dc20   92-31374
                                                                 CIP

The programs and applications presented in this book have been included for their instructional value. They have been tested with care but are not guaranteed for any particular purpose. The publisher does not offer any warranties or representations, nor does it accept any liabilities with respect to the programs or applications.

Many of the designations used by manufacturers and sellers to distinguish their products are claimed as trademarks. Where those designations appear in this book, and Addison-Wesley was aware of a trademark claim, the designations have been printed in initial caps or all caps.

1 2 3 4 5 6 7 8 9 10—MU—9695949392

*To our families
Brian, Eric, and
Kevin Hanly;
Caryn, Richard,
Deborah, and
Robin Koffman;
Martha, Shelley
and
Dara Friedman*

This textbook teaches a disciplined approach to solving problems and to applying widely accepted software engineering methods to design program solutions as cohesive, readable, and reusable modules. We present as an implementation vehicle for these modules a subset of ANSI C—a standardized, industrial-strength programming language known for its power and portability. Because this text assumes no prior knowledge of computers or programming, it can be used for a first course in programming methods. The text's broad selection of case studies and exercises allows an instructor to design an introductory programming course in C for computer science majors or for students from a wide range of engineering and scientific disciplines.

Using C to Teach Program Development

Our two goals—teaching program development and teaching C—may be regarded by some as contradictory. C is widely perceived as a language to be tackled only after one has learned the fundamentals of programming in some other, friendlier language. The perception that C is excessively difficult is traceable to the history of the language. Designed as a vehicle for programming the UNIX operating system, C found its original clientele among programmers who understood the complexities of the operating system and the underlying machine, and who considered it natural to exploit this knowledge in their programs. Therefore, it is not surprising that textbooks whose primary goal is to teach C typically expose the student to program examples requiring an understanding of machine concepts that are not in the syllabus of a standard introductory programming course.

In this text, we are able to teach both a rational approach to program development and an introduction to ANSI C because we have chosen the first goal as our primary one. One might fear that this choice would lead to a watered-down treatment of ANSI C. On the contrary, we find that the blended presentation of programming concepts and of the implementation of these concepts in C captures a focused picture of the power of ANSI C as a high-level programming language, a picture that is often blurred in texts whose foremost objective is the coverage of all of ANSI C. Even following this approach of giving program development precedence over discussion of C language features, we have arrived at a coverage of the essential constructs of C that is quite comprehensive.

Pointers and the Organization of the Book

The order in which topics are presented is dictated by our view of the needs of the beginning programmer rather than by the structure of the C programming language. You may be surprised to discover that there is no chapter entitled "Pointers." This missing chapter title follows from our treatment of C as a high-level language, not from a lack of awareness of the critical role of pointers in C.

Whereas other high-level languages have separate language constructs for output parameters, arrays, and heap references, C openly folds all three of these concepts into its notion of a pointer, drastically increasing the complexity of learning the language. We simplify the learning process by discussing pointers in stages at the points where output parameters, arrays, and strings normally arise when teaching programming using other languages, thus allowing a student to absorb the intricacies of pointer usage a little at a time. Our approach makes possible the presentation of fundamental concepts using traditional high-level language terminology—output parameter, array, array subscript, string—and makes it easier for students without a background in assembly language to master the many facets of pointer usage.

Therefore, this text has not one, but three chapters that present pointers. Chapter 6 discusses the use of pointers as simple output and input/output parameters, Chapter 8 deals with arrays, and Chapter 9 presents strings and arrays of pointers.

Software Engineering Concepts

This text presents many aspects of software engineering. Some are explicitly discussed and others are taught only by example. The connection between good problem-solving skills and effective software development is established early in Chapter 1 with a section that discusses a step-by-step approach to problem solving. The five-phase software development method introduced in Chapter 1 is used in Chapter 2 to solve the first case study and is applied subsequently to case studies throughout the text. Major program style issues are highlighted in special displays, and the coding style used in examples is based on guidelines followed in segments of the C software industry. The concept of a program as a sequence of control structures is introduced in Chapter 3. There are sections in several chapters that discuss algorithm tracing, program debugging, and testing.

Chapter 3 introduces procedural abstraction through structure charts, parameterless void functions, and selected C library functions. Chapter 6 completes the study of functions that have simple parameters. This chapter includes sections for functions returning a value, void functions, input parameters, output parameters, and input/output parameters. Function definitions are preceded by interface sections that include informal preconditions and postconditions.

Case studies in Chapters 9, 10, and 11 introduce by example the concepts of data abstraction and of encapsulation of a data type and operators. Chapter 13 presents C's facilities for formalizing procedural and data abstraction in personal libraries defined by separate header and implementation files.

The use of visible function interfaces is emphasized throughout the text. We do not mention the possibility of using a global variable until Chapter 13, and then we carefully describe both the dangers and the value of global variable usage.

Pedagogical Features

Several pedagogical features serve to enhance the usefulness of this book as a teaching tool. Some of these features are discussed below.

End-of-Section Exercises   Most sections end with several self-check exercises. These include exercises that require analysis of program fragments as well as short programming exercises. Answers to selected self-check exercises appear at the back of the book; answers to the remaining exercises are provided in the instructor's manual.

End-of-Chapter Exercises   A set of quick-check exercises with answers follows each chapter review. There are also review exercises whose solutions appear in the instructor's manual.

End-of-Chapter Projects   Each chapter ends with a set of programming projects. Answers to selected projects appear in the instructor's manual.

Examples and Case Studies   The book contains a wide variety of programming examples. Whenever possible, examples contain complete programs or functions rather than incomplete program fragments. Each chapter contains one or more substantial case studies that are solved following the software development method. Numerous case studies give the student glimpses of important applications of computing: DNA mapping, image enhancement, numerical approximation, and database search, to name a few.

Syntax Display Boxes   The syntax displays describe the syntax and semantics of new C features and provide examples.

Program Style Displays   The program style displays discuss major issues of good programming style.

Error Discussions and Chapter Review   Each chapter concludes with a section that discusses common programming errors. A chapter review includes a table of new C constructs.

Appendixes and Supplement

A reference table of ANSI C constructs appears on the inside covers of the book, and the first two appendixes consist of character set tables and an alphabetized list of information about selected C library functions. Because this text covers only a subset of ANSI C, the remaining appendixes play an especially vital role in increasing the value of the book as a reference. Appendix C gives a table showing the precedence and associativity of all ANSI C operators; the operators not previously defined are explained in this appendix. The only C numeric types used in the text are `int` and `double`; Appendix D discusses the range of numeric types available in ANSI C, and Appendix E presents how to define an enumerated data type. Throughout the book, array referencing is done with subscript notation; Appendix F is the only coverage of pointer arithmetic. Appendix G lists all ANSI C reserved words.

An instructor's manual with accompanying program disk is available for this book. To order it from your Addison-Wesley sales representative, please use the reference number 54606.

Acknowledgments

Many people participated in the development of this book. We thank especially Masoud Kermani and Thayne Routh, University of Wyoming graduate students who served as first reviewers of the manuscript, verified the programming examples, and provided answer keys for the host of exercises. Their contribution to the quality of the textbook is immeasurable. We are also grateful to Professor Sharon Salveter and to the computer science and engineering students at Boston University and at the University of Wyoming who class-tested the manuscript.

The principal reviewers were enormously helpful in suggesting improvements and in finding errors. They include Steve Allan, *Utah State University;* P. K. Andersen, *Purdue University;* Bart Childs, *Texas A&M University;* Gary Fostel, *University of Wisconsin;* Sharon Salveter, *Boston University;*

James G. Schmolze, *Tufts University;* Bob Signorile, *Boston College;* Lynda A. Thomas, *Carroll College;* and Nai-kuan Tsao, *Wayne State University.*

We truly appreciate the support of the University of Wyoming Department of Computer Science, Stanley R. Petrick, Chair, and the willingness of Jeri's colleagues to share their expertise and their libraries. We thank especially Thomas A. Bailey, Henry R. Bauer, III, John R. Cowles, Rex E. Gantenbein, Michael J. Magee, John H. Rowland, and Jeffrey VanBaalen.

We are grateful to those who assisted in producing the photographs used in our flat washer and image enhancement case studies: to Steven L. Miller, University of Wyoming botany professor, for the original mushrooms photograph; and to Thayne Routh, Bruce Henry, and the Western Research Institute of Laramie, Wyoming, for the processed images.

It has been a pleasure to work with the Addison-Wesley team in this endeavor. Andrea Danese and Peter Shepard played critical roles in initiating the project. The sponsoring editor, Lynne Doran Cote, was closely involved in all phases of the manuscript preparation and provided much guidance and encouragement. Her assistant, Andrea Danese, coordinated the review process and the preparation of the instructor's manual, and handled a great variety of other details. Loren Hilgenhurst Stevens supervised the design and production of the book, while Denise Descoteaux developed the marketing campaign. Martha Morong and Geri Davis of Quadrata, Inc., coordinated the conversion of the manuscript to a finished book.

J.R.H.
E.B.K.
F.L.F.

CONTENTS

1. Introduction to Computers and Programming   1

1.1 Electronic Computers Then and Now 2
1.2 Components of a Computer 8
1.3 Problem Solving and Software Development 13
1.4 Programming Languages 15
1.5 Processing a High-Level Language Program 17
1.6 Using the Computer 20
Chapter Review 23

2. Problem Solving and C   26

2.1 Applying the Software Development Method 27
Case Study: Converting Units of Measurement 28
2.2 Overview of C 33
2.3 Variable Declarations in C Programs 38
2.4 Executable Statements 41
2.5 General Form of C Programs 52
2.6 Data Types and Expressions 56
2.7 Formatting Numbers in Program Output 69
2.8 Interactive Mode, Batch Mode, and Data Files 72
2.9 Common Programming Errors 75
Chapter Review 81

3. Top-Down Design with Functions   88

3.1 The Art and Science of Problem Solving 89
Case Study: Finding the Area and Circumference of a Circle 93
3.2 Extending a Problem Solution 96
Case Study: Quality Control in Manufacturing Flat Washers 96
3.3 Structured Programming and Control Structures 101

3.4 Structure Charts 104
Case Study: Drawing Simple Diagrams 105
3.5 Functions 107
3.6 Displaying User Instructions 115
3.7 Functions as Program Building Blocks 116
3.8 Functions and Code Reuse 118
3.9 Common Programming Errors 126
Chapter Review 127

4. Selection Structures: if and switch Statements   132

4.1 Logical Expressions and the if Statement 133
4.2 if Statements with Compound Tasks 139
4.3 Decision Steps in Algorithms 143
Case Study: Water Bill Problem 143
Case Study: Finding the First Letter 151
4.4 Tracing an Algorithm 155
4.5 More Problem-Solving Strategies 157
*Case Study: Computing a Water Bill with
Conservation Requirements* 158
4.6 Nested if Statements and Multiple-Alternative
Decisions 161
Case Study: Computing Compass Bearings 167
4.7 The switch Statement for Multiple Alternatives 175
4.8 Common Programming Errors 180
Chapter Review 182

5. Repetition and Loop Statements   191

5.1 Repetition in Programs: Using Loops to Solve
Problems 192
5.2 Computing a Sum or a Product in a Loop 195
5.3 Counting Loops 201
5.4 Conditional Loops 208
5.5 Loop Design 214
5.6 Nested Control Structures 225
5.7 Problem Solving Illustrated 232
Case Study: Computing Radiation Levels 232
5.8 How to Debug and Test Programs 236
5.9 Common Programming Errors 239
Chapter Review 242

6. Modular Programming   251

6.1 Functions That Return a Single Result 253
         Case Study: Finding Prime Numbers 269
6.2 void Functions with Input Parameters 276
         Case Study: Computing Maximum Tensile Loads 281
6.3 Functions with Simple Output Parameters 287
6.4 Multiple Calls to a void Function with Input/Output
         Parameters 295
         Case Study: Simple Sorting Problem 296
6.5 Introduction to Scope of Names 303
6.6 Formal Output Parameters as Actual Arguments 305
6.7 Top-Down Design Illustrated 310
         *Case Study: Performing Arithmetic Operations on
         Common Fractions* 310
6.8 Debugging and Testing a Program System 320
6.9 Common Programming Errors 323
         Chapter Review 323

7. Data Types and Operators   333

7.1 Representation and Conversion of Numeric Types int
         and double 334
7.2 Representation and Conversion of Type char 343
7.3 Logical Expressions and the Operators &&, ||,
         and ! 346
7.4 Loops Revisited 354
7.5 Operators with Side Effects 362
7.6 Iterative Approximations 365
         Case Study: Approximating the Value of e 366
         Case Study: Newton's Method for Finding Roots 369
7.7 Common Programming Errors 375
         Chapter Review 376

8. Arrays   383

8.1 Declaring and Referencing Arrays 384
8.2 Array Subscripts 388
8.3 Using Indexed for loops to Process Arrays 390

8.4 Using Individual Array Elements as Input Arguments 395
8.5 Using Individual Array Elements as Output Arguments 400
8.6 Using Arrays as Input Arguments 404
8.7 Using Arrays as Output or Input/Output Arguments 412
8.8 Array Processing Illustrated 423
Case Study: Finding the Area of a Polygon 423
8.9 Multidimensional Arrays 430
8.10 Common Programming Errors 436
Chapter Review 437

9. Strings   448

9.1 String Basics 449
9.2 String Assignment and Substrings 458
9.3 Longer Strings: Concatenation and Whole-Line Input 465
9.4 String Comparison 470
9.5 Arrays of Pointers 473
9.6 Character Operations 479
9.7 String-to-Number and Number-to-String Conversions 484
9.8 String Processing Illustrated 491
Case Study: Cryptogram Generator 491
Case Study: Finding Palindromes in Nucleotide Sequence 497
9.9 Living Dangerously: String Library Functions for Assignment, Substring Extraction, and Concatenation 501
9.10 Common Programming Errors 504
Chapter Review 506

10.   Recursion   515

10.1 The Nature of Recursion 516
10.2 Tracing a Recursive Function 521
10.3 Recursive Mathematical Functions 529
10.4 Recursive Functions with Array and String Parameters 535

Case Study: Finding Capital Letters in a String 535
Case Study: Recursive Selection Sort 539
10.5 Problem Solving with Recursion 543
Case Study: Operations on Sets 543
10.6 A Classic Case Study in Recursion: Towers of Hanoi 552
10.7 Picture Processing with Recursion 557
Case Study: Counting Cells in a Blob 557
10.8 Common Programming Errors 562
Chapter Review 563

11. Structure and Union Types 569

11.1 User-Defined Structure Types 570
11.2 Structure Type Data as Input and Output Parameters 576
11.3 Functions Whose Result Values Are Structured 582
11.4 Problem Solving with Structure Types 585
Case Study: A User-Defined Type for Complex Numbers 586
11.5 Parallel Arrays and Arrays of Structures 593
Case Study: Universal Measurement Conversion 595
11.6 Union Types 604
11.7 Common Programming Errors 611
Chapter Review 611

12. File Input and Output 621

12.1 Review of Batch Processing 622
12.2 Standard Input/Output Files: Review and Further Study 623
12.3 Additional Text Files 625
12.4 Problem Solving Illustrated 631
Case Study: Land Boundary Survey 632
12.5 Binary Files 642
12.6 Searching a Database 649
Case Study: Database Inquiry 649
12.7 Common Programming Errors 659
Chapter Review 660

13. Programming in the Large   669

13.1 Using Abstraction to Manage Complexity 670
13.2 Personal Libraries: Header Files 673
13.3 Personal Libraries: Implementation Files 680
13.4 Defining Macros with Parameters 686
13.5 Storage Classes 692
13.6 Modifying Functions for Inclusion in a Library 697
Case Study: Developing an Image Enhancement Library 700
13.7 Conditional Compilation 713
13.8 Arguments to Function main 718
13.9 Common Programming Errors 721
Chapter Review 722

Appendixes

A Character Sets AP1
B Quick Reference Table: Selected Standard C Library Facilities AP3
C C Operators AP8
D C Numeric Types AP14
E Enumerated Types AP16
F Pointer Arithmetic AP18
G ANSI C Reserved Words AP20

Answers   A1

Index   I1

PROBLEM
SOLVING
A · N · D
PROGRAM
DESIGN
IN C

CHAPTER 1

INTRODUCTION TO COMPUTERS AND PROGRAMMING

1.1
Electronic Computers Then and Now

1.2
Components of a Computer

1.3
Problem Solving and Software Development

1.4
Programming Languages

1.5
Processing a High-Level Language Program

1.6
Using the Computer
Chapter Review

From the 1940s to the present—a period of only 50 years—the computer's development has spurred the growth of technology into realms only dreamed of at the turn of the century. Computers have changed the way we live and how we do business. Today we depend on computers to process our paychecks, send rockets into space, build cars and machines of all types, and help us do our shopping and banking. The computer program's role in this technology is essential; without a list of instructions to follow, the computer is virtually useless. Programming languages allow us to write those programs and thus to communicate with computers.

You are about to begin the study of computer science using one of the most versatile programming languages available today: the C language. This chapter introduces you to the computer and its components and to the major categories of programming languages.

1.1 ELECTRONIC COMPUTERS THEN AND NOW

It is difficult to live in today's society without having some contact with computers. Computers are used to provide instructional material in schools, find library books, send out bills, reserve airline and concert tickets, play games, send and receive electronic mail, and help authors write books. Several kinds of computers cooperate in dispensing cash from an automatic teller machine; *embedded* or *hidden* computers help control the ignition, fuel, and transmission systems of modern automobiles. At the supermarket, computer devices scan the bar codes on the packages you buy, total your purchases, and help manage the store's inventory. Even a microwave oven has a special-purpose computer built into it.

Computers were not always so pervasive in our society. Just a short time ago, computers were fairly mysterious devices that only a small percentage of the population knew much about. Computer know-how spread when advances in solid-state electronics led to cuts in the size and the cost of electronic computers. In the mid-1970s, a computer with the computational power of one of today's personal computers would have filled a 9-by-12-foot room and cost $100,000. Today an equivalent personal computer costs less than $2,000 and sits on a desktop (see Fig. 1.1).

If we take the literal definition for *computer* as "a device for counting or computing," then we could consider the abacus to be the first computer. The first electronic digital computer was designed in the late 1930s by Dr. John Atanasoff at Iowa State University. Atanasoff designed his computer to perform mathematical computations for graduate students.

Figure 1.1   IBM Personal Computer with Mouse

The first large-scale, general-purpose electronic digital computer, called the ENIAC, was built in 1946 at the University of Pennsylvania. Its design was funded by the U.S. Army, and it was used to compute ballistics tables, predict the weather, and make atomic energy calculations. The ENIAC weighed 30 tons and occupied a 30-by-50-foot space (see Fig. 1.2).

Figure 1.2   The ENIAC Computer (Photo Courtesy of Unisys Corporation)

Although we are often led to believe otherwise, computers cannot reason as we do. Basically, computers are devices that perform computations at incredible speeds (more than one million operations per second) and with great accuracy. However, to accomplish anything useful, a computer must be *programmed,* that is, given a sequence of explicit instructions (*a program*) to perform.

To program the ENIAC, engineers had to connect hundreds of wires and arrange thousands of switches in a certain way. In 1946, Dr. John von Neumann of Princeton University proposed the concept of a *stored-program computer*—a computer whose program was stored in computer memory rather than being set by wires and switches. Von Neumann knew programmers could easily change the contents of computer memory, so he reasoned that the stored-program concept would greatly simplify programming a computer. Von Neumann's design was a success and is the basis of the digital computer as we know it today.

Brief History of Computing

Table 1.1 lists some of the milestones along the path from the abacus to modern-day computers and programming languages. The entries before 1890 list some of the earlier attempts to develop mechanical computing devices. In 1890, the first special-purpose computer that used electronic sensors was designed; this invention eventually led to the formation of the computer industry giant called International Business Machines Corporation (IBM).

As we look at the table from 1939 on, we see a variety of new computers introduced. The computers prior to 1975 were all very large, general-purpose computers called *mainframes*. The computers listed in the table after 1975 are all smaller computers. A number of important events in the development of programming languages and environments are also listed in the table. These include Fortran (1957), CTSS (1965), C (1972), VisiCalc (1978), and Windows (1989).

We often use the term *first generation* to refer to electronic computers that used vacuum tubes (1939–1958). The *second generation* began in 1958 with the changeover to transistors. The *third generation* began in 1964 with the introduction of integrated circuits and the *fourth generation* began in 1975 with the advent of large-scale integration.

Table 1.1   Milestones in Computer Development

Date	Event
2000 B.C.	The abacus is first used for computations.
1642 A.D.	Blaise Pascal creates a mechanical adding machine for tax computations. It is unreliable.
1670	Gottfried von Leibniz creates a more reliable adding machine. It adds, subtracts, multiplies, divides, and calculates square roots.
1842	Charles Babbage designs an analytical engine to perform general calculations automatically. Ada Augusta (aka Lady Lovelace) is a programmer for this machine.
1890	Herman Hollerith designs a system to record census data. The information is stored on cards as holes that are interpreted by machines with electrical sensors. Hollerith starts a company that will eventually become IBM.
1939	John Atanasoff, with graduate student Clifford Berry, designs and builds the first electronic digital computer. His project is funded by a grant for $650.
1946	J. Presper Eckert and John Mauchly design and build the ENIAC computer. It uses 18,000 vacuum tubes and costs $500,000 to build.
1946	John von Neumann proposes that a program be stored in a computer in the same way that data are stored. His proposal (called "von Neumann architecture") is the basis of modern computers.

(continued)

Table 1.1   *(continued)*

Date	Event
1951	Eckert and Mauchly build the first general-purpose commercial computer, the UNIVAC.
1957	An IBM team designs the first successful programming language, Fortran, for solving engineering and science problems.
1957	John Backus and his team at IBM complete the first Fortran compiler.
1958	IBM introduces the first computer to use the transistor as a switching device, the IBM 7090.
1958	Seymour Cray builds the first fully transistorized computer, the CDC 1604, for Control Data Corporation.
1964	IBM announces the first computer using integrated circuits, the IBM 360.
1965	The CTSS (Compatible Time-Sharing System) operating system is introduced. The system allows several users to use or share a single computer simultaneously.
1971	Nicklaus Wirth designs the Pascal programming language as a language for teaching structured programming concepts.
1972	Dennis Ritchie of AT&T Bell Laboratories designs the programming language C as the implementation language for the UNIX operating system.
1975	The first microcomputer, the Altair, is introduced.
1975	The first supercomputer, the Cray-1, is announced.
1976	Digital Equipment Corporation introduces its popular minicomputer, the VAX 11/780.
1977	Steve Wozniak and Steve Jobs found Apple Computer.
1978	Dan Bricklin and Bob Frankston develop the first electronic spreadsheet, VisiCalc, for the Apple computer.
1981	IBM introduces the IBM PC.
1982	Sun Microsystems introduces its first workstation, the Sun 100.
1984	Apple introduces the Macintosh, the first widely available computer with a "user-friendly" graphical interface using icons, windows, and a mouse device.
1989	Microsoft Corporation introduces Windows, a Macintosh-like user interface for IBM computers.
1989	ANSI (the American National Standards Institute) publishes its first standard for the C programming language.

Categories of Computers

Modern-day computers are classified according to their size and performance. The three major categories of computers are microcomputers, minicomputers, and mainframes.

Many of you have seen or used *microcomputers* such as the IBM PC (see Fig. 1.1). Microcomputers are also called *personal computers* (PCs) or *desktop computers* because they are used by one person at a time and are small enough to fit on a desk. The smallest general-purpose microcomputers are often called *notebooks* or *laptops* because they are small enough to fit into a briefcase and are often used on one's lap in an airplane. The largest microcomputers, called *workstations,* are commonly used by engineers to produce engineering drawings and to assist in the design and development of new products (see Fig. 1.3).

Minicomputers are larger than microcomputers; they generally operate at faster speeds and can store larger quantities of information. Minicomputers can serve several different users simultaneously. The computer that you will use to solve problems for the course you are taking might well be a minicomputer, such

Figure 1.3   SUN Microsystems SPARCstation 370 (Photo Courtesy of Sun Microsystems, Inc.)

as a VAX computer from Digital Equipment Corporation. A small- or medium-sized company might use a minicomputer to perform payroll computations and to keep track of its inventory. Engineers often use minicomputers to control a chemical plant or a production process.

The largest computers are called *mainframes*. A large company might have one or more mainframes at its central computing facility for performing business-related computations. Mainframes are also used as *number crunchers* to generate solutions to systems of equations that characterize an engineering or scientific problem. A mainframe can solve in seconds equations that might take hours to solve on a minicomputer or even days on a microcomputer. The largest mainframes are called *supercomputers* and are used to solve the most complex systems of equations.

In the late 1950s, mainframe computers could perform only 50 instructions per second. Now we commonly see much smaller workstations that can perform over 20 million instructions per second. It is obvious that in a relatively short time there have been tremendous changes in the speed and size of computers.

1.2 COMPONENTS OF A COMPUTER

Despite large variations in cost, size, and capabilities, modern computers are remarkably similar to each other in a number of ways. Basically, a computer consists of the components shown in Fig. 1.4. The arrows connecting the computer components show the direction of information flow. These computer components are called the *hardware*.

All information that is to be processed by a computer must first be entered into the computer's *main memory* via an *input device*. The information in main memory is manipulated by the *central processor unit* (CPU) and the results of this manipulation are stored in main memory. Information in main memory can be displayed through an *output device*. *Secondary memory* is often used for storing large quantities of information in a semipermanent form.

Computer Memory

A computer's main memory stores information of all types: instructions, numbers, names, lists, and pictures. Think of a computer's memory as an ordered sequence of storage locations called *memory cells*. To be able to store and then *retrieve* or access information, we must have some way to identify the individual memory cells. Each memory cell has a unique *address* associated with it. The address indicates the cell's relative position in memory. The sample computer memory in Fig. 1.5 consists of 1000 memory cells, with addresses 0

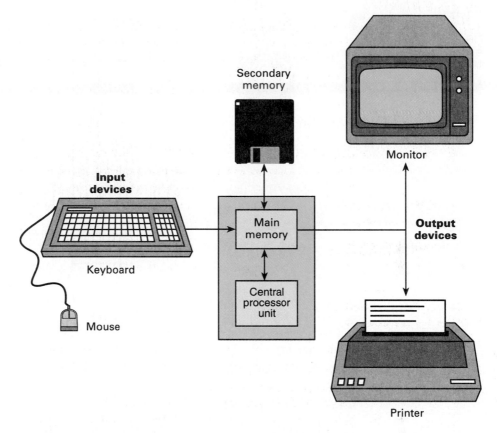

Figure 1.4
Components of
a Computer

through 999 (most computers have memories that consist of millions of individual cells).

The information stored in a memory cell is called its *contents*. Every memory cell always contains some information, although we may have no idea what that information is. Whenever new information is placed in a memory cell, any information already there is destroyed and cannot be retrieved. In Fig. 1.5, the contents of memory cell 3 is the number −26, and the contents of memory cell 4 is the letter H.

The memory cells shown in Fig. 1.5 are actually collections of smaller units called *bytes*. (The number of bytes in a memory cell varies from computer to computer.) A byte is the amount of storage required to store a single character and is composed of a sequence of even smaller units of storage called *bits*, which are single binary digits (0 or 1). Generally, there are eight bits to a byte.

To store a value, the computer sets each bit of a selected memory cell to 0 or 1, thereby destroying what was previously in that bit. Each value is represented by a particular pattern of zeros and ones. To retrieve a value from a

Figure 1.5
A Computer
Memory with
1000 Cells

Memory

Address	Contents
0	−27.2
1	354
2	0.005
3	−26
4	H
.	.
.	.
.	.
998	X
999	75.62

memory cell, the computer copies the pattern of zeros and ones stored in that cell to another storage area, the *memory buffer register,* where the bit pattern can be processed. The copy operation does not destroy the bit pattern currently in the memory cell. This process is the same regardless of the kind of information—character, number, or program instruction—stored in a memory cell.

Central Processor Unit

The CPU performs the actual processing or manipulation of information stored in memory; it also retrieves information from memory. This information can be data or instructions for manipulating data. The CPU can also store the results of those manipulations in memory for later use.

The *control unit* within the CPU coordinates all activities of the computer by determining which operations to perform and in what order they are to be carried out. The control unit then transmits coordinating control signals to the computer components.

Also found within the CPU are the *arithmetic-logic unit* (ALU) and special storage locations called *registers*. The ALU consists of electronic circuitry to perform arithmetic operations (addition, subtraction, multiplication, and division) and to make comparisons. The control unit copies the next program instruction from memory into the *instruction register* in the CPU. The ALU then performs the operation specified by the next instruction on data that are copied from memory into registers, and the computational results are copied to memory. The ALU can perform each arithmetic operation in less than a millionth of a second. The ALU can also compare data stored in its registers (for example, Which value is larger? Are the values equal?); the operations that are performed next depend on the results of the comparison.

Input and Output Devices

Input/output (I/O) devices enable us to communicate with the computer. Specifically, I/O devices provide us with the means to enter data for a computation and to observe the results of that computation.

A common I/O device used with large computers is the *computer terminal,* which is both an input and an output device. A terminal consists of a *keyboard* (used for entering information) and a *monitor* (used for displaying information). Because a computer terminal has no capability to do any local processing, it is often called a *dumb terminal.*

Frequently microcomputers are connected to larger computers and are used as terminals. Because a microcomputer can also do local processing, a microcomputer connected to another computer is called a *smart terminal.*

A computer keyboard is similar to a typewriter keyboard except that it has some extra keys for performing special functions. On the IBM keyboard shown in Fig. 1.6, the 12 keys labeled F1 through F12 in the top row are *function keys.* The function performed by pressing one of these keys depends on the program that is executing.

Most PCs are equipped with *graphics capability* that enables the output to be displayed as a two-dimensional graph or picture (see Fig. 1.3). With some graphics systems, the user can communicate with the computer by using a *mouse,* an input device that moves an electronic pointer.

The only problem with using a monitor as an output device is that it leaves no written record of the computation. If you want *hard-copy output,* you have to send your computational results to an output device such as a *printer* (see Fig. 1.7).

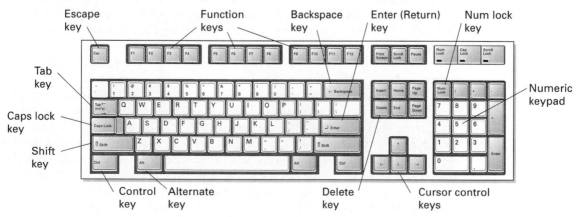

Figure 1.6 IBM Keyboard

Secondary Storage

Because computers have only a limited amount of main memory, *secondary storage* provides additional data-storage capability on most computer systems. For example, a *disk drive,* which stores data on a disk, is a common secondary storage device for today's PCs (Fig. 1.7).

There are two kinds of disks, *hard disks* and *floppy disks,* and a computer may have one or more drives of each kind. A hard disk normally cannot be removed from its drive, so the storage area on a hard disk is often shared by all the users of a computer. However, each computer user may have his or her own floppy disks that can be inserted into a disk drive as needed. Hard disks can store much more data and can operate much more quickly than floppy disks, but they are also much more expensive.

Information stored on disk is organized into collections called *files.* The data for a program can be stored in a *data file* in advance rather than being entered at the keyboard while the program is executing. Results generated by the computer can be saved as *output files* on disk. Most of the programs that you write will be saved as *program files* on disk.

The names of all the files stored on a disk are listed in the disk's *directory.* This directory may be broken into one or more levels of *subdirectories.* The

Figure 1.7 **Printer (on left) and Inserting a Floppy Disk into a Disk Drive**

details of how files are named and grouped in directories vary from one computer system to another. The names of your files must follow the conventions that apply on your system.

Main Memory versus Secondary Memory

Main memory is much faster and more expensive than the secondary memory provided by secondary storage devices. You must transfer data from secondary memory to main memory before it can be processed. Data in main memory is *volatile;* it disappears when you switch off the computer. Data in secondary memory is *permanent;* it does not disappear when the computer is switched off.

Computer Networks

Often several microcomputers in a laboratory are interconnected in what is called a *local area network* (LAN), so that they can share the use of a large hard disk and high-quality printers. The microcomputers in the network can also access common programs and data stored on the disk.

EXERCISES FOR SECTION 1.2

Self-Check

1. What are the contents of memory cells 0 and 999 in Fig. 1.5? Which memory cells contain the letter X and the fraction 0.005?
2. Explain the purpose of memory, the central processor unit, and the disk drive and disk. What input and output devices do you use with your computer?

1.3 PROBLEM SOLVING AND SOFTWARE DEVELOPMENT

We mentioned earlier that a computer cannot think; therefore, to get it to do any useful work, a computer must be provided with a *program*—that is, a list of instructions. Programming a computer is a lot more involved than simply writing a list of instructions. Problem solving is a crucial component of programming. Before we can write a program to solve a particular problem, we must consider carefully all aspects of the problem and then develop and organize its solution.

Plan and Check Your Programs Carefully

Like most programming students, initially you will probably spend a great deal of time in the computer laboratory entering your programs. Later you will spend more time removing the errors that inevitably will be present in your programs.

You may be tempted to rush to the computer laboratory and start entering your program as soon as you have some idea of how to write it. Resist this temptation. Instead, think carefully about the problem and its solution before you write any program instructions. When you have a potential solution in mind, plan it out beforehand, using either paper and pencil or a word processor, and modify the solution if necessary before you write the program.

Once you have written the program out, *desk check* your solution by carefully performing each instruction much as the computer would. To desk check a program, simulate the result of each program instruction using sample data that are easy to manipulate (for example, small whole numbers). Compare these results with the expected results, and make any necessary corrections to your program. Only then should you go to the computer laboratory and enter your program. A few extra minutes spent evaluating the proposed solution using the process summarized in Fig. 1.8 often saves hours of frustration later.

In this text, we stress a methodology for problem solving that has proved useful in helping students to learn to program. We will describe this technique next.

A Problem-Solving Method for Software Development

Students in many subject areas receive instruction in specific problem-solving methods. For example, business students are encouraged to follow a *systems approach* to problem solving; engineering and science students are encouraged

**Figure 1.8
A Problem-
Solving and
Programming
Strategy**

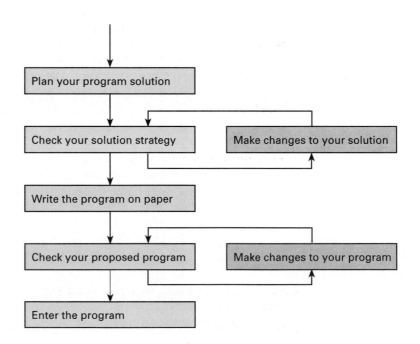

to follow the *engineering and scientific method*. Although these problem-solving methods are associated with very different fields of study, their essential ingredients are quite similar. We will outline one such method and explore it in more detail in subsequent chapters.

A *software engineer* is someone involved in the design and implementation of reliable software systems. As this title implies, programmers, like engineers, are concerned with developing practical, reliable solutions to problems. However, the product produced by a programmer is a software system rather than a physical system. Software engineers and software developers use the *software development method* for solving programming problems.

Software Development Method

1. *Requirements Specification.* State the problem and gain a clear understanding of what is required for its solution. Although this step sounds easy, it can be the most critical part of problem solving. You must study the problem carefully, eliminating aspects that are unimportant and zeroing in on the root problem. If the problem is not totally defined, you should request more information from the person posing the problem.
2. *Analysis.* Identify the problem's inputs, desired outputs, and any additional requirements or constraints on the solution. Identify what information is to be supplied as the problem's data and what results should be computed and displayed. Determine the required form and units in which the results should be displayed (for example, as a table with specific column headings).
3. *Design.* Develop a list of steps called an *algorithm* to solve the problem, and verify that the algorithm solves the problem as intended. Writing the algorithm is often the most difficult part of the problem-solving process. Once you have an algorithm, you should verify that it is correct before proceeding further.
4. *Implementation.* Implement the algorithm as a program. A knowledge of a particular programming language is required because each algorithm step must be converted into a statement in that programming language.
5. *Verification and Testing.* Test the completed program and verify that it works as expected. Don't rely on just one test case; run the program using several different sets of data.

1.4 PROGRAMMING LANGUAGES

Programming languages fall into three broad categories: machine, assembly, and high-level languages. *High-level languages* are more popular with programmers than the other two programming language categories because they are much easier to use than machine and assembly languages. In addition, a high-level language program is *portable*—it can be used without modification on many different types of computers. An *assembly language* or *machine language program,* on the other hand, can be used on only one type of computer.

Some common high-level languages are Fortran, BASIC, COBOL, C, Ada, and Lisp. Each language was designed with a specific purpose in mind. Fortran is an acronym for **FOR**mula **TRAN**slation; its principal users are engineers and scientists. BASIC (**B**eginners **A**ll-purpose **S**ymbolic **I**nstructional **C**ode) was designed to be easily learned and used by students. COBOL (**CO**mmon **B**usiness **O**riented **L**anguage) is used primarily for business data-processing operations. C combines the power of an assembly language with the ease of use and portability of a high-level language. Ada is a language designed by the Department of Defense for real-time distributed systems. Lisp is a language used primarily in artificial intelligence applications.

Each of these high-level languages has a *language standard* that describes the *syntax,* the grammatical form, of the language. Every high-level language instruction must conform to the syntax rules specified in the language standard. These rules are very precise—no allowances are made for instructions that are *almost* correct.

An important feature of high-level languages is that they allow us to write program instructions called *statements* that resemble English. We can reference data stored in memory using descriptive names like `height` and `width` rather than the numeric memory-cell addresses discussed in Section 1.2. We can also use familiar symbols to describe operations that we want performed. For example, in several high-level languages, the statement

```
value = value + delta;
```

means add `value` to `delta` and store the result back in `value`. `value` and `delta` are called *variables*. An example of numbers stored in `value` and `delta` before and after the execution of this instruction follows.

Before		After	
value	delta	value	delta
5	2	7	2

In *assembly language,* we can also use descriptive names to reference data; however, we must specify the operations to be performed on the data more explicitly. The high-level language instruction just shown might be written as

```
LOAD  value
ADD   delta
STORE value
```

in an assembly language.

Machine language is the native tongue of a particular kind of computer. Each instruction in machine language is a *binary string* (a string of zeros and ones). Some of you may be familiar with the use of binary numbers to represent decimal integers (for example, binary 11011 corresponds to decimal 27). In an analogous way, a binary string can be used to indicate an operation to be performed and the memory cell or cells that are involved. The assembly language instructions just given could be written in a machine language as

```
0010 0000 0000 0100
0100 0000 0000 0101
0011 0000 0000 0110
```

Obviously, what is easiest for a computer to understand is most difficult for a person to understand and vice versa.

A computer can understand only programs that are written in its own language. Consequently, each instruction in an assembly language program or a high-level language program must first be translated into machine language. Section 1.5 discusses the steps required to process a high-level language program.

EXERCISE FOR SECTION 1.4

Self-Check

1. What do you think the following high-level language statements mean?

```
x   = a + b + c;
x   = y / z;
d   = c - b + a;
x   = x + 1;
kelvins = celsius + 273.15;
```

1.5 PROCESSING A HIGH-LEVEL LANGUAGE PROGRAM

Before the computer can process a high-level language program, the programmer must enter it at the terminal. The program is stored on a disk as a file called the *program file* or *source file* (see Fig. 1.9). The programmer uses an *editor* or *word-processor* program to enter the program and to save it as a source file.

Once the source file is saved, it can be translated into machine language. A *compiler* program processes the source file and attempts to translate each statement. One or more statements in the source file may contain a *syntax error,* meaning that the statement does not correspond exactly to the syntax of the high-level language. In this case, the compiler causes an error message to be dis

**Figure 1.9
Preparing a
Program for
Execution**

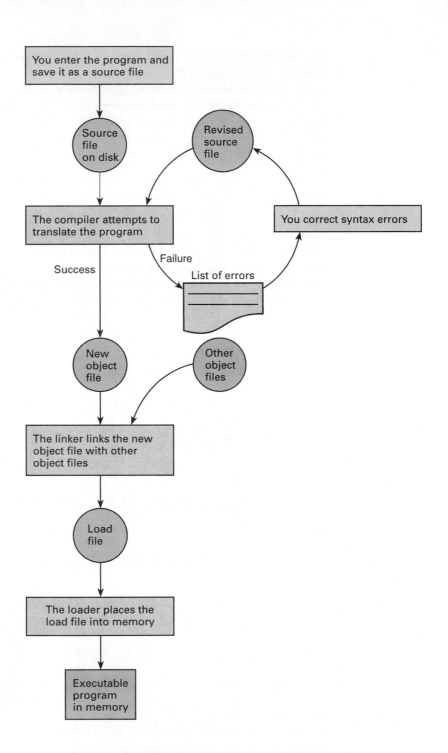

played on the monitor screen and does not attempt to create a machine-language version of the program.

At this point, you can make changes to your source file and have the compiler process the files again. If there are no more errors, the compiler creates an *object file,* which is your program translated into the target computer's machine language. The object file and any additional object files—for example, programs for input and output operations—that may be needed are combined by the *linker* program into a *load file.* Finally, the *loader* program places the load file into memory, ready for execution. The editor, compiler, linker, and loader programs are part of your computer system. The entire process of preparing a program for execution is shown in Fig. 1.9.

Executing a Program

To execute a program, the CPU must examine each program instruction in memory and send out the command signals required to carry out the instruction. Normally, the instructions are executed in sequence; however, as we will discuss

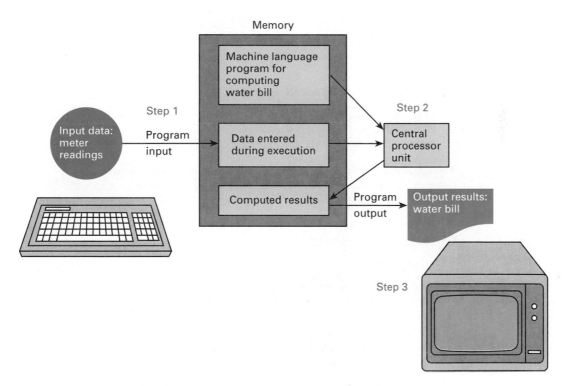

Figure 1.10   Flow of Information during Program Execution

later, it is possible to have the CPU skip over some instructions or to have it execute some instructions more than once.

During execution, data can be entered into memory and manipulated in some specified way. Program instructions are used to copy a program's data (called *input data*) into memory. After the input data are processed, instructions for displaying or printing values in memory can be executed to display the program results. The lines displayed by a program are called the *program output*.

Let's use the situation illustrated in Fig. 1.10—executing a water bill program stored in memory—as an example. In the first step, the program copies into memory data that describe the amount of water used and the water rate. In Step 2, the program manipulates the data and stores the results of the computations in memory. In the final step, the computational results are displayed as a water bill. Chapter 3 takes a closer look at such a program.

EXERCISES FOR SECTION 1.5

Self-Check

1. What is a source file? An object file? A load file? Which do you create and which does the compiler create? Which does the linker create and which is processed by the loader? What do the compiler, linker, and loader programs do?
2. What is a syntax error? In which file (source, object, or load) would a syntax error be found?

1.6 USING THE COMPUTER

The mechanics of entering a program as a source file and translating and executing a program differ from system to system. Although we cannot give specific details for a particular computer system, we will describe the general process in this section.

Operating Systems

Some of you will be using a *timeshared computer*. Universities often use timeshared computers for instructional purposes. In a timeshare environment, many users are connected by terminals to one central computer, and all users share the central facilities.

Many of you will be using a personal computer, which is a small desktop computer used by one individual at a time. Regardless of what type of computer you use, you will need to interact with a supervisory program called the *operating system* within the computer. In timeshared computers, the operating system allocates the central resources among many users. Some operating

Figure 1.11   Booting a PC

```
MS-DOS Version 3.3
Current date is Tue 1-01-1980
Enter new date: 4-05-92
Current time is 0:01:43.53
Enter new time: 10:30
C>
```

system tasks are

- validating user identification and account number (system shared by several users)
- making the editor, compiler, linker, and loader programs available to users
- allocating memory and processor time
- providing input and output facilities
- retrieving needed files
- saving new files

The operating system for a PC performs all but the first task.

Each computer has its own special *control language* for communicating with its operating system. Although space does not allow us to provide the details here, we will discuss the general process. Your instructor will provide the specific commands for your system.

Creating a Program or File

Before you can use a PC, you first need to boot up the computer. *Booting* a PC involves switching on the computer, and it may require inserting an operating system disk into a disk drive. The operating system may prompt you for the date and time. Once booted, the operating system displays a prompt (for example, C>) to indicate that it is ready to accept commands. Figure 1.11 demonstrates booting an IBM PC using MS-DOS, the Microsoft operating system. The computer user enters the characters that are in color; the other characters are those that the operating system displays.

Before you can use a timeshared computer, you must *log on,* or *connect,* to the computer. To log on, enter your account name and password (given to you by your instructor). For security reasons, your password is not displayed. Figure 1.12 demonstrates this process for the Digital Equipment Corporation™ VAX computer. The computer user enters the characters that are in color; the other characters are those that the operating system displays. The timeshared operating system shown, Ultrix-32 Version 3.1, displays the symbol > as a prompt.

Figure 1.12 Logging on to a Computer

```
Ultrix-32 V3.1 (rev. 9) (ranger.uwyo.edu)
login: hanly
Password: madaket

Last login: Sat Apr 13 09:57:55 from
posse.uwyo.edu
Ultrix-32 V3.0 (rev. 9) System #4: Tue Apr 16
14:28:36 MDT 1992

Fri Apr 19 20:39:13 MDT 1992
>
```

Once you have booted your PC or logged on to a timeshared computer, you can begin to create your program. In most cases, you will use a special program called a *word processor* or *editor* to enter your C program. After accessing the editor or word processor, you can start to enter a new C program. If you want a record of the program once it is entered, you must save it as a permanent file on disk; otherwise, your program disappears when your session with the word processor or editor is over. Follow these steps to create and save a program file:

1. Log on to a timeshared computer or boot up a PC.
2. Access the word processor or editor program, and indicate that you are creating a new file.
3. Enter each line of the program file.
4. Name your program file (if not named in Step 2), and save it as a permanent file in secondary memory.
5. Exit from the editor or word processor.

When you have created your program and are satisfied that each line is entered correctly, you can attempt to compile, link, and execute the program. On some systems you must give three separate commands; on other systems one command, such as RUN or the name of the load file, initiates this sequence of operations.

If your program will not compile because it contains syntax errors, you must edit, or correct, the program. Follow these steps to correct and re-execute a program file:

1. Re-access the editor or word processor program and access your program file.
2. Correct the statements containing syntax errors.
3. Save your edited program file.
4. Compile, link, and execute the new program file.

Interactive and Batch Input

When a correctly compiled program is executing, it must receive input data to process. The program can receive these data in two basic modes: interactive and batch.

If the program is running in *interactive mode,* the user can interact with the program by using the keyboard or another input device to enter data while the program is executing. A program that is designed to run in interactive mode will display messages called *prompts* to advise the program user as to what type of information to enter. For example, the Ultrix-32 system program shown in Fig. 1.12 is running in interactive mode. The words `login:` and `Password:` are examples of prompts that this program displays to notify the user of the type of information needed as input.

When a program runs in *batch mode,* all data must be supplied in advance, that is, the program user cannot interact with the program while it is executing. To use batch mode, you must prepare a batch data file before you execute your program. You will create and save this data file using the same steps listed for creation of a program or source file.

CHAPTER REVIEW

This chapter described the basic components of a computer: main and secondary memory, the CPU, and I/O devices. Remember these important facts about computers:

1. A memory cell is never empty, although its initial contents may be meaningless to your program.
2. The current contents of a memory cell are destroyed whenever new information is placed in that cell.
3. Programs must first be placed in the memory of the computer before they can be executed.
4. Data cannot be manipulated by the computer without first being copied into memory.
5. A computer cannot think for itself; you must use a programming language to instruct a computer to perform a task in a precise and unambiguous manner.
6. Programming a computer can be fun—if you are patient, organized, and careful.

We reviewed the history of computing and discussed the four generations of computers. We also described the different categories of computers: microcomputers, minicomputers, and mainframes, noting that a computer's size and performance capability determine its category.

We discussed problem solving and its importance in programming. We provided a method for software development that stresses a careful, organized approach to solving programming problems. The five phases of the software development method are requirements specification, analysis, design, implementation, and testing and verification.

We described the three different categories of programming languages: machine, assembly, and high-level, and showed the differences between these categories. We investigated how a high-level language source program is translated into a machine-language object file by a compiler, is linked with other object files by a linker, and finally is loaded into memory by a loader. We discussed how to use a computer and its operating system to accomplish the tasks of entering a new program and running it on a computer.

QUICK-CHECK EXERCISES

1. The ____ translates a ____ language program into ____ .
2. After a C program is executed, all program results are automatically displayed. True or false?
3. Specify the correct order for these four operations: execution, linking, translation, loading.
4. A high-level language program is saved on disk as a(n) ____ file or a(n) ____ file.
5. The ____ finds syntax errors in the ____ file.
6. A machine language program is saved on disk as a(n) ____ file.
7. A(n) ____ program is used to create and save the source file.
8. The ____ creates the load file.
9. The ____ program is used to place the ____ file into memory.
10. Computers are becoming (more/less) expensive and (bigger/smaller) in size.
11. The first large-scale, general-purpose electronic computer was called the ____ . It (was/was not) a stored-program computer.
12. A list of the names of all the files stored on a disk is found in the ____ .

ANSWERS TO QUICK-CHECK EXERCISES

1. compiler, high-level, machine language
2. false
3. translation, linking, loading, execution
4. source, program
5. compiler, source

6. object
7. word processor or editor
8. linker
9. loader, load
10. less, smaller
11. ENIAC, was not
12. directory

REVIEW QUESTIONS

1. List at least three kinds of information stored in a computer.
2. List two functions of the CPU.
3. List two input/output devices and two secondary storage devices.
4. A computer can think. True or false?
5. List the three categories of programming languages.
6. Give three advantages of programming in a high-level language such as C.
7. What processes are needed to transform a C program into a machine-language program that is ready for execution?
8. What are three characteristics of a structured program?
9. What is the difference between the requirements specification and analysis phases of the software development method?
10. In which phase of the software development method is the algorithm for a solution developed?

CHAPTER 2

PROBLEM SOLVING AND C

2.1
Applying the Software Development Method
Case Study: Converting Units of Measurement
2.2
Overview of C
2.3
Variable Declarations in C Programs
2.4
Executable Statements
2.5
General Form of C Programs
2.6
Data Types and Expressions
2.7
Formatting Numbers in Program Output
2.8
Interactive Mode, Batch Mode, and Data Files
2.9
Common Programming Errors
Chapter Review

Programming is a problem-solving activity; if you are a good problem solver, you are likely to become a good programmer. Therefore one important goal of this book is to help you improve your problem-solving ability. We believe that it is beneficial to approach each programming problem in a systematic and consistent way. This chapter shows how to apply the software development method to solve programming problems.

This chapter also introduces the programming language C, a high-level, general-purpose programming language developed in 1972 at AT&T Bell Laboratories. (A *general-purpose programming language* is one that can be used in writing many different applications.) Since C was designed by Dennis Ritchie as a language in which to write the UNIX® operating system, it was originally used primarily for systems programming. Over the years, however, the power and flexibility of C, together with the availability of high-quality C compilers for computers of all sizes, have made it a popular language in industry for a wide variety of applications.

A *language standard,* which describes all C language constructs and specifies their syntax, ensures that a C program written on one computer will also execute on another. The C language standard, usually called "ANSI C," was adopted by the American National Standards Institute (ANSI) in 1989. The examples we use in this text conform to the ANSI C standard. However, the great majority of these examples use basic language features that are also available in traditional C.

It is now accepted practice in industry to design systems using principles of structure and style that produce programs that are easy to read, understand, and keep in good working order. In this text, we strongly emphasize the use of C structures and style standards that contribute to the clarity of the program code.

This chapter describes C statements for performing computations and for getting input data and displaying results. Besides introducing problem solving and C, the chapter describes how to run C programs in interactive mode as well as in batch mode.

2.1 APPLYING THE SOFTWARE DEVELOPMENT METHOD

In this textbook we provide case solutions for a number of programming problems, following the software development method outlined in Section 1.3. We begin each case study with a statement of the problem. Then, as part of the analysis of the problem, we identify the data requirements for the problem, indicating the problem inputs and the desired outputs. Next, we develop and refine the initial algorithm. Finally, we implement this algorithm as a C program. We provide a sample run of the program and discuss how we might perform a more complete test of the program. As we walk you through a sample case study, we provide a running commentary on the process being followed so that you will be able to apply it to other situations.

Case Study: Converting Units of Measurement

PROBLEM

Your surveying job calls for you to study some maps that give distances in kilometers and some that use miles. Because you and your co-workers prefer to deal in metric measurements, you are asked to write a program that performs the necessary conversion.

ANALYSIS

The first step in understanding this problem is to determine what you are asked to do. It should be clear that you must convert from one system of measurement to another, but are you supposed to convert from kilometers to miles or miles to kilometers? Because the problem states that you prefer to work with metric measurements, the distances that are given in kilometers are already acceptable. However, the distances that are given in miles are not metric and must be converted. Therefore the problem input is *distance in miles*. You and your colleagues want to know the *equivalent distance in metric units of kilometers;* this must be your problem output. To write the program, we need to know the relationship between miles and kilometers. By examining a metric table, we find that one mile equals 1.609 kilometers.

The data requirements and relevant formulas are summarized below. The name `miles` identifies the memory cell that will contain the problem input, and the name `kms` identifies the memory cell that will contain the program result or the problem output.

Data Requirements and Formulas

Problem Inputs
```
miles    /* the distance in miles        */
```

Problem Outputs
```
kms      /* the distance in kilometers   */
```

Relevant Formula
1 mile equals 1.609 kilometers

◀ **DESIGN** ▶

Next, we try to formulate the algorithm that we must follow to solve the problem. We begin by listing the three major steps, or subproblems, of the algorithm.

Algorithm

1. Get the distance in miles.
2. Convert the distance to kilometers.
3. Display the distance in kilometers.

Now we must decide whether any steps of the algorithm need further refinement or whether they are perfectly clear as stated. Step 1 (getting the data) and Step 3 (displaying a value) are basic steps and require no further refinement. Step 2 is fairly straightforward, but it might help to add some detail that explicitly states the conversion formula to be used. The refinement of Step 2 follows.

Step 2 Refinement

2.1 The distance in kilometers is 1.609 times the distance in miles.

The complete algorithm with refinements resembles an outline for a paper. The refinement of Step 2 is numbered Step 2.1 and is indented under Step 2. We list the complete algorithm with refinements to show you how it all fits together.

Algorithm with Refinements

1. Get the distance in miles.
2. Convert the distance to kilometers.
   2.1 The distance in kilometers is 1.609 times the distance in miles.
3. Display the distance in kilometers.

◀ **IMPLEMENTATION** ▶

To implement the solution, we must write the algorithm as a C program that contains all the information needed for a complete machine-language translation. Figure 2.1 shows the C program along with a sample execution (the last two lines of the figure). For easy identification, the program statements representing algorithm steps are in color, as is the input data value typed in by the program user in the sample execution. Don't worry about understanding the details of this program yet. We will give an overview of the main points of the program here and go into more detail later in the chapter.

Figure 2.1 **Miles-to-Kilometers Conversion Program**

```
/*
 * Converts distances from miles to kilometers.
 */

#include <stdio.h>            /* printf, scanf definitions  */
#define KMS_PER_MILE 1.609 /* conversion constant          */

int
main(void)
{
      double miles, /* distance in miles                    */
             kms;   /* equivalent distance in kilometers    */

      /* Get the distance in miles.                         */
      printf("Enter the distance in miles> ");
      scanf("%lf", &miles);

      /* Convert the distance to kilometers.                */
      kms = KMS_PER_MILE * miles;

      /* Display the distance in kilometers.                */
      printf("That equals %f kilometers.\n", kms);

      return (0);
}

Enter the distance in miles> 112.0
That equals 180.208000 kilometers.
```

In Fig. 2.1, you might notice a number of lines containing text with the characters /* at the beginning and */ at the end such as

```
/* Convert the distance to kilometers.    */
```

In C, the slash-star and star-slash surround a program comment. A program *comment* is like a parenthetical remark in a sentence; its purpose is to provide supplementary information to the person reading the program. Program comments are ignored by the C compiler and are not translated into machine language. We will study various forms of comments in Section 2.5.

For the C language there are two steps in the translation process: First the C *preprocessor* revises and completes the text of the source code; then the C compiler generates the machine-language equivalent of the revised source file. The first part of our C program contains directives that are used by the preprocessor, directives that begin with a number sign (#). In the next section of the program, we tell the C compiler about the problem data requirements—that is, what memory cell names we are using and what kind of data will be stored in each memory cell. In the final section of the program, we write one or more C statements for each algorithm step. If an algorithm step has been refined, we convert its refinements into C statements.

The program in Fig. 2.1 consists of two parts: the preprocessor directives and the main function. The preprocessor directives specify the meanings of some names and tell the preprocessor where to find the meanings of others. For example, the #define directive in Fig. 2.1 informs the preprocessor that the name KMS_PER_MILE means 1.609. The #include directive notifies the preprocessor that additional names that will be needed are defined in the C standard input/output library. A *library* is a collection of named operations called *functions*. For the program in Fig. 2.1, the definitions of printf (for printing) and scanf (for scanning input data) are found in <stdio.h>. Because you will always need to use these input/output functions, your programs will begin with this same

```
#include <stdio.h>
```

The two-line heading

```
int
main(void)
```

marks the beginning of the *main function*. The remaining lines of the program form the *body* of the function. The two major sections of the function body are the *declaration part* and the *executable statements*.

The declaration part tells the compiler what memory cells are needed in the program and is based on the problem data requirements identified previously during the problem analysis. Memory cells are needed for storing the variables miles and kms.

The executable statements following the declaration part are translated into machine language and later executed. Each statement that begins with the word printf causes some program output to be displayed. The first such line

```
printf("Enter the distance in miles> ");
```

displays the first output line in the sample execution, which asks the user to type in a value in miles. The next line

```
scanf("%lf", &miles);
```

copies the data value typed by the program user (112.0) into the memory cell named miles. The & operator allows scanf to change the value of the variable miles. The program statement

```
kms = KMS_PER_MILE * miles;
```

computes the equivalent distance in kilometers by multiplying the distance in miles by 1.609. The product is stored in memory cell kms. The program statement

```
printf("That equals %f kilometers.\n", kms);
```

displays a message composed of a *string* of characters including the value of kms. The last program line,

```
return (0);
```

ends execution of the function.

Some punctuation symbols appear in Fig. 2.1. For example, commas separate items in a list, a semicolon appears at the end of several lines, and braces ({}) mark the beginning and end of the body of function main. We will give guidelines for the use of these symbols later.

TESTING

The last two lines of Fig. 2.1 show one sample run of this program, but how do we know that the program result is correct? We should always examine program results carefully to make sure that they make sense. In this run, a distance of 112.0 miles is converted to 180.208 kilometers, as it should be. To verify that the program works properly, we should enter a few more test values of miles. We really don't need to try more than a few test cases to verify that a simple program like this is correct.

EXERCISES FOR SECTION 2.1

Self-Check

1. List the five steps of the software development method.
2. What would be the data requirements and formulas for a computer program that converts a weight in pounds to a weight in kilograms?

2.2 OVERVIEW OF C

The rest of this chapter provides a description of some basic features of the C programming language. We will base our discussion on the programs in Fig. 2.1 and in the next example.

EXAMPLE 2.1    Figure 2.2 contains a C program and a sample execution of that program (see the last three lines of the figure). The program asks for a nickname and the current year and then displays a personalized message to the program user.

Figure 2.2   Printing a Welcoming Message

```
/*
 * Displays the user's nickname and the current year
 * in a welcoming message.
 */

#include <stdio.h> /* printf, scanf definitions */

int
main(void)
{
      char letter_1, letter_2, letter_3;   /* three letters */
      int  year;                           /* current year  */

      printf("Enter a 3-letter nickname and press return> ");
      scanf("%c%c%c", &letter_1, &letter_2, &letter_3);
      printf("Enter the current year and press return> ");
      scanf("%d", &year);
      printf("Welcome, %c%c%c. %d is a great year to study C!\n",
             letter_1, letter_2, letter_3, year);

      return (0);
}

Enter a 3-letter nickname and press return> Bob
Enter the current year and press return> 1993
Welcome, Bob. 1993 is a great year to study C!
```

(handwritten annotations): KEYWORD (integer) ; KEYWORD (character)

The program line starting with `char` identifies the names of three memory cells (`letter_1`, `letter_2`, `letter_3`) that will be used to store each letter of the nickname. The program instruction

```
scanf("%c%c%c", &letter_1, &letter_2, &letter_3);
```

copies the three letters `Bob` (typed by the program user) into the three memory cells, one letter per cell. After prompting the user to enter a year and storing this value in the memory cell `year`, the program displays the welcoming message shown as the last line of the sample execution. The final program line

```
return (0);
```

is a statement that completes the execution of function `main` by returning a value that indicates that the function ran normally.

One of the nicest things about C is that it lets us write programs that resemble English. At this point, you probably can read and understand the two sample programs, even though you do not know how to write your own programs. In the following sections, you'll learn more details about the two C programs we've looked at so far. ←

C Program Outline

When you review these sample programs, you will note that they both follow the simple program outline shown in Fig. 2.3.

All *preprocessor directives* use commands that have a number-sign symbol (#) as the first nonblank character on the line. These directives give instructions to the C preprocessor whose job it is to modify the text of a C program before it is compiled. The two most commonly used directives are the ones seen in Fig. 2.1 and Fig. 2.2: `#include` and `#define`.

The C language explicitly defines only a small number of operations: Many actions that are necessary in a computer program are not defined directly by C. Instead, every C implementation contains collections of useful functions

Figure 2.3   Outline of a Simple C Program

preprocessor directives
main function prototype
{
declarations
statements
}

and symbols called *libraries*. The ANSI standard for C requires that certain *standard libraries* be provided in every ANSI C implementation. A C system may expand the number of operations available by supplying additional libraries; an individual programmer can also create libraries of functions.

It is the `#include` directive that gives a program access to one of these libraries. This directive causes the preprocessor to insert definitions from a library file into a program before compilation. The sample programs we have seen must include definitions from the standard I/O library `<stdio.h>` so the compiler will know the meanings of `printf` and `scanf`.

The other preprocessor directive that we saw in Fig. 2.1 was `#define` which was used to create the constant macro[†] `KMS_PER_MILE` with the meaning `1.609`. This directive instructs the preprocessor to replace the name defined by its meaning every time the name appears in your program. For example, the preprocessor would respond to

```
#define KMS_PER_MILE 1.609
```

by replacing the symbol `KMS_PER_MILE` by the value `1.609` throughout the text of the program. As a result, the line

```
kms = KMS_PER_MILE * miles;
```

would read

```
kms = 1.609 * miles;
```

by the time it was sent to the C compiler. Only data values that never change or change very rarely should be given names using a `#define`, because an executing C program cannot change the value of a name defined as a constant macro.

Main Function Prototype

One valid *prototype* (header) for the main function of a simple C program is

```
int
main(void)
```

This prototype marks the function where program execution begins.

....

[†] What we refer to as a "constant macro" in this text is officially termed a "manifest" in C standard vocabulary.

Main Function Body

The remaining parts of the simple C program outline form the body of the main function. The curly braces mark the beginning and end of this function body. The declarations identify the memory cells used by the function, and the statements list instructions to manipulate data according to the program's purpose.

Now that we have an idea of the overall structure of a simple C program, let's look in detail at the components of the body of the main function.

Reserved Words and Identifiers

Each line of the programs in Fig. 2.1 and Fig. 2.2 satisfies the syntax rules for the C language. Each line contains a number of different elements such as reserved words, identifiers from standard libraries, special symbols, and names for memory cells. Let's look at the first two elements. All the *reserved words* appear in lowercase; they have special meaning in C and cannot be used for other purposes. A complete list of ANSI C reserved words is found in Appendix G. The reserved words appearing in Fig. 2.1 and Fig. 2.2 are

```
int, void, double, char, return
```

Two identifiers in these programs are defined by the standard libraries that we access by using the #include directive. Although these names can be used by the programmer for other purposes, we don't recommend this practice. The standard identifiers appearing in Fig. 2.1 and Fig. 2.2 are

```
printf, scanf
```

What is the difference between reserved words and standard identifiers? Although you cannot use a reserved word as the name of a memory cell used by your program, you may use a standard identifier. However, once you use a standard identifier to name a memory cell, the C compiler no longer associates the standard library definition with that identifier. For example, you could decide to use printf as the name of a memory cell, but then you would not be able to use printf to display program output, its usual purpose. Because standard identifiers lose a valuable purpose, we don't recommend using them to name memory cells. (Other identifiers appearing in the programs in Fig. 2.1 and Fig. 2.2 are described in more detail in the next section.)

The preprocessor directives and the main function prototype introduced in this section are summarized in the following displays. Each display describes the syntax of the statement and provides examples and an interpretation of the statement.

#include Directive for Defining Identifiers from Standard Libraries

SYNTAX: #include <*standard header file*>

EXAMPLES: #include <stdio.h>
             #include <math.h>

INTERPRETATION: #include directives tell the preprocessor where to find the meanings of standard identifiers used in the program. These meanings are collected in files called *standard header files*. The header file stdio.h contains information about standard input and output functions such as scanf and printf. Descriptions of common mathematical functions are found in the header file math.h. We will investigate header files associated with other standard libraries in later chapters.

#define Directive for Creating Constant Macros

SYNTAX: #define *NAME value*

EXAMPLES: #define MILES_PER_KM 0.62137
             #define PI 3.141593
             #define MAX_LENGTH 100

INTERPRETATION: The C preprocessor is notified that it is to replace each use of the identifier *NAME* by *value*. C program statements cannot change the value associated with *NAME*.

main Function Prototype

SYNTAX: int
        main(void)

INTERPRETATION: The main prototype marks the function where program execution begins.

EXERCISES FOR SECTION 2.2

Self-Check

1. What part of a C implementation changes the text of a C program just before it is compiled? Name two directives that give instructions about these changes.
2. Why shouldn't we use identifiers from standard libraries as names of memory cells in a program? Can we use reserved words instead?
3. Why should PI (3.141593) be defined as a constant macro?

2.3 VARIABLE DECLARATIONS IN C PROGRAMS

We have seen that we can associate names with constant values by using the C preprocessor directive #define. How do we tell C what names will be used to identify other data in a program?

The memory cells used for storing a program's input data and its computational results are called *variables* because the values stored in variables may change (and usually do) as the program executes. The *variable declaration*

```
double miles, /* distance in miles               */
       kms;   /* equivalent distance in kilometers */
```

in Fig. 2.1 gives the names of two memory cells used to store double-precision real numbers (for example, 112.0, 180.208).

The declarations

```
char letter_1,letter_2,letter_3; /* three  letters  */
int  year;                       /* current  year   */
```

provide names for three memory cells used to store single characters and for one memory cell used to store an integer (for example, 1993). These variable names are also identifiers.

In a variable declaration, the identifier (for example, double, char, int) that begins the statement tells the C compiler the *data type* (for example, a real number, a character, or an integer) of the information that is stored in a particular variable. A variable that is used for storing an integer value, that is, a number without a decimal point, has data type int.

You have quite a bit of freedom in selecting the identifiers that you use in a program. The rules for forming user-defined ANSI C identifiers are as follows:

1. An identifier cannot begin with a digit.
2. An identifier must consist only of letters, digits, or underscores.
3. A C reserved word cannot be used as an identifier.
4. An identifier defined in a C standard library should not be redefined.[†]

Valid Identifiers for a User Program

```
letter_1, UserName, NUM_STUDENTS, c3po
```

Invalid Identifiers for a User Program

```
1letter, int, Two-by-Four, scanf†
```

[†] Rule 4 is actually advice from the authors rather than ANSI C syntax.

Although the syntax rules for identifiers do not place a limit on length, some ANSI C compilers do not consider two names different unless there is a variation within the first 31 characters. The two identifiers

```
per_capita_meat_consumption_in_1980
per_capita_meat_consumption_in_1990
```

would be viewed as identical by a C compiler that considered only the first 31 characters to be significant.

Uppercase and Lowercase Letters

The C programmer must take great care in the use of uppercase and lowercase letters because the C compiler considers such usage significant. The names `Rate`, `rate`, and `RATE` are viewed by the compiler as *different* identifiers. Adopting a consistent pattern in the way you use uppercase and lowercase letters is helpful to the readers of your programs. You will see that all reserved words in C and the names of all standard library functions use only lowercase letters. One style that has been widely adopted in industry uses all uppercase letters in the names of constant macros. We follow this convention in this text; for variables we use all lowercase letters.

Program Style   *Choosing Names of Variables and Constant Macros*

Throughout the text, issues of good programming style are discussed in displays such as this one. These displays provide guidelines for improving the appearance and readability of programs. Because most programs will be examined or studied by someone other than the writer, programs that follow some consistent style conventions will be easier to read and understand than those that are sloppy or inconsistent. Although these conventions make it easier for humans to understand programs, they have no effect whatsoever on the computer.

Pick meaningful names for variables and constant macros so that your program is easy to read. For example, `weight` would be a good name for a variable used to store the weight of an object; the identifiers w and `bagel` would be poor choices. If an identifier consists of two or more words, placing the underscore character (_) between words will improve the readability of the name (`lbs_per_sq_in` rather than `lbspersqin`).

Choose identifiers long enough to convey your meaning, but avoid excessively long names because you are more likely to make a typing error in a longer name. For example, the shorter `lbs_per_sq_in` is preferable to the longer `lbs_per_square_inch` since both names are meaningful.

If you mistype a name so that the identifier looks like the name of another variable, often the compiler cannot help you detect your error. For this reason and to avoid confusion, do not choose names that are similar to each other. Especially avoid selecting two names that are different only in their use of

Table 2.1   Reserved Words and Identifiers in Figs. 2.1 and 2.2

Reserved Words	Identifiers from Standard Libraries	User-Defined Identifiers
`int, void, double, char`	`printf, scanf`	`KMS_PER_MILE, main, miles, letter_1, letter_2, letter_3, kms, year`

uppercase and lowercase letters such as `LARGE` and `large`. Also try not to use two names that differ only in the presence or absence of an underscore (`xcoord` and `x_coord`).

C requires that the user supply a declaration or definition for every identifier used in a program unless that identifier is defined in a standard library file mentioned in a `#include` preprocessor directive. The reserved words and identifiers used in Fig. 2.1 and Fig. 2.2 are shown in Table 2.1.

This section introduced the variable declaration; the syntax of this statement is summarized in the display that follows.

Syntax Display for Declarations

SYNTAX:
```
int variable_list;
double variable_list;
char variable_list;
```

EXAMPLES:
```
int     count,
        large;
double x, y, z;
char    first_initial;
char    ans;
```

INTERPRETATION: A memory cell is allocated for each name in the *variable_list*. The type of data (`double`, `int`, `char`) to be stored in each variable is specified at the beginning of the statement. One statement may extend over multiple lines. A single data type can appear in more than one variable declaration, so the following two declaration sections are equally acceptable ways of declaring the variables `rate`, `time`, and `age`.

```
double rate, time;        double rate;
int    age;               int    age;
                          double time;
```

Self-Check

1. Indicate which of the following words are C reserved words, which are identifiers conventionally used as names of constant macros, which are other valid identifiers, and which are invalid identifiers.

```
int    MAX_ENTRIES   double    time   G   Sue's
this_is_a_long_one   xyz123    part#2    "char"
```

2. Write an outline of a C program that has variables of type `double` representing the radius, area, and circumference of a circle and a constant macro for π. The program should have access to the I/O functions `printf` and `scanf`. Include in your outline the entire program except for the executable statements of the main function.

2.4 EXECUTABLE STATEMENTS

One of the main purposes of a computer is to perform arithmetic computations and to display the results of the computations. These operations are specified by the *executable statements* that appear in the program body, following the variable declarations. Each executable statement is translated by the C compiler into one or more machine language instructions that are copied to the object file and later executed. The declarations, on the other hand, describe to the C compiler the meaning of each user-defined identifier; these declarations are not translated into machine language instructions and do not appear in the object file.

Programs in Memory

Before examining each kind of executable statement in detail, let's see what computer memory looks like after a program is first loaded into memory and again after that program executes. Figure 2.4(a) shows the miles-to-kilometers conversion program loaded into memory along with the program memory area before execution of the program body. The question marks in memory cells `miles` and `kms` indicate that these variables are undefined—that is, the value is unknown—before program execution begins. During program execution, the data value `112.0` is copied from the input device into the variable `miles` by the execution of the statement

```
scanf("%lf", &miles);
```

Figure 2.4
(a) Memory
before Execution
of a Program;
(b) Memory
after Execution
of a Program

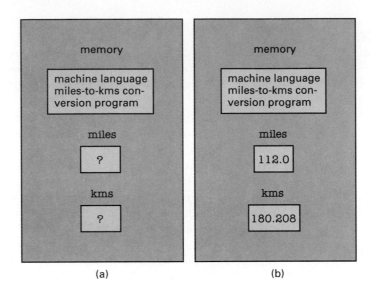

(a)   (b)

After the assignment statement

```
kms = KMS_PER_MILE * miles;
```

executes, the variables are defined as shown in Fig. 2.4(b). We will study these statements next.

Assignment Statements

In C, one use of the *assignment statement* is to store in a variable the result of a computation. The assignment statement

```
kms = KMS_PER_MILE * miles;
```

in Fig. 2.1 assigns a value to the variable `kms`. In this case, `kms` is being assigned the result of multiplying (* means multiply) the value of the constant macro `KMS_PER_MILE` by the value of the variable `miles`. Valid information must be stored in `miles` before the assignment statement is executed. As shown in Fig. 2.5, only the value of `kms` is affected by the assignment statement; the definition of the constant macro `KMS_PER_MILE` and the value of the variable `miles` remain unchanged.

The symbol = is the *assignment operator* in C and should be read "becomes" or "gets" or "takes the value of" rather than "equals" since it is *not*

Figure 2.5
Effect of `kms = KMS_PER_MILE * miles;`

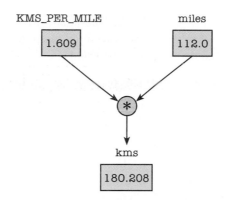

equivalent to the "equal sign" of mathematics. In mathematics, this symbol states a relationship between two values, but in C it represents an action to be carried out by the computer. The general form of the assignment statement is shown in the next display.

Syntax Display for Assignment Statements

SYNTAX: *result = expression*;

EXAMPLE: `x = x + z + 2.0;`

INTERPRETATION: The variable specified by *result* is assigned the value of *expression*. The previous value of *result* is destroyed. The *expression* can be a single variable or a single constant, or it may involve variables, constants, and the arithmetic operators listed in Table 2.2.

Table 2.2   Some Arithmetic Operators

Arithmetic Operator	Meaning
+	addition
−	subtraction or negation
*	multiplication
/	division

The division operator can yield surprising and even unpredictable results when it is used to find the quotient of two integers. We will explore assignment statements and expressions in greater detail in Section 2.6.

EXAMPLE 2.2   In C, you can write assignment statements of the form

```
sum = sum + item;
```

where the variable `sum` is used on both sides of the assignment operator. This is obviously not an algebraic equation, but it illustrates a common programming practice. The statement instructs the computer to add the current value of the variable `sum` to the value of `item`; the result is saved temporarily and then stored back into `sum`. The previous value of `sum` is destroyed in the process; however, the value of `item` is unchanged (see Fig. 2.6). ◀

Figure 2.6
Effect of `sum = sum + item;`

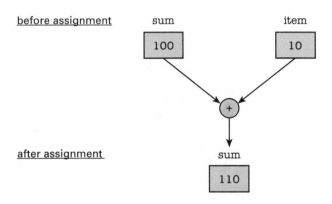

EXAMPLE 2.3   In C, you can also write assignment statements with an expression part that consists of a single variable or constant. The statement

```
new_x = x;
```

instructs the computer to copy the value of `x` into `new_x`. The statement

```
new_x = -x;
```

instructs the computer to get the value of `x`, negate this value, and store the result in `new_x` (for example, if `x` is `3.5`, `new_x` is `−3.5`). Neither of the assignment statements involving `new_x` changes the value of `x`. ◀

Input/Output Operations

Data can be stored in variables in two different ways: either through an assignment operation or through the use of a function like `scanf`. We have already introduced the assignment operator. The second method, copying data from an input device into a variable, is necessary if you want the program to manipulate different data each time the program executes. This data transfer from the outside world into memory is called an *input operation*.

As a program executes, it performs computations and assigns new values to variables. These program results can be displayed to the program user by an *output operation*.

All input/output operations in C are performed by executing special program units called *input/output functions*. The most common input/output functions are supplied in the C standard input/output library to which we gain access through use of the preprocessor directive

```
#include <stdio.h>
```

In this section, we will discuss how to use the input function named `scanf` and the output function named `printf`.

Using the scanf Function

In C, a *function call* is used to invoke or activate a function. Calling a function is analogous to asking a friend to perform an urgent task. You tell your friend what to do, but not how to do it. Then you wait for your friend to report back that the task is finished. After you hear from your friend, you can proceed with doing something else.

In Fig. 2.1, the function call statement

```
scanf("%lf", &miles);
```

causes the function `scanf` (pronounced "scan-eff") to copy input data into the variable `miles`. What is the source of the data that `scanf` stores in the variable `miles`? The source is the *standard input device*—in most cases, the keyboard. Consequently, the computer attempts to store in `miles` whatever information is typed at the keyboard by the program user. Because `miles` is declared as type `double`, the input operation will proceed without error only if the program user types in a number. The program user should press the key labeled <return> or <enter> after typing the number. The effect of the `scanf` operation is shown in Fig. 2.7.

Figure 2.2 contains a similar example of the use of the `scanf` function for copying into a variable a number input by the user. The statement

```
scanf("%d", &year);
```

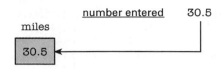

copies a whole number from the standard input device into the variable `year`. Let's compare the following two function calls that copy numbers from the input device:

```
scanf("%lf", &miles);
scanf("%d", &year);
```

What is the meaning of the quoted strings of characters `"%lf"` and `"%d"`? Each percent sign followed by one or two letters is a *placeholder* or *conversion specification* that tells `scanf` what type of data to copy into one variable. The `%lf` is a placeholder for a real number to be copied into a variable of type `double`.[†] The `%d` is a placeholder for a *d*ecimal integer. As we will see in Fig. 2.8, `%c` is a placeholder for a single *c*haracter. Since a string of placeholders gives the `scanf` function information about the format of the input data it is to process, we refer to such a string as a *format*.

The program in Fig. 2.2 also gets a person's nickname as input data. Each person using the program may have a different nickname, so the function call statement

```
scanf("%c%c%c", &letter_1, &letter_2, &letter_3);
```

causes the `scanf` function to copy data into each of the three variables, and the format includes one `%c` placeholder for each variable. Since these variables are declared as type `char`, one character will be stored in each variable. The next three characters that are entered at the keyboard are stored in these variables. Note that case is important for character data so the letters B and b have different representations in memory. Again, the program user should press the <return> or <enter> key after typing in three characters. Figure 2.8 shows the effect of this statement when the letters `Bob` are entered.

The number of input characters consumed by the `scanf` function depends on the current format placeholder which should reflect the type of the variable in which the data will be stored. Only one input character is used for a `%c` (type `char` variable); for a `%lf` or `%d` (type `double` or `int` variable), the program first skips any spaces and then scans characters until it reaches a character that

[†] Before the standardization of C, the type `double` was also called `long float`, hence `lf`.

**Figure 2.8
Effect of**
`scanf("%c%c%c",
&letter_1,
&letter_2,
&letter_3);`

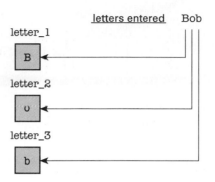

cannot be part of the number. Usually the program user, that is, the person entering the data, indicates the end of a number by typing the blank character or by pressing the <return> or <enter> key.

Notice that in a call to `scanf`, the name of each variable that is to be given a value is preceded by the ampersand character (`&`). The `&` is the C *address-of* operator. In the context of this input operation, the `&` operator tells the `scanf` function *where* to find each variable into which it is to store a new value. If the ampersand were omitted, `scanf` would know only a variable's current value, not its location in memory, so `scanf` would be unable to store a new value in the variable.

How do we know when to enter the input data and what data to enter? Your program should print a prompting message that informs you of what data to enter and when. (Prompting messages are discussed in more detail in the next section.) Each character entered by the program user is *echoed* on the screen and is also processed by the `scanf` function.

Syntax Display for scanf Function call

SYNTAX: scanf(*format, input list*);

EXAMPLE: scanf(`"%d%c"`, `&age`, `&first_initial`);

INTERPRETATION: The `scanf` function copies into memory data typed at the keyboard by the program user during program execution. The *format* is a quoted string of placeholders, one placeholder for each variable in the *input list*. Placeholders for `char`, `double`, and `int` variables are

variable type	scanf placeholder
char	%c
double	%lf
int	%d

(continued)

Each int, double, or char variable in the *input list* is preceded by an ampersand (&). Commas are used to separate variable names. The order of the placeholders must correspond to the order of the variables in the *input list*.

The data must be entered in the same order as the variables in the *input list*. The data entered should insert one or more blank characters or carriage returns between numeric items. No blanks should be inserted between consecutive character data items unless the blank character is one of the data items to be stored.

Using the printf Function

In order to see the results of a program's execution, we must have some way of specifying what variable values should be displayed. In Fig. 2.1, the function call statement

```
printf("That equals %f kilometers.\n", kms);
```

causes the function printf (pronounced "print-eff") to display a line of program output. This line is the result of printing the format string "That equals %f kilometers.\n" after substituting the values of the variables in the *print list* for their placeholders in the format string and replacing special combinations of characters called *escape sequences* by their meanings.

The format string we are considering contains one placeholder, %f, which must be replaced by the value of the variable in the print list, kms. It also contains the *newline* escape sequence \n. Like all C escape sequences, \n begins with the backslash character. Including this sequence at the end of the format string terminates the current output line. The complete line that is displayed when the value of kms is 180.208 is

```
That equals 180.208000 kilometers.
```

This sentence completes a line of output. Notice that the quotation marks surrounding the printf format were not printed. The format used in a call to the scanf or printf function is an example of a *string literal,* a sequence of characters enclosed in quotation marks. The quotation marks are the indicators of the beginning and end of the string literal and are not part of its value. The placeholders used in printf formats are like those in scanf formats except for variables of type double. These use a %f placeholder in a printf format and a %lf placeholder in a scanf format.

**Figure 2.9
Substitution of
Print List Values
for Placeholders**

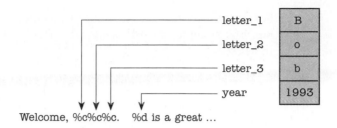

In Fig. 2.2, the function call statement

```
printf
  ("Welcome, %c%c%c. %d is a great year to study C!\n",
   letter_1, letter_2, letter_3, year);
```

displays the line

```
Welcome, Bob. 1993 is a great year to study C!
```

In Fig. 2.9, we see the values of the four variables of the print list of the printf function call substituted for the placeholders of the format string.

In addition to observing the use of the printf function to print program results, we have also seen it called to display prompts or prompting messages in Fig. 2.1 and Fig. 2.2.

```
printf("Enter the distance in miles> ");
printf("Enter a 3-letter nickname and press return> ");
printf("Enter the current year and press return> ");
```

Notice that because the format strings of these calls to printf contain no placeholders, no print list of variables is needed. In an interactive program, you should always display a prompting message just before a call to the function scanf to remind the program user to enter data. The prompt may also describe the format of the data expected. It is very important to precede each scanf operation with a printf that prints a prompt; otherwise, the program user may have no idea that the program is waiting for data or what data to enter.

More about \n

We often end a printf format string with a \n so that the call to printf produces a completed line of output. If no characters are printed on the next line before another newline character is printed, a blank line will appear in the output. For example, the following calls produce two lines of text with a blank line in between.

```
printf("Here is the first line\n");
printf("\nand this is the second.\n");
```

Here is the first line

and this is the second.

If a `printf` format string contains a `\n` in the middle of the string, the characters after the `\n` appear on a new output line as we see in this example.

```
printf("This sentence appears \non two lines.\n");
```

This sentence appears
on two lines.

The *cursor* is a moving place marker that indicates on the screen the next position where information will be displayed. When executing a `printf` function call, the cursor is advanced to the start of the next line on the screen if the `\n` escape sequence is encountered in the format string. Most of our `printf` calls include format strings ending in `\n`, so the cursor moves to the next line. However, the newline escape sequence is frequently omitted from the format strings of `printf` calls that display prompting messages. This omission allows the user to enter data on the same line with the prompt. The cursor is advanced to the next line when the user presses the <return> or <enter> key.

Syntax Display for printf Function Call

SYNTAX: `printf(`*format, print list*`);`
              or
          `printf(`*format*`);`

EXAMPLES: `printf("I am %d years old, and my gpa is %f\n",`
                  `age, gpa);`
          `printf("Enter the object weight in grams> ");`

INTERPRETATION: The `printf` function displays the value of its *format* string after substituting in order the values of the expressions in the *print list* for their placeholders in the *format* and after replacing escape sequences such as `\n` by their meanings. Placeholders for

(continued)

char, double, and int variables are

variable type	printf placeholder
char	%c
double	%f
int	%d

EXERCISES FOR SECTION 2.4

Self-Check

1. Show the output displayed by the program lines below when the data entered are 5 and 7.

```
printf("Enter two integers> ");
scanf("%d%d", &m, &n);
m = m + 5;
n = 3 * n;
printf("m = %d\nn = %d\n", m, n);
```

2. Show the contents of memory before and after the execution of the program lines shown in Exercise 1.
3. Show the output displayed by the lines below if the value of exp is 11.

```
printf("My name is ");
printf("Jane Doe.");
printf("\n");
printf("I live in ");
printf("Ann Arbor, MI\n");
printf("and I have %d years ", exp);
printf("of programming experience.\n");
```

4. How could you modify the code in Exercise 3 so that a blank line would be displayed between the two sentences?

Programming

1. Write a statement that asks the user to type three integers and another statement that stores the three user responses into first, second, and third.
2. Write a statement that displays the value of the type double number x as indicated in the line below.

```
The value of x is _____
```

3. Write a program that will ask the user to enter the radius of a circle and that will compute and display the circle's area and circumference. Use the formulas

$$area = PI * radius * radius$$
$$circumference = 2 * PI * radius$$

where `PI` is the constant macro meaning 3.14159.

2.5 GENERAL FORM OF C PROGRAMS

The programs shown so far in this text have the general form described in Fig. 2.3. Each program begins with preprocessor directives that serve to provide definitions of functions from standard libraries and definitions of necessary program constants. Examples of such directives are `#include` and `#define.` Unlike the declarations and executable statements of the main function body, the preprocessor directives we have seen do not end in semicolons. A simple C program places the prototype of the main function after the preprocessor directives. Then, an open curly brace (`{`) signals the beginning of the main function body. Within this body, we first see the declarations of all the variables to be used by the main function. These variables are followed by the statements that are translated into machine language and are eventually executed. The statements we have looked at so far perform computations or input/output operations. The end of the main function body is marked by a closing curly brace (`}`).

As shown in Fig. 2.1 and Fig. 2.2, a C statement can extend over more than one line. For example, in the statement that follows from Fig. 2.1, the declaration of the variables `miles` and `kms` extends over two lines so that comments describing the meanings of the variables can be inserted.

```
double miles, /* distance in miles                */
       kms;   /* equivalent distance in kilometers */
```

In this statement from Fig. 2.2, a call to the function `printf` extends over two lines.

```
printf("Welcome, %c%c%c. %d is a great year to study C!\n",
       letter_1, letter_2, letter_3, year);
```

Notice that in both of these examples, the statement is split at a point where there is a natural break, and the indentation of the second part of the statement helps the reader see the structure of the statement. Although ANSI C provides a means of splitting a statement even in the middle of an identifier, a reserved word, a number, or a string, we recommend against this practice since dividing a statement in mid-word makes the statement more difficult to read.

It is also possible to write more than one statement on a line. For example, the line

```
printf("Enter a letter> "); scanf("%c", &let_1);
```

contains a statement that displays a prompt message and a statement that gets the data requested. We recommend that you place only one statement on a line.

Program Style *Use of Blank Space*

The consistent and careful use of blank spaces can significantly enhance the style of a program. Blanks are needed to separate many parts of a C statement in much the same way that blanks are used to separate words in an English sentence. For example, a blank space is required to separate the data type name from the first variable name in a variable declaration. If this space were omitted—if we wrote `doublemiles` in Fig. 2.1 instead of `double miles`—the statement would appear to begin with the identifier `doublemiles`.

The compiler ignores extra blanks between words and symbols. You may insert space to improve the style and appearance of a program. In the examples in this book, we have adopted a style which calls for leaving a blank space after a comma and before and after operators such as `*`, `−`, `=`. We indent the body of the main function and use blank lines between sections of the program.

We take all of these measures for the sole purpose of improving the style—hence the clarity—of our programs. Stylistic issues have no effect whatever on the meaning of the program as far as the computer is concerned; however, they can make reading and understanding the program easier for people.

Be careful not to insert blank spaces where they do not belong. For example, a space is not allowed between the `/` and `*` characters when they form the sequence marking the opening (`/*`) or closing (`*/`) of a comment. Also, the identifier `MAXLEN` cannot be written as `MAX LEN`.

Comments in Programs

The programs in Fig. 2.1 and Fig. 2.2 contain some English phrases enclosed in slash-star and star-slash brackets; these phrases are *program comments*. Refer to these figures also to see how programmers use comments to make the program easier to understand. Comments describe the purpose of the program (the first comment line), the use of identifiers (the comments in the variable declarations), and the purpose of each major program step (the comments in the program body). Comments are an important part of the *documentation* of a program because they help others read and understand the program. The compiler, however, ignores comments; they are not translated into machine language.

As shown in Fig. 2.1, a comment can appear by itself on a program line, can be at the end of a line after a statement, or can be embedded in a statement. In the following variable declarations, the first comment is embedded in the declaration, and the second comment follows the declaration statement.

```
double miles, /* distance in miles                  */
       kms;   /* equivalent distance in kilometers   */
```

We will document the use of most variables in this way. The next displays describe the syntax and use of comments.

Syntax Display for a Program Comment

SYNTAX: /* *comment text* */

EXAMPLES: /* This is a one-line or partial-line comment */
```
            /*
             * This is a multiple-line comment in which the stars
             * not immediately preceded or followed by slashes have
             * no special syntactic significance, but simply help
             * the comment to stand out as a block. This style is
             * often used to document the purpose of a program.
             */
```

INTERPRETATION: A slash-star indicates the start of a *comment*; a star-slash indicates the end of a comment. Comments are listed with the program, but they are otherwise ignored by the C compiler. A comment may be put in a C program any place where a blank space would be valid.

NOTE: ANSI C does not permit the placement of one comment inside another.

Program Style   *Using Comments*

Comments make a program more readable by describing the purpose of the program and the use of each identifier. For example, the comment shown in the declaration

```
double miles, /* distance in miles                  */
```

describes the use of variable `miles`.

You should also place comments within the program body to describe the purpose of each section of the program. Generally, you will include one comment in the program body for each major algorithm step. A comment within the program body should describe what the step does rather than simply restate the step in English. For example, the comment

```
/* Convert the distance to kilometers. */
kms = KMS_PER_MILE * miles;
```

is more descriptive and, hence, preferable to

```
/* Multiply KMS_PER_MILE by miles and save the
    result in kms. */
kms = KMS_PER_MILE * miles;
```

Before you implement each step in the initial algorithm, you should write a comment that summarizes the purpose of the algorithm step.

Each program should begin with a documentation section that consists of a series of comments specifying

- the programmer's name
- the date of the current version
- a brief description of what the program does

If you write the program for a class assignment, you should also list the class identification and your instructor's name as shown.

```
/*
 * Programmer: William Bell    Date completed: May 9, 1993
 * Instructor: Janet Smith     Class: CIS61
 *
 * This program gets a value in miles and converts
 * it to kilometers.
 */
```

EXERCISES FOR SECTION 2.5

Self-Check

1. Explain what is wrong with the comments below.

```
/* This is a comment? *)
/* How about this one /* it seems like a comment
*/ doesn't it */
```

2. What is the purpose of including comments in a computer program?
3. Correct the syntax errors in the program below, and rewrite the program so that it follows our style conventions. What does each statement of your corrected program do? What output does it print?

```
/*
 * Compute and print the difference of two input values
 */

#include <stdio.h>

int
main(void) {int X, /* first input value */ x, /* second
   input value */
sum; /* sum of inputs */
scanf("%i%i"; X; x); X + x = sum;
printf("%d + %d = %d\n"; X; x; sum); return (0);}
```

2.6 DATA TYPES AND EXPRESSIONS

An *abstraction* is a model or simplification of a physical object. We frequently use abstractions in problem solving and programming. For example, in problem solving we sometimes make simplifying assumptions that enable us to solve a limited version of a more general problem. In programming, *abstraction* is the process of focusing on what we need to know, ignoring irrelevant details.

Data Type double

A *data type* is a set of values and a set of operations on those values. A *standard data type* in C is a data type that is predefined, such as char, double, int. In C, we use the standard data type double as an abstraction for the real numbers (in the mathematical sense). The data type double is an abstraction because it does not include all the real numbers. Some real numbers are too large or too small, and some real numbers cannot be represented precisely because of the finite size of a memory cell. However, we can certainly represent enough of the real numbers in C to carry out most of the computations we wish to perform with sufficient accuracy.

The normal arithmetic operators for real numbers (+, −, *, /) can be performed on type double objects in C where * means multiply. The assignment operator (=) is another operator that can be used with type double objects, and we can also use the standard I/O functions scanf and printf with type double objects.

Objects of a data type may be variables or constants. A type `double` constant is a number that contains a decimal point, an exponent, or both. The exponent is an uppercase or lowercase `'E'` followed by a positive or negative integer. To pronounce a constant containing an exponent, simply read the letter `'E'` as "times 10 to the power." Thus, `456.0E-2` means "456.0 times 10 to the power -2"; that is, 456.0×10^{-2} or 4.56. Examples of some constants of type `double` are shown in Table 2.3.

As shown by the last number in Table 2.3, `1.15E-3` means the same as 1.15×10^{-3} where the exponent -3 causes the decimal point to be moved left three digits. A positive exponent causes the decimal point to be moved to the right; the + sign may be omitted when the exponent is positive.

Numeric constants in C are non-negative numbers. Although it is perfectly legitimate to use a number like `-273.15` in a program, C views the minus sign as the negation operator rather than as a part of the constant.

Table 2.3   Constants of Type double (Real Numbers)

```
3.14159
0.005
12345.
15.0e-6     (value of 15.0 × 10⁻⁶ or 0.000015)
2.345E2     (value of 2.345 × 10² or 234.5)
.12e+6      (value of .12 × 10⁶ or 120000.)
1.15E-3     (value of 1.15 × 10⁻³ or 0.00115)
```

Data Type int

Another standard data type, or data abstraction, in C is type `int`, which is used to represent the integer numbers (for example, -77, 0, 999, +999). The data types `double` and `int` differ in one basic way: type `double` objects represent numbers with a decimal point and a fractional part; type `int` objects represent only whole numbers. For this reason, type `int` objects are more restricted in their use. We often use them to represent a count of items (for example, the number of children in a family) because a count must always be a whole number.

The data type of the object stored in a particular memory cell determines how the *bit pattern,* or *binary string,* in that cell is interpreted. For example, a bit pattern that represents a type `double` object is interpreted differently from a bit pattern that represents a type `int` object. However, we do not need to be concerned with this detail in order to use these data types in C. We can use arithmetic operators and the assignment operator with type `int` operands. When applied to integer operands, these operators, including the division operator (/), always give an integer result. An additional operator, the remainder operator (%), can be used with integer operands to find the remainder of longhand division. We will discuss the division and remainder operators in the next subsection.

Operators / and %

When applied to two positive integers, the division operator (/) computes the integral part of the result of dividing its first operand by its second. For example, the value of 7.0 / 2.0 is 3.5, but the value of 7 / 2 is the integral part of this result, 3. Similarly, the value of 299.0 / 100.0 is 2.99, but the value of 299 / 100 is the integral part of this result, 2. If the / operator is used with a negative and a positive integer, the result may vary from one C implementation to another. For this reason, you should avoid using division with negative integers. The / operation is undefined when the divisor (the second operand) is 0. Table 2.4 shows some examples of the integer division.

Table 2.4   Results of Integer Division

```
3 / 15 = 0      18 / 3 = 6
15 / 3 = 5      16 / −3 varies
16 / 3 = 5       0 / 4 = 0
17 / 3 = 5       4 / 0 is undefined
```

Compare the values of the expressions 6.0 / 2.0 and 6 / 2. The value of 6.0 / 2.0 is the real number 3.0; the value of 6 / 2 is the integer 3. Although these two results are equivalent in a mathematical sense, they are not the same in C and are stored in memory as different binary strings.

The remainder operator (%) returns the *integer remainder* of the result of dividing its first operand by its second. For example, the value of 7 % 2 is 1 because the integer remainder is 1.

```
     7 / 2                    299 / 100
       |                          |
       ↓                          ↓
       3                          2
    2 ⎯7                    100 ⎯299
       6                        200
      ⎯⎯                        ⎯⎯⎯
       1 ←— 7 % 2                99 ←— 299 % 100
```

The diagram on the left shows the effect of dividing 7 by 2; that is, we get a quotient of 3 (7 / 2) and a remainder of 1 (7 % 2). The diagram on the right shows that 299 % 100 is 99 because we get a remainder of 99 when we divide 299 by 100.

The magnitude of m % n must always be less than the divisor n, so if m is positive, the value of m % 100 must be between 0 and 99. The % operation is undefined when n is zero and varies from one implementation to another if n is negative. Table 2.5 shows some examples of the % operator.

Table 2.5 The % Operator

```
3 % 5 = 3     5 % 3 = 2
4 % 5 = 4     5 % 4 = 1
5 % 5 = 0     15 % 5 = 0
6 % 5 = 1     15 % 6 = 3
7 % 5 = 2     15 % -7 varies
8 % 5 = 3     15 % 0 is undefined
```

The formula

$$m \text{ equals } (m / n) * n + (m \% n)$$

defines the relationship between the operators / and % for an integer dividend of m and an integer divisor of n. We can see that this formula holds for the two problems discussed earlier by plugging in values for m, n, m / n, and m % n. In the first example that follows, m is 7 and n is 2; in the second, m is 299 and n is 100.

```
7    equals (7 / 2) * 2 + (7 % 2)
     equals   3    * 2 +   1

299  equals (299 / 100) * 100 + (299 % 100)
     equals     2       * 100 +    99
```

Type of an Expression

The data type of each variable must be specified in its declaration, but how does C determine the data type of an expression? The data type of an expression depends on the type of its operands. Let's consider the types of expressions involving operands that are integers of type `int` or reals of type `double`.[†] For example, the expression

```
ace + bandage
```

is type `int` if both `ace` and `bandage` are type `int`; otherwise, it is type `double`. In general, an expression of the form

```
ace arithmetic_operator bandage
```

is of type `int` if *both* `ace` and `bandage` are of type `int`; otherwise, it is of type `double`.

   An expression that has operands of both type `int` and type `double` is called a *mixed-type expression*. The data type of such a mixed-type expression will be `double`.

Mixed-type Assignment Statement

When an assignment statement is executed, the expression is first evaluated; then the result is assigned to the variable listed to the left of the assignment operator (=). Either a type `double` or a type `int` expression may be assigned to a type `double` variable, so if m and n are type `int` and p, x, and y are type `double`, all assignment statements in the examples that follow are valid.

```
m = 3;
n = 2;
p = 2.0;
x = m / p;
y = m / n;
```

m	n	p	x	y
3	2	2.0	1.5	1.0

In a mixed-type assignment such as

```
y = m / n;
```

a common error is to assume that the type of y (the variable being assigned) causes the expression to be evaluated as if its operands were that type too.

[†] C defines additional integer and real data types besides `int` and `double`, but these two types are adequate for representing numbers in the great majority of programming applications.

Remember, the expression is evaluated before the assignment is made, and the type of the variable being assigned has no effect whatsoever on the expression value. The expression m / n evaluates to the integer 1. This value is converted to type double (1.0) before it is stored in y.

Assignment of a type double expression to a type int variable causes the fractional part of the expression to be lost since it cannot be represented in the integer variable. The expression in the assignment statements

```
x = 9 * 0.5;
n = 9 * 0.5;
```

evaluates to the real number 4.5. If x is of type double, the number 4.5 is stored in x, as expected. If n is of type int, only the integral part of the expression value is stored in n as shown.

Expressions with Multiple Operators

In our programs so far, most expressions have involved a single arithmetic operator; however, expressions with multiple operators are common in C. Expressions can include both unary and binary operators. *Unary operators* take only one operand. In these expressions, we see the unary negation (−) and plus (+) operators.

```
x = -y;
p = +x * y;
```

Binary operators require two operands. When + and − are used to represent addition and subtraction, they are binary operators.

```
x = y + z;
z = y - x;
```

To understand and write expressions with multiple operators, we must know the C rules for evaluating expressions. For example, in the expression x + y / z, is + performed before / or is + performed after /? Is the expression x / y * z evaluated as (x / y) * z or as x / (y * z)? Verify for yourself that the order of evaluation does make a difference by substituting some simple values for x, y, and z. In both of these expressions, the / operator is evaluated first; the reasons are explained in the C rules for evaluation of arithmetic expressions which follow. These rules are based on standard algebraic rules.

Rules for Evaluation of Arithmetic Expressions

a. All parenthesized subexpressions must be evaluated separately. Nested parenthesized subexpressions must be evaluated inside out, with the innermost subexpression evaluated first.
b. *The operator precedence rule.* Operators in the same subexpression are evaluated in the following order:

```
unary +, -      first
*, /, %         next
binary +, -     last
```

c. *The associativity rule.* Unary operators in the same subexpression and at the same precedence level (such as + and –) are evaluated right to left (*right associativity*). Binary operators in the same subexpression and at the same precedence level (such as + and –) are evaluated left to right (*left associativity*).

Knowledge of these rules will help you understand how C evaluates expressions. Use parentheses as needed to specify the order of evaluation. Often, it is a good idea to use extra parentheses to clearly document the order of operator evaluation in complicated expressions. For example, the expression

```
x * y * z + a / b - c * d
```

can be written using parentheses in the more readable form

```
(x * y * z) + (a / b) - (c * d)
```

 **EXAMPLE 2.4**   The formula for the area of a circle

$$a = \pi \times r^2$$

may be written in C as

```
area = PI * radius * radius
```

where the meaning of the constant macro `PI` is 3.14159. Figure 2.10 shows the *evaluation tree* for this formula. In this tree, the arrows connect each operand

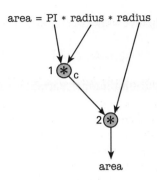

**Figure 2.10
Evaluation Tree
for** `area = PI *
radius * radius`

with its operator. The order of operator evaluation is shown by the number to the
left of each operator; the rules that apply are shown to the right.

In Fig. 2.11, we see a step-by-step evaluation of the same expression for a
`radius` value of 2.0. You may want to use a similar notation when computing
by hand the value of an expression with multiple operators.

**Figure 2.11
Step-by-step
Expression
Evaluation**

```
area   =   PI    *   radius   *   radius
          3.14159     2.0          2.0
              6.28318
                          12.56636
```

EXAMPLE 2.5

The formula for the average velocity, v, of a particle traveling on a line between
points p_1 and p_2 in time t_1 to t_2 is

$$v = \frac{p_2 - p_1}{t_2 - t_1}$$

This formula can be written and evaluated in C as shown in Fig. 2.12.

**Figure 2.12
Evaluation Tree
and Step-by-
step Evaluation
for** `v = (p2 -
p1) / (t2 - t1)`

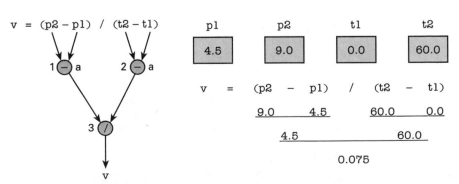

EXAMPLE 2.6 Consider the expression

```
z - (a + b / 2) + w * -y
```

containing integer variables only. The parenthesized subexpression

```
(a + b / 2)
```

is evaluated first (see Rules for Evaluation of Arithmetic Expressions, rule a) beginning with `b / 2` (rule b). Once the value of `b / 2` is determined, it can be added to `a` to obtain the value of `(a + b / 2)`. Next, `y` is negated (rule b). The multiplication operation can now be performed (rule b) and the value for `w * -y` is determined. Then, the value of `(a + b / 2)` is subtracted from `z` (rule c). Finally, this result is added to `w * -y`. The evaluation tree and step-by-step evaluation for this expression are shown in Fig. 2.13.

Figure 2.13
Evaluation Tree
and Step-by-
step Evaluation
for z - (a + b
/ 2) + w * -y

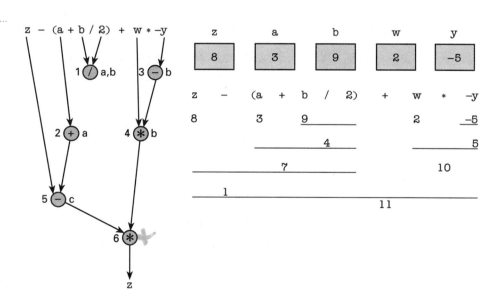

Writing Mathematical Formulas in C

The two problem areas in writing a mathematical formula in C concern multiplication and division. Multiplication can often be implied in a mathematical formula by writing the two items to be multiplied next to each other; for example, $a = bc$. In C, however, you must always use the $*$ operator to indicate multiplication, as in

```
a = b * c;
```

Another difficulty arises in formulas involving division. We normally write the numerator and denominator on separate lines, as in

$$m = \frac{y - b}{x - a}$$

In C, however, all assignment statements must be written in a linear form. Consequently, parentheses are often needed to mark the numerator and the denominator so as to clearly indicate the correct order of evaluation of the operators in the expression. The formula just shown would be written in C as

```
m = (y - b) / (x - a)
```

EXAMPLE 2.7

This example illustrates how several mathematical formulas can be written in C.

Mathematical Formula	C Expression
1. $b^2 - 4ac$	`b * b - 4 * a * c`
2. $a + b - c$	`a + b - c`
3. $\dfrac{a + b}{c + d}$	`(a + b) / (c + d)`
4. $\dfrac{1}{1 + x^2}$	`1 / (1 + x * x)`
5. $a \times -(b + c)$	`a * -(b + c)`

The points illustrated are summarized as follows:

- Always specify multiplication explicitly by using the operator $*$ where needed (1).
- Use parentheses when required to control the order of operator evaluation (3, 4).
- Two arithmetic operators can be written in succession if the second is a unary operator (5).

Data Type char

Another standard data type in C is type `char`. We have already seen that type `char` variables can be used to store any single character value (see Fig. 2.2). A type char literal must be enclosed in single quotes (for example, 'A'); however, you don't use quotes when you enter character data at a terminal. When the scanf function is called to get an input value for a type char variable, the next character you enter at the terminal is stored in that variable. You enter the blank character by pressing the space bar; in a program the blank character is written as the literal ' '.

EXAMPLE 2.8

First, the program in Fig. 2.14 gets and echoes three characters entered at the keyboard. Next, it prints them in reverse order enclosed in asterisks. Each character is stored in a variable of type char; the character value '*' is associated with the constant macro BORDER.

The line

```
printf("%c%c%c%c%c\n", BORDER, third, second,
        first, BORDER);
```

Figure 2.14   Program for Example 2.8

```
/*
 * Gets three input characters and displays them in
 * reverse order
 */

#include <stdio.h>
#define BORDER '*'

int
main(void)
{
      char first, second, third; /* 3 characters */

      printf("Enter 3 characters> ");
      scanf("%c%c%c", &first, &second, &third);
      printf("%c%c%c%c%c\n", BORDER, third, second,
              first, BORDER);

      return (0);
}

Enter 3 characters> J H
*H J*
```

displays an asterisk, the three characters in reverse order, and another asterisk. As shown in the program output, each character value is printed in a single print position. The second character entered in the sample run of Fig. 2.14 is a blank. ⬅

In Fig. 2.14, the string literal `"Enter 3 characters> "` is displayed as a prompt. In this example and in earlier examples, we use strings as prompts and to clarify program output. Only single characters, not strings, can be stored in type `char` variables; we will see how to process strings later in the text.

EXERCISES FOR SECTION 2.6

Self-Check

1. Indicate which of the following values are legal constants in C and which are not. Identify the data type of each valid constant value.

15	'XYZ'	'*'	$	25.123	15.
-999	.123	'x'	'9'	'-5'	32e-4

2. a. Evaluate the following expressions with 7 and 22 as operands.

   ```
   22 / 7      7 / 22      22 % 7      7 % 22
   ```

   Repeat this exercise for the following pairs of integers:

   b. 15, 16   c. 3, 23   d. -3, 16

3. Do a step-by-step evaluation of the expressions that follow if the value of `celsius` is 3 and `salary` is 12400.00.

   ```
   1.8 * celsius + 32.0
   (salary - 5000.00) * 0.20 + 1425.00
   ```

4. Given the constants and variable declarations

   ```
   #define PI 3.14159
   #define MAX_I 1000
   . . .
   double x, y;
   int a, b, i;
   ```

   indicate which of the following statements are valid, and find the value stored by each valid statement. Also indicate which are invalid and why.

Assume that a is 3, b is 4, and y is -1.0.

a. i = a % b;   j. i = (MAX_I - 990) / a;
b. i = (989 - MAX_I) / a;   k. x = a / y;
c. i = b % a;   l. i = PI * a;
d. x = PI * y;   m. x = PI / y;
e. i = a / -b;   n. x = b / a;
f. x = a / b;   o. i = (MAX_I - 990) % a;
g. x = a % (a / b);   p. i = a % 0;
h. i = b / 0;   q. i = a % (MAX_I - 990);
i. i = a % (990 - MAX_I);

5. What values are assigned by the legal statements in Exercise 4, assuming a is 5, b is 2, and y is 2.0?

6. Assume that you have the following variable declarations:

```
int     color, lime, straw, yellow, red, orange;
double black, white, green, blue, purple, crayon;
```

Evaluate each of the statements below using the following values: color is 2, black is 2.5, crayon is -1.3, straw is 1, red is 3, purple is 0.3E+1.

a. white = color * 2.5 / purple;
b. green = color / purple;
c. orange = color / red;
d. blue = (color + straw) / (crayon + 0.3);
e. lime = red / color + red % color;
f. purple = straw / red * color;

7. Let a, b, c, and x be the names of four type double variables; and let i, j, and k be the names of three type int variables. Each of the following statements contains one or more violations of the rules for forming arithmetic expressions. Rewrite each statement so that it is consistent with these rules.

a. x = 4.0 a * c;   d. k = 3(i + j);
b. a = ac;   e. x = 5a + bc;
c. i = 5j3;

Programming

1. Write an assignment statement that might be used to implement the following

equation in C.

$$q = \frac{kA(T_1 - T_2)}{L}$$

2. Write a program that stores the values `'X'`, `'0'`, `1.345E10`, and `35` in separate memory cells. Your program should get the first three values as input data, but use an assignment statement to store the last value.

2.7 FORMATTING NUMBERS IN PROGRAM OUTPUT

In the sample program output shown so far, all numbers were printed in C's default notation. Consequently, we had limited control over the appearance or format of each output line. In this section, we will learn how to specify the format of an output item.

Formatting Values of Type int

Specifying the format of an integer value displayed by a C program is fairly easy. All that we need to do is add a number between the `%` and the `d` of the `%d` placeholder for the integer in the `printf` format string. This number specifies how many columns are to be used for the display of digits, the *field width*. For example, the statement

```
printf("Results: %3d meters = %4d ft. %2d in.\n",
        meters, feet, inches);
```

indicates that 3 columns will be used to display the value of the first variable in the print list (`meters`), 4 columns will be used for the second variable (`feet`), and 2 columns will be used for the third (`inches`), a variable that in this context will always have a value between 0 and 11. If `meters` is 21, `feet` is 68, and `inches` is 11, the program output will be

```
Results:  21 meters =   68 ft. 11 in.
```

Note that in this line there is one extra space before the value of `meters` (21), and there are two extra spaces before the value of `feet` (68). The reason is that the placeholder for `meters` (`%3d`) allows space for 3 digits to be printed. Because the value of `meters` is between 10 and 99, its two digits are displayed *right-justified,* preceded by one blank space. Because the placeholder for `feet` (`%4d`) allows room for 4 digits, printing its two-digit value right-justified

Table 2.6   Printing 234 and −234 Using Different Placeholders

Value	Placeholder	Printed Output
234	%4d	#234
234	%5d	##234
234	%6d	###234
−234	%4d	−234
−234	%5d	#−234
−234	%6d	##−234
234	%2d	234
234	%1d	234
−234	%2d	−234

leaves two extra blank spaces. We can use the placeholder %2d to display any integer output value between −9 and 99. The placeholder %4d works for values in the range −999 to 9999. For negative numbers, the minus sign is included in the count of digits displayed.

Table 2.6 shows how two integer values are printed using different format string placeholders. The character # represents a blank character. The last three lines show that when a field width that is too small is used, the number is printed with no blanks preceding it, and the number of print columns used varies with the size of the number (i.e., the display field expands as needed).

Formatting Values of Type double

To describe the format specification for a value of type `double`, we must indicate both the total field width needed and the number of decimal places desired. The total field width should be large enough to accommodate all digits, both those before and those after the decimal point. There will be at least one digit before the decimal point since a zero is printed as the whole-number part of fractions that are less than 1.0 and greater than −1.0. We should also leave a display column for the decimal point and, for negative numbers, a column for the minus sign. The form of the necessary format string placeholder is %$n.m$f where n is a number representing the total field width, and m is the desired number of decimal places.

If x is a type `double` variable whose value will be between −99.99 and 999.99, we could use the placeholder %6.2f to display the value of x accurate to two decimal places. Table 2.7 shows different values of x displayed using this format specification. The values shown in Table 2.7 are displayed right-justified in

Table 2.7 Displaying x Using Format String Placeholder %6.2f

x	Output Displayed
−99.42	−99.42
0.123	##0.12
−9.536	#−9.54
−25.554	−25.55
99.999	100.00
999.4	999.40

6 columns, and all values are rounded to two decimal places. When you round to two decimal places, if the third digit of the value's fractional part is 5 or greater, the second digit is incremented by 1 (−9.536 becomes −9.54). Otherwise, the digits after the second digit in the fraction are simply dropped (−25.554 becomes −25.55).

Table 2.8 shows some values that were printed using other placeholders. As shown in the table, it is legal to omit the total field width in the format string placeholder, specifying only the number of decimal places. Such a placeholder has the form %.*m*f, and it causes the value to be printed with no leading blanks.

Table 2.8 Formatting Values of Type double

Value	Placeholder	Printed Output
3.14159	%5.2f	#3.14
3.14159	%4.2f	3.14
3.14159	%3.2f	3.14
3.14159	%5.1f	##3.1
3.14159	%5.3f	3.142
3.14159	%8.5f	#3.14159
3.14159	%.4f	3.1416
0.1234	%4.2f	0.12
−0.006	%4.2f	−0.01
−0.006	%.4f	−0.0060
−0.006	%8.5f	−0.00600
−0.006	%8.3f	##−0.006

Program Style   *Eliminating Leading Blanks*

As shown in Tables 2.6–2.8, a value whose whole-number part requires fewer display columns than are specified by the format field width is displayed with leading blanks. To eliminate extra leading blanks, omit the field width from the format string placeholder. The simple placeholder `%d` will cause an integer value to be displayed with no leading blanks. A placeholder of the form `%.`*m*`f` has the same effect for values of type `double`, and this placeholder still allows you to choose the number of decimal places you wish.

EXERCISES FOR SECTION 2.7

Self-Check

1. Correct the statement

   ```
   printf("Salary is %2.10f\n", salary);
   ```

2. Show how the value −15.564 would be printed using the formats `%8.4f`, `%8.3f`, `%8.2f`, `%8.1f`, `%8.0f`, `%.2f`.
3. Assuming `x` (type `double`) is `12.335` and `i` (type `int`) is `100`, show the output lines for the following statements. For clarity, use the symbol # to denote a blank space.

   ```
   printf("x is %6.2f  i is %4d\n", x, i);
   printf("i is %d\n", i);
   printf("x is %.1f\n", x);
   ```

Programming

1. If the variables a, b, and c are `504`, `302.558`, and `−12.31`, respectively, write a statement that will display the following line (for clarity, a # denotes a blank space).

   ```
   ##504#####302.56####-12.3
   ```

2.8 INTERACTIVE MODE, BATCH MODE, AND DATA FILES

In Section 1.7, we discussed the two basic modes of computer operation: batch and interactive. The programs that we have written so far are intended to be run in *interactive mode*. Our programs have included prompting messages so the program user can interact with the program and can enter data while the program is executing.

Input Redirection

Figure 2.15 shows the miles-to-kilometers conversion program rewritten as a batch program. In Fig. 2.15, we assume that the standard input device is associated with a batch data file instead of with the keyboard. In most systems, this association can be accomplished relatively easily through *input-output redirection* using operating system commands. For example, in the UNIX® and MS-DOS® operating systems, you can instruct your program to take its input from file `mydata` instead of from the keyboard by placing the symbols `<mydata` at the end of the command line that causes your compiled and linked program to execute. If you normally used the command line

```
metric
```

Figure 2.15   Batch Version of Miles-to-Kilometers Conversion Program

```
/* Converts distances from miles to kilometers.    */

#include <stdio.h>    /* printf, scanf definitions */
#define KMS_PER_MILE 1.609 /* conversion constant */

int
main(void)
{
    double miles, /* distance in miles */
           kms; /* equivalent distance in kilometers */

    /* Get the distance in miles. */
    scanf("%lf", &miles);
    printf("The distance in miles is %.2f.\n", miles);

    /* Convert the distance to kilometers. */
    kms = KMS_PER_MILE * miles;

    /* Display the distance in kilometers. */
    printf("That equals %.2f kilometers.\n", kms);

    return (0);
}

The distance in miles is 112.00.
That equals 180.21 kilometers.
```

to execute this program, your new command line would be

```
metric <mydata
```

Program Style   *Echo Prints versus Prompts*

In Fig. 2.15, the statement

```
scanf("%lf", &miles);
```

gets a value for `miles` from the first (and only) line of the data file. Because the program input comes from a data file, there is no need to precede this statement with a prompting message. Instead, we follow the call to `scanf` with the statement

```
printf("The distance in miles is %.2f.\n", miles);
```

This statement *echo prints* or displays the value just stored in `miles` and provides a record of the data manipulated by the program. Without it, we would have no easy way of knowing what value `scanf` obtained for `miles`. Whenever you convert an interactive program to a batch program, make sure you replace each prompt with an echo print that follows the call to `scanf`.

Output Redirection

You can also redirect program output to a disk file instead of to the screen. Then you can send the output file to the printer (using an operating system command) to obtain a hard copy of the program output. In UNIX or MS-DOS, use the symbols `>myoutput` to redirect output from the screen to file `myoutput`. These symbols should also be placed on the command line that causes your program to execute. The command line

```
metric >myoutput
```

executes the compiled and linked code for program `metric`, taking program input from the keyboard and writing program output to file `myoutput`. However, interacting with the running program will be difficult because all program output, including any prompting messages, will be sent to the output file. It would be better to use the command line

```
metric <mydata >myoutput
```

which takes program input from data file `mydata` and sends program output to output file `myoutput.`

If the operating system you are using does not provide input-output redirection, you can still create a program that runs in batch mode by handling the input and output files directly in the program. You can read about this type of file manipulation in Section 12.3.

EXERCISES FOR SECTION 2.8

Self-Check

1. Explain the difference in placement of calls to `printf` used to display prompts and calls to `printf` used to echo data. Which calls are used in interactive programs, and which are used in batch programs?
2. How is input data provided to an interactive program? How is input data provided to a batch program?

Programming

1. Rewrite the program in Fig. 2.14 as a batch program; assume that the data file will be made accessible through input redirection. Improve the program's output by printing an explanatory label (`"Reversed, this is "`) on the results.

2.9 COMMON PROGRAMMING ERRORS

One of the first things you will discover in writing programs is that a program very rarely runs correctly the first time that it is submitted. Murphy's Law—"If something can go wrong, it will"—seems to be written with the computer programmer or programming student in mind. In fact, errors are so common that they have their own special name (*bugs*), and the process of correcting them is called *debugging a program.* To alert you to potential problems, we will provide at the end of each chapter a section on common errors.

When the compiler detects an error, the computer will display an *error message,* which indicates that you have made a mistake and what the cause of the error might be. Unfortunately, error messages are often difficult to interpret and are sometimes misleading. However, as you gain some experience, you will become more proficient at understanding them.

Two basic categories of error messages will occur: syntax error messages and run-time error messages. *Syntax errors,* or *compilation errors,* are detected and displayed by the compiler as it attempts to translate your program. If a statement has a syntax error, it cannot be translated and your program will not be executed.

Run-time errors are detected by the computer and are displayed during execution of a program. A run-time error occurs when the program directs the computer to perform an illegal operation, such as dividing a number by zero. When a run-time error occurs, the computer will stop executing your program and will print a diagnostic message that indicates the line where the error was detected.

Syntax Errors

Figure 2.16 shows a *compiler listing* of the miles-to-kilometers conversion program that is a listing produced by the compiler during program translation. The listing shows each line of the source program (preceded by a line number) and displays any syntax errors detected by the compiler. The errors are indicated by lines in the program listing that begin with five asterisks. The program contains the following syntax errors:

- missing semicolon at the end of the variable declaration (in line 271)
- undeclared variable miles (detected in lines 275 and 278)
- last comment is not closed because of blank in * / close-comment sequence (in line 280)

The actual format of the listing and the error messages produced by your compiler may differ from the format in Fig. 2.16. Indeed, many C compilers do not produce a listing at all, but merely display error messages. In this listing, whenever an error is detected, the compiler prints a line starting with five asterisks in which the error message is displayed. You probably have already noticed that the line in which an error is detected is not always the line in which the programmer's mistake occurred. Also, you see that the compiler attempts to correct errors wherever it can. Look at line 271 in the listing. You probably noticed immediately the semicolon missing at the end of the declaration. However, the compiler cannot be sure that this semicolon is missing until it processes the `printf` symbol on line 274. Because the `printf` is not a comma or a semicolon, the compiler then knows that the variable declaration statement begun on line 271 is not being continued to another line.

We see several cases in this listing where one mistake of the programmer leads to the generation of multiple error messages. For example, our not declaring the variable `miles` causes an error message to be printed each time `miles` is used in the program. This message would also occur if we remembered to declare `miles` but mistyped it (perhaps as `milles`) in the declaration statement. The fact that `miles` is not declared as a variable is also the cause of the second error message on line 275. Because the address-of operator must have a

Figure 2.16   Compiler Listing of a Program with Syntax Errors

```
  1    /* Converts distances from miles to kilometers. */
  2
  3    #include <stdio.h>              /* printf, scanf definitions */
266    #define KMS PER MILE 1.609 /* conversion constant        */
267
268    int
269    main(void)
270    {
271          double kms
272
273          /* Get the distance in miles. */
274          printf("Enter the distance in miles> ");
***** Semicolon added at the end of the previous source line

275          scanf("%lf", &miles);
***** Identifier "miles" is not declared within this scope
***** Invalid operand of address-of operator

276
277          /* Convert the distance to kilometers. */
278          kms = KMS_PER_MILE * miles;
***** Identifier "miles" is not declared within this scope

279
280          /* Display the distance in kilometers. * /
281          printf("That equals %f kilometers.\n", kms);

282
283          return (0);
284    }
***** Unexpected end-of-file encountered in a comment
***** "}" inserted before end-of-file
```

variable as its operand, the fact that miles is not declared as a variable makes it an invalid operand.

Another case of one error causing multiple messages is seen in the messages caused by the mistyped close-comment character sequence. Since any text is valid inside a comment, the compiler is unaware that there is a problem until the point when it comes to the end of the source file without having encountered a } to end the program! After complaining about this unexpected turn of events (see line following line 284), it does what it can to correct the situation by closing the comment at the end of the source file text and adding a } to end the program properly. Mistyping a close-comment sequence can cause errors that are very difficult to find. If the comment that is not correctly closed is in the middle of a program, the compiler will simply continue to view source lines as comment text until it comes to the */ that closes the *next* comment. When you begin getting error messages that make you think your compiler isn't seeing part of your program, recheck your comments carefully. In the worst case, the executable statements that the compiler is viewing as comments may not affect the syntax of your program at all—then the program will simply run incorrectly. Mistyping the open-comment sequence /* will make the compiler attempt to process the comment as a C statement, causing a syntax error.

Your strategy for correcting syntax errors should take into account the fact that one error can lead to many error messages. It is often a good idea to concentrate on correcting the errors in the declaration part of a program first. Then recompile the program before you attempt to fix other errors. Many of the other error messages will disappear once the declarations are correct.

Syntax errors are often caused by the improper use of quotation marks with format strings. Make sure that you always use a quote (") to begin and end a string.

Run-time Errors

Figure 2.17 shows an example of a run-time error. The program compiles successfully but cannot run to completion if the first integer entered is greater than the second. In this case, integer division causes the value assigned to `temp` in line 271 to be zero. Using `temp` as a divisor in line 272 causes the `divide by zero` error shown.

Undetected Errors and lint

Many execution errors may not prevent a C program from running to completion, but they may simply lead to incorrect results. Therefore it is essential that you predict the results your program should produce and verify that the actual output is correct. A very common source of incorrect results in C programs is the input of a mixture of character and numeric data. Errors can be avoided if the programmer always keeps in mind `scanf`'s different treatment of the `%c` placeholder on the one hand, and of the `%d` and `%lf` placeholders on the other. We noted that `scanf` first skips any blanks and carriage returns in the input when a numeric value is scanned. In contrast, `scanf` skips nothing when it

Figure 2.17   A Program with a Run-time Error

```
  1   #include <stdio.h>
262
263   int
264   main(void)
265   {
266         int    first, second;
267         double temp, ans;
268
269         printf("Enter two integers> ");
270         scanf("%d%d", &first, &second);
271         temp = second / first;
272         ans = first / temp;
273         printf("The result is %.3f\n", ans);
274
275         return (0);
276   }
```

```
Enter two integers> 14 3
Arithmetic fault, divide by zero at line 272 of routine
    main
```

scans a character. Figure 2.18 shows what appears to be a minor revision of our welcoming message program from Fig. 2.2. We have merely reversed the order in which we ask for the nickname and year. However, the program in Fig. 2.18 prints a garbled welcoming message.

Figure 2.19 shows the status of memory at the time of the final call to printf. The value of year is correct, but the three characters stored are not 'B', 'o', 'b', but '\n', 'B', and 'o'. The '\n' in letter_1 is the character that results from the user's pressing the <return> key after entering the number 1993. The scan of 1993 stopped at this character, so it was the first character processed by the statement

```
scanf("%c%c%c", &letter_1, &letter_2, &letter_3);
```

The character 'b' was never scanned.

One way to repair the welcome message program would be to declare an additional character variable and to explicitly scan the extra character.

```
scanf("%c%c%c%c", &extra, &letter_1, &letter_2,
      &letter_3);
```

Figure 2.18   Program with Incorrect Results Due to Character and Numeric Scanning Problem

```
/*
 * Incorrect revision of welcoming message program
 */
#include <stdio.h> /* printf, scanf definitions */

int
main(void)
{
      char letter_1, letter_2, letter_3; /* three letters */
      int  year; /* current year */

      printf("Enter the current year and press return> ");
      scanf("%d", &year);
      printf("Enter a 3-letter nickname and press return> ");
      scanf("%c%c%c", &letter_1, &letter_2, &letter_3);
      printf("Welcome, %c%c%c. %d is a great year to study C!\n",
            letter_1, letter_2, letter_3, year);

      return (0);
}
Enter the current year and press return> 1993
Enter a 3 letter nickname and press return> Bob
Welcome,
Bo. 1993 is a great year to study C!
```

Figure 2.20 shows another error that does not cause the program to abort with a run-time error message. The programmer has left out the & (address-of) operators on the variables in the call to scanf. Because scanf does not know where to find first and second, it is unable to store in them the values entered by the user. In this instance, the program runs to completion using whatever "garbage" values were originally in the memory locations named first and second.

**Figure 2.19
Memory
Contents during
Execution of
Faulty Welcome
Message
Program**

letter_1	\n
letter_2	B
letter_3	o
year	1993

Figure 2.20   A Program That Produces Incorrect Results Due to & Omission

```
#include <stdio.h>

int
main(void)
{
      int    first, second, sum;

      printf("Enter two integers> ");
      scanf("%d%d", first, second); /* ERROR!! should be &first, &second */
      sum = first + second;
      printf("%d + %d = %d\n", first, second, sum);

      return (0);
}

Enter two integers> 14   3
5971289 + 5971297 = 11942586
```

If a lint program is available on your computer system, you should learn how to use it. The C source code analyzer, lint, issues warnings for many constructs that, although legal, are suspicious. For example, in the program of Fig. 2.20, lint would observe that the variables first and second are used in an expression before their values are set. In a C program, one can make countless errors resulting in statements that generate no syntax or run-time error messages, so the rigorous checking of a lint program can be very helpful. Since lint complains about *legal* as well as *illegal* constructs, one does need to be aware that some of its warnings will mark statements that truly are correct and are exactly what the programmer intends.

As we indicated earlier, debugging a program can be very time-consuming. The best approach is to plan your programs carefully and to desk check them to eliminate bugs before running the program. If you are not sure of the syntax for a particular statement, look it up in the text or in the reference guide provided on the inside covers. If you follow this approach, you will save yourself much time and trouble.

CHAPTER REVIEW

In this chapter, you saw how to use the C programming language to perform some very fundamental operations. You learned how to instruct the computer to copy information into memory from the keyboard or a data file, to perform some simple computations, and to print the results of the computations. All of this was done using symbols (punctuation marks, variable names, and special operators such as *, −, and +) that are familiar, easy to remember, and easy to use. You do not have to know very much about your computer in order to understand and use the basics of C.

The remainder of this text introduces more features of the C language and provides rules for using these features. You must remember throughout that, unlike the rules of English, the rules of C are precise and allow no exceptions. The compiler will be unable to translate C instructions that violate these rules. Remember to declare every identifier used as a variable and to end program statements with semicolons.

New C Constructs

Table 2.9 describes the new C constructs introduced in this chapter.

Table 2.9 Summary of New C Constructs

Construct	Effect
#include directive	
`#include <stdio.h>`	Tells the preprocessor to give the program access to definitions from the standard I/O library. These include definitions of the `printf` and `scanf` functions.
#define directive for naming constant macros	
`#define PI 3.14159` `#define STAR '*'`	Tells the preprocessor to use `3.14159` as the definition of the name `PI` and `'*'` as the meaning of the identifier `STAR`.
main function prototype	
`int` `main(void)`	Marks the start of the function where program execution begins.
variable declaration	
`double pct, wt;` `int    high, mid, low;`	Allocates memory cells named `pct` and `wt` for storage of double-precision real numbers and cells named `high`, `mid`, and `low` for storage of integers.
assignment statement	
`distance = speed * time;`	Stores the product of `speed` and `time` as the value of the variable `distance`.

(continued)

Table 2.9 *(continued)*

Construct	Effect
call to scanf function	
`scanf("%lf%d", &pct,` `        &high);`	Copies input data into the type `double` variable `pct` and the type `int` variable `high`.
call to printf function	

`printf`
` ("Percentage is %.3f\n",`
` pct);`
	Displays a line with the string `"Percentage is"` followed by the value of `pct` rounded to three decimal places.

return statement	
`return (0);`	Final statement of function `main`.

QUICK-CHECK EXERCISES

1. What value is assigned to the type `double` variable `x` by the statement

   ```
   x = 25.0 * 3.0 / 2.5;
   ```

2. What value is assigned to `x` by the following statement, assuming `x` is `10.0`?

   ```
   x = x - 20.0;
   ```

3. Show the exact form of the output line displayed when `x` is `3.456`.

   ```
   printf("Three values of x are %4.1f*%5.2f*%.3f\n",
           x, x, x);
   ```

4. Show the exact form of the output line when `n` is `345`.

   ```
   printf("Three values of n are %4d*%5d*%d\n",
           n, n, n);
   ```

5. What data types would you use to represent the following items: number of children at school, a letter grade on an exam, the average number of school days a child is absent each year?

6. In which step of the software development method are the problem inputs and outputs identified?

7. If function `scanf` is getting two numbers from the same line of input, what characters should be used to separate them?
8. How does the computer determine how many data values to get from the input device when a `scanf` operation is performed?
9. In an interactive program, how does the program user know how many data values to enter when the `scanf` function is called?
10. The compiler listing shows which kind of errors (syntax or run-time)?

ANSWERS TO QUICK-CHECK EXERCISES

1. `30.0`
2. `-10.0`
3. `Three values of x are #3.5*#3.46*3.456` (# = 1 blank)
4. `Three values of n are #345*##345*345`
5. `int`, `char`, `double`
6. analysis
7. blanks
8. It depends on the number of placeholders in the format string.
9. from reading the prompt
10. syntax errors

REVIEW QUESTIONS

1. What type of information should be specified in the block comment at the very beginning of the program?
2. Put a check mark next to the variables that are syntactically correct.

```
____ income     ____ two fold
____ 1time      ____ c3po
____ int        ____ income#1
____ Tom's      ____ item
```

3. What is illegal about the following program fragment?

```
#include <stdio.h>
#define PI 3.14159

int
main(void)
```

```
        {
             double c, r;

             scanf("%lf%lf", c, r);
             PI = c / (2 * r * r);
             . . .
        }
```

4. Stylistically, which of the following identifiers would be good choices for names of constant macros?

```
   gravity   G   MAX_SPEED   Sphere_Size
```

5. Write the data requirements, necessary formulas, and algorithm for Programming Project 6 in the next section.
6. The average pH of citrus fruits is 2.2, and this value has been stored in the variable `avg_citrus_pH`. Provide a statement to display this information in a readable way.
7. List three standard data types of C.
8. Convert the program statements below to take input data and echo it in batch mode.

```
   printf("Enter two characters> ");
   scanf("%c%c", &c1, &c2);
   printf("Enter three integers separated by spaces> ");
   scanf("%d%d%d", &n, &m, &p);
```

9. Write an algorithm that allows for the input of an integer value, doubles it, subtracts 10, and displays the result.

PROGRAMMING PROJECTS

1. Write a program to convert a temperature in degrees Fahrenheit to degrees Celsius.

Data Requirements

Problem Input
```
int fahrenheit /* temperature in degrees Fahrenheit   */
```

> **Problem Output**
> ```
> double celsius /* temperature in degrees Celsius      */
> ```
>
> **Relevant Formula**
> *celsius* = 5/9 (*fahrenheit* − 32)

2. Write a program to take two numbers as input data and print their sum, their difference, their product and their quotient.

Data Requirements

> **Problem Inputs**
> ```
> double x, y        /* two items                       */
> ```
>
> **Problem Outputs**
> ```
> double sum         /* sum of x and y                  */
> double difference  /* difference of x and y           */
> double product     /* product of x and y              */
> double quotient    /* quotient of x divided by y      */
> ```

3. Write a program to take the weight (in pounds) of an object as input data; compute and print the object's weight in kilograms and grams. (Hint: One pound is equal to 0.453592 kilogram or 453.59237 grams.)
4. Write a program that prints your first initial as a block letter. (Hint: Use a 6 × 6 grid for the letter and print six strings. Each string should consist of asterisks [*] interspersed with blanks.)
5. If a human heart beats on the average of once a second, how many times does the heart beat in a lifetime of 78 years? (Use 365.25 for days in a year.) Rerun your program for a heart rate of 75 beats per minute.
6. Write a program that takes the length and width of a rectangular yard and the length and width of a rectangular house situated in the yard. Your program should compute the time required to cut the grass at the rate of two square feet a second.
7. Write a program that takes as input the numerators and denominators of two fractions. Your program should print the numerator and denominator of the fraction that represents the product of the two fractions. Also, print the percent equivalent of the resulting product.
8. Redo Project 7; this time compute the sum of the two fractions.
9. The Pythagorean theorem states that the sum of the squares of the sides of a right triangle is equal to the square of the hypotenuse. For example, if two sides of a right triangle have lengths of 3 and 4, then the hypotenuse must have a length of 5. Together the integers 3, 4, and 5 form a *Pythagorean triple*. There are an infinite number of such triples. Given two positive integers, *m* and *n*, where *m* > *n*, a Pythagorean triple can be generated by the

following formulas:

$$side1 = m^2 - n^2$$
$$side2 = 2mn$$
$$hypotenuse = m^2 + n^2$$

The triple (3, 4, 5) is generated by this formula when $m = 2$ and $n = 1$. Write a program that takes values for m and n as input and prints the values of the Pythagorean triple generated by the formulas above.

10. Write a program to compute the rate of growth, expressed as a percentage, of an insect population. Take as input the initial size of the population and its size one week later. Then predict the size of the population in yet another week, assuming that growth continues at the same rate.

CHAPTER 3

TOP-DOWN DESIGN WITH FUNCTIONS

3.1
The Art and Science of Problem Solving
Case Study: Finding the Area and
Circumference of a Circle

3.2
Extending a Problem Solution
Case Study: Quality Control in Manufacturing
Flat Washers

3.3
Structured Programming and Control Structures

3.4
Structure Charts
Case Study: Drawing Simple Diagrams

3.5
Functions

3.6
Displaying User Instructions

3.7
Functions as Program Building Blocks

3.8
Functions and Code Reuse

3.9
Common Programming Errors
Chapter Review

In this chapter, we continue our discussion of problem solving. We will focus on a methodology that helps us develop solutions by giving us direction when we are puzzled by questions such as "Where do I start?" and "So far, so good, but now what?" We investigate how a top-down approach to system design makes it possible for us to solve complex problems by breaking them into more manageable chunks.

We also show how to represent the relationship between a problem and its subproblems (the manageable chunks) using a structure chart. We introduce an important system structure, the function, that enables us to implement the solution to a subproblem as a separate program entity.

As we work with one of our major phases of program development, the coding of an algorithm, we discuss the importance of structured programming and why it is practiced. We describe the three types of control structures that are used in structured programming.

Finally, we discuss how the use of functions enables us to more easily reuse code that has already been tested and debugged in new programs. We introduce additional standard library functions of C and show how to use these functions to perform mathematical computations.

3.1 THE ART AND SCIENCE OF PROBLEM SOLVING

You must be able to solve problems in order to succeed in academics or in the real world. Problem solving ability is a combination of art and science. The art of problem solving is the transformation of a problem given in word form into another form permitting a mechanical solution. An example of this process is the transformation of an algebra word problem into a set of algebraic equations that can then be solved for one or more unknowns.

In the real world, this process is more difficult because problem descriptions are often incomplete, imprecise, or ambiguous. The successful problem solver must be able to ask the right questions in order to clarify the problem and obtain any information that is missing from the problem statement. Next, the problem solver must analyze the problem and attempt to extract its essential features, identifying what is provided (the problem inputs) and what is required (the problem outputs). The problem solver must also be able to determine whether any constraints or simplifying assumptions can be applied to facilitate the problem solution. Often, we cannot solve the most general case of a problem; we must make some realistic assumptions that limit or constrain the problem so that it can be solved.

The science part of problem solving involves knowledge of the problem environment, knowledge of the formulas or equations that characterize the environment, and the ability to apply and manipulate those formulas. The problem solver can use this knowledge to develop a series of steps, the successful completion of which will lead to the solution of the problem. Once the solution is reached, the problem solver must verify its accuracy by comparing the computed results with observed results.

The Engineering and Scientific Method

Engineers and scientists are problem solvers. As part of the problem-solving process, they must follow these problem-analysis steps:[†]

1. *Recognize and understand the problem.* Perhaps the most difficult part of problem solving is developing the ability to recognize and define the problem precisely. You must study the problem carefully, eliminating aspects that are unimportant and zeroing in on the root problem.
2. *Accumulate facts.* Ascertain all pertinent physical facts, such as sizes, temperatures, voltages, weights, and costs. Some problems require that Steps 1 and 2 be done simultaneously.
3. *Select the appropriate theory or principle.* Select appropriate theories or scientific principles that apply to the problem solution. Understand and identify limits or constraints that apply.
4. *Make necessary assumptions.* Perfect solutions to many real problems do not exist. Simplifications need to be made if problems are to be solved. Make sure your simplifications do not significantly affect the accuracy of the solution.
5. *Solve the problem.* If Steps 3 and 4 result in a set of mathematical equations (a model), you can solve the problem by applying mathematical theory, a trial-and-error solution, or some form of graphical solution.
6. *Verify and check results.* In engineering practice, the work is not finished merely because a solution has been reached. The solution must be checked to ensure that it is mathematically correct and that units have been properly specified.

Systems designers in the computer industry have found that the engineering and scientific method of problem solving can be adapted to the development of reliable software systems as well. In recent years the term *software engineering* has been used to identify such a systematic approach to programming. In Chapter 1, we noted five phases in solving programming problems. Let's see how each aspect of the engineering and scientific method fits into these phases.

[†] Adapted with permission from Arvid Eide et al., *Engineering Fundamentals and Problem Solving,* 2d ed. (New York: McGraw-Hill, 1986).

1. *Requirements Specification.* This phase includes elements of several steps of the engineering and scientific method. To determine completely what a program is required to do, we must fully understand the whole problem, accumulate facts about the problem environment, and make any necessary assumptions that pin down which part of the whole problem we are to solve. This phase may require further clarification from the person posing the problem, clarification obtained by asking the person detailed questions.

2. *Analysis.* During the analysis phase, we study the completed problem specification and attempt to identify the problem inputs and the desired outputs. We also look for appropriate theories or scientific principles that apply to the problem solution, and we list any formulas or relationships that might be relevant.

3. *Design.* Step 5 of the engineering method, "solve the problem," breaks down into two phases of software development: design and implementation (coding). These phases take into account that two entities—the human problem solver and the computer—must ultimately be able to solve the problem. During the design phase, the human figures out a way to solve the problem and writes an algorithm that lists major subproblems. Using a process called "divide and conquer," the problem solver solves these subproblems separately. For each subproblem, refinements are added to the initial algorithm until there is a clear, complete solution.

   We should note here that only for *very* simple problems is there likely to be a unique solution. When you solve a problem for which an answer is given in the back of this book, do not assume your solution is *wrong* if it differs from the answer shown. Simply use the answer key as a guide to improving your solutions, but be ready to recognize where your algorithm is better than the given "answer."

4. *Implementation.* During the implementation phase, we take the algorithm that is our refined solution and represent it as a C program, permitting a computer to solve the problem too. For this coding of the solution, the data requirements that are identified in the analysis phase form the basis of the constant definitions and declaration part of the program; the refined algorithm forms the basis for the executable statements of the program body.

5. *Verification and Testing.* The purpose of this fifth phase is the same as the last step of the engineering and scientific method—to verify that our solution is correct. Although we list this step last, verification really applies to all four previous steps. Verification of our requirements and analysis may call for us to interact with the person posing the problem and with other experts in the field. It is essential that we try out by hand the algorithm that is the product of Step 3 (Design) before we start to code it so we won't waste time implementing a faulty solution. Running the program that we produce in Step 4 is the final part of the whole verification process. As we test and debug this pro-

gram, we first remove all obvious errors. Then, we run the program several times with a variety of test data to ensure that the program works properly. Finally, we check the program results against computations that are done by hand or by using a calculator.

Caution: Failure Is Part of the Process

Although having a step-by-step approach to problem solving is helpful, we must avoid jumping to the conclusion that if we follow these steps, we are *guaranteed* a correct solution the first time, every time. The fact that verification is so important implies an essential truth of problem solving: The first (also the second, the third, or the twentieth) attempt at a solution *may be wrong*. Probably the most important distinction between outstanding problem solvers and less proficient ones is that the outstanding problem solver is not discouraged by initial failures. Rather, the successful problem solver sees the faulty and near-correct early solutions as a means of gaining a better understanding of the problem. One of the most inventive problem solvers of all time, Thomas Edison, is noted for his positive interpretation of the thousands of failed experiments that contributed to his incredible record of inventions. His friends report that he always saw those failures in terms of the helpful data they yielded about what did *not* work.

Understanding the Problem

In this section, we will apply our problem-solving method to a programming problem. The first step is to recognize and understand the problem. The ability to listen carefully is an important skill in human communication. Often, we are too busy thinking of what our response will be to really hear what another person is saying. This can lead to a lack of understanding between a speaker and a listener.

Many of us suffer from a similar difficulty when we attempt to solve problems that are presented in either verbal or written form. We do not pay close enough attention to the problem statement to determine what really is being asked; consequently, either we are unable to solve the stated problem or we reach an incorrect solution because we solve the wrong problem.

You should analyze a problem statement carefully before attempting to solve it. Read each problem statement two or three times if necessary. The first time you read a problem, you should get a general idea of what is being asked; the second time you read it, you should try to answer these questions:

- What information should the solution provide?
- What data do I have to work with?

The answer to the first question will tell you the desired results, or the *problem outputs*. The answer to the second question will tell you what data are provided, or the *problem inputs*. You may find it helpful to underline in the problem statement the phrases that identify the inputs and the outputs. In the problem statement that follows, inputs are in italics and outputs are in boldface.

Case Study: Finding the Area and Circumference of a Circle

PROBLEM

Take the *radius* of a circle and compute and print its **area** and **circumference.**

ANALYSIS

Clearly, the problem input is the circle radius. There are two outputs requested: the area of the circle and its circumference. These variables should be type `double` because the inputs and outputs may contain fractional parts.

From our knowledge of geometry, we know the relationship between the radius of a circle and its area and circumference; we list these formulas along with the data requirements. Note that we have written the English description of each variable as a C comment to make it easier to produce the declaration part of our solution program.

Data Requirements

Problem Constant
```
PI 3.14159
```

Problem Input
```
double radius   /* radius of a circle          */
```

Problem Outputs
```
double area     /* area of a circle            */
double circum   /* circumference of a circle   */
```

Relevant Formulas
area of a circle = $\pi \times radius^2$
circumference of a circle = $2\pi \times radius$

DESIGN

Once you know the problem inputs and outputs, you should list the steps necessary to solve the problem. It is very important that you pay close attention to the order of the steps. The initial algorithm follows.

Initial Algorithm

1. Get circle radius.
2. Find area.
3. Find circumference.
4. Print area and circumference.

Algorithm Refinements

Next, we should refine any steps that do not have an obvious solution (for instance, Steps 2 and 3).

> **Step 2 Refinement**
> 2.1 Assign `PI * radius * radius` to `area`
>
> **Step 3 Refinement**
> 3.1 Assign `2 * PI * radius` to `circum`

◄ IMPLEMENTATION ►

To write the program, we must convert the refinements (Steps 2.1 and 3.1) to C, and write C code for the unrefined steps (Steps 1 and 4). Figure 3.1 shows the final program. Note that we have included the major steps of our design as program comments.

Figure 3.1   Finding the Area and Circumference of a Circle

```
/*
 * Finds and prints the area and circumference of a circle
 */

#include <stdio.h>
#define PI 3.14159

int
main(void)
{
      double radius,  /* input - radius of a circle          */
             area,    /* output - area of a circle           */
             circum;  /* output - circumference of a circle  */
```

(continued)

Figure 3.1 *(continued)*

```
        /* Get the circle radius                    */
        printf("Enter radius> ");
        scanf("%lf", &radius);

        /* Find the area                             */
        area = PI * radius * radius;

        /* Find the circumference                    */
        circum = 2 * PI * radius;

        /* Print the area and circumference          */
        printf("The area is %.2f\n", area);
        printf("The circumference is %.2f\n", circum);

        return (0);
}

Enter radius> 5.0
The area is 78.54
The circumference is 31.42
```

████ **TESTING**

The sample output shown in Fig. 3.1 provides a good test of the solution because it is relatively easy to compute the area and circumference by hand for a radius value of 5.0. The radius squared is 25.0, so the value of the area appears correct. The circumference should be ten times PI, also an easy number to compute by hand.

EXERCISES FOR SECTION 3.1

Self-Check

1. Describe the problem inputs, outputs, and algorithm for computing the sum and average of three numbers.
2. Describe the problem inputs, outputs, and algorithm for this problem: Predict the population of an insect colony at the end of a week, given the current population and the weekly growth rate (a percentage).

Programming

1. Write a C program for the algorithm you developed for Self-check exercise 2.

3.2 EXTENDING A PROBLEM SOLUTION

Quite often the solution of one problem turns out to be the basis for the solution to another problem. For example, we can easily solve the next problem by building on the solution to the previous problem.

Case Study: Quality Control in Manufacturing Flat Washers

PROBLEM

High Plains Hardware is gradually automating its manufacturing plant. The company recently installed both a camera to photograph metal parts as they pass on a conveyor belt and image processing software to compute the area of each part as it appears in the photographs. You have been asked to establish an initial quality control check for 1/2-in. flat washers (a washer is identified by the diameter of its hole). The program will compute the difference between the expected and observed areas and will print the difference as a percentage of the expected area.

ANALYSIS

How would we find the percentage difference between the expected area of the rim of a 1/2-in. washer and the actual area of the rim of a washer photographed on a conveyor belt? Let's consider an example. In Fig. 3.2(a), we see a digitized photograph of a 1/2-in. washer. Figure 3.2(b) is an image in which the part of the photograph that is one washer is marked in color. The area of the marked washer, as computed by the image processing program, is 0.6942 sq. in.

How does the expected rim area of a 1/2-in. flat washer differ from the observed rim area of the washer (0.6942 sq. in.)? Clearly, we need to compute the area between the circle that represents the washer's outer edge and the circle that represents the hole. If we can calculate the area of the two circles, we can find the area of the rim by subtracting the area of the smaller circle from the area of the larger one. At this point, we realize that our requirements specification does not contain all the facts we need to solve the problem. We must ask the High Plains Hardware representative the size of the entire washer, including the rim. Eventually, we learn that the diameter of the outer circle is 17/16 in. We can now compute the expected size of the washer rim by subtracting the area of the inner circle (the hole) from the area of the outer circle (see Fig. 3.3).

Next, we must see how the expected area (0.6903 sq. in.) differs from the observed area (0.6942 sq. in.). We can apply the formula for computing the

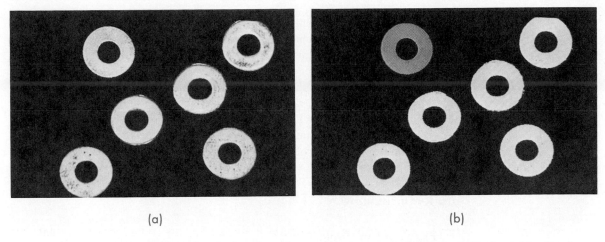

(a)   (b)

Figure 3.2   (a) Photograph of Flat Washers; (b) Image with One Washer Marked

relative error in an approximation:

$$\frac{actual\ value - approximate\ value}{actual\ value}$$

Using our expected area as the *actual value* and our observed area as the *approximate value,* we have

$$\frac{-0.0039}{0.6903} \ = \ -0.0056 \ = \ -0.56\%$$

**Figure 3.3
Computing the
Expected Rim
Area of a 1/2-
in. Washer**

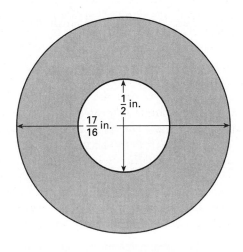

Washer rim area $= \pi\left(\dfrac{17/16}{2}\right)^2 - \pi\left(\dfrac{1/2}{2}\right)^2$

$= 0.6903$

In the Data Requirements listed next, we see that problem constants come from two major sources. Some of the constants needed in a program's computation are numerical constants from mathematics—for example, π. Other constants appear in the requirements specification: "quality control check for 1/2-in. flat washers." The radius of the washer (the hole) and the radius of the outer rim circle are listed as program variables because we need these values to compute the expected area of the washer. However, they are neither problem inputs nor explicitly stated problem constants. The expected area, another value that we need to compute, is not a problem output.

Data Requirements

Problem Constants
```
PI                 3.14159

WASHER_DIAMETER    (1.0/2.0) /* diameter in inches
                               of the hole of a
                               flat washer*/

OUTER_DIAMETER     (17.0/16.0) /* diameter in inch-
                                 es of the circu-
                                 lar outer edge*/
```

Problem Input
```
double observed_area    /* observed area (in square
                           inches) of a washer rim */
```

Problem Output
```
double pct_differ    /* how much difference there is
                        between expected area and
                        observed area (as a per-
                        centage of expected area)*/
```

Program Variables
```
double washer_radius    /* expected radius of washer
                           hole     */

double outer_radius     /* expected radius of circular
                           outer edge     */

double rim_area         /* expected area of washer rim */
```

Relevant Formulas

$$area\ of\ a\ circle = \pi \times radius^2$$

$$radius\ of\ a\ circle = 1/2\ diameter$$

$$percentage\ difference\ of\ 2\ areas = \frac{expected - observed}{expected} \times 100$$

DESIGN

Initial Algorithm

1. Get observed area of washer rim.
2. Compute expected area of rim.
3. Compute percentage difference between expected and observed areas.
4. Display percentage difference.

The algorithm refinements follow. The refinement of Step 2 shows that we must compute the radii of the washer and its outer edge before we can compute the washer's rim area.

Step 2 Refinement
2.1 Assign 1/2 `WASHER_DIAMETER` to `washer_radius`
2.2 Assign 1/2 `OUTER_DIAMETER` to `outer_radius`
2.3 `rim_area is PI * outer_radius * outer_radius`
    `- PI * washer_radius * washer_radius`

Step 3 Refinement
3.1 `pct_differ` is
    `(observed_area - rim_area) / rim_area * 100`

IMPLEMENTATION

Figure 3.4 shows the C program. We will base this program on our analysis and design by using the data requirements to develop the declaration part and by taking the initial algorithm with refinements as the starting point for the executable statements of the program body. This example is the first we have seen in which a constant macro's meaning is an expression, and it is perfectly legitimate provided that the expression is enclosed in parentheses and all of the expression's operands are constants. In this program, we use the expressions `(1.0/2.0)` and `(17.0/16.0)` rather than the decimal equivalents `0.5` and

Figure 3.4 Quality Control Program for 1/2-in. Washers

```c
/*
 * Compute the percentage difference between the expected area of the rim
 * of a WASHER_DIAMETER-inch washer (with an outer rim diameter of
 * OUTER_DIAMETER inches) and the observed area of such a washer's rim
 */

#include <stdio.h>
#define WASHER_DIAMETER (1.0/2.0)   /* diameter in inches of a flat washer
                                               (diameter of the hole)       */
#define OUTER_DIAMETER  (17.0/16.0) /* diameter of edge of outer rim of a
                                       WASHER_DIAMETER-inch flat washer   */
#define PI              3.14159

int
main(void)
{
      double observed_area;  /* input - observed area (in square inches)
                                      of a washer rim                       */
      double pct_differ;     /* output - amount of difference between
                                      observed and expected rim size, as a per-
                                      centage of expected size              */
      double washer_radius;  /* expected washer radius (radius of hole)   */
      double outer_radius;   /* expected radius of washer rim's outer edge */
      double rim_area;       /* expected area of washer rim               */

      /* Get observed area of washer rim                                  */
      scanf("%lf", &observed_area);
      printf("Observed area = %.4f sq. in.\n", observed_area);

      /* Compute expected area of rim                                     */
      washer_radius = 0.5 * WASHER_DIAMETER;
      outer_radius = 0.5 * OUTER_DIAMETER;
      rim_area = PI * outer_radius * outer_radius
                 - PI * washer_radius * washer_radius;

      /* Compute percentage difference between expected and observed
         rim area                                                         */
      pct_differ = (rim_area - observed_area) / rim_area * 100;

      /* Display percentage difference.                                   */
      printf("Expected area differs from observed area by %.2f percent.\n",
             pct_differ);

      return (0);
}
Observed area = 0.6942 sq. in.
Expected area differs from observed area by -0.56 percent.
```

`1.0625` in order to maintain an obvious correspondence between the implementation and the specification of the problem.

You will notice that we have used the names of our constant macros wherever we need to refer to the washer's dimensions, even in our comments. We do this so that a revision of the program to handle a different size of washer will require only a change of the constant macro definitions. Pay careful attention to the fact that we *do not* use WASHER_DIAMETER everywhere we need the constant 1/2, but only where the 1/2 needed is actually the diameter of the washer.

TESTING

To test this program, run it with data files containing a few different observed sizes, some of which are larger and some of which are smaller than the expected size. As you test the program, you will find that not quite enough information is printed to make it easy for you to prove the answers correct. How can you prove any relationship between the expected and observed areas when the output does not show the expected area? We could quickly modify the program to provide more information by changing the final `printf` to

```
printf("Expected area (%.4f sq. in) differs from ",
       rim_area);
printf("observed area by %.2f percent.\n", pct_differ);
```

EXERCISE FOR SECTION 3.2

Self-Check

1. What changes are required to revise the program in Fig. 3.4 to handle a 5/16-in. flat washer when the diameter of the washer rim's outer edge is 5/8 in.?

3.3 STRUCTURED PROGRAMMING AND CONTROL STRUCTURES

In this course, we teach *structured programming,* a disciplined approach to programming that results in programs that are easy to read and understand and are less likely to contain errors. The emphasis is on following accepted program style guidelines (such as using meaningful names for identifiers) to write code that is adequately documented with comments and is clear and readable. Obscure tricks and programming shortcuts are strongly discouraged. Government organizations and industry are strong advocates of structured programming because structured programs are much more cost effective in the long term.

Program maintenance involves modifying a program to remove previously undetected bugs and to keep it up-to-date as government regulations, company policies, or computer systems change. It is not uncommon to maintain a program for five years or more, often after the programmers who originally coded it have left the company or have moved on to other positions.

Control Structures

Structured programming utilizes *control structures* to control the flow of statement execution in a program. Some control structures allow a program to choose one of several possible courses of action; others make it possible to repeat a sequence of actions as many times as it is needed. The control structures of a programming language enable us to combine individual C statements into a single program entity with one entry point and one exit point. We can then write a program as a sequence of control structures rather than as a sequence of individual statements (see Fig. 3.5).

Compound Statements

There are three categories of control structures: sequence, selection, and iteration. So far, we have illustrated sequential control using *compound statements* in C. A compound statement is a group of statements enclosed by braces.

**Figure 3.5
A Program as a
Sequence of
Three Control
Structures**

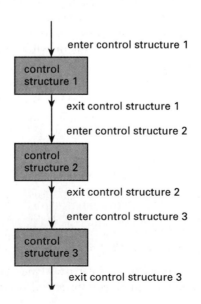

```
{
    statement₁;
    statement₂;
        •
        •
        •
    statementₙ;
}
```

Control flows from *statement*₁ to *statement*₂ and so on. A program body consists of a single compound statement usually with declarations. Later in this chapter, we will introduce a system structure called a function that also contains a body consisting of a single compound statement. We will describe the control structures for selection in Chapter 4 and the control structures for repetition in Chapter 5.

Motivation for Selection and Repetition Control Structures

In Section 3.2, we used part of the solution to one problem (finding a circle's area) in solving a second related problem (checking the area of the rim of a 1/2-in. washer). We are not quite finished with the problem yet because our goal was to be able to accept or reject a sequence of washers depending on whether or not the rim areas of the washers are close enough to the expected rim area.

One way to accomplish our larger goal is to run this program several different times, once for each flat washer, and to record the results. We can then scan the list of results, accepting or rejecting each washer based on whether it meets our quality control criterion (perhaps acceptance would require the percentage difference in areas to be between −1% and 1%).

A better solution would be to write a program that would repeat the computation steps and would also compare each result to the quality control criterion, displaying an acceptance or rejection message for each washer. Let's write an algorithm that will give us this improved solution.

Initial Algorithm for Improved Solution

1. Compute expected area of washer rim.
2. For each washer, get observed rim area and compute percentage difference between expected area and observed area. If this percentage is between −1% and 1%, accept the washer; otherwise, reject it.

Because every washer must be processed using the same procedure, Step 2 of our initial algorithm contains all the steps from our previous solution except the expected area computation, which needs to be done only once. We don't know how to do Step 2 in C yet because it involves the use of repetition and selection control structures. However, we can write a refinement of this step to give you some idea of where we are heading in the next few chapters.

Step 2 Refinement

2.1 Repeat the following steps for each washer:
    2.2 Get observed area of washer rim.
    2.3 Compute percentage difference between expected and observed areas.
    2.4 Display percentage difference.
    2.5 If percentage difference is in the range −1% to 1%, display acceptance message; otherwise, display rejection message.

Step 2.1 specifies the *repetition* of a group of steps: Step 2.2 (get the data), Step 2.3 (compute percentage difference), Step 2.4 (display percentage difference), Step 2.5 (accept or reject washer). We will repeat these steps as many times as necessary until all washers are checked. Step 2.5 is a *selection step* because it selects between the two possible outcomes: accept the washer or reject the washer.

EXERCISES FOR SECTION 3.3

Self-Check

1. Why would a repetition step be used in an algorithm?
2. Show how the washer algorithm and problem inputs described in Section 3.2 could be modified to allow the quality check of a dime based on its area and its weight. (A dime is 17.9 mm in diameter and weighs 2.27 g.)

3.4 STRUCTURE CHARTS

As we mentioned earlier, one of the most fundamental ideas in problem solving is dividing a problem into subproblems and solving each subproblem independently. In attempting to solve a subproblem at one level, we often introduce new subproblems at a lower level. The splitting of a problem into its related subproblems is analogous to the process of refining an algorithm. Each time we refine an algorithm step (subproblem), we generate new refinements (subproblems) at a lower level. This section uses a case study to introduce a design documentation tool that will enable you to keep track of the relationships between subproblems.

Case Study: Drawing Simple Diagrams

PROBLEM

You would like to be able to draw some simple diagrams or figures on your printer or screen. Two examples are the diagram for a house and a stick figure of a person in Fig. 3.6.

ANALYSIS

The figure on the left of Fig. 3.6 consists of a triangle without its base on top of a rectangle. The figure on the right consists of something that resembles a circle, a triangle, and a triangle without its base. We should be able to draw both diagrams using the four basic graphical components below.

```
                      *
•  a circle       *       *
                      *   *

•  a base line        - - - - - - -


                      |       |
•  parallel lines     |       |
                      |       |

                          / \
•  intersecting lines   /     \
                       /       \
```

**Figure 3.6
House and
Stick Figure**

Let's focus on the stick figure. We can divide the problem of drawing this figure into the following three problems:

Initial Algorithm

1. Draw a circle.
2. Draw a triangle.
3. Draw intersecting lines.

Algorithm Refinements

Because a triangle is not one of our basic components, we must refine Step 2.

Step 2 Refinement
2.1 Draw intersecting lines.
2.2 Draw a base.

We can use a diagram called a *structure chart* to show the relationship between the original problem and its subproblems. The structure chart corresponding to the initial algorithm is shown in Fig. 3.7.

As we trace down this diagram, we go from an abstract original problem to a more detailed subproblem. The original problem is shown at the top, level 0, of the structure chart. The major subproblems appear at level 1. The different subproblems resulting from the refinement of a level 1 step are shown at level 2 and are connected to their level 1 subproblem. The structure chart shows that the

**Figure 3.7
Structure Chart
for Drawing a
Stick Figure**

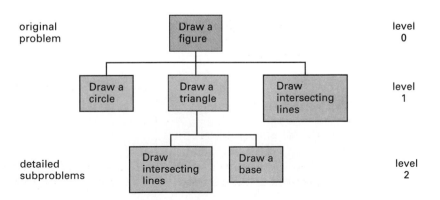

subproblem *Draw a triangle* (at level 1) is dependent on the solutions to the subproblems *Draw intersecting lines* and *Draw a base* (both at level 2). Because the subproblem *Draw a circle* is not further refined, no level 2 subproblems are connected to it.

Structure charts are intended to show the structural relationship between subproblems. The algorithm (not the structure chart) shows the order in which we must carry out each step to solve the problem.

EXERCISES FOR SECTION 3.4

Self-Check

1. Draw a structure chart for the problem of drawing the house shown in Fig. 3.6.
2. Draw a structure chart for the problem of drawing a triangle and a rectangle with a circle between them.
3. Draw a structure chart for the flat washer case study in Section 3.2.

3.5 FUNCTIONS

A structure chart proceeds from the original problem at the top level down to its detailed subproblems at the bottom level. We would like to follow this *top-down* approach when we code a program by using the function system structure.

A C *function* is a grouping of program statements into a single program unit. Just like `scanf` and `printf`, each C function that we write can be activated through the execution of a function call. If we assume that we have functions available that implement each of the level 2 subproblems in Fig. 3.7, we can use the following code fragment to implement the level 1 subproblem *Draw a triangle*.

```
/* Draw a triangle. */
draw_intersect();
draw_base();
```

This code fragment contains two function call statements. During program execution, the function call statement

```
draw_intersect();
```

causes the statements contained in the body of function `draw_intersect` to be executed. We will see how to write function `draw_intersect` in the next section.

Figure 3.8 shows the main function of the program that draws a stick figure, assuming that the solution to each subproblem at the lowest level in Fig. 3.7 is implemented as a separate function. This main function implements our original algorithm. The function body begins with the code for Step 1 (*Draw a circle*) consisting of a call to function `draw_circle`. The code for Step 2 (*Draw a triangle*) consists of the two function call statements above. The code for Step 3 (*Draw intersecting lines*) consists of a second call to function `draw_intersect`.

Function Call Statement

SYNTAX: *fname*( );

EXAMPLE: `draw_circle();`

INTERPRETATION: The function call statement initiates the execution of function *fname*. After *fname* has finished executing, the program statement that follows the function call will be executed.

Figure 3.8   Main Function for Drawing a Stick Figure

```
/*
 * Draw a stick figure
 */
int
main(void)
{
     /* Draw a circle.            */
     draw_circle();

     /* Draw a triangle.          */
     draw_intersect();
     draw_base();

     /* Draw intersecting lines.  */
     draw_intersect();

     return (0);
}
```

Figure 3.9   Function draw_circle

```
/*
 * Draws a circle
 */
void
draw_circle(void)
{
      printf("   *  \n");
      printf(" *   *\n");
      printf("  * * \n");
}
```

Declaring Functions

Just like other identifiers in C, a function must be declared before it can be referenced in a program body. One way to declare a function is to give its full definition. Figure 3.9 shows the definition of function draw_circle.

The definition of a simple function like draw_circle is similar to the definition of a main function: It consists of a prototype followed by the function body. We recommend that you place a block comment explaining the purpose of the function immediately before the function's prototype. The prototype for draw_circle consists of the keyword void, the function name draw_circle, and then the keyword void again in parentheses. The function body always starts with { and ends with }. In Fig. 3.9, the function body contains the three calls to the function printf that cause the computer to print asterisks in a shape resembling a circle. The function call statement

```
draw_circle();
```

causes these printf statements to execute.

Function Definition

SYNTAX: void
       fname(void)
       {
              local declarations
              executable statements
       }

(continued)

```
EXAMPLE: /*
         * Print a block-letter H
         */
        void
        print_h(void)
        {
               printf("** **\n");
               printf("** **\n");
               printf("*****\n");
               printf("** **\n");
               printf("** **\n");

        }
```

INTERPRETATION: The function *fname* is defined. Any identifiers that are declared in the optional *local declarations* are defined only during the execution of the function and can be referenced only within the function. The *executable statements* of the function body describe the data manipulation to be performed by the function.

Each function body may contain declarations for its own variables. These identifiers are considered *local* to the function; in other words, they can be referenced only within the function. There will be more on this topic later.

Placement of Function Declarations in a Program

C provides more than one way to include function declarations in a program. We consider one very simple method here and will study other methods in Chapter 13. Since function declarations must appear before any calls to the functions, we place the definitions of the functions called in Fig. 3.8 between the preprocessor directives and the definition of the main function. Any of the three functions may be declared first; their order of execution is determined by the order of function call statements in the body of the main function. Figure 3.10 shows the complete program with its functions.

Program Style   *Use of Comments in a Program with Functions*

Figure 3.10 includes several comments. Each function begins with a comment that describes its purpose. If the function subprograms were more complex, we would include comments on each major algorithm step just as we do in function `main.` From now on throughout this text, the block comment and prototype of each function definition are in color to help you locate functions in the program listing.

Figure 3.10   Program to Draw a Stick Figure

```c
/* Prints a stick figure */

#include <stdio.h>

/*
 * Draws a circle
 */
void
draw_circle(void)
{
      printf("    *    \n");
      printf("  *   *  \n");
      printf("   * *   \n");
}

/*
 * Draws intersecting lines
 */
void
draw_intersect(void)
{
      printf(" / \   \n");
      printf(" /   \ \n");
      printf("/     \ \n");
}

/*
 * Draws a base line
 */
void
draw_base(void)
{
      printf("-------\n");
}

int
main(void)
{
      /* Draw a circle.          */
      draw_circle();

      /* Draw a triangle.        */
      draw_intersect();
      draw_base();

      /* Draw intersecting lines. */
      draw_intersect();

      return (0);
}
```

Relative Order of Execution of Function Subprograms and Function main

In the stick figure problem, we wrote the main function body as a sequence of function call statements before we specified the details of all functions. Next, we provided the missing function definitions and placed them in the source file before the main function. The compiler must know about the function subprogram declarations before it translates the main function where the function subprograms are called. As it translates each function subprogram, when the compiler reaches the end of the function body, it inserts a machine-language statement that causes a *transfer of control* back from the function to the calling statement. In the main function body, the compiler translates a function call statement as a transfer of control to the function.

Figure 3.11 shows the main function body and the function `draw_circle` of the stick figure program in separate areas of memory. Although for simplicity the original C statements are shown in Fig. 3.11, the object code (the machine-language translation) corresponding to each statement is what is actually stored in memory.

When we run the program, the first statement in the main function body (the call to `draw_circle` in Fig. 3.11) is the first statement executed. When the computer executes a function call statement, it transfers control to the function that is referenced (the colored line in Fig. 3.11). The computer allocates any memory that may be needed for the function's local data and then performs the statements in the function body. After the last statement in the function body is executed, control returns to the main program (the black line in Fig. 3.11), and the computer releases any memory that was allocated to the function. After the return to the main function, the next statement will be executed (the call to `draw_intersect` in Fig. 3.11).

Procedural Abstraction

One important advantage of function subprograms is that their use allows us to remove from the main function the code representing the detailed procedure for solving a subproblem. Since these details are provided separately in the function

Figure 3.11
Flow of Control Between Function main and Function Subprogram

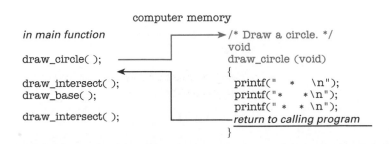

subprograms and not in the main function, we can write the main function as soon as we have specified the initial algorithm. However, we should delay writing the function for an algorithm step until we have finished refining that step. This approach to program design, called *procedural abstraction,* enables us to defer implementation details and to write our program in logically independent sections in the same way that we develop the solution algorithm.

Advantages of Using Function Subprograms

Another advantage of using functions is that they may be executed more than once in a program. For example, function `draw_intersect` is called twice in Fig. 3.10. Each time `draw_intersect` is called, the list of output statements shown in the definition of `draw_intersect` is executed and a pair of intersecting lines is drawn. If we were not using functions, the calls to `printf` that draw the lines would have to be listed twice in the program body, thereby increasing the main function's length and the chance of an error.

Finally, once you have written and tested a function subprogram, you may use it in other programs or other functions. For example, the functions we created for our stick-figure program could easily be used in programs that draw other diagrams.

Many diagrams contain triangles and rectangles. We can use functions `draw_intersect`, `draw_parallel`, and `draw_base` to define two new functions, `draw_triangle` and `draw_rectangle` (see Fig. 3.12). The initial comment in Fig. 3.12 reminds us that we must precede our two new functions with the definitions of the three functions that they call.   ◀

Figure 3.12   Functions draw_triangle and draw_rectangle

```
/* Insert functions draw_intersect, draw_parallel, and
   draw_base. */

/*
 * Draws a triangle
 */
void
draw_triangle(void)
{
      draw_intersect();
      draw_base();
}
```

(continued)

Figure 3.12   *(continued)*

```
/*
 * Draws a rectangle
 */
void
draw_rectangle()
{
      draw_base();
      draw_parallel();
      draw_base();
}
```

Self-check

1. Assume that you have functions `print_h`, `print_i`, `print_m`, and
   `print_o`, each of which draws a large block letter (for example, `print_o`
   draws a block-letter O). What is the effect of executing the following main
   function?

```
int
main(void)
{
      print_h();
      print_i();
      printf("\n\n\n");
      print_m();
      print_o();
      print_m();

      return (0);
}
```

Programming

1. Write function `draw_parallel`.
2. Write the main function for a program to print "HI HO" in block letters
   using three function subprograms. First, provide a structure chart for this
   problem.
3. Write functions `print_i`, `print_m`, and `print_o` (`print_h` was shown
   in the syntax display for function definitions).

3.6 DISPLAYING USER INSTRUCTIONS

For the time being, our use of function subprograms will be limited because we do not yet know how to pass information into or out of a function that we define. Until we have this knowledge, we will use functions only to display multiple lines of program output, such as instructions to a program user or a title page or a special message that precedes a program's results.

EXAMPLE 3.2

The function in Fig. 3.13 displays instructions to a user of our earlier program that computed the area and circumference of a circle (see Fig. 3.1). If function `instruct` is placed before the main function of the original program, the main function's executable statements can begin with the function call statement

```
instruct();
```

The rest of the program body will consist of the executable statements shown earlier. Figure 3.13 shows the output lines displayed by calling function

Figure 3.13   Function instruct and the Output Produced by a Call

```
/*
 * Displays instructions to a user of program to compute
 * the area and circumference of a circle.
 */
void
instruct(void)
{
      printf("This program computes the area\n");
      printf("and circumference of a circle.\n\n");
      printf("To use this program, enter the radius of\n");
      printf("the circle after the prompt: Enter radius>\n");
}

This program computes the area
and circumference of a circle.

To use this program, enter the radius of
the circle after the prompt: Enter radius>
```

instruct. The rest of the program output will be the same as the output shown earlier.   ⬅

Self-Check

1. Why is it better to place the user instructions in a function rather than to insert the calls to `printf` in the program body itself?

Programming

1. Write a function similar to `instruct` for the flat washer program shown in Fig. 3.4.
2. Rewrite the miles-to-kilometers conversion program shown in Fig. 2.1, so that it includes a function that displays instructions to its user.
3. Show the revised area and circumference of a circle program that calls function `instruct`.

3.7 FUNCTIONS AS PROGRAM BUILDING BLOCKS

Programmers use functions like building blocks to construct large programs. When you were very young, you probably used alphabet blocks to demonstrate your potential as a budding architect. These blocks were big so that they would be difficult to swallow. Two sides were smooth and two sides were ribbed to enable you to build towers of blocks. Unfortunately, you could not place very many blocks on a tower without having it topple over.

As you grew older, many of you started to play with Lego blocks (see Fig. 3.14). Instead of ribs, each Lego block has one surface with little protrusions and one surface with little cups. By pushing the protrusions into the cups, you could build rather elaborate Lego structures.

What does this discussion have to do with designing software systems? Well, functions `draw_circle` and `draw_parallel` are like alphabet blocks. You can write some cute little programs with these functions, but they are not particularly useful. To be able to construct interesting programs, we must provide functions with protrusions and cups so that they can be easily interconnected.

The *arguments* of a function fulfill this purpose. The function call statement

```
printf("The area is %.2f\n", area);
```

consists of two parts: the name of the C function being called, `printf`, and an argument list enclosed in parentheses. The argument list contains two argu-

**Figure 3.14
Lego Blocks**

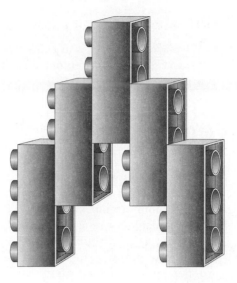

ments (a string and a variable name) separated by a comma. Because it has an argument list, function printf, like the Lego blocks, is more versatile and, hence, more useful than function print_x. Function print_x can display only a large block-letter X, whereas function printf can display whatever we want it to.

The arguments of a function are used to carry information into the function subprogram from the main function (or from another function subprogram) or to return to the calling function multiple results computed by the function subprogram. Arguments that carry information from the main function into the function subprogram are called *input arguments*; arguments that return results to the main function are called *output arguments*. Figure 3.15 is a diagram of a function with multiple inputs and outputs.

We provide a complete discussion of input and output arguments for functions in Chapter 6. For the time being, we will use only functions without arguments to display lengthy messages or instructions to program users. We will also continue to use the C standard I/O functions scanf and printf for data entry and display.

**Figure 3.15
Function with
Inputs and
Outputs**

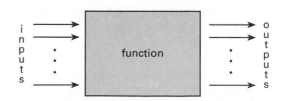

Self-Check

1. Why are `printf`'s arguments considered to be input arguments and `scanf`'s arguments (other than the format string) considered to be output arguments?

3.8 FUNCTIONS AND CODE REUSE

We have seen how functions can receive many data items through input arguments as `printf` does, and how functions can send back multiple result values through output arguments as `scanf` does. However, a C function has another option available for returning a result value making it possible to write functions that behave as arithmetic operators. When we speak of "the result" of a function, we are referring to a single result value that is returned directly to the calling program without the use of an output argument. Since this single result is considered the value of the function call, the call does not have to be a separate statement, but can appear anywhere that its result value would be appropriate. Figure 3.16 is a diagram of a function that produces a single result.

**Figure 3.16
Function with
Multiple Inputs
and a Single
Output**

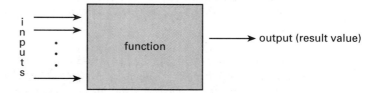

As an example, let's see how we might use a function named `sqrt` that performs the square root computation. This function is available in C's standard math library. If `x` is `16.0`, the assignment statement

```
y = sqrt(x);
```

is evaluated as follows:

1. Because `x` is `16.0`, function `sqrt` computes the $\sqrt{16.0}$ or `4.0`.
2. The function result, `4.0`, is assigned to `y`.

The expression part of the assignment statement is a function call consisting of the function name, `sqrt`, followed by the function *argument,* `x`, enclosed in parentheses.

A function can be thought of as a "black box" that is passed one or more input values and then automatically returns a single output value. Figure 3.17 illustrates this sequence for the call to function `sqrt` above. The value of `x`

**Figure 3.17
Function sqrt as
a "Black Box"**

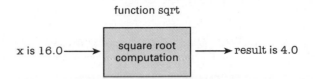

(16.0) is the function input, and the function result or output is the square root of 16.0 (the result is 4.0).

Functions are called into execution by writing a function call in an expression. After the function executes, its result is substituted for the function call. If w is 9.0, the assignment statement

```
z = 5.7 + sqrt(w);
```

is evaluated as follows:

1. Because w is 9.0, function sqrt computes the $\sqrt{9.0}$ or 3.0.
2. The values 5.7 and 3.0 are added together.
3. The sum, 8.7, is stored in z.

The two calls to function sqrt discussed so far have different arguments (x and w). We will illustrate this capability of functions again in the next example.

EXAMPLE 3.3 ▶

The program in Fig. 3.18 displays the square root of two numbers that are provided as input data (first and second) and also displays the square root of their sum. To accomplish this, the program must call the math library function sqrt three times:

```
first_sqrt = sqrt(first);
second_sqrt = sqrt(second);
sum_sqrt = sqrt(first + second);
```

For the first two calls, the function arguments are variables (first and second). The third call shows that a function argument may also be an expression (first + second). For each of the three calls, the result returned by function sqrt is assigned to a variable. The program begins with a call to function instruct, which displays some user instructions. Since the definition of the standard sqrt function is found in the standard math library, you will note that the program has an additional #include directive.

If we look closely at the program in Fig. 3.18, we will see that each statement contains a call to either a library function (printf, scanf, sqrt) or a user-defined function (instruct). Therefore we have been successful in using C functions as building blocks to construct a new program. ◀

Figure 3.18 Square Roots Program

```c
/*
 * Performs three square root computations
 */

#include <stdio.h> /* definitions of printf, scanf */
#include <math.h>  /* definition of sqrt */

/*
 * Displays user instructions
 */
void
instruct(void)
{
      printf("This program demonstrates the use of the \n");
      printf("math library function sqrt (square root).\n");
      printf("You will be asked to enter two numbers --\n");
      printf("the program will display the square root of \n");
      printf("each number and the square root of their sum.\n\n");
}

int
main(void)
{
      double first, second,   /* input - two data values                 */
             first_sqrt,      /* output - square root of first input value */
             second_sqrt,     /* output - square root of second input     */
             sum_sqrt;        /* output - square root of sum              */

      /* Display instructions.                                           */
      instruct();

      /* Get first number and display its square root.                   */
      printf("Enter the first number> ");
      scanf("%lf", &first);
      first_sqrt = sqrt(first);
      printf("The square root of the first number is %.2f\n",
             first_sqrt);

      /* Get second number and display its square root.                  */
      printf("Enter the second number> ");
      scanf("%lf", &second);
      second_sqrt = sqrt(second);
      printf("The square root of the second number is %.2f\n",
             second_sqrt);
```

(continued)

Figure 3.18   *(continued)*

```
      /* Display the square root of the sum of the two numbers.          */
      sum_sqrt = sqrt(first + second);
      printf("The square root of the sum of the two numbers is %.2f\n",
             sum_sqrt);

      return (0);
}

This program demonstrates the use of the
math library function sqrt (square root).
You will be asked to enter two numbers --
the program will display the square root of
each number and the square root of their sum.

Enter the first number> 9.0
The square root of the first number is 3.00
Enter the second number> 16.0
The square root of the second number is 4.00
The square root of the sum of the two numbers is 5.00
```

Predefined Functions and Code Reuse

A primary goal of software engineering is to write error-free code. *Code reuse,* reusing program fragments that have already been written and tested whenever possible, is one way to accomplish this goal. Stated more simply, "Why reinvent the wheel?"

C promotes reuse by providing numerous library functions like sqrt that can be called to perform complicated mathematical computations. Table 3.1 lists the names and descriptions of some of the most commonly used functions along with the name of the file to #include in order to have access to each function. A more extensive list of standard library functions appears in Appendix B.

If one of the functions in Table 3.1 is called with a numeric argument that is not of the argument type listed, this value is converted to the required type before it is used. Conversions of type int to type double cause no problems, but a conversion of type double to type int leads to the loss of any fractional part, just as in a mixed-type assignment. For example, if we call the abs function with the type double value −3.47, the result returned is the type int value 3. This result is the reason the library has a separate absolute value function (fabs) for type double arguments.

Table 3.1   Some Mathematical Library Functions

Function	Library File	Purpose: Example	Argument(s)	Result
abs(x)	<stdlib.h>	Returns the absolute value of its integer argument: if x is −5, abs(x) is 5	int	int
ceil(x)	<math.h>	Returns the smallest whole number that is not less than x: if x is 45.23, ceil(x) is 46.0	double	double
cos(x)	<math.h>	Returns the cosine of angle x: if x is 0.0, cos(x) is 1.0 (radians)	double	double
exp(x)	<math.h>	Returns e^x where $e = 2.71828\ldots$: if x is 1.0, exp(x) is 2.71828	double	double
fabs(x)	<math.h>	Returns the absolute value of its type double argument: if x is −8.432, fabs(x) is 8.432	double	double
floor(x)	<math.h>	Returns the largest whole number that is not greater than x: if x is 45.23, floor(x) is 45.0	double	double
log(x)	<math.h>	Returns the natural logarithm of x for x > 0.0: if x is 2.71828, log(x) is 1.0	double	double
log10(x)	<math.h>	Returns the base-10 logarithm of x for x > 0.0: if x is 100.0, log10(x) is 2.0	double	double
pow(x, y)	<math.h>	Returns x^y. If x is negative, y must be a whole number: if x is 0.16 and y is 0.5, pow(x, y) is 0.4	double, double	double
sin(x)	<math.h>	Returns the sine of angle x: if x is 1.5708, sin(x) is 1.0	double (radians)	double
sqrt(x)	<math.h>	Returns the non-negative square root of x ($\sqrt{x}$) for x ≥ 0.0: if x is 2.25, sqrt(x) is 1.5	double	double
tan(x)	<math.h>	Returns the tangent of angle x: if x is 0.0, tan(x) is 0.0	double (radians)	double

Most of the functions in Table 3.1 perform common mathematical computations. The arguments for `log` and `log10` must be positive; the argument for `sqrt` cannot be negative. The arguments for `sin`, `cos`, and `tan` must be expressed in radians, not in degrees.

EXAMPLE 3.4

We can use the C functions `pow` (power) and `sqrt` to compute the roots of a quadratic equation in x of the form

$$ax^2 + bx + c = 0$$

The two roots are defined as

$$root_1 = \frac{-b + \sqrt{b^2 - 4ac}}{2a} \qquad root_2 = \frac{-b - \sqrt{b^2 - 4ac}}{2a}$$

when the *discriminant* ($b^2 - 4ac$) is greater than zero. If we assume that this is the case, we can use these assignment statements to assign values to `root_1` and `root_2`.

```
/* Compute two roots, root_1 and root_2, for disc > 0.0 */
disc = pow(b,2) - 4 * a * c;
root_1 = (-b + sqrt(disc)) / (2 * a);
root_2 = (-b - sqrt(disc)) / (2 * a);
```

EXAMPLE 3.5

If we know the lengths of two sides (b and c) of a triangle and the angle between them in degrees (α), we can compute the length of the third side (a) using the following formula (see Fig. 3.19);

$$a^2 = b^2 + c^2 - 2bc \cos \alpha$$

To use the math library cosine function (`cos`), we must express its argument angle in radians instead of degrees. To convert an angle from degrees to radians, we multiply the angle by $\pi/180$. If we assume `PI` represents the constant π, the C assignment statement that follows computes the unknown side length.

```
a = sqrt(pow(b,2) + pow(c,2)
    - 2 * b * c * cos(alpha * PI / 180.0));
```

**Figure 3.19
Triangle with
Unknown Side *a***

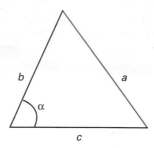

A Look at Where We Are Heading

C provides us with the capability to write our own functions. Let's assume that we have already written functions `find_area` and `find_circum`:

- Function `find_area(r)`, which returns the area of a circle with radius `r`
- Function `find_circum(r)`, which returns the circumference of a circle with radius `r`.

We can reuse these functions in the two programs shown at the beginning of this chapter (see Fig. 3.1 and Fig. 3.4). For example, Fig. 3.1 shows a program that displays the area and circumference of a circle whose radius is provided as input data. Figure 3.20 shows a revised version that uses our two functions. This program contains the two assignment statements

```
area = find_area(radius);
circum = find_circum(radius);
```

The expression part of each assignment statement is a function call with argument `radius` (the circle radius). The result returned by each function execution is stored in an output variable (`area` or `circum`).

The comment

```
/* Insert functions find_area and find_circum. */
```

appears immediately after the preprocessor directives in Fig. 3.20, reminding us to insert the functions that we assume have been written and tested. In Chapter 6, we will see how to write our own functions that can be called with arguments, and in Chapter 13, we will study how to package our own functions in personal libraries.

Besides the advantage of reusing "tried and true" code, the use of these two functions frees us from having to be concerned with the details of computing a circle's area or circumference when we write the main program. In this way, we can manage and reduce the complexity of writing programs.

Figure 3.20 **Finding Area and Circumference with Functions**

```
/*
 * Finds and prints the area and circumference of a
 * circle
 */

#include <stdio.h>
#define PI 3.14159

/* Insert functions find_area and find_circum here. */

int
main(void)
{
      double radius, /* input - radius of a circle      */
             area,   /* output - area of a circle       */
             circum; /* output - circumference of a
                        circle                          */

      /* Get the circle radius */
      printf("Enter radius> ");
      scanf("%lf", &radius);

      /* Find the area */
      area = find_area(radius);

      /* Find the circumference */
      circum = find_circum(radius);

      /* Print the area and circumference */
      printf("The area is %.2f\n", area);
      printf("The circumference is %.2f\n", circum);

      return (0);
}
Enter radius> 5.0
The area is 78.54
The circumference is 31.42
```

Self-Check

1. Rewrite the following mathematical expressions using C functions. Assume all variables should be of type double.

   a. $\sqrt{u + v} \times w^2$

   b. $\log_{10}(x^y)$

   c. $\sqrt{(x - y)^2}$

   d. $\left| xy - \dfrac{w}{z} \right|$

2. Evaluate the following:
   a. `floor(15.8)`
   b. `floor(15.8 + 0.5)`
   c. `ceil(-7.2) * pow(4.0,2.0)`
   d. `sqrt(floor(fabs(-16.8)))`
   e. `log10(1000.0)`

Programming

1. Write statements that compute and display the absolute difference of two type `double` variables, x and y ($|x - y|$).
2. Write a complete C program that prompts the user for the Cartesian coordinates of two points $(x1, y1)$ and $(x2, y2)$ and displays the distance between them computed using the following formula:

$$distance = \sqrt{(x1 - x2)^2 + (y1 - y2)^2}$$

3.9 COMMON PROGRAMMING ERRORS

Remember to use a `#include` preprocessor directive for every standard library from which you are using functions. For the time being, place the definitions of your own functions in the source file preceding any calls to these functions, and use such functions only to display messages.

Syntax or run-time errors may occur when you use C standard library functions. Make sure that each function argument is the correct type or that conversion to the correct type will lose no information. Also be careful in using functions that are undefined on some range of values. For example, if the argument for function `sqrt`, `log`, or `log10` is negative, a run-time error will occur and the function will return meaningless results.

CHAPTER REVIEW

The first part of this chapter discussed more aspects of problem solving. We reviewed the top-down approach to solving problems and showed how we could use a solution to one problem as part of the solution for another problem. We also discussed how structure charts are used to show the relationship between different levels of subproblems or between algorithm steps and their refinements.

We discussed the importance of using structured programming techniques to write programs that are easy to read, understand, and maintain. We explained that structured programs consist of sequences of control structures, and we described the compound statement as a control structure for sequential execution.

We showed how to use a system structure, the function, as a means of implementing the solution to a subproblem as a separate program module. We also introduced additional C standard library functions, and we discussed how functions enable us to reuse code that has been previously written and tested to perform mathematical computations.

New C Constructs in Chapter 3

The new C constructs introduced in this chapter are described in Table 3.2.

Table 3.2   Summary of New C Constructs

Function Definition

```
void
display(void)
{
      printf("*\n*\n*\n*\n*\n");
}
```

Function `display` is defined and may be called to print a vertical line of five asterisks.

Function Call Statement (No Arguments)

```
display();
```

Calls function `display` and causes it to begin execution.

Function Call (with Arguments)

```
sqrt(x + y)
```

Calls function `sqrt` to compute the square root of expression `x + y`.

QUICK-CHECK EXERCISES

1. The principle of code reuse states that every function in your program must be used more than once. True or false?
2. Are arguments to `printf` input arguments or output arguments?
3. Each function is executed in the order in which it is defined in the program source file. True or false?
4. How is a function executed in a program?
5. What is the purpose of a function argument?
6. Explain how a structure chart differs from an algorithm.
7. Write this equation as a C statement:

$$y = (e^{\,a\,\ln b})^2$$

8. What does the following function do?

```
void
nonsense(void)
{
      printf("*****\n");
      printf("*    *\n");
      printf("*****\n");
}
```

9. What does the following main function do?

```
int
main(void)
{
      nonsense();
      nonsense();
      nonsense();

      return (0);
}
```

ANSWERS TO QUICK-CHECK EXERCISES

1. false
2. input
3. false

4. It is called into execution by a function call, that is, the function name followed by its arguments in parentheses.
5. A function argument is used to take information into a function or to carry results back from a function to its caller.
6. A structure chart shows the relationship between subproblems; an algorithm lists the sequence in which subproblems are solved.
7. `y = pow(exp(a * log(b)),2);`
8. It displays a rectangle of asterisks.
9. It displays three rectangles of asterisks on top of each other.

REVIEW QUESTIONS

1. The diagram that shows subproblems and their interdependencies is called a(n) _____ .
2. What are three advantages of using functions?
3. When is a function executed, and where should it appear in the program source file?
4. Write a program that prompts the user for the lengths of two legs of a right triangle and makes use of the `pow` and `sqrt` functions to compute the length of the hypotenuse using the Pythagorean theorem.
5. Write a program that draws a rectangle made of a double border of asterisks. Use two functions: `draw_sides` and `draw_line`.
6. Draw a structure chart for the program described in Review Question 5.

PROGRAMMING PROJECTS

1. Write a function that displays a triangle and another one that displays a rectangle. Use these functions to write a complete C program from the basic algorithm below.
   1. Draw triangle.
   2. Draw rectangle.
   3. Print two blank lines.
   4. Draw triangle.
   5. Draw rectangle.
2. Write functions that display each of your initials in block-letter form. Use these functions to display your initials.
3. Write a computer program that computes the duration of a projectile's flight and its height above ground when it reaches the target. As part of your solution, write and call a function that displays instructions to the program user.

Problem Constant

```
G 32.17 /* gravitational constant                    */
```

Problem Inputs

```
double theta /* input - angle (radians) of elevation  */
double distance /* input - distance (ft) to target */
double velocity /* input - projectile velocity
                    (ft/sec)                         */
```

Problem Outputs

```
double time    /* output - time (sec) of flight    */
double height /* output - height at impact         */
```

Relevant Formulas

$$time = \frac{distance}{velocity \times cos(theta)}$$

$$height = velocity \times sin(theta) \times time - \frac{g \times time^2}{2}$$

Try your program on these data sets.

Inputs	Data Set 1	Data Set 2
angle of elevation	0.3 radian	0.71 radian
velocity	800 ft/sec	1,600 ft/sec
distance to target	11,000 ft	78,670 ft

4. Write a program that takes a positive number with a fractional part and rounds it to two decimal places. For example, 32.4851 would round to 32.49, and 32.4431 would round to 32.44. (*Hint:* See problem 2b in the Self-check Exercises for Section 3.8.)

5. Four track stars entered the mile race at the Penn Relays. Write a program that will take the race time in minutes and seconds for a runner, and compute and print the speed in feet per second (fps) and in meters per second (mps). (*Hint:* One mile equals 5280 feet and one kilometer equals 3282 feet.) Test your program on each of the following times:

Minutes	Seconds
3	52.83
3	59.83
4	00.03
4	16.22

Write and call a function that displays instructions to the program user.

6. A cyclist coasting on a level road slows from a speed of 10 mi/hr to 2.5 mi/hr in one minute. Write a computer program that calculates the cyclist's

constant rate of acceleration and determines how long the cyclist will take to come to rest, given an initial speed of 10 mi/hr. (*Hint:* Use the equation

$$a = \frac{v_f - v_i}{t}$$

where a is acceleration, t is time interval, v_i is initial velocity, and v_f is the final velocity.) Write and call a function that displays instructions to the program user.

7. In shopping for a new house, you must consider several factors. In this problem the initial cost of the house, the estimated annual fuel costs, and the annual tax rate are available. Write a program that will determine the total cost after a five-year period for each set of house data below. You should be able to inspect your program output to determine the best buy.

Initial House Cost	Annual Fuel Cost	Tax Rate
$67,000	$2,300	0.025
$62,000	$2,500	0.025
$75,000	$1,850	0.020

To calculate the cost of the house, add the initial cost to the fuel cost for five years; then add the taxes for five years. Taxes for one year are computed by multiplying the tax rate by the initial cost. Write and call a function that displays instructions to the program user.

8. A manufacturer wishes to determine the cost of producing an open-top cylindrical container. The surface area of the container is the sum of the area of the circular base plus the area of the outside (the circumference of the base times the height of the container). Write a program to take the radius of the base, the height of the container, the cost per square centimeter of the material (cost), and the number of containers to be produced (quantity). Calculate the cost of each container and the total cost of producing all the containers. Write and call a function that displays instructions to the user.

CHAPTER 4

SELECTION STRUCTURES: if AND switch STATEMENTS

4.1
Logical Expressions and the if Statement

4.2
if Statements with Compound Tasks

4.3
Decision Steps in Algorithms
Case Study: Water Bill Problem
Case Study: Finding the First Letter

4.4
Tracing an Algorithm

4.5
More Problem-Solving Strategies
Case Study: Computing a Water Bill with
Conservation Requirements

4.6
Nested if Statements and Multiple-Alternative
Decisions
Case Study: Computing Compass Bearings

4.7
The switch Statement for Multiple Alternatives

4.8
Common Programming Errors
Chapter Review

This chapter shows how to represent decisions in algorithms by writing steps with two or more alternative courses of action. You will see how to implement conditional execution in C by using logical expressions and the C `if` and `switch` statements. We continue our study of problem solving and study how to speed up the process by reusing solutions to problems already solved. We describe how to use data flow information in structure charts to provide additional system documentation. We also show how to hand-trace or desk-check the execution of an algorithm or program to ensure that it does what we expect.

4.1 LOGICAL EXPRESSIONS AND THE if STATEMENT

In all the algorithms illustrated in previous chapters, we execute each algorithm step exactly once in the order in which it appears. Often, we are faced with situations in which we must provide alternative steps that may or may not be executed, depending on the input data. For example, one indicator of the health of a person's heart is the resting heart rate. If this rate is 56 beats per minute or less, the heart is in excellent health. A resting heart rate between 57 and 65 beats per minute is evidence of good health, and a resting rate between 66 and 75 is average. Higher resting heart rates are a warning that the heart's condition is probably below average. A program that evaluates a person's health must be able to draw the correct conclusion from an input of the resting heart rate.

To accomplish this goal, a program must be able to determine whether the right answer to the question "Is resting heart rate more than 56 beats per minute?" is yes or no. In C, this goal is accomplished by evaluating a logical expression. Assume that the resting heart rate is stored in the type `int` variable `rst_hrt_rate`; then the logical expression corresponding to this question is

```
rst_hrt_rate > 56
```

There are only two possible values for a C expression that uses a relational or equality operator: 0 stands for false; 1 means true. If `rst_hrt_rate` is greater than `56`, the expression above evaluates to 1 (true); if `rst_hrt_rate` is not greater than `56`, the expression evaluates to 0 (false).

Most logical expressions or *conditions* that we use will have one of the following forms:

variable *relational-operator* *variable*
variable *relational-operator* *constant*
variable *equality-operator* *variable*
variable *equality-operator* *constant*

133

Relational operators are the familiar symbols < (less than), <= (less than or equal to), > (greater than), and >= (greater than or equal to). The *equality operators* are == (equal to) and != (not equal to). Take careful note of the difference between the "equal to" symbol == and the assignment operator =. These symbols are easy to confuse because we are accustomed to using = to mean "equal to" in mathematics. Unfortunately, the syntax rules of C permit the use of the assignment operator in most contexts where the "equal to" operator is legal, so the compiler often cannot recognize the substitution of an assignment operator for an equality operator as an error. Therefore, a program containing such a mistake will frequently run to completion, but it will produce incorrect results.

EXAMPLE 4.1

Table 4.1 shows the relational and equality operators and some sample conditions. Each condition is evaluated assuming these variable values and constant macro meanings.

x	power	MAX_POW	y	item	MIN_ITEM	mom_or_dad	num	SENTINEL
−5	1024	1024	7	1.5	−999.0	'M'	999	999

Table 4.1   C Relational and Equality Operators and Sample Conditions

Operator	Condition	English Meaning	Value
<=	x <= 0	x less than or equal to 0	1 (true)
<	power < MAX_POW	power less than MAX_POW	0 (false)
>=	x >= y	x greater than or equal to y	0 (false)
>	item > MIN_ITEM	item greater than MIN_ITEM	1 (true)
==	mom_or_dad == 'M'	mom_or_dad equal to 'M'	1 (true)
!=	num != SENTINEL	num not equal to SENTINEL	0 (false)

The if Statement

We now know how to write in C an expression that is the equivalent of a question such as "Is resting heart rate more than 56 beats per minute?" Next, we need to investigate a way to use the value of the expression to select a course of action. The if statement

```
if (rst_hrt_rate > 56)
      printf("Keep up your exercise program!\n");
else
      printf("Your heart is in excellent health!\n");
```

selects one of the two calls to printf. It selects the statement following the parenthesized condition if the condition evaluates to 1 representing true (i.e., rst_hrt_rate is greater than 56), and it selects the statement following the keyword else if the condition evaluates to 0 representing false.

The condition in this particular if statement always evaluates to 1 or 0 because of the way the relational operators are defined. However, C does not require the logical value true to be represented by the integer 1; instead, C always uses the integer 0 to represent the value false and accepts *any nonzero value* as a representation of true. For now, we will always use the integer 1 when we need the value true, but knowing how C really views conditions will help you understand why some common mistakes that you may make will not be seen by the C compiler as syntax errors.

Figure 4.1 is a graphical description, called a *flowchart,* of the if statement just given. Figure 4.1 shows that the condition enclosed in the diamond-shaped box (rst_hrt_rate > 56) is evaluated first. If the condition is true (that is, has a nonzero value), the arrow labeled *true* is followed, and the output on the right is executed. If the condition is false, the arrow labeled *false* is followed, and the output on the left is executed.

More if Statement Examples

The if statement shown in Fig. 4.1 has two alternatives, but only one alternative will be executed for a given value of rst_hrt_rate. Example 4.2 illustrates that an if statement can also have a single alternative executed only when the condition is true.

**Figure 4.1
Flowchart of
if Statement
with Two
Alternatives**

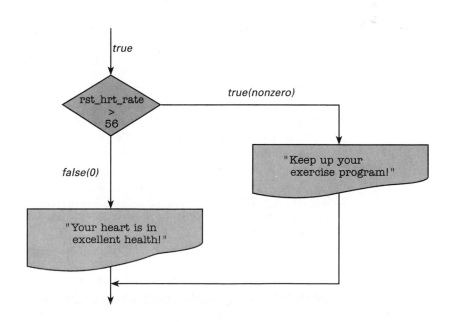

**Figure 4.2
Flowchart of if
Statement with
One Alternative**

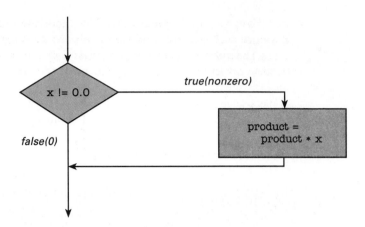

EXAMPLE 4.2

The `if` statement that follows has one alternative executed only when `x` is not equal to zero. This alternative causes `product` to be multiplied by `x`; the new value is saved in `product`, replacing the old value. If `x` is equal to zero, the multiplication is not performed. Figure 4.2 is a flowchart of this `if` statement.

```
/* Multiply product by a nonzero x only */
if (x != 0.0)
        product = product * x;
```

The assignment statement in the rectangle on the right is carried out only if `x` is not zero.

EXAMPLE 4.3

The `if` statement below has two alternatives. It displays either `Cruiser` or `Frigate`, depending on the character stored in the type `char` variable `crsr_or_frgt`.

```
if (crsr_or_frgt == 'C')
        printf("Cruiser\n");
else
        printf("Frigate\n");
```

EXAMPLE 4.4

The `if` statement that follows has one alternative; it displays the message `Cruiser` only when `crsr_or_frgt` has the value `'C'`. Regardless of whether `Cruiser` is displayed or not, the message `Combatant ship` is displayed.

```
if (crsr_or_frgt == 'C')
        printf("Cruiser\n");
printf("Combatant ship\n");
```

The program fragments that follow contain incorrect versions of the single-alternative `if` statement above. The error in the first fragment, missing parentheses around the condition, violates C syntax rules and will be detected and possibly corrected by the compiler.

```
if crsr_or_frgt == 'C' /* error - missing
                              parentheses */
      printf("Cruiser\n");
printf("Combatant ship\n");
```

The extra semicolon in the second fragment does not cause a violation of C syntax rules because the compiler translates the first line as a single-alternative `if` statement in which there is no action to perform on the true branch (i.e., an *empty statement* follows the condition). The first `printf` loses its dependency on the value of the condition; so both calls to `printf` are executed unconditionally.

```
if (crsr_or_frgt == 'C'); /* mistake - improper
                                placement of ; */
      printf("Cruiser\n");
printf("Combatant ship\n");
```

Syntax Displays for if Statement

The following display summarizes the forms of the `if` statement we have used so far. Section 4.2 considers the use of `if` statements where multiple tasks are to be performed on either the true branch or the false branch.

---

if Statement (One Alternative)

SYNTAX: `if` (*condition*)
                    statement$_T$

EXAMPLE: `if (x > 0.0)`
                    `pos_prod = pos_prod * x;`

INTERPRETATION: If the *condition* evaluates to true, then *statement*$_T$ is executed; otherwise, it is skipped.

(continued)

if Statement (Two Alternatives)

SYNTAX: if (*condition*)
            statement$_T$
      else
            statement$_F$

EXAMPLE: if (x >= 0.0)
          printf("Positive");
      else
          printf("Negative");

INTERPRETATION: If the *condition* evaluates to true, then *statement*$_T$ is executed and *statement*$_F$ is skipped; otherwise, *statement*$_T$ is skipped and *statement*$_F$ is executed.

EXERCISES FOR SECTION 4.1

Self-Check

1. What do the following statements display?
   a. ```
   if (12 < 12)
           printf("Never\n");
   else
           printf("Always\n");
   ```
   b. ```
   var1 = 15.0;
   var2 = 25.12;
   if (var2 <= 2 * var1)
           printf("O.K.\n");
   else
           printf("Not O.K.\n");
   ```

2. What value is assigned to x for each of the following segments when y is 15.0?
   a. ```
   x = 25.0;
   if (y != (x - 10.0))
           x = x - 10.0;
   else
           x = x / 2.0;
   ```
   b. ```
   if (y < 15.0)
           if (y >= 0.0)
                   x = 5 * y;
           else
                   x = 2 * y;
   else
           x = 3 * y;
   ```

3. What value is assigned to the type `int` variable `ans` in this statement if the value of `p` is `100` and `q` is `50`?

```
ans = (p > 95) + (q < 95);
```

This statement is not shown as an example of a reasonable assignment statement; rather, it is a sample of a statement that makes little sense to the reader. The statement is still legal and executable in C, however, because of the language's use of integers to represent the logical values true and false.

Programming

1. Write C statements to carry out the following steps:
   a. If `item` is nonzero, then multiply `product` by `item` and save the result in `product`; otherwise, skip the multiplication. In either case, print the value of `product`.
   b. Store the absolute difference of `x` and `y` in `z`, where the absolute difference is `(x - y)` or `(y - x)`, whichever is positive. Do not use the `abs` or `fabs` functions in your solution.
   c. If `x` is zero, add `1` to `zero_count`. If `x` is negative, add `x` to `minus_sum`. If `x` is greater than zero, add `x` to `plus_sum`.

4.2 if STATEMENTS WITH COMPOUND TASKS

In the `if` statements we have seen so far, the *statement* following the condition or the keyword `else` has always been a single executable statement such as an assignment statement or a function call statement. If multiple tasks are to be performed dependent on a condition, they can be grouped together within braces to form a single compound statement. Another `if` statement, whether a single- or double-alternative `if`, is also considered a single statement. The next three examples use `if` with compound statements following the condition or the `else`.

 **EXAMPLE 4.5**

Suppose you are a biologist writing a program to report statistics about the growth rate of a fruit fly population. You could use the `if` statement that follows to compute the percentage of population increase over a one-day period if there was, in fact, some growth. The statement first determines the amount of growth by subtracting today's population (`pop_today`) from yesterday's population (`pop_ystday`). Then it computes what percentage of the original (yesterday's) population this growth represents. The compound statement is not executed when today's population is no larger than yesterday's.

```
if (pop_today > pop_ystday) {
    growth = pop_today - pop_ystday;
    gth_pct = 100.0 * growth / pop_ystday;
}
```

In later chapters, we will see that it is useful to be able to order a pair of data values in memory so that the smaller value is stored in one variable (for example, x) and the larger value in another (for example, y). The if statement in Fig. 4.3 rearranges any two values stored in x and y so that the smaller number will always be in x and the larger number will always be in y. If the two numbers are already in the proper order, the compound statement will not be executed.

The variables x, y, and temp should all be the same data type. Although the values of x and y are being switched, an additional variable, temp, is needed for storage of a copy of one of these values.

Figure 4.3   if Statement to Order x and y

```
if (x > y) {
    temp = x;        /* Store old x in temp    */
    x = y;           /* Store old y in x       */
    y = temp;        /* Store old x in y       */
}
```

Table 4.2 is a step-by-step simulation of the execution of the if statement when x is 12.5 and y is 5.0. The table shows that temp is initially undefined (indicated by ?). Each line of the table shows the part of the if statement that is

Table 4.2   Step-by-step Simulation of if Statement

Statement Part	x	y	temp	Effect
	12.5	5.0	?	
if (x > y){				12.5 > 5.0 — true
temp = x;			12.5	Store old x in temp
x = y;	5.0			Store old y in x
y = temp;		12.5		Store old x in y
}				

being executed, followed by its effect. If any variable gets a new value, the new value is shown on that line. The last value stored in x is 5.0, and the last value stored in y is 12.5 as desired. ←

EXAMPLE 4.7

As manager of a company's automobile fleet, you may want to keep records of the safety ratings of the fleet cars. In the if statement that follows, the true task makes a record of an automobile (auto_id) whose crash test rating index (ctri) is at least as low (good) as the cutoff you have established for acceptably safe cars (MAX_SAFE_CTRI). The false task records an auto whose ctri does not meet your standard. In either case, an appropriate message is printed, and one is added to the count of safe or unsafe cars. Both the true and false statements are compound statements.

```
if (ctri <= MAX_SAFE_CTRI) {
      printf("Car #%d: safe\n", auto_id);
      safe = safe + 1;
} else {
      printf("Car #%d: unsafe\n", auto_id);
      unsafe = unsafe + 1;
}
```

If the braces enclosing the compound statements were omitted, the first printf call would end the if statement. The increment of safe would be translated as an unconditionally executed statement, and the compiler would mark the keyword else as an error, since a statement cannot begin with else. ←

Program Style *Format of the if Statement*

In all our if statement examples, the true and false tasks are indented. For double-alternative if statements, we place the else keyword (not indented) on a separate line. The purpose of the indentation is to increase *our* ability to read and understand an if statement; the C compiler ignores indentation.

When the true or false task of an if is a compound statement, the placement of the braces is a matter of personal preference. The style we use in our examples is one that is prevalent in major segments of the computer industry. We recommend using braces on both the true and the false tasks if *either* is a compound statement. Some C programmers prefer to always use the braces in if statements, even when only single-statement tasks are involved. This way all of the if statements in the program have a consistent style. The most important aspect of style standards is the adoption of the *same* set of standards by all programmers working together so that they can easily read each other's code.

Self-Check

1. Insert braces where they are needed so the meaning matches the indentation.

```
if (x > y)
      x = x + 10.0;
      printf("x Bigger\n");
else
      printf("x Smaller\n");
      printf("y is %.2f\n", y);
```

2. Correct the following `if` statement; assume the indentation is correct.

```
if (num1 < 0);
      product = num1 * num2 * num3;
      printf("Product is %d\n", product);
else;
      sum = num1 + num2 + num3;
      printf("Sum is %d\n", sum);
printf("Data: %d, %d, %d\n", num1, num2, num3);
```

3. Revise the style of the following `if` statement to improve its readability.

```
if (engine_type == 'J') {printf("Jet engine");
speed_category = 1;}
else{printf("Propellers"); speed_category
= 2;}
```

Programming

1. Write an `if` statement that might be used to compute and print the average of a set of *n* numbers whose sum is stored in variable `total`. This average should be found only if *n* is greater than 0; otherwise, an error message should be printed.
2. Write an interactive program that contains a compound `if` statement and that may be used to compute the area of a square (*area = side²*) or a triangle (*area = 1/2 × base × height*) after prompting the user to type the first character of the figure name (S or T).

4.3 DECISION STEPS IN ALGORITHMS

In the problem that follows, we will see how to write a program that can be used to compute an individual's water bill based on current usage.

Case Study: Water Bill Problem

▬◤ **PROBLEM** ◢▬

Write a program that computes a customer's water bill. The bill includes a $35 water demand charge plus a consumption (use) charge of $1.10 for every thousand gallons used. Consumption is figured from meter readings in thousands of gallons taken recently and during the previous quarter. If the customer's unpaid balance is greater than zero, a $2 late charge is assessed as well.

▬◤ **ANALYSIS** ◢▬

The total water bill is the sum of the demand and use charges, the unpaid balance, and a possible late charge. The demand charge is a program constant ($35), but the use charge must be computed. To do this, we must know the previous and current meter readings (the problem inputs). After obtaining these data, we can compute the use charge by multiplying the difference between the two meter readings by the charge for 1000 gallons, the problem constant $1.10. Next, we can determine the applicable late charge, if any, and finally compute the water bill by adding the four components.

Data Requirements

Problem Constants
```
DEMAND_CHG 35.00   /* basic water demand charge        */
PER_1000_CHG 1.10  /* charge per thousand gallons
                        used                            */
LATE_CHG 2.00      /* surcharge on an unpaid balance   */
```

Problem Inputs
```
int previous   /* meter reading from previous quarter
                    in thousands of gallons            */
int current    /* meter reading from current quarter   */
double unpaid  /* unpaid balance of previous bill      */
```

Problem Outputs

```
double bill    /* water bill    */
```

Relevant Formulas

used = current meter reading − previous meter reading
use charge = used × charge per thousand gallons
water bill = demand charge + use charge + unpaid balance
        + applicable late charge

DESIGN

The initial algorithm follows, and because the relevant formulas and initial algorithm use data in addition to the values named as problem constants, inputs and outputs, we add some program variables to our data requirements. The structure chart shown in Fig. 4.4 includes *data flow* information that shows the inputs and the outputs of each individual algorithm step. The structure chart shows that Step 2 "Get data," provides values for unpaid, previous, and current

Figure 4.4   Structure Chart for Water Bill Problem

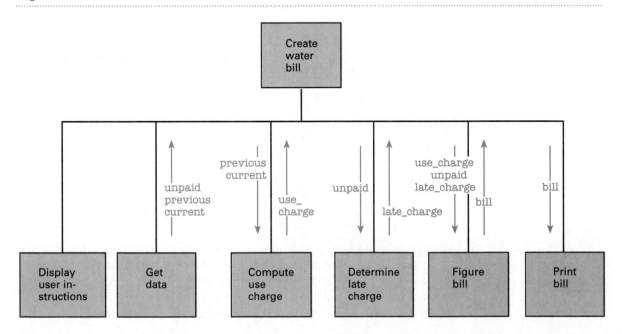

as its outputs (data flow arrow points up). Similarly, Step 3, "Compute use charge," uses `previous` and `current` as its inputs (data flow arrow points down) and provides `use_charge` as its output. We will discuss the relevance of the data flow information after we complete the problem solution.

Initial Algorithm

1. Display user instructions.
2. Get data: unpaid balance, previous and current meter readings.
3. Compute use charge.
4. Determine applicable late charge.
5. Figure bill.
6. Print bill.

Additional Data Requirements

Program Variables
```
int used /* thousands of gallons used this quarter   */
double use_charge  /* charge for actual water use    */
double late_charge /* charge for non-payment of part
                      of previous balance             */
```

Algorithm Refinements

Now let's write refinements of Steps 3 and 4 of the initial algorithm. Although Step 3 is the same for all customers, Step 4 will require a *decision*.

Step 3 Refinement
```
3.1 used is current − previous
3.2 use_charge is used × PER_1000_CHG
```

Step 4 Refinement
```
4.1 if unpaid > 0
        assess late charge
    else
        assess no late charge
```

The decision step above is expressed in *pseudocode,* which is a mixture of English and C used to describe algorithm steps. In the pseudocode for a decision step, we use indentation and the reserved words `if` and `else` to show the logical structure of the decision step. The decision step condition may be written in English or C; similarly, the true and false tasks may be written in English or C.

The program, shown in Fig. 4.5, begins with a block comment explaining the program purpose.

Figure 4.5   Program for Water Bill Problem

```
/*
 * Computes and prints a water bill given an unpaid
 * balance and previous and current meter readings.
 * Bill includes a demand charge of $35.00, a use
 * charge of $1.10 per thousand gallons, and a surcharge
 * of $2.00 if there is an unpaid balance.
 */

#include <stdio.h>

#define DEMAND_CHG   35.00 /* basic water demand charge              */
#define PER_1000_CHG 1.10  /* charge per thousand
                              gallons used                          */
#define LATE_CHG      2.00 /* surcharge assessed on unpaid balance  */

/*
 * Displays user instructions
 */
void
instruct_water(void)
{
     printf("This program figures a water bill ");
     printf("based on the demand charge/n");
     printf("($%.2f) and a $%.2f per 1000 ",
            DEMAND_CHG, PER_1000_CHG);
     printf("gallons use charge.\n\n");
     printf("A $%.2f surcharge is added to ",
            LATE_CHG);
     printf("accounts with an unpaid balance.\n");
     printf("\nEnter unpaid balance, previous ");
     printf("and current meter readings\n");
     printf("on separate lines after the prompts.\n");
     printf("Press <return> or <enter> after ");
     printf("typing each number.\n\n");
}
```

(continued)

Figure 4.5 *(continued)*

```
int
main(void)
{
        int     previous;    /* input - meter reading from
                                previous quarter in thousands of
                                gallons                          */
        int     current;     /* input - meter reading from current
                                quarter                          */
        double unpaid;       /* input - unpaid balance of
                                previous bill                    */
        double bill;         /* output - water bill             */
        int     used;        /* thousands of gallons used this
                                quarter                          */
        double use_charge;   /* charge for actual water
                                use                              */
        double late_charge;  /* charge for non-payment of part of
                                previous balance                 */

        /* Display user instructions.                           */
        instruct_water();

        /* Get data: unpaid balance, previous and current meter
           readings.                                            */
        printf("Enter unpaid balance> $");
        scanf("%lf", &unpaid);
        printf("Enter previous meter reading> ");
        scanf("%d", &previous);
        printf("Enter current meter reading> ");
        scanf("%d", &current);

        /* Compute use charge.                                  */
        used = current - previous;
        use_charge = used * PER_1000_CHG;

        /* Determine applicable late charge                     */
        if (unpaid > 0) {
             late_charge = LATE_CHG; /* Assess late charge on unpaid
                                        balance.                 */
```

(continued)

Figure 4.5   *(continued)*

```
            printf("\nBill includes $%.2f late charge",
                    late_charge);
            printf(" on unpaid balance of $%.2f\n",
                    unpaid);
    } else {
            late_charge = 0; /* Assess no late charge.              */
    }

    /* Figure bill.                                                 */
    bill = DEMAND_CHG + use_charge + unpaid + late_charge;

    /* Print bill.                                                  */
    printf("\nTotal due = $%.2f\n", bill);

    return (0);
}
```

This program figures a water bill based on the demand charge
($35.00) and a $1.10 per 1000 gallons use charge.

A $2.00 surcharge is added to accounts with an unpaid balance.

Enter unpaid balance, previous and current meter readings
on separate lines after the prompts.
Press <return> or <enter> after typing each number.

Enter unpaid balance> $71.50
Enter previous meter reading> 4198
Enter current meter reading> 4238

Bill includes $2.00 late charge on unpaid balance of $71.50

Total due = $152.50

The program begins by calling function `instruct_water` to display the user instructions (the first six lines of program output). After getting the input data, the program computes the use charge and then uses this `if` statement to implement the decision step which determines the applicable late charge:

```
if (unpaid > 0) {
    late_charge = LATE_CHG; /* Assess late charge on
                                unpaid balance.       */
    printf("\nBill includes $%.2f late charge",
        late_charge);
    printf(" on unpaid balance of $%.2f\n",
        unpaid);
} else {
    late_charge = 0; /* Assess no late charge.        */
}
```

The comments on the right are embedded in the `if` statement. Although the task on the false branch of the `if` statement (following the keyword `else`) is only a single statement, we have chosen to enclose it in braces so the style balances the style of the true branch.

━━━━ **TESTING** ━━━━

To test this program, run it with data sets that cause each branch of the decision to execute. One data set should include a positive unpaid balance, and another should have an unpaid balance of zero.

Program Style   *Using Constant Macros to Enhance Readability and Ease Maintenance*

The names of the constant macros `DEMAND_CHG`, `PER_1000_CHG`, and `LATE_CHG` appear in the user instructions, in the use and late charge computations, and in the bill calculation of the program in Fig. 4.5. We could just as easily have placed the values that these names represent (`35.00`, `1.10`, and `2.00`) directly in the statements where they are needed. The resulting statements would be

```
printf("This program figures a water bill ");
printf("based on the demand charge\n");
printf("($%.2f) and a $%.2f per 1000 ";
    35.00, 1.10);
printf("gallons use charge.\n\n");
printf("A $%.2f surcharge is added to ",
    2.00);
printf("accounts with an unpaid balance.\n");
```

```
use_charge = used * 1.10;
late_charge = 2.00; /* Assess late charge on unpaid
                             balance. */
bill = 35.00 + use_charge + unpaid + late_charge;
```

However, use of constant macro names rather than actual values has two advantages. First, the original statements are easier to understand because they use the descriptive names DEMAND_CHG, PER_1000_CHG, and LATE_CHG rather than numbers, which have no intrinsic meaning. Second, a program written using constant macros is much easier to maintain than one written with constant values. For example, if we want to use different constant values in the water bill program in Fig. 4.5, we need to change only the constant macro definitions and the statement of the program's purpose. However, if we inserted constant values directly in the statements, we would have to change any statements that manipulate the constant values.

Note that the names of the constant macros also appear in two calls to printf in function instruct_water. It is perfectly permissible to reference such names in any function body that appears later in the same source file as the constant macro definitions.

Adding Data Flow Information to Structure Charts

In Fig. 4.4, we added data flow information to the structure chart showing the inputs and outputs of each individual algorithm step. The data flow information is an important part of the system documentation; it shows which program variables are processed by each step and the manner in which these variables are processed. If a step gives a new value to a variable, then the variable is considered an *output of the step*. If a step displays a variable's value or uses it in a computation without changing its value, the variable is considered an *input to the step*. For example, the step "Determine late charge" in Fig. 4.4 processes variables unpaid and late_charge. This step uses the value of unpaid (its input) to determine late_charge (its output).

Figure 4.4 shows that a variable may have different roles for different subproblems in the structure chart. For example, when previous and current are considered in the context of the original problem statement, they are problem inputs (data supplied by the program user). When they are considered in the context of the subproblem "Get data," since the task of the subproblem is to deliver values for previous and current (as well as unpaid) to the main function, they are considered outputs from this step. When previous and current are considered in the context of the subproblem "Compute use charge," the task of the subproblem is to use them to compute a value of use_charge, so previous and current are considered inputs to this step. In the same way, the roles of the variables unpaid, use_charge, late_charge, and bill change as we go from step to step in the structure chart.

Case Study: Finding the First Letter

Of three letters, find and display the one that comes first in the alphabet.

ANALYSIS

From our prior experience with conditions and decision steps, we know how to compare two numbers to see which one is smaller using the relational operator <. In C, we can also use this operator to determine whether one letter precedes another in the alphabet, provided that the two letters being compared are both uppercase or both lowercase letters. For example, the condition 'A' < 'F' is true because A precedes F in the alphabet. Because we have no direct way to compare three items, our strategy will be to do a sequence of pairwise comparisons. We will start by comparing the first two letters to find the smaller of that pair. Next, we can compare this result to the third letter, finding the smaller of that pair. The result of the second comparison will be the smallest of all three letters.

Data Requirements

Problem Inputs
```
char ch1, ch2, ch3 /* three letters all uppercase
                      or all lowercase          */
```

Problem Outputs
```
char alpha_first    /* the alphabetically first
                       character                */
```

DESIGN

The initial algorithm follows. Figure 4.6 shows the structure chart that corresponds to the algorithm.

Initial Algorithm

1. Get three letters for variables ch1, ch2, and ch3.
2. Save the alphabetically first of ch1, ch2, and ch3 in alpha_first.
3. Display the alphabetically first letter.

**Figure 4.6
Structure Chart
for Finding the
Alphabetically
First Letter**

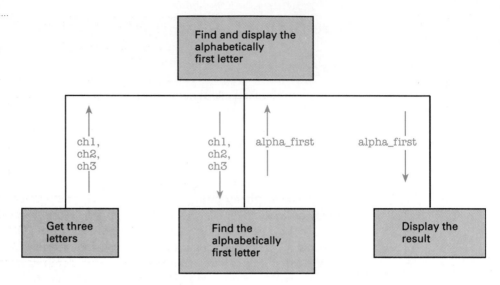

Algorithm Refinements

You can perform Step 2 by first comparing `ch1` and `ch2` and saving the alphabetically first letter in `alpha_first`; this result can then be compared to `ch3`. The refinements of Step 2 follow.

Step 2 Refinement
2.1 Save the alphabetically first of `ch1` and `ch2` in `alpha_first`.
2.2 Save the alphabetically first of `ch3` and `alpha_first` in `alpha_first`.

Step 2.1 Refinement
2.1.1 if `ch1` precedes `ch2`
   2.1.2 `alpha_first` gets `ch1`.
  else
   2.1.3 `alpha_first` gets `ch2`.

Step 2.2 Refinement
2.2.1 if `ch3` precedes `alpha_first`
   2.2.1 `alpha_first` gets `ch3`.

Figure 4.7 is a structure chart that shows the relationship between Step 2 and its refinements. The double-headed arrow on the far right indicates that `alpha_first` is both an input to and an output from this step.

◀ IMPLEMENTATION ▶

A program that implements this algorithm is shown in Fig. 4.8. The `if` statement with two alternatives saves either `ch1` or `ch2` in `alpha_first`. The `if`

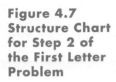

**Figure 4.7
Structure Chart
for Step 2 of
the First Letter
Problem**

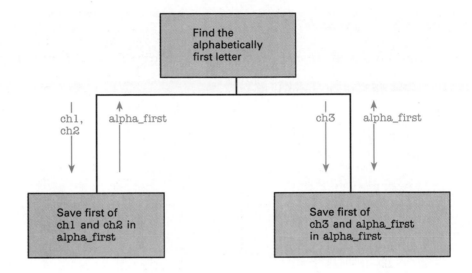

Figure 4.8   Finding the Alphabetically First Letter

```
/*
 * Finds and displays the alphabetically first letter
 */

#include <stdio.h>

int
main(void)
{
      char ch1, ch2, ch3; /* three letters (all uppercase or all
                             lowercase)                          */
      char alpha_first;   /* alphabetically first letter         */

      /* Get three letters.                                      */
      printf("Enter three uppercase or three lowercase letters> ");
      scanf("%c%c%c", &ch1, &ch2, &ch3);

      /* Save the alphabetically first of ch1 and ch2 in alpha_first.  */
      if (ch1 < ch2)
            alpha_first = ch1; /* ch1 comes before ch2           */
      else
            alpha_first = ch2; /* ch2 comes before ch1           */
```

(continued)

Figure 4.8   *(continued)*

```
    /* Save the alphabetically first of ch3 and alpha_first in
       alpha_first.                                                  */
    if (ch3 < alpha_first)
          alpha_first = ch3; /* ch3 comes before alpha_first          */

    /* Display result.                                               */
    printf("%c is the first letter alphabetically.\n", alpha_first);

    return (0);
    }

Enter three uppercase or three lowercase letters> EBK
B is the first letter alphabetically.
```

statement with one alternative stores ch3 in alpha_first if ch3 precedes the value already in alpha_first. Later in the chapter, we will see that if statements with more than two alternatives are also possible in C.

TESTING

To test this program, put the alphabetically first letter in each of the three possible positions. However, three test cases will not try out all the possible paths through the code. Section 4.4 discusses four cases that should be tested. You will also see what happens when one of the letters is repeated.

Using Functions

The program in Fig. 4.8 is an example in which we could use functions to improve the structured programming process by facilitating top-down design. As a result, we would generate code that was more concise and readable. Let's assume we have a function named choose_first that returns the alphabetically first of its two type char arguments. Rather than using if statements in the main function to compare ch1 and ch2 and then to compare ch3 and alpha_first, we can call function choose_first.

```
/* Save the alphabetically first of ch1 and ch2 in
   alpha_first */
alpha_first = choose_first(ch1, ch2);
```

```
/* Save the alphabetically first of ch3 and
   alpha_first in alpha_first                      */
alpha_first = choose_first(ch3, alpha_first);
```

These two assignment statements would replace the two if statements that appear in Fig. 4.8 resulting in a much shorter and more readable main function. The first call to choose_first returns the smaller of ch1 and ch2, which is saved in alpha_first. The second call to choose_first returns the smaller of ch3 and the current value of alpha_first, which is also saved in alpha_first. After both statements execute, alpha_first contains the smallest of all three letters as required. Of course, function choose_first must contain an if statement that compares its arguments, and choose_first must be inserted in the source file.

EXERCISES FOR SECTION 4.3

Self-Check

1. Draw a structure chart for the washer problem in Section 3.2; show the relationship between the main function and its four subproblems. Add data flow information to this structure chart. Discuss how the role of the variable representing percentage difference in area (a problem output) changes from one subproblem to another.

Programming

1. Modify the structure chart and program for the first letter problem to find the first of four letters.
2. Write a structure chart and program to find the alphabetically last of three letters.

4.4 TRACING AN ALGORITHM

A critical step in the design of an algorithm or program is to verify that it is correct before you spend a lot of time entering or debugging it. Often a few extra minutes spent in verifying the correctness of an algorithm will save hours of testing time later.

One important technique, called a hand trace or desk check, consists of a careful, step-by-step simulation on paper of how the computer would execute the algorithm or program. The results of this simulation should show the effect of each step's execution using data that are relatively easy to process by hand. In Section 4.2, we simulated the execution of an if statement that switches the values of two variables. Next, we will simulate the execution of the refined algorithm for the first letter problem.

Refined Algorithm

1. Get three letters for ch1, ch2, and ch3.
2. Save the alphabetically first of ch1, ch2, and ch3 in alpha_first.
   2.1 Save the alphabetically first of ch1 and ch2 in alpha_first.
      2.1.1 if ch1 precedes ch2
             2.1.2 alpha_first gets ch1.
      else
             2.1.3 alpha_first gets ch2.
   2.2 Save the alphabetically first of ch3 and alpha_first in alpha_first.
      2.2.1 if ch3 precedes alpha_first
             2.2.2 alpha_first gets ch3.
3. Display the alphabetically first letter.

     Table 4.3 shows a trace of the algorithm for the data string THE. Each step is listed at the left in order of its execution. If an algorithm step changes the value of a variable, the table shows the new value. The effect of each step is described at the far right. For example, the table shows that the step

     1. Get three letters for ch1, ch2, and ch3.

stores the letters T, H, and E in the variables ch1, ch2, and ch3.

Table 4.3   Trace of Algorithm for Program in Figure 4.8

Algorithm Step	ch1	ch2	ch3	alpha_first	Effect
	?	?	?	?	
1. Get three letters...	T	H	E		Gets the data
2.1.1 if ch1 precedes ch2					Is 'T' < 'H' ? value is false
2.1.3 alpha_first gets ch2.				H	'H' is first so far
2.2.1 if ch3 precedes alpha_first					Is 'E' < 'H' ? value is true
2.2.2 alpha_first gets ch3.				E	'E' is first
3. Display alpha_first.					Prints E is the first letter...

The trace in Table 4.3 clearly shows that the alphabetically first letter of the input string, E, is stored in `alpha_first` and printed. In order to verify that the algorithm is correct, you would need to select other data that cause the two conditions to evaluate to different combinations of their values. Because there are two conditions and each has two possible values (true and false), there are 2×2, or 4, different combinations that should be tried. (What are they?) An exhaustive desk check would show that the algorithm works for all of these combinations.

In addition to these four possible combinations, you should verify that the algorithm works correctly for unusual data. For example, what would happen if all three letters or a pair of letters were the same? Would the algorithm still produce the correct result? To complete the desk check, you would need to show that the algorithm does indeed handle these special situations properly.

In tracing each case, you must be very careful to execute the algorithm exactly as the computer would execute it. Often programmers assume that a particular step will be executed without explicitly testing each condition and tracing each step; however, a trace performed in this way is of little value.

EXERCISES FOR SECTION 4.4

Self-Check

1. Provide sample data and traces for the remaining three cases of the first letter problem.
   a. Case 1, both conditions are true.
   b. Case 2, first condition is true, second is false.
   c. Case 3, both conditions are false.
2. Consider a special case of the alphabetically first letter problem. Determine the value of the conditions when all three letters are the same.
3. Trace the water bill program in Fig. 4.5 when:
   a. `unpaid` is `40.00`, `previous` is `3222`, and `current` is `3242`.
   b. `unpaid` is `0`, `previous` is `4000`, and `current` is `4030`.

4.5 MORE PROBLEM-SOLVING STRATEGIES

Often what appears to be a new problem will turn out to be a variation of one that you already solved. Consequently, an important skill in problem solving is the ability to recognize that one problem is similar to another solved earlier. As you progress through this course, you will start to build up a *library* of programs and functions. Whenever possible, you should try to adapt or reuse parts of successful programs.

Modifying a Problem Solution

Writing programs that can be easily changed or modified to fit other situations is advisable; programmers and program users will often want to make slight improvements to a program after they use it. If the original program is well designed, the programmer will be able to accommodate changing specifications with a minimum of effort. As you will find by working through the next problem, when changes are needed it may be possible to modify one or two control statements rather than having to rewrite the entire program.

Case Study: Computing a Water Bill with Conservation Requirements

◄ PROBLEM ►

We need to modify the water bill program so that customers who fail to meet conservation requirements are charged for all their water use at twice the rate of customers who meet the guidelines. Residents of this water district are required to use no more than 95% of the amount of water they used in the same quarter last year in order to qualify for the lower use rate of $1.10 per thousand gallons.

◄ ANALYSIS ►

This problem is a modification of the water bill problem solved in Fig. 4.5. Customers who meet the conservation guidelines should be charged the basic use rate of $1.10 per thousand gallons; those who do not should be charged at twice this rate. We can solve this problem by adding the use figure from last year to our problem inputs and replacing Step 3.2 (the use charge calculation) in the original algorithm with a decision step that selects either the basic rate or the penalty rate for computing the use charge.

Data Requirements

Problem Constants
```
DEMAND_CHG 35.00        /*basic water demand charge */
PER_1000_CHG 1.10       /*charge per thousand gallons
                          used                     */
LATE_CHG 2.00           /*surcharge on an unpaid
                          balance                  */
```
(additional constants)
```
OVERUSE_CHG_RATE 2.0 /* double use charge as non-
                        conservation penalty    */
CONSERV_RATE 95      /* percent of last year's use
                        allowed this year        */
```

Problem Inputs

```
int previous        /* meter reading from previous
                       quarter in thousands of
                       gallons                     */
int current         /* meter reading from current
                       quarter                     */
double unpaid       /* unpaid balance of previous
                       bill                        */
(additional input)
int use_last_year   /* use same quarter last year */
```

Problem Outputs

```
double bill         /* water bill                  */
```

Program Variables

```
int used            /* thousands of gallons used
                       this quarter                */
double use_charge   /* charge for actual water use */
double late_charge  /* charge for non-payment of
                       part of previous balance    */
```

Relevant Formulas

used = current meter reading − previous meter reading
use charge = used × charge per thousand gallons
*water bill = demand charge + use charge + unpaid balance
        + applicable late charge*
(additional formulas)

$$allowed\ use = \frac{CONSERV\_RATE}{100.0} \times use\ last\ year$$

overuse use charge = used × OVERUSE_CHG_RATE *× charge per
        thousand gallons*

DESIGN

The critical changes to the algorithm involve adding last year's use to Step 2, the input step, and modifying the details of Step 3. The updated algorithm is shown followed by a new refinement for Step 3.

Initial Algorithm

1. Display user instructions.
2. Get data: unpaid balance, previous and current meter readings, and last year's use.

3. Compute use charge.
4. Determine applicable late charge.
5. Figure bill.
6. Print bill.

Algorithm Refinements

Step 3 Refinement
3.1 used = current − previous
3.2 if guidelines met
     use_charge is used × PER_1000_CHG.
   else
       notify customer of overuse
       use_charge is used × OVERUSE_CHG_RATE ×
                   PER_1000_CHG.

IMPLEMENTATION

To write the program, we should build on the program presented in Fig. 4.5, adding the necessary constants and input variable, revising the user instruction function and "Get data" step to reflect the need for last year's use data, and replacing the assignment statement that computes the use charge

```
use_charge = used * PER_1000_CHG;
```

with the if statement

```
if (used <= CONSERV_RATE / 100.0 * use_last_year) {
     use_charge = used * PER_1000_CHG;
       /* conservation requirements met */
} else {
     printf("Use charge is at %.2f times ",
           OVERUSE_CHG_RATE);
     printf("normal rate since use of\n");
     printf("%d units exceeds %d percent ",
           used, CONSERV_RATE);
     printf("of last year's %d-unit use.\n",
           use_last_year);
     use_charge = used * OVERUSE_CHG_RATE * PER_1000_CHG;
}
```

   If the condition

```
(used <= CONSERV_RATE / 100.0 * use_last_year)
```

is true, the conservation guidelines have been met and the use charge is computed as before; otherwise, the customer is notified of the overuse, and the overuse charge rate is factored into the computation of the use charge.

EXERCISES FOR SECTION 4.5

Self-Check

1. Draw a structure chart for Programming Exercise 2; include data flow information.

Programming

1. Provide the complete program for the water bill problem with conservation requirements.
2. Rewrite the miles-to-kilometers conversion program from Section 2.7 so the user may elect to convert miles to kilometers or kilometers to miles.

4.6 NESTED if STATEMENTS AND MULTIPLE-ALTERNATIVE DECISIONS

Until now, we used if statements to implement decisions involving up to two alternatives. In this section, we will see how the if statement can be used to implement decisions involving more than two alternatives.

A nested if statement occurs when the true or false statement of an if statement is itself an if statement. A nested if statement can be used to implement decisions with several alternatives, as shown in the next examples.

EXAMPLE 4.8

The nested if statement that follows has three alternatives. The statement causes one of three variables (num_pos, num_neg, or num_zero) to be increased by one depending on whether x is greater than zero, less than zero, or equal to zero, respectively.

```
/* increment num_pos, num_neg, or num_zero depending on x */
if (x > 0)
      num_pos = num_pos + 1;
else
      if (x < 0)
            num_neg = num_neg + 1;
      else /* x equals 0 */
            num_zero = num_zero + 1;
```

**Figure 4.9
Flowchart of
Nested if
Statement in
Example 4.8**

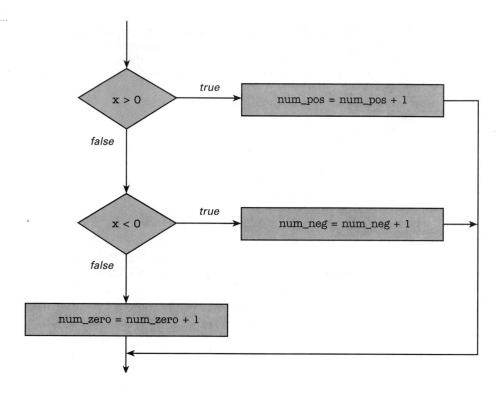

The execution of this `if` statement proceeds as follows: The first condition (`x > 0`) is tested; if it is true, `num_pos` is incremented and the rest of the `if` statement is skipped. If the first condition is false, the second condition (`x < 0`) is tested; if it is true, `num_neg` is incremented; otherwise, `num_zero` is incremented. It is important to realize that the second condition is tested only when the first condition is false.

Figure 4.9 is a flowchart that shows the execution of this `if` statement. This diagram shows that one (and only one) of the statements in rectangular boxes will be executed. Table 4.4 traces the execution of this statement when `x` is −7. ◄━

Table 4.4   Trace of if Statement in Example 4.8 for x = −7

Statement Part	Effect
`if (x > 0)`	−7 > 0: false
`else if (x < 0)`	−7 < 0: true
`    num_neg = num_neg + 1;`	Add 1 to num_neg

Program Style   *Nested if Statements Versus a Sequence of if Statements*

Beginning programmers sometimes prefer to use a sequence of if statements rather than a single nested if statement. For example, the nested if statement in Example 4.8 is rewritten below as a sequence of if statements.

```
if (x > 0)
    num_pos = num_pos + 1;
if (x < 0)
    num_neg = num_neg + 1;
if (x == 0)
    num_zero = num_zero + 1;
```

Although this sequence is logically equivalent to the original, it is not nearly as readable or as efficient as the original. Unlike the nested if statement, the sequence does not clearly show that exactly one of the three assignment statements is executed for a particular x. It is less efficient because all three of the conditions are always tested. In the nested if statement, only the first condition is tested when x is positive.

Writing a Nested if as a Multiple-Alternative Decision

Nested if statements may become quite complex. If there are more than three alternatives and indentation is not done consistently, one may have difficulty determining the if to which a given else belongs (in C, typically the closest if without an else). We find it easier to write the nested if statement in Example 4.8 as the *multiple-alternative decision* described in the next syntax display.

Multiple-Alternative Decision

SYNTAX: if (*condition$_1$*)
              statement$_1$
       else if (*condition$_2$*)
              statement$_2$
              .
              .
              .
       else if (*condition$_n$*)
              statement$_n$
       else
              statement$_e$

(continued)

EXAMPLE: /* increment num_pos, num_neg, or num_zero depending
         on x */
    if (x > 0)
        num_pos = num_pos + 1;
    else if (x < 0)
        num_neg = num_neg + 1;
    else /* x equals 0 */
        num_zero = num_zero + 1;

INTERPRETATION: The conditions in a multiple-alternative decision are evaluated in sequence until a true condition is reached. If a condition is true, the statement following it is executed, and the rest of the multiple-alternative decision is skipped. If a condition is false, the statement following it is skipped, and the next condition is tested. If all conditions are false, then $statement_e$ following the final else is executed.

NOTES: In a multiple-alternative decision, the word else and the next condition appear on the same line. All the words else align, and each dependent *statement* is indented under the condition that controls its execution.

Order of Conditions

Very often the conditions in a multiple-alternative decision are not *mutually exclusive*; in other words, more than one condition may be true for a given data value. If this is the case, then the order of the conditions becomes very important because only the statement sequence following the first true condition is executed.

EXAMPLE 4.9

Suppose you want to associate noise loudness measured in decibels with the effect of the noise. The following table shows the relationship between noise levels and human perceptions of noises.

Loudness in Decibels (db)	Perception
50 or lower	quiet
51 – 70	intrusive
71 – 90	annoying
91 – 110	very annoying
above 110	uncomfortable

The multiple-alternative decision in the following display prints the perception of noise according to this table. If the noise were measured at 62 decibels, the last three conditions would be true if evaluated; however, the perception 62-decibel noise is intrusive. would be displayed because the first true condition is noise_db <= 70.

```
/* Display perception of noise loudness */

if (noise_db <= 50)
      printf("%d-decibel noise is quiet.\n", noise_db);
else if (noise_db <= 70)
      printf("%d-decibel noise is intrusive.\n",
             noise_db);
else if (noise_db <= 90)
      printf("%d-decibel noise is annoying.\n",
             noise_db);
else if (noise_db <= 110)
      printf("%d-decibel noise is very annoying.\n",
             noise_db);
else
      printf("%d-decibel noise is uncomfortable.\n",
             noise_db);
```

The order of conditions can also have an effect on program efficiency. If we know that loud noises are much more likely than soft ones, it would be more efficient to test first for noise levels above 110 db, next for levels between 91 and 110 db, and so on.

Writing the decision as follows would be incorrect. All but the loudest sounds (those 110 db or less) would be incorrectly categorized as "very annoying" because the first condition would be true and the rest would be skipped.

```
/* incorrect perception of noise loudness */

if (noise_db <= 110)
      printf("%d-decibel noise is very annoying.\n",
             noise_db);
else if (noise_db <= 90)
      printf("%d-decibel noise is annoying.\n",
             noise_db);
else if (noise_db <= 70)
      printf("%d-decibel noise is intrusive.\n",
             noise_db);
else if (noise_db <= 50)
      printf(%d-decibel noise is quiet.\n", noise_db);
else
      printf("%d-decibel noise is uncomfortable.\n",
             noise_db);
```

Table 4.5   Decision Table for Example 4.10

Range	Salary ($)	Base Tax ($)	Percentage of Excess
1	0.00 – 14,999.99	0.00	15%
2	15,000.00 – 29,999.99	2,250.00	18%
3	30,000.00 – 49,999.99	5,400.00	22%
4	50,000.00 – 79,999.99	11,000.00	27%
5	80,000.00 – 150,000.00	21,600.00	33%

EXAMPLE 4.10

You could use a multiple-alternative `if` statement to implement any *decision table* that describes several alternatives. For instance, let's say you are an accountant setting up a payroll system for a small firm. Each line of Table 4.5 indicates an employee's salary range and a corresponding base tax amount and tax percentage. Given an employee's salary, you can calculate the tax by adding the *base tax* for that salary range and the product of the *percentage of excess* and the amount of salary over the minimum salary for that range.

For example, the second line of the table specifies that the tax due on a salary of $20,000.00 is $2,250.00 plus 18% of the excess salary over $15,000.00 (i.e., 18% of $5,000.00, or $900.00). Therefore, the total tax due is $2,250.00 plus $900.00, or $3,150.00.

The `if` statement in Fig. 4.10 implements the tax table. If the value of `salary` is within the table range (0.00 to 150,000.00), exactly one of the state-

Figure 4.10   if Statement for Table 4.5

```
if (salary < 0.0)
     printf("Error! Negative salary $%.2f\n", salary);
else if (salary < 15000.00)              /* first range   */
     tax = 0.15 * salary;
else if (salary < 30000.00)              /* second range  */
     tax = (salary - 15000.00) * 0.18 + 2250.00;
else if (salary < 50000.00)              /* third range   */
     tax = (salary - 30000.00) * 0.22 + 5400.00;
else if (salary < 80000.00)              /* fourth range  */
     tax = (salary - 50000.00) * 0.27 + 11000.00;
else if (salary <= 150000.00)            /* fifth range   */
     tax = (salary - 80000.00) * 0.33 + 21600.00;
else
     printf("Error! Salary outside range of table: $%.2f\n",
            salary);
```

Table 4.6 Trace of if Statement in Fig. 4.10 for salary = $25,000.00

Statement Part	salary	tax	Effect
	25000.00	?	
if (salary < 0.0)			25000.0 < 0.0 is false
else if (salary < 15000.00)			25000.0 < 15000.0 is false
else if (salary < 30000.00)			25000.0 < 30000.0 is true
tax = (salary - 15000.00)			Evaluates to 10000.00
* 0.18			Evaluates to 1800.00
+ 2250.00		4050.00	Evaluates to 4050.00

ments assigning a value to `tax` will be executed. A trace of the `if` statement for `salary` = $25,000.00 is shown in Table 4.6. You can see that the value assigned to `tax`, $4,050.00, is correct. ⬅

Program Style *Validating the Values of Variables*

It is important to validate the value of a variable to avoid performing computations using invalid or meaningless data. Instead of computing an incorrect tax amount, the `if` statement in Fig. 4.10 prints an error message if the value of `salary` is outside the range covered by the table (0.00 to 150,000.00). The first condition detects negative salaries: An error message is printed if `salary` is less than zero. All conditions evaluate to false if `salary` is greater than 150,000.00 and the alternative following `else` also displays an error message.

In the next case study, a multiple-alternative decision structure is used to convert compass headings to compass bearings. This problem also demonstrates the use of expressions as values to be printed. Such usage is advisable only if the value of an expression will not be needed later in the program and if the expression's presence in a call to `printf` does not harm the program's readability.

Case Study: Computing Compass Bearings

PROBLEM

While spending the summer as a surveyor's assistant, you decide to write a program that automates the table you use to transform compass headings in degrees (0 to 360 degrees) to compass bearings. The program should require entry of a compass heading, such as 110 degrees, and should display the corresponding bearing (south 70 degrees east).

Figure 4.11
Compass
Headings

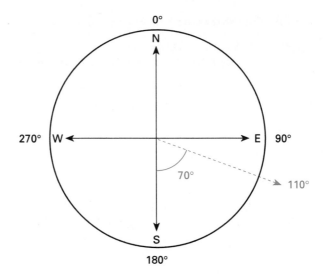

ANALYSIS

The compass bearing indicates a direction of travel corresponding to a compass heading. In this example, if you have a compass heading of 110 degrees, you should first face due south and then turn 70 degrees toward the east (see Fig. 4.11). Each compass bearing consists of three parts: the direction you face (north or south), an angle between 0 and 90 degrees, and the direction you turn before walking (east or west). Table 4.7 indicates how to transform compass headings into compass bearings. From the second line of this table, we see that a heading of 110 degrees corresponds to a bearing of south (180.0 − 110.0) east, or south 70 degrees east.

Table 4.7   Computing Compass Bearings

Heading in Degrees	Bearing Computation
0 − 89.999...	north (heading) east
90 − 179.999...	south (180.0 − heading) east
180 − 269.999...	south (heading − 180.0) west
270 − 360	north (360.0 − heading) west

Data Requirements

Problem Input

```
double heading /* the compass heading in degrees        */
```

Problem Output

equivalent bearing message

Initial Algorithm

1. Get the compass heading.
2. Display the equivalent compass bearing.

Algorithm Refinements

To refine Step 2, we must specify Table 4.7 as a multiple-alternative decision step.

Step 2 Refinement

2.1 if heading is less than zero
      2.2 bearing is undefined
   else if heading is less than 90.0
      2.3 display the bearing north (heading) east
   else if heading is less than 180.0
      2.4 display the bearing south (180.0 − heading) east
   else if heading is less than 270.0
      2.5 display the bearing south (heading − 180.0) west
   else if heading is less than or equal to 360.0
      2.6 display the bearing north (360.0 − heading) west
   else
      2.7 bearing is undefined

We could introduce an output variable, `bearing`, to hold the results of the bearing computation. However, this is not essential since the value is never used again after it is displayed. When we consider the impact that the introduction of such a variable would have on readability, we see that the code we write will actually more closely resemble the table we are implementing if the table's original expressions appear in the calls to `printf`.

> ◀ **TESTING** ▶

To test the program in Fig. 4.12, try compass headings in each of the four quadrants. Also, try compass headings at the quadrant boundaries: 0, 90, 180, 270, and 360 degrees. Finally, see what happens when the heading value is out of range.

Figure 4.12   Program to Compute Compass Bearings

```
/*
 * Transforms a compass heading to a compass bearing using this table:
 *
 *      HEADING
 *      IN DEGREES          BEARING COMPUTATION
 *
 *      0   - 89.999...     north (heading) east
 *      90  - 179.999...    south (180.0 - heading) east
 *      180 - 269.999...    south (heading - 180.0) west
 *      270 - 360           north (360.0 - heading) west
 */

#include <stdio.h>

int
main(void)
{
      double heading; /* Input - compass heading in degrees        */

      /* Get compass heading.                                       */
      printf("Enter a compass heading (0.0 - 360.0 degrees)> ");
      scanf("%lf", &heading);

      /* Display equivalent compass bearing.                        */
      if (heading < 0.0)
            printf("Error--negative heading (%.1f)\n",
                   heading);
      else if (heading < 90.0)
            printf("The bearing is north %.1f degrees east\n",
                   heading);
      else if (heading < 180.0)
            printf("The bearing is south %.1f degrees east\n",
                   180.0 - heading);
```

(continued)

Figure 4.12 *(continued)*

```
    else if (heading < 270.0)
        printf("The bearing is south %.1f degrees west\n",
            heading - 180.0);
    else if (heading <= 360.0)
        printf("The bearing is north %.1f degrees west\n",
            360.0 - heading);
    else
        printf("Error--heading > 360 (%.1f)\n", heading);

    return (0);
}


Enter a compass heading (0.0 - 360.0 degrees)> 110.0
The bearing is south 70.0 degrees east
```

Nested if Statements with More Than One Variable

All the nested if statements seen so far have involved testing different ranges of the value of a single variable; consequently, we were able to write each nested if statement as a multiple-alternative decision. In other situations, we will be able to use a multiple-alternative decision statement only if a flowchart of the decision process shows that each intermediate decision step is on the false branch of the previous decision. The next example requires decisions on true branches. Here we use a nested if statement as a "filter" to select out data that satisfy several different criteria.

EXAMPLE 4.11

The Department of Defense would like a program that identifies single males between the ages of 18 and 26 inclusive. One way to select such individuals is to use a nested if statement. In the nested if that follows, we assume that all variables already have values.

```
/* Print a message if all criteria are met. */
if (marital_status == 'S')
    if (gender == 'M')
        if (age >= 18)
            if (age <= 26)
                printf("All criteria are met.\n");  ⬅
```

The call to `printf` at the end of the `if` statement executes only when all of the conditions listed above it are true.

EXAMPLE 4.12 ➤ You are developing a program to control the warning signs at the exits of major tunnels. If roads are slick (`road_status` is `'S'`), you want to advise drivers that stopping times are doubled or quadrupled, depending on whether the roads are wet or icy. Your program will also have access to the current temperature in degrees Celsius (`temp`), so a check as to whether the temperature is above or below freezing would allow you to choose the correct message. The nested `if` statement below summarizes the decision process you should follow; the flow-chart in Fig. 4.13 diagrams the process.

```
if (road_status == 'S')
    if (temp > 0) {
        printf("Wet roads ahead\n");
        printf("Stopping time doubled\n");
    } else {
        printf("Icy roads ahead\n");
        printf("Stopping time quadrupled\n");
    }
else
    printf("Drive carefully!\n");
```

To verify that the nested `if` statement in Example 4.12 is correct, we trace its execution for all possible combinations of road status values and temperatures. The flowchart's rightmost output is executed only when both conditions are

**Figure 4.13
Flowchart of
Road Sign
Decision
Process**

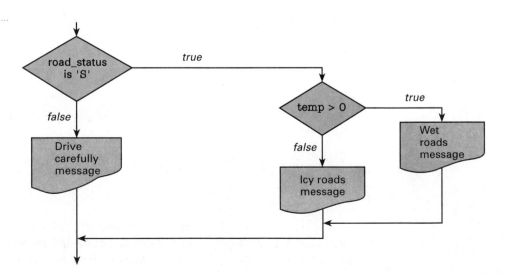

true. The leftmost output is always executed when the condition involving `road_status` is false. The output in the middle occurs when the condition involving `road_status` is true, but the condition involving `temp` is false.

When you are writing a nested if statement, it is important to be aware that C associates an `else` with the most recent incomplete `if`. For example, if the first `else` of the road sign decision were omitted, the following would be left:

```
if (road_status == 'S')
    if (temp > 0) {
        printf("Wet roads ahead\n");
        printf("Stopping time doubled\n");
    }
else
    printf("Drive carefully!\n");
```

Although the indentation would lead you to believe that the `else` remains the false branch of the first `if`, the C compiler actually sees it as the false branch of the second `if`. Indentation like this would match the actual meaning of the statement.

```
if (road_status == 'S')
    if (temp > 0) {
        printf("Wet roads ahead\n");
        printf("Stopping time doubled\n");
    } else
        printf("Drive carefully!\n");
```

To force the `else` to be the false branch of the first `if`, we use braces around the true task of this first decision.

```
if (road_status == 'S') {
    if (temp > 0) {
        printf("Wet roads ahead\n");
        printf("Stopping time doubled\n");
    }
} else {
    printf("Drive carefully!\n");
}
```

Note that we could not use a multiple-alternative decision statement to implement the flowchart in Fig. 4.13 because the intermediate decision (`temp > 0`) falls on the true branch of the initial decision. However, if we were to change the initial condition so the branches were switched, a multiple-alternative structure would work. We could do this simply by checking if the road is dry.

```
if (road_status == 'D') {
    printf("Drive carefully!\n");
} else if (temp > 0) {
    printf("Wet roads ahead\n");
    printf("Stopping time doubled\n");
} else {
    printf("Icy roads ahead\n");
    printf("Stopping time quadrupled\n");
}
```

The first condition is true only if the road is dry. The second condition is tested only when the first condition fails, so its dependent statement executes only when the road is not dry and the temperature is above freezing. Finally, the else clause executes only when the two conditions fail; then we know that the roads are not dry and the temperature is not above freezing.

EXERCISES FOR SECTION 4.6

Self-Check

1. Trace the execution of the nested if statement in Fig. 4.10 for a salary of $23,500.00.
2. What would be the effect of reversing the order of the first two conditions in the if statement in Fig. 4.12?
3. Write a nested if statement for the decision diagrammed in the flowchart at the top of the following page. Use a multiple-alternative if for intermediate decisions where possible.

Programming

1. Rewrite the if statement for Example 4.9 using only the relational operator > in all conditions.
2. Implement the following decision table using a nested if statement. Assume that the grade point average is within the range 0.0 through 4.0.

Grade Point Average	Transcript Message
0.0 – 0.99	Failed semester — registration suspended
1.0 – 1.99	On probation for next semester
2.0 – 2.99	(no message)
3.0 – 3.49	Deans list for semester
3.5 – 4.00	Highest honors for semester

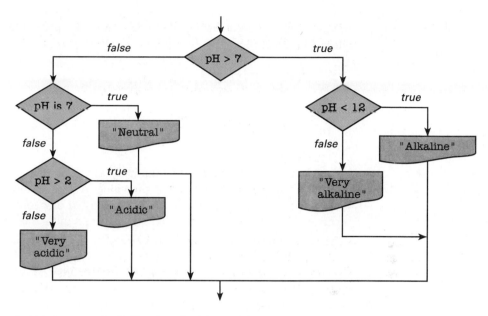

3. Implement the following decision table using a multiple-alternative if statement. Assume that the wind speed is given as an integer.

Wind Speed (mph)	Category
below 25	not a strong wind
25 – 38	strong wind
39 – 54	gale
55 – 72	whole gale
above 72	hurricane

4. The Air Force has asked you to write a program to label supersonic aircraft as military or civilian. Your program is to be given the plane's observed speed in km/h and its estimated length in meters. For planes traveling in excess of 1100 km/h, you will label those longer than 52 meters "civilian" and shorter aircraft as "military." For planes traveling at slower speeds, you will issue an "aircraft type unknown" message.

4.7 THE switch STATEMENT FOR MULTIPLE ALTERNATIVES

The switch statement may also be used in C to select one of several alternatives. The switch statement is especially useful when the selection is based on the value of a single variable or of a simple expression (called the *controlling expression*). The value of this expression may be of type int or char, but not of type double.

EXAMPLE 4.13 ▶

The `switch` statement in Fig. 4.14 is one way of implementing the following decision table.

Class ID	Ship Class
B or b	Battleship
C or c	Cruiser
D or d	Destroyer
F or f	Frigate

The message displayed by the `switch` statement depends on the value of the controlling expression, that is, the value of the variable `class` (type `char`). First, this expression is evaluated; then, the list of `case` labels (`case 'B':`, `case 'b':`, `case 'C':`, etc.) is searched until one label that matches the

Figure 4.14 Example of a switch Statement with Type char Case Labels

```
switch (class) {
case 'B':
case 'b':
      printf("Battleship\n");
      break;

case 'C':
case 'c':
      printf("Cruiser\n");
      break;

case 'D':
case 'd':
      printf("Destroyer\n");
      break;

case 'F':
case 'f':
      printf("Frigate\n");
      break;

default:
      printf("Unknown ship class %c\n", class);
}
```

value of the controlling expression is found. Statements following the matching `case` label are executed until a `break` statement is encountered. The `break` causes an exit from the `switch` statement, and execution continues with the statement that follows the closing brace of the `switch` statement body. If no `case` label matches the value of the `switch` statement's controlling expression, the statements following the `default` label are executed, if there is a `default` label. If not, the entire `switch` statement body is skipped. ◄

EXAMPLE 4.14 ►

The `switch` statement that follows finds the average life expectancy of a standard light bulb based on the bulb's wattage. Since the value of the variable `watts` controls the execution of the `switch` statement, `watts` must have a value before the statement executes.

```
/* Determine average life expectancy of a
   standard light bulb */
switch (watts) {
case 25:
     life = 2500;
     break;

case 40:
case 60:
     life = 1000;
     break;

case 75:
case 100:
     life = 750;
     break;

default:
     life = 0;
}
printf("Life expectancy of %d-watt bulb: ",
       watts);
if (life == 0)
     printf("unknown\n");
else
     printf("%d hours\n", life);
```
◄

Using a string such as `"Cruiser"` or `"Frigate"` as a case label is a common error. It is important to remember that type `int` and `char` values may be used as `case` labels, but strings and type `double` values cannot be used. Another common error is the omission of the `break` statement at the end of one alternative. In such a situation, execution "falls through" into the next alternative. We use a blank line after each `break` statement to emphasize the fact that there is no "fall-through."

Forgetting the closing brace of the `switch` statement body is also easy to do. If the brace is missing and the `switch` has a `default` label, the statements following the `switch` statement become part of the default case.

The following syntax display shows the form of the `switch` statement as a multiple-alternative decision structure.

Multiple-Alternative Decisions Using the switch Statement

SYNTAX: `switch` (*controlling expression*) {
    label set$_1$
        statements$_1$
    `break;`

    label set$_2$
        statements$_2$
    `break;`

        .
        .
        .

    label set$_n$
        statements$_n$
    `break;`

    `default:`
        statements$_d$
    `}`

EXAMPLE:
```
/* nursery rhyme decisions      */
switch (num) {
case 1:
case 2:
      printf("Buckle my shoe\n");
      break;
```

(continued)

```
case 3:
case 4:
     printf("Shut the door\n");
     break;

case 5:
case 6:
     printf("Pick up sticks\n");
     break;

default:
     printf("Number out of range: %d\n", num);
}
```

INTERPRETATION: The *controlling expression,* an expression with a value of type `int` or type `char`, is evaluated and compared to each of the `case` labels in the *label sets* until a match is found. A *label set* is made of one or more labels of the form `case` keyword followed by a constant value and a colon. When a match between the value of the controlling expression and a `case` label value is found, the statements following the `case` label are executed until a `break` statement is encountered. Then the rest of the `switch` statement is skipped. The *statements* may be *one or more* C statements, so it is not necessary to make multiple statements into a single compound statement as you must in an `if` statement. If no `case` label value matches the *controlling expression,* the entire `switch` statement body is skipped unless it contains a `default` label. If so, the statements following the `default` label are executed when no other `case` label value matches the *controlling expression.*

Comparison of Nested if Statements and the switch Statement

You can use a nested `if` statement, which is more general than the `switch` statement, to implement any multiple-alternative decision. The `switch` as described in the syntax display is more readable in many contexts, and should be used whenever practical. Case labels that contain type `double` values or strings are not permitted.

You should use the `switch` statement when each label set contains a reasonable number of `case` labels (a maximum of ten). However, if the number of values is large, use a nested `if` statement. You should include a `default` label in `switch` statements wherever possible. The discipline of trying to define a default will help you to always consider what will happen if the value of your `switch` statement's controlling expression falls outside your set of `case` label values.

EXERCISES FOR SECTION 4.7

Self-Check

1. What will be printed by this carelessly constructed `switch` statement if the value of `color` is `'R'`?

```
switch (color) { /* break statements missing */
case 'R':
      printf("red\n");
case 'B':
      printf("blue\n");
case 'Y':
      printf("yellow\n");
}
```

2. Why can't we rewrite our multiple-alternative `if` statement code from Examples 4.9 and 4.10 using `switch` statements?

Programming

1. Write a `switch` statement that assigns to the variable `lumens` the expected brightness of a standard light bulb whose wattage has been stored in `watts`. Use this table:

Watts	Brightness (in Lumens)
15	125
25	215
40	500
60	880
75	1000
100	1675

Assign −1 to `lumens` if the value of `watts` is not in the table.

2. Write a nested `if` statement equivalent to the `switch` statement described in the first programming exercise.

4.8 COMMON PROGRAMMING ERRORS

The fact that C relational and equality operators give a result of 1 for true and 0 for false means that C interprets some common mathematical expressions in a way that seems surprising at first. The casual reader of the following statement would probably not anticipate the fact that `Condition is true` will be printed for all nonnegative values of x.

```
if (0 <= x <= 4)
    printf("Condition is true\n");
```

For example, let's consider the case when x is 5. The value of 0 <= 5 is 1, and 1 is certainly less than or equal to 4! In order to check if x is in the range 0 to 4, we could write a nested if statement such as

```
if (0 <= x)
    if (x <= 4)
        printf("x is in the range 0-4\n");
```

Remember that the C equality operator is ==. It is easy to slip and use =, the mathematical equal sign. The compiler can detect this error only if the first operand is not a variable. Otherwise, your code will simply produce incorrect results. For example, the code fragment that follows always prints x is 10, regardless of the value of x when the statement is encountered.

```
if (x = 10)
    printf("x is 10");
```

The assignment operator stores the value 10 in x. The value of an assignment expression is the value assigned, so in this case the value of the if condition of the statement is 10. Since 10 is nonzero, C views it as meaning true and executes the true task.

Don't forget to parenthesize the condition of an if statement and to enclose in braces a single-alternative if used as a true task within a double-alternative if. The braces will force the else to be associated with the correct if. Also enclose in braces a compound statement used as a true task or false task. If the braces are missing, only the first statement will be considered part of the task. This can lead to a syntax error if the braces are omitted from the true task of a double-alternative if. Leaving out the braces on the false task of a double-alternative if or on the true task of a single-alternative if will not usually generate a syntax error; the omission will simply lead to incorrect results. In the example that follows, the braces around the true task are missing. The compiler assumes that the semicolon at the end of the assignment statement terminates the if statement.

```
if (x > 0)
    sum = sum + x;
    printf("Greater than zero\n");
else
    printf("Less than zero\n");
```

An `unexpected symbol` syntax error may be generated when the keyword `else` is encountered.

When you write a nested `if` statement, try to select the conditions so that the multiple-alternative format shown in Section 4.6 can be used. When possible, the logic should be constructed so each intermediate condition falls on the false branch of the previous decision. If the conditions are not mutually exclusive (i.e., more than one condition may be true), the most restrictive condition should come first.

When using a `switch` statement, make sure the controlling expression and `case` labels are of the same permitted type (`int` or `char` but not `double`). Remember that if the controlling expression evaluates to a value not listed in any of the `case` labels, the entire body of the `switch` statement will be skipped unless it contains a `default` label. It is wise to include such a `default` case whenever practical. Don't forget that the body of the `switch` statement is a single compound statement, enclosed in one set of braces. However, the statements of each alternative within the `switch` are not enclosed in braces; instead, each alternative is ended by a `break` statement.

CHAPTER REVIEW

In this chapter, we discussed how to represent decision steps in an algorithm using pseudocode and how to implement them in C using `if` and `switch` statements. We continued our discussion of problem solving and showed how to solve a new problem by reusing part of a solution to an earlier problem. We also explained how to add data flow information to structure charts to improve system documentation. We showed that a variable processed by a subproblem is classified as either an input or an output, based on how it is used by that subproblem and that the same variable may be an input to one subproblem and an output from another.

We also showed how to use traces to verify that an algorithm or a program is correct. Carefully tracing an algorithm or a program before entering the program in the computer will uncover errors in logic and will save you time in the long run.

A second selection structure, the `switch` statement, was introduced in this chapter as a convenient means of implementing decisions with several alternatives. We showed how to use the `switch` statement to implement decisions that are based on the value of a variable or simple expression (the controlling expression). This expression can be of type `int` or `char`, but not type `double`.

New C Constructs in Chapter 4

The new C constructs introduced in this chapter are described in Table 4.8.

Table 4.8   Summary of New C Constructs

Construct	Effect
if Statement	

Single-alternative
`if (x != 0.0)`
`        product = product * x;`
	Multiplies product by x only if x is nonzero.

Double-alternative
`if (tmp > 32.0)`
`        printf("%.1f: above freezing", tmp);`
`else`
`        printf("%.1f: freezing", tmp);`
	If `tmp` is greater than 32.0, it is labeled as `above freezing`; otherwise, it is labeled `freezing`

Multiple-alternative
`if (x < 0) {`
`        printf("negative");`
`        abs_x = -x;`
`} else if (x == 0) {`
`        printf("zero");`
`        abs_x = 0;`
`} else {`
`        printf("positive");`
`        abs_x = x;`
`}`
	One of three messages is printed, depending on whether x is negative, positive, or zero. `abs_x` is set to represent the absolute value or magnitude of x.

switch Statement	

`switch (next_ch) {`
`case 'A':`
`case 'a':`
`        printf("Excellent");`
`        break;`
 	
`case 'B':`
`case 'b':`
`        printf("Good");`
`        break;`
	Prints one of five messages based on the value of `next_ch` (type char). If `next_ch` is `'D'`, `'d'`, `'F'`, or `'f'`, the student is put on probation. Gives an error message if the value of `next_ch` is an invalid letter grade.

(continued)

Table 4.8   *(continued)*

Construct	Effect

```
case 'C':
case 'c':
      printf("O.K.");
      break;

case 'D':
case 'd':
case 'F':
case 'f':
      printf("Poor, student is ");
      printf("on probation");
      break;

default:
      printf("Invalid letter grade");
}
```

QUICK-CHECK EXERCISES

1. An `if` statement implements _____ execution.
2. What is a compound statement?
3. A `switch` statement is often used instead of _____ .
4. What can be the values of an expression with a relational operator?
5. The relational operator `<=` means _____ .
6. A hand trace is used to verify that a(n) _____ is correct.
7. A(n) _____ checks whether a program is grammatically correct.
8. Correct the syntax errors.

```
if x > 25.0 {
      y = x
else
      y = z;
}
```

9. What value is assigned to `fee` by the `if` statement when `speed` is 75?

```
if (speed > 35)
      fee = 20.0;
else if (speed > 50)
      fee = 40.00;
else if (speed > 75)
      fee = 60.00;
```

10. Answer Exercise 9 for the `if` statement that follows. Which `if` statement seems reasonable?

```
if (speed > 75)
        fee = 60.0;
else if (speed > 50)
        fee = 40.00;
else if (speed > 35)
        fee = 20.00;
```

11. What output line(s) are displayed by the statements that follow when grade is `'I'`? When grade is `'B'`? When grade is `'b'`?

```
switch (grade) {
case 'A':
        points = 4;
        break;

case 'B':
        points = 3;
        break;

case 'C':
        points = 2;
        break;

case 'D':
        points = 1;
        break;

case 'E':
case 'I':
case 'W':
        points = 0;
}

if (points > 0)
        printf("Passed, points earned = %d\n", points);
else
        printf("Failed, no points earned\n");
```

12. Explain the difference between the statements on the left and the statements on the right. For each group of statements, give the final value of **x** if the initial value of **x** is 1.

```
if (x >= 0)                  if (x >= 0)
      x = x + 1;                   x = x + 1;
else if (x >= 1)             if (x >= 1)
      x = x + 2;                   x = x + 2;
```

ANSWERS TO QUICK-CHECK EXERCISES

1. conditional
2. one or more statements surrounded by braces
3. nested **if** statements or a multiple-alternative **if** statement
4. 0 and 1
5. less than or equal to
6. algorithm
7. compiler
8. Parenthesize condition, remove braces (or add them around else: **} else {**), and add a semicolon to the first assignment statement.
9. **20.00**, first condition is met
10. **40.00**, the one in 10
11. when **grade** is **'I'**:
    ```
    Failed, no points earned
    ```
    when **grade** is **'B'**:
    ```
    Passed, points earned = 3
    ```
    when **grade** is **'b'**:
    The **switch** statement is skipped so the output printed depends on the previous value of **points** (which may be garbage).
12. A nested **if** statement is on the left; a sequence of **if** statements is on the right. On the left **x** becomes **2**; on the right **x** becomes **4**.

REVIEW QUESTIONS

1. Making a decision between two alternative courses of action is usually implemented with a(n) _____ statement in C.
2. Trace the following program fragment; indicate which function will be called

if a data value of 27.34 is entered.

```
printf("\Enter a temperature> ");
scanf("%lf", &temp);
if (temp > 32.0)
      not_freezing();
else
      ice_forming();
```

3. Write a multiple-alternative if statement to display a message indicating the educational level of a student based on the student's number of years of schooling (none; 1–5, elementary school; 6–8, middle school; 9–12, high school; more than 12, college). Print a message to indicate bad data as well.

4. Write a switch statement to select an operation based on the value of inventory. Increment total_paper by paper_order if inventory is 'B' or 'C'; increment total_ribbon by ribbon_order if inventory is 'E', 'F', or 'D'; increment total_label by label_order if inventory is 'A' or 'X'. Do nothing if inventory is 'M'. Display an error message if the value of inventory is not one of these eight letters.

5. Implement the following flow diagram using a nested if structure.

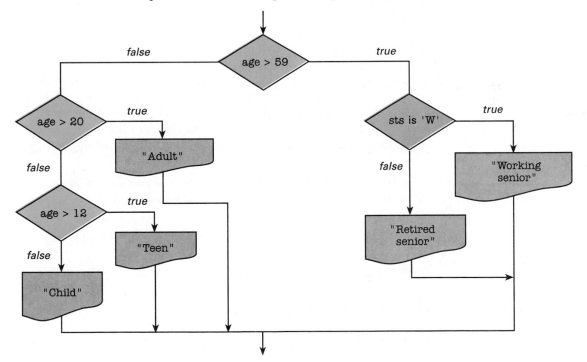

PROGRAMMING PROJECTS

1. Write a program that displays a message consisting of three block letters; each letter is either an X or an O. The program user's data determines whether a particular letter will be an X or O. For example, if the user enters the three letters XOX, the block letters X, O, and X will be displayed.
2. Write a program to simulate a state police radar gun. The program should take an automobile speed and print the message speeding if the speed exceeds 65 mph.
3. The National Earthquake Information Center has asked you to write a program implementing the following decision table to characterize an earthquake based on its Richter scale number.

Richter Scale Number (n)	Characterization
n < 5.0	Little or no damage
5.0 ≤ n < 5.5	Some damage
5.5 ≤ n < 6.5	Serious damage: walls may crack or fall
6.5 ≤ n < 7.5	Disaster: houses and buildings may collapse
higher	Catastrophe: most buildings destroyed

Could you handle this problem with a switch statement? If yes, use a switch statement; if not, explain why.

4. Write a program that takes a classroom number, its capacity, and the size of the class enrolled so far and prints an output line showing the classroom number, the capacity, both the number of seats filled and the number available, and a message indicating whether the class is filled or not. Call a function to display the following heading before the requested output line.

Room   Capacity   Enrollment   Empty seats   Filled/Not Filled

Display each part of the output line under the appropriate column heading. Test your program four times using the following classroom data:

Room	Capacity	Enrollment
426	25	25
327	18	14
420	20	15
317	100	90

5. Write a program that takes the x–y coordinates of a point in the Cartesian plane and prints a message telling either an axis on which the point lies or the quadrant in which it is found.

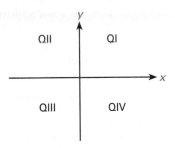

Sample lines of output:
```
(-1.0, -2.5) is in quadrant III
(0.0, 4.8) is on the y axis
```
6. Write a program that finds and prints the reciprocal of an integer, both as a common fraction and as a decimal fraction. A typical output line would be

```
The reciprocal of 2 is 1/2 or 0.500.
```

The program should print a `Reciprocal undefined` message for an input of zero.
7. The New Telephone Company has the following rate structure for long-distance calls:
   a. Any call started after 6:00 P.M. (1800 hours) but before 8:00 A.M. (0800 hours) is discounted 50%.
   b. Any call started after 8:00 A.M. (0800 hours) but before 6:00 P.M. (1800 hours) is charged full price.
   c. All calls are subject to a 4% federal tax.
   d. The regular rate for a call is $0.40 per minute.
   e. Any call longer than 60 minutes receives a 15% discount on its cost (after any other discount is subtracted but before tax is added).
   Write a program that takes the start time for a call based on a 24-hour clock and the length of the call in minutes. The gross cost (before any discounts or tax) should be printed followed by the net cost (after discounts are deducted and tax is added). Use a function to print instructions to the program user.
8. Write a program that will calculate and print bills for the city power company. The rates vary depending on whether the use is residential, commercial, or industrial. A code of R means residential use, a code of C means commercial use, and a code of I means industrial use. Any other code should be treated as an error.

The rates are computed as follows:

R: $6.00 plus $0.052 per kwh used
C: $60.00 for the first 1000 kwh and
   $0.045 for each additional kwh
I: Rate varies depending on time of usage.
   Peak hours: $76.00 for first 1000 kwh
   and $0.065 for each additional kwh
   Off-peak hours: $40.00 for first 1000 kwh
   and $0.028 for each additional kwh.

Your program should prompt the user to enter an integer account number, the use code (type `char`), and the necessary consumption figures in whole kilowatt-hours. Your program should print the amount due from the user.

CHAPTER 5

REPETITION AND LOOP STATEMENTS

5.1
Repetition in Programs: Using Loops to
Solve Problems
5.2
Computing a Sum or a Product in a Loop
5.3
Counting Loops
5.4
Conditional Loops
5.5
Loop Design
5.6
Nested Control Structures
5.7
Problem Solving Illustrated
Case Study: Computing Radiation Levels
5.8
How to Debug and Test Programs
5.9
Common Programming Errors
Chapter Review

Chapters 3 and 4 introduced you to C control statements that allow programs to call functions and to make decisions as to which of several courses of action to take, based on current data values. The control statements of a programming language enable a programmer to control the sequence and frequency of execution of program segments. Control statements cause functions to carry out their tasks when needed and also implement decisions and repetition in programs. In this chapter, you will see how to specify the repetition of a group of program statements called a *loop* using the `while` and `for` statements. This ability to rapidly repeat groups of actions on vast quantities of information gives computers the awesome data processing power that has revolutionized both scientific research and many industries. This chapter describes how to design loops in C programs as well as how to place one control structure inside another. Numerous examples and a case study will be presented.

5.1 REPETITION IN PROGRAMS: USING LOOPS TO SOLVE PROBLEMS

Just as the ability to make decisions is an important programming tool, so is the ability to specify repetition of a group of operations. For example, a company that has seven employees will want to repeat the gross pay and net pay computations in its payroll program seven times, once for each employee. The repetition of steps in a program is called a loop. The *loop body* contains the steps to be repeated. In Chapter 3, we mentioned that writing out a solution to a specific case of a problem can be helpful in preparing you to define an algorithm to solve the same problem in general. After you solve the sample case, ask yourself some of the following questions to determine if loops will be required in the general algorithm:

1. Were there any steps I repeated as I solved the problem? If so, which ones?
2. If the answer to question 1 is yes, did I know in advance how many times to repeat the steps?
3. If the answer to question 2 is no, how did I know how long to keep repeating the steps?

Your answer to the first question indicates whether or not your algorithm needs a loop and what steps to include in the loop body if it does need one. Your answers to the other questions will help you determine which loop structure to choose for your solution. Keep these questions in mind as we explore the kinds of loops available in C. Later in the chapter we will summarize the relationship between your answers to these questions and the design of a correct loop for your algorithm.

The while Statement

The program segment shown in Fig. 5.1 computes and displays gross pay for seven employees. The loop body (the steps that are repeated) is the compound statement that starts on the third line. The loop body gets an employee's payroll data and computes and displays that employee's pay. After seven pay amounts are displayed, the last statement in Fig. 5.1 calls function `printf` to display the message `All employees processed`.

The three lines in color in Fig. 5.1 control the looping process. The first statement

```
count_emp = 0; /* no employees processed yet */
```

stores an initial value of 0 in the variable `count_emp`, which represents the count of employees processed so far. The next line evaluates the logical expression `count_emp < 7`. If the expression is true, the compound statement representing the loop body is executed, calling for a new pair of data values to be input and a new pay amount to be computed and displayed. The last statement in the loop body

```
count_emp = count_emp + 1; /* increment count_emp */
```

adds 1 to the value of `count_emp`. After executing the last step in the loop body, control returns to the line beginning with `while`, and the condition is reevaluated for the next value of `count_emp`. The loop body is executed once for each value of `count_emp` from 0 to 6. Eventually, `count_emp` becomes

Figure 5.1   Loop to Process the Pay of Seven Employees

```
count_emp = 0;                  /* no employees processed yet */
while (count_emp < 7) {         /* test value of count_emp     */
    printf("Hours> ");
    scanf("%d", &hours);
    printf("Rate> ");
    scanf("%lf", &rate);
    pay = hours * rate;
    printf("Pay is $%6.2f\n", pay);
    count_emp = count_emp + 1; /* increment count_emp     */
}
printf("\nAll employees processed\n");
```

7, and the logical expression evaluates to false (0). When this happens, the loop body is not executed and control passes to the display statement that follows the loop body. The logical expression following the reserved word `while` is called the *loop repetition condition*. The loop is repeated when this condition is true, that is, when its value is not 0. We say that the *loop is exited* when this condition is false (see Fig. 5.2).

The flowchart in Fig. 5.2 summarizes what we have explained so far about `while` loops. In the flowchart, the logical expression in the diamond-shaped box is evaluated first. If that expression is true, the loop body is executed, and the process is repeated. The `while` loop is exited when the expression becomes false. If the loop repetition condition is false when it is first tested, then the loop body is not executed at all.

Make sure you understand the difference between the `while` statement in Fig. 5.1 and the following `if` statement:

```
if (count_emp < 7) {
    . . .
}
```

In an `if` statement, the compound statement after the parenthesized condition executes at most only once. In a `while` statement, the compound statement can execute more than once.

Syntax of the while Statement

In Fig. 5.1, the variable `count_emp` is called the *loop control variable* because its value determines whether the loop body is repeated. Three critical steps

**Figure 5.2
Flowchart of a
while Loop**

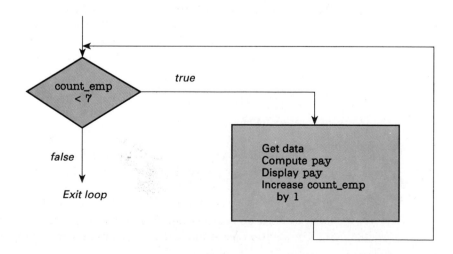

involve the loop control variable `count_emp`:

1. `count_emp` is set to an initial value of 0 (initialized to 0) before the `while` statement is reached.
2. `count_emp` is tested before the start of each loop repetition (called an *iteration* or a *pass*).
3. `count_emp` is updated (its value increases by 1) during each iteration.

Steps similar to these three steps (initialization, test, and update) must be performed for every `while` loop. If the first step is missing, the initial test of `count_emp` will be meaningless. The last step ensures that we progress toward the final goal (`count_emp >= 7`) during each repetition of the loop. If the last step is missing, the value of `count_emp` cannot change, so the loop will execute "forever" (an *infinite loop*). The syntax for the `while` statement is described in the next display.

---

while Statement

SYNTAX: while (*loop repetition condition*)
          statement

EXAMPLE:
```
/* Display N asterisks. */
count_star = 0;
while (count_star < N) {
      printf("*");
      count_star = count_star + 1;
}
```

INTERPRETATION: The *loop repetition condition* (a condition to control the loop process) is tested; if it is true, the *statement* is executed, and the *loop repetition condition* is retested. The *statement* is repeated as long as (`while`) the *loop repetition condition* is true. When this condition is tested and found to be false, the `while` loop is exited, and the next program statement after the `while` statement is executed.

5.2 COMPUTING A SUM OR A PRODUCT IN A LOOP

Often we use loops to compute a sum or a product by repeating an addition or multiplication operation. The next example uses a loop to accumulate a sum.

 **EXAMPLE 5.1**

The program in Fig. 5.3 has a `while` loop similar to the loop in Fig. 5.1. Besides displaying each employee's pay, the program accumulates the total payroll (`total_pay`) for a company. The assignment statement

```
total_pay = total_pay + pay;
```

adds the current value of `pay` to the sum being accumulated in `total_pay`. Figure 5.4 on p. 198 traces the effect of repeating this statement for the three values of `pay` shown in the sample run.

Figure 5.3 Program to Compute Company Payroll

```c
/* Compute the payroll for a company */

#include <stdio.h>

int
main(void)
{
      double total_pay;          /* company payroll      */
      int    count_emp;          /* current employee     */
      int    number_emp;         /* number of employees  */
      double hours;              /* hours worked         */
      double rate;               /* hourly rate          */
      double pay;                /* pay for this period  */

      /* Get number of employees. */
      printf("Enter number of employees> ");
      scanf("%d", &number_emp);

      /* Compute each employee's pay and add it to the payroll. */
      total_pay = 0.0;
      count_emp = 0;
      while (count_emp < number_emp) {
          printf("Hours> ");
          scanf("%lf", &hours);
          printf("Rate > $");
          scanf("%lf", &rate);
          pay = hours * rate;
          printf("Pay is $%6.2f\n\n", pay);
          total_pay = total_pay + pay;
          count_emp = count_emp + 1;
      }
```

(continued)

Figure 5.3   *(continued)*

```
        printf("All employees processed\n");
        printf("Total payroll is $%8.2f\n", total_pay);

        return (0);
}
```

```
Enter number of employees> 3
Hours> 50
Rate > $5.25
Pay is $262.50

Hours> 6
Rate > $5.00
Pay is $ 30.00

Hours> 15
Rate > $7.00
Pay is $105.00

All employees processed
Total payroll is $  397.50
```

Prior to loop execution, the statement

```
total_pay = 0.0;
```

initializes the value of `total_pay` to zero. This step is critical; if it is omitted, the final sum will be off by whatever value happens to be stored in `total_pay` when the program begins execution.   ←

Generalizing a Loop

The first loop shown in Fig. 5.1 has a serious deficiency: It can be used only when the number of employees is exactly seven. The loop in Fig. 5.3 is better because it can be used for any number of employees. This program begins by copying from the input device the total number of employees and storing this value in the variable `number_emp`. Before each execution of the loop body, the loop repetition condition compares the number of employees processed so far (`count_emp`) to the total number of employees (`number_emp`).

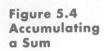

Figure 5.4
Accumulating
a Sum

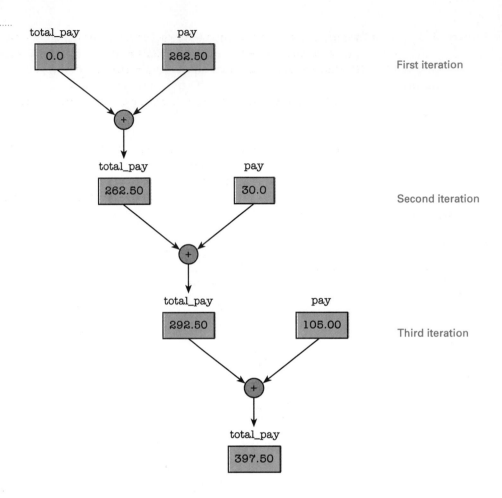

Multiplying a List of Numbers

In a similar way, we can use a loop to compute the product of a list of numbers as shown in the next example.

EXAMPLE 5.2 The loop that follows multiplies data items together as long as the product remains less than 10,000. It displays the product calculated up to this point just before asking for the next data value. The product of the data seen so far is updated on each iteration by executing the statement

```
product = product * item; /* Update product. */
```

Figure 5.5 traces the change in the value of `product` with each execution of the statement just shown. If the data items are 10, 500, and 3, the products 1 (initial value of `product`), 10, and 5000 are displayed.

```
/* Multiply data while product remains less than 10000 */
product = 1;
while (product < 10000) {
    printf("%d\n", product); /* Display product so far */
    printf("Enter next item> ");
    scanf("%d", &item);
    product = product * item; /* Update product */
}
```

**Figure 5.5
Computing a
Product in
a Loop**

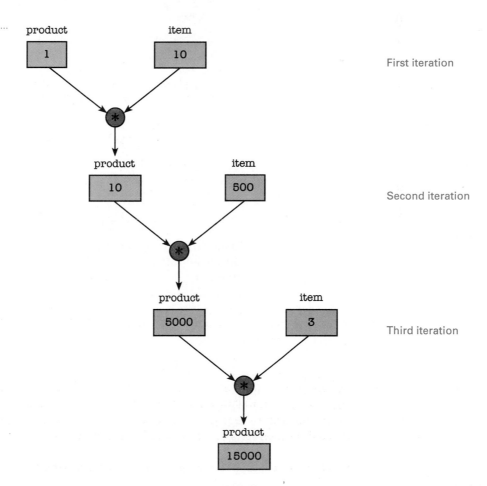

Loop exit occurs when the value of `product` is greater than or equal to 10,000. Consequently, the last value assigned to `product` (in Fig. 5.5, 15,000) is not displayed. ⬅

The loop in this example differs from other loops in this section. Its repetition condition involves a test of the variable `product`. Besides controlling loop repetition, the variable `product` also holds the result of the computation that is performed in the loop. The other loops involve a test of `count_emp`, a variable that represents the count of loop repetitions. The computation being performed in the loop does not directly involve `count_emp`. We will discuss these differences further in Section 5.4.

EXERCISES FOR SECTION 5.2

Self-Check

1. What output values are displayed by the following `while` loop for a data value of 5? of 6? of 7?

```
printf("Enter an integer> ");
scanf("%d", &x);
product = x;
count = 0;
while (count < 4) {
    printf("%d\n", product);
    product = product * x;
    count = count + 1;
}
```

In general, for a data value of any number *n,* what does this loop display?

2. What values are displayed if the call to `printf` comes at the end of the loop instead of at the beginning?

3. The following segment needs some revision. Insert braces where they are needed and correct the errors. The corrected code should take five integers and display their sum.

```
count = 0;
while (count <= 5)
count = count + 1;
printf("Next number> ");
scanf("%d", &next_num);
next_num = sum + next_num;
printf("%d numbers were added; \n", count);
printf("their sum is %d.\n", sum);
```

4. How would the program in Fig. 5.3 need to be modified to display the average employee pay, in addition to the total payroll amount?

Programming

1. Write a program segment that computes $1 + 2 + 3 + \cdots + (n - 1) + n$, where n is a data value. Follow the loop body with an `if` statement that compares this value to `(n * (n + 1)) / 2` and displays a message that indicates whether the values are the same or different. What message do you think will be displayed?

5.3 COUNTING LOOPS

The `while` loop shown in Fig. 5.3 is called a *counter-controlled loop* (or *counting loop*) because its repetition is managed by a *loop control variable* whose value represents a count. A counter-controlled loop follows this general format described in pseudocode.

> Set *loop control variable* to an initial value of 0.
> while *loop control variable* < *final value*
>   . . .
>   Increase *loop control variable* by 1.

We use a counter-controlled loop when we can determine prior to loop execution exactly how many loop repetitions will be needed to solve the problem. This number should appear as the *final value* in the `while` condition.

The for Statement

C provides the `for` statement as another form for implementing loops. The loops we have seen so far are typical of most repetition structures in that they have three major components in addition to the loop body:

1. initialization of the *loop control variable,*
2. *loop repetition condition,* and
3. change (update) of the *loop control variable.*

An important feature of the `for` statement in C is that it supplies a designated place for each of these three components. A `for` statement implementation of the loop from Fig. 5.3 is shown in Fig. 5.6.

The effect of this `for` statement is exactly equivalent to the execution of the comparable `while` loop section of the program in Fig. 5.3. Because the `for`

Figure 5.6 **Using a for Statement in a Counting Loop**

```
/* Process payroll for all employees */
total_pay = 0.0;
for  (count_emp = 0; /* initialization */
        count_emp < number_emp; /* loop repetition condition */
        count_emp = count_emp + 1) { /* update */
     printf("Hours> ");
     scanf("%lf", &hours);
     printf("Rate > $");
     scanf("%lf", &rate);
     pay = hours * rate;
     printf("Pay is $%6.2f\n\n", pay);
     total_pay = total_pay + pay;
}
printf("All employees processed\n");
printf("Total payroll is $%8.2f\n", total_pay);
```

statement's heading

```
for (count_emp = 0;            /* initialization             */
        count_emp < number_emp; /* loop repetition condition */
        count_emp = count_emp + 1) { /* update               */
```

combines the three loop control steps of initialization, testing, and update in one place, separate steps to initialize and update `count_emp` must not appear elsewhere. The `for` statement can be used to count up or down by any interval. The program in Fig. 5.7 "counts down" from a specified starting value (an input variable) to "blast-off." Since the `for` statement update expression subtracts one from the variable `time`, the value of the loop control variable decreases by one each time the loop is repeated. Because the loop body is a single statement, we could omit the braces surrounding it. However, we would then need to be very careful if a later modification of the program called for the addition of another statement to the loop body. At that point, braces forming a compound statement would be essential.

> **for Statement**
>
> SYNTAX: for (*initialization expression*;
>   *loop repetition condition*;
>   *update expression*)
>   *statement*

(continued)

EXAMPLE: /* Display N asterisks. */
```
        for  (count_star = 0;
              count_star < N;
              count_star = count_star + 1)
            printf("*");
```

INTERPRETATION: First, the *initialization expression* is executed. Then, the *loop repetition condition* is tested. If it is true, the statement is executed, and the *update expression* is evaluated. Then the *loop repetition condition* is retested. The *statement* is repeated as long as the *loop repetition condition* is true. When this condition is tested and found to be false, the `for` loop is exited, and the next program statement after the `for` statement is executed.

Caution: Although C permits the use of fractional values for counting loop control variables of type `double`, we strongly discourage this practice. Counting loops with type `double` control variables will not always execute the same number of times on different computers.

Figure 5.7   A Countdown Program

```c
/* Counting down to blast-off */

#include <stdio.h>

int
main(void)
{
   int time, start;

   printf("Enter starting time (an integer) in seconds> ");
   scanf("%d", &start);
   printf("\nBegin countdown\n");
   for  (time = start;
         time > 0;
         time = time - 1) {
      printf("T - %d\n", time);
   }
   printf("Blast-off!\n");

   return (0);
}
```

(continued)

Figure 5.7 *(continued)*

```
Enter starting time (an integer) in seconds> 5

Begin countdown
T - 5
T - 4
T - 3
T - 2
T - 1
Blast-off!
```

Program Style   *Formatting the for Statement*

For clarity, we usually place each expression of the `for` heading on a separate line. If all three expressions are very short, we may place them together on one line. Here is an example:

```
/* print natural numbers < max */
for  (i = 0;  i < max;  i = i + 1)
    printf("%d\n", i);
```

The body of the `for` loop is indented. If the loop body is a compound statement or if we are using a style in which we bracket all loop bodies, we place the opening brace at the end of the `for` heading, and terminate the statement by placing the closing brace on a separate line. This closing brace should be aligned with the "f" of the `for` that it is ending.

We have seen `for` statement counting loops that count up by one and down by one. Now we will use a loop that counts down by five to print a Celsius-to-Fahrenheit conversion table. Because of the values of the constant macros named `CBEGIN` and `CLIMIT`, the table printed by the program in Fig. 5.8 runs from 10 degrees Celsius to −5 degrees Celsius. Since the loop update step subtracts `CSTEP` (5) from `celsius`, the value of the counter `celsius` decreases by five after each repetition. Loop exit occurs when `celsius` becomes less than `CLIMIT`, that is, when `celsius` is −10. Table 5.1 on p. 206 traces the execution of this counting `for` loop.

The trace in Table 5.1 shows that the loop control variable `celsius` is initialized to `CBEGIN` (10) when the `for` loop is reached. Since 10 is greater than or equal to `CLIMIT` (−5), the loop body is executed. After each loop rep-

Figure 5.8   Printing a Celsius-to-Fahrenheit Conversion Table

....

```c
/* Conversion of Celsius to Fahrenheit temperatures */

#include <stdio.h>

/* Constant macros */
#define CBEGIN 10
#define CLIMIT -5
#define CSTEP 5

int
main(void)
{
      /* Variable declarations */
      int    celsius;
      double fahrenheit;

      /* Print the table heading */
      printf(" Celsius    Fahrenheit\n");

      /* Print the table */
      for  (celsius = CBEGIN;
            celsius >= CLIMIT;
            celsius = celsius - CSTEP) {
         fahrenheit = 1.8 * celsius + 32.0;
         printf("     %3d    %7.2f\n",   celsius, fahrenheit);
      }

      return (0);
}
   Celsius    Fahrenheit
                     10        50.00
                      5        41.00
                      0        32.00
                     -5        23.00
```

....

etition, `CSTEP` (`5`) is subtracted from `celsius`, and `celsius` is tested in the loop repetition condition to see whether its value is still greater than or equal to `CLIMIT`. If the condition is true, the loop body is executed again, and the next value of `fahrenheit` is computed and printed. If the condition is false, the loop is exited.

Table 5.1 Trace of Program Loop in Figure 5.8

Statement	celsius	fahrenheit	Effect
`for (celsius = CBEGIN;`	10		Initialize `celsius` to 10
`celsius >= CLIMIT;`			`10 >= -5` is true
`. . .`			
`fahrenheit = 1.8 *`			
`celsius + 32.0;`		50.0	Assign 50.0 to `fahrenheit`
`printf . . .`			Print 10 and 50.0
Update and test `celsius`			
`. . . celsius = celsius -`			
`CSTEP`	5		Subtract 5 from `celsius` giving 5
`celsius >= CLIMIT;`			`5 >= -5` is true
`fahrenheit = 1.8 *`			
`celsius + 32.0;`		41.0	Assign 41.0 to `fahrenheit`
`printf . . .`			Print 5 and 41.0
Update and test `celsius`			
`. . . celsius = celsius -`			
`CSTEP`	0		Subtract 5 from `celsius` giving 0
`celsius >= CLIMIT;`			`0 >= -5` is true
`fahrenheit = 1.8 *`			
`celsius + 32.0;`		32.0	Assign 32.0 to `fahrenheit`
`printf . . .`			Print 0 and 32.0
Update and test `celsius`			
`. . . celsius = celsius -`			
`CSTEP`	-5		Subtract 5 from `celsius` giving -5
`celsius >= CLIMIT;`			`-5 >= -5` is true
`fahrenheit = 1.8 *`			
`celsius + 32.0;`		23.0	Assign 23.0 to `fahrenheit`
`printf . . .`			Print -5 and 23.0
Update and test `celsius`			
`. . . celsius = celsius -`			
`CSTEP`	-10		Subtract 5 from `celsius` giving -10
`celsius >= CLIMIT;`			`-10 >= -5` is false, so exit loop

Because the structure of the `for` statement makes it easy for the reader of a program to identify the major loop control elements, we will use it in the remainder of our study of repetition whenever a loop requires simple initialization, testing, and updating of a loop control variable.

EXERCISES FOR SECTION 5.3

Self-Check

1. Trace the execution of the loop that follows for n = 8. Show values of `odd` and `sum` after the update of the loop counter for each iteration.

```
sum = 0;
for  (odd = 1;
      odd < n;
      odd = odd + 2)
    sum = sum + odd;

printf("Sum of positive odd numbers less than %d is %d.\n",
        n, sum);
```

2. Given the constant macro definitions of Fig. 5.8 (repeated here)

```
#define CBEGIN 10
#define CLIMIT -5
#define CSTEP  5
```

indicate what values of `celsius` would appear in the conversion table printed if the `for` loop header of Fig. 5.8 were rewritten as shown:

```
a. for  (celsius = CLIMIT;
          celsius >= CBEGIN;
          celsius = celsius + CSTEP)
b. for  (celsius = CLIMIT;
          celsius <= CBEGIN;
          celsius = celsius - CSTEP)
c. for  (celsius = CLIMIT;
          celsius <= CSTEP;
          celsius = celsius + CBEGIN)
d. for  (celsius = CSTEP;
          celsius >= CBEGIN;
          celsius = celsius + CLIMIT)
```

3. What is the smallest number of times that the body of a `while` loop can be executed? The body of a `for` loop?

4. What errors do you see in the following segment? Correct the code so it prints all multiples of 5 from 0 through 100.

```
for mult5 = 0;
mult5 < 100;
mult5 = mult5 + 5;
printf("%d\n", mult5);
```

5. a. Trace the following program segment:

```
j = 10;
for  (i = 1;  i <= 5;  i = i + 1) {
    printf("%d  %d\n", i, j);
    j = j - 2;
}
```

b. Rewrite the previous program segment so that it produces the same output but uses 0 as the initial value of i.

Programming

1. Write a loop that prints a table of angle measures along with their sine and cosine values. Assume that the initial and final angle measures (in degrees) are available in `init_degree` and `final_degree` (type `int` variables), and that the change in angle measure between table entries is given by `step_degree` (also a type `int` variable). Remember that the math library's `sin` and `cos` functions take arguments that are in radians. You may want to look back at Example 3.5 in Chapter 3.
2. Write a program to print an inches-to-centimeters conversion table. The smallest and largest number of inches in the table are input values. Your table should give conversions in 6-inch intervals.

5.4 CONDITIONAL LOOPS

In many programming situations, you will not be able to determine the exact number of loop repetitions before loop execution begins. When we multiplied a list of numbers in Example 5.2, the number of repetitions depended on the data entered. Although we did not know in advance how many times the loop would execute, we were still able to write a condition to control the loop. Here is another case of this type of repetition. You want to continue writing checks as long as your bank balance is positive, as indicated by the following pseudocode description:

> while the balance is still positive
>> Get the next check amount.
>> Write a check for that amount.
>> Update and print the balance.

The actual number of loop repetitions performed depends on the type of each transaction (deposit or withdrawal) and its amount. Another situation in which one does not know in advance how many times a loop should repeat is when asking the user for data and verifying that the response is reasonable.

> Print an initial prompting message.
> Get the number of observed values.
> while the number of values is negative
>> Print a warning and another prompting message.
>> Get the number of observed values.

Like the counting loops we considered earlier, these conditional loops typically have three parts that control repetition: initialization, testing of a loop repetition condition, and an update. Let's analyze the algorithm for ensuring valid input. Clearly, the loop repetition condition is

number of values < 0

Because it makes no sense to test this condition unless *number of values* has a meaning, getting this value must be the initialization step. The update action—the statement that, if left out, would cause the loop to repeat infinitely—remains to be identified. Getting a new number of observed values within the loop body is just such a step. Since we have found these three essential loop parts, we can write this validating input loop in C using a `for` statement.

```
printf("Enter number of observed values> ");
for  (scanf("%d", &num_obs);    /* initialization          */
      num_obs < 0;   /* loop repetition condition        */
      scanf("%d", &num_obs))    /* update                 */
    printf("Negative number invalid; try again> ");
```

At first, it may seem odd that the initialization and update steps are identical. In fact, this is very often the case for loops performing input operations in situations where the number of input values is not known in advance.

EXAMPLE 5.3 The program in Fig. 5.9 is designed to assist in monitoring the gasoline supply in a storage tank at the Super Oil Company refinery. The program is to alert the supervisor when the supply of gasoline in the tank falls below 10% of the tank's 80,000-barrel storage capacity. Although the supervisor always deals with the contents of the tank in terms of a number of *barrels,* the pump that is used to fill tanker trucks gives its measurements in *gallons.* The barrel used in the petroleum industry equals 42 U.S. gallons.

The program first requests that the operator enter the amount of gasoline currently stored in the tank. Then, after gasoline is pumped into each tanker, the

Figure 5.9   Program to Monitor Gasoline Storage Tank

```
/*
 * Monitor gasoline supply in storage tank. Issue warning when supply falls
 * below MIN_PCT % of tank capacity.
 */

#include <stdio.h>

/* constant macros */
#define CAPACITY      80000.0 /* number of barrels tank can hold        */
#define MIN_PCT       10      /* warn when supply falls below this percent
                                    of capacity                         */
#define GALS_PER_BRL 42.0     /* number of U.S. gallons in one barrel    */

int
main(void)
{
        double start_supply, /* initial supply in barrels              */
               min_supply,   /* minimum number of barrels left without
                                    warning                            */
               current,      /* current supply in barrels              */
               remov_gals,   /* amount of current delivery in          */
               remov_brls;   /*    barrels and gallons                 */

        /* Compute minimum supply without warning                       */
        min_supply = MIN_PCT / 100.0 * CAPACITY;

        /* Get initial supply and subtract amounts removed as long as
           minimum supply remains                                      */
        printf("Number of barrels currently in tank> ");
```

(continued)

Figure 5.9 *(continued)*

```
        scanf("%lf", &start_supply);
        for  (current = start_supply;
              current >= min_supply;
              current = current - remov_brls) {
            printf("%.2f barrels are available.\n\n", current);
            printf("Enter number of gallons removed> ");
            scanf("%lf", &remov_gals);
            remov_brls = remov_gals / GALS_PER_BRL;

            printf("After removal of %.2f gallons (%.2f barrels),\n",
                    remov_gals, remov_brls);
        }

        /* Issue warning                                            */
        printf("only %.2f barrels are left.\n\n", current);
        printf("*** WARNING ***\n");
        printf("Available supply is less than %d percent of tank's ",
                MIN_PCT);
        printf("%.2f-barrel capacity.\n", CAPACITY);

        return (0);
}

Number of barrels currently in tank> 8500.5
8500.50 barrels are available.

Enter number of gallons removed> 5859.0
After removal of 5859.00 gallons (139.50 barrels),
8361.00 barrels are available.

Enter number of gallons removed> 7568.4
After removal of 7568.40 gallons (180.20 barrels),
8180.80 barrels are available.

Enter number of gallons removed> 8400.0
After removal of 8400.00 gallons (200.00 barrels),
only 7980.80 barrels are left.

*** WARNING ***
Available supply is less than 10 percent of tank's 80000.00-barrel capacity.
```

operator enters the number of gallons removed, and the program updates the number of barrels still available. When the supply drops below the 10% limit, the program issues a warning.

A counting loop would not be appropriate in this program because we do not know in advance how many tanker deliveries will need to be processed before the warning is issued. However, the `for` statement is still a good choice because we do have initialization, testing, and update steps.

Let's take a close look at the loop in the program of Fig. 5.9. Logically, we want to continue to record amounts of gasoline removed as long as the supply in the tank does not fall below the minimum. The loop repetition condition, the second expression in the `for` loop heading, states that we stay in the loop as long as

```
current >= min_supply;
```

Since `min_supply` does not change, `current` is the variable that controls the loop. Therefore the first and third expressions of the `for` statement's heading handle the initialization and update of this variable's value.

Walking through this program with the data shown, we come first to the assignment statement that computes a value for `min_supply` of `8000.0`, based on the tank capacity and minimum percentage. The call to `printf` just before the call to `scanf` generates the prompting message for entering the tank's initial supply. Next, the starting supply entered by the program operator is scanned into variable `start_supply`. The initialization expression of the `for` statement copies the starting supply into `current`, the loop control variable, giving `current` the value `8500.5`. When the loop repetition condition

```
current >= min_supply;
```

is first tested, it evaluates to true, causing the loop body (the compound statement in braces) to execute. The current supply is displayed followed by a prompting message. A value is obtained for gallons removed (`5859.0`), the value is converted to barrels, and this amount is displayed. When execution of the loop body is complete, the update expression of the `for` statement

```
current = current - remov_brls;
```

is executed, subtracting from the current supply the amount removed. The loop repetition condition is retested with the new value of `current` (`8361.00`). Since `8361.00 > 8000.0` is true, the loop body once again displays the current supply and processes a delivery of `7568.4` gallons or `180.20` barrels. The value of `current` is then updated to `8180.80` barrels, which is still not below the minimum, so the loop body executes a third time, processing removal of 200.00 barrels. This time execution of the `for` statement update expression brings the value of `current` to 7980.80. The loop repetition condition is tested again: Since 7980.8 >= 8000.0 is false, loop exit occurs, and the statements following the closing brace of the loop body are executed.

Just as in the counting loop shown in Fig. 5.9, there are three critical steps in Fig. 5.9 that involve the loop control variable `current`.

1. `current` is *initialized* to the starting supply in the `for` statement initialization expression.
2. `current` is *tested* before each execution of the loop body.
3. `current` is *updated* (by subtraction of the amount removed) during each iteration. ←

Remember that steps similar to these appear in virtually every loop you write. The C `for` statement heading provides you with a designated place for each of the three steps.

EXERCISES FOR SECTION 5.4

Self-Check

1. Give an example of data the user could enter for the storage tank monitoring program that would cause the body of the `for` loop to be completely skipped.
2. Correct the syntax and logic of the code that follows so that it prints all multiples of 5 from 0 through 100.

```
for sum = 0;
    sum < 100;
    sum = sum + 5;
printf("%d", sum);
```

3. What output is displayed if this list of data is used for the program in Fig. 5.9?

```
8350.8
7581.0
7984.2
```

4. How would you modify the program in Fig. 5.9 so that it also determines the number of deliveries (`count_deliv`) made before the gasoline supply drops below the minimum? Which is the loop control variable, `current` or `count_deliv`?

Programming

1. There are 9,870 people in a town whose population increases by ten percent each year. Write a loop that prints the annual population and determines how many years (`count_years`) it will take for the population to go over 30,000.

5.5 LOOP DESIGN

Being able to analyze the operation of a loop is one thing; designing your own loops is another. In this section, we will consider the latter. The comment that begins the program in Fig. 5.9 is a good summary of the purpose of the loop in this program.

```
/*
 * Monitor gasoline supply in storage tank. Issue
 * warning when supply falls below MIN_PCT% of tank
 * capacity.
 */
```

Let's see how the problem-solving questions suggested in Sections 3.1 and 5.1 can help us formulate a valid loop structure. As always, the columns labeled "Answer" and "Implications . . ." in Table 5.2 represent an individual problem solver's thought processes and are not offered as the "one and only true path" to a solution.

Table 5.2   Problem-Solving Questions for Loop Design

Question	Answer	Implications for the Algorithm

What are the inputs?	Current supply of gasoline (barrels). Amounts removed (gallons).	Input variables needed:
		  `current`
		  `remov_gals`
		Value of `current` must be input once, but amounts removed are entered many times.

(continued)

Table 5.2   *(continued)*

Question	Answer	Implications for the Algorithm
What are the outputs?	Amounts removed in gallons and barrels, the current supply of gasoline, and warning when current supply drops too low.	Values of `current` and `remov_gals` are echoed in the output. Output variable needed: `remov_brls`
Is there any repetition?	Yes. One repeatedly 1. gets amount removed 2. converts the amount to barrels 3. subtracts the amount removed from the current supply 4. checks to see if the supply has fallen below the minimum.	Program variable needed: `min_supply`
Do I know in advance how many times steps will be repeated?	No.	Loop will not be controlled by a counter.
How do I know how long to keep repeating the steps?	As long as the current supply is not below the minimum.	The loop repetition condition is `current >= min_supply`

Displaying a Table of Values

The next program is an example of using a conditional loop to display a table of values.

EXAMPLE 5.4   Your physics professor wants you to write a program that displays the effect of gravity on a free-falling object. Your instructor would like a table showing the height of an object dropped from a tower for every second that it is falling.

If we assume that t is the time of free-fall, we can make the following observations about the height of an object dropped from a tower:

1. At $t = 0.0$, the object height is the same as the tower height.
2. While the object is falling, its height is the tower height minus the distance that the object has traveled.
3. Free-fall ends when the object height is less than or equal to 0.0.

These considerations are the basis of the `for` loop shown in Fig. 5.10. The object height is initialized to the tower height. The loop repetition condition

```
height > 0.0
```

ensures that loop exit occurs when the object hits the ground. As the loop control variable update step, the assignment expression

```
height = tower - 0.5 * G * t * t
```

computes the object height where distance traveled is represented by the formula

$$distance = \frac{1}{2}gt^2$$

and g is the gravitational constant. The number of lines in the table depends on the time interval between lines (`delta_t`) and the tower height (`tower`), both of which are data values. During each loop iteration, the current object height, `height`, and the current elapsed time, `t`, are displayed and new values are assigned to these variables. The message following the table is displayed when the object hits the ground.   ←

Figure 5.10   Program to Follow an Object Dropped from a Tower

```
/*
 * Displays the height of an object dropped from a tower
 * until it hits the ground.
 */

#include <stdio.h>

#define G    9.80665    /* gravitational constant */

int
main(void)
{
```

(continued)

Figure 5.10   *(continued)*

```
            double height,     /* height of object */
                   tower,      /* height of tower  */
                   t,          /* elapsed time     */
                   delta_t;    /* time interval    */

            /* Enter tower height and time interval.          */
            printf("Tower height in meters> ");
            scanf("%lf", &tower);
            printf("Time in seconds between lines of table> ");
            scanf("%lf", &delta_t);

            /* Display table of object heights as it falls.   */
            printf("\n      Time    Height\n\n");
            t = 0.0;
            for  (height = tower;
                  height > 0.0;
                  height = tower - 0.5 * G * t * t) {
               printf("    %6.2f  %7.2f\n", t, height);
               t = t + delta_t;
            }

            /* Object hits the ground                          */
            printf("\nSPLAT!!!\n");

            return (0);
}

Tower height in meters> 100.0
Time in seconds between lines of table> 1.0

      Time    Height

      0.00    100.00
      1.00     95.10
      2.00     80.39
      3.00     55.87
      4.00     21.55

SPLAT!!!
```

Program Style *Displaying a Table*

The programs in Figs. 5.8 and 5.10 display tables of output values. In each case, before the loop is reached, a `printf` statement displays a string that forms the table heading.

Within the loop body, another `printf` statement displays a pair of output values each time it is executed. The `\n` in the `printf` control string ends the line on which each pair appears, so a table consisting of two columns of numbers is created.

Working Backward to Determine Loop Initialization

It is not always easy to come up with the initialization steps for a loop. In some cases, you may be able to work backward from the results that you know are required in the first pass to determine what initial values will produce those results.

Your younger cousin is learning the binary number system and has asked you to write a program that displays powers of 2 that are less than a certain value (for example, 10,000). Assuming that each power of 2 is stored in the variable `power`, you can make the following observations about the loop:

1. `power` during pass i is 2 times `power` during pass i − 1 (for i > 1).
2. `power` must be between `10000` and `20000` just after loop exit.

Statement 1 follows from the fact that the powers of 2 are all multiples of 2, and Statement 2 follows from the fact that only powers less than 10,000 are displayed. From Statement 1, you know that `power` must be multiplied by 2 in the loop body. From Statement 2, you know that the loop exit condition is `power >= 10000`, so the loop repetition condition is `power < 10000`. These considerations lead us to the outline.

1. Initialize `power` to ___ .
2. while `power  <  10000`
    3. Display `power`.
    4. Multiply `power` by `2`.

One way to complete Step 1 is to ask what value should be displayed during the first loop repetition. The value of *n* raised to the power zero is one for any number *n*. Therefore if we initialize `power` to 1, the value displayed during the first loop repetition will be correct (1. Initialize `power` to `1`.).

Sentinel-Controlled Loops

Frequently, you will not be able to determine exactly how many data items a program will process until after the program begins execution. There may be too many data items to count beforehand, or the number of data items provided may depend on how the computation proceeds. One way to handle this situation is to require the user to enter a unique data value to mark the end of the data. The program can compare each value to the *sentinel value* and terminate after this special value is input.

The typical form of a loop that is processing data until the sentinel value is entered is

1. Get a line of data.
2. while the sentinel value has not been encountered
    3. Process the data line.
    4. Get another line of data.

Note that this loop, like other loops we have studied, has an *initialization* (Step 1), a *loop repetition condition* (Step 2), and an *update* (Step 4). Step 1 gets the first line of data; Step 4 gets all the other data lines and then tries to obtain one more line. This attempted extra input permits entry of the sentinel value. The sentinel must be a value that would not be entered as a normal data item. For program readability, we usually name the sentinel by defining a constant macro.

EXAMPLE 5.6

This example shows a sentinel-controlled loop that accumulates the sum of a collection of exam scores, where each score is copied from the input device into the variable `score`. The outline for this solution is as follows:

Sentinel Loop

1. Initialize `sum` to zero.
2. Get first `score`.
3. while `score` is not the `sentinel`
    4. Add `score` to `sum`.
    5. Get next `score`.

One is tempted to try the following algorithm that reverses the order of Steps 4 and 5 so as to be able to omit the duplication of Step 5 in Step 2.

Incorrect Sentinel Loop

1. Initialize `sum` to zero.

2. while `score` is not the `sentinel`
  3. Get `score`.
  4. Add `score` to `sum`.

There are two problems associated with this strategy. First, with no initializing input statement, you will have no value for `score` on which to judge the loop repetition condition when it is first tested. Second, consider the last two iterations of the loop. On the next-to-last iteration, the last data value is copied into `score` and added to the accumulating `sum`; on the last iteration, the attempt to get another score obtains the sentinel value. However, this fact will not cause the loop to exit until the loop repetition condition is tested again. Before exit occurs, the sentinel is added to `sum`. For these reasons, it is important to set up sentinel-controlled loops using the recommended structure: one input to get the loop going (the *initialization* input), and a second to keep it going (the *update* input). The following program uses a `for` structure to implement the sentinel-controlled loop (Fig. 5.11). It also shows that the declaration of a variable may include an initialization.

The following sample dialogue would be used to enter the scores 55, 33, and 77:

```
Enter first score (or -99 to quit)> 55
Enter next score (-99 to quit)> 33
Enter next score (-99 to quit)> 77
Enter next score (-99 to quit)> -99

Sum of exam scores is 165
```

Figure 5.11   Program Showing a Sentinel-Controlled Loop

```
/* Compute the sum of a list of exam scores. */

#include <stdio.h>

#define SENTINEL -99

int
main(void)
{
      int sum = 0,    /* sum of scores input so far    */
          score;      /* current score                 */
```

(continued)

Figure 5.11 *(continued)*

```
        printf("Enter first score (or %d to quit)> ",
               SENTINEL);
        for   (scanf("%d", &score);
                  score != SENTINEL;
                  scanf("%d", &score)) {
           sum = sum + score;
           printf("Enter next score (%d to quit)> ",
                  SENTINEL);
        }

        printf("\nSum of exam scores is %d\n", sum);

        return (0);
}
```

It is usually instructive (and often necessary) to question what happens when there are no data items to process. In this case, the sentinel value would be entered at the first prompt. Loop exit would occur right after the first and only test of the loop repetition condition, so the loop body would not be executed—that is, it is a loop with zero iterations. The variable sum would correctly retain its initial value of zero.   ←

Endfile-Controlled Loops

In Section 2.8, we discussed writing programs to run in batch mode using data files made accessible by input redirection. A data file is always terminated by an endfile character that can be detected by the scanf function. Therefore it is possible to write a batch program that processes a list of data of any length without requiring a special sentinel value at the end of the data.

To write such a program, you must set up your input loop so it notices when scanf encounters the endfile character. So far we have discussed only the effect scanf has on the variables passed to it as arguments. However, scanf also returns a result value just like the functions we studied in Section 3.7. When scanf is successfully able to fill its argument variables with values from the standard input device, the result value that it returns is the number of data items it actually obtained. For example, successful execution of the scanf in this statement returns a 3, which is assigned to input_status.

```
input_status = scanf("%d%d%lf", &age, &weight, &wage);
```

However, if `scanf` runs into difficulty with invalid or insufficient data (for instance, if it comes across the letter `'o'` instead of a zero when trying to get a decimal integer), the function returns as its value the number of data items scanned before encountering the error or running out of data. This means that for the example shown, a nonnegative value less than 3 returned by `scanf` indicates an error. The third situation `scanf` can encounter is detecting the endfile character before getting input data for any of its arguments. In this case, `scanf` returns as its result the value of the standard constant `EOF` (a negative integer).

It is possible to design a repetition statement very similar to the sentinel-controlled loop that uses the status value returned by the `scanf` function to control repetition rather than using the values `scanf` stores in its argument variables. An example of such a loop is shown in Fig. 5.12, which is a batch version of the exam scores program in Fig. 5.11.

Figure 5.12   Batch Version of Sum of Exam Scores Program

```
/*
 * Compute the sum of a list of exam scores.
 * (batch version)
 */

#include <stdio.h>        /* defines printf, scanf, and EOF */

int
main(void)
{
      int sum = 0,      /* sum of scores input so far     */
          score,        /* current score                  */
          input_status; /* status value returned by scanf */

      printf("Scores\n");

      for  (input_status = scanf("%d", &score);
            input_status != EOF;
            input_status = scanf("%d", &score)) {
         printf("%5d\n", score);
         sum = sum + score;
      }
```

(continued)

Figure 5.12 *(continued)*

```
        printf("\nSum of exam scores is %d\n", sum);

        return (0);
}
```

```
Scores
    55
    33
    77

Sum of exam scores is 165
```

Infinite Loops on Faulty Data

The behavior of the `scanf` function when it encounters faulty data can quickly make infinite loops of the `for` statements in Fig. 5.11 and Fig. 5.12. For example, let's assume the user responds to the prompt

```
Enter next score (-99 to quit)>
```

in Fig. 5.11 with the faulty data `7o` (the second character is the letter `'o'` rather than a zero). The function `scanf` would stop at the letter `'o'`, storing just the value 7 in `score` and leaving the letter `'o'` unprocessed. On the next loop iteration, there would be no wait for the user to respond to the prompt, for `scanf` would find the letter `'o'` awaiting processing. However, since this letter is not part of a valid integer, the `scanf` function would then leave the variable `score` unchanged and the letter `'o'` unprocessed, returning a status value of zero as the result of the function call. Because the sentinel-controlled loop of Fig. 5.11 does not use the value returned by `scanf`, the printing of the prompt and the unsuccessful attempt to process the letter `'o'` would repeat over and over.

Even though the loop of the batch program in Fig. 5.12 does use the status value returned by `scanf`, it too would go into an infinite loop on faulty data. The only status value that causes this loop to exit is the negative integer meaning EOF. However, the endfile-controlled loop could be easily modified to exit when encountering end of file or faulty data. Changing the loop repetition condition to

```
input_status == 1
```

would cause the loop to exit on either end of file (`input_status` negative) or faulty data (`input_status` zero). We would also need to add an `if` statement after the loop to decide whether to simply print the results or to warn of bad input.

```
if (input_status == EOF) {
      printf("Sum of exam scores is %d\n", sum);
} else {
      scanf("%c", &bad_char);
      printf("*** Error in input: %c ***\n", bad_char);
}
```

EXERCISES FOR SECTION 5.5

Self-Check

1. Identify these three steps in the pseudocode that follows: the initialization of the loop control variable, the loop repetition condition, and the update of the loop control variable.
   a. Get a value for n.
   b. Give p the value 1.
   c. while n is positive
           d. Multiply p by n.
           e. Subtract 1 from n.
   f. Print p with a label.
2. What would be the behavior of the loop in Fig. 5.12 if the braces around the loop body were omitted?

Programming

1. Translate the pseudocode from Exercise 1 using a `for` loop. Which of these three labels would it make sense to print along with the value of p?

   ```
   n*i =       n! =       n to the ith power =
   ```

2. Modify the loop in Fig. 5.3 so that it is a sentinel-controlled loop. Get an input value for `hours` as both the initialization and update steps of the loop. Use the value −99 as the sentinel.
3. Rewrite the program in Fig. 5.3 to run in batch mode with an endfile-controlled loop.
4. Write a program segment that allows the user to enter values and prints out the number of positive and the number of negative values entered. Design this segment as a sentinel-controlled loop using zero as the sentinel value.

5.6 NESTED CONTROL STRUCTURES

In many programming situations, it is necessary to nest one control structure inside another. We discussed the nested `if` structure in Section 4.7 and considered several examples. It is also possible to nest `if` statements within loops and to nest loops within other control structures. The program in Fig. 5.13 contains an `if` statement nested within a loop that finds the product of all nonzero data items. Each data item is tested, the nonzero values are included in the product being computed, and the loop is exited after the sentinel is encountered.

Figure 5.13   **Program to Find the Product of Nonzero Data Items**

```
/* Finds the product of nonzero data. */

#include <stdio.h>

#define SENT -9999.0

int
main(void)
{
      double product = 1.0; /* product so far of nonzero data          */
      int    status;        /* status of input operation               */
      double data_item;     /* current data value                      */

      printf("Enter a data item (%.1f to quit)> ", SENT);
      for  (scanf("%lf", &data_item);
            data_item != SENT;
            scanf("%lf", &data_item)) {
         if (data_item != 0)
             product = product * data_item;
         printf("Enter next data item (%.1f to quit)> ", SENT);
      }

      printf("The product of nonzero data is %8.3f.\n", product);

      return (0);
}
```

(continued)

Figure 5.13 *(continued)*

```
Enter a data item (-9999.0 to quit)> 3.0
Enter next data item (-9999.0 to quit)> 0.0
Enter next data item (-9999.0 to quit)> -1.0
Enter next data item (-9999.0 to quit)> -9999.0
The product of nonzero data is   -3.000.
```

Nested Loops

The last category of nested structures that we will consider is nested loops, the most difficult of all nested structures to deal with. For each iteration of the outer loop, the control structure that is the inner loop is entered and repeated until done.

 **EXAMPLE 5.7**   The program in Fig. 5.14 contains a sentinel loop nested within a counting loop. This structure is being used to tally by month the local Audubon Club members' sightings of bald eagles for the past year. The data for this program consists of a group of positive integers followed by a zero, then a second group of positive inte-

Figure 5.14 **Program to Process Bald Eagle Sightings for a Year**

```
/*
 * Tally by month the bald eagle sightings for the year. Each month's
 * sightings are terminated by the sentinel zero.
 */

#include <stdio.h>

#define SENTINEL    0
#define NUM_MONTHS 12

int
main(void)
{
```

(continued)

Figure 5.14 *(continued)*

```
   int month,      /* number of month being processed          */
      mem_sight,  /* one member's sightings for this month      */
      sightings;  /* total sightings so far for this month      */

   printf("BALD EAGLE SIGHTINGS\n");
   for (month = 1;
        month <= NUM_MONTHS;
        month = month + 1) {
      sightings = 0;

      for (scanf("%d", &mem_sight);
           mem_sight != SENTINEL;
           scanf("%d", &mem_sight)) {
         sightings = sightings + mem_sight;
      }
      printf("  month %2d: %2d\n", month, sightings);
   }

   return (0);
}
```

Input data
2 1 4 3 0
1 2 0
0
5 4 1 0
. . .

Results
BALD EAGLE SIGHTINGS
  month 1: 10
  month 2: 3
  month 3: 0
  month 4: 10
  . . .

gers followed by a zero, then a third group, and so on, for twelve groups of numbers. The first group of numbers represents sightings in January, the second represents sightings in February, and so on, for all twelve months. ←

EXAMPLE 5.8 ► In Fig. 5.15, we see a sample run of a program with two nested counting loops. The outer loop is repeated three times (for `i = 1, 2,` and `3`). Each time the outer loop is repeated, the statement

```
printf("Outer %6d\n", i);
```

displays the string `"Outer"` and the value of `i` (the outer loop control vari-

Figure 5.15   Nested Counting Loop Program

```
/*
 * Illustrates a pair of nested counting loops
 */

#include <stdio.h>

int
main(void)
{
      int i, j;   /* loop control variables */

      printf("         I    J\n");              /* prints column labels */

      for  (i = 1;  i < 4;  i = i + 1)   { /* heading of outer for loop */
          printf("Outer %6d\n", i);
          for  (j = 0;  j < i;  j = j + 1)    { /* heading of inner loop */
              printf("  Inner%9d\n", j);
          }  /* end of inner loop */
      }   /*  end of outer loop */

      return (0);

}
```

(continued)

Figure 5.15   *(continued)*

	I	J
Outer	1	
Inner		0
Outer	2	
Inner		0
Inner		1
Outer	3	
Inner		0
Inner		1
Inner		2

able). Next, the inner loop is entered, and its loop control variable j is reset to 0. The number of times the inner loop is repeated depends on the current value of i. Each time the inner loop is repeated, the statement

```
printf("   Inner %9d\n", j);
```

displays the string "Inner" and the value of j.

A compound statement executes each time the outer for loop is repeated. This statement displays the value of the outer loop control variable and then executes the inner for loop. The body of the inner for loop is a single statement displaying the value of the inner loop control variable. This statement executes i times where i is the outer loop control variable.

The outer loop control variable i appears in the condition that determines the number of repetitions of the inner loop. Although this usage is perfectly valid, it is not legitimate to use the same variable as the loop control variable of both an outer and an inner for loop in the same nest. ⬅

EXAMPLE 5.9

The program in Fig. 5.16 prints the addition table for integer values between 0 and 9. For example, the line beginning with the digit 9 in the table shows the result of adding to 9 each of the digits 0 through 9. The initial loop prints the list of digits from 0 through 9 as part of the table heading.

The nested counting loops are used to print the table body. The outer loop (loop control variable addend_1) first prints the current value of addend_1. In the inner loop, each value of addend_2 (0 through 9) is added to addend_1 and the individual sums are printed. Each time the outer loop is repeated, ten additions are performed so the program prints 100 sums. ⬅

Figure 5.16   Program to Print an Addition Table

```c
/*
 * Prints an addition table
 */

#include <stdio.h>

#define NUM_DIGITS   10

int
main(void)
{
      int addend_1,    /* first addend       */
          addend_2,    /* second addend      */
          sum;         /* sum of addends     */

      /* Prints the table heading.            */
      printf("+");
      for  (addend_2 = 0;
            addend_2 < NUM_DIGITS;
            addend_2 = addend_2 + 1)
         printf("%3d", addend_2);   /* Prints each digit
                                       in heading. */

      /* Prints the table body. */
      for  (addend_1 = 0;
            addend_1 < NUM_DIGITS;
            addend_1 = addend_1 + 1) {
         printf("\n%d", addend_1);   /* Starts a row with
                                        first addend. */

            for  (addend_2 = 0;
                  addend_2 < NUM_DIGITS;
                  addend_2 = addend_2 + 1) {
               sum = addend_1 + addend_2;
               printf("%3d", sum);
            }

      }
      printf("\n");

      return (0);
}
```

(continued)

Figure 5.16   *(continued)*

+	0	1	2	3	4	5	6	7	8	9
0	0	1	2	3	4	5	6	7	8	9
1	1	2	3	4	5	6	7	8	9	10
2	2	3	4	5	6	7	8	9	10	11
3	3	4	5	6	7	8	9	10	11	12
4	4	5	6	7	8	9	10	11	12	13
5	5	6	7	8	9	10	11	12	13	14
6	6	7	8	9	10	11	12	13	14	15
7	7	8	9	10	11	12	13	14	15	16
8	8	9	10	11	12	13	14	15	16	17
9	9	10	11	12	13	14	15	16	17	18

EXERCISES FOR SECTION 5.6

Self-Check

1. What is displayed by the following program segments, assuming m is 3 and n is 5?

   a. ```
   for (i = 1; i <= n; i = i + 1) {

       for (j = 0; j < i; j = j + 1) {
           printf("*");
       }

       printf("\n");
   }
   ```
   b. ```
   for  (i = n;  i > 0;  i = i - 1) {

       for  (j = m;  j > 0;  j = j - 1) {
           printf("*");
       }

       printf("\n");
   }
   ```

2. Show the output printed by these nested loops.

   ```
   for  (i = 0;  i < 2;  i = i + 1) {
       printf("Outer %4d\n", i);
   ```

```
for  (j = 0;  j < 3;  j = j + 1) {
   printf("  Inner%3d%3d\n", i, j);
}

for  (k = 2;  k > 0;  k = k - 1) {
   printf("  Inner%3d%3d\n", i, k);
}
}
```

Programming

1. Write a program that prints the multiplication table for numbers 0 to 9.
2. Write nests of loops that cause the following output to be printed.

```
0
0 1
0 1 2
0 1 2 3
0 1 2 3 4
0 1 2 3
0 1 2
0 1
0
```

5.7 PROBLEM SOLVING ILLUSTRATED

In this section, we will examine a programming problem that illustrates many of the concepts discussed in this chapter. The *top-down design* process will be demonstrated in solving this programming problem. The program will be implemented in a stepwise manner, starting with a list of major algorithm steps and continuing to add detail through refinement until the program can be written.

Case Study: Computing Radiation Levels

▸ **PROBLEM**

In a certain building at a top secret research lab, some yttrium-90 has leaked into the computer analysts' coffee room. The leak would currently expose personnel to 150 millirems of radiation a day. The half-life of the substance is about three days, that is, the radiation level is only half of what it was three days ago. The analysts want to know how long it will be before the radiation is down to a safe level of 0.466 millirem a day. They would like a chart that displays the radiation level for every three days with the message `Unsafe` or `Safe` after every line. The chart should stop just before the radiation level is one-tenth of the safe level, because the more cautious analysts will require a safety factor of 10.

ANALYSIS

Printing the chart will require the use of a loop that displays a line with a day number and a radiation level for each iteration. The loop should continue to repeat as long as the radiation level is above one-tenth of the safe level. The data requirements and algorithm follow.

Data Requirements

Problem Constants
```
SAFE_RAD         0.466 /* the safe radiation level in
                           millirems                  */
SAFETY_FACT      10.0  /* the safety factor           */
```

Problem Input
```
int init_radiation    /* the initial radiation level */
```

Problem Outputs
```
int day             /* the day number                     */
int radiation_lev /* the radiation level in millirems */
```

DESIGN

Initial Algorithm

1. Initialize `day` to zero.
2. Compute the stopping level of radiation, that is, the safe level divided by the safety factor.
3. Prompt the user to enter the initial radiation level.
4. Compute and display the day number and the radiation level every three days that the radiation level exceeds the stopping radiation level. Also, indicate whether each level is safe or unsafe.

Algorithm Refinements

We will introduce a new variable (`min_radiation`) to hold the stopping level of radiation referred to in Step 1 of our initial algorithm. Since it is clear that some steps of our solution will be repeated, we will first use a `while` loop in our pseudocode for Step 4 and then look for the initialization and update steps that would permit us to use a `for` loop in our final implementation.

Additional Program Variable

```
double min_radiation  /* the stopping level of radiation  */
```

Step 4 Refinement

4.1 Initialize `radiation_lev` to `init_radiation`
4.2 while `radiation_lev` exceeds `min_radiation`
      4.3 Display the value of `day`, `radiation_lev`, and the string "Unsafe" or "Safe".
      4.4 Add 3 to the value of `day`.
      4.5 Compute `radiation_lev` for the next period.

Let's see if our new refinements make it possible to identify initialization and update steps for our loop. We note that our loop repetition condition is a comparison between the variables `radiation_lev` and `min_radiation`. Since `min_radiation` does not change after it is first initialized, it must be `radiation_lev` that is our loop control variable; therefore Steps 4.1 and 4.5 are the initialization and update steps we need in order to use a `for` statement in our implementation. Now we can further refine Step 4.3 as shown below.

Step 4.3 Refinement

4.3.1 if `radiation_lev` exceeds `SAFE_RAD`
      Display `day`, `radiation_lev`, and "Unsafe".
  else
      Display `day`, `radiation_lev`, and "Safe".

◀ IMPLEMENTATION ▶

The program appears in Fig. 5.17.

◀ TESTING ▶

The only data item for this program is the initial radiation level. One run with a data value of `150.0` (millirems) will give you output that you can use to show correctness on valid, middle-of-the-road data. Check that each radiation value in the table displayed is one-half the previous value and that the number of days

Figure 5.17   Program to Compute Radiation Levels

```
/*
 * Calculates and prints a chart showing the safety level of
 * a coffee room.
 */

#include <stdio.h>

#define SAFE_RAD     0.466  /* safe level of radiation            */
#define SAFETY_FACT  10.0   /* safety factor                      */

int
main(void)
{
      int    day;            /* days elapsed since substance leak   */
      double init_radiation, /* radiation level right after leak    */
             radiation_lev,  /* current radiation level             */
             min_radiation;  /* safe level divided by safety factor */

      /* Initializes day and min_radiation           */
      day = 0;
      min_radiation = SAFE_RAD / SAFETY_FACT;

      /* Prompts user to enter initial radiation level   */
      printf("Enter the radiation level (in millirems)> ");
      scanf("%lf", &init_radiation);

      /* Displays table                              */
      printf("\n  Day   Radiation   Status\n      (millirems)");
      for  (radiation_lev = init_radiation;
            radiation_lev > min_radiation;
            radiation_lev = radiation_lev / 2.0) {
          if  (radiation_lev > SAFE_RAD)
                printf("  %3d     %9.4f Unsafe\n", day, radiation_lev);
          else
                printf("  %3d     %9.4f Safe\n", day, radiation_lev);

          day = day + 3;
      }
```

(continued)

Figure 5.17 *(continued)*

```
    return (0);

}
```

Enter the radiation level (in millirems)> 150.0

Day	Radiation (millirems)	Status
0	150.0000	Unsafe
3	75.0000	Unsafe
6	37.5000	Unsafe
9	18.7500	Unsafe
12	9.3750	Unsafe
15	4.6875	Unsafe
18	2.3438	Unsafe
21	1.1719	Unsafe
24	0.5859	Unsafe
27	0.2930	Safe
30	0.1465	Safe
33	0.0732	Safe

always increases by three. Also check that the first safe value is less than 0.466 millirem. Verify that your loop exited correctly by dividing the last radiation value displayed by 2.0. You must get a value that is less than or equal to 0.0466 (0.466/10.0 is 0.0466).

EXERCISES FOR SECTION 5.7

Self-Check

1. Replace the for statement in Fig. 5.17 with a while loop.
2. How would you get the program in Fig. 5.17 to stop the table display *after*, instead of before, the radiation level becomes less than or equal to the safe level divided by the safety factor?

5.8 HOW TO DEBUG AND TEST PROGRAMS

In Section 2.9, we described the general categories of error messages that you are likely to see: syntax errors and run-time errors. We also noted that it is possible for a program to execute without generating any error messages but still produce incorrect results. Sometimes the cause of a run-time error or the origin of incorrect results is apparent, and the error can easily be fixed. However, very often the error is not obvious and may require considerable effort to locate.

The first step in attempting to find a hidden error is to examine the program output to determine which part of the program is generating incorrect results. Then you can focus on the statements in that section to determine which one(s) are at fault. To help you locate problem areas, you may need to insert extra debugging statements that display intermediate results at different points in your program. You may also want to insert extra calls to `printf` to trace the values of certain critical variables during program execution. For example, if the loop in Fig. 5.11 is not computing the correct sum, you might want to insert an extra diagnostic call to `printf` as shown by the line in color in the loop below.

```
for  (scanf("%d", &score);
       score != SENTINEL;
       scanf("%d", &score)) {
    sum = sum + score;
    printf("***** score is %d, sum is %d\n", score, sum);
    printf("Enter next score (%d to quit)> ",
            SENTINEL);
}
```

The diagnostic call to `printf` will display each partial sum that is accumulated along with the current value of `score`. This call displays a string of asterisks at the beginning of its output line, making it easier to identify diagnostic output in the debugging runs. The string of asterisks also simplifies locating the diagnostic `printf` calls in the source program. We usually include a \n at the end of every `printf` format string. It is especially critical that you do this in diagnostic print statements so your output will be printed immediately; otherwise, if a run-time error occurs before a \n is encountered in another format string, you may never see the diagnostic message.

Take care when inserting extra diagnostic `printf` calls. Sometimes it will be necessary to add a set of braces if a single statement inside an `if` statement or a loop becomes a compound statement because of the additional call.

Once it appears that you have located an error, you will want to take out the extra diagnostic statements. As a temporary measure, it is sometimes advisable to make these diagnostic statements into comments by enclosing them in /* */. If these errors crop up again in later testing, it is easier to remove the comment symbols than to retype the diagnostic statements.

Off by One Loop Errors

A fairly common error in programs with loops is a loop that executes one time more, or one time less, than it should. If a sentinel-controlled loop performs an extra iteration, it may erroneously process the sentinel value as if it were a data value.

If a loop performs a counting operation, make sure that the initial and final values of the loop control variable are correct and that the loop repetition condition is right. For example, the loop body below executes n + 1 times instead of n times. If your intention is to execute the loop body n times, change the loop repetition condition to `count < n`.

```
for  (count = 0;  count <= n;  count = count + 1) {
    sum = sum + count;
    count = count + 1;
}
```

You can get a good idea as to whether a loop is correct by checking what happens at the *loop boundaries,* that is, at the initial and final values of the loop control variable. For a counting `for` loop, you should carefully evaluate the expression in the initialization step, substitute this value everywhere the counter variable appears in the loop body, and verify that it makes sense as a beginning value. Then choose a value for the counter that still causes the loop repetition condition to be true but that will make this condition false after one more evaluation of the update expression. Check the validity of this boundary value wherever the counter variable appears. As an example, in the `for` loop,

```
sum = 0;
k = 1;
for  (i = -n;  i < n - k;  i = i + 1)
    sum = sum + i * i;
```

check that the first value of the counter variable i is supposed to be $-n$ and that the last value should be $n - 2$. Next, check that the assignment statement

```
sum = sum + i * i;
```

is correct at these boundaries. When i is $-n$, sum gets the value of n^2. When i is $n - 2$, the value of $(n - 2)^2$ is added to the previous sum. As a final check, pick some small value of n (for example, 2) and trace the loop execution to see that it computes sum correctly for this case.

Using Debugger Programs

Many computer systems have *debugger programs* available to help you debug a C program. The debugger program lets you execute your program one statement at a time (*single-step execution*) so that you can see the effect of each statement.

You can select several variables whose values will be automatically displayed after each statement executes. This feature allows you to trace the program's execution. Besides printing a diagnostic when a run-time error occurs, the debugger indicates the statement that caused the error and displays the values of the variables you selected.

You can also separate your program into segments by setting *breakpoints* at selected statements. A breakpoint is like a fence between two segments of a program. You can ask the debugger to execute all statements from the last breakpoint up to the next breakpoint. When the program stops at a breakpoint, you can select variables to examine, in this way determining whether the program segment executed correctly. If a program segment executes correctly, you will want to execute through to the next breakpoint. If it does not, you may want to set more breakpoints in that segment or perhaps perform single-step execution through that segment.

Testing

After all errors have been corrected and the program appears to execute as expected, the program should be tested thoroughly to make sure that it works. In Section 4.4, we discussed tracing an algorithm and suggested that enough sets of test data be provided to ensure that all possible paths are traced. The same is true for a simple completed program; make enough test runs to verify that the program works properly for representative samples of all possible data combinations.

EXERCISES FOR SECTION 5.8

Self-Check

1. For the first counting loop in the subsection "Off by One Loop Errors," add debugging statements to show the value of the loop control variable at the start of each repetition. Also add debugging statements to show the value of sum at the end of each loop repetition.
2. Repeat Exercise 1 for the second loop in the same subsection.

5.9 COMMON PROGRAMMING ERRORS

Students sometimes confuse decision steps with while loops because the header for both structures contains a parenthesized condition. If the statements depending on the condition value are to be executed at most one time, you are dealing with a decision step and should use an if statement. You should use a while loop only if the statements depending on the condition may need to be executed more than once. The syntax of the `for` statement header is repeated.

```
for    (initialization expression;
        loop repetition condition;
        update expression)
```

Remember to end the initialization expression and the loop repetition condition with semicolons. Be careful not to put a semicolon before or after the closing parenthesis of the `for` statement header. A semicolon after this parenthesis would have the effect of ending the `for` statement without making execution of the loop body dependent on its condition.

Another common mistake in using `while` and `for` statements is to forget that the structure assumes that the loop body is a single statement. Remember to use braces around a loop body consisting of multiple statements. Some C programmers always use braces around a loop body, whether it contains one or many statements. Keep in mind that your compiler ignores indentation, so a loop defined as shown (with braces around the loop body left out)

```
while (x > xbig)
     x = x - 2;
     xbig = xbig + 1;
/* end while */
```

really executes as

```
while (x > xbig)
     x = x - 2; /* only this statement is repeated */

xbig = xbig + 1;
```

The C compiler can easily detect that there is something wrong with code in which a closing brace has been omitted on a compound statement. However, the error message noting the symbol's absence may be far from the spot where the brace belongs, and other error messages often appear as a side effect of the omission. When compound statements are nested, the compiler will associate the first closing brace encountered with the innermost structure. Even if it is the terminator for this inner structure that is left out, the compiler may complain about the outer structure. In the example that follows, the body of the `for` statement is missing a brace. However, the compiler will associate the closing brace before the keyword `else` with the body of the `for` loop and then proceed to mark the `else` as improper.

```
printf("Experiment successful?(Y/N)> ");
scanf("%c", &ans);
```

```
if (ans == 'Y') {
    printf("Enter data one value per line (%d to quit)\n> ",
            SENT);
    for  (scanf("%d", &data);
            data != SENT;
            scanf("%d", &data)) {
        sum = sum + data;
        printf("> ");
                    /* <— missing } */
} else {
    printf("Try it again tomorrow.\n");
    printf("Now follow correct shutdown procedure.\n");
}
```

Be very careful when using tests for inequality to control the repetition of a loop. The following loop is intended to process all transactions for a bank account while the balance is positive.

```
for  (scanf("%d%lf", &code, &amount);
        balance != 0.0;
        scanf("%d%lf", &code, &amount) {
   . . .
}
```

If the bank balance goes from a positive to a negative amount without ever being exactly 0.0, the loop will not terminate as planned. The loop that follows would be much safer:

```
for  (scanf("%d%lf", &code, &amount);
        balance > 0.0;
        scanf("%d%lf", &code, &amount) {
   . . .
}
```

You should verify that a loop's repetition condition will eventually become false (0); otherwise, an infinite loop may result. If a sentinel value is used to control loop repetition in an interactive program, make sure that the program's prompting messages tell what value to enter to stop loop repetition. Also, be careful when you are entering a list of data interactively; as we discussed in Section 5.5, an invalid character received by the scanf function can cause an infinite loop. In Chapter 7, we will study how to construct programs that are not easily broken by a user's poor typing skills!

Another common cause of a nonterminating loop is the use of a loop repetition condition in which an equality test is mistyped as an assignment operation.

Table 5.3 Summary of Loop Statements from Chapter 5

Statement	Effect

Counting for Loop

```
for (num = 0;
     num < 26;
     num = num + 1) {
   square = num * num;
   printf("%5d %5d\n", num,
          square);
}
```

Prints 26 lines, each containing an integer from 0 to 25 and its square.

Counting for Loop with a Negative Step

```
for (volts = 20;
     volts >= -20;
     volts = volts - 10) {
   current = volts / resistance;
   printf("%5d %8.3f\n", volts,
          current);
}
```

For values of volts equal to 20, 10, 0, −10, −20, computes value of current and displays volts and current.

Sentinel-controlled for Loop

```
product = 1;
printf("Enter %d to quit\n",
       SENVAL);
printf("Enter first number> ");
for  (scanf("%d", &dat);
      dat != SENVAL;
      scanf("%d", &dat)) {
   product = product * dat;
   printf("Next number> ");
}
```

Computes the product of a list of numbers. The product is complete when the user enters the sentinel value (SENVAL).

Endfile-controlled for Loop

```
sum = 0;
for  (status = scanf("%d", &num);
      status != EOF;
      status = scanf("%d", &num)) {
   sum = sum + num;
}
```

Accumulates the sum of a list of numbers. The sum is complete when scanf detects the endfile character.

Conditional Loop Using while Statement

```
printf("Balloon's diameter> ");
scanf("%d", &diameter);
while (diameter < RIGHT_SIZE) {
   printf("Keep blowing!\n");
   printf("New diameter> ");
   scanf("%d", &diameter);
}
printf("Stop blowing!\n");
```

Instructs user to continue blowing as long as a balloon's diameter is below the desired size (RIGHT_SIZE).

Consider the following loop that expects the user to type the number 0 (actually any integer other than 1) to exit.

```
for  (again = 1; /* initialization        */
      again = 1; /* should be: again == 1 */
      scanf("%d", &again)) {
   . . .
   printf("One more time? (1 to continue/ 0 to quit)> ");
}
```

The value of the second assignment statement will always be 1, never 0 (false), so this loop will not exit on an entry of zero or of any other number.

CHAPTER REVIEW

This chapter described how to repeat steps in a C program. You learned two repetition constructs: the while statement, which repeats its loop body as long as the condition in its header is true; and the for statement, whose header provides places for the three aspects of loop control—initialization, testing, and update of the loop control variable. You also studied how to write counting loops that allow you to repeat program segments a predetermined number of times, and you saw that the counters in these loops can count up or down in steps of any size. This chapter introduced how to use a for statement to implement a loop whose exact number of repetitions is not known before the loop begins executing. Two techniques were presented for input and processing of lists of data of varying lengths. In both approaches, for statements are used with calls to scanf for initialization and update of the loop control variable. If the data is terminated by a special sentinel value, the for statement's loop repetition condition is a comparison of the input variable and the sentinel value. If the end of the list coincides with the end of the input file, the value returned by the scanf function is assigned to a status variable in the initialization and update sections of the for statement header, and the loop repetition condition is a comparison of the status variable and the standard EOF value.

Examples of the loops introduced in this chapter are described in Table 5.3.

QUICK-CHECK EXERCISES

1. A loop that continues to process input data until a special value is entered is called a _____-controlled loop.

2. Some `for` loops cannot be rewritten as code using a `while` loop. True or false?

3. It is an error if the body of a `for` loop never executes. True or false?

4. In an endfile-controlled `for` loop, the initialization and update expressions typically include calls to the function _____ if the data file is made accessible through input redirection.

5. In a counter-controlled loop, the number of loop repetitions may not be known until the loop is executing. True or false?

6. During execution of the following program segment, how many lines of asterisks are displayed?

```
for  (i = 0;  i < 10;  i = i + 1)
    for  (j = 0;  j < 5;  j = j + 1)
        printf("**********\n");
```

7. During execution of the following program segment,
   a. How many times does the first call to `printf` execute?
   b. How many times does the second call to `printf` execute?
   c. What is the last value displayed?

```
for  (i = 0;  i < 7;  i = i + 1) {
    for  (j = 0;  j < i;  j = j + 1)
        printf("%4d", i * j);
    printf("\n");
}
```

ANSWERS TO QUICK-CHECK EXERCISES

1. sentinel
2. false
3. false
4. `scanf`
5. false
6. 50
7. a. 0 + 1 + 2 + 3 + 4 + 5 + 6 = 21
   b. 7
   c. 30

REVIEW QUESTIONS

1. In what ways are the `for` loop headings alike in a sentinel-controlled loop and an endfile-controlled loop? How are they different?

2. Write a program to compute and print the sum of a collection of Celsius temperatures entered at the terminal until a sentinel value of −275 is entered.
3. Hand-trace the program that follows given the following data:

```
4 2 8 4    1 4 2 1    9 3 3 1    −22 10 8 2    3 3 4 5
```

```c
#include <stdio.h>
#define SPECIAL_SLOPE   0.0
int
main(void)
{
      double slope, y2, y1, x2, x1;

      printf("Enter four numbers separated by spaces.");
      printf("\nThe last two numbers cannot be the ");
      printf("same, but\nthe program terminates if ");
      printf("the first two are.\n");

      printf("\nEnter four numbers> ");
      scanf("%lf%lf%lf%lf", &y2, &y1, &x2, &x1);

      for (slope = (y2 - y1) / (x2 - x1);
           slope != SPECIAL_SLOPE;
           slope = (y2 - y1) / (x2 - x1)) {
         printf("Slope is %5.2f.\n", slope);
         printf("\nEnter four more numbers> ");
         scanf("%lf%lf%lf%lf", &y2, &y1, &x2, &x1);
      }

      return (0);
}
```

4. Rewrite the program in Review Question 3 so it uses a `while` loop.
5. Rewrite the program segment that follows, using a `for` loop.

```c
count = 0;
i = 0;
while (i < n) {
    scanf("%d", &x);
    if (x == i)
         count = count + 1;
    i = i + 1;
}
```

6. Rewrite this `for` loop heading, omitting any invalid semicolons.

```
for (i = n;
     i < max;
     i = i + 1;);
```

PROGRAMMING PROJECTS

1. Write a program that will find the smallest, largest, and average value in a collection of *n* numbers when the value of *n* is the first data item.
2. Write a program to take a collection of integer data items and find and print the index of the first occurrence and the last occurrence of the number 12. Your program should print index values of 0 if the number 12 is not found. The index is the sequence number of the data item 12. For example, if the eighth data item is the only 12, then the index value 8 should be printed for the first and last occurrence.
3. Write a program to process a data file containing a collection of daily high temperatures. Your program should count and print the number of hot days (high temperature 85 or higher), the number of pleasant days (high temperature 60–84), and the number of cold days (temperatures less than 60). The program should also display the category of each temperature.

    Test your program on the following data:

    ```
    55   62   68   74   59   45   41   58   60   67   65   78   82
    88   91   92   90   93   87   80   78   79   72   68   61   59
    ```

4. a. The Fibonacci sequence is a sequence of numbers beginning

    $$1, 1, 2, 3, 5, 8, 13, 21, \ldots$$

    The first two elements are defined to be 1. Each of the other elements is the sum of its two predecessors. Write a program that takes a value for *n* in the range 1 to 30 and displays the first *n* elements of the Fibonacci sequence.

    b. Modify your program to display the elements eight per line.

5. It is a dark and stormy night. Our secret agent, 008, is behind enemy lines at a fuel depot. She walks over to a cylindrical fuel tank, which is 20 feet tall and 8 feet in diameter. The tank is full. Our agent opens a 2-inch-diameter circular nozzle. She knows that the volume of the fuel leaving the tank is

    volume lost (ft^3) = *velocity* × (*area of the nozzle*) × *time* and that

$$velocity \ (ft/sec) = 8.02 \ \times \ \sqrt{height \ of \ fluid \ in \ the \ tank}$$

Our agent must radio in a report giving the approximate height of the fluid in the tank minute by minute until the tank is empty. She can first calculate the volume lost over one minute and assume that the loss of fluid is constant. Next she can then subtract the volume from the tank and determine the new height of the fluid inside the tank at the end of the minute. Then she can calculate the loss for the next minute. These calculations must be repeated over and over until the tank is dry.

Design a program that would save 008 a lot of computation the next time this kind of situation comes up. Print a table showing the elapsed time in seconds, the volume lost, and the height of the fluid remaining. At the very end, convert the total seconds elapsed to minutes. Your table could look like this one:

Time (seconds)	Volume Lost (cubic feet)	Fluid Height (feet)
60	46.95	19.07
120	45.84	18.15
180	44.73	17.26
. . .		
2340	3.93	0.06
2400	2.62	0.01

After 41.0 minutes, tank is empty.

6. Let n be a positive integer consisting of up to ten digits, d_{10}, d_9, ... , d_1. Write a program to list in one column each of the digits in the number n. The rightmost digit, d_1, should be listed at the top of the column. Hint: If n is 3704, what is the value of the digit as computed according to the formula

```
digit = n % 10;
```

Test your program for values of n equal to 6, 3704, and 170498.
7. An integer n is divisible by 9 if the sum of its digits is divisible by 9. Use the algorithm developed for Project 6, and write a program to determine whether or not the following numbers are divisible by 9.

154368   621594   123456

8. The pressure of a gas changes as the volume and temperature of the gas vary. Write a program that shows in tabular form the relationship between the

pressure and the volume of n moles of carbon dioxide at a constant absolute temperature. Inputs to the program include n, the temperature (in Kelvins), the initial and final volumes (in milliliters), and the volume increment between lines of the table. Your program will print a table that varies the volume of the gas from the initial to the final volume in steps prescribed by the volume increment. Use a variant of the following formula based on the Van der Waals equation of state for a gas:

$$\left(P + \frac{3.6n^2}{V^2}\right)(V - 0.428n) = 0.08023nT$$

P is the pressure in atmospheres, V is the volume in liters, and T is the temperature in Kelvins. Here is a sample run:

```
Please enter at the prompts the number of moles of carbon
dioxide, the absolute temperature, the initial volume in
milliliters, the final volume, and the increment volume
between lines of the table.

Amount of carbon dioxide (moles)> .02
Temperature (Kelvins)> 300
Initial volume (milliliters)> 400
Final volume (milliliters)> 600
Volume increment (milliliters)> 50

0.0200 moles of carbon dioxide
at an absolute temperature of 300. degrees
```

Volume (milliliters)	Pressure (atmospheres)
400	1.1970
450	1.0646
500	0.9587
550	0.8718
600	0.7994

9. A concrete channel to bring water to Crystal Lake is being designed. It will have vertical walls and be 15 feet wide. It will be 10 feet deep, have a slope of .0015 feet/foot, and a roughness coefficient of .014. How deep will the water be when 1,000 cubic feet per second is flowing through the channel?

To solve this problem, we can use Manning's equation

$$Q = \frac{1.49}{N} AR^{2/3}S^{1/2}$$

where Q is the flow of water (cubic feet per second), N is the roughness coefficient (unitless), A is the area (square feet), S is the slope (feet/foot), and R is the hydraulic radius (feet).

The hydraulic radius is the cross-sectional area divided by the wetted perimeter. For square channels like the one in this example,

$$Hydraulic\ radius = depth \times width / (2.0 \times depth + width)$$

To solve this problem, design a program that allows the user to guess a depth and then calculates the corresponding flow. If the flow is too little, the user should guess a depth a little higher; if the flow is too high, the user should guess a depth a little lower. The guessing is repeated until the computed flow is within 0.1 percent of the flow desired.

To help the user make an initial guess, the program should display the flow for half the channel depth. Note the example run:

```
At a depth of 5.0 feet, the flow is 643.0518 cubic feet
per second.

Enter your initial guess for the channel depth
when the flow is 1000.0 cubic feet per second
Enter guess> 6.0

Depth: 6.000000  Flow: 827.8129 cfs  Target: 1000.0 cfs
Difference: 172.1871  Error: 17.21871 percent

Enter guess> 7.0

Depth: 7.000000  Flow: 1020.5180 cfs  Target: 1000.0 cfs
Difference: -20.5180  Error: -2.05180 percent

Enter guess> 6.8
. . .
```

10. Bunyan Lumber Co. needs to create a table of the engineering properties of its lumber. The dimensions of the wood are given as base and height in inches. Engineers need to know the following information about lumber:

cross-sectional area: $base \times height$

moment of inertia: $\dfrac{base \times height^3}{12}$

section modulus: $\dfrac{base \times height^2}{6}$

The owner, Paul, makes lumber with base sizes of 2, 4, 6, 8, 10, and 12 inches. The height sizes are 2, 4, 6, 8, and 10 inches. Produce a table with appropriate headings to show these values and the computed engineering properties. Do not duplicate a 2-by-6-inch board with a 6-by-2-inch board. The first part of the table's outline is shown.

```
Lumber      Cross-sectional    Moment of    Section
Size             Area          Inertia      Modulus

  2 x  2
  2 x  4
  2 x  6
  2 x  8
  2 x 10
  4 x  4
  4 x  6
  4 x  8
  4 x 10
  6 x  6
     .
     .
     .
```

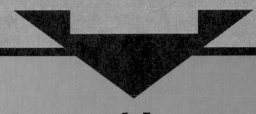

CHAPTER 6

MODULAR PROGRAMMING

6.1
Functions That Return a Single Result
Case Study: Finding Prime Numbers

6.2
void Functions with Input Parameters
Case Study: Computing Maximum Tensile Loads

6.3
Functions with Simple Output Parameters

6.4
Multiple Calls to a void Function with
Input/Output Parameters
Case Study: Simple Sorting Problem

6.5
Introduction to Scope of Names

6.6
Formal Output Parameters as Actual Arguments

6.7
Top-Down Design Illustrated
Case Study: Performing Arithmetic Operations
on Common Fractions

6.8
Debugging and Testing a Program System

6.9
Common Programming Errors
Chapter Review

Chapter 3 introduced you to functions, separate program modules corresponding to the individual steps in a problem solution. We have not yet used functions extensively because we have not discussed how to pass information between our own function subprograms or between our own function subprograms and the main function.

Chapter 3 also introduced you to the idea that a function can be a module that returns a single result. You saw how to write expressions that call C library functions, and you did pass information into these functions through arguments. In addition, Chapter 3 discussed how functions could be used to facilitate structured design.

The use of arguments is a very important concept in programming. Arguments make function subprograms more versatile because they enable a module to manipulate different data each time the module is called. For example,

```
printf("%d", m);
```

displays the value of its argument m; whereas

```
printf("%d", n);
```

displays the value of its argument n.

Our goal throughout this course will be to use functions as building blocks of larger program systems. As you progress through the course, your programming skills and own personal *library* of functions will grow. You should be able to reuse functions written for earlier applications in new programs.

We can make an analogy between a carefully designed program that uses functions and a stereo system. Each stereo component is an independent device that performs a specific operation. The stereo receiver and compact disc (CD) player are "black boxes" that we connect together. We know the purpose of each component, but we have no idea what electronic parts are used inside each box or how they function, nor do we need to have this knowledge in order to use the stereo system.

Information in the form of electronic signals is sent back and forth between these components over wires. If you look at the back of a stereo receiver, you will find that some connection points or plugs are marked as inputs and others are marked as outputs. The wires attached to the plugs marked inputs carry electronic signals into the receiver where they are processed. (These signals may come from a cassette deck, tuner, or CD player.) New electronic signals, generated by the receiver, come out of the receiver from the plugs marked outputs and go to the speakers or back to the cassette deck for recording.

Currently, we know how to design the separate components (functions) of a programming system, but we don't know how to pass data between the main function and a function subprogram that we write. In this chapter, we will learn how to use arguments to provide communication paths between the main function and the other modules we write or between two function subprograms just as we used arguments with library functions.

6.1 FUNCTIONS THAT RETURN A SINGLE RESULT

The mathematical library functions we have seen are convenient in that they permit us to perform a particular computation as often as we wish simply by referencing a function name in an expression. Each time we perform this computation, different arguments can be passed to the function. In the following example, we write our own function to compute the factorial of *n, n*!. The ANSI C math library includes no function that computes factorial, but we can have all the same conveniences if we write our own function.

The function `factorial` in Fig. 6.1 computes the factorial of an integer. The number whose factorial will be computed is represented by the variable n; its value is passed as an argument when the function is called.

The factorial function in Fig. 6.1 resembles the `void` functions we discussed in Chapter 3. The differences are these:

- The function prototype begins with the data type of the result value that the function computes. In parentheses, after the function name, is a list of type declarations for the *formal parameters* that are the inputs to the function. The prototype has the form

    ftype
    fname(type$_1$ param$_1$, type$_2$ param$_2$, . . . , type$_n$ param$_n$)

    Function `factorial` has a single formal parameter, n.
- The function does not print its result; instead, it executes a `return` statement to communicate its result back to the module that called it.

The variables i and `product` are called *local variables* because they are declared in the function and can be manipulated only within the function body. The local variables and formal parameters of a function cannot be referenced by name in any other function. For example, function `factorial` could not reference a variable declared in function `main`. However, all functions are allowed to use any names defined as constant macros in the same file, provided that the `#define` directive precedes the function definition.

Figure 6.1   Function to Compute Factorial

```
/*
 * Computes n!
 * Pre: n is greater than or equal to zero
 */
int
factorial(int n)
{
      int i,            /* local variables */
          product = 1;

      /* Computes the product n x (n-1) x (n-2) x ... x 2 x 1 */
      for  (i = n;  i > 1;  i = i - 1) {
          product = product * i;
      }

      /* Returns function result */
      return (product);
}
```

The syntax display that follows describes the form of a function definition.

Definition of a Function That Computes a Single Result

SYNTAX: *function interface comment*
ftype
fname (*formal parameter declaration list*)
{
　　local variable declarations
　　executable statements
}

EXAMPLE: `/*`
`  * Finds the larger of two numbers`
`  * Pre: input parameters n1 and n2 are defined`
`  */`

(continued)

```
        double
        bigger(double n1, double n2)
        {
                double larger;

                if (n1 > n2)
                        larger = n1;
                else
                        larger = n2;

                return (larger);
        }
```

INTERPRETATION: The *function interface comment* is described in the next Program Style display. The next two lines are the function *prototype,* which specifies the function name, *fname,* and the type of the result returned, *ftype.* It also indicates the names and types of the *formal parameters* in the *formal parameter declaration list.* Note that the lines of the prototype do not end in semicolons. The braces enclose a block that forms the body of the function. The type of any additional variable needed should be declared in the *local variable declarations.* The *executable statements* describe the data manipulation that the function performs on the parameters and local variables in order to compute the result value. Execution of a `return` statement causes the value of the expression following the keyword `return` to be returned as the function's result value. The parentheses around this expression that are shown in the example above are optional.

NOTE: If the function does not have any formal parameters, the keyword `void` is used as the *formal parameter declaration list* in the function prototype.

Program Style   *Function Interface Comment*

The block comment and prototype that begin function `factorial` in Fig. 6.1 contain all the information that anyone needs to know in order to use this function. The function interface block comment begins with a statement of what the function does. Then the line

```
* Pre: n is greater than or equal to zero
```

describes the condition that should be true before the function is called; this condition is known as the *precondition.* You will also want to include a statement describing the condition that must be true after the function completes execution, if some details of this *postcondition* are not included in the initial statement of the function's purpose. We will see an example of such a postcondition later in this chapter in Fig. 6.20.

We recommend that you begin all function definitions in this way. The function interface comment combined with the prototype provide valuable documentation to other programmers who might want to reuse your functions in a new program without having to read the function code.

Figure 6.2 shows a complete program file that includes the function subprogram `factorial` and a main function that takes an integer input value, calls the `factorial` function, and prints the result returned by `factorial`. This program calls function `factorial` only with arguments that are no larger than 10. Even 10! is such a large number (3,628,800) that it cannot be represented as an integer on some computer systems.

Figure 6.2   Complete Program Using Function factorial

```
/*
 * Computes and prints the factorial of a number to demonstrate a user-
 * defined function that has an input parameter and returns a result.
 */

#include <stdio.h>

/*
 * Computes n!
 * Pre: n is greater than or equal to zero
 */
int
factorial(int n)
{
      int i,                  /* local variables */
          product = 1;

      /* Computes the product n x (n-1) x (n-2) x ... x 2 x 1 */
      for  (i = n;   i > 1;   i = i - 1) {
          product = product * i;
      }
```

(continued)

Figure 6.2   *(continued)*

```
      /* Returns function result */
      return (product);
}

/*
 * Demonstrates a call from the main function which passes an argument to a
 * user-defined function.
 */
int
main(void)
{
      int num, fact;

      printf("Enter an integer between 0 and 10> ");
      scanf("%d", &num);
      if (num < 0) {
            printf("The factorial of a negative number (%d) is undefined\n",
                     num);
      } else if (num <= 10) {
            fact = factorial(num);
            printf("The factorial of %d is %d\n", num, fact);
      } else {
            printf("Number out of range: %d\n", num);
      }

      return (0);
}
```

If the input value stored in the variable num of function main is between 0 and 10, the statement

```
fact = factorial(num);
```

is executed. The expression references function factorial; therefore, function factorial is called into execution, and the assignment statement in the main function waits for the function result. Figure 6.3 illustrates how the value of num, the *actual argument* in the function call, is used as the actual value of the *formal parameter* n when the body of function factorial is executed. The result of the execution of factorial is returned to the main function, assigned to the variable fact, and printed.

Figure 6.3
Effect of
Execution of
factorial When
num is 6

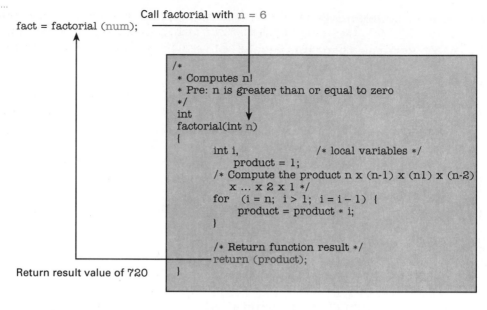

Call factorial with n = 6

fact = factorial (num);

```
/*
 * Computes n!
 * Pre: n is greater than or equal to zero
 */
int
factorial(int n)
{
      int i,                    /* local variables */
          product = 1;
      /* Compute the product n x (n-1) x (n1) x (n-2)
         x ... x 2 x 1 */
      for  (i = n;  i > 1;  i = i - 1) {
          product = product * i;
      }

      /* Return function result */
      return (product);
}
```

Return result value of 720

EXAMPLE 6.2 ▷ A formula from probability theory can be used to compute the number of different ways in which *r* items can be selected from a collection of *n* items without regard to order. The formula is written as

$$C(n, r) = \frac{n}{r!(n - r)!}$$

This formula represents the number of different combinations of *n* items taken *r* at a time. For example, if we have a class of five students and we want to know the number of different pairs of students that can be selected, we perform the computation

$$C(5, 2) = \frac{5!}{2!(5 - 2)!} = \frac{5!}{2!3!} = \frac{120}{2 \times 6} = 10$$

The answer is ten different pairs of students.

The program in Fig. 6.4 uses function `factorial` to perform this computation. The user is first asked to enter n and r. If r is not greater than n, the statement

```
c = factorial(n) / (factorial(r) * factorial(n-r));
```

calls function `factorial` with three different actual arguments: the variable n, the variable r, and the expression n−r. The results of these calls are manipulated as previously described, and the number of different combinations of n items taken r at a time is saved in variable c.

In the main program of Fig. 6.4, a different actual argument is passed in each call to function `factorial`; consequently, a different result is computed each time. The effect of each call to function `factorial` is summarized in Table 6.1.

Table 6.1 illustrates one of the most important reasons for using functions. A function may be called several times in a program, each time with a different actual argument. Each call to the function causes the program statements associated with the function definition to be executed. Without using functions, these program statements would have to be listed several times in the main function. It is certainly easier to insert a function reference in a program than to insert the entire function body.

Figure 6.4   Program to Find Combinations of *n* Items Taken *r* at a Time

```
/*
 * Computes the number of combinations of n items taken r at a time
 */

#include <stdio.h>

/*
 * Computes n!
 * Pre: n is greater than or equal to zero
 */
int
factorial(int n)
{
      int  i,              /* local variables */
           product = 1;

      /* Computes the product n x (n-1) x (n-2) x ... x 2 x 1 */
      for (i = n;  i > 1;  i = i - 1) {
          product = product * i;
      }

      /* Returns function result */
      return (product);
}
```

(continued)

Figure 6.4   *(continued)*

```
/*
 * Demonstrates multiple calls from the main function passing different
 * actual arguments to a user-defined function.
 */
int
main(void)
{
      int n, r, c;

      printf("Enter number of items in the collection> ");
      scanf("%d", &n);
      printf("Enter number of items to be selected> ");
      scanf("%d", &r);

      if (r <= n) {
            c = factorial(n) / (factorial(r) * factorial(n-r));
            printf("The number of combinations is %d\n", c);
      } else {
            printf("Items to be selected cannot exceed total items\n");
      }

      return (0);
}
```

Table 6.1   Effect of Each Call to factorial

Call	Actual Argument	Formal Parameter Value	Function Result
1	n	5	120
2	r	2	2
3	n-r	3	6

The Function Data Area

Each time a function call statement is executed, an area of memory is allocated to store that function's data. Included in the data area are storage cells for the formal parameters and any local variables that may be declared in the function. The function data area is erased when the function terminates; it is recreated when the function is called again. When a function's data area is created, each local variable is undefined unless its declaration includes an initialization. Each formal parameter is assigned the value of the corresponding actual argument. Figure 6.5 shows the data storage areas for functions main and factorial just after factorial is called with actual argument n–r and before it executes. There is a memory cell in main allocated for variable n (value 5) and a memory cell in factorial's data area for the formal parameter n, whose value 3 is the result of evaluating the actual argument n–r. Even though they have the same names, the formal parameter n of factorial and the local variable n of main are unrelated. In fact, at the time when the scanf function stores the value 5 in main's n, factorial's n has not yet been created. Only when a call to factorial is being executed is a cell allocated for the formal parameter n. Each call to factorial recreates and redefines its parameter n.

By the same reasoning, local variables i and product in factorial are unrelated to any other use of these names either in function main or in any other function subprogram. Moreover, variables c and r declared in function main may be manipulated *only* in function main. It would be illegal for function factorial to attempt to reference either c or r.

**Figure 6.5
Data Areas for
Functions main
and factorial**

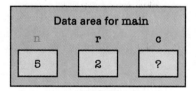
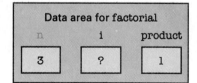

Source File Structure

For now, always organize your program source files according to the pattern shown in our examples. Begin with a block comment identifying the program's purpose; then include any preprocessor directives. Next place the definitions of your function subprograms ordered so a function's definition precedes any call to it from another function. Include your main function last.

Functions with Multiple Input Parameters and a Single Result Value

Our next example is similar to `factorial` in that it returns a single result value, but it has more than one input parameter. Figure 6.6 is a diagram of such a function.

When designing a function of your own, you may wish to draw a diagram like this as part of your analysis of the problem. For every input arrow of your diagram, you will need a formal parameter in your function prototype. A question you can ask yourself to help identify the input parameters of your function is this: What information do I need to know before I can start to carry out this function's purpose?

**Figure 6.6
Function with
Multiple Inputs
and a Single
Result**

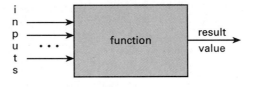

EXAMPLE 6.3

Function `round` in Fig. 6.7 is used to round its first input argument to the number of places indicated by its second argument. This means that the function reference

```
round(2.51863, 3)
```

returns the value 2.519. To compute the rounded value, the function first isolates the sign of x. It represents the sign by -1 for negative values of x and by 1 for nonnegative values. Then `round` works on rounding $|x|$, recognizing that multiplying the result by the value of variable `sign` will restore the sign of the number.

Rounding the number 2.51863 to three decimal places is equivalent to rounding 2518.63 (2.51863×10^3) to the nearest integer and then moving the decimal point three places to the left. The standard C math library does not include a "nearest integer" function. However, we can compute the integer nearest to a positive value by adding 0.5 and then finding the largest whole number not greater than this sum.

$$
\begin{array}{r}
2518.63 \\
+ \ 0.50 \\
\hline
2519.13
\end{array}
$$

Figure 6.7   Function That Rounds Its Argument

```
#include <stdio.h>
#include <math.h>

/*
 * Rounds the value of x to designated number of decimal places
 * Pre:  x is defined and places is greater than or equal to zero.
 */
double
round(double x, int places)
{
      int    sign;          /* -1 if x negative, 1 otherwise        */
      double power,         /* 10 raised to the places power        */
             temp_x,        /* copy of |x| with decimal point moved places
                               places to the right.                 */
             x_rounded;     /* function result                      */

      /* Saves sign of x  */
      if (x < 0)
            sign = -1;
      else
            sign = 1;

      /* Computes rounded value */
      if (places >= 0) {
            power = pow(10.0, places);
            temp_x = fabs(x) * power;
            x_rounded = floor(temp_x + 0.5) / power * sign;
      } else {
            printf("\nError: second argument to round cannot be negative.\n");
            printf("No rounding done.\n");
            x_rounded = x;
      }
      return (x_rounded);
}
```

The `floor` function that we studied in Chapter 3 finds exactly the whole number we need. Moving the decimal point is accomplished by dividing the number by 10^3.

Table 6.2 traces the execution of the function call above. The function result is `2519/1000.0`, or 2.519, as desired.

Function `round` illustrates that a user-defined function can call a C standard library function. Since the functions `pow` and `floor` are both from the math library, the source file in which the definition of `round` appears must have a `#include` directive for `<math.h>`. It is also possible for one user-defined function to call another or even to call itself.

When using multiple-argument functions, you must be careful to include the correct number of arguments in the function call. Also, the order of the actual arguments used in the function reference must correspond to the order of the formal parameters listed in the prototype of the function definition.

Finally, if the function is to return meaningful results, assignment of each actual argument to the corresponding formal parameter must not cause any loss of information. Usually, you should use an actual argument of the same data type as the corresponding formal parameter, although this is not always essential. For example, the `<math.h>` library description indicates that both parameters of the function `pow` are of type `double`. In our function `round` in Fig. 6.7, we call `pow` with a second actual argument that is of type `int` (`places`). This call does not cause a problem because there is no loss of information when an `int` is

Table 6.2 Trace of round(2.51863, 3)

Statement	x	places	power	temp_x	x_rounded	Effect
	2.51863	3	?	?	?	
if (places >= 0)						True: does true task
power = pow(10.0, places);			1000.0			Assigns 10^3 to power
temp_x = x * power;				2518.63		Copies x with decimal point moved 3 places to the right
x_rounded = floor(temp_x+0.5) / power;					2.519	Assigns floor(2519.13) / 1000.0 to x_rounded
return (x_rounded);						Returns 2.519 as function result

assigned to a type `double` variable. If we were to try to pass an actual argument of type `double` to a formal parameter of type `int`, loss of the fractional part of our actual argument would likely lead to an unexpected function result. The rules for argument list correspondence are summarized next. ←

Argument List Correspondence

- The number of actual arguments used in a call to a function must be the same as the number of formal parameters listed in the function prototype.
- Each actual argument must be of a data type that can be assigned to the corresponding formal parameter with no unexpected loss of information. The first actual argument corresponds to the first formal parameter, the second actual argument corresponds to the second formal parameter, and so on.

Program Style   *Validating Function Arguments*

The `if` structure in Fig. 6.7 validates the value of the second formal parameter, `places`. The function cannot be executed in accordance with its purpose if `places` is negative. Rather than computing an answer that makes no sense, the function prints an error message and returns its first argument as the result. In this way, the program user is warned that the computation did not take place; however, the program is able to continue execution since a reasonable value is returned as the function result.

Testing Functions

A function is an independent program module, and as such, it can be tested separately from the program that uses it. To run such a test, you should write a short *driver* program that defines the function arguments, calls the function, and prints the value returned. For example, the function `main` in Fig. 6.8 could act as a driver program to test function `round`.

Figure 6.8   Driver Program to Test Function round

```
/*
 * Tests function round
 */

#include <stdio.h>
#include <math.h>
```

(continued)

Figure 6.8 *(continued)*

```
/*
 * Rounds the value of x to designated number of decimal places
 * Pre:  x is defined and places is greater than or equal to zero.
 */
double
round(double x, int places)
{
      int    sign;       /* -1 if x negative, 1 otherwise        */
      double power,      /* 10 raised to the places power         */
             temp_x,     /* copy of |x| with decimal point moved places
                            places to the right.                  */
             x_rounded;  /* function result                       */

      /* Saves sign of x */
      if (x < 0)
            sign = -1;
      else
            sign = 1;

      /* Computes rounded value */
      if (places >= 0) {
            power = pow(10.0, places);
            temp_x = fabs(x) * power;
            x_rounded = floor(temp_x + 0.5) / power * sign;
      } else {
            printf("\nError: second argument to round cannot be negative.\n");
            printf("No rounding done.\n");
            x_rounded = x;
      }
      return (x_rounded);
}

int
main(void)
{
      double num,        /* number to round                       */
             dec_places; /* number of decimal places to round to  */
```

(continued)

Figure 6.8   *(continued)*

```
     printf("Enter a number to round or zero to quit> ");
     for  (scanf("%lf", &num);
            num != 0;
            scanf("%lf", &num)) {
         printf("Round to how many decimal places?> ");
         scanf("%d", &dec_places);
         printf("%.6f rounded to %d decimal places is %.6f\n", num,
                 dec_places, round(num, dec_places));
         printf("\nEnter another number to round or zero to quit> ");
     }

     return (0);
}

Enter a number to round or zero to quit> 38.56
Round to how many decimal places?> 1
38.560000 rounded to 1 decimal places is 38.600000

Enter another number to round or zero to quit> -5.98476
Round to how many decimal places?> 3
-5.984760 rounded to 3 decimal places is -5.985000

Enter another number to round or zero to quit> 84.9
Round to how many decimal places?> -2
Error: second argument to round cannot be negative
No rounding done
84.900000 rounded to -2 decimal places is 84.900000

Enter another number to round or zero to quit> 84.9
Round to how many decimal places?> 0
84.900000 rounded to 0 decimal places is 85.000000

Enter another number to round or zero to quit> 38.71
Round to how many decimal places?> 2
38.710000 rounded to 2 decimal places is 38.710000

Enter another number to round or zero to quit> 0
```

You should build a source file containing any necessary preprocessor directives, the function(s) to be tested, and the driver. Execute the driver program on a variety of data until you are satisfied that each function tested is working correctly.

Logical Functions

In Chapter 4, we saw that C uses integers to represent the logical concepts true and false. This means that a type `int` result returned by a function can be interpreted as a logical value. Such functions are often used to make conditions more readable.

EXAMPLE 6.4

Function `even` in Fig. 6.9 returns the integer 1 meaning true if its integer argument is an even number; otherwise, it returns 0 for false.

Function `even` is called in the following `if` statement which could be used inside a loop to count even and odd numbers.

```
if (even(x))
      even_nums = even_nums + 1;
else
      odd_nums = odd_nums + 1;
```

Figure 6.9   Function That Checks Whether a Value is Even

```
/*
 * Indicates whether or not num is even (divisible by 2):
 *    returns 1 if it is, 0 if not
 * Pre:  num is defined
 */
int
even(int num)
{
      int ans;

      ans = ((num % 2) == 0);
      return (ans);
}
```

Case Study: Finding Prime Numbers

PROBLEM

Prime numbers have been studied by mathematicians for many years. A prime number is an integer that has no divisors other than 1 and itself (for example, the integers 2, 3, 5, 7, and 11). Write a program that finds the smallest divisor of a number or determines that the number is a prime number.

ANALYSIS

To determine whether an integer n is a prime number, our program will test integers smaller than n until it finds an integer that is a divisor. We will limit the number we test to 1000 or less. The data requirements are as follows:

Data Requirements

Problem Constant
```
1000 (NMAX)      /* largest number that can be tested    */
```

Problem Input
```
int n            /* number to be tested                  */
```

Problem Output
```
int min_div      /* smallest divisor greater than 1      */
```

DESIGN

Initial Algorithm

1. Get the number to be checked to see if it is prime.
2. Find the smallest divisor other than 1, or determine that the number is prime.
3. Print the smallest divisor or a message that the number is prime.

Algorithm Refinements

Since n must be an integer greater than 1, we will check the value entered to see if it is in the valid range for the problem. The refinement of Step 1 follows.

Step 1 Refinement
1.1 Get a value for n.
1.2 if n < 2
         Print an error message.
     else if n <= NMAX
         Do Steps 2 and 3.
     else
         Print an error message.

We will write a new function, `find_div`, to implement Step 2. This function will return the smallest divisor of n that is greater than 1—that is, if n is prime, `find_div` will return n. Our decision to write a function for Step 2 establishes this step as a subproblem to be solved separately. For now, we will assume we have a function that accomplishes the purpose of `find_div`. The value returned by this function will be stored in `min_div` and tested in Step 3. The refinement for Step 3 is

Step 3 Refinement
3.1 if the smallest divisor is n
         Print a message that n is prime.
     else
         Print the smallest divisor of n.

IMPLEMENTATION

We can now write the main function (see Fig. 6.10). The statement

```
min_div = find_div(n);
```

calls the function `find_div` to perform Step 2 of the algorithm. The outer `if` statement implements Step 1, and the inner `if` implements Step 3. We can now turn our attention to function `find_div`.

Subproblem: Function find_div

Function `find_div` finds the smallest divisor of *n* that is greater than 1.

ANALYSIS

Function `find_div` finds a divisor of *n* by testing each integer that is a possible divisor, starting with 2. If 2 does not divide *n,* then no other even integer divides *n;* consequently, only 2 and the odd integers need to be tested. The data requirements for `find_div` follow.

Figure 6.10   Function main of Prime Numbers Program

```
/*
 * Finds and prints the smallest divisor (other than 1) of the integer n.
 * Prints that n is a prime number if no divisor smaller than n is found.
 */

#include <stdio.h>
#define NMAX 1000
...

int
main(void)
{
      int n,        /* number to check to see if it is prime         */
          min_div; /* minimum divisor (greater than 1) of n          */

      /* Gets a number to test.                                       */
      printf("Enter a number that you think is a prime number> ");

      /* Checks that the number is in the range 2...1000              */
      if (n < 2) {
            printf("Error: number too small. The smallest prime is 2.\n");
      } else if (n <= 1000) {

            /* Finds the smallest divisor (> 1) of n */
            min_div = find_div(n);

            /* Prints the smallest divisor or a message that n is prime.  */
            if (min_div == n)
                  printf("%d is a prime number.\n", n);
            else
                  printf("%d is the smallest divisor of %d.\n", min_div, n);
      } else {
            printf("Error: largest number accepted is %d.\n", NMAX);

      }

      return (0);
}
```

Data Requirements

Problem Input (formal parameter)
```
int n          /* number to check to see if it is prime */
```

Problem Output (result to return)
```
int divisor  /* smallest divisor found;
                0 means no value found yet      */
```
Program Variables (other local variables)
```
int trial    /* each trial divisor beginning
                with 2                          */
```

DESIGN

Algorithm

1. if n is even

   Set divisor to 2.

   else

   Set divisor to 0 (meaning no divisor found).

   Set trial to 3.
2. As long as divisor is 0, keep trying odd integers (trial). If a divisor is found, store it in divisor. If trial exceeds $\sqrt{n}$, store n in divisor.
3. Return divisor.

First, we find out if 2 divides n. If n is even, the 2 is stored in divisor, causing Step 2 to be skipped. Since we have already defined a function even, we can call it in our implementation of Step 1. If n is odd, divisor is set to 0, trial is set to the smallest odd integer greater than 1 (3), and the loop in Step 2 is executed. Step 2 is used to test each odd integer less than or equal to $\sqrt{n}$ as a possible divisor. The refinement of Step 2 follows.

Step 2 Refinement

2.1 Repeat as long as a divisor has not been found

   if trial > $\sqrt{n}$

   Set divisor to n.

   else if trial is a divisor of n

   Set divisor to trial.

   else

   Store the next odd integer in trial.

It is necessary to test as possible divisors only integers less than or equal to $\sqrt{n}$.

IMPLEMENTATION

In our code for `find_div`, we check to see if `trial` is a divisor of n by determining if the remainder of n divided by `trial` is zero (see Fig. 6.11). We use a `while` statement rather than a `for` statement to implement this loop because the initialization and update steps are not simple, unconditional statements.

Functions `even` and `find_div` should be inserted in the prime number program right after the preprocessor directives. In Fig. 6.10, an ellipsis (. . .) at this point notes the omission of part of the program. Function `even` should precede function `find_div` so the compiler will see its definition before meeting `find_div`'s call to it.

Figure 6.11   Function to Find the Smallest Divisor Greater Than 1 of an Integer

```
/*
 * Finds the smallest divisor of n between 2 and n
 * Pre:  n is greater than 1
 */
int
find_div(int n)
{
      int trial,    /* current candidate for smallest divisor of n         */
          divisor;  /* smallest divisor of n; zero means divisor not yet
                       found                                                */

      /* Chooses initialization of divisor and trial depending on whether
         n is even or odd.                                                  */
      if (even(n)) {
            divisor = 2;
      } else {
            divisor = 0;
            trial = 3;
      }
```

(continued)

Figure 6.11 *(continued)*

```
/* Tests each odd integer as a divisor of n until a divisor is found
   this way or until trial is so large that it is clear that n is the
   smallest divisor other than 1.
 */
 while (divisor == 0) {
        if (trial > sqrt(n))
              divisor = n;
        else if ((n % trial) == 0)
              divisor = trial;
        else
              trial = trial + 2;
 }

 /* Returns problem output to calling module. */
 return (divisor);
}
```

TESTING

The complete program should be tested for both small and large integers that are prime numbers. You should be able to find a table of primes to help you select sample cases. Make sure you test odd numbers that are nonprimes, even numbers, and data values that are out of range.

Several sample runs of the prime number program are shown in Fig. 6.12. The test values used for n were selected to exercise all parts of the program and to verify that the program works for numbers that are prime as well as numbers that are not prime. The operation of the program at the boundaries (2 and 1000) was also checked, as was the operation of the program for invalid data values (0 and 1001). A very large prime number (997) was used as a test case as well as odd and even numbers that were not prime. Although a very large percentage of the valid data values were *not* tested, the sample selected is representative and provides a fair indication that the program is correct.

You should use a similar strategy when selecting test data to try out your programs. Avoid choosing sample test data that are very much alike; be sure to include select test data that are at or near any boundary values.

Figure 6.12   Six Sample Runs of Prime Number Program

```
Enter a number that you think is a prime number> 1000
2 is the smallest divisor of 1000.

Enter a number that you think is a prime number> 997
997 is a prime number.

Enter a number that you think is a prime number> 35
5 is the smallest divisor of 35.

Enter a number that you think is a prime number> 0
Error: number too small. The smallest prime is 2.

Enter a number that you think is a prime number> 1001
Error: largest number accepted is 1000.

Enter a number that you think is a prime number> 2
2 is a prime number.
```

EXERCISES FOR SECTION 6.1

Self-Check

1. What value would be returned by function one_more for this reference?

```
        one_more(85.76)

int
one_more(int num)
{
        return (num + 1);
}
```

Programming

1. Write a function that checks a positive integer to see if it is prime. Your function should return a 1 for true if its argument is prime, and a 0 for false if it is not. You may call the function find_div in prime.
2. Write a function that computes the speed (km/h) one must average to reach a certain destination by a designated time. You need to deal only with arrivals occurring later on the same day as the departure. Function inputs include departure and arrival times as integers on a 24-hour clock (8:30 P.M. = 2030) and the distance to the destination in kilometers. Also write a driver program to test your function.

6.2 void FUNCTIONS WITH INPUT PARAMETERS

In Chapter 3, we wrote several `void` functions that did not return a result but simply produced some output. Such `void` functions are much more useful when they have input parameters. In the next example, we will reuse our function `find_div` to simplify the problem of factoring a number.

EXAMPLE 6.5

Function `factor` in Fig. 6.13 has a return type of `void` because its purpose is not to compute a value to return to the calling module. Rather, its intent is to print a message showing the prime factors of the argument passed to its formal parameter n. For example, in response to the call

```
factor(84);
```

the function would print

```
84 = 2 x 2 x 3 x 7
```

In keeping with our plan to reuse proven modules whenever possible, we call function `find_div` to find each factor. It is possible to use `find_div` here because the first factor printed, 2, is the smallest divisor of 84; the second

Figure 6.13   void Function That Factors an Integer

```
/*
 * Prints a message displaying the prime factors of n.
 * Example:  factor(12) would print  12 = 2 x 2 x 3
 * Pre:  n is greater than 1
 */
void
factor(int n)
{
      int to_factor,  /* product of unprinted factors of n        */
          cur_factor; /* current factor of n                      */

      /* Prints initial part of message including the smallest prime
         factor.                                                   */
      cur_factor = find_div(n);
      printf("%d = %d", n, cur_factor);
```

(continued)

Figure 6.13 *(continued)*

```
      /* Finds and prints remaining factors preceded by x signs.        */
      for (to_factor = n / cur_factor;
              to_factor > 1;
              to_factor = to_factor / cur_factor) {
          cur_factor = find_div(to_factor);
          printf(" x %d", cur_factor);
      }
      printf("\n");
}
```

Table 6.3 **Trace of factor(84) Which Prints 84 = 2 × 2 × 3 × 7**

Statement	n	to_factor	cur_factor	Effect
	84	?	?	
cur_factor = find_div(n);			2	find_div finds 84's smallest divisor > 1, and result is stored in cur_factor
printf("%d = %d", n, cur_factor);				Prints 84 = 2
for (to_factor = n / cur_factor;		42		Stores 84/2 = 42 in to_factor
to_factor > 1				True: loop continues
cur_factor = find_div(to_factor);			2	Smallest divisor of 42 (> 1) stored in cur_factor
printf(" x %d", cur_factor);				Prints x 2
to_factor = to_factor / cur_factor		21		Stores 42/2 = 21 in to_factor
to_factor > 1				True: loop continues
cur_factor = find_div(to_factor);			3	Smallest divisor of 21 (> 1) stored in cur_factor

(continued)

Table 6.3   *(continued)*

Statement	n	to_factor	cur_factor	Effect
	84	21	3	
`printf(" x %d",` `    cur_factor);`				Prints x 3
`to_factor = to_factor /` `        cur_factor`		7		Stores 21/3 = 7 in to_factor
`to_factor > 1`				True: loop continues
`cur_factor =` `  find_div(to_factor);`			7	Smallest divisor of 7 (> 1) stored in cur_factor
`printf(" x %d",` `    cur_factor);`				Prints x 7
`to_factor = to_factor /` `        cur_factor`		1		Stores 7/7 = 1 in to_factor
`to_factor > 1`				False: loop exits
`printf("\n");`				Completes output line

factor, 2, is the smallest divisor of 42 (84/2); the third factor, 3, is the smallest divisor of 21 (42/2); and 7 is the smallest divisor of 7 (21/3). Our function will deal only with numbers greater than 1. Table 6.3 traces the call

`factor(84);`

In the next example, we see a **void** function with two input arguments of different types.

 **EXAMPLE 6.6**

Sometimes, to dress up the appearance of a report, one can print whole lines of a single character. One can also generate simple graphic output by computing how many copies of a character to print rather than using a string that has a fixed length in a **printf** statement as we did in Chapter 3. In Fig. 6.14 the void function `duplicate` is used repeatedly by a program that prints rectangles based on dimensions entered by the user.

Function `duplicate` has two input parameters: a character and an integer. The integer determines how many copies of the character are printed. ⬅

Figure 6.14   **Program to Print a Rectangle Using Character-Duplicator Function**

```
/*
 * Prints a rectangle given its length in characters and its width in lines
 */
#include <stdio.h>
#include <math.h>

#define MIN_LEN 10
#define MAX_LEN 100
#define MIN_WID 2

/*
 * Prints n copies of sym
 */
void
duplicate(char sym, int n)
{
      int i;

      for   (i = 0;  i < n;  i = i + 1) {
          printf("%c", sym);
      }
}

int
main(void)
{
      int len, /* length of rectangle in characters  */
          wid, /* width of rectangle in lines         */
          i;
```

(continued)

Figure 6.14 *(continued)*

```
    /* Gets dimensions */
    printf("Enter dimensions of rectangle within the limits shown.\n");
    printf("Length in the range %d .. %d characters> ", MIN_LEN, MAX_LEN);
    scanf("%d", &len);
    printf("Width in lines (at least %d)> ", MIN_WID);
    scanf("%d", &wid);

    /* Prints top side */
    printf("\n\n");
    duplicate('*', len);
    printf("\n");

    /* Prints vertical sides */
    for  (i = 0;  i < wid - 2;  i = i + 1) {
        printf("**");
        duplicate(' ', len - 4);
        printf("**\n");
    }

    /* Prints bottom side and a blank line */
    duplicate('*', len);
    printf("\n\n");

    /* Prints dimensions (centered) */
    duplicate(' ', floor(len / 2.0) - 4);
    printf("%d X %d\n", len, wid);

    return(0);
}

Enter dimensions of rectangle within the limits shown.
Length in the range 10 .. 100 characters> 45
Width in lines (at least 2)> 8
```

(continued)

Figure 6.14   *(continued)*

```
*******************************************
**                                    **
**                                    **
**                                    **
**                                    **
**                                    **
**                                    **
*******************************************

          45 X 8
```

Case Study: Computing Maximum Tensile Loads

Superb Steel Company produces steel reinforcing bars called rebars. The size of
a rebar is designated by a number that, when divided by 8, gives the diameter of
the cylindrical bar in inches (e.g., a number 5 rebar is 5/8 of an inch in diameter). The company needs to produce a chart showing the maximum tensile load
of the bars when they are made from certain grades of steel. Superb makes
number 2 to number 11 rebars. Each chart should have the following form:

```
*****************************************************************
                     SUPERB STEEL COMPANY
                      Rebar Load Chart
            For bars with a steel strength of 8000.00 psi
        Bar              Cross-sectional              Max. Load
       Number            Area (sq. in.)                (lbs.)
       ------            ---------------              ---------
         2                    0.05                      393.
         3                    0.11                      884.
         4                    0.20                     1571.
         5                    0.31                     2454.
         6                    0.44                     3534.
         7                    0.60                     4811.
         8                    0.79                     6283.
         9                    0.99                     7952.
        10                    1.23                     9817.
        11                    1.48                    11879.
*****************************************************************
```

ANALYSIS

The maximum tensile load on a bar is the amount of force the bar can hold in tension. It is calculated by multiplying the cross-sectional area of the bar by the tensile strength of the steel. For a given tensile strength, we can display each line of the preceding chart by first determining the cross-sectional area corresponding to that number rebar. We can then use the formula given to compute the maximum load.

Data Requirements

Problem Constants
```
MIN_REBAR 2        /* smallest rebar Superb makes    */
MAX_REBAR 11       /* largest rebar Superb makes     */
```

Problem Input
```
double strength   /* tensile strength of the steel  */
```

Problem Outputs
```
int bar_num       /* the rebar number               */
double area       /* the cross-sectional area        */
double load       /* the maximum tensile load        */
```

Relevant Formula
load = area × steel strength

DESIGN

Initial Algorithm

1. Get the steel strength.
2. Display the table heading.
3. Repeat for each rebar from number 2 (`MIN_REBAR`) to 11 (`MAX_REBAR`).
    4. Compute cross-sectional area.
    5. `load = area * strength`
    6. Display rebar number, area, and load.

Structure Chart and Refinements

We will implement Steps 2 and 4 using function subprograms and write the rest of the algorithm as part of the main function. We will implement Step 2 as

**Figure 6.15
Structure Chart
for Maximum
Tensile Load
Problem**

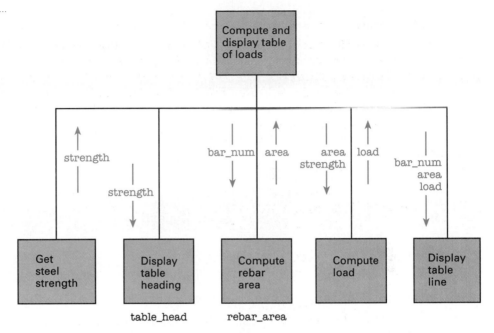

function `table_head` whose type is `void` because its purpose is not to compute and return a result value. The fact that the structure chart in Fig. 6.15 shows the value of `strength` flowing into the table heading module means that our `void` function will have one input parameter. We will implement Step 4 as function `rebar_area` that returns a value of type `double` (the cross-sectional area). Again, there will be a single input parameter since the structure chart shows the `bar_num` value flowing into the module. We will write the remaining steps in line (in the main function) since they are relatively straightforward and involve one or two lines of code.

The structure chart shows each of the major subproblems in the algorithm. For subproblems implemented with functions, we have shown the function name below the rectangle that represents the algorithm step.

◀ **IMPLEMENTATION** ▶

With the structure chart in mind, we can write the function `main` shown in Fig. 6.16. Because the details of the table heading output and the cross-sectional area computation are handled in functions, this main function is very concise and readable. The statement

`table_head(strength);`

Figure 6.16   Function main for Maximum Tensile Load Program

```
/*
 * Prints a table of maximum tensile loads for rebars.
 */
#include <stdio.h>

/* Insert functions duplicate, table_head, rebar_area along with associated
   constant macros here.
 */

#define MIN_REBAR 2  /* smallest rebar Superb makes                         */
#define MAX_REBAR 11 /* largest rebar Superb makes                          */

int
main(void)
{
      double strength; /* tensile steel strength                            */
      int    bar_num;  /* size number of rebar                              */
      double area,     /* cross-sectional area of rebar                     */
             load;     /* maximum tensile load of rebar                     */

      /* Gets steel strength                                                */
      printf("Enter steel tensile strength in psi> ");
      scanf("%lf", &strength);

      /* Writes table heading                                              */
      table_head(strength);

      /* Prints table of cross-sectional areas and tensile loads           */
      for  (bar_num = MIN_REBAR;
           bar_num <= MAX_REBAR;
           bar_num = bar_num + 1) {
        area = rebar_area(bar_num);
        load = area * strength;
        printf("  %2d                        %4.2f", bar_num, area);
        printf("                   %6.0f\n",  load);
      }
      duplicate('*', 60);

      return (0);
}
```

calls function `table_head` to display the table heading. Within the `for` loop, the statement

```
area = rebar_area(bar_num);
```

calls function `rebar_area`, passing the current value of `bar_num` as the actual argument. The function result is returned to the main function and is stored in the variable `area`.

Solving the Subproblems

Now we can turn our attention to solving the problems that are the purposes of functions `table_head` and `rebar_area`. The first function is a simple collection of calls to `printf` as shown in Fig. 6.17. Function `rebar_area` computes the cross-sectional area (`csarea`) for a cylindrical bar whose rebar number is the value of the input parameter. This function uses the formulas

$$radius = \frac{rebar\ number}{16.0}$$

$$area = \pi \times radius^2$$

Figure 6.17 also shows function `rebar_area`. Notice that the variables `radius` and `csarea` are declared locally in function `rebar_area` and not in the main function because `radius` and `csarea` are used only in the cross-sectional area computation and are not needed in `main`. The `duplicate` function from Fig. 6.14, together with all of Fig. 6.17 which shows functions `table_head` and `rebar_area`, can be inserted in Fig. 6.16 at the indicated spot to form a complete program source file.

Figure 6.17   Functions table_head and rebar_area

```c
/*
 * Displays a heading for a table showing the maximum tensile loads of
 * rebars of different sizes made from steel whose tensile strength is
 * indicated by the value of the input parameter.
 */
void
table_head(double strength)
{
```

(continued)

Figure 6.17 *(continued)*

```
      duplicate('*', 60);
      printf("                SUPERB STEEL COMPANY\n");
      printf("                 Rebar Load Chart\n");
      printf("          For bars with a steel strength of %.2f psi\n\n",
            strength);
      printf(" Bar                  Cross-sectional          Max. Load\n");
      printf("Number                 Area (sq. in.)            (lbs.)\n");
      printf("------                 ---------------          ---------\n");
}

#define PI 3.14159

/*
 * Calculates the cross-sectional area of a circular rebar identified by
 * number bar_num
 * Pre:  bar_num is greater than zero
 */
double
rebar_area(int bar_num)
{
      double radius,  /* radius of rebar cross-section */
             csarea;  /* cross-sectional area          */

      /* Computes radius                                 */
      radius = bar_num / 16.0;

      /* Computes and returns cross-sectional area       */
      csarea = PI * radius * radius;

      return (csarea);
}
```

Self-Check

1. What output would be printed by the rectangle program in Fig. 6.14 if the data entered were 16 for length and 3 for width?
2. Write a `void` function `blast_off` to be called by function `main` in order to accomplish the same purpose as the countdown program in Fig. 5.7.

```
int
main(void)
{
    int start;

    printf("Enter starting time (an integer) in seconds> ");
    scanf("%d", &start);
    blast_off(start);

    return (0);
}
```

6.3 FUNCTIONS WITH SIMPLE OUTPUT PARAMETERS

So far, we know how to pass inputs into a function and how to use the `return` statement to send back, at most, one result value from a function. In this section, we will learn how to return multiple results from a function. The `return` statement cannot accomplish the return of more than one value.

We have seen how when a function call executes, the computer allocates memory space in the function data area for each formal parameter. The value of each actual parameter is stored in the memory cell allocated to its corresponding formal parameter. The function body can manipulate this value. Next, we will discuss how a function sends back multiple outputs to the function that calls it.

EXAMPLE 6.7

Function `separate` in Fig. 6.19 finds the sign, whole number magnitude, and fractional parts of its first parameter. In our previous examples, all the formal parameters of a function represent inputs to the function from the calling module. In function `separate`, however, only the first formal parameter, `num`, is an input; the other three formal parameters — `signp`, `wholep`, and `fracp` — are output parameters, used to carry multiple results from function `separate` back to the module calling it. Figure 6.18 gives a diagram of the function as a box with an input and several outputs.

**Figure 6.18
Diagram of
Function
separate that
Computes
Multiple Results**

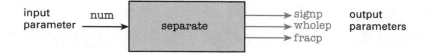

The actual argument value passed to the formal parameter `num` is used to determine the values to be sent back through `signp`, `wholep`, and `fracp`. Notice that in Fig. 6.19 the declarations of these output parameters in the function prototype have asterisks before the parameter names. In the assignment statements that use these parameters to send back the function results, there are also asterisks in front of the parameter names. The function type is `void` as it is for functions returning no result, and the function body does not include a `return` statement to send back a single value as we saw in functions `factorial`, `round`, `even`, and `find_div`.

Figure 6.19   Function separate Which Has Input and Output Parameters

```
/*
 * Separates a number into three parts: a sign (+, -, or blank),
 * a whole number magnitude, and a fractional part.
 */
void
separate(double  num,       /* input - value to be split          */
         char   *signp,     /* output - sign of num               */
         int    *wholep,    /* output - whole number magnitude of num   */
         double *fracp)     /* output - fractional part of num    */
{
      double magnitude; /* local variable - magnitude of num      */

      /* Determines sign of num */
      if (num < 0)
            *signp = '-';
      else if (num == 0)
            *signp = ' ';
      else
            *signp = '+';
```

(continued)

Figure 6.19 *(continued)*

```
    /* Finds magnitude of num (its absolute value) and
       separates it into whole and fractional parts */
    magnitude = fabs(num);
    *wholep = floor(magnitude);
    *fracp = magnitude - *wholep;
}
```

Let's focus for a moment on the prototype of the function in Fig. 6.19.

```
void
separate(double   num,     /* input - value to be split   */
         char    *signp,   /* output - sign of num        */
         int     *wholep,  /* output - whole number
                                       magnitude of num    */
         double *fracp)    /* output - fractional part
                                       of num              */
```

A declaration of a simple output parameter such as `char *signp` tells the compiler that `signp` will contain the *address* of a type `char` variable. Another way to express the idea that `signp` is the address of a type `char` variable is to say that the parameter `signp` is a *pointer* to a type `char` variable. Similarly, the output parameters `wholep` and `fracp` are pointers to variables of types `int` and `double`. We have chosen names for these output parameters that end in the letter 'p' because they are all pointers.

Figure 6.20 shows a complete program including a brief function `main` that calls function `separate`. Function `separate` is defined as it was in Fig. 6.19, but pre- and postconditions have been added to its block comment. It is the responsibility of the calling function to provide variables in which function `separate` can store the multiple results it computes. Function `main` in our example declares three variables to receive these results — a type `char` variable `sn`, a type `int` variable `whl`, and a type `double` variable `fr`. Notice that no values are placed in these variables prior to the call to function `separate`, for it is the job of `separate` to define their values. This change of the values of memory cells in the data area of the calling function is considered a *side effect* of the call to function `separate`.

Figure 6.20   Program That Calls a Function with Output Arguments

```
/*
 * Demonstrates the use of a function with input and output parameters.
 */

#include <stdio.h>
#include <math.h>

/*
 * Separates a number into three parts: a sign (+, -, or blank),
 * a whole number magnitude, and a fractional part.
 * Pre:   num is defined; signp, wholep, and fracp contain addresses
 *        of memory cells where results are to be stored
 * Post: function results are stored in cells pointed to by signp
 *        wholep, and fracp
 */
void
separate(double  num,        /* input - value to be split              */
         char    *signp,     /* output - sign of num                   */
         int     *wholep,    /* output - whole number magnitude of num */
         double *fracp)      /* output - fractional part of num        */
{
      double magnitude;  /* local variable - magnitude of num          */

      /* Determines sign of num */
      if (num < 0)
            *signp = '-';
      else if (num == 0)
            *signp = ' ';
      else
            *signp = '+';

      /* Finds magnitude of num (its absolute value) and
         separates it into whole and fractional parts                  */
```

(continued)

Figure 6.20   *(continued)*

```
      magnitude = fabs(num);
      *wholep = floor(magnitude);
      *fracp = magnitude - *wholep;
}

int
main(void)
{
      double value; /* input - number to analyze              */
      char    sn;    /* output - sign of value                */
      int     whl;   /* output - whole number magnitude of value */
      double fr;     /* output - fractional part of value      */

      /* Gets data                                            */
      printf("Enter a value to analyze> ");
      scanf("%lf", &value);

      /* Separates data value into three parts                */
      separate(value, &sn, &whl, &fr);

      /* Prints results                                       */
      printf("Parts of %.4f\n  sign: %c\n", value, sn);
      printf("  whole number magnitude: %d\n", whl);
      printf("  fractional part:  %.4f\n", fr);

      return (0);
}

Enter a value to analyze> 35.817
Parts of 35.8170
  sign: +
  whole number magnitude: 35
  fractional part: 0.8170
```

Figure 6.21 shows the data areas of `main` and `separate` as they are set up by the function call statement

```
separate(value, &sn, &whl, &fr);
```

This statement causes the number stored in the actual argument `value` to be copied into the input parameter `num` and the addresses of the arguments `sn`, `whl`, and `fr` to be stored in the corresponding output parameters `signp`, `wholep`, and `fracp`. The small numbers in color represent possible actual addresses in memory. Since it makes no difference to our program which specific cells are used, we normally diagram an address stored in a memory cell simply as a pointer like the arrow from `signp` to `sn`. Note that the use of the address-of operator `&` on the actual arguments `sn`, `whl`, and `fr` is essential. If the operator were omitted, we would be passing to `separate` the *values* of `sn`, `whl`, and `fr`, information that is worthless from the perspective of `separate`. The only way `separate` can store values in `sn`, `whl`, and `fr` is if it knows where to find them in memory. The purpose of `separate` with regard to its second, third, and fourth arguments is comparable to the purpose of the library function `scanf` with regard to all of its arguments except the first (the format string).

In addition to the fact that the *values* of the actual output arguments in the call to `separate` are useless, these values are also of data types that do not

**Figure 6.21
Correspondence
of Input and
Output
Parameters for**
`separate(value,
&sn, &whl,
&fr);`

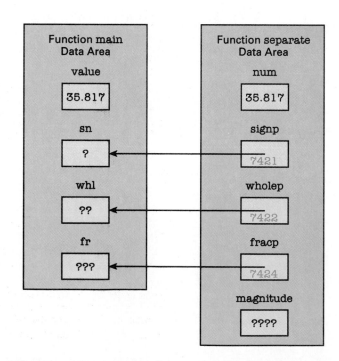

Table 6.4 Effect of & Operator on the Data Type of a Reference

Declaration	Data Type of x	Data Type of &x
char x	char	char * (pointer to char)
int x	int	int * (pointer to int)
double x	double	double * (pointer to double)

match the types of the corresponding formal parameters. Table 6.4 shows the effect of the address-of operator & on the data type of a reference. You see that in general if a reference x is of type "whatever-type", the reference &x is of type "pointer to whatever-type", that is, "whatever-type *".

So far, we have examined how to declare simple output parameters in a function prototype and how to use the address-of operator & in a function call statement to pass pointers of appropriate types. Now we need to study how the function manipulates these pointers in order to send back multiple results. The statements in function separate that cause the return of results follow.

```
*signp = '-';
*signp = ' ';
*signp = '+';
*wholep = floor(magnitude);
*fracp = magnitude - *wholep;
```

In each case, the name of the formal parameter is preceded by the *indirection operator,* unary *. When the unary * operator is applied to a reference that is of some pointer type, it has the effect of following the pointer referenced by its operand. Figure 6.22 shows the difference between a *direct* reference to a variable of type "pointer to int" and an *indirect* or "pointer-following" reference to the same variable using the indirection operator.

Figure 6.22 Comparison of Direct Reference and Indirect Reference

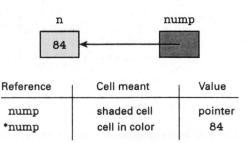

Reference	Cell meant	Value
nump	shaded cell	pointer
*nump	cell in color	84

For the data pictured in Fig. 6.21, the statement

```
*signp = '+';
```

follows the pointer in `signp` to the cell that function `main` calls `sn` and stores in it the character `'+'`. The statement

```
*wholep = floor(magnitude);
```

follows the pointer in `wholep` to the cell called `whl` by `main` and stores the integer 35 there. Similarly, the statement

```
*fracp = magnitude - *wholep;
```

uses two indirect references: One accesses the value in `main`'s local variable `whl` through the pointer in `wholep`, and another accesses `fr` of `main` through the pointer `fracp` to give the final output argument the value `0.817`.

EXERCISES FOR SECTION 6.3

Self-Check

1. Write a prototype for a function `sum_n_avg` that has three type `double` input parameters and two output parameters.

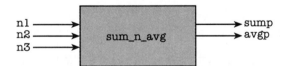

The function computes the sum and the average of its three input arguments and relays its results through two output parameters.

2. The following code fragment is from a function preparing to call `sum_n_avg` (see Exercise 1). Complete the function call statement.

```
{
     double one, two, three, sum_of_3, avg_of_3;
     printf("Enter three numbers> ");
     scanf("%lf%lf%lf", &one, &two, &three);
     sum_n_avg(_____);
. . .
```

3. Given the memory setup shown, fill in the chart by indicating the data type and value of each reference as well as the name of the function in which the reference would be legal. Give pointer values by referring to cell attributes.

For example, the value of `valp` would be "pointer to color shaded cell," and the value of `&many` would be "pointer to gray shaded cell."

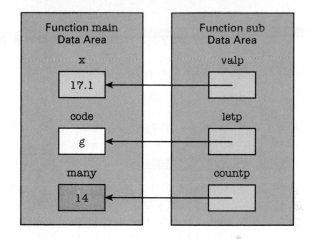

Reference	Where Legal	Data Type	Value
valp	sub	double *	pointer to color shaded cell
code			
&code			
countp			
*countp			
*valp			
letp			
&x			

Programming

1. Define the function `sum_n_avg` whose prototype you wrote in Self-check Exercise 1. The function should compute both the sum and the average of its three input parameters and relay these results through its output parameters.

6.4 MULTIPLE CALLS TO A void FUNCTION WITH INPUT/OUTPUT PARAMETERS

We have seen in Sections 6.1 and 6.2 how input parameters are used to bring information into a function; in Section 6.3 we studied how output parameters transmit results back to the calling module. Our next case study demonstrates the use of a single parameter both to bring a data value into a function and to carry a result value out of the function.

Case Study: Simple Sorting Problem

◄ PROBLEM ►

Write a program that takes any three numbers and rearranges the data so that the smallest number is stored in `num1`, the next larger number is in `num2`, and the largest number is in `num3`.

◄ ANALYSIS ►

This sorting problem is a special case of the more general problem of sorting a data list of any length. Since there are only three items to be sorted, we can solve this relatively simple case now; the general sorting problem is a bit more complicated and will be considered later.

Data Requirements

Problem Inputs
```
double num1, num2, num3       /* three numbers   */
```

Problem Outputs
the three numbers stored in increasing order in `num1, num2, num3`

◄ DESIGN ►

Initial Algorithm

1. Get three numbers for `num1`, `num2`, and `num3`.
2. Place the smallest number in `num1`, the next larger number in `num2`, and the largest number in `num3`.
3. Print `num1`, `num2`, and `num3`.

Algorithm Refinements

We can think of the three variables `num1`, `num2`, `num3` as representing a list of consecutive storage cells. To perform Step 2, we can compare pairs of numbers, always moving the smaller number in the pair closer to the front of the list (`num1`) and the larger number closer to the end of the list (`num3`). It should take three comparisons to sort the numbers in the list; one possible sequence of comparisons is shown next.

Table 6.5 Trace of Step 2 Refinement for Input Data 8, 10, 6

Algorithm Step	num1	num2	num3	Effect
	8.0	10.0	6.0	
2.1	8.0	10.0	6.0	num1, num2 are in order.
2.2	6.0	10.0	8.0	Switches num1 and num3.
2.3	6.0	8.0	10.0	Switches num2 and num3.

Step 2 Refinement
2.1 Compare num1 and num2 and store the smaller number in num1 and the larger number in num2.
2.2 Compare num1 and num3 and store the smaller number in num1 and the larger number in num3.
2.3 Compare num2 and num3 and store the smaller number in num2 and the larger number in num3.

Table 6.5 traces this refinement for the input sequence: 8.0, 10.0, 6.0. The final order is correct.

Figure 6.23 on p. 298 shows the structure chart for this algorithm. The data-flow information for subproblem "Order num1 and num2" shows that function order uses num1 and num2 both for input and output when performing this step.

◀ IMPLEMENTATION ▶

This is the first example we have seen of a function with parameters that serve both to bring input into the function and to carry results out of the function. The double-headed data-flow arrows in our structure chart are associated with parameters serving this double purpose. You will notice in the final program shown in Fig. 6.24 that these parameters are handled like the output parameters discussed in the previous section. Each output parameter is declared as a pointer, and every parameter reference uses the * indirection operator. In the calls to the function, the function is given the capability to access variables in the calling function's data area by means of the & address-of operator. The three statements that call function order have different argument lists; they are

```
order(&num1, &num2);
order(&num1, &num3);
order(&num2, &num3);
```

Consequently, a different pair of variables is manipulated each time function order executes.

**Figure 6.23
Structure Chart
for Three-Item
Sorting Problem**

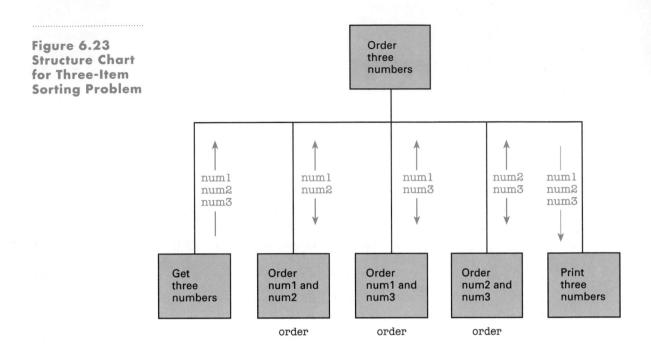

Figure 6.24   Program to Order Three Numbers

```
/*
 * Tests function order by ordering three numbers
 */
#include <stdio.h>

/*
 * Arranges arguments in ascending order.
 * Pre:  smp and lgp are addresses of defined type double variables
 * Post: variable pointed to by smp contains the smaller of the type
 *       double values; variable addressed by lgp contains the larger
 */
void
order(double *smp, double *lgp)/* input/output */
{
      double temp; /* temporary variable to hold one number during swap */
```

(continued)

Figure 6.24 *(continued)*

```
        /* Compares values pointed to by smp and lgp and switches if necessary   */
        if (*smp > *lgp) {
                temp = *smp;
                *smp = *lgp;
                *lgp = temp;
        }
}

int
main(void)
{
        double num1, num2, num3; /* three numbers to put in order                */

        /* Gets test data                                                         */
        printf("Enter three numbers separated by blanks> ");
        scanf("%lf%lf%lf", &num1, &num2, &num3);

        /* Orders the three numbers                                               */
        order(&num1, &num2);
        order(&num1, &num3);
        order(&num2, &num3);

        /* Prints results                                                         */
        printf("The numbers in ascending order are: %.2f %.2f %.2f\n",
                num1, num2, num3);

        return (0);
}

Enter three numbers separated by blanks> 7.5 5.5 9.6
The numbers in ascending order are: 5.50 7.50 9.60
```

In Fig. 6.25, we see the values in memory in the middle of the execution of the first of the three calls to function `order`. The formal parameter `smp` contains the address of the actual argument `num1`, and formal parameter `lgp` contains the address of the actual argument `num2`. Testing the condition

```
(*smp > *lgp)
```

causes both of these pointers to be followed, resulting in the condition

`(7.5 > 5.5)`

which evaluates to true. Executing the first assignment statement in the true task,

`temp = *smp;`

causes the `7.5` to be copied into the local variable `temp`. Figure 6.25 shows us a snapshot of the values in memory immediately after execution of this assignment statement.

Execution of the next assignment statement,

`*smp = *lgp;`

would cause the `7.5` in the variable referenced through `smp` to be replaced by `5.5`, the value of the variable referenced by `lgp`. The final assignment statement,

`*lgp = temp;`

copies the contents of the temporary variable (`7.5`) into the variable referenced by `lgp`. This completes the swap of values.

**Figure 6.25
Function Data
Areas for
Sorting
Program after
Assignment
Statement
temp = *smp;
During First
Call to order**

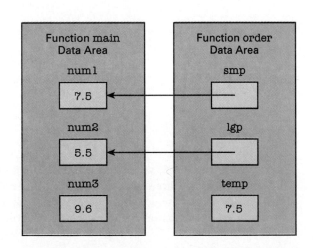

In this chapter, we have seen four kinds of functions, and we have studied how formal parameters are used in all of them. Table 6.6 compares the various kinds of functions and indicates the circumstances when each kind should be used.

Table 6.6 Kinds of Function Subprograms Seen So Far and Where to Use Them

Purpose	Function Type	Parameters	To Return Result
To compute or obtain as input a single numeric or character value.	Same as type of value to be computed or obtained.	Input parameters hold copies of data provided by calling function.	Function code includes a `return` statement with an expression whose value is the result.
To produce printed output containing values of numeric or character arguments.	`void`	Input parameters hold copies of data provided by calling function.	No result is returned.
To compute multiple numeric or character results.	`void`	Input parameters hold copies of data provided by calling function. Output parameters are pointers to actual arguments.	Results are stored in the calling function's data area by indirect assignment through output parameters. No `return` statement is required.
To modify argument values.	`void`	Input/output parameters are pointers to actual arguments. Input data is accessed by indirect reference through parameters.	Results are stored in the calling function's data area by indirect assignment through output parameters. No `return` statement is required.

Program Style   *Preferred Kinds of Functions*

Although all the kinds of functions we consider in this chapter are useful in developing computer systems, we recommend that you use the first kind shown in Table 6.6 whenever it is possible to do so. Functions that return a single value are the easiest functions for a program reader to deal with. You will note that all the mathematical functions we discussed in Section 3.7 are of this variety. Since such functions take only input arguments, the programmer is not concerned with using such complexities as indirect referencing in the function definition or applying the address-of operator in the function call. If the value returned by the function is to be stored in a variable, the reader sees an assignment statement in the code of the calling function. If a function subprogram has a meaningful name, the reader can often get a good idea of what is happening in the calling function without feeling obliged to read the function subprogram's code.

EXERCISES FOR SECTION 6.4

Self-Check

1. What would be the effect of the following sequence of calls to function `order`? Hint: Trace the calls for `num1 = 8, num2 = 12, num3 = 10`.

   ```
   order(&num3, &num2);
   order(&num2, &num1);
   order(&num3, &num2);
   ```

2. Show the table of values for x, y, and z that is the output displayed by the following program. You will notice that the function `sum` does not follow the suggestion in the last Program Style segment of Section 6.4. You can improve this program in the programming exercise that follows.

   ```
   #include <stdio.h>

   void
   sum(int a, int b, int *cp)
   {
           *cp = a + b;
   }

   int
   main(void)
   {
   ```

```
        int x, y, z;

        x = 5; y = 3;

        printf("   x    y   z\n\n");

        sum(x, y, &z);
        printf("%4d%4d%4d\n", x, y, z);

        sum(y, x, &z);
        printf("%4d%4d%4d\n", x, y, z);

        sum(z, y, &x);
        printf("%4d%4d%4d\n", x, y, z);

        sum(z, z, &x);
        printf("%4d%4d%4d\n", x, y, z);

        sum(y, y, &y);
        printf("%4d%4d%4d\n", x, y, z);

        return (0);
}
```

Programming

1. Rewrite the sum function in Self-check Exercise 2 as a function that takes just two input arguments. The sum computed should be returned as the function's type int result. Also, write an equivalent function main that calls your sum function.

6.5 INTRODUCTION TO SCOPE OF NAMES

The *scope* of a name refers to the region of a program in which the name has a particular meaning. Let's consider the names in the program outline shown in Fig. 6.26. The scope of the constant macro names MAX and LIMIT begins at their definition and continues to the end of the source file. This means that all three functions can use MAX, but only fun_two and main can use LIMIT.

The scope of each function name with the associated formal parameter types begins with its prototype and continues to the end of the source file,

Figure 6.26 Outline of Program for Studying Scope of Names

```
#define MAX   950

void
one(int anarg, double second)    /* prototype 1          */
{
        int onelocal;            /* local 1              */
        . . .
} /* end one */

#define LIMIT 200

int
fun_two(int one, char anarg)     /* prototype 2          */
{
        int localvar;            /* local 2              */
        . . .
} /* end fun_two */

int
main(void)                       /* prototype 3          */
{
        int localvar;
        . . .
} /* end main */
```

except for functions that have a local meaning for the same name. For example, even though function `one` is defined before function `fun_two`, `fun_two` cannot call `one` because it has its own meaning for the identifier `one`. Notice that `one` is the name of its first formal parameter. Therefore function `one` can be called only by itself and `main`. Function `fun_two` with one integer and one character parameter can also be called by itself and `main`.

　　All of the formal parameters and local variables in Fig. 6.26 are visible only from their declaration to the closing brace of the function in which they are declared. For example, from the line that is marked with the comment `/* prototype 1 */` to the line marked `/* end  one */` the identifier `anarg` means an integer variable in the data area of function `one`. From the line with the comment `/* prototype 2 */` through the line marked `/* end  fun_two */` this name refers to a character variable in the data area of `fun_two`. In the rest of the file, the name `anarg` is not visible.

Table 6.7   Scope of Names in Fig. 6.26

Name	Visible in one	Visible in fun_two	Visible in main
MAX	yes	yes	yes
one (the function)	yes	no	yes
anarg (int)	yes	no	no
second	yes	no	no
onelocal	yes	no	no
LIMIT	no	yes	yes
fun_two	no	yes	yes
one (the formal parameter)	no	yes	no
anarg (char)	no	yes	no
localvar (inside fun_two)	no	yes	no
main	no	no	yes
localvar (inside main)	no	no	yes

Table 6.7 shows which identifiers are visible within each of the three functions.

6.6 FORMAL OUTPUT PARAMETERS AS ACTUAL ARGUMENTS

So far, all of our actual arguments in calls to functions have been either local variables or input parameters of the calling function. However, sometimes we need to pass our output parameters as arguments. In Fig. 6.27, which we have left incomplete, we rewrite our simple sorting program so that main calls order_three, a function that places three numbers in ascending order. Function order_three calls order three times to make the necessary exchanges.

You may want to turn back to Fig. 6.24 to verify that the situation inside function order_three in Fig. 6.27 is not an exact match with the situation in function main of the earlier figure. In function main of Fig. 6.24, we have three type double variables whose contents we want to arrange in ascending order. The fact that these variables are of type double — even though the formal parameters of the function we are about to call are of type pointer to double (double *) — immediately suggests to us the need for the address-of operator on the actual arguments in the function call. The situation is clearly different in order_three, for the variables to be passed to order are them-

Figure 6.27 **Program Using Output Parameters as Actual Arguments**

```c
/*
 * Function subprogram orders three numbers to demonstrate
 * the use of output parameters as actual arguments.
 */
#include <stdio.h>

/*
 * Arranges arguments in ascending order.
 * Pre:  smp and lgp are addresses of defined type double variables
 * Post: variable pointed to by smp contains the smaller of the type
 *       double values; variable addressed by lgp contains the larger
 */
void
order(double *smp, double *lgp)
{
      double temp; /* temporary variable to hold one number during swap    */

      /* Compares values pointed to by smp and lgp and switches if necessary */
      if (*smp > *lgp) {
            temp = *smp;
            *smp = *lgp;
            *lgp = temp;
      }
}

void
order_three(double *sp, double *mp, double *lp)
{
      order(_____, _____); /* order first and second */
      order(_____, _____); /* order second and third */
      order(_____, _____); /* order first and second */
}

int
main(void)
{
      double num1, num2, num3; /* three numbers to put in order */
```

(continued)

Figure 6.27 *(continued)*

```
    /* Gets test data                                                    */
    printf("Enter three numbers separated by blanks> ");
    scanf("%lf%lf%lf", &num1, &num2, &num3);

    /* Orders the three numbers                                          */
    order_three(&num1, &num2, &num3);

    /* Prints results                                                    */
    printf("The numbers in ascending order are: %.2f %.2f %.2f\n",
           num1, num2, num3);

    return (0);
}
```

selves of type pointer to `double`. Figure 6.28 gives us a look at the data areas of `main` and `order_three` at the point where the first call to `order` occurs. In addition, we show the data area of `order` before its parameter values have been assigned.

Let's consider this memory setup in the context of what `order_three` needs function `order` to do. The first call to `order` should rearrange the `7.5` and `5.5` in `num1` and `num2`. For that to be possible, the formal parameters of `order` must contain the addresses of `num1` and `num2`. These addresses are the

Figure 6.28 Function Data Areas for Sorting Program at Time of First Call to order from order_three

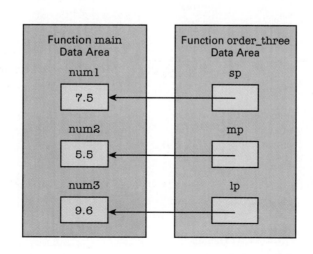
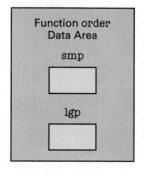

current values of the formal parameters `sp` and `mp` of `order_three`, so it is these values that must be passed to `order`. The correct calls to `order` to complete the program in Fig. 6.27 are

```
order(sp, mp);
order(mp, lp);
order(sp, mp);
```

Passing a formal output parameter to another function requires careful consideration of the purpose of the function being called. It is often advisable to sketch the data areas of the affected functions before determining the correct references to use in the function calls. When the arguments involved are simple variables of types `int`, `double`, and `char`, the usage pattern described in Table 6.8 works well. Unfortunately, these rules do not generalize to cover all arguments of the composite types we will study in later chapters. In the interest of completeness, Table 6.8 includes some cases for which we have not yet seen any examples.

Table 6.8   Passing to Function some_fun an Argument x of Simple Base Type int, double or char

Actual Argument Type	Use in Calling Function	Purpose in Called Function (some_fun)	Formal Parameter Type	Call to some_fun	Example
int char double	local variable or input parameter	input parameter	int char double	some_fun(x)	Fig. 6.2, main: `factorial(num)`
int char double	local variable	output or input/output parameter	int * char * double *	some_fun(&x)	Fig. 6.20, main: `separate(value, &sn, &whl, &fr);` (2nd–4th arguments)
int * char * double *	output or input/output parameter	output or input/output parameter	int * char * double *	some_fun(x)	Fig. 6.27 completed, order_three: `order(sp, mp);`
int * char * double *	output or input/output parameter	input parameter	int char double	some_fun(*x)	Self-Check Ex. 2 in 6.6, trouble: `double_trouble (y, *x);` (2nd argument)

**EXERCISES FOR
SECTION 6.6**

Self-Check

1. Box models of functions `onef` and `twof` follow. Do not try to define the complete functions; write only the portions described.

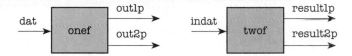

Assume that these functions are concerned only with integers, and write *prototypes* for `onef` and `twof`. Begin the body of function `onef` with a declaration of an integer local variable `tmp`. Show a call from `onef` to `twof` in which the input argument is `dat`, and `tmp` and `out2p` are the output arguments. Function `onef` intends for `twof` to store one integer result in `tmp` and one in the variable pointed to by `out2p`.

2. a. Classify each formal parameter of `double_trouble` and `trouble` as input, output, or input/output.

   b. What values of `x` and `y` are printed by this program? Hint: Sketch the data areas of `main`, `trouble`, and `double_trouble` as the program executes.

```c
void
double_trouble(int *p, int y)
{
        int x;
        x = 14;
        *p = 2 * x - y;
}

void
trouble(int *x, int *y)
{
        double_trouble(x, 5);
        double_trouble(y, *x);
}

int
main(void)
{
        int x, y;
        trouble(&x, &y);
        printf("x = %d, y = %d\n", x, y);
        return (0);
}
```

What naming convention introduced in Section 6.3 is violated in the prototype of `trouble`?

6.7 TOP-DOWN DESIGN ILLUSTRATED

In our next case study, we manipulate numeric data of a type not provided as one of C's base types. In order to do this, we must write our own functions to perform many operations that we take for granted when using types `int` and `double`.

Case Study: Performing Arithmetic Operations on Common Fractions

▶ **PROBLEM** ◀

You are working problems in which you must display your results as integer ratios; therefore you need to be able to compute using common fractions and get results that are common fractions in reduced form. You want to write a program that will allow you to add, subtract, multiply, and divide common fractions. The program will prompt you for a fraction, an operator, and another fraction and then print the problem and the result. The process will be repeated until you enter an `n` to answer the question, `Continue? (y/n)`.

▶ **ANALYSIS** ◀

Because the problem specifies that results are to be in reduced form, we will need to include a fraction-reducing function in addition to the computational functions. If we break the problem into small enough chunks, there should be an opportunity to reuse code by calling the same function multiple times. The in-depth analysis of the problem is actually distributed through the development of these modules.

Data Requirements

Problem Inputs
```
int n1, d1 /* numerator, denominator of first fraction */
int n2, d2 /* numerator, denominator of second fraction */
char op    /* arithmetic operator + - * or /         */
char again /* y or n depending on user's desire to
              continue                                */
```

Problem Outputs
```
int n_ans  /* numerator of answer                      */
int d_ans  /* denominator of answer                    */
```

As we develop an algorithm through stepwise refinement, we will look for instances in which a definition of a new function would simplify the design.

Initial Algorithm

1. Initialize `again` to `y`.
2. As long as user wants to continue,
   3. Get a fraction problem.
   4. Compute the result.
   5. Print problem and result.
   6. Check if user wants to continue.

Step 3 Refinement
3.1 Get first fraction.
3.2 Get operator.
3.3 Get second fraction.

Step 4 Refinement
4.1 Select a task based on operator:
    '+': 4.1.2 Add the fractions.
    '−': 4.1.3 Add the first fraction and the negation of the second.
    '*': 4.1.4 Multiply the fractions.
    '/': 4.1.5 Multiply the first fraction and the reciprocal of the second.
4.2 Put the result fraction in reduced form.

Step 4.2 Refinement
4.2.1 Find the greatest common divisor (gcd) of the numerator and denominator.
4.2.2 Divide the numerator and denominator by the gcd.

The structure chart in Fig. 6.29 shows the data flow among the steps we have identified.

We plan to implement `scan_fraction` (Steps 3.1 and 3.3), `get_operator` (Step 3.2), `op_invalid` (refinement of Step 3.2), `add_fractions` (Steps 4.1.2 and 4.1.3), `multiply_fractions` (Steps 4.1.4 and 4.1.5), `reduce_fraction` (Step 4.2), `find_gcd` (Step 4.2.1), and `print_fraction` (refinement of Step 5) as function subprograms. As a result, coding func-

**Figure 6.29
Structure Chart
for Common
Fraction
Problem**

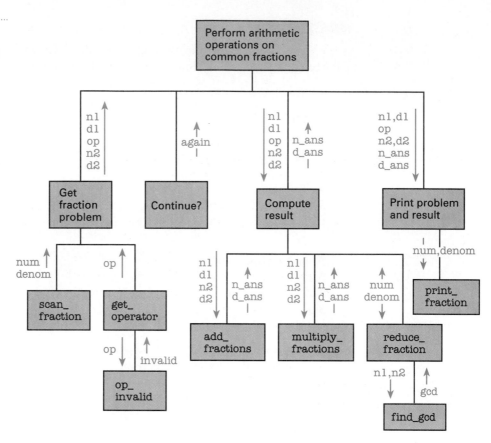

tion **main** is quite straightforward. Figure 6.30 shows most of the program; however, the functions **multiply_fractions** and **find_gcd** have been left as exercises. In their places, we have inserted *stubs,* skeleton functions that have complete comments and prototypes but merely assign values to their output parameters to allow testing of the partial system. Debugging and testing the system will be explained in Section 6.8.

TESTING

We have chosen to leave portions of our fraction system for you to write, but we would still like to test the functions that are complete. We have inserted a stub for each function not yet completed. Each stub prints an identification message and assigns values to its output parameters. We have made the **find_gcd** stub interactive so we can enter a correct greatest common divisor and see if this leads to correct results.

Figure 6.30   Program to Perform Arithmetic Operations on Common Fractions

```
/*
 * Adds, subtracts, multiplies and divides common fractions, displaying
 * results in reduced form.
 */

#include <stdio.h>
#include <stdlib.h>    /* provides function abs */

/*
 * Prompts the user to type in a fraction as <integer>/<integer>.
 * Gives the user an example and allows reentry if the fraction's form
 * is invalid.
 * Pre:  nump and denomp contain addresses of type int variables
 * Post: fraction's numerator and denominator are stored in variables
 *       pointed to by nump and denomp
 */
void
scan_fraction(int  *nump,    /* output - numerator    */
              int  *denomp) /* output - denominator */
{
      int  numerator;
      char delimiter;
      int  denominator;

      printf("Enter a fraction> ");
      for  (scanf("%d%c%d", &numerator, &delimiter, &denominator);
            delimiter != '/';
            scanf("%d%c%d", &numerator, &delimiter, &denominator)) {
          printf("Please reenter fraction.\n");
          printf("One-half would be entered as 1/2\n> ");
      }

      *nump = numerator;
      *denomp = denominator;
}

/*
 * Returns 1 for true if op is not one of the four characters + - * /.
 * Returns 0 otherwise.
 */
```

(continued)

Figure 6.30   *(continued)*

```
int
op_invalid(char op) /* input - arithmetic operator candidate          */
{
      int invalid;

      switch (op) {
      case '+':
      case '-':
      case '*':
      case '/':
            invalid = 0;
            break;

      default:
            invalid = 1;
      }

      return (invalid);
}

/*
 * Gets and returns a valid arithmetic operator.  Skips over newline
 * characters and permits re-entry of operator in case of error.
 */
char
get_operator(void)
{
      char op;

      printf("Enter an arithmetic operator (+,-,*, or /)\n> ");
      for  (scanf("%c", &op);
            op_invalid(op);
            scanf("%c", &op)) {
         if (op != '\n')
               printf("%c invalid, reenter operator (+,-, *,/)\n> ",
                      op);
      }
```

(continued)

Figure 6.30   *(continued)*

```
      return (op);
}

/*
 * Adds fractions represented by pairs of integers.
 * Pre:  n1, d1, n2, d2 are defined;
 *       n_ansp and d_ansp are addresses of type int variables.
 * Post: sum of n1/d1 and n2/d2 is stored in variables pointed
 *       to by n_ansp and d_ansp.  Result is not reduced.
 */
void
add_fractions(int    n1,     int    d1,     /* input - first fraction     */
              int    n2,     int    d2,     /* input - second fraction    */
              int    *n_ansp, int   *d_ansp) /* output - sum of two fractions*/
{
      int denom,       /* common denominator used for sum
                          (may not be least)                */
          numer,       /* numerator of sum                  */
          sign_factor; /* -1 for a negative, 1 otherwise    */

      /* Finds a common denominator                                      */
      denom = d1 * d2;

      /* Computes numerator                                              */
      numer = n1 * d2 + n2 * d1;

      /* Adjusts sign (at most, numerator should be negative)            */
      if (numer * denom >= 0)
            sign_factor = 1;
      else
            sign_factor = -1;

      numer = sign_factor * abs(numer);
      denom = abs(denom);

      /* Returns result                                                  */
      *n_ansp = numer;
      *d_ansp = denom;
}
```

(continued)

Figure 6.30   *(continued)*

```
/*
 ***** STUB *****
 * Multiplies fractions represented by pairs of integers.
 * Pre:  n1, d1, n2, d2 are defined;
 *       n_ansp and d_ansp are addresses of type int variables.
 * Post: product of n1/d1 and n2/d2 is stored in variables pointed
 *       to by n_ansp and d_ansp.  Result is not reduced.
 */
void
multiply_fractions(int    n1,     int  d1, /* input - first fraction     */
                   int    n2,     int  d2, /* input - second fraction    */
                   int    *n_ansp,         /* output -                   */
                   int    *d_ansp)         /* product of two fractions   */
{
      /* Prints trace message                                           */
      printf("\nEntering multiply_fractions with\n");
      printf("n1 = %d, d1 = %d, n2 = %d, d2 = %d\n", n1, d1, n2, d2);

      /* Defines output arguments                                       */
      *n_ansp = 1;
      *d_ansp = 1;
}

/*
 ***** STUB *****
 * Finds greatest common divisor of two integers
 */
int
find_gcd (int n1, int n2) /* input - two integers                       */
{
      int gcd;

      /* Prints trace message                                           */
      printf("\nEntering find_gcd with n1 = %d, n2 = %d\n", n1, n2);

      /* Asks user for gcd                                              */
      printf("gcd of %d and %d?> ", n1, n2);
      scanf("%d", &gcd);
```

(continued)

Figure 6.30   *(continued)*

```
                                                                        */
      /* Prints exit trace message
      printf("find_gcd returning %d\n", gcd);
      return (gcd);
}

/*
 * Reduces a fraction by dividing its numerator and denominator by their
 * greatest common divisor.
 */
void
reduce_fraction(int  *nump,     /* input/output -                        */
                int  *denomp)   /*      numerator and denominator of
                                        fraction                         */
{
      int gcd;    /* greatest common divisor of numerator and
                          denominator                                    */

      gcd = find_gcd(*nump, *denomp);

      *nump = *nump / gcd;
      *denomp = *denomp / gcd;
}

/*
 * Prints pair of integers as a fraction.
 */
void
print_fraction(int num, int denom) /* input - numerator and
                                          denominator                    */
{
      printf("%d/%d", num, denom);
}

int
main(void)
{
      int  n1, d1;        /* numerator, denominator of first fraction    */
      int  n2, d2;        /* numerator, denominator of second fraction   */
      char op;            /* arithmetic operator + - * or /              */
      char again;         /* y or n depending on user's desire to
                                 continue                                */
      char endline;       /* endline character to ignore                 */
      int  n_ans, d_ans;  /* numerator, denominator of answer            */
```

(continued)

Figure 6.30 *(continued)*

```
    /* As long as user wants to continue, takes and solves arithmetic
       problems with common fractions                               */
    for  (again = 'y';
          again != 'n';
          scanf("%c%c", &endline, &again)) {

        /* Gets a fraction problem                                 */
        scan_fraction(&n1, &d1);
        op = get_operator();
        scan_fraction(&n2, &d2);

        /* Computes the result                                     */
        switch (op) {
        case '+':
             add_fractions(n1, d1, n2, d2, &n_ans, &d_ans);
             break;

        case '-':
             add_fractions(n1, d1, -n2, d2, &n_ans, &d_ans);
             break;

        case '*':
             multiply_fractions(n1, d1, n2, d2, &n_ans, &d_ans);
             break;

        case '/':
             multiply_fractions(n1, d1, d2, n2, &n_ans, &d_ans);
        }
        reduce_fraction(&n_ans, &d_ans);

        /* Prints problem and result                               */
        printf("\n");
        print_fraction(n1, d1);
        printf(" %c ", op);
        print_fraction(n2, d2);
        printf(" = ");
        print_fraction(n_ans, d_ans);

        /* Asks user about doing another problem                   */
        printf("\nDo another problem? (y/n)> ");
    }

    return (0);
}
```

[handwritten note: ✶ WHEN DOING A SCANF FOR A TYPE CHAR VARIABLE, WHITESPACE (OR RETURN) IS EVALUATED AS CHARACTERS (WHICH IS IGNORED WHEN USING A NUMERIC VARIABLE)]

Figure 6.31 shows a run of the program in its present form. Notice that when the operator + is chosen and a correct greatest common divisor is entered interactively, the fraction problem's result is correct. However, when operator * is chosen, although the program continues execution by calling the stubs, the answer printed is incorrect.

Figure 6.31   Sample Run of a Partially Complete Program Containing Stubs

```
Enter a fraction> 3 4
Please reenter fraction.
One-half would be entered as 1/2
> 3/4
Enter an arithmetic operator (+,-,*, or /)
> +
Enter a fraction> 5/8
Entering find_gcd with n1 = 44, n2 = 32
gcd of 44 and 32?> 4
find_gcd returning 4

3/4 + 5/8 = 11/8
Do another problem? (y/n)> y
Enter a fraction> 1/2
Enter an arithmetic operator (+,-,*, or /)
> 5
5 invalid, reenter operator (+,-,*,/)
> *
Enter a fraction> 5/7
Entering multiply_fractions with
n1 = 1, d1 = 2, n2 = 5, d2 = 7

Entering find_gcd with n1 = 1, n2 = 1
gcd of 1 and 1?> 1
find_gcd returning 1

1/2 * 5/7 = 1/1
Do another problem? (y/n)> n
```

Self-Check

1. Why are pointer types used for the parameters of `scan_fraction`?
2. Why was it not necessary to include a default case in the `switch` statement that calls `add_fractions` and `multiply_fractions`?

Programming

1. Implement the following algorithm as the `find_gcd` function needed in the common fraction system of Fig. 6.30. Your function will find the greatest common divisor (that is, the product of all common factors) of integers `n1` and `n2`.

    1. Put the absolute value of `n1` in `q` and of `n2` in `p`.
    2. Store the remainder of `q` divided by `p` in `r`.
    3. As long as `r` is not zero
        4. Copy `p` into `q` and `r` into `p`.
        5. Store the remainder of `q` divided by `p` in `r`.
    6. `p` is the `gcd`.

2. Write the function `multiply_fractions`. If your result has a zero denominator, print an error message and change the denominator to `1`.

6.8 DEBUGGING AND TESTING A PROGRAM SYSTEM

As the number of statements in a program system grows, the possibility of error also increases. If we keep each module to a manageable size, the likelihood of error will increase much more slowly. It will also be easier to read and test each module.

In the last case study, we inserted stubs in the program for functions that were not yet written. When a team of programmers is working on a problem, using stubs is a common practice. Obviously, not all modules will be ready at the same time, and the use of stubs enables us to test and debug the main program flow and those modules that are available.

Each stub displays an identification message and assigns values to its output parameters to prevent execution errors caused by undefined values. We show the stub for function `multiply_fractions` again in Fig. 6.32. If a program contains one or more stubs, the message printed by each stub when it is called provides a trace of the call sequence and allows the programmer to determine whether the flow of control within the program is correct. The process of testing a program in this way is called *top-down testing*.

Figure 6.32   Stub for Function multiply_fractions

```
/*
 ***** STUB *****
 * Multiplies fractions represented by pairs of integers.
 * Pre:  n1, d1, n2, d2 are defined;
 *       n_ansp and d_ansp are addresses of type int variables.
 * Post: product of n1/d1 and n2/d2 is stored in variables pointed
 *       to by n_ansp and d_ansp. Result is not reduced.
 */
void
multiply_fractions(int   n1,    int  d1, /* input - first fraction     */
                   int   n2,    int  d2, /* input - second fraction    */
                   int  *n_ansp,         /* output -                   */
                   int  *d_ansp)         /*    product of two fractions */
{
    /* Prints trace message                                            */
    printf("\nEntering multiply_fractions with\n");
    printf("n1 = %d, d1 = %d, n2 = %d, d2 = %d\n", n1, d1, n2, d2);

    /* Defines output arguments                                        */
    *n_ansp = 1;
    *d_ansp = 1;
}
```

When a module is completed, it can be substituted for its stub in the program. However, we often perform a preliminary test of a new module before substitution because it is easier to locate and correct errors when dealing with a single module rather than with a complete program system. We can perform such a *unit test* by writing a short driver program to call it.

Don't spend a lot of time creating an elegant driver program because you will discard it as soon as the new module is tested. A driver program should contain only the declarations and executable statements necessary to perform a test of a single module. A driver program should begin by giving values to all input and input/output parameters. Next comes the call to the function being tested. After calling the module, the driver program should display the module results. A driver program for function scan_fraction is shown in Fig. 6.33.

Once we are confident that a module works properly, it can then be substituted for its stub in the program system. The process of separately testing

Figure 6.33 **Driver for Function scan_fraction**

```
/* Driver for scan_fraction */

int
main(void)
{
      int num, denom;
      printf("To quit, enter a fraction with a zero numerator\n");
      for   (scan_fraction(&num, &denom);
             num != 0;
             scan_fraction(&num, &denom))
          printf("Fraction is %d/%d\n", num, denom);

      return (0);
}
```

individual modules before inserting them in a program system is called *bottom-up testing*. Tests of individual functions are called *unit* tests, and tests of the entire system are *system integration* tests.

By following a combination of top-down and bottom-up testing, a programming team can be fairly confident that the complete program system will be relatively free of errors when it is finally put together. Consequently, the final debugging sessions should proceed quickly and smoothly.

Debugging Tips for Program Systems

A list of suggestions for debugging a program system follows.

1. Carefully document each module parameter and local variable using comments as you write the code. Also describe the module operation using comments.
2. Create a trace of execution by printing the module name as you enter it.
3. Print the values of all input and input/output parameters upon entry to a module. Check that these values make sense.
4. Print the values of all module outputs after returning from a module. Verify that these values are correct by hand computation. Make sure that all input/output and output parameters are declared as pointer types.
5. Make sure that a module stub assigns a value to the variable pointed to by each output parameter.

It is a good idea to plan for debugging as you write each module rather than to wait for the whole program to be complete. Unless you plan to use a debugger program, include the output statements mentioned in Debugging Tips 2 through 4 in the original C code for the module. When you are satisfied that the module works as you want it to work, you can remove the debugging statements. One way to remove them is to change them to comments by enclosing them within the symbols /*, */. If you have a problem later, you can remove these symbols and change the comments to executable statements.

6.9 COMMON PROGRAMMING ERRORS

Many opportunities for error arise when you use functions with parameter lists, so be extremely careful. The proper use of parameters is difficult for beginning programmers to master, but it is an essential skill. One obvious pitfall occurs in ensuring that the actual argument list has the same number of items as the formal parameter list. Each actual input argument must be of a type that can be assigned to its corresponding formal parameter. An actual output argument must be of the same pointer data type as the corresponding formal parameter.

If a function produces a single result, the function name should be declared in its prototype to be the type of the result, and the value should be returned using a `return` statement. It is easy to introduce errors in a function that produces multiple results. If the output parameters are not of pointer types or if the calling module neglects to send correct variable addresses, the program results will be incorrect.

The C scope rules determine where a name is visible and can therefore be referenced. If an identifier is referenced outside its scope, an `undeclared symbol` syntax error will result.

CHAPTER REVIEW

We discussed the use of parameters for passing data to and from functions. The parameter list provides a highly visible communication path between a module and its calling program. By using parameters, we can cause different data to be manipulated by a module each time we call it, making it easier to reuse the module in another program system.

Parameters may be used for input to a function, for output or sending back results, and for both input and output. An input parameter is used only for passing data into a module. The parameter's declared type is the same as the type of the data. Output and input/output parameters must be able to access variables in the calling module's data area so they are declared as pointers to the result data types. The actual argument corresponding to an input parameter may be an expression or a constant; the actual argument corresponding to an output or input/output parameter must be the address of a variable.

We also discussed the scope of identifiers. A parameter or local variable is visible and can be referenced anywhere within the function that declares it. Names of functions and of constant macros are visible from their definitions to the end of the source file except within functions that have local variables of the same names.

New C Constructs

Table 6.9 summarizes the definition and calling of the various kinds of functions with parameters that were described in this chapter.

Table 6.9   Summary of Functions in Chapter 6

Function Example	Effect and Sample Call
Function That Returns a Single Result	

```
char
sign(double x)
{
     char sign_symbol;

     if (x > 0)
          sign_symbol = '+';
     else if (x == 0)
          sign_symbol = ' ';
     else
          sign_symbol = '-';

     return (sign_symbol);
}
```

Returns a character value indicating the sign of its type `double` input argument.

```
double day;
char day_sign;
   . . .
day_sign = sign(day);
```

Function That Returns No Result

```
void
print_boxed(int num)
{
     printf("********\n");
     printf("*      *\n");
     printf("* %3d  *\n", num);
     printf("*      *\n");
     printf("********\n");
}
```

Prints its type `int` input argument inside a rectangle.

```
int score;
   . . .
print_boxed(score + 3);
```

(continued)

Table 6.9   *(continued)*

Function Example	Effect and Sample Call

Function That Returns Multiple Results

```
void
make_change(double   change,        /* input  */
            double   token_val,     /* input  */
            int     *num_tokenp,    /* output */
            double  *leftp)         /* output */
{
     *num_tokenp = floor(change /
                          token_val);
     *leftp = change - *num_tokenp *
                          token_val;
}
```

Determines how many of a certain bill or coin (`token_val`) should be included in change amount. This number is sent back through the output parameter `num_tokenp`. The amount of change remaining to be made is sent back through the output parameter `leftp`. The call below assigns a 3 to `num_twenties` and 11.50 to `remaining_change`.

```
int     num_twenties;
double  remaining_change;
    . . .
make_change(71.50, 20.00,
      &num_twenties,
      &remaining_change);
```

Function with Input/Output Parameters

```
void
correct_fraction(int *nump,      /* input/ */
                 int *denomp)    /* output */
{
     if ((*nump * *denomp) > 0)
           *nump = abs(*nump);
     else
           *nump = -abs(*nump);
     *denomp = abs(*denomp);
}
```

Corrects the form of a common fraction so the denominator is always positive (e.g. −5/3 rather than 5/−3).

```
int num, denom;

num = 5;
denom = -3;
correct_fraction(&num, &denom);
```

QUICK-CHECK EXERCISES

1. The items passed in a function call are the _____ _____. The corresponding _____ _____ appear in the function prototype.
2. Constants and expressions can be actual arguments corresponding to formal parameters that are _____ parameters.
3. Formal parameters that are output parameters must have actual arguments that are _____.
4. If an actual argument of −35.7 is passed to a type `int` formal parameter, what will happen?
5. If an actual argument of 17 is passed to a type `double` formal parameter, what will happen?
6. Which of the following is used to test a function: a driver or a stub?
7. Which of the following is used to test program flow in a partially complete system: a driver or a stub?
8. What are the values of main function variables `x` and `y` at the point marked `/* values here */` in the following program?

```
/* nonsense */
void
silly(int x)
{
      int y;

      y = x + 2;
      x = 2 * x;
}

int
main(void)
{
      int x, y;

      x = 10; y = 11;
      silly(x);
      silly(y);    /* values here */
       . . .
}
```

9. Let's make some changes in our nonsense program. What are `main`'s `x` and `y` at `/* values here */` in this version?

```
/* nonsense */
void
silly(int *x)
{
      int y;

      y = *x + 2;
      *x = 2 * *x;
}

int
main(void)
{
      int x, y;

      x = 10;   y = 11;
      silly(&x);
      silly(&y);   /* values here */
       . . .
}
```

ANSWERS TO QUICK-CHECK EXERCISES

1. actual arguments; formal parameters
2. input
3. addresses of variables/ pointers
4. The formal parameter's value will be −35.
5. The formal parameter's value will be 17.0.
6. driver
7. stub
8. x is 10, y is 11
9. x is 20, y is 22

REVIEW QUESTIONS

1. Write the prototype for a function called `script` that has three input parameters. The first parameter will be the number of spaces to print at the beginning of a line. The second parameter will be the character to print after the

spaces, and the third parameter will be the number of times to print the second parameter on the same line.

2. Write a function called `letter_grade` that has a type `int` parameter called `points` and returns the appropriate letter grade using a straight scale (90 – 100 is an A, 80 – 89 is a B, and so on).

3. Why would you choose to write a function that computes a single numeric or character value as a `nonvoid` function that returns a result through a `return` statement rather than to write a `void` function with an output parameter?

4. Explain the allocation of memory cells when a function is called.

5. Which of the functions in the following program outline *can* call the function `grumpy`? All prototypes and declarations are shown; only executable statements are omitted.

```
int
grumpy(int dopey)
{
      double silly;
      . . .
}

char
silly(double grumpy)
{
      double happy;
      . . .
}

double
happy(int goofy, char greedy)
{
      char grumpy;
      . . .
}

int
main(void)
{
      double p,q,r;
      . . .
}
```

6. Sketch the data areas of functions `main` and `silly` as they appear immediately before the return from the first call to `silly` in Quick-Check Exercise 9.

7. Present arguments against these statements:
   a. It is foolish to use function subprograms because a program written with functions has many more lines than the same program written without functions.
   b. The use of function subprograms leads to more errors because of mistakes in using argument lists.

PROGRAMMING PROJECTS

1. Two positive integers i and j are considered to be *relatively prime* if there exists no integer greater than 1 that divides them both. Write a function `relprm` that has two input parameters, i and j, and returns a value of 1 for true if and only if i and j are relatively prime. Otherwise, `relprm` should return a value of 0 for false.

2. Given the lengths a, b, c of the sides of a triangle, write a function to compute the area A of the triangle. The formula for computing A is given by

$$A = \sqrt{s(s-a)\,(s-b)\,(s-c)}$$

where s is the semiperimeter of the triangle

$$s = \frac{a+b+c}{2}$$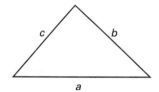

Write a driver program to get values for $a, b,$ and c and call your function to compute A. The driver should print $A, a, b,$ and c.

3. Determine the following information about each value in a list of positive integers.
   a. Is the value a multiple of 7, 11, or 13?
   b. Is the sum of the digits odd or even?
   c. What is the positive square root of the value?
   d. Is the value a prime number?
   You should have at least four function subprograms; label all output. Some sample input data might be 104   3773   13   121   77   30751.

4. To design a square timber column in a structure, three formulas must be satisfied:
   a. Buckling load:

$$maximum\ load = (0.30 \times E \times area) / (length/width)^2$$

b. Compressive stress:

$$maximum\ load = area \times maximum\ compressive\ strength$$

c. Slenderness limits:

$$length/width \le 50$$

where E is the modulus of elasticity (1,700,000 psi), the area is the cross-sectional area in square inches, and

$$maximum\ compressive\ strength = 445\ psi\ (Douglas\ fir).$$

Write a program that uses these three formulas to give an initial design to a structural engineer. Assume the columns to be used are square and are available in intervals of 2 inches (i.e., 2 by 2, 4 by 4, and so on). Have the output look like the following:

```
Please enter the expected load in pounds> 9000
Please enter the length of the column in inches> 120
. . .Testing a beam with width of 2.0 inches -- failed the
       tests
. . .Testing a beam with width of 4.0 inches -- failed the
       tests
. . .Testing a beam with width of 6.0 inches -- OK
For a load of 9000.0 pounds and a length of 120.0 inches,
recommended square beam has sides of 6.0 inches.
```

Write a function for each of the three tests. Each function should return a 1 if the test is passed, a 0 otherwise.

5. The square root of a number N can be approximated by repeated calculation using the formula

$$NG = 0.5(LG + N/LG)$$

where NG stands for next guess and LG stands for last guess. Write a function that calculates the square root of a number using this method.

The initial guess will be the starting value of LG. The program will compute a value for NG using the formula given. The difference between NG and LG is checked to see whether these two guesses are almost identical. If they are, NG is accepted as the square root; otherwise, the new guess (NG) becomes the last guess (LG) and the process is repeated (another value is computed for *NG*, the difference is checked, and so on). The loop should be repeated until the difference is less than 0.005. Use an initial guess of 1.0.

Write a driver function and test your square root function for the numbers 4, 120.5, 88, 36.01, 10000.

6. The electric company charges according to the following rate schedule:

9 cents per kilowatt-hour (kwh) for the first 300 kwh
8 cents per kwh for the next 300 kwh (up to 600 kwh)
6 cents per kwh for the next 400 kwh (up to 1000 kwh)
5 cents per kwh for all electricity used over 1000 kwh

Write a function to compute the total charge for each customer. Write a main function to call the charge calculation function using the following data:

Customer Number	Kilowatt-hours Used
123	725
205	115
464	600
596	327
601	915
613	1011
722	47

The program should print a three-column chart listing the customer number, the kilowatt-hours used, and the charge for each customer. The program should also compute and print the number of customers, the total kilowatt-hours used, and the total charges.

7. Write a function `ln_approx` that computes an approximation of the natural logarithm of a number between 1 and 2 by summing a given number of terms of this series:

$$\ln(1 + x) = \sum_{n=1}^{\infty} \frac{(-1)^{n+1} x^n}{n}$$

Also, write a driver that calls `ln_approx` twice with the same value, requesting first the sum of four terms of the series and then requesting seven terms. The program should print a message comparing the results of the two calls to the value returned by the math library function `log`.

8. Write a function that computes the necessary score on a 100-point final exam to achieve the desired grade in a course. The function inputs are the final exam weight, the student's average in all other course work, and the desired letter grade. Use a grading scale of 90–100 is an A, 80–89 is a B, and so on.

For example, if the test weight were 0.25, the student's average were 88.4, and the desired grade were an A, the necessary score would be

$$\text{ceil}\left(\frac{90 - .75(88.4)}{.25}\right) = 95 \text{ points}$$

9. Write a function that computes and prints a table of negative powers of two $(2^{-1}, 2^{-2}, \text{and so on})$ as both common fractions and decimals as shown. The range of powers printed should be determined by the function's input arguments. Test your function using a driver.

Power of 2	Fraction	Decimal Value
−1	1/2	0.5000
−2	1/4	0.2500
−3	1/8	0.1250

CHAPTER 7

DATA TYPES AND OPERATORS

7.1
Representation and Conversion of Numeric
Types int and double
7.2
Representation and Conversion of Type char
7.3
Logical Expressions and the Operators &&, ||,
and !
7.4
Loops Revisited
7.5
Operators with Side Effects
7.6
Iterative Approximations
Case Study: Approximating the Value of *e*
Case Study: Newton's Method for Finding Roots
7.7
Common Programming Errors
Chapter Review

So far, we have used three data types: `int`, `double`, and `char`. We have seen how type `int` values are used in C to represent both the numeric concept of an integer and the logical concepts true and false. In this chapter, we take a closer look at these data types and introduce new operations that can be performed on them.

You will also meet a new looping structure. You will see how to use this structure in several contexts including input validation and implementation of Newton's method for finding a root of a function.

7.1 REPRESENTATION AND CONVERSION OF NUMERIC TYPES int AND double

We have seen many examples of the representation of numeric information in C using the data types `int` and `double`. We used type `int` variables as loop counters and to represent data that were whole numbers, such as numbers of bald eagles. In most other instances, we used type `double` numeric data.

Differences Between Numeric Types

You may wonder why having more than one numeric type is necessary. Can the data type `double` be used for all numbers? Yes, but on many computers, operations involving integers are faster than those involving numbers of type `double`. Less storage space is needed to store type `int` values. Also, operations with integers are always precise, whereas some loss of accuracy or *round-off error* may occur when dealing with type `double` numbers.

These differences result from the way the numeric data types are represented internally in your computer's memory. All data are represented in memory as *binary strings,* strings of 0s and 1s. However, the binary string stored for the type `int` value 13 is not the same as the binary string stored for the type `double` number 13.0. The actual internal representation is computer dependent, and type `double` numbers usually require more bytes of computer memory than type `int`. Compare the sample `int` and `double` formats shown in Fig. 7.1.

Positive integers are represented by standard binary numbers. If you are familiar with the binary number system, you know that the integer 13 is represented as the binary number 01101.

The format of type `double` values is analogous to scientific notation. The storage area occupied by the number is divided into two sections: the *mantissa* and the *exponent*. The mantissa is a binary fraction between 0.5 and 1.0 for positive numbers and between −0.5 and −1.0 for negative numbers. The expo-

Figure 7.1 Internal Formats of Type int and Type double

type int format

binary number

type double format

| mantissa | exponent |

nent is an integer. The mantissa and exponent are chosen so that the following formula is correct.

$$real\ number = mantissa \times 2^{exponent}$$

Because of the finite size of a memory cell, not all real numbers in the range allowed can be represented precisely as type double values. We will discuss this concept later.

We have seen that type double values may include a fractional part, whereas type int values cannot. An additional advantage of the type double format is that a much larger range of numbers can be represented as compared to type int. Actual ranges vary from one implementation to another, but the ANSI standard for C specifies that the minimum range of positive values of type int is from 1 to 32,767 (approximately 3.3×10^4). The minimum range specified for positive values of type double is from 10^{-37} to 10^{37}. To understand how small 10^{-37} is, consider the fact that the mass of one electron is approximately 10^{-27} grams, and 10^{-37} is one ten-billionth of 10^{-27}. The enormity of 10^{37} may be clearer when you realize that if you multiply the diameter of the Milky Way galaxy in kilometers by a trillion, your numeric result is just one ten-thousandth of 10^{37}.

You can determine the exact ranges of the (ANSI-conforming) C implementation you are using by running the program in Fig. 7.2.

Figure 7.2   Program to Print Implementation-Specific Ranges for Positive Numeric Data

```
/*
 * Find implementation's ranges for positive numeric data
 */

#include <stdio.h>
#include <limits.h>  /* definition of INT_MAX                          */
#include <float.h>   /* definitions of DBL_MIN, DBL_MAX                */
```

(continued)

Figure 7.2 *(continued)*

```
int
main(void)
{
      printf("Range of positive values of type int: 1 . . %d\n",
             INT_MAX);
      printf("Range of positive values of type double: %e . . %e\n",
             DBL_MIN, DBL_MAX);

      return (0);
}
```

The %e format specifier in the second call to printf calls for the values associated with the names DBL_MIN and DBL_MAX to be printed in scientific notation (see Section 2.6).

Numerical Inaccuracies

One of the problems in processing data of type double is that sometimes an error occurs in representing real numbers. Just as certain fractions cannot be represented exactly in the decimal number system (e.g., the fraction 1/3 is 0.333333. . .), so some fractions cannot be represented exactly as binary numbers in the mantissa of the type double format. The *representational error* (sometimes called *round-off error*) will depend on the number of binary digits (bits) used in the mantissa: the more bits, the smaller the error. Because of this kind of error, an equality comparison of two type double values can lead to surprising results.

The number 0.1 is an example of a number that has a representational error as a type double value. The effect of a small error is often magnified through repeated computations. Therefore the result of adding 0.1 one hundred times is not exactly 10.0, so the following loop may fail to terminate on some computers.

```
for (trial = 0.0;
     trial != 10.0;
     trial = trial + 0.1) {
   . . .
}
```

If the loop repetition test is changed to trial < 10.0, the loop may execute 100 times on one computer and 101 times on another. For this reason, it is best to use integer variables for loop control whenever you can predict the exact number of times a loop body should be repeated.

Other problems occur when manipulating very large and very small real numbers. When you add a large number and a small number, the larger number may "cancel out" the smaller number, resulting in a *cancellation error*. If x is much larger than y, then $x + y$ may have the same value as x (for example, 1000.0 + 0.0000001234 is equal to 1000.0 on some computers).

If two very small numbers are multiplied, the result may be too small to be represented accurately, so it will be represented as zero. This phenomenon is called *arithmetic underflow*. Similarly, if two very large numbers are multiplied, the result may be too large to be represented. This phenomenon, called *arithmetic overflow*, is handled in different ways by different C compilers. (Arithmetic overflow can occur when processing very large integer values as well.)

EXAMPLE 7.1

The program in Fig. 7.3 draws a sine curve. It uses the math library function `sin`, which returns the trigonometric sine of its parameter, an angle expressed in radians. As an illustration of the numerical inaccuracy that may result when performing computations with type `double` values, examine the sine value displayed for angles of 180 and 360 degrees. The actual sine should be zero; the magnitude of the sine value computed is quite small (less than 10^{-5}) in both cases, but it is not zero. Because the value of the constant representing π is imprecise, the result of any computation involving π will have a small numerical error.

The `for` loop in Fig. 7.3 executes for values of `theta` equal to 0, 18, 36, . . . , 360 degrees. For each `theta`, the first of the following assignment statements

```
radians = theta * RAD_PER_DEGREE;
indent = 1 + floor(SCALE * (1.0 + sin(radians)) + 0.5);
```

computes the number of radians corresponding to `theta`. Then, the variable `indent` is assigned a value based on `sin(radians)`. This value increases from 1 when `sin(radians)` is −1.0 to 41 (1 + SCALE * 2.0) when `sin(radians)` is 1.0. The call to function `duplicate` prints from 1 to 41 blanks as determined by the value of `indent`. Finally, the statement

```
printf("%c%20e\n", PLOT_SYM, sin(radians));
```

places an asterisk on the output line immediately after the blanks and follows the asterisk by the numeric value of `sin(radians)` printed in scientific notation in a field of 20 columns.

Figure 7.3   Program to Plot a Sine Curve

```
/*
 * Plots a sine curve, labeling each point plotted.
 */

#include <stdio.h>
#include <math.h>

#define PI              3.14159
#define RAD_PER_DEGREE (PI / 180.0) /* degrees to radians conversion
                                       constant                       */
#define PLOT_SYM        '*'         /* symbol being plotted           */
#define SCALE           20          /* scale factor for plot          */
#define MIN_ANGLE       0           /* smallest angle (in degrees)    */
#define MAX_ANGLE       360         /* largest angle (in degrees)     */
#define STEP_ANGLE      18          /* increment in degrees           */

/* Reuse function duplicate from Section 6.2 here.                    */

int
main(void)
{
      int    theta;        /* angle in degrees                        */
      double radians;      /* angle in radians                        */
      int    indent;       /* number of blanks to print before PLOT_SYM */

      printf("Theta              Sine Curve Plot\n");

      for  (theta = MIN_ANGLE;
            theta <= MAX_ANGLE;
            theta = theta + STEP_ANGLE) {
         printf("%4d|   ", theta);
         radians = theta * RAD_PER_DEGREE;
         indent = 1 + floor(SCALE * (1.0 + sin(radians)) + 0.5);
         duplicate(' ', indent);
         printf("%c%20e\n", PLOT_SYM, sin(radians));
      }

      return (0);
}
```

(continued)

Figure 7.3 *(continued)*

```
Theta                       Sine Curve Plot
    0|                              *          0.000000e+00
   18|                                *          3.090167e-01
   36|                                 *          5.877848e-01
   54|                                  *          8.090165e-01
   72|                                   *          9.510562e-01
   90|                                    *          1.000000e+00
  108|                                   *          9.510570e-01
  126|                                  *          8.090181e-01
  144|                                 *          5.877870e-01
  162|                                *          3.090193e-01
  180|                              *          2.653590e-06
  198|                          *          -3.090142e-01
  216|                       *          -5.877827e-01
  234|                    *          -8.090150e-01
  252|                  *          -9.510554e-01
  270|                 *          -1.000000e+00
  288|                 *          -9.510578e-01
  306|                  *          -8.090196e-01
  324|                   *          -5.877891e-01
  342|                      *          -3.090218e-01
  360|                         *          -5.307180e-06
```

Automatic Conversion of Data Types

In Chapter 2, we saw several cases in which data of one numeric type was automatically converted to another numeric type. Table 7.1 summarizes the automatic conversions we have seen. The variables in the table are declared and initialized as follows:

```
int    k = 5, m = 4, n;
double x = 1.5, y = 2.1, z;
```

In Chapter 3 and Chapter 6, we studied what happens when an actual argument of one numeric data type is passed to a formal parameter of a different type. We saw that the actual argument value is converted to the format of the formal parameter just as if the assignment operator were used.

Table 7.1   Automatic Conversion of Numeric Data

Context of Conversion	Example	Explanation
expression with binary operator and operands of different numeric types	`k + x` value is `6.5`	Value of `int` variable k is converted to type `double` format before operation is performed.
assignment statement with type `double` target variable and type `int` expression	`z = k / m;` expression value is `1;` value assigned to z is `1.0`	Expression is evaluated *first*. Then, the result is converted to type `double` format for assignment.
assignment statement with type `int` target variable and type `double` expression	`n = x * y;` expression value is `3.15;` value assigned to n is `3`	Expression is evaluated *first*. Then, the result is converted to type `int` format for assignment, and fractional part is lost.

Explicit Conversion of Data Types

In addition to automatic conversions, C also provides an explicit type conversion operation called a *cast*. The function in Fig. 7.4 uses cast operations to prevent integer division. Because both `total_score` and `num_students` are of type `int`, evaluation of the expression

```
total_score / num_students
```

would result in a loss of the fractional part of the average. Placing the name of the desired type in parentheses immediately before the value to be converted causes the value to be changed to the desired data format before it is used in computation. Because this explicit conversion is a very high-precedence operation, it is performed before the division.

Although we show explicit casts of both operands of the division operator in the expression in Fig. 7.4, explicitly converting only one would be sufficient because the rules for evaluation of mixed-type expressions would then cause the other to be converted as well. However, we could *not* achieve our goal

Figure 7.4   Using Casts to Prevent Integer Division

```
/*
 * Averages a list of scores terminated by a sentinel
 */

#include <stdio.h>

#define SENT -99

int
main(void)
{
      int     score,
              total_score = 0,
              num_students = 0;
      double average;

      for  (scanf("%d", &score);
            score != SENT;
            scanf("%d", &score)) {
         total_score = total_score + score;
         num_students = num_students + 1;
      }

      average = (double)total_score / (double)num_students;
      printf("Average score is %.2f\n", average);

      return (0);
}
```

by writing the expression as

average = (double)(total_score / num_students);

In this case, the quotient total_score / num_students is computed first, resulting in the loss of the fractional part. The cast to double simply converts this whole number quotient to type double format.

In addition to using casts to prevent the loss of a fractional part in integer division, we sometimes include casts that do not affect the result but simply make clear to the reader the conversions that would occur automatically. For example, evaluation of the following assignment statement causes two automatic conversions if m and `sqrt_m` are type int variables.

```
sqrt_m = sqrt(m);
```

The formal parameter of the `sqrt` library function is of type `double`, so a type int actual argument, such as the value of m, will automatically be converted to type `double` format for assignment to the formal parameter. The `sqrt` function also returns a value of type `double` that will automatically be converted to type int format for assignment to `sqrt_m`. One has the option of emphasizing to the reader the fact that these conversions are occurring by including explicit casts as in this statement:

```
sqrt_m = (int)sqrt((double)m);
```

When a cast operation is applied to a variable, the conversion carried out determines the value of the expression, but the conversion does not change what is stored in the variable. For example, if x is a type int variable whose value is 5, the following statements will first print 5.00 and then print 5. The value of the expression

```
(double)x
```

is 5.0, but the value stored in x is still the integer 5.

Statements	Output
`printf("%.2f", (double)x);`	
`printf("%4d\n", x);`	5.00 5

In the next section, we study the representation of type char and see how we can convert from type char to type int and vice versa.

EXERCISES FOR SECTION 7.1

Self-Check

1. How does cancellation error differ from representational error?
2. If squaring 10^{-20} gives a result of zero, the type of error that has occurred is called _____ .
3. Evaluate the following expressions if x is 10.5, y is 7.2, m is 5, and n is 2.
   a. `x / (double)m`   d. `(double)(n / m) + y`
   b. `x / m`   e. `(double)(n / m)`
   c. `(double)(n * m)`

Programming

1. Run the program from Fig. 7.2 to determine the largest type int value and the largest type double value that can be used on your computer system's implementation of C.

7.2 REPRESENTATION AND CONVERSION OF TYPE char

We have seen C's data type `char` that allows us to store and manipulate individual characters such as those that comprise a person's name, address, and other personal data. We have declared variables of type `char` and have used type `char` constants consisting of a single character (for example, a letter, digit, or punctuation mark) enclosed in apostrophes. We have assigned a character value to a character variable and have associated a character value with an identifier in a constant macro, as shown.

```
#define STAR '*'
    .
    .
    .
char next_letter;
next_letter = 'A';
```

The character variable `next_letter` is assigned the character value `'A'` by the assignment statement just shown. A single character variable or value may appear on the right-hand side of a character assignment statement. Character values may also be compared, scanned, printed, and converted to type `int`.

Using Relational Operators with Characters

Assuming `next` and `first` are type `char`, the logical expressions

```
next == first
next != first
```

determine whether two character variables have the same or different values. Order comparisons can also be performed on character variables using the relational operators <, <=, >, and >=.

To understand the result of an order comparison, we must know something about the way characters are represented internally within your computer. Each character has its own unique numeric code; the binary form of this code is stored in a memory cell that has a character value. These binary numbers are compared by the relational operators in the normal way.

Three common character codes are shown in Appendix A. The digit characters are an increasing sequence of consecutive characters in all three codes. For example, in ASCII (American Standard Code for Information Interchange), the digit characters `'0'` through `'9'` have code values of 48 through 57 (decimal). The order relationship that follows holds for the digit characters (i.e., `'0'` < `'1'`, `'1'` < `'2'`, and so on).

```
'0'<'1'<'2'<'3'<'4'<'5'<'6'<'7'<'8'<'9'
```

The uppercase letters are also an increasing sequence of characters, but they are not necessarily consecutive. In ASCII, uppercase letters do have consecutive codes, namely the decimal code values 65 through 90. The order relationship that follows holds for uppercase letters.

```
'A'<'B'<'C'< ... <'X'<'Y'<'Z'
```

The lowercase letters are also an increasing, but not necessarily consecutive, sequence of characters. In ASCII, lowercase letters have the consecutive decimal code values 97 through 122, and the following order relationship holds.

```
'a'<'b'<'c'< ... <'x'<'y'<'z'
```

In our examples and programs, we will assume that the letters are consecutive characters.

In ASCII, the *printable characters* have codes from 32 (code for a blank or space) to 126 (code for the symbol ~). The other codes represent nonprintable *control characters*. Sending a control character to an output device causes the device to perform a special operation such as returning the cursor to column one, advancing the cursor to the next line, or ringing a bell.

Since characters are represented by integer codes, C permits conversion of type `char` to type `int` and vice versa. For example, you could use the following to find out the code your implementation uses for a question mark:

```
qmark_code = (int)'?';
printf("Code for ? = %d\n", qmark_code);
```

EXAMPLE 7.2

A *collating sequence* is a sequence of characters arranged by character code number. The program in Fig. 7.5 uses explicit conversion of type `int` to type `char` and `char` to `int` to print part of the C collating sequence. The program lists the portion of the sequence between the blank and the uppercase `'Z'` inclusive. The sequence shown is for the ASCII code; the first character printed is a blank.

Figure 7.5   Program to Print Part of the Collating Sequence

```
/*
 * Prints part of the collating sequence
 */
```

(continued)

Figure 7.5   *(continued)*

```
#include <stdio.h>

#define START_CHAR ' '
#define END_CHAR   'Z'

int
main(void)
{
     int char_code; /* numeric code of each character printed */

     for  (char_code = (int)START_CHAR;
           char_code <= (int)END_CHAR;
           char_code = char_code + 1)
        printf("%c", (char)char_code);
     printf("\n");

     return (0);
}
```

```
 !"#$%&'()*+,-./0123456789:;<=>?-ABCDEFGHIJKLMNOPQRSTUVWXYZ
```

EXERCISES FOR SECTION 7.2

Self-Check

1. Evaluate the following, assuming that letters have consecutive character codes.
   a. `(int)'D' - (int)'A'`
   b. `(char)((int)'C' + 2)`
   c. `(int)'6' - (int)'7'`
2. Write a `for` loop that would print the alphabet in lowercase letters, assuming that letters have consecutive codes.

Programming

1. Write a function `next_char` that returns as its type `char` value the character that follows in the collating sequence the value passed as the argument for `next_char`. (For now, ignore the possibility of a boundary error.)
2. Rewrite the loop from Self-check Exercise 2 so it uses function `next_char` and has a type `char` loop control variable.

7.3 LOGICAL EXPRESSIONS AND THE OPERATORS &&, ||, AND !

In earlier chapters, we saw how C uses type int values to represent the logical concepts true and false. Our study included examples of logical expressions that use relational and equality operators (<, <=, >, >=, ==, !=) and expressions that call a function returning a 1 for true and a 0 for false.

Actually, the simplest form of logical expression is a single type int value or variable intended to represent the value true or false. In this code fragment, such a variable is used to represent the concept of whether or not a person's age places him or her in the category of senior citizen.

```
int senior_citizen;
. . .
senior_citizen = age >= 65;
```

A variable such as senior_citizen is a perfectly legitimate condition to use in a decision or as a loop repetition test. Consider this example:

```
if (senior_citizen)
        printf("Send senior discount brochure.\n");
```

If we assume that the identifier TRUE has been defined to mean 1, then any one of the following assignment statements results in the variable senior_citizen having the value 1, meaning true.

```
senior_citizen = 1;
senior_citizen = TRUE;
senior_citizen = 66 >= 65;
```

In Section 4.8, we saw how C's use of type int values to represent the logical concepts true and false leads to surprising values for some expressions. Specifically, we saw that it was *not* possible to check if the value of x falls in the range 0 through 4 by using the test if (0 <= x <= 4). Just as it is often necessary to combine results of arithmetic expressions using other arithmetic operators, it is also helpful to be able to combine results of logical expressions such as those using the relational and equality operators. C's logical operators are && (read "and"), || (read "or"), and ! (read "not"). Some logical expressions formed using these operators are

```
salary < min_sal || num_depend > 5
temp > 90.0 && humidity > 0.90
winning_record && !probation
0 <= n && n <= 100
```

The first logical expression determines whether an employee is eligible for special scholarship funds. The expression evaluates to true if *either* the expression

```
salary < min_sal
```

or the expression

```
num_depend > 5
```

is true. The second logical expression describes an unbearable summer day with both temperature and humidity in the nineties. The expression evaluates to true only when *both* conditions are true. The third expression manipulates two type int variables that represent logical concepts (winning_record, probation). A college team for which this expression is true may be eligible for the postseason tournament. The final expression is true if n is between 0 and 100 inclusive.

The logical operators that are used to form complex logical expressions are described in Tables 7.2, 7.3, and 7.4.

Table 7.2 shows that the && operator yields a true result of 1 only when both its operands are true (nonzero); Table 7.3 shows that the || operator yields a false result of zero only when both its operands are false (zero). The && operator requires that *both* operands evaluate to true in order to produce a result of 1; therefore if the first operand is zero, evaluating the second operand is not really necessary in order to know the result. In this case, C evaluates only the

Table 7.2 && Operator

operand1	operand2	operand1 && operand2 (read *operand1* and *operand2*)
nonzero	nonzero	1
nonzero	0	0
0	nonzero	0
0	0	0

Table 7.3 || Operator

operand1	operand2	operand1 || operand2 (read *operand1* or *operand2*)
nonzero	nonzero	1
nonzero	0	1
0	nonzero	1
0	0	0

Table 7.4   ! Operator

operand1	!operand1	(read not *operand1*)
nonzero	0	
0	1	

first (leftmost) operand. Similarly, since the | | operator requires both operands to be zero to produce a result of zero, the value of the second operand is not needed and is not computed if the value of the first operand is nonzero. This evaluation of only as much of the logical expression as is needed to determine its value is called *short-circuit evaluation.*

The ! operator has a single operand. Table 7.4 shows that the ! operator yields the *logical complement,* or *negation,* of its operand—that is, if `shift` is true, `!shift` is false and vice versa.

The precedence of an operator determines its order of evaluation. Table 7.5 shows the precedence of all the C operations we have seen to this point.

As you can see, function calls have the highest precedence. They are followed by the unary arithmetic and logical operators, along with the address-of and indirection operators. Next are the cast operations for explicit type conversions; casts are also unary operations. The binary arithmetic operations follow with the multiplicative operators `*`, `/`, and `%`, one level higher in precedence than the additive operators `+` and `−`. After the binary arithmetic operations are the comparison operators, with relational operators applied before equality operators. The binary logical operators `&&` (and) and `| |` (or) have quite low precedence, with `&&` having the higher precedence of the two. The lowest precedence operator we have

Table 7.5   Precedence of Operations

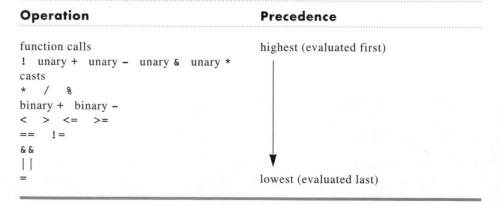

Operation	Precedence
function calls	highest (evaluated first)
! unary + unary − unary & unary *	
casts	
* / %	
binary + binary −	
< > <= >=	
== !=	
&&	
| |	
=	lowest (evaluated last)

Figure 7.6   Step-by-Step Evaluation of Expression with Operations of Many Precedence Levels

```
ans = 2 + (int)ceil(80.2) % 9 > 10          level
                     81.0                      1
              81                               2
                                0              3
          2                                    4
                                    0          5
      0                                        6
```

studied is the assignment operator. The precedence shown can always be overridden by use of parentheses, and parentheses can often make a complex expression more readable even when the parentheses do not change the order of evaluation.

Figure 7.6 shows a step-by-step evaluation for an expression that illustrates the application of several aspects of the precedence rules. Operations at six different precedence levels are shown. At the highest level, we see a call to the library function ceil. At level 2, we apply the conversion to type int due to a cast. At level 3, we evaluate the expression with the integer remainder operator %, and at 4, the addition operation. At level 5, the relational operator > is applied; the last operation is the assignment to ans.

Testing for a Range of Values

Expressions similar to the following are common in programming.

```
min_x <= x && x <= max_x
```

If min_x represents the lower bound of a range of values, and max_x represents the upper bound (min_x is less than max_x), this expression tests whether x lies within the range min_x through max_x inclusive. In Fig. 7.7, this range of values is shaded. The expression is true if x lies within this range and false if x is outside this range.

Figure 7.7   Range of True Values for min_x <= x && x <= max_x

More Logical Expressions

EXAMPLE 7.3

If x, y, and z are type double and flag is type int, the following expressions are all legal. The value of each expression, shown in brackets, assumes that x is 3.0, y is 4.0, z is 2.0, and flag is 0.

Expression	Value
1. x > z && y > z	[1]
2. x + y / z <= 3.5	[0]
3. z > x || z > y	[0]
4. !flag	[1]
5. x == 1.0 || x == 3.0	[1]
6. z < x && x < y	[1]
7. x <= z || x >= y	[0]
8. !flag || y + z >= x - z	[1]
9. !(flag || y + z >= x - z)	[0]

Expression 1 gives the C form of the relationship "x and y are greater than z." It is often tempting to write this as

x && y > z

However, if we apply the operator precedence rules to this expression, we quickly see that it does not have the intended meaning. Moreover, the type double variable x is an invalid operand for the logical operator &&. Expression 5 shows the correct way to express the relationship "x is equal to 1.0 or to 3.0."

Expression 6 is the C form of the relationship z < x < y (that is, "x is in the range 2.0 to 4.0"). The boundary values, 2.0 and 4.0, are excluded from the range of x values that yield a true result. Expression 7 is true if the value of x lies outside the range bounded by z and y.

In Fig. 7.8, the shaded areas represent the values of x that yield a true result. Both y and z are included in the set that yields a true result.

To verify the results, you may want to do step-by-step evaluations of Expressions 8 and 9 in a way similar to that shown in Fig. 7.6.

Figure 7.8   Range of True Values for x <= z \|\| x >= y

Logical Assignment

At the beginning of this section, we saw how type int variables can be assigned the results of expressions representing logical concepts. Let's consider some additional examples of this type of assignment statement.

The assignment statements that follow assign values to two type int variables representing logical ideas, in_range and is_letter. Variable in_range gets the value 1 (for true) if n satisfies both of the conditions listed (n is greater than −10 and less than 10); otherwise, the expression's value is 0 for false. The expression in the second assignment statement uses the logical operators && and ||. The subexpression before the || is true if the value of ch is an uppercase letter; the subexpression after the || is true if ch is a lowercase letter. Consequently, the value assigned to is_letter represents true if ch is a letter (assuming consecutive character codes); otherwise, the value assigned represents false. The parentheses in this expression do not affect the order of evaluation; they are included for clarity.

```
in_range = n > -10 && n < 10;
is_letter = ('A' <= ch && ch <= 'Z') ||
            ('a' <= ch && ch <= 'z');
```

EXAMPLE 7.5

Either of the following assignment statements assigns a value meaning true to variable even if n is an even number.

```
even = n % 2 == 0;     even = !(n % 2 == 1);
```

The statement on the left assigns a value of 1 to even when the remainder of n divided by 2 is zero. (All even numbers are divisible by 2.) In the statement on the right, the expression in parentheses (n % 2 == 1) evaluates to true if n is an odd number—that is, if the remainder of n divided by 2 is 1. Applying the ! (not) operator to this expression yields the negation of "n is odd"—that is, n is even.

Complementing a Condition

In algorithm development, forming the complement or negation of a condition is often necessary. If a logical expression is true, its complement must be false and vice versa. Occasions when we need to complement a condition arise both in determining loop repetition conditions and in writing decision structures. Often we find it easy to state a condition that will be true when a loop should exit.

Since our loop repetition condition must be true when the loop body should be executed, we need the complement of the exit condition. In the development of complex decision structures in Chapter 4, we saw that we can usually use a multiple-alternative `if` when a flowchart of the decision structure has all intermediate decisions falling on false branches of previous decisions. We can sometimes achieve this structure by changing the true/false branches of one or two decisions. Such a switch of the branches is made possible by complementing the condition.

There is always more than one way to complement a condition. One approach is to apply the `!` (not) operator to the entire condition. In the next two examples, we compare this approach to other ways of complementing conditions.

EXAMPLE 7.6 ▶

Two forms of the complement of the condition

```
item == SENT
```

are

```
item != SENT       and       !(item == SENT)
```

The form on the left is obtained by complementing the equality operator (changing `==` to `!=`); the complement on the right is obtained by applying the `!` operator (meaning negation) to the original condition.

Generally, changing the equality or relational operator when you are dealing with simple conditions like the one shown in Example 7.6 is easy to do. The relational operator `<=` should be changed to `>`, `<` should be changed to `>=`, and so on. To complement more complicated conditions, it is easier to place the `!` operator in front of the entire condition. ◀

EXAMPLE 7.7 ▶

The condition

```
age > 25 && status == 's'
```

is true for a single person over 25. The complement of this condition is

```
! (age > 25 && status == 's')
```
◀

DeMorgan's Theorem

DeMorgan's theorem can also be used to form the complement of a logical expression. DeMorgan's theorem states

- The complement of *expr1* && *expr2* is written as *comp1* || *comp2*, where *comp1* is the complement of *expr1*, and *comp2* is the complement of *expr2*.
- The complement of *expr1* || *expr2* is written as *comp1* && *comp2*, where *comp1* is the complement of *expr1*, and *comp2* is the complement of *expr2*.

EXAMPLE 7.8

Using DeMorgan's theorem, we can write the complement of

```
age > 25 && (status == 's' || status == 'd')
```

as

```
age <= 25 || (status != 's' && status != 'd')
```

The original condition is true for anyone who is over 25 and is either single or divorced. The complement would be true for anyone who is 25 or younger or anyone who is currently married.

EXERCISES FOR SECTION 7.3

Self-Check

1. Assuming x is 15.0 and y is 25.0, what are the values of the following conditions?

   ```
   x != y
   x < x
   x >= y - x
   x == y + x - y
   ```

2. Evaluate each of the following expressions if a is 5, b is 10, c is 15, and flag is 1. Which parts of these expressions are not computed at all due to short-circuit evaluation?
   a. c == a + b || !flag
   b. a != 7 && flag || c >= 6
   c. !(b <= 12) && a % 2 == 0
   d. !(a > 5 || c < a + b)
3. Show step-by-step evaluations of Expressions 8 and 9 in Example 7.3.

Programming

1. Write an expression for each relationship described.
    a. x is in the range −1.5 to 3.2, excluding end points.
    b. a is in the range 17 to 23 inclusive.
    c. y is greater than x and less than z.
    d. w is either equal to 6 or not greater than 3.
2. Write the following assignment statements:
    a. Assign a 1 to `between` if n is in the range −k to +k inclusive; otherwise, assign a zero.
    b. Assign a value of 1 to `uppercase` if ch is an uppercase letter; otherwise, assign a zero.
    c. Assign a value of 1 to `divisor` if m is a divisor of n; otherwise, assign a zero.

7.4 LOOPS REVISITED

In all the loops we have seen up to this point, we have viewed the loop initialization and update steps as two distinct entities. In many situations where repetition is used, this procedure is essential because not all the repeated steps are to be executed the same number of times. For example, when we first list the steps to be performed in a sentinel loop that is processing a list of numbers, we have

1. Get a number.
2. Process the number.

However, when we begin to use these steps as the basis of a loop body repeated as long as the number is not the sentinel, we soon realize that some revision is necessary. In fact, it is not true that all numbers in our list are to receive identical processing. The number that is the sentinel must *not* be processed like the other numbers. We saw that an efficient way to accomplish this was to designate Step 1 as both the initialization and update steps of a `for` loop, leaving only Step 2 as the loop body.

In some circumstances, however, *all* elements of a list should actually be processed identically. In such cases, C's `do-while` statement is an excellent loop structure to choose. In Fig. 7.9, we see a function that repeatedly prompts the user for a value falling in the range from n_min to n_max inclusive. Function `get_inrange` uses two `do-while` structures. The outer `do-while` implements the stated purpose of the function; the inner `do-while` skips the rest of a line of input by repeatedly scanning a character and checking the input value to see if it is the newline character `'\n'`.

Figure 7.9   Validating Input Function Using do-while Statement

```c
/*
 * Gets an integer input value in the range from n_min to n_max inclusive.
 * Gives an error message on input of an invalid data type, and clears
 * character causing error.
 * Pre:   n_min <= n_max
 */
int
get_inrange(int n_min, int n_max)
{
      int   inval,          /* data value which user enters             */
            status;         /* status value returned by scanf           */
      char skip_ch;         /* character to skip                        */
      int   error;          /* error flag for bad input                 */

      do {
          printf("Enter an integer in the range from %d to %d inclusive> ",
                  n_min, n_max);
          status = scanf("%d", &inval);
          if (status == 1) {
                error = 0;
          } else {
                error = 1;
                scanf("%c", &skip_ch);
                printf("\nInvalid character>>%c>> Skipping rest of line.\n",
                        skip_ch);

                do {
                    scanf("%c", &skip_ch);
                } while (skip_ch != '\n');

          }
      } while (error || inval < n_min || inval > n_max);

      return (inval);
}
```

Execution of function `get_inrange` using the call statement

```
num = get_inrange(10, 20);
```

would proceed as shown below, assuming that the user responds to the first prompt by mistyping the number 10 as a 1 followed by the letter o. Notice that when the program first encounters the o, it does not flag the character as an error. The program simply scans up to the o, stops scanning, and then stores the 1. Because the number 1 is outside the acceptable range of values for \get_inrange, the do-while does not exit. Instead, it prompts again for input, but then `scanf` tries to convert the o to an integer. At this point, the error message is printed.

```
Enter an integer in the range from 10 to 20 inclusive> 1o
Enter an integer in the range from 10 to 20 inclusive>
Invalid character >>o>> Skipping rest of line.
Enter an integer in the range from 10 to 20 inclusive> 10
```

Getting a prompt with no opportunity to respond to it is annoying, but at least the prompts do not keep appearing indefinitely. Table 7.6 traces the execution of this call to function `get_inrange`.

Figure 7.10 shows a flowchart of an input validation loop like the do-while loop of Fig. 7.9. Notice that the first iteration of the loop body occurs unconditionally, and all input values receive the same processing.

Checking for valid input is one situation in which the do-while is often the structure to choose. The do-while used in Fig. 7.9 also shows one way to

**Figure 7.10
Flowchart of
Input Validation
Loop**

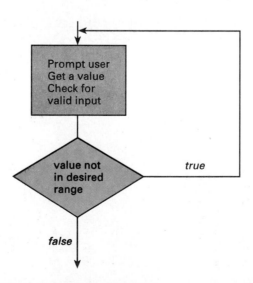

Table 7.6 Trace of Call to Function get_inrange

Statement	n_min	n_max	inval	status	skip_ch	error	Effect
...get_inrange (10, 20);	10	20	?	?	?	?	Formal parameters initialized to 10 and 20.
printf("Enter...							Prompting message printed.
status = scanf("%d", &inval);			1	1			Assuming the characters 1 and o are typed, the 1 is stored in inval and the scanf function returns a 1. Scanning stops at the letter o.
if (status == 1)							Condition is true.
error = 0;						0	Error flag is set to false.
while (error || inval < n_min || inval > nmax)							1 < 10 so loop repetition condition is true.
printf("Enter...							Prompting message is printed again.
status = scanf("%d", &inval);				0			scanf encounters the unprocessed letter o and returns an error code of 0.
if (status == 1)							Condition is false.
error = 1;						1	Error flag is set to true.

(continued)

Table 7.6 (continued)

Statement	n_min	n_max	inval	status	skip_ch	error	Effect
`scanf("%c", &skip_ch); printf("Invalid...`					o		Letter causing a problem is copied into skip_ch and printed.
`do { scanf(... } while (...`					\n		Remainder of input line is scanned.
`while (error || inval < n_min || inval > nmax)`							error is true, so loop repetition condition is true.
`printf("Enter...`							Prompting message is printed again.
`status = scanf("%d", &inval);`			10	1			This time user types 10 correctly, so 10 is stored in inval and scanf returns 1, which is stored in status.
`if (status == 1)`							Condition is true.
`error = 0;`						0	Error flag is set to false.
`while (error || inval < n_min || inval > nmax)`							error is false, 10 is not less than 10, and 10 is not greater than 20, so loop exits
`return (inval);`							in_range returns 10

avoid the infinite input loops one can easily get into when using `scanf` if the user types an invalid character. In Chapter 5, we saw how an input loop trying to rescan an erroneous character can get bogged down indefinitely. The input loop of Fig. 7.9 will not hang in this way because as soon as it receives a status code from `scanf` indicating an error, the loop body explicitly scans and echoes the bad character, skips the rest of the input line, and sets the error flag so the loop will execute again permitting fresh (and hopefully valid) input.

The syntax of the `do-while` follows.

---

do-while Statement

SYNTAX: do

                statement

            while (*loop repetition condition*);

EXAMPLE: /* Find first capital letter input */
            do
                status = scanf("%c", &alpha);
            while (status >= 0 && (alpha < 'A' || alpha > 'Z'));

INTERPRETATION: First, the *statement* is executed. Then, the *loop repetition condition* is tested, and if it is true, the *statement* is re-executed and the *condition* retested. The *statement* is executed repeatedly as long as the *loop repetition condition* is true. When this condition is tested and found to be false, the loop is exited and the next statement after the `do-while` is executed.

NOTE: If the loop body contains more than one statement, the group of statements must be surrounded by braces.

Flag-Controlled Loops for Input Validation

Sometimes a loop repetition condition becomes so complex that placing the full expression in its usual spot is awkward. In many cases, the condition may be simplified by using a *flag*. A *flag* is a type `int` variable used to represent whether or not a certain event has occurred. The `get_inrange` function of Fig. 7.9 uses the variable `error` as a flag to record whether or not a bad character has been encountered in the input.

Frequently, a flag is initialized to 0 (false) at the beginning of processing and is changed to 1 (true) when the anticipated event occurs. The function in Fig. 7.11 uses another flag named `error` to represent whether or not any type of error in the form of the current input has been detected. The module is a more

Figure 7.11   Function with Flag-Controlled Input Validation Loop

```
/*
 * Get a valid fraction
 * Pre:  nump and denomp are addresses of type int variables
 * A valid fraction is of this form: integer/positive integer
 */
void
scan_fraction(int *nump,     /* output - numerator                    */
              int *denomp)   /* output - denominator                  */
{
      int  num, den;         /* local variables for fraction          */
      char slash;            /* local - character between numerator and
                                   denominator                        */
      int  status;           /* status code returned by scanf indicating
                                   number of valid values obtained     */
      int  error;            /* flag indicating whether or not an error has
                                   been detected in current input      */
      char discard;          /* unprocessed character from input line  */

      do {
          /* No errors detected yet                                    */
          error = 0;

          /* Get a fraction from the user                              */
          printf("Enter a common fraction as two integers separated by ");
          printf("a slash\nand press <enter> or <return>\n> ");
          status = scanf("%d%c%d", &num, &slash, &den);

          /* Validate the fraction                                     */
          if (status < 3) {
                error = 1;
                printf("Input invalid--please read directions carefully\n");
          } else if (slash != '/') {
                error = 1;
                printf("Input invalid--separate numerator and denominator");
                printf(" by a slash (/)\n");
          } else if (den <= 0) {
                error = 1;
                printf("Input invalid--denominator must be positive\n");
          }
```

(continued)

Figure 7.11   *(continued)*

```
     /* Discard extra input characters                        */
     do {
          scanf("%c", &discard);
     } while (discard != '\n');
} while (error);

/* Return validated fraction                                  */
*nump = num;
*denomp = den;
}
```

robust version of the function `scan_fraction` used in our fraction-manipu-
lating case study at the end of Chapter 6.

Let's see why the validation process shown in Fig. 7.11 needs a step to
clear a line of invalid input. If the input provided were

85.0/3<return>

the format specifiers of the statement

status = scanf("%d%c%d", &num, &slash, &den);

would process the line as follows. The first `%d` would be used to scan the 85.
Then, the decimal point would be processed using `%c`, and the 0 would be used
by the second `%d`. If the remaining characters (/3<return>) are not discarded,
they will be processed on the next iteration of the input loop. The input-dis-
carding loop takes one character at a time until the newline character '\n' is
recognized. This character results from the user's typing the <enter> or <return>
key. On valid input this character should be the very next one after the valid
fraction's denominator.

EXERCISES FOR SECTION 7.4

Self-Check

1. If you want a loop to exit when n has a value that is a positive even number,
   what is your loop repetition condition? Give two valid answers—one that
   uses the `!` operator to complement a statement of the exit condition and one
   that applies DeMorgan's theorem to complement the exit condition.

2. Rewrite the following code using a `do_while` statement with no decisions in the loop body.

```
sum = 0;
for  (odd = 1;  odd < n;  odd = odd + 2)
     sum = sum + odd;
printf("Sum of the positive odd numbers less than %d is %d\n",
       n, sum);
```

In what situations will the rewritten code print an incorrect sum?

3. Which of the following code segments is a better way to implement a sentinel-controlled loop? Why?

```
for  (scanf("%d", &num);        do {
     num != SENT;                   scanf("%d", &num);
     scanf("%d", &num)) {           if (num != SENT) {
  /* process num */                      /* process num */}
}                               } while (num != SENT);
```

Programming

1. Design an interactive input loop that scans pairs of integers until it reaches a pair in which the first integer evenly divides the second.
2. Write a type `int` function `get_positive` that has no arguments. The function is to prompt for and take input repeatedly until the user enters a positive integer. This value is to be returned as the function result; the function should be able to reject input of an invalid data type without falling into an infinite loop.

7.5 OPERATORS WITH SIDE EFFECTS

We use some operators in an expression as much for their effect on memory cells as for the values they compute. In fact, you may have been surprised to see that the assignment operator, like other binary operators, produces a value (the value assigned). Usually, we don't really care about an assignment expression's computed value; rather, we use the operator for its *side effect*, the fact that it changes the value of its left operand in memory. In many programming languages, the assignment operator is the *only* operator that has a side effect. However, C has several other operators with this property. These operators make it possible to use fewer keystrokes and, in some instances, less computer time to carry out operations that we can already perform in other ways.

Increment and Decrement Operators

You have seen many occasions when we write assignment statements of the form

```
counter = counter + 1;
```

The increment operator ++ takes a single variable of type int or type **char** as its operand. The side effect of applying the ++ operator is that the value of its operand is incremented by one. Frequently, ++ is used just for this side effect as in the following loop in which the counter ct is to run from 0 up to limit.

```
for (ct = 0;  ct < limit;  ++ct)
    . . .
```

The *value* of the expression in which the ++ operator is used depends on the position of the operator. When the ++ is placed immediately in front of its operand (*prefix increment*), the value of the expression is the variable's value *after* incrementing. When the ++ comes immediately after the operand (*postfix increment*), the expression's value is the value of the variable *before* it is incremented. Compare the action of the two code segments in Fig. 7.12, given an initial value of 2 in i.

C also provides a decrement operator that can be used in either the prefix or postfix position. For example, if the initial value of n is 4, the code fragment on the left prints

    3   3

and the one on the right prints

    4   3

```
printf("%3d", --n);          printf("%3d", n--);
printf("%3d", n);            printf("%3d", n);
```

**Figure 7.12
Comparison of
Prefix and
Postfix
Increments**

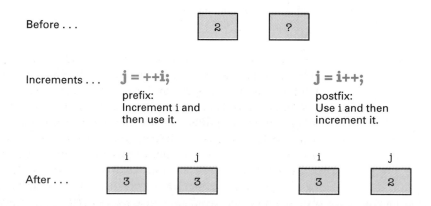

You should avoid using the increment and decrement operators in complex expressions in which the variables to which they are applied appear more than once. C compilers are expected to exploit the commutativity and associativity of various operators in order to produce efficient code. The user must not depend on side effects that will vary from one compiler to another.

Compound Assignment Operators

We have seen many instances of assignment statements of the form

$$variable = variable \; op \; expression;$$

These include increments and decrements of loop counters

```
ct = ct + 1;
time = time - 1;
```

as well as statements accumulating a sum or computing a product in a loop, such as

```
total_pay = total_pay + pay;
product = product * data;
```

C provides special assignment operators that make possible a more concise notation of statements of this type. For the operations +, -, *, /, and %, C defines the compound *op*= assignment operators +=, -=, *=, /=, and %=. A statement of the form

$$variable \; op= \; expression;$$

is an alternate way of writing the statement

$$variable = variable \; op \; (expression);$$

Table 7.7 lists the assignment statements just noted along with their equivalents using compound assignment operators. In addition, the table shows one assignment that demonstrates the relevance of the parentheses around *expression* in the definition of an assignment statement with a compound operator.

Compound assignment operators are especially useful when the target of the assignment is a single component of one of the composite data structures that we will study in Chapters 8, 9, and 11. In these cases, the use of a compound assignment operator is not only more concise but also more efficient.

Table 7.7 Using Compound Assignment Operators

Statement with Simple Assignment Operator	Equivalent Statement with Compound Assignment Operator
ct = ct	1;	ct += 1;
time = time - 1;	time -= 1;
total_pay = total_pay + pay;	total_pay += pay;
product = product * data;	product *= data;
n = n * (x + 1);	n *= x + 1;

EXERCISES FOR SECTION 7.5

Self-Check

1. What values are assigned to n, m, and p, given these initial values?

i	j
3	9

```
n = ++i * --j;
m = i + j--;
p = i + j;
```

2. Rewrite the code shown in Exercise 1 so the effect is equivalent but no increment/decrement operator appears in an expression with another arithmetic operator.
3. Where possible, write equivalents for the following statements using compound assignment operators.

```
r = r / 10;
z = z * x + 1;
q = q + r * m;
m = m - (n + p);
```

Programming

1. Write a version of function `factorial` that uses the decrement operator and a compound assignment operator (see Fig. 6.1).
2. Write a function that takes two integer parameters, n and m (m $\geq$ 0), and computes n^m without calling the `pow` function from the math library.

7.6 ITERATIVE APPROXIMATIONS

Numerical analysis is the field of study concerned with developing methods to use the computer to solve computational problems in mathematics. Some examples of numerical methods include finding solutions to sets of equations, performing operations on matrices, finding roots of equations, and performing numerical integration. This section contains two case studies that illustrate methods for iteratively approximating solutions to computational problems.

Case Study: Approximating the Value of *e*

PROBLEM

A number of mathematical quantities can be represented using a series approximation in which a series is represented by a summation of an infinite number of terms. We are interested in using this technique to compute *e* (value is 2.71828...), the base of the natural logarithms.

ANALYSIS

We can compute an approximation to the value of *e* by evaluating the series

$$\frac{1}{0!} + \frac{1}{1!} + \frac{1}{2!} + \frac{1}{3!} + \cdots + \frac{1}{n!}$$

where *n*! is the factorial of *n*. This expression can be represented using *summation notation* as

$$\sum_{i=0}^{n} \frac{1}{i!}$$

where the first term is obtained by substituting 0 for *i* (1/0! is 1/1), the second term is obtained by substituting 1 for *i* (1/1!), and so on. The larger the value of *n* we use, the more terms will be included in the series, resulting in increased accuracy. The value of *n* will be a problem input.

Data Requirements

Problem Input
```
int n          /* number of terms, n, in the sum    */
```

Problem Output
```
double e      /* approximate value of e               */
```

DESIGN

Although we could design a solution that repeatedly calls the factorial function we defined in Chapter 6, we can find a much more efficient algorithm by observing the relationship between successive denominators of terms of the series. Consider the first 5 denominators.

$$
\begin{array}{ccccc}
0! & 1! & 2! & 3! & 4! \\
1 & 1 & 2 & 6 & 24
\end{array}
$$

Notice that 4! (24) is $3! \times 4$. Similarly, 3! is $2! \times 3$ and 2! is $1! \times 2$. In general, $n!$ is $(n-1)! \times n$, as long as n is greater than 0. Therefore our summation could be rewritten as

$$
\frac{1}{0!} + \sum_{i=1}^{n} \frac{1}{(i-1)! \times i} = 1 + \sum_{i=1}^{n} \frac{1}{(i-1)!} \times \frac{1}{i}
$$

This form means that given an initial term of 1, a counting `for` loop with i as the index can compute each new term of the series, $1/i!$ by dividing the previous term $1/(i-1)!$ by i.

Program Variables
```
double ith_term /* ith term of the series */
int i            /* loop control variable */
```

Initial Algorithm

1. Get the value of n.
2. Initialize the ith term to 0! = 1.0.
3. Initialize e to 1.0.
4. Repeat for each i from 1 through n.
   5. Compute the ith term in the series by dividing the previous term by i.
   6. Add the ith term to e.
7. Print the value of e.

IMPLEMENTATION

The program is shown in Fig. 7.13. Inside the `for` loop, the statement

```
ith_term /= i;
```

computes the value of the ith term in the series by dividing the previous term by the loop control variable i. The statement

```
e += ith_term;
```

adds the new value of `ith_term` to the sum being accumulated in **e**. Trace the execution of this loop to satisfy yourself that `ith_term` takes on the values 1/1!, 1/2!, 1/3!, and so on, during successive loop iterations.

Figure 7.13   Program to Approximate e

```
/*
 * Computes the value of e by a series approximation.
 */
#include <stdio.h>

int
main(void)
{
      int n;                   /* number of terms in series */
      double e = 1.0,          /* value being approximated  */
             ith_term = 1.0; /* ith term of the series    */
      int    i;                /* loop counter              */

      printf("Enter the number of terms in the series> ");
      scanf("%d", &n);

      /* Compute each term and add it to the accumulating sum */
      for (i = 1;   i <= n;   ++i) {
         ith_term /= i;
         e += ith_term;
      }

      printf("The approximate value of e is %.10e\n", e);

      return (0);
}


Enter the number of terms in the series> 15
The approximate value of e is 2.7182818284e+00
```

To determine whether this algorithm works, run the program for a particular value of n and compare the result with the frequently used approximation of e, 2.71828183. Obviously, the value computed when n equals 15 is very close to the actual value. It would be interesting to see the effect of the value of n on the accuracy of the final computed result. Programming Exercise 1 at the end of this section asks you to compute and display such a table.

Case Study: Newton's Method for Finding Roots

Your calculus instructor would like you to write a program that uses Newton's method for finding a root of an equation, $y = f(x)$, where k is a root if $f(k)$ equals zero. Newton's method starts with an initial guess for a root, x_0, and then generates successive approximate roots $x_1, x_2, \ldots, x_j, x_{j+1}, \ldots$, using the iterative formula

$$x_{j+1} = x_j - \frac{f(x_j)}{f'(x_j)}$$

where $f'(x_j)$ is the derivative of function f evaluated at $x = x_j$. The formula generates a new guess, x_{j+1}, from a previous one, x_j. Newton's method terminates when successive guesses are sufficiently close in value, that is, when

$$\left| x_{j+1} - x_j \right| < epsilon$$

where *epsilon* is a very small constant (for example, 0.00001).

Sometimes Newton's method will fail to converge to a root. In this case, the program should terminate after many trials, perhaps 100.

Figure 7.14 shows the geometric interpretation of Newton's method where x_0, x_1, and x_2 represent successive guesses for the root. At each point x_j, the derivative, $f'(x_j)$, is the slope of the tangent to the curve, $f(x)$. The next guess for the root, x_{j+1}, is the point at which the tangent crosses the x axis.

From geometry, we get the equation

$$\frac{y_{j+1} - y_j}{x_{j+1} - x_j} = m$$

**Figure 7.14
Geometric
Interpretation
of Newton's
Method**

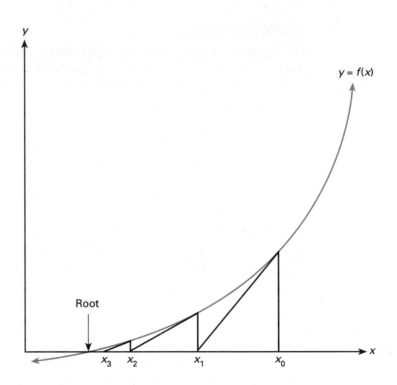

where m is the slope of the line between points (x_{j+1}, y_{j+1}) and (x_j, y_j). In Fig. 7.14, we see that y_{j+1} is zero, y_j is $f(x_j)$, and m is $f'(x_j)$; therefore by substituting and rearranging terms, we get

$$-f(x_j) = f'(x_j) \times (x_{j+1} - x_j)$$

leading to the formula shown at the beginning of the case study. In the data requirements that follow, **x_previous** corresponds to x_j and **x_guess** corresponds to x_{j+1}.

Data Requirements

Problem Constants
```
EPSILON 0.00001   /* the maximum difference between
                     successive guesses to decide on
                     an approximation                 */
MAX_GUESS 100     /* the maximum number of guesses    */
```

Problem Outputs

```
double x_guess      /* the next guess for a root
                       (initialized as an input)     */
int num_guess       /* the count of guesses          */
```

Program Variables

```
double x_previous   /* previous guess for a root     */
```

Functions

```
f(x)                /* the function whose root is being
                       determined                     */
fprime(x)           /* the derivative of function f(x) */
```

DESIGN

The initial guess for the root is an input. Inside a loop, we compute the next guess for the root value, **x_guess**, from the last guess, **x_previous**. The loop must continue to execute until the difference between successive guesses is less than EPSILON. In this algorithm, we see an example of a very common situation: Two possible reasons for exiting the loop exist, and which of the two applies does matter. Therefore the statement immediately after the loop checks to determine the reason for exit. The algorithm follows.

Algorithm for Newton's Method

1. Get the initial **x_guess** and set **num_guess** to one.
2. Repeat
   3. Set **x_previous** to the previous guess that is stored in **x_guess**.
   4. Compute the next guess, **x_guess**, from **x_previous** by evaluating $f($**x_previous**$)$ and $f'($**x_previous**$)$.
   5. Increment **num_guess**.
   as long as $|$**x_guess** - **x_previous**$|$ >= EPSILON
   and **num_guess** <= MAX_GUESS
6. If a root was found, then
   7. Display the root and the function value at the root.
8. Display the number of guesses.

> **IMPLEMENTATION**

The program must contain declarations for function $f(x)$, the function whose root is being computed, and function $fprime(x)$, the derivative of $f(x)$. The program in Fig. 7.15 computes the root for the function

$$f(x) = 5x^3 - 2x^2 + 3$$

with derivative

$$f'(x) = 15x^2 - 4x$$

Figure 7.15   Program to Apply Newton's Method

```
/*
 * Finds a root of an equation using Newton's method
 */

#include <stdio.h>
#include <math.h>

#define EPSILON    0.00001   /* maximum difference between successive
                                guesses to decide on an approximation   */
#define MAX_GUESS 100        /* maximum number of guesses               */

/*
 * Function whose root is being found.
 */
double
f(double x)
{
      double f_of_x;

      /* insert function here */
      f_of_x = 5 * pow(x, 3) - 2 * pow(x, 2) + 3;

      return (f_of_x);
}

/*
 * Derivative of f
 */
```

(continued)

Figure 7.15 *(continued)*

```c
double
fprime(double x)
{
      double fp of_x;

      fp_of_x = 15 * pow(x, 2) - 4 * x;

      return (fp_of_x);
}

int
main(void)
{
      double x_previous,
             x_guess;
      int    num_guess;

      printf("Initial guess for a root> ");
      scanf("%lf", &x_guess);
      num_guess = 1;

      do {
          x_previous = x_guess;
          x_guess = x_previous - f(x_previous) / fprime(x_previous);
          ++num_guess;
      } while (fabs(x_guess - x_previous) >= EPSILON
                  && num_guess <= MAX_GUESS);

      /* Display the root and function value if a root was found */
      if (fabs(x_guess - x_previous) < EPSILON) {
            printf("The approximate root is %.10e\n", x_guess);
            printf("The function value f(%.10e) is %.10e\n",
                    x_guess, f(x_guess));
      } else {
            printf("Root not found.\n");
      }

      printf("%d guesses made.\n", num_guess);
```

(continued)

Figure 7.15 *(continued)*

```
      return (0);
}

Initial guess for a root> 1.0
The approximate root is -7.2900142869e-01
The function value f(-7.2900142869e-01) is -6.3025307195e-11
9 guesses made.
```

TESTING

The function value in Fig. 7.15 is sufficiently close to zero that we can feel confident that we have found a root. To test Newton's method, run the program on several mathematical functions and with several different starting points for each function. In most cases, Newton's method should find a solution relatively quickly.

You may find situations in which Newton's method will not work; the program will cycle until `MAX_GUESS` guesses are made. At other times, Newton's method will fail because `fprime(x_previous)` becomes zero, and a division by zero causes a run-time error. In these cases, you must try a different technique for finding function roots.

EXERCISES FOR SECTION 7.6

Self-check

1. Determine the output from the program that implements Newton's method in Fig. 7.15 if

$$f(x) = 2x^2 - 2x - 1.5$$
$$f'(x) = 4x - 2$$

Try initial guesses of 1.0, −1.0, 10.0, and −10.0. Do the results make sense? Can you suggest a more direct way to compute these results?

Programming

1. Display a table showing approximations of e computed using values of n between 3 and 15.
2. The value of e^x is represented by the series

$$1 + x + \frac{x^2}{2!} + \frac{x^3}{3!} + \cdots + \frac{x^n}{n!} + \cdots$$

Define a function named `e_to_the_x` to compute the value of this series for any *x* and *n*. Write a main function that prints the result and compares it to the value of `exp(x)`, printing the message `OK` or `Not OK`, depending on whether the difference between these results is less than 0.0001.

7.7 COMMON PROGRAMMING ERRORS

A good deal of care is required when working with complicated expressions because it is easy to omit parentheses or operators. If an operator or a single parenthesis is omitted, a syntax error will be detected. If a pair of parentheses is omitted, the expression, although syntactically correct, will compute the wrong value.

Do not use operators with side effects as subexpressions in complex expressions. At best, such usage leads to expressions that are difficult to read; at worst, to expressions that produce varying results in different implementations of C.

Remember the parentheses that are assumed to be around any expression that is the second operand of a compound assignment operator. Since the statement

`a *= b + c;`   is equivalent to   `a = a * (b + c);`

there is no shorter way to write

`a = a * b + c;`

Be sure that the operand of an increment or decrement operator is a variable and that this variable is referenced after executing the increment or decrement operation. Without a subsequent reference, the operator's side effect of changing the value of the variable is pointless. Do not use a variable twice in an expression in which it is incremented/decremented. Applying the increment/decrement operators to constants or expressions is illegal.

With three looping constructs from which to choose, selecting one not best suited to the needs of your algorithm is easy to do. Before selecting the `do-while` statement, be sure that there is no possible situation in which you would want to skip execution of the loop body completely. If you ever find yourself adding an `if` statement to patch your code with a result like this:

```
if (condition₁)
     do {
       . . .
     } while (condition₁);
```

be ready to replace the segment with a `while` or `for` statement. Both of these statements automatically test the loop repetition condition *before* executing the loop body. Another misuse of the `do_while` has this general outline:

```
do   {
     first statement
     if (condition₁) {
          rest of loop body
     }
} while (condition₁);
```

This segment is essentially a sentinel loop that is better implemented using a `for` statement with *first statement* as both the initialization and update expressions. The `for` loop version tests $condition_1$ only once per iteration of the loop.

CHAPTER REVIEW

This chapter reviewed the manipulation of simple data types. We discussed the internal representation of simple types and investigated the differences between the numeric types `int` and `double`. We explained that arithmetic with type `double` values is inherently less precise than integer arithmetic because not all real numbers can be represented exactly. We described other sources of numerical errors, such as cancellation errors and arithmetic overflow and underflow. We also studied cast operations that allow explicit conversion from one simple type to another.

We presented the logical operators `!`, `&&`, and `||` which are used to form complex logical expressions. We also introduced DeMorgan's theorem, which describes how to form the complement of a logical expression. We saw that complex logical expressions are often used as loop repetition conditions, and we met a third repetition statement available in C—the `do-while`. Because this structure always executes its loop body at least once, we used it to create an input verification loop and to compute an approximation iteratively.

In this chapter, we also studied two groups of C operators that have side effects: the unary increment/decrement operators and the binary compound assignment operators. We noted reasons why all of these operators should be used with care, and we also cited cases where they should not be used at all.

Finally, we discussed numerical analysis, the branch of mathematics and computer science concerned with developing techniques for mathematical computation. We showed how to use iterative approximation to evaluate a series and to find a root of an equation.

New C Constructs

Table 7.8 summarizes the looping construct and the operators with side effects introduced in this chapter.

Table 7.8   Summary of New Constructs from Chapter 7

Construct	Effect

do-while loop
``do {
   printf("Enter positive number < 10> ");
   scanf("%d", &num);
} while (num < 1 || num >= 10);```
	Repeatedly prints prompt and stores a number in num until user enters a number that is in range.

increment / decrement ```z = ++j * k--;```	Stores in z the product of the incremented value of j and the current value of k. Then k is decremented.
compound assignment ```ans *= a - b;```	Assigns to ans the value of ans * (a - b).

QUICK-CHECK EXERCISES

1. a. Evaluate the expression

   ```
   1 && (30 % 10 >= 0) && (30 % 10 <= 3)
   ```

   b. Is either set of parentheses required?
   c. Write the complement of the expression two ways: First, add one operator and one set of parentheses. For the second version, apply DeMorgan's theorem.
2. Assuming an ASCII character set, evaluate these expressions.
   a. `(char)((int)'z' - 2)`
   b. `(int)'F' - (int)'A'`
   c. `(char)(5 + (int)'M')`

3. If the value of n is 4 and m is 5, is the value of the following expression 21?

```
++(n * m)
```

Explain your answer.

4. What values are assigned to n, m, and p, given these initial values?

```
n = j - ++k;
m = j-- + k--;
p = k + j;
```

5. What values are assigned to x, y, and z?

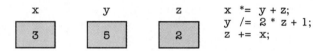

```
x *= y + z;
y /= 2 * z + 1;
z += x;
```

6. What does the following code segment print? Try each of these inputs: 345, 82, 6. Then, describe the action of the code.

```
printf("\nEnter a positive integer> ");
scanf("%d", &num);
do {
    printf("%d   ", num % 10);
    num /= 10;
} while (num > 0);
printf("\n");
```

7. What does this segment print?

```
for  (ch = (int)'d';
      ch < (int)'n';
      ch += 3)
    printf("%c", (char)ch);
printf("\n");
```

ANSWERS TO QUICK-CHECK EXERCISES

1. a. 1
   b. no
   c. !(1 && (30 % 10 >= 0) && (30 % 10 <= 3))
      0 || (30 % 10 < 0) || (30 % 10 > 3)

2. a. `'x'`
   b. `5`
   c. `'R'`
3. No. The expression is illegal. The increment operator cannot be applied to an expression such as `(n * m)`.
4. `n=2, m=8, p=6`
5. `x=21, y=1, z=23`
6. ```
   Enter a positive integer> 345
   5  4  3
   Enter a positive integer> 82
   2  8
   Enter a positive integer> 6
   6
   ```

   The code prints the digits of an integer in reverse order and separated by spaces.
7. `dgjm`

REVIEW QUESTIONS

1. What are the advantages of data type `int` over data type `double`? What are the advantages of type `double` over type `int`?
2. List and explain three computational errors that may occur in type `double` expressions.
3. Assume you are using the ASCII character set, and write a `for` loop that runs from the code for `'Z'` down to the code for `'A'` and prints only the consonants. Define a function `is_vowel` that returns a 1 if its character argument is a vowel and a 0 otherwise. Call this function from your loop.
4. Write an assignment statement that gives the variable `overtime` the value 1 for true if a worker's hours are greater than `40` and assigns value 0 for false otherwise.
5. Write an `if` statement that prints an acceptance message for an astronaut candidate if the person's weight is between the values of `opt_min` and `opt_max` inclusive, the person's age is between `age_min` and `age_max` inclusive, and the person is not a smoker (the value of the `smoker` flag is false).
6. Write a `do-while` loop that repeatedly prompts for and takes input until a value in the range 0 through `1.5` inclusive is input. Include code that prevents the loop from cycling indefinitely on input of a wrong data type.
7. Write a C function with type `int` argument n and type `double` argument x that returns as its value the sum of the first n terms of the series

$$x + \frac{x^2}{2} + \frac{x^3}{3} + \frac{x^4}{4} + \cdots + \frac{x^n}{n}$$
   ```

8. Write a nest of loops that will print the following output. Use increment/decrement operators and compound assignment operators wherever possible.

```
 1 10 9 8 7 6 5 4 3 2
 2 10 9 8 7 6 5 4 3
 4 10 9 8 7 6 5
 8 10 9
16
```

PROGRAMMING PROJECTS

1. A number is said to be *perfect* if the sum of its divisors (except for itself) is equal to itself. For example, 6 is a perfect number because the sum of its divisors (1 + 2 + 3) is 6. The number 8 is said to be *deficient* because the sum of its divisors (1 + 2 + 4) is only 7. The number 12 is said to be *abundant* because the sum of its divisors (1 + 2 + 3 + 4 + 6) is 16. Write a program that lists all the divisors of the numbers between 1 and 100 and classifies each number as perfect, deficient, or abundant.

2. Write a program that processes an input list of 12 numbers representing the number of inches of rainfall in Springfield for each month of one year. Create a bar graph like the one shown that prints six asterisks per inch. Assume that the maximum monthly rainfall will not exceed 12 inches. Follow your graph with a line showing the average monthly rainfall and the maximum monthly rainfall. Design your program for batch processing; use input redirection to provide access to your data file.

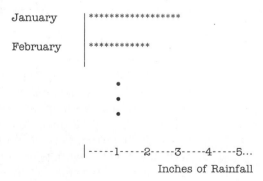

Include in your solution functions corresponding to the prototypes that follow.

```
/* Write the month name corresponding to the value of
   month (integer from 1-12)*/
void
write_month(int month) /* input - month number */

/* Draw a bar whose length is computed from inches with
   label determined by month */
void
draw_bar(int     month,    /* input - month number       */
         double inches)  /* input - amount of rainfall */

/* Draw scale and label at bottom of graph */
void
draw_scale_line(int max_inches) /* input - maximum number
                                          of inches on scale */
```

3. Experiments that are either too expensive or too dangerous to perform are
   often simulated on a computer when the computer is able to provide a good
   representation of the experiment. Write a program that uses a random number
   generator to simulate the dropping of glass rods that break into three pieces.

   The purpose of the experiment is to estimate the probability that the
   lengths of the three pieces are such that they might form the sides of a triangle. For the purposes of this experiment, you may assume that the glass rod
   always breaks into three pieces and that a break is equally likely to occur at
   any point along the rod. If you use the line segment 0 to 1 on the real number
   line as a mathematical model of the glass rod, a random number generator
   function can be used to generate two numbers between 0 and 1 to represent
   the coordinates of the breaks. The triangle inequality—that is, the sum of the
   lengths of two sides of a triangle is always greater than the length of the third
   side—may be used to test the length of each piece against the lengths of the
   other two pieces.

   To estimate the probability that the pieces of the rod form a triangle,
   you will need to repeat the experiment many times and count the number of
   times a triangle can be formed from the pieces. The probability estimate is
   the number of successes divided by the total number of rods dropped. Your
   program should prompt the user for the number of rods to drop and allow the
   experiment to be repeated. Use a sentinel value of −1 to halt execution of the
   program.

   ANSI C has a function rand defined in <stdlib.h>. This function
   returns an integer between 0 and the value associated with RAND_MAX, a
   constant macro that is defined in the same library. You can use this function
   in defining your own pseudorandom number generator that will return values
   in the range 0 to 1.

4. The rate of decay of a radioactive isotope is given in terms of its half-life H, the time lapse required for the isotope to decay to one-half of its original mass. The isotope strontium 90 (Sr^{90}) has a half-life of 28 years. Compute and print in table form the amount of this isotope that remains after each year for n years, given the initial presence of an amount in grams. The values of n and *amount* should be provided interactively. The amount of Sr^{90} remaining can be computed by using the following formula:

$$r = amount \times C^{(y/H)}$$

where *amount* is the initial amount in grams, C is expressed as $e^{-0.693}$ ($e = 2.71828$), y is the number of years elapsed, and H is the half-life of the isotope in years.

5. The value for π can be determined by the series equation

$$\pi = 4 \times \left(1 - \frac{1}{3} + \frac{1}{5} + \frac{1}{7} + \frac{1}{9} - \frac{1}{11} + \frac{1}{13} - \cdots \right)$$

Write a program to calculate the value of π using the formula given including terms up through 1/99.

6. Write a program to create a chart showing the underwater pressure in pounds per square inch (psi) of depths from 1 foot to 30 feet. Water weighs 62.4 pounds per cubic foot, so a column 1 foot high and 1 inch square will weigh 0.433 pound. Have your chart look something like the following Underwater Pressure Chart:

Depth (ft)	Pressure (psi)
1	0.4333333
2	0.8666667
3	1.3000000
.	.
.	.
.	.
29	12.5666667
30	13.0000000

ARRAYS

8.1
Declaring and Referencing Arrays
8.2
Array Subscripts
8.3
Using Indexed for Loops to Process Arrays
8.4
Using Individual Array Elements as
Input Arguments
8.5
Using Individual Array Elements as
Output Arguments
8.6
Using Arrays as Input Arguments
8.7
Using Arrays as Output or
Input/Output Arguments
8.8
Array Processing Illustrated
Case Study: Finding the Area of a Polygon
8.9
Multidimensional Arrays
8.10
Common Programming Errors
Chapter Review

$\mathbf{I}$n all previous programs in this text, each variable was associated with a single memory cell; such variables are called *simple variables*. In this chapter, we study a C *data structure*. A data structure is a grouping of related data items in memory. The items in a data structure can be processed individually, although some operations may be performed on the structure as a whole.

An *array* is a data structure used for storage of a collection of data items that are all the same type (for example, all the exam scores for a class). By using an array, we will be able to associate a single variable name (`scores`) with a group of related data items (exam scores). The individual data items in an array are stored in adjacent cells of main memory (one item per memory cell). Since each item is saved in a separate memory cell, we can process the individual items more than once and in any order we wish.

In earlier programs, we reused the same memory cell to store each exam score. Each time a new item was placed in the cell, its previous value was lost. Consequently, we could no longer access the third score after getting the fourth score. This inability to work with earlier data values after seeing the entire list severely limited the analysis we could do of the data. By using an array to store each data value in a separate memory cell, accessing earlier data will no longer be a problem.

8.1 DECLARING AND REFERENCING ARRAYS

An array is a collection of two or more adjacent memory cells, called *array elements*, that are associated with a particular symbolic name. To set up an array in memory, we must declare both the name of the array and the number of cells associated with it.

The declaration

```
double x[8];
```

instructs the compiler to associate eight memory cells with the name `x`; these memory cells will be adjacent to each other in memory. Each element of array `x` may contain a single type `double` value, so a total of eight such numbers may be stored and referenced using the array name `x`.

In order to process the data stored in an array, we reference each individual element by specifying the array name and identifying the element desired (for example, element 3 of array `x`). The *subscripted variable* `x[0]` (read as `x` sub zero) may be used to reference the initial or 0th element of the array `x`, `x[1]` the next element, and `x[7]` the last element. The integer enclosed in brackets is the *array subscript*, and its value must be in the range from zero to one less than the number of memory cells in the array.

Figure 8.1 The Eight Elements of Array x

double x[8];

Array x

x[0]	x[1]	x[2]	x[3]	x[4]	x[5]	x[6]	x[7]
16.0	12.0	6.0	8.0	2.5	12.0	14.0	−54.5

EXAMPLE 8.1

Let x be the array shown in Fig. 8.1. Notice that x[1] is the second array element and x[7], not x[8], is the last array element. A sequence of statements that manipulate this array is shown in Table 8.1. The contents of array x after execution of these statements are shown after Table 8.1. Only x[2] and x[3] are changed.

Table 8.1   Statements That Manipulate Array x

Statement	Explanation
`printf("%.1f", x[0]);`	Displays the value of x[0], which is 16.0.
`x[3] = 25.0;`	Stores the value 25.0 in x[3].
`sum = x[0] + x[1];`	Stores the sum of x[0] and x[1], which is 28.0 in the variable sum.
`sum += x[2];`	Adds x[2] to sum. The new sum is 34.0.
`x[3] += 1.0;`	Adds 1.0 to x[3]. The new x[3] is 26.0.
`x[2] = x[0] + x[1];`	Stores the sum of x[0] and x[1] in x[2]. The new x[2] is 28.0.

Array x

x[0]	x[1]	x[2]	x[3]	x[4]	x[5]	x[6]	x[7]
16.0	12.0	28.0	26.0	2.5	12.0	14.0	−54.5

EXAMPLE 8.2

Two arrays are declared as follows:

```
int    id[50];
double gpa[50];
```

The arrays id and gpa each have fifty elements. Each element of array id can be used to store an integer value; each element of array gpa can be used to store a value of type double. If these declarations are used in a problem to assess the range and distribution of grade point averages, the first student's id can be stored in id[0], and the same student's gpa can be stored in gpa[0]. Because the data stored in `id[i]` and `gpa[i]` relate to the `i`th student, the two arrays are called *parallel arrays*. Samples of these arrays are shown next.

id[0]	609465503		gpa[0]	2.71
id[1]	512984556		gpa[1]	3.09
id[2]	323415691		gpa[2]	2.98
	. . .			. . .
id[49]	512009146		gpa[49]	1.92

EXAMPLE 8.3 The statement

```
char answer[10];
```

declares an array `answer` with ten elements; each element can store a single character. This array could be used to store the ten answers for a true-false quiz (e.g., `answer[0]` is `'T'`, `answer[1]` is `'F'`). A sample array is shown next.

answer[0]	T
answer[1]	F
answer[2]	F
	. . .
answer[9]	T

EXAMPLE 8.4 More than one array may be declared in a single type declaration. The statements

```
double cactus[5], needle, pins[6];
int    factor[12], n, index;
```

declare `cactus` and `pins` to be arrays with five and six type `double` elements, respectively. The variable `factor` is an array with 12 type `int` elements. In addition, individual memory cells will be allocated for storage of the simple variables `needle`, `n`, and `index`.

Naming the constant that specifies the number of array elements to allocate is advisable. By doing so, one can easily change the size of an array. ⬅

EXAMPLE 8.5 ▶ The statements

```
#define NUM_READINGS 20
. . .
double gauge[NUM_READINGS];
int    time[NUM_READINGS];
```

allocate storage for two arrays of numbers. The array `gauge` can hold 20 type `double` values, and array `time` can hold 20 integers. ⬅

Array Initialization

A simple variable can be initialized when it is declared, as we see in the statement

```
int sum = 0;
```

an array can also be initialized in its declaration. The size of an array that is being fully initialized can optionally be omitted from the declaration since it can be deduced from the initialization list. For example, in the following statement, a 25-element array is initialized with the prime numbers less than 100.

```
int prime_lt_100[25] = {2, 3, 5, 7, 11, 13, 17, 19, 23, 29,
                        31, 37, 41, 43, 47, 53, 59, 61, 67,
                        71, 73, 79, 83, 89, 97};
```

All the points illustrated so far are summarized in the next display.

Array Declaration

SYNTAX: *element-type aname*[*size*];   /* uninitialized */
element-type aname[*size*] = {*initialization list*};/* initialized */

EXAMPLE: #define A_SIZE 5
. . .
double a[A_SIZE];
char vowels[] = {'A', 'E', 'I', 'O', 'U'};

(continued)

INTERPRETATION: The general uninitialized array declaration just given allocates storage space for array *aname* consisting of *size* memory cells. Each memory cell can store one data item whose data type is specified by *element-type* (i.e., `double`, `int`, or `char`). The individual array elements are referenced by the subscripted variables *aname*[0], *aname*[1], . . . , *aname*[*size*-1]. A constant expression of type `int` is used to specify an array's *size*.

In the initialized array declaration shown, the *size* shown in brackets is optional since the array's size can also be indicated by the length of the *initialization list*. The *initialization list* consists of constant expressions of the appropriate *element-type* separated by commas. Element 0 of the array being initialized is set to the first entry in the *initialization list*, element 1 to the second, and so forth.

EXERCISES FOR SECTION 8.1

Self-Check

1. What is the difference between `x3` and `x[3]`?
2. For the declaration

   `char grades[5];`

   how many memory cells are allocated for data storage? What type of data can be stored there? How does one refer to the initial array element? To the final array element?
3. Allocate one array for storing the square roots of the integers from 0 through 10 and a second array for storing the cubes of the same integers.

8.2 ARRAY SUBSCRIPTS

A subscript is used to differentiate between the individual array elements and to allow us to specify which array element is to be manipulated. Any expression of type `int` may be used as an array subscript. However, to create a valid reference, the value of this subscript must lie between 0 and one less than the declared size of the array.

Understanding the distinction between an array subscript value and an array element value is essential. The original array `x` from Fig. 8.1 follows. The subscripted variable `x[i]` references a particular element of this array. If `i` has the value 0, the subscript value is 0, and `x[0]` is referenced. The value of `x[0]` in this case is `16.0`. If `i` has the value 2, the subscript value is 2, and the value of x[i] is 6.0. If i has the value 8, the subscript value is 8, and we cannot predict the value of x[i] because the subscript value is out of the allowable range.

Array x

x[0]	x[1]	x[2]	x[3]	x[4]	x[5]	x[6]	x[7]
16.0	12.0	6.0	8.0	2.5	12.0	14.0	–54.5

EXAMPLE 8.6

Table 8.2 lists some sample statements involving the array x above. The variable i is assumed to be of type int with value 5. Make sure you understand each statement.

The two attempts to display element x[10], which is not in the array, may result in a run-time error, but they are more likely to print incorrect results. Consider the call to printf that uses (int)x[4] as a subscript expression. Since this expression evaluates to 2, the value of x[2] (and *not* x[4]) is printed. If the value of (int)x[4] were outside the range 0 through 7, its use as a subscript expression would not reference a valid array element.

Table 8.2   Some Statements That Manipulate Array x When i is 5

Statement	Explanation
`printf("%d  %.1f", 4, x[4]);`	Displays 4 and 2.5 (value of x[4])
`printf("%d  %.1f", i, x[i]);`	Displays 5 and 12.0 (value of x[5])
`printf("%.1f", x[i] + 1);`	Displays 13.0 (value of x[5] plus 1)
`printf("%.1f", x[i] + i);`	Displays 17.0 (value of x[5] plus 5)
`printf("%.1f", x[i + 1]);`	Displays 14.0 (value of x[6])
`printf("%.1f", x[i + i]);`	Invalid attempt to display x[10]
`printf("%.1f", x[2 * i]);`	Invalid attempt to display x[10]
`printf("%.1f", x[2 * i - 3]);`	Displays –54.5 (value of x[7])
`printf("%.1f", x[(int)x[4]]);`	Displays 6.0 (value of x[2])
`printf("%.1f", x[i++];`	Displays 12.0 (value of x[5]); then assigns 6 to i
`printf("%.1f", x[--i];`	Assigns 5 (6 - 1) to i and then displays 12.0 (value of x[5])
`x[i - 1] = x[i];`	Assigns 12.0 (value of x[5]) to x[4]
`x[i] = x[i + 1];`	Assigns 14.0 (value of x[6]) to x[5]
`x[i] - 1 = x[i];`	Illegal assignment statement

Array Subscripts

SYNTAX: *aname* [*subscript*]

EXAMPLE: `b[i + 1]`

INTERPRETATION: The *subscript* may be any expression of type `int`. Each time a subscripted variable is encountered in a program the subscript is evaluated and its value determines which element of array *aname* is referenced.

NOTE: It is the programmer's responsibility to verify that the *subscript* is within the declared range. If the subscript is in error, an invalid reference will be made. Although occasionally a run-time error message will be printed, more often an invalid reference will cause a side effect whose origin is difficult for the programmer to pinpoint. The side effect can also lead to incorrect program results.

EXERCISES FOR SECTION 8.2

Self-Check

1. Show the contents of array `x` after executing the valid statements in Table 8.2.
2. For the new array derived in Exercise 1, describe what happens when the valid statements in Table 8.2 are executed for `i = 3`.

8.3 USING INDEXED for LOOPS TO PROCESS ARRAYS

Very often, we wish to process the elements of an array in sequence, starting with element zero. An example would be scanning data into the array or printing its contents. In C, we can accomplish this processing easily using an *indexed* `for` loop, a counting loop whose loop control variable runs from zero to one less than the array size. Using the loop counter as in an array *index* (subscript) gives access to each array element in turn.

EXAMPLE 8.7

The following array `square` will be used to store the squares of the integers 0 through 10 (e.g., `square[0]` is 0, `square[10]` is 100). We assume that the name `SIZE` has been defined to be 11.

```
int square[SIZE], i;
```

The `for` loop

```
for  (i = 0;  i < SIZE;  ++i)
    square[i] = i * i;
```

initializes this array, as shown.

Array square

[0]	[1]	[2]	[3]	[4]	[5]	[6]	[7]	[8]	[9]	[10]
0	1	4	9	16	25	36	49	64	81	100

Statistical Computations Using Arrays

One common use of arrays is for storage of a collection of related data values. Once the values are stored, some simple statistical computations may be performed. In Fig. 8.2, the array x is used for this purpose.

The program in Fig. 8.2 uses three `for` loops to process the array x. The constant macro `MAX_ITEM` determines the size of the array. The variable i is used as the loop control variable and array subscript in each loop.

The first `for` loop,

```
for  (i = 0;  i < MAX_ITEM;  ++i)
    scanf("%lf", &x[i]);
```

stores one input value into each element of array x (the first item is placed in x[0], the next in x[1], and so on). The call to `scanf` is repeated for each value of i from 0 to 7; each repetition gets a new data value and stores it in x[i]. The subscript i determines which array element receives the next data value.

The second `for` loop is used to accumulate (in sum) the sum of all values stored in the array. The loop also accumulates (in sum_sqr) the sum of the squares of all element values. The formulas implemented by this loop are

$$sum = \texttt{x[0]} + \texttt{x[1]} + \cdots + \texttt{x[6]} + \texttt{x[7]} = \sum_{i=0}^{\texttt{MAX\_ITEM}-1} \texttt{x[i]}$$

$$sum\_sqr = \texttt{x[0]}^2 + \texttt{x[1]}^2 + \cdots + \texttt{x[6]}^2 + \texttt{x[7]}^2 = \sum_{i=0}^{\texttt{MAX\_ITEM}-1} \texttt{x[i]}^2$$

This loop will be discussed in detail later.

Figure 8.2   Program to Print a Table of Differences

```c
/*
 * Computes the mean and standard deviation of an array of data and prints  */
 * the difference between each value and the mean.
 */

#include <stdio.h>
#include <math.h>

#define MAX_ITEM  8  /* maximum number of items in list of data              */

int
main(void)
{
      double x[MAX_ITEM], /* data list                                       */
             mean,        /* mean (average) of the data                      */
             st_dev,      /* standard deviation of the data                  */
             sum,         /* sum of the data                                 */
             sum_sqr;     /* sum of the squares of the data                  */
      int    i;

      /* Gets the data                                                       */
      printf("Enter %d numbers separated by blanks or <return>s\n> ",
             MAX_ITEM);
      for  (i = 0;  i < MAX_ITEM;  ++i)
          scanf("%lf", &x[i]);

      /* Computes the sum and the sum of the squares of all data             */
      sum = 0;
      sum_sqr = 0;
      for  (i = 0;  i < MAX_ITEM;  ++i) {
          sum += x[i];
          sum_sqr += x[i] * x[i];
      }

      /* Computes and prints the mean and standard deviation                 */
      mean = sum / MAX_ITEM;
      st_dev = sqrt(sum_sqr / MAX_ITEM - mean * mean);
      printf("The mean is %.2f.\n", mean);
      printf("The standard deviation is %.2f.\n", st_dev);

      /* Displays the difference between each item and the mean              */
      printf("\nTable of differences between data values and mean\n");
      printf("Index      Item      Difference\n");
      for  (i = 0;  i < MAX_ITEM;  ++i)
          printf("%3d    %9.2f      %9.2f\n", i, x[i], x[i] - mean);
```

(continued)

Figure 8.2 *(continued)*

```
      return (0);
}
```

```
Enter 8 numbers separated by blanks or <return>s
> 16   12   6   8   2.5   12   14   -54.5
The mean is 2.00.
The standard deviation is 21.75.

Table of differences between data values and mean
Index        Item        Difference
  0          16.00          14.00
  1          12.00          10.00
  2           6.00           4.00
  3           8.00           6.00
  4           2.50           0.50
  5          12.00          10.00
  6          14.00          12.00
  7         -54.50         -56.50
```

The last `for` loop,

```
for  (i = 0;  i < MAX_ITEM;  ++i)
     printf("%3d      %9.2f      %9.2f\n", i, x[i],
              x[i] - mean);
```

prints a table. Each line of the table displays an array subscript, an array element, and the difference between that element and the mean, `x[i]` − `mean`. Note how the placeholders in the format string of the call to `printf` cause each column of values in the output table to be lined up under its respective column heading.

Now that we have seen the entire program, we will take a closer look at the computation `for` loop:

```
/* Computes the sum and the sum of the squares of all data */
sum = 0;
sum_sqr = 0;
for  (i = 0;  i < MAX_ITEM;  ++i) {
    sum += x[i];
    sum_sqr += x[i] * x[i];
}
```

This loop accumulates the sum of all eight elements of array x in the variable
sum. Each time the loop body is repeated, the next element of array x is added
to sum. Then this array element value is squared, and its square is added to the
sum being accumulated in sum_sqr. The execution of this program fragment is
traced in Table 8.3 for the first three repetitions of the loop.

The *standard deviation* of a set of data is a measure of the spread of the
data values around the mean. A small standard deviation indicates that the data
values are all relatively close to the average value. For MAX_ITEM data items, if
we assume that x is an array whose lowest subscript is 0, the standard deviation
is given by the formula

$$standard\ deviation = \sqrt{\frac{\displaystyle\sum_{i=0}^{MAX\_ITEM-1} x[i]^2}{MAX\_ITEM} - mean^2}$$

Table 8.3   Partial Trace of Computing for Loop

Statement	i	x[i]	sum	sum_sqr	Effect
sum = 0;			0.0		Initializes sum
sum_sqr = 0;				0.0	Initializes sum_sqr
for (i = 0;	0	16.0			Initializes i to 0
i < MAX_ITEM;					which is less than 8
...					
sum += x[i];			16.0		Adds x[0] to sum
sum_sqr +=					
x[i] * x[i];				256.0	Adds 256.0 to sum_sqr
increment and test i	1	12.0			1 < 8 is true
sum += x[i];			28.0		Adds x[1] to sum
sum_sqr +=					
x[i] * x[i];				400.0	Adds 144.0 to sum_sqr
increment and test i	2	6.0			2 < 8 is true
sum += x[i];			34.0		Adds x[2] to sum
sum_sqr +=					
x[i] * x[i];				436.0	Adds 36.0 to sum_sqr

In Fig. 8.2, this formula is implemented by the statement

```
st_dev = sqrt(sum_sqr / MAX_ITEM - mean * mean);
```

Program Style   *Using Loop Control Variables as Array Subscripts*

In Fig. 8.2, the variable `i`, which is the counter of each indexed `for` loop, determines which array element is manipulated during each loop repetition. The use of the loop control variable as an array subscript is common, because it allows the programmer to specify easily the sequence in which the elements of an array are to be manipulated. Each time the value of the loop control variable is increased, the next array element is automatically selected. Note that the same loop control variable is used in all three loops. This reuse is not necessary but is permitted since the loop control variable is always initialized at loop entry. Thus, `i` is reset to 0 when each loop is entered.

EXERCISE FOR SECTION 8.3

Self-Check

1. Write indexed `for` loops to fill the arrays described in Exercise 3 at the end of Section 8.1. Each array element should be assigned the value specified for it.

8.4 USING INDIVIDUAL ARRAY ELEMENTS AS INPUT ARGUMENTS

We have seen that we can use individual elements of numeric arrays in expressions for computation just as we would use simple numeric variables. We can also use array elements as actual arguments in function calls. However, array elements *cannot* be used as formal parameters in function prototypes. An array element used as an actual input argument should correspond to a formal parameter that is a simple variable of the same type as the array element. For example, the program in Fig. 8.3 assigns to array `rounded_x` the result of calling function `round` on each element of `x`. The definition of function `round` is taken from Fig. 6.7.

The call to function `round` in Fig. 8.3

```
x_rounded[i] = round(x[i], FRAC_PLACES);
```

uses the array element `x[i]` as an actual input argument. This call is valid because each element of array `x` is of type `double` and the first formal para-

**Figure 8.3   Program to Compute Differences from Mean
with Original and Rounded Data**

```
/*
 * Rounds each element of data list leaving FRAC_PLACES digits to the
 * right of the decimal point. Investigates the effect of the rounding on
 * a table of differences from the mean.
 */
#include <stdio.h>
#include <math.h>

#define X_SIZE      8
#define FRAC_PLACES 2

/*
 * Rounds the value of x to designated number of decimal places
 * Pre:  x is defined and places is greater than or equal to zero.
 */
double
round(double x, int places)
{
    int    sign;      /* -1 if x negative, 1 otherwise              */
    double power,     /* 10 raised to the places power              */
           temp_x,    /* copy of |x| with decimal point moved places
                            places to the right.                    */
           x_rounded; /* function result                           */

    /* Saves sign of x  */
    if (x < 0)
        sign = -1;
    else
        sign = 1;

    /* Computes rounded value */
    if (places >= 0) {
        power = pow(10.0, places);
        temp_x = fabs(x) * power;
        x_rounded = floor(temp_x + 0.5) / power * sign;
    } else {
        printf("\nError:  second argument to round cannot be negative.\n");
```

(continued)

Figure 8.3   *(continued)*

```
            printf("No rounding done.\n");
            x_rounded = x;
      }
      return (x_rounded);
}

int
main(void)
{
      double x[X_SIZE],          /* data list                  */
             x_rounded[X_SIZE], /* rounded data list          */
             sum, rd_sum,        /* sums of two lists          */
             mean, rd_mean;      /* means of the two lists     */
      int    i;

      /* Gets data                                             */
      printf("Enter %d values> ", X_SIZE);
      for (i = 0;  i < X_SIZE;  ++i)
         scanf("%lf", &x[i]);

      /* Rounds the data and computes means                    */
      sum = 0;
      rd_sum = 0;
      for (i = 0;  i < X_SIZE;  ++i) {
         x_rounded[i] = round(x[i], FRAC_PLACES);
         sum += x[i];
         rd_sum += x_rounded[i];
      }
      mean = sum / X_SIZE;
      rd_mean = round(rd_sum / X_SIZE, FRAC_PLACES);

      /* Prints table of differences from the means            */
      printf
        ("\n Original    Difference       Rounded    Difference from\n");
      printf("    data        from mean         data     rounded mean\n");
      for (i = 0;  i < X_SIZE;  ++i)
         printf("%10.4f     %9.4f   %11.2f      %10.2f\n", x[i],
                 x[i] - mean, x_rounded[i], x_rounded[i] - rd_mean);
```

(continued)

Figure 8.3   *(continued)*

```
    /* Compares means                                          */
    printf("\nmean of original data:          %.4f\n", mean);
    printf("rounded mean of rounded data:  %.2f\n", rd_mean);
    printf("Original is %.4f ", fabs(mean - rd_mean));
    if (mean > rd_mean)
          printf("greater than rounded mean\n");
    else
          printf("less than rounded mean\n");

    return (0);
}
```

Enter 8 values> 1.111 2.222 3.333 4.444 5.555 6.666 7.777 8.888

Original data	Difference from mean	Rounded data	Difference from rounded mean
1.1110	-3.8885	1.11	-3.89
2.2220	-2.7775	2.22	-2.78
3.3330	-1.6665	3.33	-1.67
4.4440	-0.5555	4.44	-0.56
5.5550	0.5555	5.56	0.56
6.6660	1.6665	6.67	1.67
7.7770	2.7775	7.78	2.78
8.8880	3.8885	8.89	3.89

```
mean of original data:          4.9995
rounded mean of rounded data:  5.00
Original is 0.0005 less than rounded mean
```

meter of function round is also of type double. The for loop in which we find this call to round

```
for  (i = 0;  i < X_SIZE;  ++i) {
    x_rounded[i] = round(x[i], FRAC_PLACES);
    sum += x[i];
    rd_sum += x_rounded[i];
}
```

causes the call to be executed once for each element of array x, since the loop control variable i takes on the values 0, 1, . . . , 6, 7, and this same variable is used as the subscript on **x**. The variable **i** is also the subscript used on array **x_rounded**, so on each iteration of the **for** loop, a rounded data value is stored in a different element of **x_rounded**.

Notice that the definition of the function **round** is exactly as it was in Fig. 6.7. No modification is necessary for **round** to process type **double** values taken one at a time from an array. It simply does not matter to function **round** whether the value of its first formal parameter comes from an actual argument that is a simple type **double** variable, from an argument that is a type **double** array element, or from an argument that is any other numeric expression.

EXERCISES FOR SECTION 8.4

Self-Check

1. Write a statement that assigns to **seg_len** the length of a line segment from $x_i y_i$ to $x_{i+1} y_{i+1}$ using the formula

$$\sqrt{(x_{i+1} - x_i)^2 + (y_{i+1} - y_i)^2}$$

Assume that x_i represents the ith element of array **x**, and y_i represents the ith element of array **y**.

2. Write a **for** loop that sums the even values from the **LIST_SIZE**-element array **list**. For example, the sum for this list would be **104** (**30 + 12 + 62**).

Array list

list[0]	list[1]	list[2]	list[3]	list[4]	list[5]
30	12	51	17	45	62

Call function **even** from Fig. 6.9.

3. Write a **for** loop that sums the even-numbered elements (elements 0, 2, and 4) from array **list**. For the list shown in Exercise 2, the sum would be **126** (**30 + 51 + 45**).

Programming

1. Write a program to store an input list of ten integers in an array; then print a table similar to the following showing each data value and what percentage each value is of the total of all ten values.

```
n       % of total

8          4.00
12         6.00
18         9.00
25        12.50
```

```
n      % of total

24       12.00
30       15.00
28       14.00
22       11.00
23       11.50
10        5.00
```

8.5 USING INDIVIDUAL ARRAY ELEMENTS AS OUTPUT ARGUMENTS

An individual array element can be used in all the ways a simple variable of the same type can be used, including as an actual output argument. We saw an example of this usage in the program of Fig. 8.2. The very first `for` loop of the program calls the `scanf` function with the address of each element of array `x` in succession.

```
for  (i = 0;  i < MAX_ITEM;  ++i)
    scanf("%lf", &x[i]);
```

Using array elements as output arguments in calls to user-defined functions is equally valid. Figure 8.4 shows the prototype of a function that converts an integer time on a 24-hour clock to a time on a 12-hour clock (e.g., 2052 to 8:52). The main program uses this function to convert a list of 24-hour-clock times to lists of the equivalent hours and minutes of 12-hour-clock times. We show only the program outline. You will be asked to complete the program in the exercises at the end of this section.

Figure 8.4   Outline of Program to Convert List of Times from 24-hour Clock to 12-hour Clock

```
/*
 * Converts a list of 24-hour-clock times to lists of the components of
 * equivalent 12-hour-clock times
 */
. . .

#define T_SIZE 20
```

(continued)

Figure 8.4 *(continued)*

```
/*
 *  Converts a 24-hour-clock time to an equivalent 12-hour-clock time.
 *  Pre:  time is a value between 1 and 2400;
 *        hrsp and minp are addresses of type int variables
 *  Post: equivalent 12-hour-clock time is expressed as integer hours and
 *        minutes and stored in the variables pointed to by hrsp and minp
 */
void
convert_to_12hr(int  time,       /* input - 24-hour-clock time        */
                int *hrsp,       /* output - hours                    */
                int *minp)       /* output - minutes                  */
{
     /* conversion code  . . . */
}

int
main(void)
{
     int  t_24[T_SIZE],        /* list of 24-hour-clock times         */
          t_12_hrs[T_SIZE],    /* lists representing equivalent 12-   */
          t_12_min[T_SIZE],    /*    hour times in hours and minutes  */
          i;

     /* Code to fill t_24 with input data  . . . */

     /* Converts 24-hour-clock times to 12-hour-clock times           */
     for  (i = 0;  i < T_SIZE;  ++i)
          convert_to_12hr(t_24[i], &t_12_hrs[i], &t_12_min[i]);

     /*  Further processing . . . */
}
```

In the for loop that converts the list of times, the argument list in the function call

```
convert_to_12hr(t_24[i], &t_12_hrs[i], &t_12_min[i]);
```

supplies the value of an element of array t_24 as an input argument and the addresses of corresponding elements of t_12_hrs and t_12_min as output arguments. Table 8.4 traces the first few calls to convert_to_12hr, assuming these contents of t_24. Figure 8.5 shows the data areas of functions main and convert_to_12hr as they appear just before the return from the third call.

Array t_24

t_24[0]	t_24[1]	t_24[2]	t_24[3]	t_24[4]	
2052	817	1925	1305	345	. . .

Table 8.4   Partial Trace of for Loop Calling convert_to_12hr

Statement	i	t_24[i]	t_12_hrs[i]	t_12_min[i]	Effect

`for (i=0; i<T_SIZE;...`
 `   convert_to_12_hr`
 `      (t_24[i],`
 `      &t_12_hrs[i],`
 `      &t_12_min[i])`
	0	2052	?
			
			 8
				?
				
				 52
					0 < 20 is true.
					
					 2052 is broken into 12-hour-clock hour and minute portions, which are stored in ith elements of t_12_hrs and t_12_min.

`Increment and test i`
 `(... i<T_SIZE   ;...`
 `   convert_to_12_hr`
 `      (t_24[i],`
 `      &t_12_hrs[i],`
 `      &t_12_min[i])`
	1	817
		
		 8
			
			 17
					1 < 20 is true.
					
					 817 is broken into 12-hour-clock hour and minute portions, which are stored in ith elements of t_12_hrs and t_12_min.

`Increment and test i`
 `(... i<T_SIZE   ;...`
 `   convert_to_12_hr`
 `      (t_24[i],`
 `      &t_12_hrs[i],`
 `      &t_12_min[i])`
	2	1925
		
		 7
			
			 25
					2 < 20 is true.
					
					 1925 is broken into 12-hour-clock hour and minute portions, which are stored in ith elements of t_12_hrs and t_12_min.

. . .		See Fig. 8.5			

**Figure 8.5
Data Areas
of Functions
main and
convert_to_12hr
Just Before
Return from
Third Call**

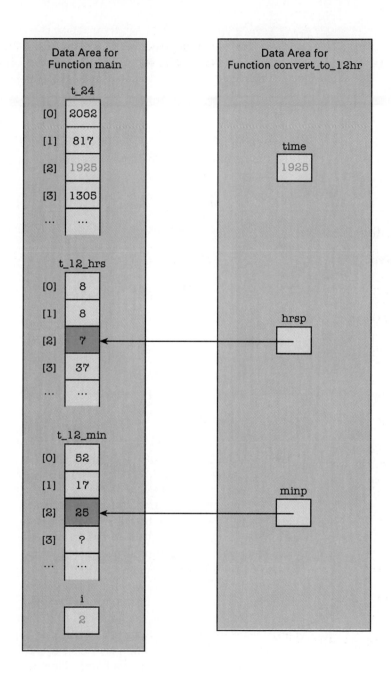

Clearly, the conversion code needed to complete function `convert_to_12hr` must contain assignment statements beginning

```
*hrsp = . . .
*minp = . . .
```

These statements use indirection to follow the pointers in `hrsp` and `minp` to send the function results back to the calling module.

EXERCISES FOR SECTION 8.5

Self-Check

1. Complete function `convert_to_12hr` from Fig. 8.4.

Programming

1. Complete the program in Fig. 8.4 so that it prints a table listing the 24-hour-clock times and the 12-hour-clock times with a colon between the hour and minute values.

8.6 USING ARRAYS AS INPUT ARGUMENTS

Until now, all input arguments to a function that we have seen have been single values that were copied into formal parameters inside the function's data area. The function then worked with its own copy of each argument value. C provides no analogous automatic copying of whole arrays used as input arguments. Rather, when an array name with no subscript appears in the argument list of a function call, what is actually stored in the function's corresponding formal parameter is the address of the initial array element. Subscripting operations can then be applied to the formal parameter to access all of the array's elements. However, the function is manipulating the original array, not its own personal copy, so an assignment to one of the array elements by a statement in the function changes the contents of the original array. ANSI C does provide a qualifier that we can include in the declaration of the array formal parameter in order to notify the C compiler that the array is only an input to the function and that the function does not intend to modify the array. This qualifier allows the compiler to mark any attempt to change an array element within the function.

EXAMPLE 8.8   Function `get_max` in Fig. 8.6 can be called to find the largest value in an array. It uses the variable `list` as an array input parameter.

Figure 8.6   Function to Find the Largest Element in an Array

```
/*
 *  Returns the largest of the first n values in array list
 *  Pre:  First n elements of array list are defined and n > 0
 */
int
get_max(const int list[], /* input - list of n integers              */
        int        n)      /* input - number of list elements to examine */
{
      int i,
          cur_large;       /* largest value so far                    */

      /*  Initial array element is largest so far.                    */
      cur_large = list[0];

      /*  Compare each remaining list element to the largest so far;
          save the larger                                             */
      for  (i = 1;  i < n;  ++i)
          if (list[i] > cur_large)
              cur_large = list[i];

      return (cur_large);
}
```

Let's focus on the declaration of the formal parameter `list` within the prototype of function `get_max`,

```
const int list[]
```

The type qualifier `const` alerts both the reader of the code and the compiler that `list` is an input argument only. Note that we have not stated in the argument declaration how many elements are in `list`. Because we are not allocating space in memory for copying the array, the compiler does not need to know the size of the array parameter. In fact, since we do not provide the size, we have the flexibility to pass to the function an array of any number of integers.

If `x` is a five-element array of type `int` values, the statement

```
x_large = get_max(x, 5);
```

causes function `get_max` to search array `x` for its largest element; this value is returned and stored in `x_large`. Figure 8.7 shows the argument correspondence for this call. Notice that what is stored in `list` is actually the address of the type `int` variable `x[0]`. In fact, this call to `get_max` would execute exactly like the call pictured in Fig. 8.7:

```
x_large = get_max(&x[0], 5);
```

However, this call using `&x[0]` leads the reader of the code to expect that `get_max` may be using `x[0]` as an output argument. For readability, you should use the name of an array (with no subscript) when you call a function that processes the list the array represents.

In Section 8.5, when we passed individual array elements as output arguments as in

```
convert_to_12hr(t_24[i], &t_12_hrs[i], &t_12_min[i]);
```

from Fig. 8.4, the formal parameters corresponding to actual arguments `&t_12_hrs[i]` and `&t_12_min[i]` were declared to be of type `int *`. Yet in the alternate form of the call to `get_max`, `get_max(&x[0], 5)`, the address of an array element is matched with a formal parameter declared as

```
const int list[]
```

**Figure 8.7
Argument
Correspondence
for** `x_large =`
`get_max(x, 5);`

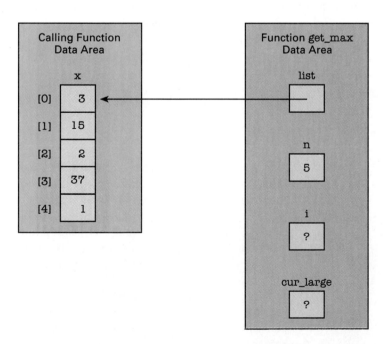

Because we have already discussed the reason that the `const` qualifier is used, let's just consider these possible parameter declarations:

```
int  list[]
int *list
```

The first tells us that the actual argument is an array. However, because C passes an array argument by passing the address of its initial element, the second declaration would be equally valid for an integer array parameter. In this text, we will usually use the first form to declare a parameter representing an array, saving the second form to represent simple output parameters. You should take care, however, to remember that a formal parameter of the form

$type_1$ `*param`

is compatible with an actual argument that is an array of $type_1$ values.   ◀

EXAMPLE 8.9   In Fig. 8.8, we have rewritten the program from Fig. 8.2 that prints a table of differences between array elements and the average of the array values. We have omitted the standard deviation computation and defined a function to find the average of the array elements.

Figure 8.8   Program with Function to Average an Array of Numbers

```
/*
 * Computes the average (mean) of a list of data and prints the difference
 * between each value and the average.
 */

#include <stdio.h>

/*
 * Computes the average of a list of numbers
 * Pre:  n > 0 and first n elements of list are defined
 */
double
average(const double list[], /* input - list of numbers                 */
        int           n)      /* input - number of list elements to process */
```

(continued)

Figure 8.8 *(continued)*

```c
{
      int    i;
      double sum = 0;

      for (i = 0;  i < n;  ++i)
          sum += list[i];

      return (sum / n);
}

#define MAX_ITEM 8

int
main(void)
{
      int    i;
      double x[MAX_ITEM], mean;

      /*  Gets the data                                                    */
      printf("Enter %d numbers> ", MAX_ITEM);
      for (i = 0;  i < MAX_ITEM;  ++i)
          scanf("%lf", &x[i]);

      /*  Computes and prints the mean                                     */
      mean = average(x, MAX_ITEM);
      printf("The mean is %.2f\n", mean);

      /*  Displays the difference between each item and the mean           */
      printf("\nTable of differences between data values and mean\n");
      printf("Index      Item      Difference\n");
      for (i = 0;  i < MAX_ITEM;  ++i)
          printf("%3d     %9.2f     %9.2f\n", i, x[i], x[i] - mean);

      return (0);
}
```

In the main function of Fig. 8.8, the statement

```
mean = average(x, MAX_ITEM);
```

calls function `average` to compute the mean of all `MAX_ITEM` elements of array `x`. The result returned is stored in `mean`. The fact that function `average` uses the value passed as its second argument to determine how many array elements to include in its computation means that we could use the same function to average just the first four array elements by executing the statement

```
mean = average(x, 4);
```

Later in this chapter, we will see that sometimes an array is only partially filled by a program, so a function's flexibility regarding the number of array elements it processes is very useful. ←

An Array Input Parameter

SYNTAX: const *element-type array-name* [ ]
                                    or
          const *element-type *array-name*

EXAMPLE: double
          find_min(const double data[], /* input - array of numbers */
                      int   data_size) /* input - number of
                                                    elements   */
          {
              int   i;
              double small; /* smallest value so far   */

              small = data[0];
              for (i = 1;   i < data_size;   ++i)
                  if (data[i] < small)
                          small = data[i];

              return (small);
          }

INTERPRETATION: The syntax shown is valid within the parameter list of a function prototype. In this context, the reserved word `const` indicates that the variable declared is strictly an input parameter and will not be modified by the function. This fact is important because the value of the declared formal parameter will be the address of the actual argument

CONST = CONSTANT

(continued)

array; if `const` were omitted, modification of the argument would be possible. The data type of an array element is indicated by *element-type*. The [ ] after *array_name* means that the corresponding actual argument will be an array. What is actually stored in the formal parameter when the function is called is the address of the initial element of the actual argument array. Since this value is a pointer to a location used to store a value of type *element-type,* the second syntax option is equivalent to the first.

Searching an Array

A common problem encountered in programming is the need to search an array in order to find the location of a desired value. For example, we might wish to search an array of student IDs to locate a particular ID called the *target*. This search can be accomplished by examining in turn each array element using a loop and by testing whether it matches the target. The search loop should be exited when the target value is found; this process is called a *linear search*. An algorithm for a linear search follows.

Algorithm

1. Assume the target has not been found.
2. Start with the initial array element.
3. Repeat while the target is not found and there are more array elements
   4. if the current element matches the target
      5. Set a flag to indicate that the target has been found.
   else
      6. Advance to the next array element.
7. if the target was found
   8. Return the target index as the search result.
   else
   9. Return −1 as the search result.

A function that implements this algorithm is shown in Fig. 8.9. This function returns the index of the target if it is present in the array; otherwise, it returns −1. The local variable `i` (initial value 0) selects the array element that is compared to the target value.

The type `int` variable `found` is used to represent the logical concept of whether the target has been found yet and is tested in the loop repetition condition. The variable is initially set to 0 for false (the target is certainly not found before we begin searching for it) and is reset to 1 for true only if the target is found. After `found` becomes true or the entire array has been searched, the loop

Figure 8.9   Function That Searches for a Target Value in an Array

```
#define NOT_FOUND -1    /*  Value returned by search function
                            if target not found */

/*
 *  Searches for target item in first n elements of array arr
 *  Returns index of target or NOT_FOUND
 *  Pre:  target and first n elements of array arr are defined and n>=0
 */
int
search(const int arr[],  /*  array to search                         */
       int       target, /*  value searched for                      */
       int       n)      /*  number of array elements to search      */
{
      int i,
          found = 0,      /*  whether or not target has been found    */
          where;          /*  index where target found or NOT_FOUND   */

      /*  Compares each element to target                            */
      i = 0;
      while (!found && i < n) {
          if (arr[i] == target)
                found = 1;
          else
                ++i;
      }

      /* Returns index of element matching target or NOT_FOUND        */
      if (found)
            where = i;
      else
            where = NOT_FOUND;

      return (where);
}
```

is exited, and the decision statement following the loop defines the value returned. If array `ids` is declared in the calling function, the assignment statement

```
index = search(ids, 4902, ID_SIZE);
```

calls function `search` to search the first `ID_SIZE` elements of array `ids` for the target ID `4902`. The subscript of the first occurrence of `4902` is saved in `index`. If `4902` is not found, then index is set to −1.

Self-Check

1. What value is returned by function `search` if array elements 1, 3, and 5 all contain the target? Modify `search` so that it returns how many times `target` is found in the array, instead of returning *where* `target` is first found.

Programming

1. Define a function `multiply` that computes and returns the product of the type `int` elements of its array input argument. The function should have a second input argument telling the number of array elements to use.
2. Define a function `abs_table` that takes an input array argument with type `double` values and prints a table displaying the data and their absolute values like the table shown.

```
    x      |x|
   38.4    38.4
 -101.7   101.7
   -2.1     2.1
    .  .  .
```

8.7 USING ARRAYS AS OUTPUT OR INPUT/OUTPUT ARGUMENTS

In C, it is not legal for a function's return type to be an array; therefore defining a function of the variety modeled in Fig. 8.10 requires use of an output argument to send the result array back to the calling module. You also have the option of returning a pointer to this array as the function value, an option we will explore in Chapter 9 when we discuss strings.

In Section 6.3, we saw that when we use simple output parameters, the calling function must declare variables into which the function subprogram will

**Figure 8.10
Diagram of a
Function That
Computes an
Array Result**

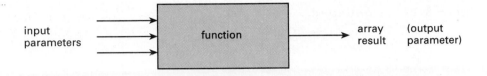

store its results. Similarly, a function computing an array result depends on its caller to provide an array variable into which the result can be stored.

EXAMPLE 8.10

Function `add_arrays` in Fig. 8.11 adds two arrays. The sum of arrays `ar1` and `ar2` is defined as `arsum` such that `arsum[i]` is equal to `ar1[i]` + `ar2[i]` for each subscript `i`. The last parameter, `n`, specifies how many corresponding elements are summed.

The formal parameter list declaration

```
const double ar1[],
const double ar2[],
double        arsum[],
int           n
```

indicates that formal parameters `ar1`, `ar2`, and `arsum` stand for actual argument arrays whose elements are of type `double` and that `ar1` and `ar2` are strictly input parameters, as is `n`. The function can process type `double` arrays of any size as long as the preconditions stated in the initial block comment are met.

Figure 8.11   Function to Add Two Arrays

```
/*
 *  Adds corresponding elements of arrays ar1 and ar2, storing the result
 *  in arsum. Processes first n elements only.
 *  Pre:  First n elements of ar1 and ar2 are defined.  arsum's
 *        corresponding actual argument has a declared size >= n (n >= 0)
 */
void
add_arrays(const double ar1[],    /* input -                              */
           const double ar2[],    /*     arrays being added               */
           double       arsum[], /* output - sum of corresponding
                                              elements of ar1 and ar2     */
           int          n)       /* input - number of element pairs summed */
```

(continued)

Figure 8.11 *(continued)*

```
{
     int i;

     /* Adds corresponding elements of ar1 and ar2                    */
     for  (i = 0;  i < n;  ++i)
          arsum[i] = ar1[i] + ar2[i];
}
```

If we assume that a calling function has declared three 5-element arrays x, y, and x_plus_y and has filled x and y with data, the call

```
add_arrays(x, y, x_plus_y, 5);
```

would lead to the memory setup pictured in Fig. 8.12.

After execution of the function, x_plus_y[0] will contain the sum of x[0] and y[0], or 3.5; x_plus_y[1] will contain the sum of x[1] and y[1], or 6.7; and so on. Input argument arrays x and y will be unchanged; output argument array x_plus_y will have these new contents:

x_plus_y after call to add_arrays

3.5	6.7	4.7	9.1	12.2

Address-of Operator Not Used

Note carefully that in the *call* to add_arrays there is no notational difference between the references to input argument arrays x and y and the reference to output argument array x_plus_y. Specifically, the & (address-of) operator is *not* applied to the name of the output array argument. We discussed earlier the fact that C always passes whole arrays used as arguments by storing the *address* of the initial array element in the corresponding formal parameter. Since the output parameter arsum is declared with no const qualifier, function add_arrays automatically has access and authority to change the corresponding actual array argument.

**Figure 8.12
Function Data
Areas for**
`add_arrays(x,
y, x_plus_y,
5);`

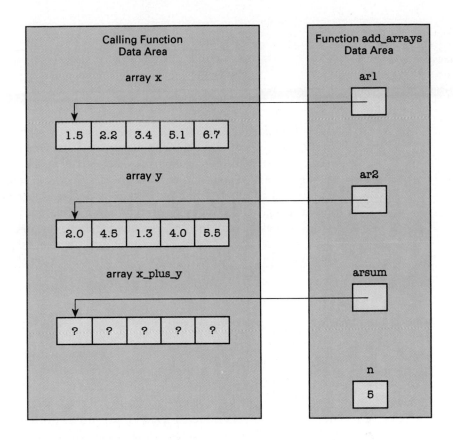

Partially Filled Arrays

Frequently, a program will need to process many lists of similar data; these lists may not all be the same length. In order to reuse an array for processing more than one data set, the programmer often declares an array large enough to hold the largest data set anticipated. This array can be used for processing shorter lists as well, provided that the program keeps track of how many array elements are actually in use.

 EXAMPLE 8.11   The purpose of function `fill_to_sentinel` is to fill a type `double` array with data until the designated sentinel value is encountered in the input data. Figure 8.13 shows both the input parameters that `fill_to_sentinel` requires and the results that are communicated through its output parameters.

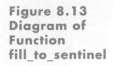

**Figure 8.13
Diagram of
Function
fill_to_sentinel**

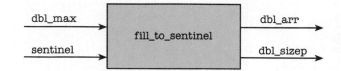

When we use an array that may be only partially filled (such as `dbl_arr` in Fig. 8.13), we must deal with *two* array sizes. One size is the array's declared size, represented by the input parameter `dbl_max`, shown in Fig. 8.13. The other is the size counting only the elements in use, represented in Fig. 8.13 by the output parameter `dbl_sizep`. The declared size is only of interest at the point in a program where the array is being filled, for it is important not to try to store values beyond the array's bounds. However, once this input step is complete, the array size relevant in the rest of the processing is the number of elements actually filled. Figure 8.14 shows an implementation of function `fill_to_sentinel`.

Figure 8.14   Function Using a Sentinel-Controlled Loop to Store Input Data in an Array

```
/*
 *  Gets data to place in dbl_arr until value of sentinel is encountered
 *  in the input. Returns number of values stored through dbl_sizep.
 *  Stops input prematurely if there are more than dbl_max data values
 *  before the sentinel or if invalid data is encountered.
 *  Pre:  sentinel and dbl_max are defined and dbl_max is the declared
 *        size of dbl_arr
 */
void
fill_to_sentinel(int     dbl_max,  /* input - declared size of dbl_arr  */
                 double  sentinel, /* input - end of data value in input
                                                list                    */
                 double  dbl_arr[],/* output - array of data            */
                 int     *dbl_sizep)/* output - number of data values
                                                stored in dbl_arr       */
{
      double data;
      int    i, status;

      /* Sentinel input loop                                            */
      i = 0;
```

(continued)

Figure 8.14 *(continued)*

```
    for  (status = scanf("%lf", &data);
          status == 1  &&  data != sentinel  &&  i < dbl_max;
          status = scanf("%lf", &data)) {
        dbl_arr[i] = data;
        ++i;
    }

    /* Issues error message on premature exit                    */
    if (status != 1) {
        printf("\n*** Error in data format ***\n");
        printf("*** Using first %d data values ***\n", i);
    } else if (data != sentinel) {
        printf("\n*** Error: too much data before sentinel ***\n");
        printf("*** Using first %d data values ***\n", i);
    }

    /* Sends back size of used portion of array                  */
    *dbl_sizep = i;
}
```

Figure 8.15 shows a main function that calls `fill_to_sentinel`. The main function is using batch mode; it issues no prompting message, but it does echo print its input data. Notice that after the call to `fill_to_sentinel`, the expression used as the upper bound on the subscripting variable in the loop that echo prints the data is not the array's declared size, `A_SIZE`. Rather, it is the variable `in_use` that designates how many elements of `arr` are currently filled.

Figure 8.15 **Driver for Testing fill_to_sentinel**

```
/* Driver to test fill_to_sentinel function */

#define A_SIZE  20
#define SENT    -1.0

int
main(void)
```

(continued)

Figure 8.15 *(continued)*

```
{
    double arr[A_SIZE];
    int    in_use,     /* number of elements of arr in use */
           i;

    fill_to_sentinel(A_SIZE, SENT, arr, &in_use);

    printf("List of data values\n");
    for  (i = 0;  i < in_use;  ++i)
        printf("%13.3f\n", arr[i]);

    return (0);
}
```

In the call to `fill_to_sentinel` in Fig. 8.15, we see another example of the difference between the way an array output argument is passed to a function and the way a simple output argument is passed. Both `arr` and `in_use` are output arguments, but the address-of operator `&` is applied only to the simple variable `in_use`. Since `arr` is an array name with no subscript, it already represents an address, the address of the initial array element. ⬅

Sorting an Array

In Section 6.4, we discussed a simple sort operation involving three numbers and we performed the sort by examining pairs of numbers and exchanging them if they were out of order. This same type of operation would be useful to sort the elements in an array. For example, we might prefer to have a grade report printed out with the student IDs in ascending order.

In this section, a fairly simple (but not very efficient) algorithm called the *bubble sort* will be discussed. A bubble sort compares adjacent array elements and exchanges their values if they are out of order. In this way, the smaller values "bubble" to the top of the array (toward element 0), while the larger values sink to the bottom of the array. The data requirements and one algorithm for a bubble sort function follow.

Problem Inputs
the array being sorted
the number of array elements

Problem Output
the sorted array

An Algorithm for a Bubble Sort

1. Repeat
    2. Examine every pair of adjacent array elements and exchange
        values that are out of order
    as long as the array is not sorted.

As an example, we will trace through one execution of Step 2, that is, we
will do one *pass* through an array being sorted. By scanning the diagrams in Fig.
8.16 from left to right, we see the effect of each comparison. The pair of array
elements being compared is shown in a darker color in each diagram. The first
pair of values (m[0] is 60, m[1] is 42) is out of order, so the values are
exchanged. The next pair of values (m[1] is now 60, m[2] is 75) is compared
in the second array; this pair is in order, as is the next pair (m[2] is 75, m[3]
is 83). The last pair (m[3] is 83, m[4] is 27) is out of order, so the values are
exchanged, as shown in the last diagram of Fig. 8.16.

**Figure 8.16
One Pass of a
Bubble Sort of
Array m**

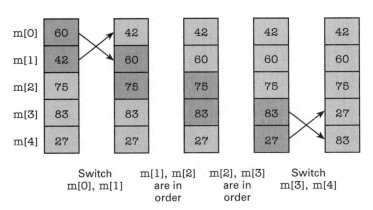

The last array shown in Fig. 8.16 is closer to being sorted than the original
is. The only value that is out of order is the number 27 in m[3]. Unfortunately,
the algorithm will need to complete three more passes through the entire array
before this value bubbles to the top of the array. In each of these passes, only
one pair of values will be out of order, so only one exchange will be made. The
contents of array m after the completion of each pass are shown in Fig. 8.17.

We can tell by looking at the contents of the array at the end of pass 4 that
the array is now sorted. However, the algorithm we have chosen calls for the
computer to recognize that the sorting is completed by making one additional
pass in which no exchanges are necessary. If no exchanges are made, then all

Figure 8.17
Array m after
Completion of
Each Pass

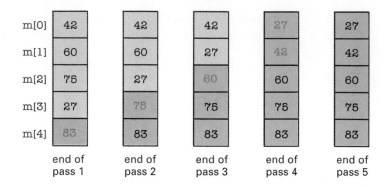

pairs must be in order. This is the reason for the extra pass shown in Fig. 8.17 and for the flag named `sorted` that is described here.

Program Variables
```
int sorted   /* flag to indicate whether any exchanges
                have been made in the current pass    */
int i        /* loop control variable and subscript   */
int pass     /* number of current pass starting with 1 */
```

Step 2 Refinement
2.1 Initialize `sorted` to 1 (for true).
2.2 Repeat for each pair of adjacent array elements
2.3   if the values in a pair are out of order
2.4   Exchange the values.
2.5   Set `sorted` to 0 (false).

Step 2 will be implemented using a `for` loop. The loop control variable `i` will also be the subscript of the first element in each pair; consequently, `i + 1` will be the subscript of the second element in each pair. During each pass, the initial value of `i` is 0. The final value of `i` must be less than the highest valid array subscript so that `i + 1` will also be in range.

For an array of n elements, the number of pairs of elements compared in a particular pass is n − `pass`, where `pass` is the number of the current pass, starting with 1 for the first pass. The reason that the number of pairs to compare decreases with each pass is that we do not need to examine array elements that are already in place. At the end of pass 1, the last array element must be in its correct place and at the end of pass 2, the last two array elements must be in their correct places, and so on. The section of the array that is already certain to be sorted is shown in a darker color in Fig. 8.17.

Function `bubble` in Fig. 8.18 performs a bubble sort on the array represented by formal parameter `list`, which is an input/output parameter. You

Figure 8.18   Bubble Sort Function for an Array of Integers

```
/*
 *   Sorts the data in array list
 *   Pre:  first n elements of list are defined and n >= 0
 */
void
bubble(int list[], /* input/output - array being sorted         */
       int n)      /* input - number of elements to sort        */
{
    int i,
        pass,     /* number of current pass through array        */
        temp,     /* temporary variable used in exchange of
                     out-of-order pairs                          */
        sorted;   /* whether or not array is definitely sorted   */

    pass = 1;
    do {
        /*  Assumes array is sorted until an out-of-order pair
            is found                                             */
        sorted = 1;

        /*  Makes a pass through possibly unsorted elements      */
        for  (i = 0;  i < n - pass;  ++i) {
            if (list[i] > list[i + 1]) {
                    /* Exchanges out-of-order pair  */
                    temp = list[i];
                    list[i] = list[i + 1];
                    list[i + 1] = temp;
                    sorted = 0;
            }
        }

        ++pass;
    } while(!sorted);
}
```

notice that its declaration is of the same form as the output parameter arrays discussed earlier in this section.

Our implementation uses the `do-while` statement for the outer loop because we can be sure the loop body must be executed at least once. There is no way to know that the array is sorted without making at least one pass through the data.

Self-Check

1. Modify function `fill_to_sentinel` from Fig. 8.14 so its return type is `int` rather than `void`. Have the function return the value 1 if no error conditions occur and 0 if there is an error. In all other respects, leave the function's purpose unchanged.

2. Can you think of a way to combine the following two statements that form the body of the `for` loop of function `fill_to_sentinel` into just one statement?

   ```
   dbl_arr[i] = data;
   ++i;
   ```

3. Modify the prototype and declarations of function `bubble` so it would sort an array of type `double` values. Be careful—some variables should still be of type `int`!

4. Assume a main function contains declarations for three type `double` arrays—c, d, and e, each with six elements. Also assume that values have been stored in all array elements. Explain the effect of each valid call to `add_arrays` (see Fig. 8.11). Explain why each invalid call is invalid.

   a. `add_arrays(ar1, ar2, c, 6);`
   b. `add_arrays(c[6], d[6], e[6], 6);`
   c. `add_arrays(c, d, e, 6);`
   d. `add_arrays(c, d, e, 7);`
   e. `add_arrays(c, d, e, 5);`
   f. `add_arrays(c, d, 6, 3);`
   g. `add_arrays(e, d, c, 6);`
   h. `add_arrays(c, c, c, 6);`
   i. `add_arrays(c, d, e, c[1]);` (if c[1] is 4.3? if c[1] is 91.7?)
   j. `add_arrays(&c[2], &d[2], &e[2], 4);`

Programming

1. Write a function that negates the type `double` values stored in an array. The first argument should be the array (an input/output parameter) and the second should be the number of elements to negate.

2. Write a function that takes two type `int` array input arguments and their effective size and produces a result array containing the absolute differences between corresponding elements. For example, for the three-element input arrays 5 −1 7 and 2 4 −2, the result would be an array containing 3 5 9.

8.8 ARRAY PROCESSING ILLUSTRATED

The next problem illustrates two common ways of selecting array elements for processing. Sometimes we need to manipulate many or all elements of an array in some uniform manner (for example, fill them with input data). In such situations, it makes sense to process the array elements in sequence (*sequential access*), starting with the first and ending with the last.

At other times, the order in which the array elements are accessed depends either on the order of the problem data or the nature of the formula that is the basis of the processing. In these situations, access to element `i + 1` of an array does not necessarily occur right after access to element `i`, so we are not using sequential access, but rather *random access*.

Case Study: Finding the Area of a Polygon

PROBLEM

You have been asked to develop a program to compute the area of a polygon represented by the (x, y) coordinates of the endpoints of the figure's sides.

ANALYSIS

Assume that the endpoints of an n-sided polygon are numbered in sequence, as shown in Fig. 8.19, where point (x_0, y_0) lies between points (x_{n-1}, y_{n-1}) and (x_1, y_1), and point (x_1, y_1) lies between points (x_0, y_0) and (x_2, y_2), and so on. We can store the coordinates of the endpoints of the polygon in a pair of parallel arrays, `x` and `y`, of size `NMAX` and then find the area of the polygon. Looking through a book on image processing, you find a formula applicable to this problem:

$$area = \frac{1}{2} \left| x_0 y_1 + x_1 y_2 + \cdots + x_{n-2} y_{n-1} + x_{n-1} y_0 \right.$$

$$\left. - y_0 x_1 - y_1 x_2 - \cdots - y_{n-2} x_{n-1} - y_{n-1} x_0 \right|$$

**Figure 8.19
Sample Polygon
with Five Sides**

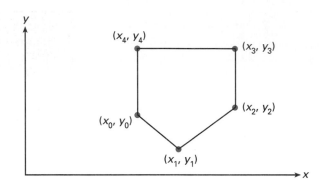

Data Requirements

Problem Constant
```
NMAX   20   /* maximum number of sides in program
                 polygons                            */
```

Problem Inputs
```
double x[NMAX]   /* array of x coordinates        */
double y[NMAX]   /* array of y coordinates        */
```

Problem Output
```
double area      /* area of the polygon           */
```

Program Variable
```
int    n         /* actual number of sides in
                    the polygon                   */
```

DESIGN

Initial Algorithm

1. Get the (x, y) coordinates and store them in arrays x and y, also defining the actual number of sides in the polygon.
2. Display the coordinates.
3. Compute the area of the polygon.
4. Display the area.

Structure Chart and Algorithm Refinements

Figure 8.20 shows the structure chart for this problem. We will implement Step 1 and Step 2 using functions get_coords and show_coords, respectively; we will implement Step 3 using function poly_area. Arrays x and y and variable n are outputs from get_coords and are passed as inputs to show_coords and poly_area.

**Figure 8.20
Structure Chart
for Finding the
Area of a
Polygon**

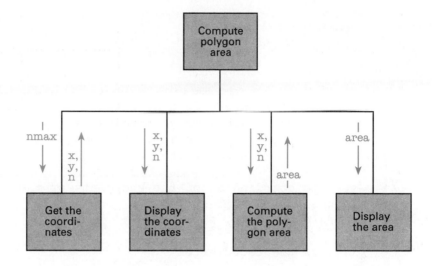

IMPLEMENTATION

Figure 8.21 shows the main function and preprocessor directives. The function begins by calling `get_coords` and `show_coords` to get and display the coordinates. Next, the statement

```
area = poly_area(x, y, n);
```

calls function `poly_area`, passing arrays `x` and `y` along with `n` as input arguments. The function result is stored in `area` and displayed by the call to `printf` in function `main`.

Figure 8.21   Main Function for Computation of Polygon Area

```
/*
 *  Computes the area of a polygon whose coordinates are taken from
 *  a data file made accessible through input redirection.
 */
#include <stdio.h>
#include <math.h>

#define NMAX  20    /* maximum number of sides                       */

/*  Function subprograms get_coords, show_coords, and poly_area
    go here.   */
```

(continued)

Figure 8.21   *(continued)*

```
int
main(void)
{
      double x[NMAX], /* array of x coordinates                       */
             y[NMAX]; /* array of y coordinates                       */
      int    n;       /* actual number of sides in the polygon        */
      double area;    /* area of the polygon                          */

      /*  Gets the coordinates of the endpoints of the polygon's sides
          and the actual number of sides                              */
      get_coords(NMAX, x, y, &n);

      /*  Displays the coordinates                                    */
      show_coords(x, y, n);

      /*  Computes area of polygon                                    */
      area = poly_area(x, y, n);

      /*  Displays area                                               */
      printf("\nPolygon area is %.2f square units\n", area);

      return (0);
}
```

▸ **IMPLEMENTATION** ▸ OF THE FUNCTION SUBPROGRAMS

Functions `get_coords` and `show_coords` are relatively straightforward; they are shown in Fig. 8.22. Function `get_coords` is similar to `fill_to_sentinel` (see Fig. 8.14) except that it fills two arrays and uses endfile checking rather than a sentinel to trigger loop exit. Since each call to `scanf` should get both an x and a y coordinate, function `scanf` will return the value 2 as the number of data items obtained on each call except on the one that hits end of file, unless there is an error in the data format. The declarations of formal parameters x, y, and np in the prototype of `get_coords`

```
double x[],
double y[],
int    *np
```

differ from the declarations of x, y, and n in the prototype of show_coords

```
const double x[],
const double y[],
int         n
```

because all three are output parameters of get_coords and input parameters of show_coords. Each function declares a local variable i to use as a loop control and subscripting variable.

Function poly_area must implement the formula for the area of a polygon given earlier and repeated here. The number of terms in this formula increases with *n*.

$$area = \frac{1}{2} \left| x_0 y_1 + x_1 y_2 + \cdots + x_{n-2} y_{n-1} + x_{n-1} y_0 \right.$$

$$\left. - y_0 x_1 - y_1 x_2 - \cdots - y_{n-2} x_{n-1} - y_{n-1} x_0 \right|$$

Rearranging terms, we get

$$area = \frac{1}{2} \left| x_0 y_1 - y_0 x_1 + x_1 y_2 - y_1 x_2 + \cdots + x_{n-2} y_{n-1} - y_{n-2} x_{n-1} + x_{n-1} y_0 - y_{n-1} x_0 \right|$$

Figure 8.22   Functions get_coords and show_coords

```
/*
 * Gets up to nmax (x, y) coordinates for storage in parallel arrays x and y.
 * Also sends back through np the actual number of coordinate pairs
 * obtained.
 * Pre:  nmax is defined and <= the declared sizes of output array
 *       parameters x and y.
 */
void
get_coords(int      nmax,   /* input - maximum number of coordinate pairs */
           double   x[],    /* output - arrays holding                    */
           double   y[],    /*             (x, y) coordinates             */
           int      *np)    /* output - actual number of coordinate pairs */
{
      int    i, status;
      double xcoord, ycoord;
```

(continued)

Figure 8.22 *(continued)*

```
      /* Input loop with exit on end of file (EOF) or invalid data    */
      i = 0;
      for  (status = scanf("%lf%lf", &xcoord, &ycoord);
            status == 2  &&  i < nmax;
            status = scanf("%lf%lf", &xcoord, &ycoord)) {
         x[i] = xcoord;
         y[i] = ycoord;
         ++i;
      }

      /* Issues error message if loop exit not triggered by end of file */
      if (status != EOF)
            if (status == 2)
                  printf("\nToo much data: first %d points used\n", nmax);
            else
                  printf("\nInvalid data: using only first %d points\n",
                          i);

      /* Defines actual number of coordinates                          */
      *np = i;
}

/*
 *  Displays the first n values in parallel array parameters x and y
 *  Pre:  First n elements of x and y must be defined
 */
void
show_coords(const double x[],  /* input - parallel arrays with        */
            const double y[],  /*             (x, y) coordinates       */
            int          n)    /* input - number of points            */
{
      int i;

      /*  Displays table heading                                       */
      printf("          x             y\n\n");

      /*  Displays n coordinate pairs                                  */
      for  (i = 0;  i < n;  ++i)
          printf("%10.2f  %10.2f\n", x[i], y[i]);
}
```

a formula we can write using summation notation.

$$area = \frac{1}{2} \left| \sum_{i=0}^{n-2} (x_i y_{i+1} - y_i x_{i+1}) + x_{n-1} y_0 - y_{n-1} x_0 \right|$$

We can use a single indexed loop to compute the sum represented by the summation notation.

Program Variables
```
int i        /* loop control and subscripting variable */
double sum   /*  sum of the xy products                */
```

Figure 8.23 shows the implementation of function `poly_area`.

Figure 8.23   Function poly_area Computing the Area of a Polygon

```
/*
 *  Computes the area of an n-sided polygon.  The coordinates of the end-
 *  points of the sides are stored in the arrays represented by x and y.
 *  Pre:   arrays x and y contain n polygon coordinates and n is greater
 *         than or equal to 3 and not greater than the declared sizes of
 *         arrays to which x and y refer.
 */
double
poly_area(const double x[],/* input - parallel arrays with (x, y)      */
          const double y[],/*          coordinates of endpoints of sides */
          int          n)  /* input - number of points                 */
{
     double sum;  /* sum of the xy products                            */
     int    i;

     sum = 0;
     for (i = 0;  i < n - 1;  ++i)
         sum += x[i] * y[i + 1]  -  y[i] * x[i + 1];

     sum  +=  x[n - 1] * y[0]  -  y[n - 1] * x[0];

     return (fabs(sum) / 2.0);
}
```

Figure 8.24 **Sample Run of Area-Computation Program**

```
        x               y

     -2.00           -2.00
      2.00           -2.00
      2.00            2.00
     -2.00            2.00
Polygon area is 16.00 square units
```

TESTING

Figure 8.24 shows a sample run of the area-computation program for a square centered around the origin of the coordinate system. For further testing, use simple polygons such as triangles and rectangles whose areas can be verified using well-known formulas. Verify that the program works for coordinates that are negative as well as positive.

Program Style   *Checking for Subscript-Range Errors*

In function `poly_area`, the indexed `for` loop adds together a collection of products of elements from arrays x and y. The array subscripts used within the loop are i and i + 1. We should verify that these subscripts are in range during all loop iterations by checking their values during the first and last repetitions of the loop. The first time through the loop, the value of i is 0, so the two subscripts are 0 and 1. On the last iteration, i is n − 2, the largest value it can take on and still remain less than n − 1. During this time through, the subscript values are n − 2 and n − 1. Since the subscript values are in range for the first and last loop repetitions, we can be fairly certain that they will be in range for all loop iterations.

8.9 MULTIDIMENSIONAL ARRAYS

In this section, we introduce *multidimensional* arrays, that is, arrays with two or more dimensions. We will use two-dimensional arrays to represent tables of data, matrices, and other two-dimensional objects. A two-dimensional object that many are familiar with is a tic-tac-toe board. The array declaration

```
char tictac[3][3];
```

**Figure 8.25
A Tic-tac-toe
Board Stored as
Array tictac**

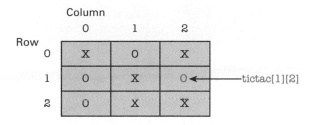

allocates storage for a two-dimensional array (`tictac`) with three rows and three columns. This array has nine elements, each of which must be referenced by specifying a row subscript (0, 1, or 2) and a column subscript (0, 1, or 2). Each array element contains a character value. The array element `tictac[1][2]` marked in Fig. 8.25 is in row 1, column 2 of the array; the element contains the character O. The diagonal line consisting of array elements `tictac[0][0]`, `tictac[1][1]`, and `tictac[2][2]` represents a win for player X because each cell contains the character X.

A function that takes a tic-tac-toe board as an input parameter will have a declaration similar to this in its prototype:

```
const char tictac[][3]
```

In the declaration of a multidimensional array parameter, only the first dimension, the number of rows, can be omitted. Including both dimensions is also permissible. Because tic-tac-toe boards do not vary in size, using the declaration that follows would probably make more sense.

```
const char tictac[3][3]
```

As in one-dimensional array parameter declarations, the `const` keyword is used on input parameters and omitted on output parameters.

Multidimensional Array Declaration

SYNTAX: *element-type aname*[*size*$_1$][*size*$_2$]...[*size*$_n$]; `/* storage`
                                                                        `allocation    */`

   `const` *element-type aname*[ ][*size*$_2$]...[*size*$_n$] `/* input parameter`
                                                                        `in prototype   */`

   element-type aname[ ][*size*$_2$]...[*size*$_n$] `/* output parameter`
                                                                        `in prototype   */`

(continued)

EXAMPLES: double table[NROWS][NCOLS]; /* storage allocation   */

```
          void
          process_matrix(const int in[][4],  /* input
                                                parameter       */
                        int        out[][4], /* output
                                                parameter       */
                        int        nrows)    /* input - number
                                                of rows         */
```

INTERPRETATION: The first form above allocates storage space for an array *aname* consisting of $size_1 \times size_2 \times \ldots \times size_n$ memory cells. Each memory cell can store one data item whose data type is specified by *element-type*. The individual array elements are referenced by the subscripted variables *aname*[0][0]...[0] through *aname*[$size_1-1$][$size_2-1$]... [$size_n-1$]. An integer constant expression is used to specify each $size_i$.

The second and third declaration forms shown are valid when declaring multidimensional array parameters in function prototypes. The size of the first dimension (the number of rows) is the only size that can be omitted. As for one-dimensional arrays, the value actually stored in an array formal parameter is the address of the initial element of the actual argument. The use of the const keyword indicates that an array parameter is an input to the function only, and the function will not modify the actual argument. Without this keyword, a function has access and authority to change an array formal parameter.

NOTE: ANSI C requires that an implementation allow multidimensional arrays of at least six dimensions.

EXAMPLE 8.12

The array table

```
double table[7][5][6];
```

consists of three dimensions: The first subscript may take on values from 0 to 6; the second, from 0 to 4; and the third, from 0 to 5. A total of $7 \times 5 \times 6$, or 210, type double values may be stored in the array table. All three subscripts must be specified in each reference to array table in order to access a single number (e.g., table[2][3][4]). ◄

EXAMPLE 8.13

Function filled checks whether a tic-tac-toe board is completely filled (see Fig. 8.26). If the board contains no cells with the value ' ', the function returns 1 for true; otherwise, it returns 0 for false. ◄

Figure 8.26   Function to Check Whether Tic-tac-toe Board is Filled

```
/* Checks whether a tic-tac-toe board is completely filled. */
int
filled(const char ttt_brd[3][3]) /*  input - tic-tac-toe board          */
{
      int r, c,  /* row and column subscripts    */
          ans;   /* whether or not board filled */

      /*  Assumes board is filled until blank is found               */
      ans = 1;

      /*  Resets ans to zero if a blank is found                     */
      for  (r = 0;  r < 3;  ++r)
          for  (c = 0;  c < 3;  ++c)
              if (ttt_brd[r][c] == ' ')
                    ans = 0;
      return (ans);
}
```

Initialization of Multidimensional Arrays

Multidimensional arrays may be initialized in their declarations in a manner similar to the initialization of one-dimensional arrays. However, instead of listing all table values in one list, the values are usually grouped by rows. For example, the following statement would allocate a tic-tac-toe board and initialize its contents to blanks.

```
char tictac[3][3] = { {' ', ' ', ' '}, {' ', ' ', ' '},
                      {' ', ' ', ' '} };
```

Arrays with Several Dimensions

The array `enroll` declared here

```
int enroll[MAXCRS][5][4];
```

course   *campus*   *year*

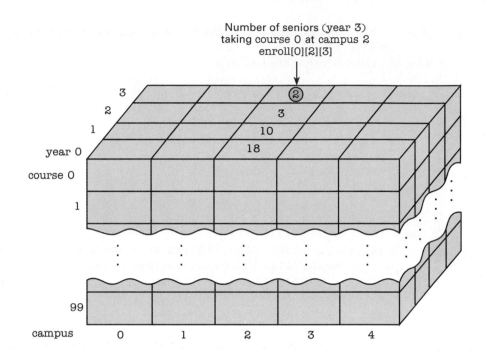

**Figure 8.27
Three-
Dimensional
Array enroll**

and pictured in Fig. 8.27 is a three-dimensional array that may be used to store the enrollment data for a college. We will assume that the college offers 100 (MAXCRS) courses at five different campuses. In keeping with C's practice of starting array subscripts with zero, we will number the freshman year 0, the sophomore year 1, and so on. Thus enroll[1][4][3] represents the number of seniors taking course 1 at campus 4.

Array enroll is composed of a total of 2000 (100 × 5 × 4) elements. A potential pitfall exists when you are dealing with multidimensional arrays: Memory space can be used up rapidly if several multidimensional arrays are declared in the same program. You should be aware of the amount of memory space required by each large array in a program.

We can answer many different questions by processing the data in Fig. 8.27. We can determine the total number of students taking a particular course, the number of juniors in course 2 at all campuses, and so on. The type of information desired determines the order in which we must reference the array elements.

 **EXAMPLE 8.14** The program fragment that follows finds and prints the total number of students in each course.

```
/*  Finds and prints number of students in each course  */
for  (course = 0;  course < MAXCRS;  ++course) {
    crs_sum = 0;
    for  (campus = 0;  campus < 5;  ++campus) {
        for  (cls_rank = 0;  cls_rank < 4;  ++cls_rank) {
            crs_sum += enroll[course][campus][cls_rank];
        }
    }
    printf("Number of students in course %d is %d\n",
           course, crs_sum);
}
```

Since we are printing the number of students in each course, the loop control variable for the outermost indexed loop is the subscript that denotes the course.

The program fragment that follows prints the number of students at each campus. This time the loop control variable for the outermost indexed loop is the subscript that denotes the campus.

```
/* Finds and prints number of students at each campus   */
for  (campus = 0;  campus < 5;  ++campus) {
    campus_sum = 0;
    for  (course = 0;  course < MAXCRS;  ++course) {
        for  (cls_rank = 0;  cls_rank < 4;  ++cls_rank) {
            campus_sum += enroll[course][campus][cls_rank];
        }
    }
    printf("Number of students at campus %d is %d\n",
           campus, campus_sum);
}
```

EXERCISES FOR SECTION 8.9

Self-Check

1. Redefine MAXCRS as 5, and write and test program segments that perform the following operations:
   a. Enter the enrollment data.
   b. Find the number of juniors in all classes at all campuses. Students will be counted once for each course in which they are enrolled.

    c. Write a function that has three input parameters: the enrollment array, a class rank, and a course number. The function is to find the number of students of the given rank who are enrolled in the given course on all campuses. Try using your function to find the number of sophomores (`rank = 1`) on all campuses who are enrolled in course `2`.

    d. Compute and print the number of upperclass students in all courses at each campus, as well as the total number of upperclass students enrolled on all campuses. (Upperclass students are juniors and seniors—ranks `2` and `3`.) Again, students will be counted once for each course in which they are enrolled.

Programming

1. Write a function that prints the values on the diagonal of its 10×10 matrix parameter.

8.10 COMMON PROGRAMMING ERRORS

The most common error in using arrays is a subscript-range error. An out-of-range reference occurs when the subscript value used is outside the range specified by the array declaration. For the array `celsius`,

```
int celsius[100];
```

a subscript-range error occurs when `celsius` is used with a subscript that has a value less than `0` or greater than `99`. If the value of `i` is `150`, a reference to the subscripted variable `celsius[i]` may cause an error message such as

```
access violation at line no. 28
```

In many situations, however, no run-time error message will be produced—the program will simply produce incorrect results. Subscript-range errors are not syntax errors; consequently, they will not be detected until program execution, and often not even then. They are most often caused by an incorrect subscript expression, a loop counter error, or a nonterminating loop. Before spending considerable time in debugging, you should check all suspect subscript calculations carefully for out-of-range errors. View the successive values of a subscripting variable in a debugger program, or insert diagnostic output statements that print subscript values that are of concern.

    If a subscript-range error occurs inside an indexed loop, verify that the subscript is in range for both the initial and the final values of the loop control variable. If these values are in range, it is likely that all other subscript references in the loop are in range as well.

If a subscript-range error occurs in a loop controlled by a variable other than the array subscript, check that the loop control variable is being updated as required. If it is not, the loop may be repeated more often than expected, causing the subscript-range error. This error could happen if the control-variable update step was inside a condition or was inadvertently omitted.

When using arrays as arguments to functions, be careful not to apply the address-of operator to the array name even if the array is an output argument. However, do remember to use the & on an array *element* that is being passed as an output argument.

Be sure to use the correct forms for declaring array input and output parameters in function prototypes. Remember when reading C code that a parameter declared as

```
int *z
```

could represent a single integer output parameter or an integer array parameter. Comment your own prototypes carefully and use the alternate declaration form

```
int z[]
```

for array parameters to assist readers of your code.

If you are working on a computer system with very limited memory, you may find that some correct C programs generate run-time error messages indicating an access violation. The use of arrays can cause a program to require large amounts of memory for function data areas. The portion of memory set aside for function data areas is called the *stack*. You may need to tell your operating system that an increased stack size is necessary in order to be able to run programs using large arrays.

CHAPTER REVIEW

In this chapter, we introduced a data structure called an *array*, which is a convenient facility for naming and referencing a collection of like items. We discussed how to declare both one-dimensional and multidimensional arrays as local variables where space is actually allocated for the structure and how to declare an array in a function prototype as an input or output parameter. We showed how to reference an individual array element by placing a square-bracketed subscript for each dimension immediately following the array name.

The indexed `for` loop enables us to reference the elements of a one-dimensional array in sequence. We saw that nesting such loops provides the same ease of reference for multidimensional arrays. We used indexed `for` loops in the input and output of arrays and in controlling the manipulation of individual array elements.

New C Constructs

Table 8.5 summarizes the declaration and manipulation of arrays as covered in this chapter.

Table 8.5   Using Arrays in C Programs

Example	Effect
Array Declarations	
Local Variables	
`double data[30];` `int    matrix[2][3];`	Allocates storage for 30 type `double` items in array `data` (`data[0]`, `data[1]`, ... , `data[29]`), and six type `int` items (2 rows of 3 columns) in two-dimensional array `matrix` (`matrix[0][0]`, `matrix[0][1]`, `matrix[0][2]`, `matrix[1][0]`, `matrix[1][1]`, `matrix[1][2]`.
Initialization	
`char vowels[5] =` `    {'A', 'E', 'I', 'O', 'U'};`	Allocates storage for five type `char` items in array `vowels` and initializes the array contents: `vowels[0]='A'`, `vowels[1]='E'`, ... `vowels[4]='U'`.
`int  id[2][2] =` `    { {1, 0}, {0, 1} };`	Allocates four locations for the 2 × 2 matrix `id`, initializing the storage so `id[0][0]=1`, `id[0][1]=0`, `id[1][0]=0`, and `id[1][1]=1`.
Input Parameter	

`void`
`print_alpha(const char alpha[],`
`            const int   m[][3],`
`            int         a_size,`
`            int         m_rows)`
`    or`
`... (const char *alpha, ...`
	States that function `print_alpha` uses arrays `alpha` and `m` as input parameters only— `print_alpha` will not change their contents.

Output or Input/Output Parameter	

`void`
`fill(int nums[], int n)`
`      or`
`... (int *nums,...`
	States that function `fill` can both look at and modify the actual argument array passed to `nums`.

Table 8.5   *(continued)*

Example	Effect
Array References	
`if (data[0] < 39.8)`	Compares value of initial element of array `data` to `39.8`.
`for (i = 0; i < 30; ++i)` `    data[i] /= 2.0;`	Divides each element of array `data` by 2, changing the array contents.

`for (i = 0; i < 2; ++i) {`
`    for (j = 0; j < 3; ++j)`
`        printf("%6d", matrix[i][j]);`
`    printf("\n");`
`}`
	Prints contents of `matrix` in 2 rows with 3 columns.

QUICK-CHECK EXERCISES

1. What is a data structure?
2. Of what data type are array subscripting expressions?
3. Can two elements of the same array be of different data types?
4. If an array is declared to have ten elements, must the program use all ten?
5. The two methods of array access are called _____ and _____ .
6. An _____ loop allows us to access easily the elements of an array in _____ order.
7. What is the difference in the use of array b that is implied by these two prototypes?

   ```
   int                 int
   fun_one(int b[], n) fun_two(const int b[], n)
   ```

8. Look again at the prototypes in Exercise 7. Why does neither array declaration indicate a size?
9. Let `nums` be an array of 12 type `int` locations. Describe how the following loop works.

   ```
   i = 0;
   for (status = scanf("%d", &n);
            status == 1 && i < 12;
            status = scanf("%d", &n))
         nums[i++] = n;
   ```

10. How many elements does array m have? Show how you would reference each one.

    ```
    double m[2][4];
    ```

11. If x is an array declared

    ```
    int x[10];
    ```

    and you see a function call like

    ```
    some_fun(x, n);
    ```

    how can you tell if x is an input or an output argument?

ANSWERS TO QUICK-CHECK EXERCISES

1. A data structure is a grouping of related values in main memory.
2. type `int`
3. no
4. no
5. sequential, random
6. indexed, sequential
7. In `fun_one`, b can be used as an output parameter or as an input/output parameter. In `fun_two`, b is strictly an input parameter array.
8. The size of b is not needed because the function does not allocate storage for copying parameter arrays. Only the starting address of the actual argument array will be stored in the formal parameter.
9. As long as `scanf` continues to return a value of 1 meaning a valid integer has been obtained for n, unless the subscript i is ≥ 12, the loop body will store the input in the next element of `nums` and will increment the loop counter. The loop exits on EOF (`scanf` returns a negative value), on invalid data (`scanf` returns zero), or on i no longer being less than 12.
10. m has 8 elements: `m[0][0], m[0][1], m[0][2], m[0][3], m[1][0], m[1][1], m[1][2], m[1][3]`
11. You can't tell by looking at the function call, nor can you rely on the prototype of `some_fun` to tell you either unless the corresponding formal parameter declaration has a `const` qualifier. If it does, x must be an input argument.

REVIEW QUESTIONS

1. Identify an error in the following C statements:

```
int x[8], i;
for  (i = 0;  i <= 8;  ++i)
    x[i] = i;
```

Will the error be detected? If so, when?

2. Declare an array of type `double` values called `exper` that can be referenced by using any day of the week as a subscript where 0 represents Sunday, 1 represents Monday, and so on.

3. The statement marked /* this one */ in the following code is valid. True or false?

```
int counts[10], i;
double x[5];
printf("Enter an integer between 0 and 4> ");
i = 0;
scanf("%d", &counts[i]);
x[counts[i]] = 8.384;  /* this one */
```

4. What are the two common ways of selecting array elements for processing?

5. Write a C program segment to print out the index of the smallest and the largest numbers in an array x of 20 integers. Assume array x already has values assigned to each element.

6. Write a C function called `reverse` that takes an array named x as an input parameter and an array named y as an output parameter. A third function parameter is n, the number of values in x. The function should copy the integers in x into y but in reverse order (i.e., y[0] gets x[n - 1], ... y[n - 1] gets x[0]).

7. Write a program segment to display the sum of the values in each row of a 5 × 3 type `double` array named `table`. How many row sums will be displayed? How many elements are included in each sum?

8. Answer Review Exercise 7 for the column sums.

PROGRAMMING PROJECTS

1. Write a program to take two numerical lists of the same length ended by a sentinel value and store the lists in arrays x and y, each of which has 20 elements. Let n be the actual number of data values in each list. Store the prod-

uct of corresponding elements of x and y in a third array, z, also of size 20. Print a three-column table displaying the arrays x, y, and z. Then compute and print the square root of the sum of the items in z. Make up your own data, and be sure to test your program on at least one data set with number lists of exactly 20 items. One data set should have lists of 21 numbers, and one set should have significantly shorter lists.

2. Let arr be an array of 20 integers. Write a program that first fills the array with up to 20 input values and then finds and prints both the *subscript* of the largest item in arr and the value of the largest item.

3. Each year the Department of Traffic Accidents receives accident-count reports from a number of cities and towns across the country. To summarize these reports, the department provides a frequency-distribution printout that gives the number of cities reporting accident counts in the following ranges: 0–99, 100–199, 200–299, 300–399, 400–499, and 500 or above. The department needs a computer program to take the number of accidents for each reporting city or town and add one to the count for the appropriate accident range. After all the data have been processed, the resulting frequency counts are to be printed.

4. Modify the area computation program in Figs. 8.21–8.23 to find the area of a piece of land that forms a polygon. The *x* and *y* coordinates (in feet) at the edges of the property are available in a data file. Compute and display the acreage (1 acre = 43,560 square feet). Use the following sample data file as one test case:

12.342	33.476
19.564	43.556
34.451	55.026
46.735	77.323
50.034	70.432
43.958	65.361
30.985	59.207
22.894	38.976
15.347	36.890

5. Generate a table that indicates the rainfall for the city of Plainview and compares the average rainfall for the city with the rainfall from the previous year. Print some summary statistics that will indicate both the annual rainfall for each year and the average monthly rainfall for each year. The input data will consist of twelve pairs of numbers. The first number in each pair will be the average rainfall for a month, and the second number will be what fell the previous year. The first data pair will represent January, the second will be

February, and so forth. If you assume the data begin

```
3.2   4     (for January)
2.2   1.6   (for February)
```

the output should resemble the following:

```
              Table of monthly rainfall

              January      February     March . . .
This year       3.2          2.2
Last year       4.0          1.6

Total rainfall this year:  35.7
Total rainfall last year:  42.8
Average monthly rainfall for this year:  3.6
Average monthly rainfall for last year:  4.0
```

6. Write an interactive program that plays a game of Hangman. Store the word to be guessed in successive elements of an array of individual characters called word. The player must guess the letters belonging to word. The program should terminate when either all letters have been guessed correctly (the player wins) or a specified number of incorrect guesses have been made (the computer wins). *Hint:* Use another array, guessed, to keep track of the solution so far. Initialize all elements of guessed to the ' * ' symbol. Each time a letter in word is guessed, replace the corresponding ' * ' in guessed with that letter.

7. The results from the mayor's race have been reported by each precinct as follows:

Precinct	Candidate A	Candidate B	Candidate C	Candidate D
1	192	48	206	37
2	147	90	312	21
3	186	12	121	38
4	114	21	408	39
5	267	13	382	29

Write a program to do the following:
a. Print the table with appropriate labels for the rows and columns.
b. Compute and print the total number of votes received by each candidate and the percentage of the total votes cast.

    c. If any one candidate received over 50 percent of the votes, the program should print a message declaring that candidate the winner.

    d. If no candidate received 50 percent of the votes, the program should print a message declaring a runoff between the two candidates receiving the highest number of votes; the two candidates should be identified by their letter names.

    e. Run the program once with the data shown and once with candidate C receiving only 108 votes in Precinct 4.

8. Write a function that will merge the contents of two sorted (ascending order) arrays of type `double` values, storing the result in an array output parameter (still in ascending order). The function should not assume that both its input parameter arrays are the same length but can assume that one array does not contain two copies of the same value. The result array should also contain no duplicate values.

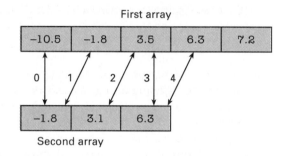

Hint: When one of the input arrays has been exhausted, do not forget to copy the remaining data in the other array into the result array. Test your function with cases in which (1) the first array is exhausted first, (2) the second array is exhausted first, and (3) the two arrays are exhausted at the same time (i.e., they end with the same value). Remember that the arrays input to this function *must already be sorted.*

9. The binary search algorithm that follows may be used to search an array when the elements are in order. This algorithm is analogous to the following approach for finding a name in a telephone book.

    a. Open the book in the middle, and look at the middle name on the page.

    b. If the middle name isn't the one you're looking for, decide whether it comes before or after the name you want.

    c. Take the appropriate half of the section of the book you were looking in and repeat these steps until you land on the name.

Algorithm for Binary Search

1. Let `bottom` be the subscript of the initial array element.
2. Let `top` be the subscript of the last array element.
3. Let `found` be false.
4. Repeat as long as `bottom` isn't greater than `top` and the target has not been found
   5. Let `middle` be the subscript of the element halfway between `bottom` and `top`.
   6. if the element at `middle` is the target
      7. Set `found` to true and `index` to `middle`.
      else if the element at `middle` is larger than the target
      8. Let `top` be `middle − 1`.
      else
      9. Let `bottom` be `middle + 1`.

   Write and test a function `binary_srch` that implements this algorithm for an array of integers. When there is a large number of array elements, which function do you think is faster: `binary_srch` or the linear search function of Fig. 8.9?

10. The selection sort is another technique for sorting an array. In the selection sort, the first pass through the array finds the largest value in the array and its subscript. The largest value is then switched with the value in the last array position, putting the largest value in the last position, where it belongs, much like the bubble sort. The process is then repeated (the second pass), but the last position is not included in the search for the largest value. After the second pass, the second largest value is known and can be switched with the value currently in the second position from the end of the array. This process continues until each item is in its correct location. It requires $n-1$ passes to sort an array of n elements (why?). Write and test a function that implements this sorting method.

11. Write a program that simulates the movement of radioactive particles in a two-dimensional shield around a reactor. A particle in the shield can move in one of four directions. The direction for the next second of travel is determined by generation of a random number between 1 and 4 (forward, backward, left, right). A change in direction is interpreted as a collision with another particle resulting in a dissipation of energy. Each particle can have only a limited number of collisions before it dies. For each particle that enters the shield, determine whether that particle exits the shield before it dies. A particle exits the shield if its net forward travel time is n seconds before k collisions occur (i.e., it takes n more forward steps than backward steps). Determine the percentage of particles that exit the shield where n, k, and the number of particles are data items. See Programming Project 3 at the end of Chapter 7 for information about the library function `ranf`.

12. Statistical analysis of data makes heavy use of arrays. One such analysis, called cross-tabulation, is used to help decide whether a relationship exists between two or more variables. For example, the following data might represent opinions from a survey concerning an amendment to the U.S. Constitution making it illegal to destroy or damage the U.S. flag in any way.

Opinion	Male	Female	Total
In Favor	63	27	90
Opposed	19	42	61
No Opinion	6	39	45
Totals	88	108	196

Write a C program that will take pairs of male/female response totals (one pair per line)

```
63   27
19   42
 6   39
```

and print out the cross-tabulation matrix including the row totals and the column totals.

   The program should also print out the percentage in each category. For example, we would want to know that the 39 females with no opinion represent 36 percent of the total females interviewed and 87 percent of those with no opinion. Make all the output as attractive as possible.

13. The game of Life, invented by John H. Conway, is supposed to model the genetic laws for birth, survival, and death (see *Scientific American*, October 1970, p. 120). We will play the game on a board that consists of 25 squares in the horizontal and vertical directions (a total of 625 squares). Each square can be empty, or it can contain an X indicating the presence of an organism. Each square (except for the border squares) has eight neighbors. The small square of asterisks shown in the following segment of the board connects the neighbors of the organism named X*.

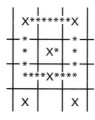

Generation 1

The next generation of organisms is determined according to the following criteria:

a. Birth—an organism will be born in each empty location that has exactly three neighbors.

b. Death—an organism with four or more organisms as neighbors will die from overcrowding. An organism with fewer than two neighbors will die from loneliness.

c. Survival—an organism with two or three neighbors will survive to the next generation. Possible generations 2 and 3 for the sample follow:

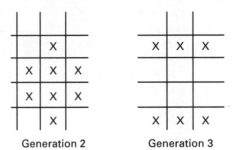

Generation 2   Generation 3

Take an initial configuration of organisms as input data. Print the original game array, calculate the next generation of organisms in a new array, copy the new array into the original game array, and repeat the cycle for as many generations as you wish. *Hint:* Assume that the borders of the game array are infertile regions where organisms can neither survive nor be born; you will not have to process the border squares.

CHAPTER 9

STRINGS

9.1
String Basics
9.2
String Assignment and Substrings
9.3
Longer Strings: Concatenation and Whole-Line Input
9.4
String Comparison
9.5
Arrays of Pointers
9.6
Character Operations
9.7
String-to-Number and Number-to-String Conversions
9.8
String Processing Illustrated
Case Study: Cryptogram Generator
Case Study: Finding Palindromes in
Nucleotide Sequences
9.9
String Library Functions for Assignment,
Substring Extraction, and Concatenation
9.10
Common Programming Errors
Chapter Review

So far, we have seen limited use of character data because most applications that process character data deal with a grouping of characters, a data structure called a *string*. Because C implements the string data structure using arrays of type `char`, we could not explore strings until we had a foundational understanding of arrays.

Strings are important in computer science because many computer applications are concerned with the manipulation of textual data rather than numerical data. Computer-based *word processing systems* enable a user to compose letters, term papers, newspaper articles, and even books at a computer terminal instead of at a typewriter. Storing the text in the computer's memory allows us to modify the text, check the spelling electronically, move whole paragraphs, and then print a fresh copy without mistakes or erasures.

Strings play an important role in science as well. The chemist works with elements and compounds whose names often combine alphabetic and numeric characters (e.g., $C_{12}H_{22}O_{11}$)—data easily represented by a string. Molecular biologists identify amino acids by name and map our DNA with strings of amino acid abbreviations. Many mathematicians, physicists, and engineers spend more time modeling our world with equations (strings of character and numeric data) than they do crunching numbers. In subsequent chapters, we will meet other representations of some of these concepts that are more easily manipulated than the string model; however, we will still need strings as the vehicle for communication between the computer system and the human user.

In the sections that follow, we will introduce some fundamental operations that can be performed on character data. We will investigate selected functions from the standard string and ctype libraries that provide most of C's facilities for working with character strings.

9.1 STRING BASICS

We have already used string constants extensively in our earlier work. Indeed, every one of our calls to `scanf` or `printf` used a string constant as the first argument. Consider this call:

```
printf("Average = %.2f", avg);
```

The first argument is the string constant `"Average = %.2f"`, a string of 14 characters. Notice that the blanks in the string are characters just as valid as those requiring ink! Like other constant values, a string constant can be associated with a symbolic name using the `#define` directive.

```
#define ERR_PREFIX    "*****Error - "
#define INSUFF_DATA   "Insufficient Data"
```

449

Declaring and Initializing String Variables

As we mentioned earlier, a string in C is implemented as an array, so declaring a string variable is the same as declaring an array of type `char`. In

```
char string_var[30];
```

the variable `string_var` will hold strings from 0 to 29 characters long. It is C's handling of this varying length characteristic that distinguishes the string data structure from other arrays. C permits initialization of string variables using either a brace-enclosed character list as shown in Chapter 8 or a string constant as shown in the following declaration of `str`.

```
char str[20] = "Initial value";
```

Let's look at `str` in memory after this declaration with initialization.

[0]				[4]					[9]					[14]					[19]
I	n	i	t	i	a	l		v	a	l	u	e	\0	?	?	?	?	?	?

Notice that `string_var[13]` contains the character `'\0'`, the *null* character that marks the end of a string. Using this marker allows the string's length within the character array to vary from 0 to one less than the array's declared size. All of C's string handling functions simply ignore whatever is stored in the cells following the null character. The following diagram shows `string_var` holding a string that is the longest it can represent—19 characters plus the null character.

[0]				[4]					[9]					[14]					[19]
n	u	m	b	e	r	s		a	n	d		s	t	r	i	n	g	s	\0

Arrays of Strings

Because one string is an array of characters, an array of strings is a two-dimensional array of characters in which each row is one string. The following are statements to declare an array to store up to 30 names, each of which is less than 25 characters long.

```
#define NUM_NAMES 30
#define NAME_LEN  25
   . . .
char names[NUM_NAMES][NAME_LEN];
```

We can initialize an array of strings at declaration in the following manner:

```
char month[12][10] = {"January", "February", "March", "April",
                      "May", "June", "July", "August",
                      "September", "October", "November",
                      "December"};
```

Input/Output with printf and scanf

Both `printf` and `scanf` can handle string arguments as long as the place-holder `%s` is used in the format string:

```
printf("Topic: %s\n", string_var);
```

The `printf` function, like other standard library functions that take string arguments, depends on finding a null character in the character array to mark the end of the string. If `printf` were passed a character array that contained no `'\0'`, the function would first interpret the contents of each array element as a character and print it. Then `printf` would continue to print as characters the contents of memory locations following the array argument until it encountered a null character or until it attempted to access a memory cell that was not assigned to the program, causing a run-time error. When we write our own string-building functions, we must be sure that a null character is inserted at the end of every string. This inclusion of the null character is automatic for constant strings.

The `%s` placeholder in a `printf` format string can be used with a minimum field width as shown.

```
printf("***%8s***%3s***\n", "Short", "Strings");
```

The first string is printed right-justified in a field of eight columns. The second string is longer than the specified field width, so the field is expanded to accommodate it exactly with no padding. We are more accustomed to seeing lists of strings printed left-justified rather than right-justified. Consider the two lists in Fig. 9.1.

Placing a minus sign prefix on a placeholder's field width causes left justification of the value printed. If `president` is a string variable, repeated execution of this call to `printf` will produce a left-justified list.

```
printf("%-20s\n", president);
```

The `scanf` function can be used for input of a string. However, when we call `scanf` with a string variable as an argument, we must remember that array

Figure 9.1
Right and Left
Justification of
Strings

Right-justified	**Left-justified**
George Washington	George Washington
John Adams	John Adams
Thomas Jefferson	Thomas Jefferson
James Madison	James Madison

output arguments are *always* passed to functions by sending the address of the initial array element. Therefore we do not apply the address-of operator to a string argument passed to `scanf` or to any other function. In Fig. 9.2, we see a brief main function performing string I/O with `scanf` and `printf`. In this program, the user is expected to type in a string representing an academic depart-

Figure 9.2   String Input/Output with scanf and printf

```
#define STRING_LEN   10

int
main(void)
{
      char dept[STRING_LEN];
      int  course_num;
      char days[STRING_LEN];
      int  time;

      printf("Enter department code, course number, days and ");
      printf("time like this:\n> COSC 2060 MWF 1410\n> ");
      scanf("%s%d%s%d", dept, &course_num, days, &time);
      printf("%s %d meets %s at %d\n", dept, course_num, days, time);

      return (0);
}

Enter department code, course number, days and time like this:
> COSC 2060 MWF 1410
> MATH 1270 TR 800
MATH 1270 meets TR at 800
```

ment, an integer course code, a string abbreviation for the days of the week the course meets, and an integer that gives the meeting time of the class.

The approach scanf takes to string input is very similar to its processing of numeric input. As shown in Fig. 9.3, when it scans a string, scanf skips leading whitespace characters such as blanks, newlines, and tabs. Starting with the first nonwhitespace character, scanf copies the characters it encounters into successive memory cells of its character array argument. When it comes across a whitespace character, scanning stops, and scanf places the null character at the end of the string in its array argument.

Because of the way scanf treats whitespace, the values could be spaced on the data lines in many ways that would result in variables dept, course_num, days, and time receiving correct values upon execution of the scanf call in Fig. 9.2. For example, the data could have been entered one value per line with extra whitespace:

```
>        MATH
  1270
     TR
                    1800
```

or two values per line:

```
> MATH 1270
  TR 1800
```

Function scanf would have difficulty if some essential whitespace between values were omitted or if a nonwhitespace separator were substituted. For example, if the data were entered as

```
> MATH1270 TR 1800
```

scanf would store the 8-character string "MATH1270" in dept and would then be unable to convert T to an integer for storage using the next parameter.

**Figure 9.3
Execution of**
scanf
   ("%s", dept);

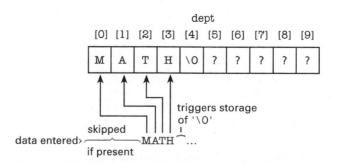

Figure 9.4 **Execution of** `scanf("%s%d%s%d", dept, &course_num,` `days, &time);` **on Entry of Invalid Data**

The situation would be worse if the data were entered as

```
> MATH,1270,TR,1800
```

Then the `scanf` function would store the entire 17-character string plus `'\0'` in the `dept` array, causing characters to be stored in eight locations not allocated to `dept` as shown in Fig. 9.4.

For easy input of predictable-length strings that have no internal blanks, `scanf` with the `%s` placeholder works well. However, in an environment in which the proper data entry format may not be observed or where even an occasional program fault is critical, a more robust string input function should be used. We will write one such function in Section 9.3.

EXAMPLE 9.1

Earlier in this chapter, we declared an array of strings suitable for holding 30 names (a two-dimensional array of type `char` values). Let's see how to use `scanf` and `printf` to fill this array and echo print it.

You will recall from our study of arrays that no address-of operator is needed when an array is passed as an output argument. Because each element `names[i]` of an array of strings represents a kind of array, it is passed as an output argument without using the `&` operator. The following code segment fills parallel arrays `names` and `ages` with data. In the call to `scanf`, note the contrasting application of the `&` operator to elements of the `ages` array since these elements are simple output arguments of type `int`.

```
#define NUM_NAMES 30
#define NAME_LEN  25
  . . .
char names[NUM_NAMES][NAME_LEN];

for (i = 0;  i < NUM_NAMES;  ++i) {
    scanf("%s%d", names[i], &ages[i]);
    printf("%-35s %3d", names[i], ages[i]);
}
```

EXAMPLE 9.2 The program in Fig. 9.5 plots the values of the function $t^2 - 4t + 5$ for values of t between 0 and 10 by storing an asterisk in the element of the string `plot` corresponding to the function value, while all other elements are blank. The character array `plot` is first initialized to all blanks. This could be done with an initialization in the declaration of `plot`. However, it is certainly easier for the computer to count 66 blanks accurately than for the programmer to do so. Within the computing `for` loop, the assignment statement

```
funval = f(t);
```

calls the function `f` and saves the value returned in `funval`. The first of the two assignment statements

```
plot[funval] = '*';
plot[funval + 1] = '\0';
```

Figure 9.5   Plot of Function $t^2 - 4t + 5$

....

```
/*                                    2
 *  Plots the function   f(t) = t   -   4t   +   5   for t between 0 and 10
 */

#include <stdio.h>

#define MAX_VAL 65   /*  maximum function value */

/*
 *                2
 *   f(t) = t   -   4t   +   5
 */
int
f (int t)
{
      return (t * t - 4 * t + 5);
}

int
main(void)
{
      char plot[MAX_VAL + 2];   /* one line of plot */
      int i, t, funval;
```

(continued)

Figure 9.5   *(continued)*

```
    /* Displays heading lines                                    */
    for  (i = 0;  i <= MAX_VAL;  i += 5)
        printf("%5d", i);
    printf("\n");

    for  (i = 0;  i <= MAX_VAL;  i += 5)
        printf("    |");
    printf("\n");

    /* Initializes plot to all blanks                            */
    for  (i = 0;  i <= MAX_VAL + 1;  ++i)
        plot[i] = ' ';

    /* Computes and plots f(t) for each value of t from 0 through 10  */
    for  (t = 0;  t <= 10;  ++t) {
        funval = f(t);
        plot[funval] = '*';
        plot[funval + 1] = '\0';
        printf("t=%2d%s\n", t, plot);
        plot[funval] = ' ';
        plot[funval + 1] = ' ';
    }

    return (0);
}
```

```
        0    5   10   15   20   25   30   35   40   45   50   55   60   65
        |    |    |    |    |    |    |    |    |    |    |    |    |    |
t= 0         *
t= 1      *
t= 2    *
t= 3      *
t= 4          *
t= 5             *
t= 6                  *
t= 7                       *
t= 8                            *
t= 9                                 *
t=10                                           *
```

places an asterisk in the string element that corresponds to the function value; the second statement ends the string immediately after this value. The call to `printf`

```
printf("t=%2d%s\n", t, plot);
```

displays a line that begins with the value of t followed by the string plot. The string contains a single asterisk; the position of the asterisk depends on the value of `funval`. After each line is printed, the assignment statements

```
plot[funval] = ' ';
plot[funval + 1] = ' ';
```

reset the nonblank elements to blanks.

There are three calls to `printf` in Fig. 9.2 that are executed repeatedly. The first of these calls prints the heading line consisting of the integers 0, 5, 10, and so on, spaced five columns apart. The second call prints a line consisting of 14 occurrences of the symbol '|' spaced five columns apart directly beneath the first line. As mentioned, the last repeated call to `printf` prints the current value of t and the corresponding function value (denoted by the symbol *). The first output line shows that f[0] is 5.   ←

EXERCISES FOR SECTION 9.1

Self-Check

1. When the `scanf` function is scanning a string, if there is more input data (with no blanks) than will fit in the array output argument, `scanf` ____ (choose one).
   a. copies in only the characters that will fit and ignores the rest.
   b. copies in the whole string overflowing the output argument because `scanf` has no way of knowing the array's declared size.
   c. scans all the characters but stores only the ones that fit, discarding the rest.
2. When `printf` is given a string argument to print using a `%s` placeholder, how does it know how many characters to print?
3. Declare a 30-character array, and initialize it at declaration to a string of 29 blanks.

Programming

1. Write a program that takes a word less than 25 characters long and prints a statement like this:

```
fractal starts with the letter f
```

Have the program process words until it encounters a "word" beginning with the character `'9'`.

9.2 STRING ASSIGNMENT AND SUBSTRINGS

We have become accustomed to using the assignment operator = to copy data into a variable. Although we do use the assignment symbol in a declaration of a string variable with initialization, this context is the *only* one in which the operator means to copy the string that is the right operand into the variable that is the left operand. We have seen that an array name with no subscript represents the address of the initial array element. This address is constant and cannot be changed through assignment, so the following code fragment will cause a compiler error message such as `Invalid target of assignment`:

```
char one_str[20];
one_str = "Test string";   /* Does not work */
```

Figure 9.6 shows a `strassign` function that we can use for string assignment. To carry out the desired assignment shown in our faulty code, we would call `strassign` in a manner such as

```
strassign(one_str, "Test string", 20);
```

Because we do not want to overflow the space allocated for the destination variable (`one_str` in the example given), the `strassign` function requires that we provide as the third argument the number of characters that can be stored. If the source string is too long, it is truncated. For example,

```
strassign(one_str, "Test string", 10);
```

would assign to `one_str` the string `"Test stri"`, i.e., nine characters of the source string plus the null character. Since `strassign` uses functions from the C string library, the file in which it is placed must have an `#include <string.h>` directive.

The first of the two functions from the C standard string library that `strassign` uses is `strlen`, a function that is extremely useful in string processing. This string length function takes a single string argument and returns the number of characters in it, not counting the null character at the end. The second function, `memmove`, copies `new_len` characters from `src` to `dest`, trusting the caller to have verified that doing this copy is reasonable.

The `strassign` function mimics the assignment operator in that the value it returns is the string assigned (specifically, the copy that is in the destination variable). The calling function actually has two ways of referencing the result of `strassign`. It can use either the first argument from the call or the function result. This characteristic of `strassign` (and of `substr` and

Figure 9.6   String Assignment Function

```
#include <string.h>
/*
 *  Copies into dest the string value of src, or as much as will fit given
 *  that dest has room for only dest_len characters, including \0.  Extra
 *  characters are truncated.
 */
char *
strassign(char       dest[],     /* output - destination string    */
          const char src[],      /* input  - source string         */
          int        dest_len)   /* input  - space available in dest */
{
      int new_len,  /* number of characters to copy into dest        */
          i;

      if (strlen(src) < dest_len)
           new_len = strlen(src);
      else
           new_len = dest_len - 1;

      /*  Copies new_len chars from src to dest using function that gives
          correct results even if src and dest overlap              */
      memmove(dest, src, new_len);

      /*  Adds null character at end of string                       */
      dest[new_len] = '\0';

      return (dest);
}
```

`concat` discussed later) is also typical of string-building functions in the C string library.

Substrings

We frequently need to reference a substring of a longer character string. For example, we might want to examine the "Cl" in the string "NaCl", or the "30" in the string "Jan. 30, 1992". In Fig. 9.7, we see a function `substr` that allows us to extract a portion of a string by specifying a starting and ending subscript.

Figure 9.7   Substring Function

```
/*
 *  Extracts a substring from src and returns it in dest, truncating if
 *  the substring contains dest_len or more characters.  The substring
 *  extracted starts with src[st] and contains characters up to but not
 *  including src[end] unless src[end - 1] is beyond the end of src, in
 *  which case the substring returned is src[st] to the end of src.  The
 *  empty string is returned if st > end or if st >= strlen(src)
 */
char *
substr(char       dest[],   /* output - destination string            */
       const char src[],    /* input  - source string                 */
       int        st,       /* input  - subscript of first character of
                                         src to include                */
       int        end,      /* input  - subscript of character following
                                         last character included       */
       int        dest_len)/* input  - space available in dest        */
{
      int sub_len;  /* length of substring returned                    */

      /*  Adjusts st and end if they are beyond the ends of src        */
      if (end > strlen(src))
            end = strlen(src);
      if (st < 0)
            st = 0;
      if (st > end) { /* if starting point is past ending point        */
            dest[0] = '\0';
      } else {
            sub_len = end - st;
            if (sub_len >= dest_len)
                  sub_len = dest_len - 1;
            memmove(dest, &src[st], sub_len);
            dest[sub_len] = '\0';
      }

      return (dest);
}
```

For now, we would like you to accept that our substr function works as described in its initial block comment. If the details of its code make sense to you, great; if not, don't worry about it right now. One of the advantages of modular programming is that all that is required to make use of a function is an understanding of its purpose and arguments.

We noted in our early study of arrays that for a function to produce an array result, the function that calls it must provide as an output argument the space into which the result can be stored. String-building functions are no exception to this rule, and both `strassign` and `substr` require this output argument from the functions that call them. These functions also require that the calling function tell them how much space has been provided so that they can prevent overflow of the output argument.

EXAMPLE 9.3 Calls to `substr` to extract three substrings of the string stored in `pres` are shown.

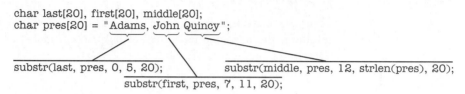

```
char last[20], first[20], middle[20];
char pres[20] = "Adams, John Quincy";
```

```
substr(last, pres, 0, 5, 20);          substr(middle, pres, 12, strlen(pres), 20);
            substr(first, pres, 7, 11, 20);
```

The `substr` call that extracts `"Quincy"` demonstrates that given a starting point all the rest of a string can be accessed if one uses `strlen(source_string)` as the ending point.

EXAMPLE 9.4 The program segment

```
char socsec[12], /* social security number  */
     ssn1[4], ssn2[3], ssn3[5];
printf("Enter social security number including dashes\n> ");
scanf("%s", socsec);
substr(ssn1, socsec, 0, 3, 4);
substr(ssn2, socsec, 4, 6, 3);
substr(ssn3, socsec, 7, strlen(socsec), 5);
```

takes a character string representing a social security number. If the string entered is `"123-45-6789"`, the program segment breaks it into substrings:

socsec	ssn1	ssn2	ssn3
1 2 3 - 4 5 - 6 7 8 9 \0	1 2 3 \0	4 5 \0	6 7 8 9 \0

EXAMPLE 9.5 The program in Fig. 9.8 breaks compounds into their elemental components, assuming that each element name begins with a capital letter and that our implementation is using the ASCII character set. For example, this program would break `"NaCl"` into `"Na"` and `"Cl"`.

The program variable `first` always contains the subscript of the beginning of the current component. During each execution of the loop, the condition

```
compound[next] >= 'A' && compound[next] <= 'Z'
```

tests to see whether the next character is a capital letter. If it is, the statements

```
printf("%s\n", substr(elem, compound, first, next,
       ELEM_LEN));
first = next;
```

cause all characters in the current component (from `first` up to, but not including, the next capital letter) to be printed, and `first` to be reset to the subscript of the next capital letter.

Figure 9.8   Program Using substr Function to Separate Compounds into Elemental Components

```
/*
 * Prints each elemental component of a compound
 */

#include <stdio.h>
#include <string.h>

#define CMP_LEN  30  /* size of string to hold a compound  */
#define ELEM_LEN 10  /* size of string to hold a component */

/*  insert function substr from Fig. 9.7 here  */

int
main(void)
{
    char compound[CMP_LEN];  /* string representing a compound */
    char elem[ELEM_LEN];     /* one elemental component        */
    int  first, next;

    /*  Gets data string representing compound                 */
    printf("Enter a compound> ");
    scanf("%s", compound);
```

(continued)

Figure 9.8   *(continued)*

```
    /*  Prints each elemental component.  These are identified
        by an initial capital letter.                         */
    first = 0;
    for  (next = 1;  next < strlen(compound);  ++next)
        if (compound[next] >= 'A' && compound[next] <= 'Z') {
            printf("%s\n", substr(elem, compound, first, next, ELEM_LEN));
            first = next;
        }

    /*  Prints the last component                             */
    printf("%s\n", substr(elem, compound, first, strlen(compound),
                        ELEM_LEN));

    return (0);
}

Enter a compound> H2SO4
H2
S
O4
```

The statement

```
printf("%s\n", substr(elem, compound, first,
                        strlen(compound), ELEM_LEN));
```

following the loop is used to print the last component. Notice that the last two calls to `printf` take advantage of the fact that `substr` returns as its value the starting address of the string it has just stored in `elem`. Rather than writing two statements

```
substr(elem, compound, . . .
printf("%s\n", elem);
```

we can simply call the function `substr` right at the spot where the value it computes is needed—that is, in the argument list for `printf`.

Also check carefully the use of `CMP_LEN` and `strlen(compound)`. In this program, we see again the use of part of an array. As we studied in Chapter 8, in situations like this, the declared size of the array is no longer the effective size once data have been stored in the array. When dealing with strings, we use the `strlen` string library function to find the number of characters in use (not counting the null character). ⬅

Self-Check

1. Given the function `substr` from Fig. 9.7 and the string variables `ssn1`, `pres`, `first`, and `last` (defined in Examples 9.3 and 9.4), show what would be printed by

```
printf("%s", substr(last, ssn1, 0, 2, 20));
printf(" %s", substr(last, pres, 7, strlen(pres), 20));
printf(" %s%s\n", substr(first, pres, 7, 9, 20),
        substr(first, pres, 14, 16, 20));
```

Programming

1. Write a program to take a product code from Millie's Mail-Order Catalog and separate it into its component parts. A MMOC product code begins with one or more letters identifying the warehouse where the product is stored. Next come the one or more digits that are the product ID. The final field of the string starts with a capital letter and represents qualifiers such as size, color, and so on. For example, ATL1203S14 stands for product 1203, size 14, in the Atlanta warehouse. Write a program that takes a code, finds the position of the first digit and of the first letter after the digits, and uses `substr` to print a report such as the following:

```
Warehouse:  ATL
Product:    1203
Qualifiers: S14
```

2. Write a function `trim_blanks` that takes a single string argument and returns the string with leading and trailing blanks removed. Use `substr` in `trim_blanks`.

a_string (before)

		a		p	h	r	a	s	e				\0

a_string (after the call: trim_blanks(a_string);)

a		p	h	r	a	s	e	\0					

9.3 LONGER STRINGS: CONCATENATION AND WHOLE-LINE INPUT

In this section, we look at a function that lets us join (concatenate) two strings to form a longer string. We also see a function that lets us scan a full line of character data even if there are internal blanks.

Concatenation

The function `concat` shown in Fig. 9.9 forms a string by joining `str1` and `str2` and returns as much of the string as will fit in `dest`. Like `strassign` and `substr`, `concat` requires the calling module to provide space for the result and to send in the size of the space.

Figure 9.9   String Concatenation Function

```
/*
 *  Concatenates str1 and str2, copying as much of the result as will fit
 *  into dest, which has space available for dest_len characters
 *  Pre:  dest_len <= MAX_STR_LEN for correct results
 */
char *
concat(char        dest[],    /* output - destination string         */
       const char str1[],     /* input  - strings                    */
       const char str2[],     /*            to concatenate           */
       int        dest_len)   /* input  - available space in dest     */
{
    char result[MAX_STR_LEN];  /* local string space for result       */

    /*  Checks if result will be wrong due to lack of local space     */
    if (dest_len > MAX_STR_LEN  &&
        strlen(str1) + strlen(str2) >= MAX_STR_LEN)
          printf("\nInsufficient local storage causing loss of data\n");

    /*  Builds result in local storage to properly handle overlap
        of dest and str1 or str2                                      */
    strassign(result, str1, MAX_STR_LEN);
    strncat(result, str2, MAX_STR_LEN - strlen(result) - 1);
    strassign(dest, result, dest_len);

    return (dest);
}
```

Function `concat` uses a local variable in which to build the result in case the destination variable overlaps one of the source strings. It calls the string library function `strncat`, which modifies its first argument by adding to the current value up to n characters of its second argument, where n is the third argument. Function `strncat` always ends the result it returns with `'\0'`, so, at most, it adds n+1 characters to the end of its output argument.

EXAMPLE 9.6 ▶

In the following expressions, we assume access to the temporary variables

```
char tmp1[40], tmp2[40], tmp3[40], tmp4[40];
```

The call to `concat`

```
concat(tmp1, "ABC", "DE", 40)
```

returns a string `"ABCDE"` that is the concatenation of `"ABC"` and `"DE"`.

Because the functions `strassign`, `substr`, and `concat` all return values of type `char *`, calls to them can be nested. For example, given a string variable named `message` containing eleven or more characters, this expression

```
concat(tmp3,
        substr(tmp1, message, 0, 5, 40),
        concat(tmp2, "*****",
               substr(tmp4, message, 10,
                        strlen(message), 40)), 40);
```

creates a new string that differs from `message` only in character positions 5 through 9 (replaced with asterisks). Although the nested expression is quite legal, many readers would find this sequence of statements easier to follow,

```
substr(tmp1, message, 0, 5, 40);
substr(tmp2, message, 10, strlen(message), 40);
concat(tmp3, tmp1, "*****", 40);
concat(tmp3, tmp3, tmp2, 40);
```

and the result of the final call to `concat` matches the result of the nested expression. ◀

Distinction between Characters and Strings

When using the concatenation function, one may be tempted to supply a single character as one of the two strings to join. A type `char` value is *not* a valid argument for a function with a corresponding parameter of type `char *`. Note the difference internally between the representations of the character `'Q'` and the string `"Q"`.

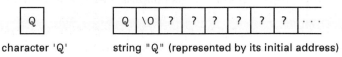

If you wish to add a single character at the end of a string, you should view the string as an array and use assignment to subscripted elements for access. Be sure to include the null character at the end of the string.

Scanning a Full Line

Although blanks are natural separators to place between numeric data values, viewing them as delimiters (as `scanf` does) when processing strings does not always make sense since a blank is a perfectly valid character element of a string. For instance, in many situations it is helpful to have the lines of a document numbered for reference. Figure 9.10 shows a program that scans the data file one line at a time and prints a new version with the lines numbered.

The function subprogram `scanline` is one you may wish to use for input of a complete line of text. Although we include an explanation of the code of `scanline` following Fig. 9.10, this function is another you could use based simply on its purpose and parameters.

Figure 9.10   Function scanline for Whole-Line Input

```
/*
 *  Numbers and double spaces lines of a document.  Lines longer than
 *  MAX_LEN - 1 characters are split on two lines.
 */

#include <stdio.h>
#include <string.h>

#define MAX_LEN 120

/*
 *  Gets one line of data from standard input.  Returns an empty string on
 *  end of file.
 */
char *
scanline(char dest[],        /* output - destination string          */
```

(continued)

Figure 9.10   *(continued)*

```
        int  dest_len)    /* input  - space available in dest       */
{
    /* Uses library function fgets to get the next input line.  If
       fgets returns 0, signals end of file by returning an empty
       string.                                                      */
    if (fgets(dest, dest_len, stdin) == 0)
        dest[0] = '\0';
    /* Removes newline character if it is present                   */
    else if (dest[strlen(dest) - 1] == '\n')
        dest[strlen(dest) - 1] = '\0';

    return (dest);
}

int
main(void)
{
    char line[MAX_LEN];
    int  i = 0;

    for  (scanline(line, MAX_LEN);
          strlen(line) > 0;
          scanline(line, MAX_LEN)) {
        printf("\n%3d>> %s\n", ++i, line);
    }

    return (0);
}
```

File used as input

In the early 1960s, designers and implementers of operating
systems were faced with a significant dilemma. As people's
expectations of modern operating systems escalated, so did
the complexity of the systems themselves. Like other
programmers solving difficult problems, the systems
programmers desperately needed the readability and
modularity of a powerful high-level programming language.

(continued)

Figure 9.10   *(continued)*

Program output

```
1>> In the early 1960s, designers and implementers of operating
2>> systems were faced with a significant dilemma. As people's
3>> expectations of modern operating systems escalated, so did
4>> the complexity of the systems themselves. Like other
5>> programmers solving difficult problems, the systems
6>> programmers desperately needed the readability and
7>> modularity of a powerful high-level programming language.
```

We could have called the string library input function `fgets` directly from our program to scan a line of up to some maximum number of characters. However, one never knows whether or not the line returned by `fgets` ends with a newline character until one checks. The first argument to `fgets` is the character array in which to store a line of text; the second argument is the maximum number of characters to store. If `fgets` encounters a `'\n'` in the input before reaching the maximum, it includes the `'\n'` in the string returned and adds a `'\0'` after it. However, if the maximum − 1 characters are scanned without seeing a `'\n'`, `fgets` stops scanning and just adds a `'\0'` to the line. The third argument to `fgets` is the source of the input. In Chapter 12, we will see how functions like `fgets` help us to use more than one input or output file in a program. In our `scanline` function, we use `stdin` as the third argument. C assigns this name to the standard input device, the source from which the basic input function `scanf` always takes data.

**EXERCISES FOR
SECTION 9.3**

Self-Check

1. Given the string `pres` (value is `"ADAMS, JOHN QUINCY"`) and the 40-character temporary variables `tmp1` and `tmp2`, what string is printed by the following code fragment?

```
substr(tmp1, pres, 7, 11, 40);
concat(tmp1, tmp1, " ", 40);
substr(tmp2, pres, 0, 5, 40);
printf("%s", concat(tmp1, tmp1, tmp2, 40));
```

2. There is an error in the second call to `concat` in the following code fragment. What is the error? Why is it wrong? What is the correct call to `concat`? What is the value of `tmp1` after execution of your corrected call?

```
substr(tmp1, pres, 12, strlen(pres), 40);
concat(tmp1, tmp1, " ", 40);
concat(tmp1, tmp1, pres[7], 40);
```

Programming

1. Write a function `bracket_by_len` that takes a word as an input argument and returns the word bracketed to indicate its length. Words less than five characters long are bracketed with << >>, words five to ten letters long are bracketed with (* *), and words over ten characters long are bracketed with /+ +/. Your function should require the calling function to provide as the first argument, space for the result, and as the third argument, the amount of space available. Consider the expected results of these calls to the function.

```
bracket_by_len(tmp, "insufficiently", 20)        =>
        "/+insufficiently+/"
bracket_by_len(tmp, "the", 20)         =>         "<<the>>"
```

9.4 STRING COMPARISON

In earlier chapters, we studied the fact that characters are represented by numeric codes, and we used relational and equality operators to compare characters. For example, the conditions

```
crsr_or_frgt == 'C'
```

and

```
ch1 < ch2
```

were used to test character variables in decision statements. Unfortunately, these operators cannot be used for comparison of strings because of C's representation of strings as arrays.

Because an array name used with no subscript represents the address of the initial array element, if `str1` and `str2` are string variables, the condition

```
str1 < str2
```

is *not* checking whether `str1` precedes `str2` alphabetically. However, the comparison *is* legal, for it determines whether the place in memory where storage of `str1` begins precedes the place in memory where `str2` begins.

The standard string library provides the `int` function `strcmp` for comparison of two strings that we will refer to as `str1` and `str2`. Function `strcmp` separates its argument pairs into three categories as shown in Table 9.1.

In this table, we are using the expression "less than" as a string generalization of the "less than" comparison of characters. We have seen that for character variables `ch1` and `ch2`, `ch1 < ch2` is true if the numeric character code value of `ch1` is less than the code in `ch2`. ANSI C extends this concept to strings by stating the following two conditions to define "less than."

1. If the first n characters of `str1` and `str2` match and `str1[n]`, `str2[n]` are the first nonmatching corresponding characters, `str1` is less than `str2` if `str1[n] < str2[n]`.

```
str1 t h r i l l          str1 e n e r g y
str2 t h r o w            str2 f o r c e
           *                   *
First 3 letters match.    First 0 letters match.
str1[3] < str2[3]         str1[0] < str2[0]
    'i' < 'o'                 'e' < 'f'
```

2. If `str1` is shorter than `str2` and all the characters of `str1` match the corresponding characters of `str2`, `str1` is less than `str2`.

```
str1  j o y
str2  j o y o u s
```

Table 9.1   Possible Results of strcmp(str1, str2)

Relationship	Value Returned	Example
`str1` is less than `str2`	negative integer	`str1` is `"marigold"` `str2` is `"tulip"`
`str1` equals `str2`	zero	`str1` and `str2` are both `"end"`
`str1` is greater than `str2`	positive integer	`str1` is `"shrimp"` `str2` is `"crab"`

Figure 9.11   Numeric and String Versions of Portion of Bubble Sort That Exchanges Out-of-Order Array Elements

```
if (list[i] > list[i + 1]){          if (strcmp(list[i], list[i + 1]) > 0) {
    temp = list[i];                      strassign(temp, list[i], STR_LEN);
    list[i] = list[i + 1];               strassign(list[i], list[i + 1], STR_LEN);
    list[i + 1] = temp;                  strassign(list[i + 1], temp, STR_LEN);
    sorted = 0;                          sorted = 0;
}                                    }
```

EXAMPLE 9.7 String comparisons are essential when alphabetizing a list. To alphabetize a list of words made up of either all uppercase or all lowercase letters, we could use the bubble sort function we developed in Section 8.7, if we made slight modifications in the prototype and in the code portion that exchanges two out-of-order values (see Fig. 8.18). Figure 9.11 compares the numeric and string versions of this code. The second version uses the string assignment function from Fig. 9.6. This version assumes that the array being alphabetized is a list of strings of up to STR_LEN characters and that **temp** is a local variable declared as

```
char temp[STR_LEN];
```
⬅

EXAMPLE 9.8 When we process a list of string data interactively, we often do not know in advance how much data will be entered. In this situation, we can use a sentinel-controlled loop, prompting the user to type in the sentinel value when entry of the data is complete. Figure 9.12 outlines such a loop, using **strcmp** to check for entry of the sentinel.
⬅

Figure 9.12   Sentinel-Controlled Loop for String Input

```
printf("Enter list of words on as many lines as you like.\n");
printf("Separate words by at least one blank.\n");
printf("When done, enter %s to quit.\n", SENT);

for  (scanf("%s", word);
      strcmp(word, SENT) != 0;
      scanf("%s", word)) {
   /* process word */
}
```

Self-Check

1. Write C code to accomplish each of the following goals. Assume that all string variables mentioned can hold up to STR_LEN characters.
   a. Write a message indicating whether name1 and name2 match.
   b. Store in the string variable word either the value of w1 or of w2. Choose the value that comes first alphabetically.
   c. Store in mtch matching initial portions of s1 and s2. For example, if s1 is "placozoa" and s2 is "placement", mtch becomes "plac". If s1 is "joy" and s2 is "sorrow", mtch becomes the empty string.

Programming

1. Write the string bubble sort function described in Example 9.7.

9.5 ARRAYS OF POINTERS

In Section 9.4, we discussed how we might modify our numeric bubble sort code to create a program that would alphabetize a list of strings composed of uppercase or lowercase letters. Let's look closely at the code that exchanges out-of-order strings in Fig. 9.13.

Figure 9.14 pictures the data area of strassign and the data area of the calling function as the second call to strassign begins. This figure reminds us that C represents every array by its starting address. Since each list[i] is a reference to an array of characters, it is passed to a function as a pointer, that is, as the address of the array's element 0. When we consider sorting a list of strings, we see a lot of copying of characters from one memory cell to another. We have three operations that copy an entire string for every exchange that the sort requires, and when the sort is complete, our original list is lost.

Figure 9.13   Exchanging Out-of-Order Strings

```
if (strcmp(list[i], list[i + 1]) > 0) {
    strassign(temp, list[i], STR_LEN);
    strassign(list[i], list[i + 1], STR_LEN);
    strassign(list[i + 1], temp, STR_LEN);
    sorted = 0;
}
```

**Figure 9.14
Executing**
```
strassign
  (list[i],
  list[i + 1],
  STR_LEN);
```

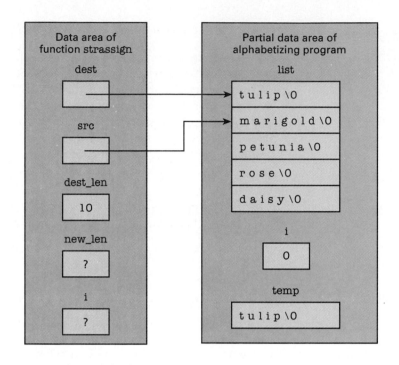

In fact, C's use of pointers to represent arrays presents us with an opportunity to develop an alternate approach to our sorting problem. Study the two arrays in Fig. 9.15.

Listing the values of the elements of `alphap`

```
alphap[0]        address of    "daisy"
alphap[1]        address of    "marigold"
alphap[2]        address of    "petunia"
alphap[3]        address of    "rose"
alphap[4]        address of    "tulip"
```

**Figure 9.15
An Array
of Pointers**

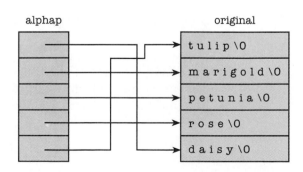

calls to our attention that daisy, marigold, petunia, rose, tulip form an alphabetized list. Therefore, if we were to execute this loop,

```
for  (i = 0;  i < 5;  ++i)
     printf("%s\n", alphap[i]);
```

we would see displayed the contents of `original` in alphabetical order, just as
if we had copied the strings into a new array and sorted them. When `printf`
sees a `%s` specifier, it *always* expects to receive the starting address of a string
as the corresponding input argument, so `alphap[i]` is just as legitimate an
argument as `original[i]`.

How would we declare the array of pointers `alphap`? Each element is the
address of a character string, and there are five elements, so the appropriate declaration is

```
char *alphap[5];
```

In our next example, we explore how to use an array of pointers to maintain two
orderings of a list of strings while keeping only one copy of each string.

EXAMPLE 9.9   The Open School admits children to its kindergarten in the order in which they
apply. However, most of the staff's use of the list of applicants is made easier if
the list is alphabetized. The program in Fig. 9.16 takes an input list of names
reflecting the order in which applications were received and creates an array of
pointers through which the list can be accessed in alphabetical order.

The array of pointers is initialized by assigning to each element the starting address of one of the strings in the `applicants` array. Then a bubble
sort is applied to the array of pointers. Although `strcmp` looks at the actual
strings whose starting addresses are in the array of pointers, the element
exchange code moves only the pointers.

Figure 9.16   Two Orderings of One List Using an Array of Pointers

```
/*
 * Maintains two orderings of a list of applicants:  the original
 * ordering of the data, and an alphabetical ordering accessed through an
 * array of pointers.
 */
```

(continued)

Figure 9.16 *(continued)*

```
#include <stdio.h>
#define STRSIZ 30  /*  maximum string length */
#define MAXAPP 50  /*  maximum number of applications accepted */

/*
 *  Orders the pointers in array list so they access strings in
 *  alphabetical order
 *  Pre:  first n elements of list reference strings of uniform case;
 *        n >= 0
 */
void
bubble_str(char *list[],  /* input/output - array of pointers being
                              reordered to access strings alphabetically */
           int   n)       /* input - number of elements to sort         */
{
    int   i,
          pass;      /* number of current pass through array          */
    char *temp;      /* temporary variable used in exchange of out-of-
                        order pairs                                    */
    int   sorted;    /* whether or not array is definitely sorted     */

    pass = 1;
    do {
        /*  Assumes array is sorted until an out-of-order pair is found */
        sorted = 1;

        /*  Makes a pass through possibly unsorted elements; strcmp
            looks at strings whose starting addresses are in list[i],
            list[i + 1]                                                 */
        for (i = 0;  i < n - pass;  ++i) {
            if (strcmp(list[i], list[i + 1]) > 0) {
                /* Exchanges pair of pointers */
                temp = list[i];
                list[i] = list[i + 1];
                list[i + 1] = temp;
                sorted = 0;
            }
        }
```

(continued)

Figure 9.16   *(continued)*

```
        ++pass;
    } while(!sorted);
}

/*  insert function scanline from Fig. 9.10 here */

int
main(void)
{
    char   applicants[MAXAPP][STRSIZ]; /* list of applicants in the
                                           order in which they applied */
    char  *alpha[MAXAPP];              /* list of pointers to
                                           applicants                   */
    int    num_app,                    /* actual number of applicants  */
           i, one_char;

    /*  Gets applicant list                                            */
    printf("Enter number of applicants (0 . . %d)\n> ", MAXAPP);
    scanf("%d", &num_app);
    do      /* skips rest of line after number */
        scanf("%c", &one_char);
    while (one_char != '\n');
    printf("Enter names of applicants on separate lines\n");
    printf("in the order in which they applied\n");
    for (i = 0;  i < num_app; ++i)
        scanline(applicants[i], STRSIZ);

    /*  Fills array of pointers and sorts                              */
    for (i = 0;  i < num_app;  ++i)
        alpha[i] = applicants[i];   /* copies ONLY address */
    bubble_str(alpha, num_app);

    /*  Prints both lists                                              */
    printf("\n\nApplication Order                ");
    printf("Alphabetical Order\n\n");
    for (i = 0;  i < num_app;  ++i)
        printf("%-30s    %-30s\n", applicants[i], alpha[i]);

    return(0);
}
```

(continued)

Figure 9.16 *(continued)*

```
Enter number of applicants (0 . . 50)
> 5
Enter names of applicants on separate lines
in the order in which they applied
SADDLER, MARGARET
INGRAM, RICHARD
FAATZ, SUSAN
GONZALES, LORI
KEITH, CHARLES

Application Order                Alphabetical Order

SADDLER, MARGARET                FAATZ, SUSAN
INGRAM, RICHARD                  GONZALES, LORI
FAATZ, SUSAN                     INGRAM, RICHARD
GONZALES, LORI                   KEITH, CHARLES
KEITH, CHARLES                   SADDLER, MARGARET
```

Using an array of pointers to represent a second or third or fourth ordering of a list of strings has several benefits. First, a pointer (an integer address) requires less storage space than a full copy of a character string. Second, our sorting function executes faster when it copies only pointers and not complete arrays of characters. Finally, because the strings themselves are stored only once, a spelling correction made in the original list would automatically be reflected in the other orderings as well.

Arrays of String Constants

C also permits the use of an array of pointers to represent a list of string constants. Two alternatives for representing the list of month names we saw in Section 9.1 follow.

```
char month[12][10] = {"January", "February", "March", April",
                      "May", "June", "July","August",
                      "September", "October", "November",
                      "December"};
char *month[12] = {"January", "February", "March", "April",
                   "May", "June", "July", "August",
                   "September", "October", "November",
                   "December"};
```

Actually, the number of rows (12) is optional in both of these declarations since the initialization list also implies this value.

Self-Check

1. Write two prototypes for a function that orders a list of strings according to string length—shortest to longest. In the first, the function should expect an input/output argument that is a two-dimensional array of characters in which strings have at most STRSIZ characters. In the second, the function should expect an input/output argument that is an array of pointers.
2. Consider the following valid call to printf. Is strs a two-dimensional array of characters or an array of pointers to strings?

```
printf("%s\n", strs[4]);
```

Programming

1. Write the function described in Exercise 1 using an array of pointers.

9.6 CHARACTER OPERATIONS

When we develop programs that involve string processing, often we must work with the individual characters that make up the string. C provides character input/output routines as part of the stdio library, and an extensive collection of facilities for character analysis and conversion is available in the library we #include as <ctype.h>.

Character Input/Output

The stdio library includes a routine named getchar that is used to get the next character from the standard input source, the same input source that scanf uses. Unlike scanf, getchar does not expect the calling module to pass as an argument the address of a variable in which to store the input character. Rather, getchar takes no arguments and returns the character as its result. Either of the following two expressions can be used to store the next available input character in ch.

```
scanf("%c", &ch)              ch = getchar()
```

There is, however, a difference between the two fragments, because the *values* of the expressions themselves are different. You will recall that scanf returns as its value an integer representing the number of values it took from the input stream for storage through its output parameters. When `scanf` encounters the end of the input file, it returns the value associated with EOF. In the expression that calls `getchar`, we have an assignment operator, so the value of the expression is the value assigned, namely the character that `getchar` found in standard input. What if there were no characters for `getchar` to take? What if `getchar` came across the end of the data? When we look up a full description of the `getchar` facility, we discover that the type of the value it returns is not `char` but `int`. We have already seen that in a computer, characters are represented by integer codes, and in Chapter 7 we used character codes that we cast as type `int` as the initial and ending values of a type `int` loop control variable.

Although character codes are, in fact, integers, in most C implementations the `char` data type is allotted only enough space to store the range of integers actually used by the implementation's character set. This range does not include the negative value associated with the name EOF. The data type `int` must be able to represent a much larger range of integers that includes both the full range of character codes and the EOF value. For this reason, we use a type `int` variable to store the result of a call to `getchar`, at least until we verify that `getchar` did not return EOF.

 **EXAMPLE 9.10**

In Fig. 9.17, we write a version of `scanline` that uses `getchar`. Like the `scanline` of Fig. 9.10, this new version takes as arguments the string variable in which to store the input line and the amount of space available. It stores in the output argument either the full input line or as much as will fit. However, when part of the line does not fit, the `scanline` of Fig. 9.17 does not leave this portion to be scanned on a later call. Rather, it discards the extra characters until `'\n'` or EOF is encountered.

Figure 9.17   Implementation of scanline Function Using getchar

```
/*
 *  Gets one line of data from standard input.  Returns an empty string on
 *  end of file.  If data line will not fit in allotted space, stores
 *  portion that does fit and discards rest of input line.
 */
char *
scanline(char dest[],     /* output - destination string              */
         int  dest_len)   /* input  - space available in dest         */
{
     int i, ch;
```

(continued)

Figure 9.17 *(continued)*

```
/*  Gets next line one character at a time.                      */
i = 0;
for  (ch = getchar();
         ch != '\n'  &&  ch != EOF   &&  i < dest_len - 1;
         ch = getchar())
    dest[i++] = ch;
dest[i] = '\0';

/*  Discards any characters that remain on input line            */
while (ch != '\n'  &&  ch != EOF)
    ch = getchar();

return (dest);
}
```

The standard library's single-character output facility is named `putchar`, and it takes a single argument of type `int`. Since type `char` can always be converted to type `int` with no loss of information, we frequently call `putchar` with arguments of type `char`.　◀

Character Analysis and Conversion

In many string-processing applications, we need to know if a character belongs to a particular subset of the overall character set. Is this character a letter? a digit? a punctuation mark? The library we `#include` as `<ctype.h>` defines facilities for answering questions like these and also provides routines to do common character conversions like uppercase to lowercase or lowercase to uppercase. Table 9.2 lists a number of these routines; each takes a single type `int` argument representing a character code. The *classification* routines (those whose names begin with "`is`") return a nonzero value (not necessarily 1) if the condition checked is true. The example given for the `isspace` routine is a loop that can be used to advance to the next nonblank input character.

EXAMPLE 9.11　When we alphabetize a list of strings, we must frequently deal with words containing a mixture of uppercase and lowercase letters. In this situation, we cannot rely on `strcmp` to give useful results. This call to `strcmp`

```
strcmp("Ziegler", "aardvark")
```

Table 9.2   Character Classification and Conversion Facilities in ctype Library

Facility	Checks	Example
isalpha	if argument is a letter of the alphabet	`if (isalpha(ch))` `    printf("%c is a letter\n", ch);`
isdigit	if argument is one of the ten decimal digits	`dec_digit = isdigit(ch);`

islower (isupper)	if argument is a lowercase (or uppercase) letter of the alphabet	`if (islower(fst_let)) {`
		`    printf("\nError:  sentence ");`
		`    printf("should begin with a ");`
		`    printf("capital letter.\n");`
		`}`

ispunct	if argument is a punctuation character, that is, a noncontrol character that is not a space, a letter of the alphabet, or a digit	`if (ispunct(ch))`
		`    printf("Punctuation mark: %c\n",`
		`            ch);`

isspace	if argument is a whitespace character such as a space, a newline, or a tab	`while (isspace(c = getchar()) &&` `        c != EOF) {}`

Facility	Converts	Example

tolower (toupper)	its lowercase (or uppercase) letter argument to the uppercase (or lowercase) equivalent and returns this equivalent as the value of the call	`if (islower(ch))`
		`    printf("Capital %c = %c\n",`
		`            ch, toupper(ch));`

will return a negative value indicating that `"Ziegler"` is less than `"aardvark"` if our system is using the ASCII character codes, since all capital letters have lower ASCII character codes than the lowercase letters. On computers that use the EBCDIC character set, we also have difficulty handling a mixture of uppercase and lowercase letters because all *lowercase* letters have smaller character codes than uppercase letters (see Appendix A). Figure 9.18 shows a function `string_greater` that could be used to find out-of-order elements when alphabetizing a list of strings in a situation where the case of the letters should be ignored. The function converts each of its arguments to all capital letters using `string_toupper` before comparing them. Since `str1` and `str2` are strictly input parameters of `string_greater`, their values must not be changed. However, `string_toupper` does change its parameter, so we first make copies of `str1` and `str2` in `s1` and `s2` and then send these copies to `string_toupper`.

Figure 9.18   Function Implementing Strings for a Greater-Than Operator That Ignores Case

```c
#include <string.h>
#include <ctype.h>

#define STRSIZ 80

/*  insert function strassign                                              */

/*
 *  Converts the lowercase letters of its string argument to uppercase
 *  leaving other characters unchanged.
 */
char *
string_toupper(char str[]) /* input/output - string whose lowercase
                                letters are to be replaced by uppercase  */
{
      int i;

      for  (i = 0;  i < strlen(str);  ++i)
          if (islower(str[i]))
               str[i] = toupper(str[i]);

      return (str);
}

/*
 *  Compares two strings of up to STRSIZ characters ignoring the case of
 *  the letters.  Returns the value 1 if str1 should follow str2 in an
 *  alphabetized list; otherwise returns 0
 */
int
string_greater(const char str1[],  /* input -                            */
               const char str2[])  /*    strings to compare              */
{
      char s1[STRSIZ], s2[STRSIZ];

      /*  Copies str1 and str2 so string_toupper can modify copies      */
      strassign(s1, str1, STRSIZ);
      strassign(s2, str2, STRSIZ);

      return (strcmp(string_toupper(s1), string_toupper(s2)) > 0);
}
```

Self-Check

1. What is wrong with the following statement? How would you rewrite it to accomplish its apparent purpose?

```
if (isupper(substr(tmp, str, 0, 1, 30)))
    printf("%s begins with a capital letter\n", str);
```

Programming

1. Write a function `scanstring` that works basically like `scanf` with a `%s` placeholder—that is, skips leading whitespace and then copies a string up to the next whitespace character—except that it uses `getchar` and takes an extra argument stating the amount of space available in the first argument. Function `scanstring` should prevent overflow of its string argument.
2. Write a batch program that takes and echoes input data one character at a time until `EOF` is encountered and then prints a summary such as

```
The 14 lines of text processed contained 20 capital
letters, 607 lowercase letters, and 32 punctuation
marks.
```

9.7 STRING-TO-NUMBER AND NUMBER-TO-STRING CONVERSIONS

Some of the most common operations in a computer program are the conversion of a string like `"3.14159"` to the type `double` numeric value it represents and the conversion of a number like −36 from its internal representation in computer memory to the three-character string `"-36"` that is our usual picture of this number. Such conversions are constantly being carried out by the library functions `scanf` and `printf`. Table 9.3 and Table 9.4 review some of the format string placeholders that we have used in earlier chapters to guide the conversion process. These tables also present some new placeholders. The last example in Table 9.4 shows the use of a maximum field width. The `%3.3s` placeholder indicates output of a string using a minimum field width of 3 (3.3) and a maximum field width of 3 (3.3). As a result, only the first three characters of the string are printed.

The functions `printf` and `scanf` are such powerful string manipulators that sometimes we would like to directly control the strings on which they work. The stdio library gives us this ability through similar functions named `sprintf` and `sscanf`. The `sprintf` function requires space for a string as

Table 9.3   Review of Use of scanf

Declaration	Statement	Data (# Means Blank)	Value Stored
char t	scanf("%c", &t);	#g \n A	# \n A
int n	scanf("%d", &n);	#32# ##-8.6 #+19#	32 -8 19
double x	scanf("%lf", &x);	###4.32# #-8# #1.76e-3#	4.32 -8.0 .00176
char str[10]	scanf("%s", str);	##hello\n overlengthy#	hello\0 overlengthy\0 (overruns length of str)

Table 9.4   Placeholders Used with printf

Value	Placeholder	Output (# Means Blank)
'a'	%c %3c %-3c	a ##a a##
-10	%d %2d %4d %-5d	-10 -10 #-10 -10##
49.76	%.3f %.1f %10.2f %10.3e	49.760 49.8 #####49.76 #4.976e+01
"fantastic"	%s %6s %12s %-12s %3.3s	fantastic fantastic ###fantastic fantastic### fan

its first argument. Consider this call to `sprintf`; assume that `s` has been declared as `char s[100]`, and the values of type `int` variables `mon`, `day`, and `year` are as shown.

```
sprintf(s, "%d/%d/%d", mon, day, year);
```

Function `sprintf` substitutes values for placeholders just as `printf` does, but instead of printing the result, `sprintf` stores it in the character array accessed by its initial argument.

s

8 / 2 3 / 1 9 1 4 \0

The `sscanf` function works exactly like `scanf` except instead of taking the data values for its output parameters from the standard input device, it takes data from the string that is its first argument. For example, the illustration that follows shows how

```
sscanf(" 85   96.2   hello", "%d%lf%s", &num, &val, word);
```

stores values from the first string.

num	val	word
85	96.2	h e l l o \0

EXAMPLE 9.12 ▶ Because `sscanf` is available, we have the option of taking an entire data line as input and verifying that it conforms to the expected format before attempting to convert and store the line's values in memory. For example, if one line of data is expected to contain two nonnegative integers and then a string of up to 15 characters, one could write a validation function that would take the entire data line as an input argument and check the line one character at a time. The validation routine would look for optional whitespace characters followed by a group of digits, more whitespace, another group of digits, more whitespace, and then up to 15 nonwhitespace characters. If the validation function discovered an error, it could print a message and return the position of the character where the error was detected. Otherwise, it could return a negative value. Figure 9.19 shows a program segment that assumes the availability of such a validation function and also of the `scanline` function defined in Fig. 9.17.   ◀

Figure 9.19   Program Segment That Validates Input Line before Storing Data Values

```
char data_line[STRSIZ], str[STRSIZ];
int n1, n2, error_mark;

scanline(data_line, STRSIZ);
error_mark = validate(data_line);

if (error_mark < 0)) {
      /*  Stores in memory values from correct data line  */
      sscanf(data_line, "%d%d%s", &n1, &n2, str);
} else {
      /*  Prints line and marks spot where error detected */
      printf("\n%s\n", data_line);
      for  (i = 0;  i < error_mark;  ++i)
          putchar(' ');
      putchar('/');
}
```

In our next example, we combine the power of sprintf/sscanf with the ability to directly access an array element to produce convenient functions for the conversion of one representation of a date to another.

EXAMPLE 9.13 The conversion of a date from a representation including a month name to a list of three numbers (12 January 1941 => 1 12 1941) and the reverse conversion are very common in everyday life. The program in Fig. 9.20 shows functions for both conversions and a driver program to test them. Arrays of pointers to strings are extremely useful for storing the constants needed in this type of conversion. Note that we could change the representation of the date string to use an abbreviation (12 JAN 1941) or a different language (12 janvier 1941) merely by

Figure 9.20   Functions That Convert Representations of Dates

```
/*
 * Functions to change the representation of a date from a string containing
 * day, month name and year to three integers (month day year) and vice versa
 */
```

(continued)

Figure 9.20 *(continued)*

```c
#include <stdio.h>
#include <string.h>

#define STRSIZ 40

/*
 *  Takes integers representing a month, day and year and produces a
 *  string representation of the same date.
 */
char *
nums_to_string_date(char         date_string[],   /* output - string
                                                          representation      */
                    int          month,           /* input  -                 */
                    int          day,             /* input  representation     */
                    int          year,            /*    as three numbers       */
                    const char   *month_names[])   /* input  - string represen-
                                                          tations of months     */
{
    sprintf(date_string, "%d %s %d", day, month_names[month - 1], year);
    return (date_string);
}

#define NOT_FOUND -1    /*  Value returned by search function if target
                            not found                                       */

/*
 *  Searches for target item in first n elements of array arr
 *  Returns index of target or NOT_FOUND
 *  Pre:  target and first n elements of array arr are defined and n>0
 */
int
search(const char *arr[],      /*  array to search                          */
       const char  target[],   /*  value searched for                       */
       int         n)          /*  number of array elements to search       */
{
    int i,
        found = 0,      /*  whether or not target has been found */
        where;          /*   index where target found or NOT_FOUND*/
```

(continued)

Figure 9.20 *(continued)*

```
        /*  Compares each element to target                         */
        i = 0;
        while (!found && i < n) {
            if (strcmp(arr[i], target) == 0)
                    found = 1;
            else
                    ++i;
        }

        /* Returns index of element matching target or NOT_FOUND    */
        if (found)
                where = i;
        else
                where = NOT_FOUND;
        return (where);
}


/*
 *  Converts date represented as a string containing a month name to
 *  three integers representing month, day, and year
 */
void
string_date_to_nums(const char  date_string[], /* input - date to convert */
                    int         *monthp,        /* output - month number */
                    int         *dayp,          /* output - day number   */
                    int         *yearp,         /* output - year number  */
                    const char *month_names[]) /* input - names used in
                                                      date string       */
{
        char mth_nam[STRSIZ];
        int  month_index;

        sscanf(date_string, "%d%s%d", dayp, mth_nam, yearp);

        /*  Finds array index (range 0..11) of month name.            */
        month_index = search(month_names, mth_nam, 12);
        *monthp = month_index + 1;
}
```

(continued)

Figure 9.20 *(continued)*

```
/*  Tests date conversion functions                                  */
int
main(void)
{
      char *month_names[12] = {"January", "February", "March", "April",
                               "May", "June", "July", "August",
                               "September", "October", "November",
                               "December"};

      int m, y, mon, day, year;
      char date_string[STRSIZ];

      for  (y = 1993;  y < 2010;  y += 10)
          for  (m = 1;  m <= 12;  ++m) {
              printf("%s", nums_to_string_date(date_string,
                                          m, 15, y, month_names));
              string_date_to_nums(date_string, &mon, &day, &year,
                                  month_names);
              printf(" = %d/%d/%d\n", mon, day, year);
          }

      return (0);
}

15 January 1993 = 1/15/1993
15 February 1993 = 2/15/1993
. . .
15 December 2003 = 12/15/1993
```

using a different initialization of our array. The conversion from a string including the month name to a group of three numbers involves a search of the list of
month names using a function that is a string adaptation of the numeric linear
search function we developed in Chapter 8.

This date conversion application is one instance where C's required use of
zero as the subscript of an initial array element is rather annoying. If we could
have an array with row subscripts 1. . .12, the conversion from month number
to name would be more direct. We have chosen to use a 12-string array and to
correct the off-by-one error in the conversion functions. In
`nums_to_string_date` we have

```
sprintf(date_string, "%d %s %d", day,
        month_names[month - 1], year);
```

and in `string_date_to_nums` we find the reference

```
*monthp = month_index + 1;
```

←

Self-Check

1. Consider the following call to `sscanf` from the `string_date_to_nums` function.

   ```
   sscanf(date_string, "%d%s%d", dayp, mth_name, yearp);
   ```

   Why is the address-of operator not applied to any of the arguments?
2. Write a code segment that uses an array of pointers to strings and `sprintf` to convert a type `double` monetary value less than `10.00` to a string for use on a check. For example, `4.83` would be converted to `"Four and 83/100 dollars"`.

Programming

1. Write a type `int` function `strtoint` and a type `double` function `strtodouble` that convert string representations of numbers to their numeric equivalents.

   ```
   strtoint("-8") => -8    strtodouble("-75.812") => -
   75.812
   ```

9.8 STRING PROCESSING ILLUSTRATED

In this section, we look at two problems that illustrate the wide range of applications in which string processing is used. First, we will consider how to encode messages. Then, we will look at how to search for palindromes in the nucleotide sequences of DNA.

Case Study: Cryptogram Generator

PROBLEM

The security division of a major corporation needs to provide a program to encode messages. One approach is to use a program that generates cryptograms, coded messages formed by substituting a code character for each letter of the original message. For example, every A is replaced by an S, every B is replaced by a P, and so forth. All punctuation (including spaces between words) remains unchanged.

ANALYSIS

The program must examine every character in the message and replace each alphabetic letter by its code symbol. We can store the code symbols as a string of letters and use a transformation of a letter's character code to generate an index for looking up the letter's code symbol in the code string.

Data Requirements

Problem Constants

```
ALPHARANGE  26   /* number of character codes in the
                    range 'A'..'Z' (26 assumes use of
                    ASCII)                              */
STRSIZ  100      /* maximum space for a line           */
```

Problem Inputs

```
char code[ALPHARANGE + 1] /* code string              */
char msgline[STRSIZ]      /* one line of original
                             message                   */
```

Problem Outputs

```
char codeline[STRSIZ]     /* one line of encrypted
                             message                   */
```

DESIGN

Initial Algorithm

1. Get code string.
2. Repeat for each line of message.
   2.1 Get message line.
   2.2 Encrypt line.
   2.3 Display encrypted line.

Algorithm Refinements and Structure Chart

As shown in the structure chart in Fig. 9.21, user-defined functions will be created for Step 1 and Step 2.2. The data requirements and algorithms for these user-defined functions follow.

**Figure 9.21
Structure Chart
for Cryptogram
Generator**

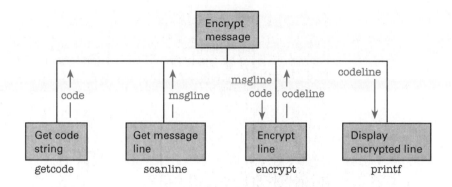

Algorithm for getcode

1. Display the alphabet and a prompt.
2. Get the string of code symbols.

Local Variables for encrypt

```
int   next        /* subscript to access next character
                     of message line                  */
char  cap         /* next message letter converted to a
                     capital letter                   */
int   code_index  /* offset of current message character
                     in alphabet                      */
```

Algorithm for encrypt

1. For each character of message
    1.1 if character is alphabetic
            1.1.1 Convert character to capital letter.
            1.1.2 Convert character code to offset in alphabet.
            1.1.3 Store encrypted character in `codeline`.
        else
            1.1.4 Store original character in `codeline`.

Step 1.1.2 Refinement

Subtract code for `'A'` from character code of capital letter.

IMPLEMENTATION

The program in Fig. 9.22 assumes that the uppercase letters are consecutive characters, as they are in the ASCII character set. This program must be modified slightly for computers that use the EBCDIC character set because this character set contains some special characters between the letters I and J and between R and S. One way to handle the EBCDIC gaps in alphabetic character codes is to define ALPHARANGE as 41 and to replace the call to scanline in getcode by this loop that stores blanks in the code string for the characters corresponding to the special characters.

```
for (next = (int)'A'; next <= (int)'Z'; ++next)
    if (isalpha(next))
        code[next - (int)'A'] = getchar();
    else
        code[next - (int)'A'] = ' ';
code[ALPHARANGE] = '\0';
```

Figure 9.22 Program to Encrypt a Message

```
/*
 *  Generates a cryptogram for a message
 */

#include <stdio.h>
#include <string.h>
#include <ctype.h>

#define ALPHARANGE 26   /* consecutive character codes for alphabet    */
#define STRSIZ     100  /* maximum string space                        */

/*  Insert scanline from Fig. 9.17                                      */

/*
 *  Gets a code symbol for each alphabetic letter                       */
 */
char *
getcode(char code[],      /* output - code string                      */
        int  codesize)    /* input-space available for code            */
{
```

(continued)

Figure 9.22   *(continued)*

```
        printf("Specify the code by entering a code symbol under each ");
        printf("letter\nABCDEFGHIJKLMNOPQRSTUUVWXYZ\n");
        scanline(code, codesize);
        return (code);
}

/*
 *  Encrypts one message line replacing each alphabetic letter by the
 *  corresponding code symbol
 */
char *
encrypt(char       codeline[],  /* output - encrypted line            */
        const char msgline[],   /* input  - message line              */
        const char code[])      /* input  - code for alphabet         */
{
      int   next;         /* subscript to access next character of message
                             line                                     */
      char cap;           /* current letter as a capital letter       */
      int  code_index;  /* offset of current message character in
                           alphabet                                   */

      for  (next = 0;  next < strlen(msgline);  ++next)
          if (isalpha(msgline[next])) {
                cap = toupper(msgline[next]);
                code_index = (int)cap - (int)'A'; /* 'A' => 0, 'B' => 1,
                                                     etc                */
                codeline[next] = code[code_index];
          } else {
                codeline[next] = msgline[next];
          }

      codeline[next] = '\0';

      return (codeline);
}

int
main(void)
{
```

(continued)

Figure 9.22 *(continued)*

```
    char code[ALPHARANGE + 1],   /* code string                        */
         msgline[STRSIZ],         /* one line of message                */
         codeline[STRSIZ];        /* one line of encrypted message      */

    getcode(code, ALPHARANGE + 1);

    printf("\nEnter your message.  It will be encrypted line by ");
    printf("line.\nEnd the message with an extra <return>.\n");
    for  (scanline(msgline, STRSIZ);
          strlen(msgline) > 0;
          scanline(msgline, STRSIZ))
        printf("%s\n", encrypt(codeline, msgline, code));

    return (0);
}

Specify the code by entering a code symbol under each letter.
ABCDEFGHIJKLMNOPQRSTUVWXYZ
CDEFGHIJKLMNOPQRSTUVWXYZAB

Enter your message. It will be encrypted line by line.
End the message with an extra <return>.
This is a
VJKU KU C
short message.
UJQTV OGUUCIG.
```

TESTING

In the preceding sample run, the user types the code symbol for each letter directly beneath that letter in response to the prompt from function `getcode`. The program follows each message line by the corresponding cryptogram. For a simple test, try using each letter as its own code symbol; then the cryptogram will simply be the original message in all capital letters. Make sure the program encodes both lowercase and uppercase letters and does not change other characters.

Case Study: Finding Palindromes in Nucleotide Sequences

PROBLEM

A molecular biologist has asked us to develop a program to identify palindromes of a certain length in strings representing the nucleotide sequences of a portion of a DNA molecule. Palindromic regions are of great interest to researchers studying the transmission of the genetic information encoded in DNA.

ANALYSIS

Although we recall that a palindrome is a string that reads the same forward and backward, such as "Madam, I'm Adam" or "Able was I ere I saw Elba," we must first see how closely this definition applies to the palindromes of DNA molecules.

DNA is a double-stranded molecule composed of pairs of the nucleotides Adenine, Thymine, Cytosine, and Guanine. Adenine always pairs with Thymine, and Cytosine pairs with Guanine. Figure 9.23 shows a portion of a DNA molecule in which the complementary strands are ATCGCAT . . . and TAGCGTA. . . .

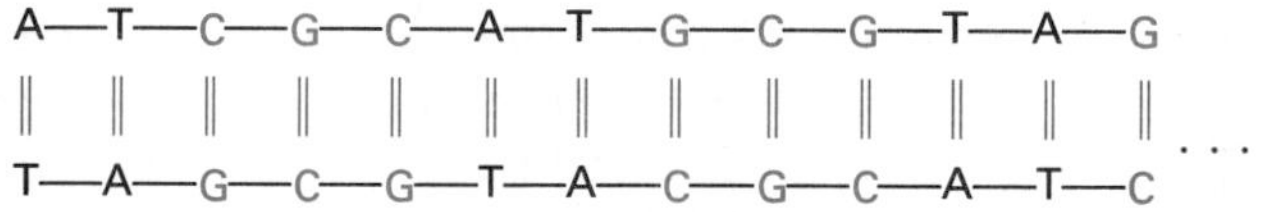

Figure 9.23 Model of a Portion of a DNA Molecule

The molecule portion shown contains a palindromic sequence of eight nucleotide pairs, the sequence inside the added color rectangle of Fig. 9.24. This region is palindromic because the sequence of nucleotides along the top strand, CGCATGCG, is exactly the reverse of the sequence along the bottom strand, GCGTACGC.

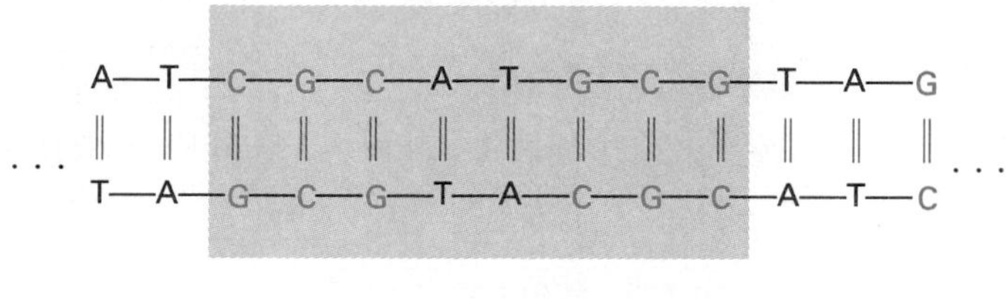

Figure 9.24 Palindromic Region of Length 8 in a DNA Molecule

Given strings representing the complementary strands and a length value, we must identify all palindromic sequences of the specified length.

Data Requirements

Problem Constant
```
STRANDSIZ  100    /*  maximum space for a strand    */
```

Problem Inputs
```
char   strand1[STRANDSIZ], /* complementary strands */
       strand2[STRANDSIZ]  /* of DNA                 */
int    palin_len           /* length of palindromic
                              sequences of interest */
```

Problem Outputs
index and value of each palindromic sequence of length `palin_len`

DESIGN

Algorithm

1. Get input data: complementary strands and palindrome length.
2. For each starting subscript of a substring of the desired length
    2.1 if the substring from `strand1` matches the reverse of the corresponding substring of `strand2`
        2.1.1 Print the position where palindrome found and the two substrings.

IMPLEMENTATION

The implementation in Fig. 9.25 reuses our `substr` function from Fig. 9.7 to extract pieces of the strands to examine. The code includes a separate function to reverse a string so the implementation of Step 2.1 closely resembles the pseudocode.

TESTING

Try the program on sequence lengths ranging from two to the full strand length. For this particular application, only palindromic sequences of even lengths are of interest. Be sure to try the program on some strands containing two or more palindromic sequences of the desired length as well as on some strands containing no palindromes of interest.

Figure 9.25   Program to Find Specified-Length Palindromic Sequences of Nucleotide Pairs

```
/*
 *  Finds specified-length palindromic sequences of nucleotide pairs in a
 *  portion of a DNA molecule whose complementary strands are represented
 *  as strings
 */

#include <stdio.h>
#include <string.h>

#define STRANDSIZ  100  /*  maximum space for storing a strand         */

/*  include code for substr here                                       */

/*
 *  Reverses a string
 *  Pre:  size of revstr is at least one more than strlen(str)
 */
char *
reverse(char        revstr[],  /* output - reversed string            */
        const char str[])      /* input  - string to reverse          */
{
     int i, len;
     len = strlen(str);
     for  (i = 1;  i <= len;  ++i)
         revstr[i - 1] = str[len - i];
     revstr[len] = '\0';

     return (revstr);
}

int
main(void)
{
     char strand1[STRANDSIZ],     /* complementary strands             */
          strand2[STRANDSIZ],     /*    of DNA                         */
          subs1[STRANDSIZ],       /* piece of strand1                  */
          subs2[STRANDSIZ],       /* piece of strand2                  */
          revstr[STRANDSIZ];      /* reversed piece of strand2         */
```

(continued)

Figure 9.25   *(continued)*

```
      int  palin_len;                 /* length of palindromic sequences of
                                                    interest                     */
      int  i;

      /* Gets input data and prints reference lines                             */
      printf("Enter one strand of DNA molecule segment\n> ");
      scanf("%s", strand1);
      printf("\nEnter complementary strand\n> ");
      scanf("%s", strand2);
      printf("\nEnter length of palindromic sequence\n> ");
      scanf("%d", &palin_len);
      printf("\n%s\n%s\n", strand1; strand2);
      for  (i = 0;  i < strlen(strand1);  ++i)
          printf("%d", i % 10);
      printf("\n\nPalindromes of length %d\n\n", palin_len);

      /* Prints palindromes of interest                                         */
      for  (i = 0;  i <= strlen(strand1) - palin_len;  ++i) {
          substr(subs1, strand1, i, i + palin_len, STRANDSIZ);
          substr(subs2, strand2, i, i + palin_len, STRANDSIZ);
          if (strcmp(subs1, reverse(revstr, subs2)) == 0) {
                printf("Palindrome at position %d\n", i);
                printf("   %s\n   %s\n", subs1, subs2);
          }
      }

      return (0);

}


Enter one strand of DNA molecule segment
> ATCGCATGCGTAG

Enter complementary strand
> TAGCGTACGCATC

Enter length of palindromic sequence
> 8
```

(continued)

Figure 9.25 *(continued)*

```
ATCGCATGCGTAG
TAGCGTACGCATC
0123456789012

Palindromes of length 8

Palindrome at position 2
CGCATGCG
GCGTACGC
```

**EXERCISES FOR
SECTION 9.8**

Self-Check

1. Trace the execution of the `reverse` function from Fig. 9.25 for the call

   ```
   reverse(rev, "glob");
   ```

2. Make changes to the input section of the palindromic nucleotide sequence program so that `strand2` is not an input, but rather is automatically created based on `strand1`.

Programming

1. Rewrite the cryptogram generation program so it prompts the user for a string of characters to substitute for blanks. If the user responds with * − +, the program should encode the first blank as *, the second as −, the third as +, the fourth as *, the fifth as −, and so on.

9.9 LIVING DANGEROUSLY: STRING LIBRARY FUNCTIONS FOR ASSIGNMENT, SUBSTRING EXTRACTION, AND CONCATENATION

In this chapter, we have studied basic string operations using three of our own protected string functions: `strassign`, `substr`, and `concat`. Our purpose in using these protected functions is to help you develop the following expectations of C string processing functions:

1. A C string function that computes a string result has a character array output argument.

2. The calling function must provide a string function with space in which to build the string result.
3. The size of the space provided by the calling function is of great importance to the string function called.

The functions we have used have, for the most part, protected you from hidden problems that can arise in string processing. You certainly can continue to use these functions for your string application programs; however, the protection these functions afford may seem too costly in terms of the space and execution time they require. Moreover, you may find that the type of string manipulation you do never calls for you to concatenate overlapping strings or to assign a string that may need to be truncated or to take a substring by specifying bounds that may be out of range for the subject string. If so, you may not want to take the trouble to include the definitions of `strassign`, `substr`, and `concat` in your programs.

In Table 9.5, we see some uses of `strassign`, `substr`, and `concat` along with selected equivalent statements using functions from the standard string library. The string library function calls shown are not the only way to accomplish the given tasks, but they do illustrate characteristics of some string library functions of which you should be aware.

Table 9.5   Some Calls to Protected Functions and String Library Equivalents

A. Calls to Protected Functions	B. Calls to Standard String Functions	When Columns A and B Are Equivalent
`strassign(dest, src,` `       DEST_SIZ);`	`strcpy(dest, src);`	When `strlen(src)` < `DEST_SIZ` and `dest` and `src` do not overlap in memory
`concat(dest, src1, src2,` `     DEST_SIZ);`	`strcpy(dest, src1);` `strcat(dest, src2);`	When `strlen(src1)` + `strlen(src2)` < `DEST_SIZ` and `dest`, `src1`, and `src2` are nonoverlapping

`substr(dest, src, st, end,`
`     DEST_SIZ);`
	`strncpy(dest, &src[st],`
	`         end - st);`
	`dest[end - st] = '\0';`
		When $0 \leq st \leq end$, $end \leq strlen(src)$, $end - st < DEST\_SIZ$, and `dest` and portion of `src` to extract do not overlap

The string copy function `strcpy` copies all the characters of `src` including the null into the output argument `dest`, so `strcpy` is a reasonable replacement for `strassign` in many cases. Function `strcpy` *assumes* there is enough room in `dest` just as `scanf` assumes enough space in a string output argument for whatever is scanned in conjunction with a `%s` placeholder. We saw in Fig. 9.4 the consequences when this assumption by `scanf` was false. Function `strcpy` is equally able to overflow its string output argument, causing program errors that are both disastrous and difficult to find.

The string library concatenation function `strcat` does not use a separate output argument for its result, but rather attaches its entire second string argument to its first, again merely *assuming* there is room in the unused portion of the first argument's allocated space for all the characters of the second argument. Like `strcpy`, `strcat` nonchalantly overflows its first argument when this assumption is false.

The "equivalent" for the `substr` function call using the library function `strncpy` suffers not only from a whole laundry list of *assumptions* but also from a significant loss of readability. The first statement shown

```
strncpy(dest, &src[st], end - st);
```

computes the length of the desired substring (`end - st`) and then tells `strncpy` that its source string is the string that starts with the `st`th character of `src` and the number of characters to copy is the computed substring length. This operation leaves us with *almost* the desired value of `dest`, although there remains the little matter of the null character to end the substring.

The standard string functions `strcpy`, `strncpy`, and `strcat` work very well provided that the programmer remembers their preconditions. We encourage you to continue to use `strassign`, `substr`, and `concat`, at least until concern for the size of their output string arguments is second nature to you. This sensitivity will serve you well in your use of functions from the string library.

EXERCISE FOR SECTION 9.9

Self-Check

1. Complete the following table by filling in the column Equivalent? with Yes or No to indicate whether the effect of the statement in Column A matches the effect of the statement(s) in Column B. For each pair marked No, explain the difference between the two options. You may assume that the destination string lengths provided in the calls to the protected string functions represent the actual amount of space allocated for the destination strings.

A	B	Equivalent?
1. `strassign(d1, "Hello", 6);`	`strcpy(d1, "Hello");`	Yes
2. `strassign(d2, "Flower", 6);`	`strcpy(d2, "Flower");`	

3. `strassign(s1, "quintessential", 25);`
`  substr(d3, s1, 7, 11, 10);`
	`strcpy(s1, "quintessential");`
	`strncpy(d3, &s1[7], 4);`
	`d3[4] = '\0';`	

4. (Use s1 from 3)
`  substr(d4, s1, 5, 14, 9);`
	(Use s1 from 3)
	`strncpy(d4, &s1[5], 9);`
	`d4[9] = '\0';`	

5. `concat(d5, "string ",` `      "functions", 15);`	`strcpy(d5, "string ");` `strcat(d5, "functions");`	

9.10 COMMON PROGRAMMING ERRORS

When manipulating string variables, the programmer must use great care in the allocation and management of memory. When we work with numeric values or single characters, we commonly compute a value of interest in a function, storing the result value temporarily in a local variable of the function until it is returned to the calling module using the `return` statement. One cannot use this approach in string functions, for such functions do not actually return a string *value* in the same way that an `int` function returns an integer value. Rather a string function returns the *address* of the initial character of a string. If we were to use the same strategy in a string function as we do in many numeric functions, we would build our result string in a local variable and return the address of the new string as the function value. The problem with this approach is that the function's data area is deallocated as soon as the `return` statement is executed, so it is not valid to access from the calling module the string the function constructed in its own local variable. Figure 9.26 shows a poor rewrite of the `concat` function from Fig. 9.9. Rather than requiring the calling function to provide space in which to construct the function result as the earlier `concat` did (and as is the practice of the functions in the C string library), this faulty `concat` returns a string built in local storage. As a consequence, the string that the `printf` function tries to print is in a section of memory that neither `main` nor `printf` has any legitimate right to access and that may be overwritten

Figure 9.26   Flawed concat Returns Address of Deallocated Space

```
/*
 *  Concatenates str1 and str2 storing result in local variable
 *  which has space available for MAX_STR_LEN characters.
 *  Error:  returns address of space that is immediately deallocated.
 */
char *
concat(const char str1[],      /* input  - strings                    */
       const char str2[])      /*                 to concatenate      */
{
     char result[MAX_STR_LEN];  /* local string space for result      */

     /*  Checks if result will be wrong due to lack of local space  */
     if (strlen(str1) + strlen(str2) >= MAX_STR_LEN)
          printf("\nInsufficient local storage causing loss of data\n");

     /*  Builds result in local storage                            */
     strassign(result, str1, MAX_STR_LEN);
     strncat(result, str2, MAX_STR_LEN - strlen(result) - 1);

     return (result);
}

int
main(void)
{
     printf("%s\n", concat("How I wish ", "this would abort!"));

     return (0);
}
```

with new values at any moment. What makes this type of error particularly grievous is that on some C implementations it will compile and pass unit testing without creating any error in the output.

To avoid creation of such "time-bomb" functions that do not "blow up" until system integration tests, follow the pattern of the C string library and have any string functions you write require the calling module to provide as the first argument a variable in which to build the string result. The error illustrated in Fig. 9.26 is one that typically *will* be flagged by a lint program; some ANSI C compilers will mark it as well.

A second error that creeps into C programs with string use is the misuse or neglect of the & operator. The fact that this operator is *not* applied to strings or to any other whole arrays used as output arguments often leads beginning users of C to forget that the address-of operator must still be used on simple output arguments such as variables of type `int`, `char`, or `double`, as well as on single array elements of these types when used as output arguments. You may want to review the use of the & on simple variables as shown in Table 6.7.

Another problem that is common with string use is the overflow of character arrays allocated for strings. Since library functions like `scanf`, `sprintf`, `strcpy`, and `strcat` just assume that the calling module has provided adequate space for whatever may need to be stored, calling these functions with inadequate storage causes errors that are really difficult to find. In Fig. 9.4, which is repeated here, we see such a situation.

Execution of scanf("%s%d%s%d", dept, &course_num, days, &time);
on Entry of Invalid Data

Whatever was stored in the cells following array `dept` has just been overwritten. If that memory was being used for other program variables, their values will appear to change spontaneously.

Most of the string functions we have written as examples (`strassign`, `substr`, `concat`, `scanline`) protect the calling function from string overflow by requiring an input argument telling how much space is available for the string result. These functions take care to prevent storage of a string that is too long. We encourage you to use protective functions like these in your string programs.

A relatively minor error that can lead to difficult bugs is forgetting that all strings end with the null character. The programmer must remember the null character both when allocating space for a string and when building a string one character at a time.

It is easy to slip and use equality or relational operators when comparing strings or the assignment operator for copying them. Remember to use `strcmp` for comparisons and library functions such as `strcpy` or `memmove` or your own protected string assignment function for copying strings.

CHAPTER REVIEW

In this chapter, we described character string manipulation. We saw C's representation of strings as arrays of characters ended by the null character `'\0'`. We studied how to declare, initialize, copy, concatenate, compare, and convert strings and how to extract substrings. Sorting and searching an array of strings were also presented. These new statements and functions are summarized in Table 9.6.

Many examples of string processing were shown. We applied string functions to generating cryptograms and to solving a problem that might arise in DNA mapping. Such problems as these that manipulate symbols rather than numbers are among the most challenging in computer science.

Table 9.6   Statements That Manipulate Strings

Statement	Effect	
Declarations		
`char str[100];`	Allocates space for a string of up to 99 characters plus the null character.	
`char str[11] = " ";`	Allocates space for a string of up to 10 characters plus the null and initializes it to all blanks.	
`char *abbrevs[10];`	Declares an array of 10 pointers to character strings.	

`const char arg1[]`
     `or`
`const char *arg1`
	Declares a string input parameter.	

`char out[]`
     `or`
`char *out`
	Declares a string output or input/output parameter.	

`char names[10][20];`	Allocates space for an array of 10 strings, each of which has up to 19 characters plus the null character.	

`char *weekdays[] =`
     `{"Mon", "Tue", "Wed",`
     `"Thu", "Fri"};`
	Declares and initializes an array of pointers to five strings.	

`char list[][20]`	Declares an output or input/output parameter that is an array of strings in which each string has up to 19 characters plus the null.	
`char *strs[]`	Declares an output or input/output parameter that is an array of pointers to strings.	
Calls to Protected Functions		**Figure Where Defined**
`strassign(str_result,` `str_src, 30);`	Copies string value of `str_src` into `str_result`, truncating if necessary.	9.6
`substr(str_result,` `str_src, 2, 5, 20);`	Copies substring consisting of `str_src[2]`, `str_src[3]`, `str_src[4]`, and the null character into `str_result`.	9.7

(continued)

Table 9.6 *(continued)*

Statement	Effect	Figure Where Defined
Calls to Protected Functions		
`concat(str_result,` `    "sym", "bolic", 20);`	Concatenates `"sym"` and `"bolic"` and stores result (`"symbolic"`) in `str_result`.	9.9
`scanline(str_result, 30);`	Stores the next full line of input (or as much as will fit) in 30-character array `str_result`.	9.17
Calls to Conversion Functions		
`sprintf(s, "%d + %d = %d", x,` `    y, x + y);`	If `x` is 3 and `y` is 4, builds and returns the string `"3 + 4 = 7"`.	
`sscanf("14.3 -5", "%lf%d",` `    &p, &n);`	Stores `14.3` in `p` and `–5` in `n`.	
Calls to String Library		
`strlen(a_string)`	Returns the number of characters in the string `a_string` up to but not including the null character.	
`strcmp(str1, str2)`	Returns a negative integer if `str1` precedes `str2` alphabetically, a positive integer if `str2` precedes `str1`, and zero if `str1` and `str2` are equal.	
`strcpy(str_result, str_src)`	Copies all the characters of `str_src` including the null character into `str_result`. Assumption is that `str_result` has enough room for all these characters.	
`strncpy (str_result,` `    str_src, 10)`	Copies first 10 characters of `str_src` into `str_result`. Assumption is that `str_result` has room for all ten. Characters stored include `'\0'` *only if* `strlen(str_src) < 10`.	
`strcat(str_result, new)`	Concatenates the complete value of `new` on the end of `str_result`. Assumption is that `str_result` has room enough for its own current value plus the added characters of `new`.	
`strncat(str_result, new, 10)`	Concatenates the value of `new` at the end of `str_result` providing `new`'s length (not counting the null character) is less than or equal to 10. Otherwise, it concatenates the first 10 characters of `new` on the end of `str_result`. It always adds a null character at the end, so at most 11 characters are added to `str_result`.	

(continued)

Table 9.6 *(continued)*

Statement	Effect
| ```
memmove(str_result,
        str_src, 12);
``` | Copies the first 12 characters of `str_src` into `str_result`. Does *not* add a null character. Assumption is that `str_src` has at least 12 characters, and `str_result` has room for all 12. |
| **Calls to String Library**<br>```
fgets(str_result, 10,
      stdin);
``` | Takes up to 9 characters from standard input for storage in `str_result`. Stores a `'\0'` as the last character. If a `'\n'` is within the first nine characters, it is the last character input, and it is stored in `str_result` followed by the null character. |

QUICK-CHECK EXERCISES

1. For each of the following functions, explain its purpose, the type(s) of its output parameters, and the type(s) of its input parameter(s). Also indicate if it is user-defined or if it is from the string library or from the ctype library.

   ```
   strassign       substr        strncat
   islower         concat        scanline
   isalpha         strlen        strcmp
   ```

2. Look at Appendix A, which lists three character sets. Which of the following expressions may yield different results on different computers?
   a. `(char)45`
   b. `'a' < 'A'`
   c. `'A' < 'Z'`
   d. `('A' <= ch && ch <= 'Z') && isalpha(ch)`
   e. `(int)'A'`
   f. `(int)'B' - (int)'A'`

3. Which of the following strings could represent space allocated for a local variable? Which could represent a formal parameter of any length?

   ```
   char str1[50]     char str2[]
   ```

4. A program you have written is producing incorrect results on your second data set, although it runs fine on the first. You discover after adding extra print statements for debugging that the value of one of your strings is spon-

taneously changing from "blue" to "al" in the following code segment. What could be wrong?

```
. . .
printf("%s\n", s1);  /* prints "blue" */
scanf("%s", s2);
printf("%s\n", s1);  /* prints "al"   */
. . .
```

5. Declare a variable `str` with as little space as would be reasonable given that `str` will hold each of the values below in turn.

```
carbon    uranium    tungsten    bauxite
```

6. What is the value of the following expression?

```
substr(t1, concat(t2, "Merry ", "Christmas", 40), 3, 8, 40)
```

7. The action of joining two strings is called _____ .
8. Write a statement that assigns to `s1` the end of the string value of `s2` starting with the fourth character (i.e., `s2[3]`). Assume `s1` has room for 35 characters.
9. Write statements that take a whole data line as input and print all the uppercase letters in the line.
10. What is the value of the following expression?

```
isdigit(9)
```

ANSWERS TO QUICK-CHECK EXERCISES

1.

Function's Purpose	Output Parameter Types	Input Parameter Types	Where Defined
`strassign` copies one string into another, truncating if necessary.	`char *` (string result)	`const char *` (input string) `int` (space available in result string)	user
`islower` checks whether its argument is the character code for a lowercase character.	none	`int`	ctype

Function's Purpose	Output Parameter Types	Input Parameter Types	Where Defined
isalpha determines if its argument is the character code for a letter of the alphabet.	none	int	ctype
substr extracts a substring from its second argument.	char * (string result)	const char * (source string) int (3 - starting and ending positions, also space available in result string)	user
concat concatenates two source strings.	char * (string result)	const char * (2 - source strings) int (amount of space available in result string)	user
strlen finds the length of its argument, counting the letters that precede the null character.	none	const char * (source string)	string
strncat concatenates two arguments by adding up to *n* characters from the second argument to the end of the first argument.	char * (input/output argument — first source string and string result)	const char * (second source string) int (maximum number of characters to copy from second string)	string
scanline (version 2) takes one line of input as a string, stores as much as will fit in its output argument, and discards the rest.	char * (string result)	int (space available in result string)	user
strcmp compares arguments and returns a negative integer if first is less than second, zero if they are equal, and a positive integer otherwise	none	const char * (2 input strings)	string

2. Results differ for a, b, e.
3. local variable: str1   parameter: str2
4. The call to scanf may be getting a string too long to fit in s2, and the extra characters could be overwriting memory allocated to s1.

5. `char str[9]` The longest value (`"tungsten"`) has eight characters, and one more is needed for the null character.
6. `"ry Ch"`
7. concatenation
8. `substr(s1, s2, 3, strlen(s2), 35)`
9. `scanline(line, 80);`
   `for  (i = 0;  i < strlen(line);  ++i)`
   `    if (isupper(line[i]))`
   `        putchar(line[i]);`
10. 0 (false)   However, `isdigit('9')` would be true.

REVIEW QUESTIONS

Refer to these declarations when evaluating the expressions in Questions 1–4.

```
char s5[5], s10[10], s20[20];
char aday[7] = "Sunday";
char another[9] = "Saturday";
```

1. `strassign(s5, another, 5)`
2. `substr(s10, aday, 1, 4, 10)`
3. `strlen(another)`
4. `concat(s20, s10, s5, 20)`
5. Write a function that pads a variable-length string with blanks to its maximum size. For example, if `s10` is a 10-character array currently holding the string `"screen"`, `blank_pad` would add three blanks (one of which would overwrite the null character) and finish the string with the null character. Be sure your function would work if no blank padding were necessary.
6. Write a function that would return a copy of its string argument with the first occurrence of a specified letter deleted.
7. Write functions `isvowel` and `isconsonant` that return true if their type `int` argument is the character code for a vowel (or consonant). *Hint:* Use a `switch` statement in `isvowel`.

PROGRAMMING PROJECTS

1. Write and test a function `deblank` that takes a string output and a string input argument and returns a copy of the input argument with all blanks removed.

2. Write a program that processes a sequence of lines, displaying a count of the total number of words in those lines as well as counts of the number of words with one letter, two letters, and so on.

3. Write and test a function `hydroxide` that returns a 1 for true if its string argument ends in the substring `OH`.

    Try the function `hydroxide` on the following data:

    KOH   H2O2   NaCl   NaOH   C9H8O4   MgOH

4. Write a program that takes nouns and forms their plurals on the basis of these rules:
    a. If noun ends in "y," remove the "y" and add "ies."
    b. If noun ends in "s," "ch," or "sh," add "es."
    c. In all other cases, just add "s."
    Print each noun and its plural. Try the following data:

    chair   dairy   boss   circus   fly   dog   church   clue   dish

5. Write a program that stores lists of names (the last name first) and ages in parallel arrays and sorts the names into alphabetical order keeping the ages with the correct names. Sample output:

    Original list

    ```
    Ryan, Elizabeth     62
    McIntyre, Osborne   84
    DuMond, Kristin     18
    Larson, Lois        35
    Hodge, Jesse        39
    Romero, Robert      56
    ```

    Alphabetized list

    ```
    DuMond, Kristin     18
    Hodge, Jesse        39
    Larson, Lois        35
    McIntyre, Osborne   84
    Romero, Robert      56
    Ryan, Elizabeth     62
    ```

6. Write a program that takes data a line at a time and reverses the words of the line. For example,

    ```
    Input: birds and bees
    Reversed: bees and birds
    ```

    The data should have one blank between each pair of words.

7. Write and test a function that finds the longest common prefix of two words (e.g., the longest common prefix of "global" and "glossary" is "glo," of "department" and "depart" is "depart," and of "glove" and "dove" is the empty string).

8. Write a program that takes a sequence of lines and displays each line with all four-letter words replaced by asterisks.

CHAPTER 10

RECURSION

10.1
The Nature of Recursion
10.2
Tracing a Recursive Function
10.3
Recursive Mathematical Functions
10.4
Recursive Functions with Array and String
Parameters
Case Study: Finding Capital Letters in a String
Case Study: Recursive Selection Sort
10.5
Problem Solving with Recursion
Case Study: Operations on Sets
10.6
A Classic Case Study in Recursion:
Towers of Hanoi
10.7
Picture Processing with Recursion
Case Study: Counting Cells in a Blob
10.8
Common Programming Errors
Chapter Review

A function that calls itself is said to be *recursive*. A function `f1` is also recursive if it calls a function `f2`, which under some circumstances calls `f1`, creating a cycle in the sequence of calls. The ability to invoke itself enables a recursive function to be repeated with different parameter values. You can use recursion as an alternative to iteration (looping). Generally, a recursive solution is less efficient than an iterative solution in terms of computer time due to the overhead for the extra function calls; however, in many instances, the use of recursion enables us to specify a very natural, simple solution to a problem that would otherwise be very difficult to solve. For this reason, recursion is an important and powerful tool in problem solving and programming.

10.1 THE NATURE OF RECURSION

Problems that lend themselves to a recursive solution have the following characteristics:

- One or more *simple cases* of the problem have a straightforward, nonrecursive solution.
- The other cases can be redefined in terms of problems that are closer to the simple cases.
- By applying this redefinition process every time the recursive function is called, eventually the problem is reduced entirely to simple cases, which are relatively easy to solve.

The recursive algorithms that we write will generally consist of an `if` statement with the following form:

if this is a simple case
    solve it
else
    redefine the problem using recursion

Figure 10.1 illustrates this approach. Let's assume that for a particular problem of size n, we can split the problem into a problem of size 1, which we can solve (a simple case), and a problem of size $n - 1$. We can split the problem of size $n - 1$ into another problem of size 1 and a problem of size $n - 2$, which we can split further. If we split the problem $n - 1$ times, we will end up with n problems of size 1, all of which we can solve.

Figure 10.1   Splitting a Problem into Smaller Problems

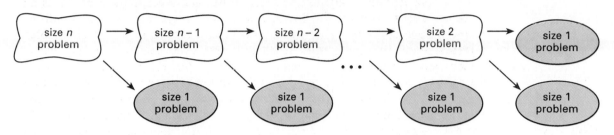

EXAMPLE 10.1

As a simple example of this approach, let's consider how we might solve the problem of multiplying 6 by 3, assuming we know our addition tables but not our multiplication tables. We do know, however, that any number multiplied by 1 gives us the original number, so if we ever come across this simple case, we'll just solve it. The problem of multiplying 6 by 3 can be split into the two problems:

1. Multiply 6 by 2.
2. Add 6 to the result of problem 1.

Because we know our addition tables, we can solve problem 2 but not problem 1. However, problem 1 is closer to the simple case than the original problem was. We can split problem 1 into the following two problems, 1.1 and 1.2, leaving us three problems to solve, two of which are additions.

1. Multiply 6 by 2.
    1.1   Multiply 6 by 1.
    1.2   Add 6 to the result.
2. Add 6 to the result of problem 1.

Problem 1.1 is one of the simple cases we were looking for. By solving problem 1.1 (the answer is 6) and problem 1.2, we get the solution to problem 1 (the answer is 12). Solving problem 2 gives us the final answer (18).

Figure 10.2 implements this approach to doing multiplication as the recursive C function `multiply` that returns the product m × n of its two arguments. The body of function `multiply` implements the general form of a recursive algorithm shown earlier. The simplest case is reached when the condition n == 1 is true. In this case, the statement

```
ans = m;     /* simple case   */
```

executes, so the answer is m. If n is greater than 1, the statement

```
ans = m + multiply(m, n - 1);   /* recursive step */
```

Figure 10.2   Recursive Function multiply

```
/*
 *  Performs integer multiplication using + operator.
 *  Pre:   m and n are defined and n > 0
 *  Post:  returns m * n
 */
int
multiply(int m, int n)
{
      int ans;

      if (n == 1)
            ans = m;        /* simple case */
      else
            ans = m + multiply(m, n - 1);  /* recursive
                                              step */

      return (ans);
}
```

executes, splitting the original problem into the two simpler problems:

* multiply m by n–1
* add m to the result

The first of these problems is solved by calling `multiply` again with n–1 as its second argument. If the new second argument is greater than 1, there will be additional calls to function `multiply`.

At first, it may seem odd that we must rely on the function `multiply` before we have even finished writing it! However, this approach is the key to developing recursive algorithms. In order to solve a problem recursively, first we must trust our function to solve a simpler version of the problem. Then we build the solution to the whole problem on the result from the simpler version.

For now, you will have to take our word that function `multiply` performs as desired. We will see how to trace the execution of a recursive function in the next section.

One group of problems for which recursive solutions seem very natural are problems involving varying-length lists. Since a string is a varying-length list of characters, this chapter contains numerous examples of recursive functions that process strings.

EXAMPLE 10.2 We need to develop a function to count the number of times a particular character appears in a string. For example,

```
count('s', "Mississippi sassafras")
```

should return the value 8. Of course, we could set up a loop to count the s's, but instead we will look for a recursive solution. Since recursion requires breaking a problem into a combination of simpler problems, our initial reaction to a problem should be something like, "This whole problem is entirely too hard. Maybe I can do a little bit of this problem, but I will definitely need help to do the whole problem." We then need to arrange things so the "help" needed is actually in solving a simpler version of the same problem. When dealing with a list of elements as we are in this problem, a recursive solution usually explicitly processes only the first list element. The recursive problem solver's thought process is illustrated in Fig. 10.3.

Looking back at the if statement that is our "generic" recursion algorithm,

if this is a simple case
    solve it
else
    redefine the problem using recursion

we see that the thought process shown in Fig. 10.3 fits into our generic else clause. We have redefined the problem "Count s's in Mississippi sassafras" as "Count s's in ississippi sassafras and add one more if the first letter is an s." Our redefinition of the general problem "Count a letter in a string" is recursive, since part of the solution is still to count a letter in a string. What has changed is that the new string is shorter. We still need to identify the simplest case of the problem, which must involve a *very* short string. Although it would be fairly easy to count a certain character in a string with only one character element, we would still need to do a comparison. If the string had *no* characters at all, we would know immediately that there were zero occurrences of the character being counted. Now that we have a simple case and a way to redefine more complex cases using recursion, we can write a

**Figure 10.3
Thought
Process of
Recursive
Algorithm
Developer**

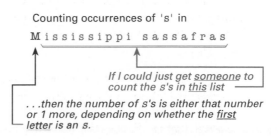

Counting occurrences of 's' in

Mississippi sassafras

If I could just get <u>someone</u> to count the s's in <u>this</u> list

. . . then the number of s's is either that number or 1 more, depending on whether the <u>first</u> letter is an s.

Figure 10.4 **Recursive Function to Count a Character in a String**

```
/*
 *  Count the number of occurrences of the character ch in the string str
 */
int
count(char ch, const char str[])
{
      char rest_str[STRSIZ];   /* local space to store str without first
                                  letter                                 */
      int ans;

      if (str[0] == '\0')                              /*  simple case  */
            ans = 0;
      else                             /*  redefine problem using recursion */
            if (ch == str[0])       /*  first character must be counted  */
                  ans = 1 + count(ch, substr(rest_str, str, 1,
                              strlen(str), STRSIZ));
            else                           /*  first character is not counted  */
                  ans = count(ch, substr(rest_str, str, 1, strlen(str),
                              STRSIZ));

      return (ans);
}
```

recursive function `count`. In the implementation shown in Fig. 10.4, we use the `substr` function from Chapter 9 to extract the portion of `str` to be processed by the recursive call. ◀

In our first example, we saw how a recursive `multiply` function broke a size n multiplication problem into n size 1 addition problems. Similarly, the effect of our recursive `count` function is to split the problem of analyzing a length n string into n problems of comparing single characters.

EXERCISES FOR SECTION 10.1

Self-Check

1. Using diagrams similar to those in Fig. 10.1, show the specific problems that are generated by the following calls.
   a. `multiply(5, 4)`
   b. `count('d', "dad");`

Programming

1. Write a recursive function `count_digits` that counts all the digits in a string.
2. Write a recursive function `add` that computes the sum of its two integer parameters. Assume `add` does not know general addition tables but does know how to add or subtract 1.

10.2 TRACING A RECURSIVE FUNCTION

Hand-tracing an algorithm's execution provides us with valuable insight into how that algorithm works. We can trace the execution of a recursive function, and now we will illustrate how to do this by first studying the execution of a recursive function that returns a value, and then studying the execution of a recursive `void` function.

Tracing a Recursive Function That Returns a Value

In Section 10.1, we wrote the recursive function `multiply` (see Fig. 10.2). We can trace the execution of the function call

`multiply(6, 3)`

by drawing an *activation frame* corresponding to each call of the function. An activation frame shows the parameter values for each call and summarizes the execution of the call.

The three activation frames generated to solve the problem of multiplying 6 by 3 are shown in Fig. 10.5. The part of each activation frame that executes before the next recursive call is in color; the part that executes after the return from the next call is in grey. The darker the color of an activation frame, the greater the depth of recursion.

The value returned from each call is shown alongside each black arrow. The return arrow from each call points to the operator + because the addition is performed just after the return.

Figure 10.5 shows three calls to function `multiply`. Parameter m has the value 6 for all three calls; parameter n has the values 3, 2, and, finally, 1. Since n is 1 in the third call, the value of m (6) is assigned to `ans` and is returned as the result of the third and last call. After returning to the second activation frame, the value of m is added to this result, and the sum (12) is returned as the result of the second call. After returning to the first activation frame, the value of m is added to this result, and the sum (18) is returned as the result of the original call to function `multiply`.

**Figure 10.5
Trace of
Function
multiply**

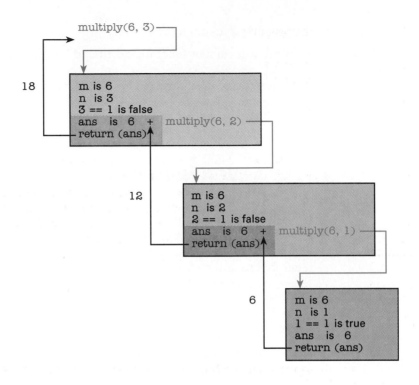

Tracing a void Function That Is Recursive

Hand-tracing a void function is somewhat simpler than tracing a function that returns a value. For both types of functions, we use activation frames to track each function call.

 **EXAMPLE 10.3**

Function reverse_input_words in Fig. 10.6 is a recursive module that takes n words of input and prints them in reverse order. If this function call statement

reverse_input_words(5)

is executed, the five words entered at the keyboard are printed in reverse order. If the words entered are

the
course
of
human
events

the program output will be

```
events
human
of
course
the
```

Like most recursive modules, the body of function reverse_input_words consists of an if statement that evaluates a *terminating condition*, n <= 1. When the terminating condition is true, the function is dealing with one of the problem's simple cases—printing in reverse order a list of just one word. Since reversing word order has no effect on a single-word list, for the simple case when n is less than or equal to one, we just get the word using scanf and print it.

Figure 10.6   Function reverse_input_words

```
/*
 *  Take n words as input and print them in reverse order on separate lines.
 *  Pre: n > 0
 */
void
reverse_input_words(int n)
{
      char word[WORDSIZ];   /*  local variable for storing one word        */

      if (n <= 1) {    /* simple case: just one word to get and print      */

            scanf("%s", word);
            printf("%s\n", word);

      } else {  /* get this word; get and print the rest of the words in
                    reverse order; then print this word                    */

            scanf("%s", word);
            reverse_input_words(n - 1);
            printf("%s\n", word);
      }
}
```

If the terminating condition is false (n > 1), the recursive step (following else) is executed. This group of statements transfers the current input word into memory, gets "someone" (i.e., reverse_input_words) to take and reverse print the remaining n – 1 words of interest, and then prints the current word.

Figure 10.7 shows a trace of the function call

reverse_input_words(3)

assuming that the words "bits" "and" "bytes" are entered as data. The trace shows three separate activation frames for function reverse_input_words. Each activation frame begins with a list of the initial values of n and word for that frame. The value of n is passed into the function when it is called; the value of the local variable word is initially undefined.

The statements that are executed for each frame are shown next. The statements in color in the activation frames are recursive function calls and result in new activation frames, as indicated by the colored arrows. A void function's return occurs when the closing brace of the function body is encountered, indicated by the word return and a black arrow that points to the statement in the calling frame to which the function returns. Tracing the colored arrows and then the black arrows in Fig. 10.7 gives us the sequence of events listed in Fig. 10.8. To help you understand this list, all the statements for a particular activation frame are indented to the same column.

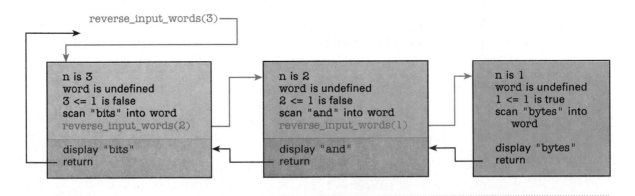

Figure 10.7   Trace of reverse_input_words(3) When the Words Entered are "bits" "and" "bytes"

Figure 10.8   Sequence of Events for Trace of reverse_input_words(3)

Call `reverse_input_words` with n equal to 3.
>   Scan the first word (`"bits"`) into `word`.
>   Call `reverse_input_words` with n equal to 2.
>>   Scan the second word (`"and"`) into `word`.
>>   Call `reverse_input_words` with n equal to 1.
>>>   Scan the third word (`"bytes"`) into `word`.
>>>   Display the third word (`"bytes"`).
>>>   Return from third call.
>>   Display the second word (`"and"`).
>>   Return from second call.
>   Display the first word (`"bits"`).
>   Return from original call.

As shown, there are three calls to function `reverse_input_words`, each with a different parameter value. The function returns always occur in the reverse order of the function calls—that is, we return from the last call first, then we return from the next to last call, and so on. After we return from a particular execution of the function, we display the string that was stored in `word` just prior to that function call.

Parameter and Local Variable Stacks

You may be wondering how C keeps track of the values of n and `word` at any given point. C uses a special data structure called a *stack* that is analogous to a stack of dishes or trays. Think of the countless times you have stood in line in a cafeteria. Recall that clean dishes are always placed on top of a stack of dishes. When we need a dish, we always remove the one most recently placed on the stack and the next to last dish placed on the stack becomes the top dish of the stack.

Similarly, whenever a new call to `reverse_input_words` occurs, the parameter value associated with that call is placed on the top of the parameter stack. A new cell whose value is initially undefined is also placed on top of the stack that is maintained for the local variable `word`. Whenever n or `word` is referenced, the value at the top of the corresponding stack is always used. When a function return occurs, the value currently at the top of each stack is removed, causing the value just below it to become the top value.

As an example, let's look at the two stacks as they appear right after the first call to `reverse_input_words`. One cell is on each stack, as shown.

After first call to reverse_input_words

n	word
3	?

The word `"bits"` is stored in `word` just before the second call to `reverse_input_words`.

n	word
3	bits

After the second call to `reverse_input_words`, the number 2 is placed on top of the stack for `n`, and the top of the stack for `word` becomes undefined again as shown next. The value in color is at the top of each stack.

After second call to reverse_input_words

n	word
2	?
3	bits

The word `"and"` is scanned and stored in `word` just before the third call to `reverse_input_words`.

n	word
2	and
3	bits

However, `word` becomes undefined again right after the third call.

After third call to reverse_input_words

n	word
1	?
2	and
3	bits

During this execution of the function, the word `"bytes"` is scanned and stored in `word`, and `"bytes"` is echo printed immediately because n is 1 (a simple case).

```
        n              word

        1             bytes
        2             and
        3             bits
```

The function return causes the values at the top of the stack to be removed, as shown next.

After first return

```
        n              word

        2              and
        3              bits
```

Because control is returned to a `printf` call, the value of `word` (`"and"`) at the top of the stack is then displayed. Another return occurs, causing the values currently at the top of the stack to be removed.

After second return

```
        n              word

        3              bits
```

Again, control is returned to a `printf` statement, and the value of `word` (`"bits"`) at the top of the stack is displayed. The third and last return exits the original function call, so there is no longer any memory allocated for n and `word`.

A stack is a data structure that you can implement and manipulate yourself using arrays. However, C automatically handles all the stack manipulation associated with function calls, we can write recursive functions without needing to worry about the stacks.

Implementation of Parameter Stacks in C

For illustrative purposes, we have used separate stacks for each parameter in our discussion; however, the compiler actually maintains a single stack. Each time a call to a function occurs, all its parameters and local variables are pushed onto the stack along with the memory address of the calling statement\. This address gives the computer the return point after execution of the function. Although multiple copies of a function's parameters may be saved on the stack, only one copy of the function body is in memory.

When and How to Trace Recursive Functions

Doing a trace by hand of multiple calls to a recursive function is helpful in understanding how recursion works but less useful when trying to develop a recursive algorithm. During algorithm development, it is best to trace a specific case simply by trusting any recursive call to return a correct value based on the function purpose. Then the hand trace can check whether this value is manipulated properly to produce a correct function result for the case under consideration.

However, if a recursive function's implementation is flawed, tracing its execution is an essential part of identifying the error. The function can be made to trace itself by inserting debugging print statements showing entry to and exit from the function. Figure 10.9 shows a self-tracing version of function `multiply` as well as output generated by the call

```
multiply(8, 3)
```

Figure 10.9 Recursive Function multiply with Print Statements to Create Trace and Output from multiply(8, 3)

```
/*
 *  ***  Includes calls to printf to trace execution ***
 *  Performs integer multiplication using + operator.
 *  Pre:   m and n are defined and n > 0
 *  Post:  returns m * n
 */
int
multiply(int m, int n)
{
     int ans;

  printf("Entering multiply with m = %d, n = %d\n", m, n);

     if (n == 1)
          ans = m;      /* simple case */
     else
          ans = m + multiply(m, n - 1); /* recursive step*/
```

(continued)

Figure 10.9   *(continued)*

```
    printf("multiply(%d, %d) returning %d\n", m, n, ans);

        return (ans);
}

Entering multiply with m = 8, n = 3
Entering multiply with m = 8, n = 2
Entering multiply with m = 8, n = 1
multiply(8, 1) returning 8
multiply(8, 2) returning 16
multiply(8, 3) returning 24
```

EXERCISES FOR SECTION 10.2

Self-Check

1. Trace the contents of stack representations of m, n, and ans for the evaluation of multiply(6,3) whose activation frames are shown in Fig. 10.5.
2. Draw activation frames showing the evaluation of count('d',"dad"), assuming that count is defined as shown in Fig. 10.4.

Programming

1. Rewrite function count from Fig. 10.4, adding calls to printf to make count self-tracing. Then show the output produced by the call count('l', "lull").

10.3 RECURSIVE MATHEMATICAL FUNCTIONS

Many mathematical functions can be defined recursively. An example is the factorial of a number *n (n!)*, a function that we defined iteratively in Chapter 6.

- 0! is 1
- *n!* is $n \times (n-1)!$, for $n > 0$

Thus 4! is $4 \times 3!$, which means $4 \times 3 \times 2 \times 1$, or 24. Implementing this definition as a recursive function in C is quite straightforward.

Figure 10.10   Recursive factorial Function

```
/*
 *  Compute n! using a recursive definition
 *  Pre:  n >= 0
 */
int
factorial(int n)
{
      int ans;

      if (n == 0)
            ans = 1;
      else
            ans = n * factorial(n - 1);

      return (ans);
}
```

EXAMPLE 10.4 ▶ Function `factorial` in Fig. 10.10 computes the factorial of its argument n. The recursive step

```
ans = n * factorial(n - 1);
```

implements the second line of the factorial definition just shown. Thus the result of the current call (argument n) is computed by multiplying by n the result of the call `factorial(n - 1)`.

A trace of

```
fact = factorial(3);
```

is shown in Fig. 10.11. The value returned from the original call, `factorial(3)`, is 6, and this value is assigned to `fact`. Be careful when using the factorial function as its value increases very rapidly and could lead to an integer overflow error (e.g., 8! is 40320).

Although the recursive implementation of function `factorial` follows naturally from its definition, we saw in Chapter 6 that this function can also be implemented easily using iteration. The iterative version we developed in that chapter is shown in Fig. 10.12.

Note that the iterative version contains a loop as its major control structure, whereas the recursive version contains an `if` statement. In the iterative version, the variable `product` is the target of repeated assignments, each of

**Figure 10.11
Trace of** `fact =`
`factorial(3);`

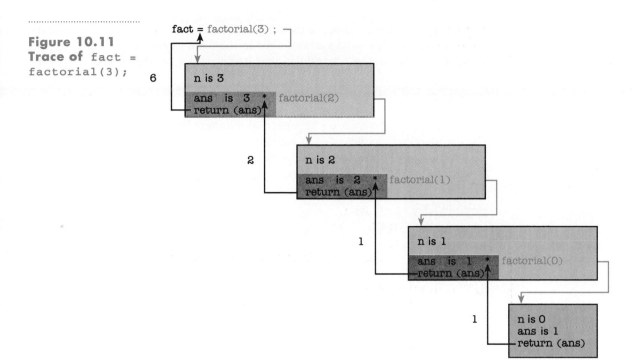

Figure 10.12   Iterative Function factorial

```
/*
 * Computes n!
 * Pre: n is greater than or equal to zero
 */
int
factorial(int n)
{
    int i,              /* local variables */
        product = 1;

    /* Compute the product n x (n-1) x (n-2) x ... x 2 x 1 */
    for  (i = n;  i > 1;  i = i - 1) {
        product = product * i;
    }

    /* Return function result */
    return (product);
}
```

which brings its value closer to the result value. Compare this use of `product` to the purpose of the local variable `ans` in the recursive version. Variable `ans` holds the answer to the subproblem that is the reason for the current call to the function. ←

EXAMPLE 10.5 ➤ The Fibonacci numbers are a sequence of numbers that have many varied uses. They were originally intended to model the growth of a rabbit colony. Although we will not go into the details of the model here, the Fibonacci sequence 1, 1, 2, 3, 5, 8, 13, 21, 34, . . . certainly seems to increase rapidly enough. The fifteenth number in the sequence is 610 (that's a lot of rabbits!). The Fibonacci sequence is defined as

- Fibonacci$_1$ is 1
- Fibonacci$_2$ is 1
- Fibonacci$_n$ is Fibonacci$_{n-2}$ + Fibonacci$_{n-1}$, for $n > 2$.

Verify for yourself that the sequence of numbers just shown is correct.

A recursive function that computes the nth Fibonacci number is shown in Fig. 10.13. Although easy to write, `fibonacci` is not very efficient because each recursive step generates two calls to function `fibonacci`. ←

Figure 10.13   Recursive Function fibonacci

```
/*
 *   Computes the nth Fibonacci number
 *   Pre: n > 0
 */
int
fibonacci(int n)
{
     int ans;

     if (n == 1 || n <= 2)
          ans = 1;
     else
          ans = fibonacci(n - 2)  +  fibonacci(n - 1);

     return (ans);
}
```

EXAMPLE 10.6  In Chapter 6, we also developed an iterative function for finding the greatest common divisor of two integers. Euclid's algorithm for finding the gcd can be defined recursively as shown. You recall that the *greatest common divisor* of two integers is the largest integer that divides them both.

- gcd(*m*,*n*) is *n* if *n* divides *m*
- gcd(*m*,*n*) is gcd(*n*, remainder of *m* divided by *n*) otherwise

This algorithm states that the gcd is *n* if *n* divides *m*. If *n* does not divide *m*, the answer is obtained by finding the gcd of *n* and the remainder of *m* divided by *n*. One of the elegant features of this definition is that it does not matter whether *m* or *n* is the larger number. If *m* is greater than *n*, the computation seems to proceed more directly to a solution; if it is not, the first application of the recursive step has the effect of exchanging *m* and *n*. This exchange is a result of the fact that when *m* is less than *n*, the remainder of *m* divided by *n* is *m*. The declaration and use of a recursive gcd function is shown in Fig. 10.14.   ←

Figure 10.14   Program Using Recursive Function gcd

```
/*
 *   Prints the greatest common divisor of two integers
 */

#include <stdio.h>

/*
 *   Finds the greatest common divisor of m and n
 *   Pre:  m and n are both > 0
 */
int
gcd(int m, int n)
{
      int ans;

      if (m % n == 0)
            ans = n;
      else
            ans = gcd(n, m % n);

      return (ans);
}
```

(continued)

Figure 10.14 *(continued)*

```
int
main(void)
{
      int n1, n2;

      printf("Enter two positive integers separated by a space> ");
      scanf("%d%d", &n1, &n2);
      printf("Their greatest common divisor is %d\n", gcd(n1, n2));

      return (0);
}


Enter two positive integers separated by a space> 24 84
Their greatest common divisor is 12
```

EXERCISES FOR SECTION 10.3

Self-Check

1. Complete the following recursive function that calculates the value of a number (**base**) raised to a power. Assume that **power** is a nonnegative integer.

```
int
power_raiser(int base, int power)
{
      int ans;

      if (power == _____)
            ans = _____;
      else
            ans = _____ * _____;

      return (ans);
}
```

2. What is the output of the following program? What does function **strange** compute when called with a positive integer?

```
#include <stdio.h>

int
strange(int n)
```

```
{
        int ans;

        if (n == 1)
                ans = 0;
        else
                ans = 1 + strange(n / 2);

        return (ans);
}

int
main(void)
{
        printf("%d\n", strange(8));
}
```

3. Explain what would happen if the terminating condition for function `fibonacci` were just (n == 1).

Programming

1. Write a recursive function `find_sum` that calculates the sum of successive integers starting at 1 and ending at n (i.e., `find_sum(n)` = (1 + 2 + · · · + (n − 1) + n).
2. Write an iterative version of the function to find the nth Fibonacci number.

10.4 RECURSIVE FUNCTIONS WITH ARRAY AND STRING PARAMETERS

In this section, we will examine two problems and will implement recursive functions to solve them. Both problems involve processing of some type of array.

Case Study: Finding Capital Letters in a String

PROBLEM

Form a string containing all the capital letters found in another string.

ANALYSIS

Just as in the problem of counting occurrences of a particular letter in a string, recursion will allow us to solve this problem by simply working out what to do with the string's first letter and then combining this processing with a recursive call handling the rest of the string. For instance, if the string in question were "Franklin Delano Roosevelt", finding capital letters in "ranklin Delano Roosevelt" would give us the string "DR". It is a simple matter to combine this string with the capital 'F' to form the full result. Of course, the simplest string in which to look for *anything* is the empty string, so checking for this simple case gives us the necessary terminating condition.

Data Requirements

Problem Input
```
char str[]     /* a string from which to extract capital
                  letters                              */
```

Problem Output
```
char caps[]    /* the capital letters from str    */
```

DESIGN

Algorithm
1. if str is the empty string
    2. Store empty string in caps (a string with no letters certainly has no caps).
  else
    3. if initial letter of str is a capital letter
        4. Store in caps this letter and the capital letters from the rest of str.
      else
        5. Store in caps the capital letters from the rest of str.

Function find_caps in Fig. 10.15 implements the recursive algorithm. Since both alternatives of the condition in Step 3 use the "rest of str," the imple-

Figure 10.15   Recursive Function to Extract Capital Letters from a String

```
/*
 * Forms a string containing all the capital letters found in the input
 * parameter str.
 * Pre:  caps has sufficient space to store all caps in str plus the null
 */
char *
find_caps(char       caps[], /* output - string of all caps found in str  */
          const char str[])  /* input  - string from which to extract caps*/
```
(continued)

Figure 10.15 *(continued)*

```
{
     char reststr[STRSIZ];  /* substring of str without initial letter    */
     char restcaps[STRSIZ]; /* caps from reststr                          */

     if (str[0] == '\0') {
          caps[0] = '\0';   /* no letters in str => no caps in str        */
     } else {
          substr(reststr, str, 1, strlen(str), STRSIZ);
          if (isupper(str[0]))
               sprintf(caps, "%c%s", str[0], find_caps(restcaps,
                                                  reststr));
          else
               find_caps(caps, reststr);
     }

     return (caps);
}
```

mentation stores this substring in a local variable before checking the initial let-ter of the string.

> **TESTING**

Given this #define directive and declaration,

```
#define STRSIZ 50
. . .
char caps[STRSIZ];
```

and the statement

```
printf("Capital letters in JoJo are %s\n",
       find_caps(caps, "JoJo"));
```

five calls to find_caps will be executed, as shown in Fig. 10.16. The string sent back from each function call is shown to the left of the arrow coming from the return statement.

Figure 10.17 shows the sequence of events that results from following first the colored arrows and then the black arrows of Fig. 10.16. There are five calls to function find_caps, each with a different input argument. The desired string of capital letters is constructed one character at a time as the function returns cause the recursion to unwind.

Figure 10.16   Trace of Call to Recursive Function find_caps

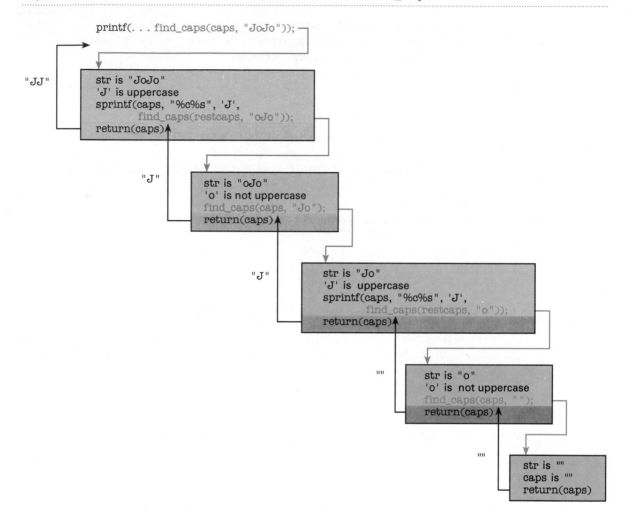

Figure 10.17   Sequence of Events for Trace of Call to find_caps from printf Statements

Call `find_caps` with input argument `"JoJo"` to determine value to print.
      Since `'J'` is a capital letter,
        prepare to use `sprintf` to build a string with `'J'`
        and the result of calling `find_caps` with input argument `"oJo"`.

(continued)

Figure 10.17   *(continued)*

```
            Since 'o' is not a capital letter,
         call find_caps with input argument "Jo".
                     Since 'J' is a capital letter,
                     prepare to use sprintf to build a string with 'J'
                     and the result of calling find_caps with input argument "o".
                         Since 'o' is not a capital letter,
                         call find_caps with input argument "".
                                 Return "" from fifth call.
                     Return "" from fourth call.
                 Complete execution of sprintf combining 'J' and "".
                 Return "J" from third call.
         Return "J" from second call.
     Complete execution of sprintf combining 'J' and "J".
     Return "JJ" from original call.
Complete call to printf to print Capital letters in JoJo are JJ.
```

Case Study: Recursive Selection Sort

In Chapter 6 and Chapter 9, we studied one algorithm for sorting data in ascending order, the bubble sort. In this section, we discuss a fairly intuitive but equally inefficient algorithm called the *selection sort*.

PROBLEM

Sort an array in ascending order using a selection sort.

ANALYSIS

To perform a selection sort of an array with n elements (subscripts $0 \ldots n-1$), we locate the largest element in the array and then switch the largest element with the element at subscript $n-1$, thereby placing the largest element in the final array position. We then locate the largest element remaining in the subarray with subscripts $0 \ldots n-2$, and switch it with the element at subscript $n-2$, thereby placing the second largest element in the next to last position $n-2$. We continue this process until the whole array is sorted.

Figure 10.18 traces the operation of the selection sort algorithm. The diagram on the left shows the original array. Each subsequent diagram shows the array after the next largest element is moved to its final position in the array. The subarray in the darker color represents the portion of the array that is sorted after each exchange occurs. Note that it will require, at most, $n-1$ exchanges to sort an array with n elements.

**Figure 10.18
Trace of
Selection Sort**

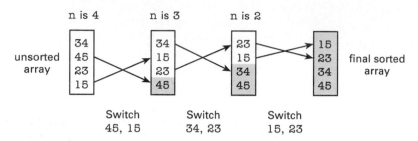

n = size of unsorted subarray

Switch 45, 15   Switch 34, 23   Switch 15, 23

DESIGN

Because the selection sort can be viewed as a sort accomplished by first placing one element and then sorting a subarray, it is a good candidate for a recursive solution.

Recursive Algorithm for Selection Sort

1. if *n* is 1
    2. The array is sorted.
else
    3. Place the largest array value in last array element.
    4. Sort the subarray which excludes the last array element
       (`array[0]..array[n-2]`).

IMPLEMENTATION

Figure 10.19 shows an implementation of our recursive algorithm that uses a function `place_largest` to perform Step 3 and a recursive function `select_sort` that carries out the overall procedure. Figure 10.20 shows an iterative selection sort for comparison. The recursive function is slightly simpler

---

Figure 10.19   Recursive Selection Sort

```
/*
 *  Finds the largest value in list array[0]..array[n-1] and exchanges it
 *  with the value at array[n-1]
 *  Pre:  n > 0 and first n elements of array are defined
 *  Post: array[n-1] contains largest value
 */
```

(continued)

Figure 10.19   *(continued)*

```
void
place_largest(int array[],    /* input/output - array in which to place
                                  largest                               */
              int n)          /* input - number of array elements to
                                  consider                              */
{
      int temp,        /* temporary variable for exchange        */
          j,           /* array subscript and loop control       */
          max_index;   /* index of largest so far                */

      /*  Save subscript of largest array value in max_index     */
      max_index = n - 1;       /* assume last value is largest    */
      for  (j = n - 2;  j >= 0;  --j)
          if (array[j] > array[max_index])
                max_index = j;

      /*  Unless largest value is already in last element, exchange
          largest and last elements                              */
      if (max_index != n - 1) {
            temp = array[n - 1];
            array[n - 1] = array[max_index];
            array[max_index] = temp;
      }
}

/*
 *  Sorts n elements of an array of integers
 *  Pre:  n > 0 and first n elements of array are defined
 *  Post: array elements are in ascending order
 */
void
select_sort(int array[],   /* input/output - array to sort          */
            int n)         /* input - number of array elements to sort */
{
      if (n > 1) {
            place_largest(array, n);
            select_sort(array, n - 1);
      }
}
```

Figure 10.20 **Iterative Selection Sort Function**

```
/*  Include function place_largest from Fig. 10.19                     */

/*
 *  Sorts n elements of an array of integers
 *  Pre:  n > 0 and first n elements of array are defined
 *  Post: array elements are in ascending order
 */
void
select_sort(int array[],  /* input/output - array to sort            */
            int n)        /* input - number of array elements to sort */
{
    int i;                /* number of elements in unsorted subarray  */

    for  (i = n;  i > 1;  --i)
          place_largest(array, i);
}
```

to understand than this second version because it contains a single `if` statement rather than a loop. The recursive function typically executes more slowly, however, because of the extra overhead due to the recursive function calls.

Notice that the logic of the `select_sort` function does not exactly match our original algorithm or our generic recursive algorithm. If you look back at the initial algorithm, you will see that if we are at the simplest case (an array of one element), no action is necessary. Rather than explicitly making the test for the simple case and having an empty true branch, we have chosen to negate the test for the simplest case so that all the actions are on the true branch of the decision. Notice that if n == 1, the selection sort function returns without doing anything. This behavior is correct because a one-element array is always sorted.

EXERCISES FOR SECTION 10.4

Self-Check

1. Using activation frames, hand-trace the execution of the `find_caps` function on the string `"DoD"`.
2. Trace the execution of both recursive and iterative `select_sort` functions on an array that has the integers 5, 8, 10, 1 stored in consecutive elements.

3. In the `find_caps` function, because `substr` is always called to extract a substring that includes the end of the original string and the substring extracted is not modified by the function to which it is passed as an argument, there is a more space-efficient way to access this portion of `str`. What could you use in place of the references to `reststr` that would make the call to `substr` unnecessary?

Programming

1. Modify the `find_caps` function to create a `find_digits` function.

10.5 PROBLEM SOLVING WITH RECURSION

Since C does not have a built-in representation of a set data structure, we would like to develop an implementation of a group of set operations using strings as our sets.

Case Study: Operations on Sets

PROBLEM

Develop a group of functions to perform the $\in$ (is an element of), $\subseteq$ (is a subset of), and $\cup$ (union) operations on sets of characters. Also develop functions to check that a certain set is valid (that is, that it contains no duplicate characters), to check for the empty set, and to print a set in standard set notation.

ANALYSIS

Character strings provide a fairly natural representation of sets of characters. Like sets, strings can be of varying sizes and can be empty. If a character array that is to hold a set is declared to have one more than the number of characters in the universal set (to allow room for the null character), then set operations should never produce a string that will overflow the array.

DESIGN

This problem is naturally divided into subproblems, each of which corresponds to a single function. Since these functions are all basic set utilities, their individual algorithms are quite straightforward. We will develop pseudocode for the simplest functions first and will refer to these functions in the more complex solutions. Since one goal of this case study is to demonstrate the use of recursion, we will ignore the existence of looping constructs for the time being.

Algorithm for `is_empty(set)`

1. Is initial character `'\0'`?

Algorithm for `is_element(ele, set)`

1. if `is_element(set)`   /* simple case 1   */
      2. Answer is false.
   else if initial character of `set` matches `ele`   /* simple case 2   */
      3. Answer is true.
   else
      4. Answer depends on whether `ele`
         is in the rest of `set`.   /* recursive step */

Algorithm for `is_set(set)`

1. if `is_empty(set)`   /* simple case 1   */
      2. Answer is true.
   else if `is_element`(initial set character,
                        rest of `set`)   /* simple case 2   */
      3. Answer is false.
   else
      4. Answer depends on whether rest of `set` is a
         valid set.   /* recursive step */

Algorithm for `is_subset(sub, set)`

1. if `is_empty(sub)`   /* simple case 1   */
      2. Answer is true.
   else if initial character of `sub` is not an element of
      `set`   /* simple case 2   */
      3. Answer is false.
   else
      4. Answer depends on whether rest of `sub` is a
         subset of `set`.   /* recursive step */

Algorithm for union of `set1` and `set2`

1. if `is_empty(set1)`   /* simple case 1   */
      2. Result is `set2`.
   else if initial character of `set1` is also an element
      of `set2`   /* recursive step */

3. Result is the union of the rest of `set1` with
`set2`.   /* case 1   */
        else   /* case 2   */
4. Result includes initial character of `set1` and the union of the rest of `set1` with `set2`.

Algorithm for `print_set(set)`

1. Output a {.
2. if `set` is not empty, print elements separated by commas.
3. Output a }.

Algorithm for `print_with_commas(set)`

1. if `set` has exactly one element
    2. Print it.
else
    3. Print initial element and a comma.
    4. `print_with_commas` the rest of `set`.

IMPLEMENTATION

Every recursive function in the collection of functions we have designed references "the rest of the set" for some set, that is, all but the first letter of the set. In all of these functions, this "rest of the set" is passed as an input argument only—the function called looks at it but does not modify it. Since this particular substring includes all the characters of the original string from the substring's starting point right through the original string's null character, in this situation we do not actually need to recopy the substring as function `substr` does. Since all string arguments are passed as addresses, specifically as the address of the string's initial character, here we can pass to a function the "rest of the set" by simply using `&set[1]` as the validating function `is_set` does. Figure 10.21 shows the data area of a main function that we assume contains a call to `is_set` that passes the string `set1` whose value is "acdfk." Also pictured are the data area of this initial call to `is_set` and the data area of the first recursive call, `is_set(&set[1])`. Figure 10.22 shows our implementation of `is_set` along with code for our other set operations.

You will notice that the name of our function that forms the union of two sets is `set_union`. We could not use the name `union` because this is a reserved word in C. In the implementation of `set_union`, we could not use the variable `result` as the output argument for both the call to `set_union` and the call to `sprintf` because `sprintf` does not guarantee correct results if there is overlap between its input and output arguments.

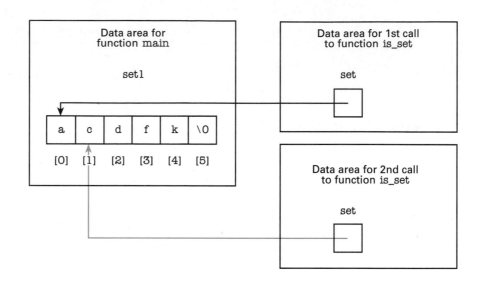

**Figure 10.21
Reference to a
Substring
without
Recopying in
Recursive Call
to is_set**

Figure 10.22   Recursive Set Operations on Sets Represented as Character Strings

```
/*
 *   Functions to perform basic operations on sets of characters
 *   represented as strings. Note: "Rest of set" is represented  as
 *   &set[1], which is indeed the address of the rest of the set excluding
 *   the first element.  This efficient representation, which does not
 *   recopy the rest of the set, is an acceptable alternative to
 *   substr(result, set, 1, strlen(set)) in these functions only because
 *   the "rest of the set" is always passed strictly as an input argument.
 */

#include <stdio.h>
#include <string.h>
#include <ctype.h>

#define SETSIZ   65   /* 52 uppercase and lowercase letters, 10 digits,
                         {, }, and '\0'                                   */
#define TRUE     1
#define FALSE    0

/*  Include strassign and substr functions from Chapter 9 here           */

/*
 *  Determines if set is empty.  If so, returns 1;  if not, returns 0.
```

(continued)

Figure 10.22   *(continued)*

```
 */
int
is_empty(const char set[])
{
      return (set[0] == '\0');
}

/*
 *  Determines if ele is an element of set.
 */
int
is_element(char        ele,     /* input - element to look for in set    */
           const char set[])    /* input - set in which to look for ele  */
{
      int ans;

      if (is_empty(set))
            ans = FALSE;
      else if (set[0] == ele)
            ans = TRUE;
      else
            ans = is_element(ele, &set[1]);

      return (ans);
}

/*
 *  Determines if string value of set represents a valid set (no duplicate
 *  elements)
 */
int
is_set(const char set[])
{
      int ans;

      if (is_empty(set))
            ans = TRUE;
      else if (is_element(set[0], &set[1]))
            ans = FALSE;
      else
            ans = is_set(&set[1]);
```

(continued)

Figure 10.22 *(continued)*

```
        return (ans);
}

/*
 *  Determines if value of sub is a subset of value of set
 */
int
is_subset(const char sub[], const char set[])
{
        int ans;

        if (is_empty(sub))
                ans = TRUE;
        else if (!is_element(sub[0], set))
                ans = FALSE;
        else
                ans = is_subset(&sub[1], set);

        return (ans);
}

/*
 *   Finds the union of set1 and set2.
 *   Pre:  size of result array is at least SETSIZ;
 *         set1 and set2 are valid sets of characters and digits
 */
char *
set_union(char        result[], /* output - space in which to store
                                            string result               */
        const char set1[],   /* input  - sets whose                     */
        const char set2[])   /*           union is being formed         */
{
        char temp[SETSIZ];        /* local variable to hold result of call
                                     to set_union embedded in sprintf call */

        if (is_empty(set1))
                strassign(result, set2, SETSIZ);
        else if (is_element(set1[0], set2))
                set_union(result, &set1[1], set2);
        else
```

(continued)

Figure 10.22   *(continued)*

```
            sprintf(result, "%c%s", set1[0],
                    set_union(temp, &set1[1], set2));

      return (result);
}

/*
 *  Prints a string so that each pair of characters is separated by a
 *  comma and a space.
 */
void
print_with_commas(const char str[])
{
      if (strlen(str) == 1) {
            putchar(str[0]);
      } else {
            printf("%c, ", str[0]);
            print_with_commas(&str[1]);
      }
}

/*
 *  Prints a string in standard set notation.
 *  e.g.  print_set("abc") outputs {a, b, c}
 */
void
print_set(const char set[])
{
      putchar('{');
      if (!is_empty(set))
            print_with_commas(set);
      putchar('}');
}

/*
 *  Gets a set input as a string with brackets (e.g., {abc})
 *  and strips off the brackets.
 */
char *
get_set(char set[])  /* output - set string without brackets {}        */
```

(continued)

Figure 10.22 *(continued)*

```
{
      char inset[SETSIZ];

      scanf("%s", inset);
      substr(set, inset, 1, strlen(inset) - 1, SETSIZ);
      return (set);
}

/*
 *   Tries out set operation functions.
 */
int
main(void)
{
      char ele, set_one[SETSIZ], set_two[SETSIZ], set_three[SETSIZ];

      printf("A set is entered as a string of up to %d letters\n",
             SETSIZ - 3);
      printf("              and digits enclosed in {} ");
      printf("(no duplicate characters)\n");
      printf("For example, {a, b, c} is entered as {abc}\n");
      printf("Enter a set to test validation function> ");
      get_set(set_one);
      putchar('\n');
      print_set(set_one);
      if (is_set(set_one))
            printf(" is a valid set\n");
      else
            printf(" is invalid\n");

      printf("Enter a single character, a space, and a set> ");
      while(isspace(ele = getchar()));   /* gets first character after
                                            white space                  */
      get_set(set_one);
      printf("\n%c ", ele);
      if (is_element(ele, set_one))
            printf("is an element of ");
      else
            printf("is not an element of ");
      print_set(set_one);
```

(continued)

Figure 10.22   *(continued)*

```
    printf("\nEnter two sets to test set_union> ");
    get_set(set_one);
    get_set(set_two);
    printf("\nThe union of ");
    print_set(set_one);
    printf(" and ");
    print_set(set_two);
    printf(" is ");
    print_set(set_union(set_three, set_one, set_two));
    putchar('\n');

    return (0);
}
```

TESTING

We have added one function to our group of set functions to make it easier to write a driver function for testing. The function `get_set` takes an input string representing a set and strips off the brackets { } that the driver program asks the user to place around the set entered. These brackets make it easy for the user to enter the empty set.

When testing this group of functions, choose data that check boundary conditions. For instance, test `is_set` with valid sets, including the empty set, and with invalid sets that have duplicate letters in various parts of the set string. For `is_element`, test an element found at the beginning of the set string, an element in the middle, an element at the end, and an element not in the string. Also try the empty set as the second argument. With `is_subset`, test using empty sets for `sub` and/or `set`, and try various orderings of letters in `sub`. Try a case where the sets are equal as well. When testing `set_union`, test equal sets, disjoint sets, and partially overlapping sets with various orderings of the elements. In addition, try the empty set as the first argument, then as the second; then call `set_union` using the empty set for both arguments.

EXERCISES FOR SECTION 10.5

Self-Check

1. Imagine that we add calls to `printf` of the type shown in Fig. 10.9 to functions `is_element` and `is_subset`. Show the tracing output that would be produced for the function call `is_subset("bc", "cebf");`

Programming

1. Define a recursive `intersection` function that computes `set1` ∩ `set2`. Then, define an iterative version of the same function.
2. Define a very short `set_equal` function that calls the `intersection` function from Programming Exercise 1.

10.6 A CLASSIC CASE STUDY IN RECURSION: TOWERS OF HANOI

The Towers of Hanoi problem involves moving a specified number of disks that are all different sizes from one tower (or peg) to another. Legend has it that the world will come to an end when the problem is solved for 64 disks.

PROBLEM

Move *n* disks from peg A to peg C using peg B as needed. The following conditions apply:

1. Only one disk at a time may be moved, and this disk must be the top disk on a peg.
2. A larger disk can never be placed on top of a smaller disk.

ANALYSIS

The version of the problem shown in Fig. 10.23 has five disks (numbered 1 through 5) and three towers or pegs (lettered A, B, and C). The goal is to move the five disks from peg A to peg C. The simplest cases of the problem involve moving one disk only (e.g., move disk 2 from peg A to peg C). A simpler problem than the original would be to move four disks subject to the conditions given or three disks, and so on. Therefore we want to split the original five-disk problem into several simpler problems, each of which involves fewer disks. Let's consider splitting the original problem into the following three problems:

**Figure 10.23
Towers of
Hanoi**

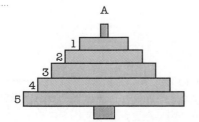

**Figure 10.24
Towers of
Hanoi after
Steps 1 and 2**

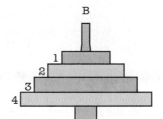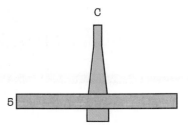

1. Move four disks from peg A to peg B.
2. Move disk 5 from peg A to peg C.
3. Move four disks from peg B to peg C.

In Step 1, we move all disks but the largest to peg B, an auxiliary peg not mentioned in the original problem. In Step 2, we move the largest disk to C, the goal peg. Then, in Step 3 we move the remaining disks from B to the goal peg where they will be placed on top of the largest disk. Let's assume that we will be able to perform Step 1 and Step 2 (a simple case); Fig. 10.24 shows the status of the three pegs after completing these steps. At this point, it should be clear that we will indeed solve the original five-disk problem if we can complete Step 3.

Unfortunately, we still don't know how to perform Step 1 or Step 3. However, both of these steps involve four disks instead of five, so they are easier than the original problem. We should be able to split each of these steps into simpler problems in the same way that we split the original problem. Step 3 involves moving four disks from peg B to peg C, so we can split this step into the following two three-disk problems and one one-disk problem:

3.1 Move three disks from peg B to peg A.
3.2 Move disk 4 from peg B to peg C.
3.3 Move three disks from peg A to peg C.

Figure 10.25 shows the status of the pegs after completing Step 3.1 and Step 3.2. We now have the two largest disks on peg C. Once we complete Step 3.3, all five disks will be on peg C as required.

**Figure 10.25
Towers of
Hanoi after
Steps 1, 2, 3.1,
and 3.2**

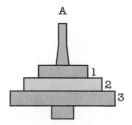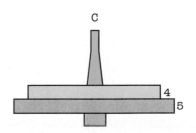

By splitting each *n*-disk problem into two problems involving *n* − 1 disks and a third problem involving only one disk, we will eventually divide our original problem into many one-disk problems. These simple cases are ones we already know how to solve.

The solution to the Towers of Hanoi problem consists of a printed list of individual disk moves. We need a recursive function that can be used to print instructions for moving any number of disks from one peg to another using the third peg as an auxiliary.

Data Requirements

Problem Inputs
```
int n           /* the number of disks to be moved   */
char from_peg   /* the from peg                       */
char to_peg     /* the to peg                         */
char aux_peg    /* the auxiliary peg                  */
```

Problem Outputs
a list of individual disk moves

DESIGN

Algorithm

1. if *n* is 1 then
   - 2. Move disk 1 from the *from* peg to the *to* peg

   else
   - 3. Move *n* − 1 disks from the *from* peg to the *auxiliary* peg using the *to* peg.
   - 4. Move disk *n* from the *from* peg to the *to* peg.
   - 5. Move *n* − 1 disks from the *auxiliary* peg to the *to* peg using the *from* peg.

If *n* is 1, we have a simple case that we can solve immediately. If *n* is greater than 1, the recursive step (the step following else) splits the original problem into three smaller subproblems, one of which is another simple case. Each simple case displays a move instruction. Verify that the recursive step generates the three problems listed below Fig. 10.24 when *n* is 5, the *from* peg is A, and the *to* peg is C.

The implementation of this algorithm is shown as function `tower` in Fig. 10.26. Function `tower` has four input parameters. The function call statement

```
tower('A', 'C', 'B', 5);
```

Figure 10.26   Recursive Function tower

```
/*
 *  Displays instructions for moving n disks from from_peg to to_peg using
 *  aux_peg as an auxiliary.  Disks are numbered 1 to n (smallest to
 *  largest). Instructions call for moving one disk at a time and never
 *  require placing a larger disk on top of a smaller one.
 */
void
tower(char from_peg,    /* input - characters naming      */
      char to_peg,      /*           the problem's        */
      char aux_peg,     /*           three pegs           */
      int  n)           /* input - number of disks to move */
{
    if (n == 1) {
        printf("Move disk 1 from peg %c to peg %c\n", from_peg,
               to_peg);
    } else {
        tower(from_peg, aux_peg, to_peg, n - 1);
        printf("Move disk %d from peg %c to peg %c\n", n, from_peg,
               to_peg);
        tower(aux_peg, to_peg, from_peg, n - 1);
    }
}
```

solves the problem that was posed earlier of moving five disks from peg A to peg C using B as an auxiliary (see Fig. 10.23).

In Fig. 10.26, when the terminating condition is true, a call to `printf` displays an instruction regarding moving disk 1. Each recursive step consists of two recursive calls to `tower` with a call to `printf` sandwiched between them. The first recursive call solves the problem of moving $n - 1$ disks to the *auxiliary* peg. The call to `printf` displays a message to move the remaining disk to the *to* peg. The second recursive call solves the problem of moving the $n - 1$ disks from the *auxiliary* peg to the *to* peg.

TESTING

The function call statement

```
tower('A', 'C', 'B', 3);
```

solves a simpler three-disk problem: Move 3 disks from peg A to peg C. Its execution is traced in Fig. 10.27 and the output generated is shown in Fig. 10.28. Verify for yourself that this list of steps does indeed solve the three-disk problem.

Comparison of Iterative and Recursive Functions

It is interesting to consider that function **tower** in Fig. 10.26 will solve the Towers of Hanoi problem for any number of disks. The three-disk problem results in a total of seven calls to function **tower** and is solved by seven disk moves. The five-disk problem would result in a total of 31 calls to function **tower** and is solved in 31 moves. In general, the number of moves required to

Figure 10.27 Trace of
`tower('A', 'C', 'B', 3);`

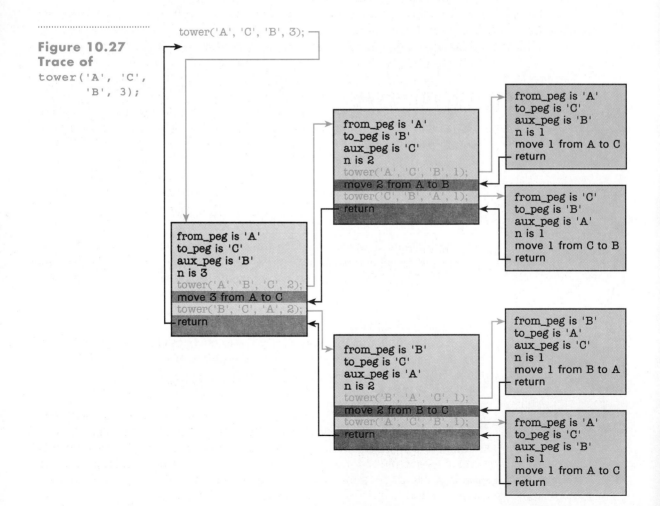

**Figure 10.28
Output
Generated by**
`tower('A', 'C',
      'B', 3);`

Move disk 1 from A to C
Move disk 2 from A to B
Move disk 1 from C to B
Move disk 3 from A to C
Move disk 1 from B to A
Move disk 2 from B to C
Move disk 1 from A to C

solve the *n*-disk problem is $2^n - 1$. Because each function call requires the allocation and initialization of a local data area in memory and the computer time increases exponentially with the problem size, be careful about running this program with a value of n that is larger than ten.

The dramatic increase in processing time for larger numbers of disks is a function of this problem, not a function of recursion. However, in general, if there are recursive and iterative solutions to the same problem, the recursive solution will require more time and space because of the extra function calls.

Although recursion was not really needed to solve the simpler problems in this section, it was extremely useful in formulating an algorithm for Towers of Hanoi. For certain problems, recursion leads naturally to solutions that are much easier to read and understand than their iterative counterparts. To researchers developing solutions to the complex problems that are at the frontiers of their research areas, the benefits gained from increased clarity far outweigh the extra cost in time and memory of running a recursive program.

**EXERCISES FOR
SECTION 10.6**

Self-Check

1. How many moves are needed to solve the six-disk problem?
2. Write a main program that takes a data value for n (the number of disks) and calls function `tower` to move n disks from A to B.

10.7 PICTURE PROCESSING WITH RECURSION

Case Study: Counting Cells in a Blob

The next problem is a good illustration of the power of recursion. Its solution is relatively easy to write recursively; however, the problem would be much more difficult without using recursion. An algorithm such as the one developed in this case study might be used to count *pixels* (picture elements) belonging to an object in a photograph, one aspect of computing the "observed area" that we used as an input to our flat washer case study in Chapter 3.

**Figure 10.29
Grid with
Three Blobs**

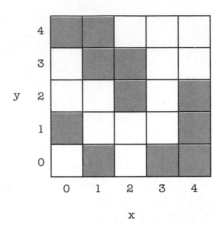

PROBLEM

We have a two-dimensional grid of cells, each of which may be empty or filled. The filled cells that are connected form a blob. There may be several blobs on the grid. We would like a function that accepts as input the coordinates of a particular cell and returns the size of the blob containing the cell.

In Fig. 10.29, three blobs are in the sample grid. If we have a function blob_check whose parameters represent the grid and the *x* and *y* coordinates of a cell, the result of blob_check(grid, 1, 3) is 5, the result of blob_check(grid, 0, 1) is 2, the result of blob_check(grid, 4, 4) is 0, and the result of blob_check(grid, 4, 0) is 4.

ANALYSIS

Function blob_check must test whether the cell specified by its arguments is filled. There are two simple cases: The cell (x, y) may not be on the grid, or the cell (x, y) may be empty. In either of these cases, the value returned by blob_check is 0. If the cell is on the grid and filled, then the value returned is 1 plus the sizes of the blobs containing each of its eight neighbors. To avoid counting a filled cell more than once, we mark it as empty once we have visited it.

Data Requirements

> **Problem Inputs**
> ```
> int grid[N_ROWS][N_COLS]    /* the grid                   */
> int x, y                    /* coordinates of the point
>                                being visited               */
> ```

> **Problem Outputs**
> the number of cells in the blob containing point (x, y)

---DESIGN---

Algorithm

1. if cell (x, y) is not in the array then
   2. The count is 0
   else if cell (x, y) is empty then
   3. The count is 0
   else
   4. Mark cell (x, y) as empty.
   5. The count is 1 + the counts of (x, y)'s
      eight neighbor cells.

---IMPLEMENTATION---

Function `blob_check`, shown in Fig. 10.30, assumes the presence of the `#define` directives that follow. N_ROWS and N_COLS are the dimensions of the grid. FILLED and EMPTY represent the possible values of the grid elements.

```
#define N_ROWS   100
#define N_COLS   100

#define FILLED   1
#define EMPTY    0
```

Figure 10.30   Function blob_size and Recursive Function blob_check

```
/*
 *  Counts the number of filled array elements in the blob to which
 *  point (x, y) belongs.  If (x, y) itself is empty or point (x, y) is
 *  not within the N_ROWS x N_COLS grid, a zero is returned.
 *
 *  Side effect:  elements of blob to which (x, y) belongs are set to
 *  EMPTY
 */
int
blob_check(int grid[N_ROWS][N_COLS], /* input/output - grid containing
                                        blob elements left to process */
           int x, int y)             /* input - coordinates of point in
                                        blob of interest              */
```

(continued)

Figure 10.30 *(continued)*

```
{
     int ct;
     if (x < 0  ||  x >= N_COLS  ||  y < 0  ||  y >= N_ROWS) {
          ct = 0;
     } else if (grid[x][y] == EMPTY) {
          ct = 0;
     } else {
          grid[x][y] = EMPTY;
          ct = 1 + blob_check(grid, x-1, y+1) + blob_check(grid, x, y+1)
                 + blob_check(grid, x+1, y+1) + blob_check(grid, x+1, y)
                 + blob_check(grid, x+1, y-1) + blob_check(grid, x, y-1)
                 + blob_check(grid, x-1, y-1) + blob_check(grid, x-1, y);
     }

     return (ct);
}

/*
 *  Counts the number of filled cells in the blob containing point (x, y).
 *  Uses blob_check to perform the counting operation.  Since blob_check
 *  resets blob cells to EMPTY, passes blob_check a "disposable" copy of
 *  grid array.
 */
int
blob_size(const int grid[N_ROWS][N_COLS], /* input - grid of blobs      */
               int x, int y)              /* input - coordinates of point
                                             in blob of interest        */
{
     int i, j;
     int grid_copy[N_ROWS][N_COLS];

     for  (i = 0;  i < N_ROWS;  ++i)
         for  (j = 0;  j < N_COLS;  ++j)
             grid_copy[i][j] = grid[i][j];

     return (blob_check(grid_copy, x, y));
}
```

In Fig. 10.30, function `blob_check` implements the counting algorithm, and function `blob_size` makes a copy of the grid to pass to `blob_check`. Because of this copying, the fact that `blob_check` marks a cell EMPTY after visiting it will not result in erasure of the blobs on the original grid. We use two functions because the creation of this grid copy needs to occur only once. Placing the copy operation at the beginning of our recursive function, `blob_check`, would lead to creation of a new grid on every recursive call—a totally unnecessary waste of time and space. Function `blob_size` passes its grid copy and parameters `x` and `y` to `blob_check` and returns the value computed by `blob_check` as its own result.

If the cell visited is off the grid or is empty, `blob_check` returns a value of 0 immediately. Otherwise, the recursive step executes, causing function `blob_check` to call itself eight times; each time, a different neighbor of the current cell is visited. The cells are visited in a clockwise manner starting with the neighbor above and to the left. The function result is defined as the sum of all values returned from these recursive calls plus 1 (for the current cell).

The sequence of operations performed in function `blob_check` is very important. The `if` statement tests whether the cell (`x`, `y`) is on the grid before testing whether cell (`x`, `y`) is empty. If the order were reversed, the condition `grid[x][y] == EMPTY` would reference an out-of-range element whenever cell (`x`, `y`) was off the grid.

Also, the recursive step resets `grid[x][y]` to EMPTY before visiting the neighbors of point (`x`, `y`). If this reset were not done first, then cell (`x`, `y`) would be counted more than once since it is a neighbor of all its neighbors. A worse problem could occur: The recursion would not terminate. When each neighbor of the current cell is visited, `blob_check` is called again with the coordinates of the current cell as arguments. If the current cell is EMPTY, an immediate return occurs. If the current cell were still FILLED, the recursive step would be executed erroneously. Eventually, the program would run out of time or memory space. Exhausting available memory is often indicated by a `stack overflow` or `access violation` error message.

EXERCISES FOR SECTION 10.7

Self-Check

1. Trace informally the execution of function `blob_check` for the coordinate pairs (0, 0) and (0, 1) in the sample grid.
2. Is the order of the two tests performed in function `blob_check` critical? What happens if we reverse them?

Programming

1. Write a function `line_len` that takes an n-element integer array whose values are either `FILLED(1)` or `EMPTY(0)`, along with an integer `p` designating a position in the array, and finds the number of cells in the line of which `array[p]` is part. Use a recursive helper function. This problem is a one-dimensional version of the blob program.

10.8 COMMON PROGRAMMING ERRORS

The most common problem with a recursive function is that it may not terminate properly. For example, if the terminating condition is not correct or is incomplete, the function may call itself indefinitely or until all available memory is used up. Frequently, a run-time error message noting stack overflow or an access violation is an indicator that a recursive function is not terminating. Make sure that you identify all simple cases and provide a terminating condition for each one. Also be sure that each recursive step redefines the problem in terms of arguments that are closer to simple cases so that repeated recursive calls will eventually lead to simple cases only.

In our examples of recursive functions that return a value, we have always used a local variable (or, in the case of string functions, an output parameter) into which the function result is placed by the function's decision structure. Then we have ended the function's code with a `return` statement. Since C permits the use of the `return` statement anywhere in the function code, a module like `is_set` from Fig. 10.22 could also have been written as follows.

```
int
is_set(const char set[])
{
      if (is_empty(set))
           return (TRUE);
      else if (is_element(set[0], &set[1]))
           return (FALSE);
      else
           return (is_set(&set[1]));
}
```

You should be aware that it is critical that every path through a `nonvoid` function lead to a `return` statement. In particular, the `return` statement to return the value of the recursive call to `is_set` is just as important as the other two `return` statements. However, when a multiple-`return` style is adopted, omitting one of these necessary `return` statements is easy to do.

The recopying of large arrays or other data structures can quickly consume all available memory. Such copying should be done inside a recursive function only when absolutely essential for data protection. If only a single copy is necessary, a nonrecursive function can be created that makes the necessary copy, passes the copy and the other arguments to the recursive function, and returns the result computed.

It is also a good idea to introduce a nonrecursive function to handle preliminaries and call the recursive function when there is error checking. Checking for errors inside a recursive function is extremely inefficient if the error is of the type that would be detected on the very first call. In such a situation, repeated checks in recursive calls are a waste of computer time.

Sometimes, it is difficult to observe the output produced when running recursive functions that you have made self-tracing as described in Section 10.2. If each recursive call generates two or more output lines and there are many recursive calls, the output will scroll down the screen more quickly than it can be read. On most systems, pressing a control character sequence (e.g., Control S) will temporarily stop output to the screen. If this is not possible, you can stop your output temporarily by printing a prompting message followed by a call to `getchar`. Your program will resume execution when you enter a data character.

CHAPTER REVIEW

In this chapter, many examples of recursive functions, along with valuable insight regarding their use, were provided. We hope that studying them has given you some appreciation of the power of recursion as a problem-solving and programming tool. Although it may take some time to feel comfortable thinking in this new way about programming, it is certainly worth the effort.

QUICK-CHECK EXERCISES

1. Explain the use of a stack in recursion.
2. Which is generally more efficient, recursion or iteration?
3. Which control statement do you typically find in a recursive function?
4. How would you improve the efficiency of the following factorial function?

```
int
fact(int n)
{
     int ans;
```

```
            if (n < 0  ||  n > 10) {
                    printf("\nInvalid argument to fact:   %d\n",
                            n);
                    ans = n;
            } else if (n == 0) {
                    ans = 1;
            } else {
                    ans = n * fact(n - 1);
            }

            return (ans);
      }
```

5. When might a programmer conceptualize a problem solution using recursion but implement it using iteration?
6. What problem do you notice in the following recursive function? Show two possible ways to correct the problem.

```
int
silly(int n)
{
      if (n <= 0)
              return (1);
      else if (n % 2 == 0)
              return (n);
      else
              silly(n - 3);
}
```

7. What is a common cause of a stack overflow error?
8. What can you say about a recursive algorithm that has the following form?

   if condition
       Perform recursive step.

ANSWERS TO QUICK-CHECK EXERCISES

1. The stack is used to hold all parameter and local variable values along with the return point for each execution of a recursive function.
2. Iteration is generally more efficient than recursion.

3. `if` statement
4. Write as two functions so error checking occurs only once.

```
int
factorial(int n)
{
      int ans;

      if (n == 0)
            ans = 1;
      else
            ans = n * factorial(n - 1);
      return (ans);
}

int
fact(int n)
{
    int ans;

    if (n < 0  ||  n > 10) {
          printf("\nInvalid argument to fact:  %d\n",
                n);
          ans = n;
    } else {
          ans = factorial(n);
    }

    return (ans);
}
```

5. When a problem's solution is much easier to conceptualize using recursion but a recursive implementation would be too inefficient.
6. One path through the function does not encounter a `return` statement. Either place a `return` statement in the final `else`

```
return (silly(n - 3));
```

or assign 1, n, `silly(n-3)` to a local variable, and place that variable in a `return` statement at the end of the function.
7. Too many recursive calls
8. Nothing is done when the simplest case is reached.

REVIEW QUESTIONS

1. Why does recursion make it easier to conceptualize a solution to a problem?
2. Discuss the efficiency of recursive functions.
3. Differentiate between a simple case and a terminating condition.
4. Write a recursive C function that accumulates the sum of the values in an *n*-element array. *Hint:* Since the "rest of the array" will be strictly an input argument, a representation like the one used for "rest of the set" in the set functions of Section 10.5 would be a good choice.
5. Write a recursive C function that counts the number of vowels in a string. You may wish to call the `is_element` function defined in Section 10.5.
6. Write the recursive helper function `check_geometric` which assists function `main` in carrying out its purpose.

```
/*
 *  Determines if an input list forms a geometric
 *  sequence, a sequence in which each term is the
 *  product of the previous term and the common
 *  ratio.  Prints the message "List forms a geometric
 *  sequence" if this is the case.  Otherwise, stops
 *  input and prints the messages "Input halted at
 *  <incorrect term value>.  List does not form a
 *  geometric sequence"
 */
int
main(void)
{
      double term1, term2,
             ratio;       /* common ratio of a geometric
                             sequence whose first two
                             terms are term1 and term2  */
      printf("Data:  \n");
      scanf("%lf", &term1);
      printf("%.2f  ", term1);
      scanf("%lf", &term2);
      printf("%.2f  ", term2);

      ratio = term2 / term1;
      check_geometric(ratio, term2);  /* gets and checks
            rest of input list, considering ratios equal
            if they differ by less than .001            */

      return (0);
}
```

7. Write a recursive function that returns the position of the last nonblank character of a string. You may assume that you are working with a disposable copy of the string.

PROGRAMMING PROJECTS

1. Write a function that takes each line of input as a string and converts it to a row of `grid` (see Fig. 10.30). The initial character of the first line of input corresponds to `grid[0][0]`, the second character corresponds to `grid[0][1]`, and so on. Set the element value to `EMPTY` if the character is blank or if the position is beyond the end of the string; otherwise, set it to `FILLED`. The number of rows in the grid is the first input value. Use this function in a program that takes cell coordinates and prints the number of cells in the blob containing each coordinate pair.

2. A palindrome consists of a word or deblanked, unpunctuated phrase that is spelled exactly the same when the letters are reversed. Write a recursive function that returns a value of 1 if its string argument is a palindrome. Notice that in palindromes such as level, deed, sees, and Madam I'm Adam (madamimadam), the first letter matches the last, the second matches the next-to-last, and so on.

3. Write a recursive function that returns the value of the following recursive definition:

$$f(x, y) = x - y \qquad \text{if } x \text{ or } y < 0$$
$$f(x, y) = f(x-1, y) + f(x, y-1) \quad \text{otherwise}$$

4. Write a recursive function that lists all of the two-element subsets of a given set of letters. For example, `two_ele_subs("ACEG") =>`

```
{A, C}
{A, E}
{A, G}
{C, E}
{C, G}
{E, G}
```

5. Write a function that accepts an 8 by 8 array of characters that represents a maze. Each position can contain either an X or a blank. Starting at position (0,1), list any path through the maze to get to location (7,7). Only horizontal and vertical moves are allowed. If no path exists, write a message indicating there is no path.

    Moves can be made only to locations that contain a blank. If an X is encountered, that path is blocked and another must be chosen. Use recursion.

6. In Programming Project 9 at the end of Chapter 8, we described an iterative algorithm for searching for a target value in a sorted list. Here again is the introduction to that problem.

   The binary search algorithm that follows may be used to search an array when the elements are in order. This algorithm is analogous to the following approach to finding a name in a telephone book.

   a. Open the book in the middle and look at the middle name on the page.

   b. If the middle name isn't the one you're looking for, decide whether it comes before or after the name you want.

   c. Take the appropriate half of the section of the book you were looking in, and repeat these steps until you land on the name.

   Iterative Algorithm for Binary Search

   1. Let bottom be the subscript of the initial array element.
   2. Let top be the subscript of the last array element.
   3. Let found be false.
   4. Repeat as long as bottom isn't greater than top and the target has not been found
        5. Let middle be the subscript of the element halfway between bottom and top
        6. If the element at middle is the target
             7. Set found to true and index to middle.
           else if the element at middle is larger than the target
             8. Let top be middle − 1.
           else
             9. Let bottom be middle + 1.

   Develop a recursive binary search algorithm, and write and test a function `binary_srch` that implements the algorithm for an array of integers.

7. Write a recursive function that prints all the binary (base 2) numbers represented by a string of x's, 0's, and 1's. The x's represent digits that can be either 0 or 1. For example, the string `1x0x` represents the numbers `1000`, `1001`, `1100`, `1101`. The string `xx1` represents `001`, `011`, `101`, `111`. *Hint:* Write a helper function `replace_first_x` that builds two strings based on its input argument. In one, the first `x` is replaced by a `0`, and in the other by a `1`. The set function `is_element` may be useful too.

8. Another version of the selection sort (see Section 10.4) places the smallest value in the initial array element, the second smallest in the next element, and so on. Implement this version both recursively and iteratively.

CHAPTER 11

STRUCTURE AND UNION TYPES

11.1
User-Defined Structure Types
11.2
Structure Type Data as Input and Output
Parameters
11.3
Functions Whose Result Values Are Structured
11.4
Problem Solving with Structure Types
Case Study: A User-Defined Type for
Complex Numbers
11.5
Parallel Arrays and Arrays of Structures
Case Study: Universal Measurement Conversion
11.6
Union Types
11.7
Common Programming Errors
Chapter Review

In previous chapters, we have seen how to represent in C numbers, characters, words, other strings, and lists (arrays) of these objects. But surely there is more to the world we live in than words and lists of numbers! Every day the role of computers in this complex universe widens, and a programming language must be able to model not only numbers and names, but also protozoa, people, and planets.

In this chapter, we will study how to broaden the modeling facilities of C by defining our own data types that represent structured collections of data pertaining to particular objects. Unlike an array, a structure can have individual components that contain data of different types. A single variable of a composite type designed for planets can store a planet's name, diameter, distance from the sun, the number of years to complete one solar orbit, and the number of hours to make one rotation on its axis. Each of these data items is stored in a separate component of the structure and can be referenced by using the component name.

11.1 USER-DEFINED STRUCTURE TYPES

A *database* is a collection of information stored in a computer's memory or in a disk file. A database is subdivided into records, which normally contain information regarding specific data objects. The structure of the record is determined by the structure of the object's data type.

Structure Type Definition

Before a structured data object can be created or saved, the format of its components must be defined. Although C provides several ways to define structures, we will explore just one approach—defining a new data type for each category of structured objects.

 **EXAMPLE 11.1**

As part of a project for our local observatory, we are developing a database of the planets in our solar system. For each planet, we need to represent the following descriptive information:

Name: Jupiter
Diameter: 142,800 km
Distance from sun (average): 778.3 million km
Orbital period: 11.9 yr
Axial rotation period: 9.925 hr

We can define a *structure type* `planet_t` to use in declaring a variable in which to store this information. There must be five *components* in the structure type, one for each data item. We must specify the name of each component and the type of information stored in each component. We choose the names in the same way we choose all other identifiers: The names describe the nature of the information represented. The contents of each component determine the appropriate data type. For example, the planet's name should be stored in a component that is an array of characters.

The structure type `planet_t` has five distinct components. One is an array of characters; the other four are of type `double`. Although the value in kilometers for distance from the sun will be a whole number, its magnitude is likely to be too great to be stored as type `int` in many C implementations.

```
#define STRSIZ 10

typedef struct planet_s {
    char    name[STRSIZ];
    double diameter,        /* equatorial diameter in
                                km                    */
           dist_sun,        /* average distance from sun
                                in km                 */
           orbital_prd,     /* years to orbit sun once */
           axial_rot_prd;   /* hours to complete one
                                revolution on axis    */
} planet_t;
```

This type definition is a template that describes the format of a planet structure and the name and type of each component. A name chosen for a component of one structure may be the same as the name of a component of another structure or the same as the name of a variable. We will see that the approach C takes to referencing these components will rule out confusion of matching names used in these different contexts. The `typedef` statement itself allocates no memory. A variable declaration is required to allocate storage space for a structured data object. The variables `current_planet` and `previous_planet` are declared next, and the variable `blank_planet` is declared and initialized.

```
{
    planet_t current_planet,
             previous_planet,
             blank_planet = {"", 0, 0, 0, 0};
    . . .
```

The structured variables `current_planet`, `previous_planet`, and `blank_planet` all have the format specified in the definition of type `planet_t`. Thus the memory allocated for each consists of storage space for five distinct values. The variable `blank_planet` is pictured as it appears after initialization.

Variable blank_planet, a structure of type planet_t

.name	\0 ? ? ? ? ? ? ? ? ?
.diameter	0.0
.dist_sun	0.0
.orbital_prd	0.0
.axial_rot_prd	0.0

A user-defined type like `planet_t` can be used to declare both simple and array variables and to declare components in other structure types. A structure containing components that are themselves structures is sometimes called a *hierarchical* structure. The following definition of a structure type includes a component that is an array of planets.

```
typedef struct solar_sys_s {
     double   diameter;
     planet_t planets[9];
     char     galaxy[STRSIZ];
} solar_sys_t;
```

Structure Type Definition

SYNTAX: typedef struct *struct_tag* {
                  type$_1$ *id_list*$_1$;
                  type$_2$ *id_list*$_2$;
                          .
                          .
                          .
                  type$_n$ *id_list*$_n$;
            } *struct_type*;

EXAMPLE: typedef struct complex_s { /* complex number structure */
                  double real_pt,
                            imag_pt;
            } complex_t;

(continued)

INTERPRETATION: The identifier *struct_type* is the name of the structure type being defined. Each *id_list*$_i$ is a list of one or more component names separated by commas; the data type of each component in *id_list*$_i$ is specified by *type*$_i$. The *struct_tag* is an identifier that is an optional part of the structure type definition. When the tag is included, the term `struct` *struct_tag* can be used interchangeably with the identifier *struct_type*.

NOTE: *type*$_i$ can be any standard or previously specified user-defined data type.

Manipulating Individual Components of a Structured Data Object

We can reference a component of a structure by using the *direct component selection* operator, which is a period. The period is preceded by the name of a structure type variable and is followed by the name of a component.

EXAMPLE 11.2 Figure 11.1 shows as an example the manipulation of the components of the variable `current_planet` listed at the beginning of Example 11.1. The statements in the figure store in the variable the data pictured earlier. We assume access to the `strassign` function that we defined in Chapter 9.

Once data are stored in a record, they can be manipulated in the same

Figure 11.1 Assigning Values to Components of Variable current_planet

```
strassign(current_planet.name, "Jupiter", STRSIZ);
current_planet.diameter = 142800;
current_planet.dist_sun = .7783e+9;
current_planet.orbital_prd = 11.9;
current_planet.axial_rot_prd = 9.925;
```

Variable current_planet, a structure of type planet_t

.name	J u p i t e r \0 ? ?
.diameter	142800.0
.dist_sun	.7783e+9
.orbital_prd	11.9
.axial_rot_prd	9.925

way as other data in memory. For example, the statement

```
printf("%s's equatorial diameter is %.1f km.\n",
       current_planet.name, current_planet.diameter);
```

prints the sentence

```
Jupiter's equatorial diameter is 142800.0 km.
```

Review of Operator Precedence

With the addition of the direct component selection operator to our repertory of operators, we will take a moment to see how this operator fits into our overall scheme of precedence rules. Table 11.1 not only shows operator precedence answering the question, In an expression with two operators, which is applied first? It also lists operator associativity answering the question, In an expression containing two of these operators in sequence, which is applied first?

In a generic expression containing two of the same operators in sequence,

$operand_1 \;\; op \;\; operand_2 \;\; op \;\; operand_3$

Table 11.1 Precedence and Associativity of Operators Seen So Far

Precedence	Symbols	Operator Names	Associativity
highest	`a[j] f(...) .`	subscripting, function calls, direct component selection	left
	`++ --`	postfix increment and decrement	left
	`++ -- !` `- + & *`	prefix increment and decrement, logical not, unary negation and plus, address of, indirection	right
	`( type name )`	casts	right
	`* / %`	multiplicative operators (multiplication, division, remainder)	left
	`+ -`	binary additive operators (addition and subtraction)	left
	`< > <= >=`	relational operators	left
	`== !=`	equality / inequality operators	left
	`&&`	logical and	left
	`||`	logical or	left
lowest	`= += -=` `*= /= %=`	assignment operators	right

if *op* has left associativity, the expression is evaluated as

(*operand*$_1$ *op* *operand*$_2$) *op* *operand*$_3$

whereas if *op* has right associativity, the implied order of evaluation is:

operand$_1$ *op* (*operand*$_2$ *op* *operand*$_3$)

Manipulating Whole Structures

The name of a structure type variable used with no component selection operator refers to the entire structure. A new copy of a structure's value can be made by simply assigning one structure to another as in the following statement:

```
previous_planet = current_planet;
```

We will see other instances of the manipulation of whole structures in the next section when we study the use of structures as input and output parameters of functions and as function result types.

Program Style *Naming Convention for Types and Structure Tags*

When we write programs that define new types, it is easy to confuse type names, structure tag names, and variable names. To help reduce confusion, in this text we choose user-defined type names that use lowercase letters and end in the suffix _t (a practice recommended in some industrial software design environments). Similarly, our structure tag names are also lowercase and end in the suffix _s.

EXERCISES FOR SECTION 11.1

Self-Check

1. Define a type named `long_lat_t` that would be appropriate for storing longitude or latitude values. Include components named `minutes` (an integer), `seconds` (an integer), and `direction` (one of the characters `'N'`, `'S'`, `'E'`, or `'W'`).
2. The following are a type to represent a geographic location and a variable of this hierarchical structure type. We will assume that `STRSIZ` means `20`.

```
typedef struct location_s {
      char        place[STRSIZ];
      long_lat_t longitude,
                  latitude;
} location_t;

location_t resort;
```

Given that the values shown have been stored in `resort`, complete the following table to check your understanding of component selection.

Variable resort, a structure of type location_t

.place	Fiji\0??...		
.longitude	18	40	S
.latitude	175	O	E

Reference	Data type of reference	Value
resort.longitude	long_lat_t	18 40 'S'
resort.place	_____	_____
resort.longitude.direction	_____	_____
_____	char	'E'
resort.place[3]	_____	_____

3. A catalog listing for a textbook consists of the authors' names, the title, the publisher, and the year of publication. Declare a structure type `catalog_entry_t` and a variable `book`, and write statements that store the relevant data for this textbook in `book`.

11.2 STRUCTURE TYPE DATA AS INPUT AND OUTPUT PARAMETERS

When a structured variable is passed as an input argument to a function, all of its component *values* are copied into the components of the function's corresponding formal parameter. When such a variable is used as an output argument, the address-of operator must be applied in the same way that we would pass output arguments of the standard types `char`, `int`, and `double`.

EXAMPLE 11.3

Our observatory program from Example 11.1 and Example 11.2 frequently needs to output as a unit all of the descriptive data about a planet. Figure 11.2 shows a function to do this.

To print the value of our structure `current_planet`, we would use the call statement

```
print_planet(current_planet);
```

Figure 11.2   Function with a Structured Input Parameter

```
/*
 * Prints with labels all components of a planet_t structure
 */
void
print_planet(planet_t pl) /* input - one planet structure */
{
      printf("%s\n", pl.name);
      printf("  Equatorial diameter: %.0f km\n", pl.diameter);
      printf("  Average distance from the sun: %.4e km\n", pl.dist_sun);
      printf("  Time to complete one orbit of the sun: %.2f years\n",
             pl.orbital_prd);
      printf("  Time to complete one rotation on axis: %.4f hours\n",
             pl.axial_rot_prd);
}
```

Having an output function like `print_planet` helps us to view the planet object as a concept at a higher level of abstraction rather than as an ad hoc collection of components.

Another function that would help us think of a planet as a data object is a function that would perform an equality comparison of two planets. Although C permits copying of a structure using the assignment operator, the equality and inequality operators cannot be applied to a structured type as a unit. Figure 11.3 shows a `planet_equal` function that takes two planets as input arguments and returns 1 or 0 depending on whether all components match.

Figure 11.3   Function Comparing Two Structured Values for Equality

```
#include <string.h>

/*
 * Determines whether or not the components of planet_1 and planet_2 match
 */
int
planet_equal(planet_t planet_1, /* input - planets to      */
             planet_t planet_2) /*          compare        */
{
```

(continued)

Figure 11.3   *(continued)*

```
       return (strcmp(planet_1.name, planet_2.name) == 0      &&
              planet_1.diameter == planet_2.diameter          &&
              planet_1.dist_sun == planet_2.dist_sun          &&
              planet_1.orbital_prd == planet_2.orbital_prd    &&
              planet_1.axial_rot_prd == planet_2.axial_rot_prd);
}
```

A planet input function would also help us to process `current_planet` as `planet_t` data. Figure 11.4 shows the function `scan_planet` that resembles `scanf` in that it takes an output argument and returns the value 1 if its single output argument is successfully filled, returns the value 0 if there is an error, and returns the negative value `EOF` if the end of the file is encountered.

As you can see from this example, manipulating a structured output argument really requires you to keep C's operator precedence rules straight. In order

Figure 11.4   **Function with a Structured Output Argument**

```
/*
 * Fills a type planet_t structure with input data. Integer returned as
 * function result is success/failure/EOF indicator.
 *     1 => successful input of one planet
 *     0 => error encountered
 *     EOF => insufficient data before end of file
 * In case of error or EOF, value of type planet_t output argument is
 * undefined.
 */
int
scan_planet(planet_t *plnp) /* output - address of planet_t structure
                                         to fill                       */
{
     int result;

     result = scanf("%s%lf%lf%lf%lf", (*plnp).name,
                                      &(*plnp).diameter,
                                      &(*plnp).dist_sun,
                                      &(*plnp).orbital_prd,
                                      &(*plnp).axial_rot_prd);
     if (result == 5)
```
(continued)

Figure 11.4   *(continued)*

```
        result = 1;
   else if (result != EOF)
        result = 0;

   return (result);
}
```

to use `scanf` to store a value in one component of the structure whose address is in `plnp`, we must carry out the following steps (in order):

1. Follow the pointer in `plnp` to the structure.
2. Select the component of interest.
3. Unless this component is an array (e.g., component `name` in Fig. 11.4), get its address to pass to `scanf`.

When we check our precedence chart (see Table 11.1), we find that this reference

```
&*plnp.diameter
```

would attempt Step 2 before Step 1. For this reason, the program in Fig. 11.4 overrides the default operator precedence by parenthesizing the application of the indirect referencing (pointer-following) operator, the unary `*`. Figure 11.5 shows the data areas of functions `main` and `scan_planet` during execution of the following statement in `main`:

```
status = scan_planet(&current_planet);
```

We are assuming that the assignment statement of `scan_planet` calling `scanf` has just finished executing and that it has successfully obtained input values for all components of the output argument structure.

In Table 11.2, we analyze the reference `&(*plnp).diameter` from our function `scan_planet`. C also provides a single operator that combines the functions of the indirection and component selection operators. This *indirect component selection* operator is represented by the character sequence `->` (a "minus" sign followed by a "greater than"). Thus these two expressions are equivalent.

```
(*structp).component        structp->component
```

We elect to use the `(*structp).component` notation in our examples in this chapter so that all nonarray output parameters will be referenced using the `*` operator.

Figure 11.5 **Data Areas of main and scan_planet during Execution of** `status = scan_planet(&current_planet);`

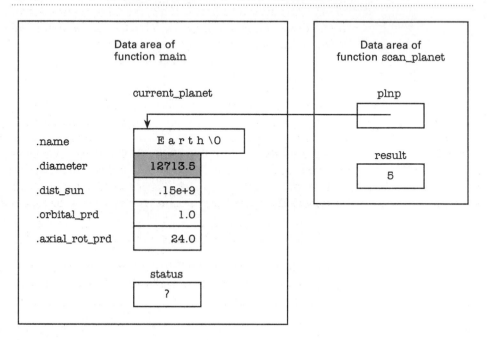

Table 11.2 **Step-by-Step Analysis of Reference &(*plnp).diameter**

Reference	Type	Value
plnp	planet_t *	address of structure that main refers to as current_planet
*plnp	planet_t	structure that main refers to as current_planet
(*plnp).diameter	double	12713.5
&(*plnp).diameter	double *	address of colored component of structure that main refers to as current_planet

In the next section, we see how to write a function that fills up a `planet_t` structure with input data and returns this structure as the function value. This alternative way of approaching input of structures avoids the need for indirect referencing, but it cannot return a status indicator as the function value in the same way `scan_planet` does.

EXERCISES FOR SECTION 11.2

Self-Check

1. Write functions `print_long_lat`, `long_lat_equal`, and `scan_long_lat` to perform output, equality comparison, and input of type `long_lat_t` data (see Self-Check Exercise 1 at the end of Section 11.1).
2. Assume that you have a function `verify_location` that manipulates a structured input/output argument of type `location_t` (see Self-Check Exercise 2 at the end of Section 11.1). The figure that follows shows the data areas of functions `main` and `verify_location` during execution of the call

```
code = verify_location(&resort);
```

Complete the table following the figure with references appropriate for use in `verify_location` (if such references were needed).

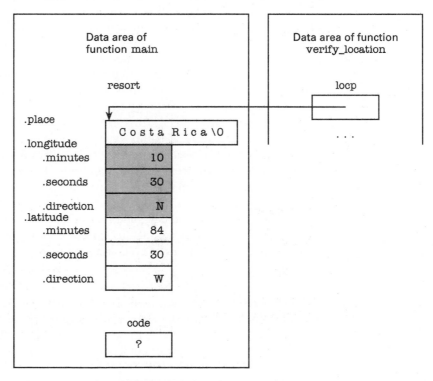

Reference in verify_location	Type of Reference	Value of Reference
locp	location_t *	address of the structure that main refers to as resort
_____	_____	the structure that main refers to as resort
_____	_____	"Costa Rica"
_____	_____	address of the colored component of the structure that main refers to as resort
_____	_____	84

11.3 FUNCTIONS WHOSE RESULT VALUES ARE STRUCTURED

In our study so far, we have seen many situations in which user-defined structured data types are treated just like C's own simple types, yet we have seen only one situation in which structures are handled differently, namely, in equality comparisons. In Chapter 8 and Chapter 9, we saw that C's processing of the array data structure differs significantly from its handling of simple data types. One of the many differences is the fact that the values of an entire array cannot be returned as a function result. Rather, functions computing array results typically require the calling module to provide an array output argument in which to store the result and then return this array's address as the function value.

Since arrays and structure types are both data *structures*, one might expect that C would handle them in a similar fashion. In fact, learning C is greatly assisted by doing away with this expectation, because C's approach to processing structure types closely resembles its facilities for working with simple data types, but is very different from its handling of arrays.

A function that computes a structured result can be modeled on a function computing a simple result. A local variable of the structure type can be allocated, filled with the desired data, and returned as the function result. The function does not return the *address* of the structure as it would with an array result; rather it returns the *values* of all components.

 **EXAMPLE 11.4**

In Fig. 11.6, we see a function that obtains from the input device values for all components of a planet_t structure and returns the structure as the function result. Like function getchar, our function get_planet requires no arguments. If we assume entry of correct data, the statement

```
current_planet = get_planet();
```

Figure 11.6   Function get_planet Returning a Structured Result Type

```
/*
 * Gets and returns a planet_t structure
 */
planet_t
get_planet(void)
{
      planet_t planet;

      scanf("%s%lf%lf%lf%lf", planet.name,
                              &planet.diameter,
                              &planet.dist_sun,
                              &planet.orbital_prd,
                              &planet.axial_rot_prd);
      return (planet);
}
```

has the same effect as

```
scan_planet(&current_planet);
```

However, the assumption of correct data entry format is frequently unjustified, so **scan_planet** with its ability to return an integer error code is the more generally useful function. ←

EXAMPLE 11.5

Before performing a potentially dangerous or costly experiment in the laboratory, we can often use a computer program to simulate the experiment. In computer simulations, we need to keep track of the time of day as the experiment progresses. Normally, the time of day is updated after a certain period has elapsed. Assuming a 24-hour clock, the structure type **time_t** is defined as follows:

```
typedef struct time_s {
        int hour, minute, second;
} time_t;
```

Function **new_time** in Fig. 11.7 returns as its value an updated time based on the original time of day and the number of seconds that have elapsed since the previous update. If **time_now** were 21:58:32 and **secs** had the value 97, the

Figure 11.7   Function to Compute an Updated Time Value

```
/*
 * Computes a new time represented as a time_t structure
 * and based on time of day and elapsed seconds.
 */
time_t
new_time(time_t time_of_day,    /* input - time to be
                                             updated             */
         int     elapsed_secs)  /* input - seconds since
                                             last update         */
{
      int new_hr, new_min, new_sec;

      new_sec = time_of_day.second + elapsed_secs;
      time_of_day.second = new_sec % 60;
      new_min = time_of_day.minute + new_sec / 60;
      time_of_day.minute = new_min % 60;
      new_hr = time_of_day.hour + new_min / 60;
      time_of_day.hour = new_hr % 24;

      return (time_of_day);
}
```

result returned by the call

```
new_time(time_now, secs)
```

would be 22:00:09. Because new_time's variable time_of_day is strictly an input parameter, the value of time_now will not be affected by the call to new_time. If the intent is to update time_now, an assignment statement is used.

```
time_now = new_time(time_now, secs);
```

Figure 11.8 traces the assignment statement just mentioned showing the structured time_t value used as an input argument and the type time_t function value.   ←

Figure 11.8 Structured Values as a Function Input Argument and as a Function Result

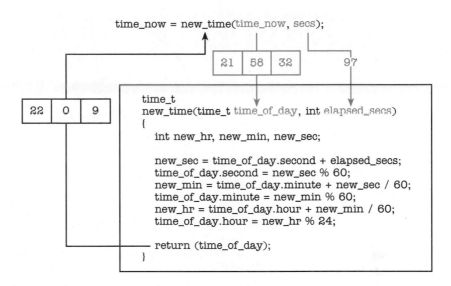

```
time_now = new_time(time_now, secs);

    21   58   32            97

22   0   9
            time_t
            new_time(time_t time_of_day, int elapsed_secs)
            {
                int new_hr, new_min, new_sec;

                new_sec = time_of_day.second + elapsed_secs;
                time_of_day.second = new_sec % 60;
                new_min = time_of_day.minute + new_sec / 60;
                time_of_day.minute = new_min % 60;
                new_hr = time_of_day.hour + new_min / 60;
                time_of_day.hour = new_hr % 24;

                return (time_of_day);
            }
```

EXERCISES FOR SECTION 11.3

Self-Check

1. Why does function `new_time`'s assignment of new values to the `second`, `minute`, and `hour` components of its formal parameter `time_of_day` have no effect on the components of actual argument `time_now` in the call `new_time(time_now, secs)`?
2. Could you modify function `get_planet` so that it would still have a type `planet_t` result but would also indicate input success or failure to the calling function?

Programming

1. Define a structure type to represent a common fraction. Write a program that gets a fraction and prints both the fraction and the fraction reduced to lowest terms using the following code fragment:

```
frac = get_fraction();
print_fraction(frac);
printf(" = ");
print_fraction(reduce_fraction(frac));
```

11.4 PROBLEM SOLVING WITH STRUCTURE TYPES

When we solve problems using C's standard data types, we take for granted the fact that C provides us with all the basic operations we need to manipulate our data. However, when we work with a problem whose data objects are more

**Figure 11.9
Data Type
planet_t
and Basic
Operations**

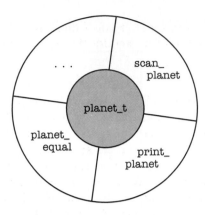

complex, we find that defining our own data types is just the first step in building a tool with which to attack the problem. In order to be able to think about the problem on the basis of our own data types, we must also provide basic operations for manipulating these types.

Combining a user-defined type with a set of basic operations that allow one truly to see the type as a unified concept creates what is called an *abstract data type* (ADT). Figure 11.9 shows one view of our data type `planet_t` combined with its operations.

If we take the time to define enough basic operations for a structure type, we then find it possible to think about a related problem at a higher level of abstraction; we are no longer bogged down in the details of manipulating the type's components.

In our next case study, we develop such a group of basic operations for processing complex numbers.

Case Study: A User-Defined Type for Complex Numbers

PROBLEM

We are working on an engineering project that uses complex numbers for modeling of electrical circuits. We need to develop a user-defined structure type and a set of operations that will make complex arithmetic virtually as straightforward as arithmetic on C's built-in numeric types.

ANALYSIS

A complex number is a number with a real part and an imaginary part. For example, the complex number $a + bi$ has a real part a and an imaginary part b, where the symbol i represents $\sqrt{-1}$. We will need to define functions for complex I/O as well as for the basic arithmetic operations (addition, subtraction, multiplication, and division) and for finding the absolute value of a complex number.

⬮ **DESIGN**

The two major aspects of our solution to this problem are defining the structure of the user-defined type and describing the function name, parameters, and purpose of each operation. Each function purpose then forms a subproblem to be solved separately. The details of these subproblems will be of interest to us as we develop our operations. However, once this group of functions is complete, we will be concerned only with *what* each function does, not with *how* it does it. In the same way, when we use C's built-in multiplication operator, we are interested only in the fact that * does multiplication, not caring in the least *how* it manages to accomplish this.

Specification of Type complex_t and Associated Operations

STRUCTURE: A complex number is an object of type `complex_t` that consists of a pair of type `double` values.

OPERATORS:

```
/*
 * Complex number input function returns standard scanning
 * error code
 */
int
scan_complex(complex_t *c)   /* output - address of complex
                                          variable to fill   */

/*
 * Complex output function prints value as a + bi or a - bi.
 * Prints only a if imaginary part is 0.
 * Prints only bi if real part is 0.
 */
void
print_complex(complex_t c)   /* input - complex number to
                                         print                 */

/*
 * Returns sum of complex values c1 and c2
 */
complex_t
add_complex(complex_t c1, complex_t c2)            /* input */
```

(continued)

```
/*
 * Returns difference c1 - c2
 */
complex_t
subtract_complex(complex_t c1, complex_t c2)      /* input */

/*
 * Returns product of complex values c1 and c2
 */
complex_t
multiply_complex(complex_t c1, complex_t c2)      /* input */

/*
 * Returns quotient of complex values (c1 / c2)
 */
complex_t
divide_complex(complex_t c1, complex_t c2)        /* input */

/*
 * Returns absolute value of complex number c
 */
complex_t
abs_complex(complex_t c)                           /* input */
```

As soon as this specification is complete, our co-workers on the circuit modeling project can begin designing algorithms that assume the availability of these operations. Then, when our implementation is complete, our code can either be added to their programs or packaged for inclusion in a way we will describe in Chapter 13.

Figure 11.10 shows a partial implementation of our specification together with a driver function. Functions `multiply_complex` and `divide_complex` have been left as an exercise. Notice that the definition of type `complex_t` is placed immediately after our preprocessor directives so that it is visible throughout the entire program. Function `abs_complex` uses the following formula to compute the absolute value of a complex number:

$$\left| a + bi \right| = \sqrt{(a + bi)(a - bi)} = \sqrt{a^2 + b^2}$$

This result always has an imaginary part of zero, so `print_complex` will print the result as a real number.

Figure 11.10   Partial Implementation of Type and Operators for Complex Numbers

```c
/*
 *  Operators to process complex numbers
 */
#include <stdio.h>
#include <math.h>

/*  User-defined complex number type */
typedef struct complex_s {
      double real, imag;
} complex_t;

/*
 *  Complex number input function returns standard scanning error code
 *     1 => valid scan, 0 => error, negative EOF value => end of file
 */
int
scan_complex(complex_t *c) /* output - address of complex variable to
                                     fill                           */
{
      int status;

      status = scanf("%lf%lf", &(*c).real, &(*c).imag);
      if (status == 2)
            status = 1;
      else if (status != EOF)
            status = 0;

      return (status);
}

/*
 *  Complex output function prints value as (a + bi) or (a - bi),
 *  dropping a or b if they round to 0 unless both round to 0
 */
void
print_complex(complex_t c) /* input - complex number to print     */
{
      double a, b;
      char   sign;

      a = c.real;
      b = c.imag;
```

(continued)

Figure 11.10   *(continued)*

```
      printf("(");

      if (fabs(a) < .005 && fabs(b) < .005) {
            printf("%.2f", 0.0);
      } else if (fabs(b) < .005) {
            printf("%.2f", a);
      } else if (fabs(a) < .005) {
            printf("%.2fi", b);
      } else {
            if (b < 0)
                  sign = '-';
            else
                  sign = '+';
            printf("%.2f %c %.2fi", a, sign, fabs(b));
      }

      printf(")");
}

/*
 *  Returns sum of complex values c1 and c2
 */
complex_t
add_complex(complex_t c1, complex_t c2) /* input - values to add    */
{
      complex_t csum;

      csum.real = c1.real + c2.real;
      csum.imag = c1.imag + c2.imag;

      return (csum);
}

/*
 *  Returns difference c1 - c2
 */
complex_t
subtract_complex(complex_t c1, complex_t c2) /* input parameters    */
{
      complex_t cdiff;
```

(continued)

Figure 11.10   *(continued)*

```
        cdiff.real = c1.real - c2.real;
        cdiff.imag = c1.imag - c2.imag;

        return (cdiff);
}

/*  ** Stub **
 *  Returns product of complex values c1 and c2
 */
complex_t
multiply_complex(complex_t c1, complex_t c2) /* input parameters    */
{
        printf("Function multiply_complex returning first argument\n");
        return (c1);
}

/*  ** Stub **
 *  Returns quotient of complex values (c1 / c2)
 */
complex_t
divide_complex(complex_t c1, complex_t c2) /* input parameters    */
{
        printf("Function divide_complex returning first argument\n");
        return (c1);
}

/*
 *  Returns absolute value of complex number c
 */
complex_t
abs_complex(complex_t c) /* input parameter                        */
{
        complex_t cabs;

        cabs.real = sqrt(c.real * c.real + c.imag * c.imag);
        cabs.imag = 0;

        return (cabs);
}
```

(continued)

Figure 11.10   *(continued)*

```
/*   Driver                                                                   */
int
main(void)
{
      complex_t com1, com2;

      /*  Gets two complex numbers                                           */
      printf("Enter the real and imaginary parts of a complex number\n");
      printf("separated by a space> ");
      scan_complex(&com1);
      printf("Enter a second complex number> ");
      scan_complex(&com2);

      /*  Forms and displays the sum                                         */
      printf("\n");
      print_complex(com1);
      printf("  +  ");
      print_complex(com2);
      printf("  =  ");
      print_complex(add_complex(com1, com2));

      /*  Forms and displays the difference                                  */
      printf("\n\n");
      print_complex(com1);
      printf("  -  ");
      print_complex(com2);
      printf("  =  ");
      print_complex(subtract_complex(com1, com2));

      /*  Forms and displays the absolute value of the first number      */
      printf("\n\n|");
      print_complex(com1);
      printf("|  =  ");
      print_complex(abs_complex(com1));
      printf("\n");

      return (0);
}
Enter the real and imaginary parts of a complex number
separated by a space> 3.5 5.2
Enter a second complex number> 2.5 1.2

(3.50 + 5.20i)  +  (2.50 + 1.20i)  =  (6.00 + 6.40i)

(3.50 + 5.20i)  -  (2.50 + 1.20i)  =  (1.00 + 4.00i)

|(3.50 + 5.20i)|  =  (6.27)
```

EXERCISES FOR SECTION 11.4

Self-Check

1. What does the following program segment display if the data entered are 6.5 5.0 3.0 -4.0?

```
complex_t a, b, c;

scan_complex(&a);
scan_complex(&b);

print_complex(a);
printf(" + ");
print_complex(b);
printf(" = ");
print_complex(add_complex(a, b));

c = subtract_complex(a, abs_complex(b));
printf("\n\nSecond result = ");
print_complex(c);
printf("\n");
```

Programming

1. Write functions `multiply_complex` and `divide_complex` to implement the operations of multiplication and division of complex numbers defined as follows:

$$(a + bi) \times (c + di) = (ac - bd) + (ad + bc)i$$

$$\frac{(a + bi)}{(c + di)} = \frac{ac + bd}{c^2 + d^2} + \frac{bc - ad}{c^2 + d^2} i$$

11.5 PARALLEL ARRAYS AND ARRAYS OF STRUCTURES

Often a data collection contains items of different types or items that, although of the same type, represent quite distinct concepts. For example, the data used to represent a list of students might consist of an integer identification number and a type `double` gpa for each student. The data representing a polygon might be a list of the (x, y) coordinates of the polygon's corners.

Parallel Arrays

In Chapter 8, we learned how to represent such data collections using *parallel arrays* like those on the following page:

```
int     id[50];      /* id numbers and               */
double  gpa[50];     /*   gpa's of up to 50 students */
double  x[NUM_PTS],  /* (x,y) coordinates of         */
        y[NUM_PTS];  /*   up to NUM_PTS points        */
```

Arrays id and gpa are called parallel arrays because the data items with the same subscript (for example, *i*) pertain to the same student (the *i*th student). Similarly, the *i*th elements of arrays x and y are the coordinates of one point. A better way to organize data collections like these is shown next.

Declaring an Array of Structures

A more natural and convenient organization of student data or polygon points is to group the information pertaining to one student or to one point in a structure whose type we define. Declarations of arrays whose elements are structures follow.

```
#define MAX_STU 50
#define NUM_PTS 10

typedef struct student_s {
    int     id;
    double gpa;
} student_t;

typedef struct point_s {
    double x, y;
} point_t;

. . .

{
    student_t stulist[MAX_STU];
    point_t   polygon[NUM_PTS];
```

A sample array stulist is shown in Fig. 11.11. The data for the first student are stored in the structure stulist[0]. The individual data items are stulist[0].id and stulist[0].gpa. As shown, stulist[0].gpa is 2.71.

If a function scan_student is available for scanning a student_t structure, the following for statement can be used to fill the entire array stulist with data.

```
for (i = 0;  i < MAX_STU;  ++i)
    scan_student(&stulist[i]);
```

**Figure 11.11
An Array of
Structures**

Array stulist

	.id	.gpa
stulist[0]	609465503	2.71
stulist[1]	512984556	3.09
stulist[2]	232415569	2.98
. . .	. . .	. . .
stulist[49]	173745903	3.98

stulist[0].gpa ← (arrow pointing to stulist[0].gpa 2.71)

This `for` statement would display all the `id` numbers.

```
for  (i = 0; i < MAX_STU;  ++i)
    printf("%d\n", stulist[i].id);
```

In our next case study, we see how to use an array of descriptive information about units of measurement in order to make possible conversion of any measurement to any other unit of the same category.

Case Study: Universal Measurement Conversion

In a day when our computer software spell-checks text and looks up synonyms for words, it seems primitive to use printed tables for hand conversion of feet to meters, liters to quarts, and so on.

PROBLEM

We would like a program that takes a measurement in one unit (e.g., 4.5 quarts) and converts it to another unit (e.g., liters). For example, this conversion request

```
450 km miles
```

would result in this program output

```
Attempting conversion of 450.0000 km to miles . . .
450.0000 km  =   279.6247 miles
```

The program should produce an error message if a conversion between two units of different classes (e.g., liquid volume to distance) is requested. The program should be able to handle both unit names (e.g., milligrams) and their abbreviations (mg).

ANALYSIS

This program's basic data objects are units of measurement. We need to define a structure type that groups all relevant attributes about one unit. We can then store a database of these structures in an array and look up conversion factors as needed. To convert a measurement, the user will need to provide the measurement as a number and a string (e.g., 5 mg or 6.5 inches). The user must also enter the name or abbreviation of the desired units.

The attributes of a unit include its name and abbreviation, its class (liquid volume, distance, and so on), and a representation of the unit in terms of the chosen standard unit for its class. If we allow the actual unit name, class names, and standard units to be determined by the input data, the program will be usable for any class of measurements and for units in any language based on our character set.

Data Requirements

Structured Data Type
```
unit_t
   components:
   name      /* character string such as "milligrams"  */
   abbrev    /* shorter character string such as "mg"   */
   class     /* character string "liquid_volume",
                   "distance", or "weight"              */
   standard /* number of standard units that are
                   equivalent to this unit              */
```

Problem Constants
```
NAME_LEN    20  /* storage allocated for a unit name   */
ABBREV_LEN  4   /* storage allocated for a unit
                     abbreviation                       */
CLASS_LEN   15  /* storage allocated for a
                     measurement class                  */
MAX_UNITS   20  /* maximum number of different units
                     handled                            */
```

Problem Inputs
```
unit_t units[MAX_UNITS]    /* array representing unit
                                conversion factors
                                database                */
```

```
double quantity          /* value to convert        */
char old_units[NAME_LEN] /* name or abbreviation of
                            units to be converted */
char new_units[NAME_LEN] /* name or abbreviation of
                            units to convert to    */
```

Problem Output

message giving conversion

DESIGN

Algorithm

1. Load units of measurement database.
2. Get value to convert and old and new unit names.
3. Repeat until EOF or data format error encountered
       4. Search for old units in database.
       5. Search for new units in database.
       6. if conversion is impossible
               7. Issue appropriate error message.
           else
               8. Compute and print conversion.
       9. Get value to convert and old and new unit names.

We will develop separate functions for Step 1 (load units), for the search used in Step 4 and Step 5, and for the conversion aspect of Step 8. We can base our `load_units` function on function `fill_to_sentinel` (see Fig. 8.14) and our `search` function on our linear search function (see Fig. 8.9).

IMPLEMENTATION

Code that implements our universal conversion program is shown in Fig. 11.12. One aspect of this program is rather awkward: Our database of units and our list of quantities to convert come from the same input source. To expect the user to enter interactively all the unit data at the beginning of each program run is unreasonable; therefore, the program is written to run in batch mode. The program assumes that the data file made accessible by input redirection will contain the units database ended by a sentinel record and followed by the conversion problems. A much more natural setup would call for the units database to come from a file and the conversion problems to be entered interactively. Our next chapter discusses the problem of how to use more than one input source or output destination.

```c
/*
 * Converts measurements of liquid volume, distance, and weight to any
 * other units of the same category that are listed in the database.
 * Handles both names and abbreviations of units.
 */
#include <stdio.h>
#include <string.h>

#define NAME_LEN    20    /* storage allocated for a unit name          */
#define ABBREV_LEN  4     /* storage allocated for a unit abbreviation  */
#define CLASS_LEN   15    /* storage allocated for a measurement class  */

typedef struct unit_s {          /* unit of measurement type           */
      char    name[NAME_LEN];        /* character string such as "milligrams" */
      char    abbrev[ABBREV_LEN]; /* shorter character string such as "mg"  */
      char    class[CLASS_LEN];   /* character string "volume","distance",
                                        or "weight"                        */
      double standard;               /* number of standard units equivalent
                                        to this unit                       */
} unit_t;

/*
 * Gets data to fill output argument
 * Returns standard error code:  1 => successful input,  0 => error,
 *                                negative EOF value => end of file
 */
int
scan_unit(unit_t *unitp)  /*  output - unit_t structure to fill */
{
      int status;

      status = scanf("%s%s%s%lf", (*unitp).name,
                                   (*unitp).abbrev,
                                   (*unitp).class,
                                   &(*unitp).standard);

      if (status == 4)
            status = 1;
      else if (status != EOF)
            status = 0;

      return (status);
}
```

(continued)

Figure 11.12 *(continued)*

```
/*
 * Gets data to place in units until value of sentinel is encountered in
 * the name component of the input structure. Stops input prematurely if
 * there are more than unit_max data values before the sentinel or if
 * invalid data is encountered.
 * Pre:  sentinel and unit_max are defined and unit_max is the declared
 *       size of units
 */
void
load_units(int          unit_max,    /* input - declared size of units   */
           const char *sentinel,     /* input - end of data value in input
                                                 list                     */
           unit_t       units[],     /* output - array of data           */
           int         *unit_sizep)  /* output - number of data values
                                                 stored in units          */
{
      unit_t data;
      int    i, status;

      /* Sentinel input loop                                              */
      i = 0;

      for  (status = scan_unit(&data);
            status == 1  &&  strcmp(data.name, sentinel) != 0  &&
               i < unit_max;
            status = scan_unit(&data)) {
         units[i++] = data;
      }

      /* Issue error message on premature exit                            */
      if (status != 1) {
            printf("\n*** Error in data format ***\n");
            printf("*** Using first %d data values ***\n", i);
      } else if (strcmp(data.name, sentinel) != 0) {
            printf("\n*** Error: too much data before sentinel ***\n");
            printf("*** Using first %d data values ***\n", i);
      }
```

(continued)

Figure 11.12   *(continued)*

```
    /* Send back size of used portion of array                    */
    *unit_sizep = i;
}

#define NOT_FOUND -1   /*  Value returned by search function if target
                            not found                             */

/*
 *  Searches for target key in name and abbrev components of first n
 *     elements of array units
 *  Returns index of structure containing target or NOT_FOUND
 *  Pre:  target and first n elements of array units are defined and n > 0
 */
int
search(const unit_t units[],  /*  array of unit_t structures to search */
       const char  *target,   /*  key searched for in name and abbrev
                                   components                      */
       int         n)         /*  number of array elements to search  */
{
    int i,
        found = 0,     /*  whether or not target has been found    */
        where;         /*  index where target found or NOT_FOUND   */

    /*  Compare name and abbrev components of each element to target */
    i = 0;
    while (!found && i < n) {
        if (strcmp(units[i].name,   target) == 0  ||
            strcmp(units[i].abbrev, target) == 0)
            found = 1;
        else
            ++i;
    }

    /* Return index of element containing target or NOT_FOUND       */
    if (found)
        where = i;
    else
        where = NOT_FOUND;
```

(continued)

Figure 11.12   *(continued)*

```
        return(where);
}

/*
 *  Converts one measurement to another given the representation of both
 *  in a standard unit.  For example, to convert 24 feet to yards given a
 *  standard unit of inches:  quantity = 24, old_stand = 12 (there are 12
 *  inches in a foot), new_stand = 36 (there are 36 inches in a yard),
 *  result is 24 * 12 / 36 which equals 8
 */
double
convert(double quantity,       /* value to convert                        */
        double old_stand,      /* number of standard units in one of
                                  quantity's original units               */
        double new_stand)      /* number of standard units in one of new
                                  units                                   */
{
        return (quantity * old_stand / new_stand);
}

#define MAX_UNITS   20         /* maximum number of different units handled */
#define SENT        "*****"    /* end of data value in units list          */

int
main(void)
{
        unit_t units[MAX_UNITS];       /* units classes and conversion
                                          factors                         */
        int    num_units;              /* number of elements of units in
                                          use                             */
        char   old_units[NAME_LEN],    /* units to be converted (name or
                                          abbrev.)                        */
               new_units[NAME_LEN];    /* units to convert to (name or
                                          abbrev.)                        */
        int    status;                 /* input status                    */
        double quantity;               /* value to convert                */
        int    old_index,              /* index of units element where
                                          old_units found                 */
               new_index;              /* index of units element where
                                          new_units found                 */
```

(continued)

Figure 11.12   *(continued)*

```
    /*  Loads units of measurement database                          */
    load_units(MAX_UNITS, SENT, units, &num_units);

    /*  Converts quantities to desired units until EOF or data format
           error                                                     */
    for  (status = scanf("%lf%s%s", &quantity, old_units, new_units);
          status == 3;
          status = scanf("%lf%s%s", &quantity, old_units, new_units)) {
        printf("Attempting conversion of %.4f %s to %s . . .\n",
                quantity, old_units, new_units);
        old_index = search(units, old_units, num_units);
        new_index = search(units, new_units, num_units);
        if (old_index == NOT_FOUND)
              printf("Unit %s not in database\n", old_units);
        else if (new_index == NOT_FOUND)
              printf("Unit %s not in database\n", new_units);
        else if (strcmp(units[old_index].class, units[new_index].class)
                  != 0)
              printf("Cannot convert %s (%s) to %s (%s)\n",
                      old_units, units[old_index].class,
                      new_units, units[new_index].class);
        else
              printf("%.4f %s  =  %.4f %s\n", quantity, old_units,
                      convert(quantity, units[old_index].standard,
                              units[new_index].standard),
                      new_units);
    }

    return (0);
}
```

████ **TESTING** ████

In addition to testing the conversion of units of liquid volume, distance, and weight using values whose conversions are easy to verify, we should also select test cases that exercise each of the error message facilities of the program. Figure 11.13 shows a small data file and the results of processing it. The database in this file assumes standard units of liters, meters, and kilograms. Note that all that is required by the program is that the database consistently use *some* standard units. It does not prescribe *what* units these must be.

Figure 11.13   Data File and Sample Run of Measurement Conversion Program

....

Data:

miles	mi	distance	1609.3
kilometers	km	distance	1000
yards	yd	distance	0.9144
meters	m	distance	1
quarts	qt	liquid_volume	0.94635
liters	l	liquid_volume	1
gallons	gal	liquid_volume	3.7854
milliliters	ml	liquid_volume	0.001
kilograms	kg	weight	1
pounds	lb	weight	0.45359
ounces	oz	weight	0.02835
grams	g	weight	0.001
*****	**	*****	0

```
2.5 qt l
450 km miles
25 km grams
35 mg g
14 qt cups
```

Output:

```
Attempting conversion of 2.5000 qt to l . . .
2.5000 qt  =  2.3659 l
Attempting conversion of 450.0000 km to miles . . .
450.0000 km  =  279.6247 miles
Attempting conversion of 25 km to grams . . .
Cannot convert km (distance) to grams (weight)
Attempting conversion of 35 mg to g . . .
Unit mg not in database
Attempting conversion of 14 qt to cups . . .
Unit cups not in database
```

....

Self-Check

1. In function `main` of our universal conversion program, we see the statement

   ```
   load_units(MAX_UNITS, SENT, units, &num_units);
   ```

   Inside `load_units` we see the function call

   ```
   scan_unit(&data);
   ```

   Variables `units`, `num_units`, and `data` are all being used as output arguments in these statements. Why is the `&` applied to `num_units` and `data`, but not to `units`?
2. Write a code fragment that would add `0.2` to all the gpa's in `stulist` (see Fig. 11.11). If the addition of `0.2` would inflate a `gpa` past `4.0`, just set the `gpa` to `4.0`.

11.6 UNION TYPES (OPTIONAL)

So far, all the variables we have seen of a particular structure type have had exactly the same components. However, sometimes we need structured types in which some components vary depending on the value of another component. For example, if we were to write a program to manipulate a variety of geometric figures, the data we would need to store would vary depending on the type of figure processed. In order to find the area and circumference of a circle, we would need to know the radius; to compute the area and perimeter of a square, we would need to know the length of a side; to figure the area and perimeter of other rectangles, we would need height and width.

   C provides a data structure called a *union* to deal with situations in which one needs a data object that can be interpreted in a variety of ways.

EXAMPLE 11.6

The following declaration shows a definition of a union structure to use as the type of one component of the physical description of a person. If the person has hair, we would like to record the hair color. However, if the person is bald, we need to note whether or not this baldness is disguised by a wig.

```
typedef union hair_u {
      int   wears_wig;
      char color[20];
} hair_t;
```

As you can see, the format of a union type definition exactly parallels a structure type definition. As before, our `typedef` statement allocates no memory. A later declaration

```
hair_t hair_data;
```

creates a variable `hair_data` built on the template of the type definition. This variable `hair_data` does not contain *both* `wears_wig` *and* `color` components. Rather, it has *either* a `wears_wig` component referenced by `hair_data.wears_wig` *or* a color component referenced by `hair_data.color`. When memory is allocated for `hair_data`, the amount of memory is determined by the largest component of the union.

In most cases, it is useful to be able to interpret a chunk of memory in more than one way only if it is possible to determine *which* way is currently the valid interpretation. For this reason, unions are most often used as types of portions of a larger structure, and the larger structure typically contains a component whose value indicates which interpretation of the union is correct at the present time. Such a structure containing a `hair_t` union component is the following:

```
typedef struct hair_info_s {
      int     bald;
      hair_t h;
} hair_info_t;
```

When we write code using a `hair_info_t` structure, we can base our manipulation of the union component h on the value of the `bald` component. This component indicates whether the subject is bald. For bald subjects, the `wears_wig` interpretation of component h is valid. For nonbald subjects, the `color` interpretation is valid and represents the color of the subject's hair. Figure 11.14 shows a function to print `hair_info_t` data.

In Fig. 11.15, we see the two possible interpretations of the h component of parameter `hair`, one that is conceptually valid when `hair.bald` is true, and one that applies when `hair.bald` is false. Referencing the appropriate union component is *always* the programmer's responsibility; C can do no checking of the validity of such a component reference. ◄

Figure 11.14   Function That Prints a Structure with a Union Type Component

```
void
print_hair_info(hair_info_t hair) /* input - structure
                                     to print       */
{
    if (hair.bald) {
        printf("Subject is bald");
        if (hair.h.wears_wig)
            printf(", but wears a wig.\n");
        else
            printf(" and does not wear a wig.\n");
    } else {
        printf("Subject's hair color is %s.\n",
            hair.h.color);
    }
}
```

Figure 11.15   Two Interpretations of Parameter hair

EXAMPLE 11.7 In Fig. 11.16, we see a partial solution to the problem of finding the area and perimeter (circumference) of a geometric figure, the problem mentioned at the beginning of our discussion of union types. First, we define structure types for each figure of interest including components for the figure's area and perimeter or circumference as well as components for those dimensions of the figure that are needed in computation of its area and perimeter. Then, we define a union type with a component for each figure type. Finally, we define a structure containing both a component of the union type and a component whose value denotes which is the correct interpretation of the union. Notice that all functions that process figure_t data contain switch statements to select the valid view of the fig component based on the value of the shape component. In

function `compute_area`, the default case of the `switch` statement prints an error message. This message will never appear as long as the function's preconditions are met.   ←

Figure 11.16   Program to Compute Area and Perimeter of Geometric Figures

```
/*
 *  Computes the area and perimeter of a variety of geometric figures.
 */

#include <stdio.h>
#define PI 3.14159

/*  Types defining the components needed to represent each shape.       */
typedef struct circle_s {
      double area,
             circumference,
             radius;
} circle_t;

typedef struct rectangle_s {
      double area,
             perimeter,
             width,
             height;
} rectangle_t;

typedef struct square_s {
      double area,
             perimeter,
             side;
} square_t;

/*  Type of a structure that can be interpreted a different way for
     each shape                                                         */
typedef union figure_data_u {
      circle_t    circle;
      rectangle_t rectangle;
      square_t    square;
} figure_data_t;
```

(continued)

Figure 11.16 *(continued)*

```c
/*  Type containing a structure with multiple interpretations along with
 *  a component whose value indicates the current valid interpretation  */
typedef struct figure_s {
      char          shape;
      figure_data_t fig;
} figure_t;

/*
 *  Prompts for and stores the dimension data necessary to compute a
 *  figure's area and perimeter.  Figure returned contains a 'Q' in the
 *  shape component when signaling end of data.
 */
figure_t
get_figure_dimensions(void)
{
      figure_t object;

      printf("Enter a letter to indicate the object's shape or Q to
             quit.\n");
      printf("C (circle),  R (rectangle),  or S (square)> ");
      object.shape = getchar();

      switch (object.shape) {
      case 'C':
      case 'c':
            printf("Enter radius> ");
            scanf("%lf", &object.fig.circle.radius);
            break;

      case 'R':
      case 'r':
            printf("Enter height> ");
            scanf("%lf", &object.fig.rectangle.height);
            printf("Enter width> ");
            scanf("%lf", &object.fig.rectangle.width);
            break;

      case 'S':
```

(continued)

Figure 11.16   *(continued)*

```
      case 's':
            printf("Enter length of a side> ");
            scanf("%lf", &object.fig.square.side);
            break;

      default:  /*  Error is treated as a QUIT  */
            object.shape = 'Q';
      }

      return(object);
}

/*
 *  Computes the area of a figure given relevant dimensions.   Returns
 *  figure with area component filled.
 *  Pre:   value of shape component is one of these letters: CcRrSs
 *         necessary dimension components have values
 */
figure_t
compute_area(figure_t object)
{
      switch (object.shape) {
      case 'C':
      case 'c':
            object.fig.circle.area = PI * object.fig.circle.radius *
                                     object.fig.circle.radius;
            break;

      case 'R':
      case 'r':
            object.fig.rectangle.area = object.fig.rectangle.height *
                                        object.fig.rectangle.width;
            break;

      case 'S':
      case 's':
            object.fig.square.area = object.fig.square.side *
                                     object.fig.square.side;
            break;
```

(continued)

Figure 11.16   *(continued)*

```
      default:
            printf("Error in shape code detected in compute_area\n");
      }

      return(object);
}

/*  Code for compute_perim and print_figure goes here  */

int
main(void)
{
      figure_t onefig;

      printf("Area and Perimeter Computation Program\n");

      for  (onefig = get_figure_dimensions();
             onefig.shape != 'Q';
             onefig = get_figure_dimensions()) {
          onefig = compute_area(onefig);
          onefig = compute_perim(onefig);
          print_figure(onefig);
      }

      return(0);
}
```

**EXERCISES FOR
SECTION 11.6**

Self-Check

1. Determine how many bytes are needed to store a structure of type
   hair_info_t, assuming two bytes for an integer and one byte for a character. How much of this space is actually in use when component
   wears_wig is valid?

Programming

1. Write functions compute_perim and print_figure to complete the
   program in Fig. 11.16.

11.7 COMMON PROGRAMMING ERRORS

When programmers manipulate structure types, their most common error is incorrect use of a component selected for processing. When using the direct selection operator (.), always be aware of the type of the component selected, and use the value in a manner consistent with its type. For example, if the component selected is an array, passing it to a function as an output argument does not require application of the address-of operator.

If a structure type output parameter is used in a function, one can easily forget that the precedence of the direct selection operator (.) is higher than the precedence of the address-of and indirection operators (& and *). When attempting to write a reference using a combination of these operators, one should first describe the operations in the order desired and compare this sequence to the order imposed by the precedence rules. If the two do not match, parentheses must be included in the reference to override the default precedence.

C allows the use of structure type values in assignment statements, as function arguments, and as function results, so one can easily forget that expressions of these types cannot be operands of equality comparators nor arguments of `printf` and `scanf`. You can select simple components from a structure to use in these contexts, or you can write your own type-specific equality and I/O functions.

When you use a union type, referencing a component that is not currently valid is easy to do. It is helpful to place the union within another structure that contains a component whose value indicates which interpretation of the union is correct. Then all manipulation of the union can fall within `if` or `switch` statements that reference the union component based on the value of the associated structure component.

CHAPTER REVIEW

This chapter examined structure and union types and C's facilities for integrating such user-defined types into its overall system of data types. We discussed how to reference each individual component of a composite type through the use of the direct selection operator (.) placed between the structure variable name and the component name.

We saw that user-defined structure types can be used in most of the situations where built-in types are valid. Structured values can be function arguments and function results, and they can be copied using the assignment operator. Structure types are legitimate in declarations of variables, of structure components, and of array elements. However, structured values cannot be compared for equality using the == and != operators.

We saw that structure types play an important role in the process of data abstraction, and we studied how to implement operator functions that assist the programmer in thinking of the structure type as a unified concept.

New C Constructs

The C constructs introduced in this chapter are described in Table 11.3.

Table 11.3   Summary of New C Constructs

Construct	Effect
Definition of a Structure Type ```typedef struct part_s { char name[20]; int quantity; double price;} part_t;```	A structure type `part_t` (or `struct part_s`) is defined with components that can store a string and two numbers, one of type `int` and one of type `double`.
Declaration of Variables to Hold One Structure or an Array of Structures ```part_t nuts, bolts, parts_list[40];part_t mouse = {"serial mouse", 30, 145.00};```	`nuts`, `bolts`, and `mouse` are structured variables of type `part_t`; `parts_list` is an array of 40 such structures. The three components of `mouse` are initialized in its declaration.
Component Reference ```cost = nuts.quantity * nuts.price;```	Multiplies two components of type `part_t` variable `nuts`.
```printf("Part: %s\n", parts_list[i].name);```	Prints `name` component of `i`th element of `parts_list`.
Structure Copy ```bolts = nuts;```	Stores in `bolts` a copy of each component of `nuts`.
Definition of a Union Type ```typedef union multi_u { char str[4]; int intger; double real;} multi_t;```	A union type `multi_t` (or `union multi_u`) is defined allowing three interpretations of the contents of a type `multi_t` variable: the contents may be seen as a four-character string, as an integer, or as a type `double` number.

(continued)

Table 11.3   *(continued)*

Construct	Effect
Definition of a Structure Type with a Union Component	
```typedef struct choose_s { char interp; multi_t val; } choose_t;```	A structure type `choose_t` is defined with a component `interp` whose value ('S' for string, 'I' for integer, 'D' for double) indicates which interpretation of union component `val` is valid.

QUICK-CHECK EXERCISES

1. What is the primary difference between a structure and an array? Which would you use to store the catalog description of a course? To store the names of students in the course?

2. How do you access a component of a structure type variable?

Exercises 3–8 refer to the following type `student_t` and to variables `stu1` and `stu2`.

```
typedef struct student_s {
     char fst_name[20],
          last_name[20];
     int  score;
     char grade;
} student_t;
. . .
student_t stu1, stu2;
```

3. Identify the following statements as possibly valid or definitely invalid. If invalid, explain why.
   a. `student_t stulist[30];`
   b. `printf("%s", stu1);`
   c. `printf("%d %c", stu1.score, stu1.grade);`
   d. `stu2 = stu1;`
   e. `if (stu2.score == stu1.score)`
      `    printf("Equal");`
   f. `if (stu2 == stu1)`
      `    printf("Equal structures");`
   g. `scan_student(&stu1);`
   h. `stu2.last_name = "Martin";`

4. Write a statement that prints the initials of `stu1` (with periods).
5. How many components does variable `stu2` have?
6. Write functions `scan_student` and `print_student` for type `student_t` variables.
7. Declare an array of 40 `student_t` structures, and write a code segment that prints on separate lines the names (*last name, first name*) of all the students in the list.
8. Identify the type of each of the following references:
   a. `stu1`
   b. `stu2.score`
   c. `stu2.fst_name[3]`
   d. `stu1.grade`
9. When should you use a union type component in a structured variable?

ANSWERS TO QUICK-CHECK EXERCISES

1. A structure can have components of different types, but an array's elements must all be of the same type. Use a structure for the catalog item and an array of strings for the list of student names.
2. Components of structures are accessed using the direct selection operator followed by a component name.
3. a. valid
   b. invalid: `printf` does not accept structured arguments
   c. valid
   d. valid
   e. valid
   f. invalid: equality operators cannot be used with structure types
   g. valid (assuming parameter type is `student_t *`)
   h. invalid: cannot copy strings with = except in declaration (this case needs `strassign` or `strcpy`)
4. `printf("%c.%c.",  stu1.fst_name[0],`
         `stu1.last_name[0]);`
5. four
6. `int`
   `scan_student(student_t *stup) /* output - student struc-`
   `                                       ture to fill */`

   `{`
   `     int  status,`
   `     char temp[4]; /* temporary storage for grade */`

```
              status = scanf("%s%s%d%s", (*stu).fst_name,
                                         (*stu).last_name,
                                         &(*stu).score,
                                         temp);

         if (status == 4) {
              status = 1;
              (*stu).grade = temp[0];
         } else if (status != EOF) {
              status = 0;
         }

         return (status);
    }

    void
    print_student(student_t stu) /* input - student structure
                                          to print */
    {
         printf("Student: %s, %s\n", stu.last_name,
              stu.fst_name);
         printf("    Score: %d     Grade: %c\n", stu.score,
              stu.grade);
    }
```

7. ```
   student_t students[40];

   for (i = 0; i < 40; ++i)
       printf("%s, %s\n", students[i].last_name,
              students[i].fst_name);
   ```

8. a. `student_t`
   b. `int`
   c. `char`
   d. `char`

9. Use a union type component in a structured variable when the needed structure components vary depending on the value of one component.

REVIEW QUESTIONS

1. Define a structure type called `subscriber_t` that contains the components `name`, `street_address`, and `monthly_bill` (i.e., how much the subscriber owes).
   ```

2. Write a C program that scans data to fill the variable `competition` declared below and then prints the contents of the structure with suitable labels.

```
#define STR_LENGTH 20

typedef struct olympic_s {
      char event[STR_LENGTH],
            entrant[STR_LENGTH],
            country[STR_LENGTH];
      int   place;
} olympic_t;
. . .
olympic_t competition;
```

3. How would you call a function `scan_olympic` passing `competition` as an output argument?

4. Identify and correct the errors in the following program:

```
typedef struct summer_s
      char    name[15],
              start_date[15],
      double hrs_worked,
summer_help_t;

/* code for function scan_sum_hlp goes here */

int
main(void)
{
      summer_s operator;

      scan_sum_hlp(operator);
      printf("Name: %s\nStarting date: %s\nHours worked:
              %.2f\n", operator);

      return(0);
}
```

5. Define a data structure to store the following student data: gpa, major, address (consisting of street_address, city, state, zip), and class_schedule (consisting of up to six class records, each of which has description, time, and days components). Define whatever data types are needed.

PROGRAMMING PROJECTS

1. Define a structure type `auto_t` to represent an automobile. Include components for the make and model (strings), the odometer reading, the manufacture and purchase dates (use another user-defined type called `date_t`), and the gas tank (use a user-defined type `tank_t` with components for tank capacity and current fuel level, giving both in gallons). Write I/O functions `scan_date`, `scan_tank`, `scan_auto`, `print_date`, `print_tank`, and `print_auto`, and also write a driver function that repeatedly fills and displays an auto structure variable until EOF is encountered in the input file.
   Here is a small data set to try:

   ```
   Mercury Sable     49842 1 18 1989 5 30 1991 16    12.5
   Ford      Bronco_II 74560 2 20 1986 6 15 1986 20.5 16.7
   ```

2. Define a structure type `element_t` to represent one element from the periodic table of elements. Components should include the atomic number (an integer); the name, chemical symbol, and class (strings); a numeric field for the atomic weight; and a 7-element array of integers for the number of electrons in each shell. The following are the components of an `element_t` structure for sodium.

   ```
   11  Sodium  Na  alkali_metal  22.9898  2 8 1 0 0 0 0
   ```

   Define and test I/O functions `scan_element` and `print_element`.

3. A number expressed in scientific notation is represented by its mantissa (a fraction) and its exponent (an integer). Define a type `sci_not_t` that has separate components for these two parts. Define a function `scan_sci` that takes from the input source a string representing a positive number in scientific notation, and breaks it into components for storage in a `sci_not_t` structure. The mantissa of an input value (m) should satisfy this condition: `0.1 <= m < 1.0`. Also write functions to compute the sum, difference, product, and quotient of two `sci_not_t` values. All these functions should have a result type of `sci_not_t` and should ensure that the result's mantissa is in the prescribed range. Define a `print_sci` function as well. Then, create a driver program to test your functions. Your output should be of this form:

   ```
   Values input:  0.25000e3  0.20000e1
   Sum:  0.25200e3
   Difference:  0.24800e3
   Product:  0.50000e3
   Quotient:  0.12500e3
   ```

4. Rewrite the program, Compute the Area of a Polygon, from Chapter 8 using an array of `point_t` structures to hold the coordinates list. Refer to Figs. 8.21–8.23.

5. The results of a survey of the households in your township have been made available. Each record contains data for one household, including a four-digit integer identification number, the annual income for the household, and the number of members of the household. You may assume that no more than 25 households were surveyed. Write a program to store the survey results into an array of user-defined structures of type `household_t`. Then perform the following analyses:

a. Print a three-column table displaying the data.

b. Calculate the average household income, and list the identification number and income of each household whose income exceeds the average.

c. Determine the percentage of households having incomes below the poverty level. The poverty level income may be computed using the formula

$$P = \$6500.00 + \$950.00 \times (m - 2)$$

where m is the number of members of each household. This formula shows that the poverty level depends on the number of family members m and the poverty level increases as m gets larger.

The following is one data set to use in testing your program.

Identification Number	Annual Income	Household Members
1041	$12,180	4
1062	13,240	3
1327	19,800	2
1483	24,458	8
1900	17,000	2
2112	19,125	7
2345	17,623	2
3210	5,200	6
3600	9,500	5
3601	11,970	2
4725	9,800	3
6217	10,000	2
9280	8,200	1

6. Expand the geometric figure program from Fig. 11.16 to handle processing of right triangles. Include components to store the base and height of a right tri-

angle. Some relevant formulas are:

$$area = \frac{1}{2} \, base \times height$$

$$hypotenuse = \sqrt{base^2 + height^2}$$

7. At a grocery store, certain categories of products sold have been established, and this information is to be computerized. Write a function to scan and store information in a structure variable whose data type is one you define— a type that includes a component that has multiple interpretations. Also write an output function and a driver function to use in testing.

   The data for each item consists of the item name (a string of less than 20 characters with no blanks), the unit cost in cents (an integer), and a character indicating the product category ('M' for meat, 'P' for produce, 'D' for dairy, 'C' for canned goods, and 'N' for nonfoods). The following additional data will depend on the product category.

Product Category	Additional Data
Meats	character indicating meat type ('R' for red meat, 'P' for poultry, 'F' for fish) date of packaging expiration date
Produce	character 'F' for fruit or 'V' for vegetable date received
Dairy	expiration date
Canned goods	expiration date (month and year only) aisle number (an integer) aisle side (letter 'A' or 'B')
Nonfoods	character indicating category ('C' for cleaning product, 'P' for pharmacy, 'O' for other) aisle number (an integer) aisle side (letter 'A' or 'B')

A data line for canned corn would be

```
corn   89C   11 94   12B
```

The corn costs 89 cents, expires in November of 1994, and is displayed on aisle 12B.

8. Rewrite the common fraction program from Chapter 6 using a structure type to represent a fraction.

9. In the Self-Check Exercises of Sections 11.1 and 11.2, you defined a data type `location_t` to represent a geographic location and some functions to process certain components of the type. Write functions `print_location`, `location_equal`, and `scan_location` for processing type `location_t` data, and develop a driver to use in testing this group of functions.

FILE INPUT AND OUTPUT

12.1
Review of Batch Processing
12.2
Standard Input/Output Files: Review and
Further Study
12.3
Additional Text Files
12.4
Problem Solving Illustrated
Case Study: Land Boundary Survey
12.5
Binary Files
12.6
Searching a Database
Case Study: Database Inquiry
12.7
Common Programming Errors
Chapter Review

This chapter explores in greater depth the use of standard input and output. It provides a complete discussion of text files and introduces binary files. Library functions for I/O from text files as well as functions for reading and writing binary files are described.

12.1 REVIEW OF BATCH PROCESSING

Although we discussed the use of data files in Section 2.8, the majority of our example programs have been interactive. Interactive programs take all input data from the keyboard and display all outputs on the screen. This mode of operation is fine for small programs. However, as you begin to write larger programs, you will see many advantages to using data files for program input and output.

You have seen that you can create a data file using a text editor in the same way that you create a program file. Once the data file is entered in computer memory, you can carefully check and edit each line and then save the final data file as a permanent disk file. When you enter data interactively, you do not always have the opportunity to examine and edit the data. The data are processed as they are entered—they are not saved permanently.

After the data file is saved on disk, you can construct your program so it takes data from the data file rather than from the keyboard. Recall from Chapter 2 that this mode of program execution is called batch processing. Because the program data are supplied before execution begins, prompting messages are not required in batch programs. Instead, batch programs must contain display statements that echo print data values in order to provide a record of the data that are scanned and processed in a particular run.

Besides giving you the opportunity to check for errors in your data, using data files provides another advantage. A data file can be processed many times. During debugging, you can rerun the program as often as you need to without re-entering the test data each time.

You can also arrange for your program to write its output to a disk file rather than to display it on the screen. When you write output to the screen, it disappears after it scrolls off the screen. However, if program output is written to a disk file, you have a permanent copy of it. You can get a hard copy of a disk file by sending it to the printer, or you can use an operating system command such as

type *filename*

to list the contents of *filename* on the screen.

Finally, you can use the output file generated by one program as a data file for another program. For example, a data collection program may prompt the user to enter and check planet information and then write the data about each planet to an output file. Later, a second program that analyzes planetary data in response to user queries could use the output of the first program as its data file.

EXERCISES FOR SECTION 12.1

Self-Check

1. List three advantages of writing your program output to a data file, rather than simply displaying it on the computer screen.
2. a. For a computer program that handles registering a student for a semester schedule of classes, would batch processing of data be preferred to interactive data processing? Explain your answer.
   b. In a program for printing student transcripts at a large university, which would be preferable, batch processing or interactive data processing?

12.2 STANDARD INPUT/OUTPUT FILES: REVIEW AND FURTHER STUDY

C can process two kinds of files: text files and binary files. We will study text files in this section and in Section 12.3; we will study binary files later in this chapter. All the files you have created using an editor or word processor have been text files. A *text file* is a collection of characters stored under the same name in secondary memory (i.e., on a disk). A text file has no fixed size. To mark the end of a text file, the computer places a special *end-of-file* character, which we will denote <eof>, after the last character in the file.

As you create a text file using an editor program, press the <return> key to separate the file into lines. Each time you press this key, the newline character (represented by C as '\n') is placed in the file.

The following lines represent a text file consisting of two lines of letters, blank characters, and the punctuation characters . and ! .

```
This is a text file!<newline>
It has two lines.<newline><eof>
```

Each line ends with the newline character, and the eof character follows the last newline in the file. For convenience in examining the file's contents, we listed each line of the file (through <newline>) as a separate line, although this would not be the case in the actual disk file. The disk file consists of a sequence of characters occupying consecutive storage locations on a track of the disk as shown next.

```
This is a text file!<newline>It has two lines.<newline><eof>
```

The first character of the second line (I) follows directly after the last character of the first line (the newline character). Because all textual input and output data are actually a continuous stream of character codes, we sometimes refer to a data source or destination as an *input stream* or *output stream*. These general terms can be applied to files, to the terminal keyboard and screen, and to any other sources of input data or destinations of output data.

The Keyboard and Screen as Text Streams

In interactive programming, C associates system names with the terminal keyboard and screen. The name `stdin` represents the keyboard's input stream. Two system streams, the "normal" output stream `stdout` and the "error" output stream `stderr`, are associated with the screen. All three streams can be treated like text files because their individual components are characters.

Normally at the keyboard, we enter one line of data at a time, pressing <return> or <enter> to indicate the end of a data line. Pressing one of these keys inserts the newline character in system stream `stdin`. Normally in interactive programming, we use a sentinel value to indicate the end of data rather than attempting to place the eof character in system stream `stdin`. However, the eof character could be used. No single key represents the eof character, so most systems use the control key followed by a letter (for example, on computers running the UNIX operating system, the stroke <control-d> would be used).

Writing characters to the streams `stdout` and `stderr` causes a display on the screen in an interactive program. We have studied the use of the `printf` and `putchar` functions to write characters to the screen. Using a '\n' in the `printf` format string causes output of a newline character that moves the cursor to the start of the next line of the screen.

Newline and EOF

We have seen that C handles the special newline character differently than the eof character, even though they have similar purposes. The newline marks the end of a line of text, and the <eof> marks the end of the entire file. The newline can be processed like any other character: It can be input using `getchar` or using `scanf` with the `%c` specifier, it can be compared to '\n' for equality, and it can be output using `printf` or `putchar`.

However, input of the special eof character is regarded as a failed operation, and the input function responsible returns as its value the negative integer associated with the identifier EOF. Because this special return value gives the calling function an indication that no more data are in the input file, the C run-time support system is under no obligation to provide an error message if the program ignores the warning value and continues to attempt to get input from the stream in question. The following is another example of the input loops that we studied that base their exit condition on the appearance of the EOF return value.

```
for  (status = scanf("%d", &num);
        status != EOF;
        status = scanf("%d", &num))
    process(num);
```

EXERCISES FOR SECTION 12.2

Self-Check

1. Summarize the purposes of the following loops:
    a. `for (c = getchar();  c != '\n';  c = getchar())`
          `if  (isupper(c))`
                `putchar(c);`
    b. `for (c = getchar();  c != EOF;  c = getchar())`
          `if  (isupper(c))`
                `putchar(c);`

Programming

1. Write a function that gets one line of text input, one character at a time, and counts the number of nonwhitespace characters in the line.

12.3 ADDITIONAL TEXT FILES

In our Universal Measurement Conversion case study in Chapter 11, we found it very awkward to be limited to a single input stream. For that program, we built an input file that contained first a database of conversion information, then a sentinel value, and finally the conversion problems for the program to process. We observed that a much more reasonable arrangement would have been to use batch input of the database and interactive input of the problems. However, we would have needed an input stream in addition to stdin. We can access this stream by declaring and manipulating a file pointer variable that gives us a way to obtain data from a second input source. A *file pointer* is the address of a structure containing the information necessary to access an input or output file.

Declaring and Initializing a File Pointer Variable

Before we can use a nonstandard text file for input or output, we must declare a file pointer variable and give it a value, allowing us to access the desired file. The system must prepare the file for input or output before permitting access. This preparation is the purpose of the stdio library function `fopen`. The statements that follow declare and initialize the file pointer variables `infilep` and `outfilep`.

```
FILE *infilep;
FILE *outfilep;

infilep = fopen("b:data.txt", "r");
outfilep = fopen("b:results.txt", "w");
```

Notice that the data type of `infilep` and `outfilep` is `FILE *`. Remember that C is case sensitive, so you must use all capital letters in writing the type name `FILE`. It is possible to declare both `infilep` and `outfilep` in the same statement, but each must be immediately preceded by the asterisk denoting "pointer to" as shown.

```
FILE *infilep, *outfilep;
```

We use the stdio library function `fopen` to open or create an additional text file. The `"r"` in the first call to `fopen` just shown indicates that we wish to use the text file opened as an input file from which we will read (scan) data. The `"w"` in the second call conveys that our intention is to write to the file, i.e., to use it as an output destination. The first argument to `fopen` is a string that is the name of the text file to manipulate. The result returned by `fopen` is the *file pointer* to be used in all further operations on the file. This pointer is the address of a structure of type `FILE` that contains the information necessary to access the file opened by `fopen`. The pointer must be saved in a variable of type `FILE *`. In a program containing the lines just shown, the variable `infilep` will be used to access the input file named `"b:data.txt"`, and the variable `outfilep` will be used to access the newly created output file named `"b:results.txt"`. The identifiers `stdin`, `stdout`, and `stderr` also name variables of type `FILE *`, variables initialized by the system prior to the start of a C program.

If the `fopen` function is unable to accomplish the requested operation, the file pointer that it returns is equal to the value associated with the identifier `NULL` by the stdio library. For example, if execution of this call to `fopen`

```
infilep = fopen("b:data.txt", "r");
```

were unsuccessful due to the nonexistence of a file named `"b:data.txt"`, then execution of the following statement would print an appropriate error message.

```
if (infilep == NULL)
      printf("Cannot open b:data.txt for input\n");
```

A pointer whose value equals `NULL` is called a *null pointer*. Take care not to confuse this concept with the *null character*, whose value is the character `'\0'`. A null pointer is *not* equivalent to a null character.

Using `fopen` with mode `"w"` to open for output a file that already exists usually causes loss of the contents of the existing file. However, if the computer's operating system automatically numbers file versions and creates a new version when it opens an output file, the contents of the existing file will not be lost.

Functions That Take File Pointer Arguments

The stdio library provides functions designed to take input from or send output to a file accessed using a file pointer. Table 12.1 compares calls to I/O functions studied in earlier chapters with calls to analogous functions for input from the file accessed by `infilep` and for output to the file accessed by `outfilep`. In this table, we assume that `infilep` and `outfilep` have been initialized as shown earlier.

Line 1 shows input of a single integer value to be stored in `num`. The call to `scanf` obtains this value from the standard input stream, typically the keyboard. The call to `fscanf` obtains the integer value from `"b:data.txt"`, the file accessed through the file pointer `infilep`. Like `scanf`, function `fscanf` returns as its result the number of input values it has successfully stored through

Table 12.1   Comparison of I/O with Standard Files and I/O with User-Defined File Pointers

Line	Functions That Access stdin and stdout	Functions That Can Access Any Text File
1	`scanf("%d", &num);`	`fscanf(infilep, "%d", &num);`

2	`printf`
	`   ("Number = %d\n",`
	`   num);`
		`fprintf(outfilep,`
		`    "Number = %d\n", num);`

3	`ch = getchar();`	`ch = getc(infilep);`
4	`putchar(ch);`	`putc(ch, outfilep);`

its output arguments. Function `fscanf` also returns the negative EOF value when it encounters the end of the file accessed by its file pointer argument.

Similarly, the behavior of `fprintf`, `getc`, and `putc` is fully comparable to the behavior of the standard I/O equivalents—`printf`, `getchar`, and `putchar`—except that each takes a file pointer argument through which to access its input source or output destination. Observe carefully that this file pointer is provided as the first argument to `fscanf`, `fprintf`, and `getc`. In contrast, `putc` takes the file pointer as its second argument.

Closing a File

When a program has no further use for a file, it should *close* the file by calling the library function `fclose` with the file pointer. The following is a statement to close the file accessed through `infilep`.

```
fclose(infilep);
```

Function `fclose` disposes of the structure that was created to store file access information and carries out other "cleanup" operations.

If necessary, a program can create an output file and can then rescan the file. The file is first opened in `"w"` mode, and data are stored using functions such as `fprintf` and `putc`. The file is then closed using `fclose` and reopened in `"r"` mode, allowing the data to be rescanned with functions such as `fscanf` and `getc`.

EXAMPLE 12.1 ▶

For security reasons, having a backup or duplicate copy of a file is a good idea, in case the original is lost. Even though operating systems typically provide a command that will copy a file, we will write our own C program to do this. The program in Fig. 12.1 copies each character in one file to a backup file and allows the user to enter interactively both the name of the file to copy and the name of the backup file.

The program in Fig. 12.1 is the first we have seen that uses more than one input source and more than one output destination. The program begins by displaying a prompting message on the screen using `printf`. Then `scanf` is executed to take the file name typed at the keyboard.

The repetition condition of the first `for` loop is

```
(inp = fopen(in_name, "r")) == NULL
```

The call to function `fopen` causes the system to try to open for input the file whose name is stored in `in_name`. If this attempt is successful, a file pointer is returned and assigned to `inp`. The value of this assignment will equal NULL only if the file could not be successfully opened; in this case, the user is asked to reenter the name of the file.

In the next program segment, the standard I/O streams are used again to issue a prompting message and scan a file name. The program's second call to fopen opens the output file and returns a file pointer for storage in outp.

The for loop that follows manipulates not the standard I/O streams but rather the input and output files accessed through the file pointers in inp and outp. Function getc is called repeatedly to take one character at a time from the input file, and putc echoes these characters to the output file. When the copy is complete, the calls to fclose release the two files after writing an <eof> on the output file.

Figure 12.2 shows the input and output streams used by the file backup program.

Figure 12.1   Program to Make a Backup Copy of a Text File

```
/*
 *  Makes a backup file.  Repeatedly prompts for the name of a file to
 *  back up until a name is provided that corresponds to an available
 *  file.  Then it prompts for the name of the backup file and creates
 *  the file copy.
 */

#include <stdio.h>
#define   STRSIZ 80

int
main(void)
{
      char  in_name[STRSIZ],  /* strings giving names                     */
            out_name[STRSIZ]; /*    of input and backup files             */
      FILE *inp,              /* file pointers for input and              */
           *outp;             /*    backup files                          */
      int   ch;               /* one character of input file              */

      /*  Get the name of the file to back up and open the file for
          input                                                           */
      printf("Enter name of file you want to back up> ");
      for  (scanf("%s", in_name);
            (inp = fopen(in_name, "r")) == NULL;
            scanf("%s", in_name)) {
```

(continued)

Figure 12.1 *(continued)*

```
        printf("Cannot open %s for input\n", in_name);
        printf("Re-enter file name> ");
    }

    /*  Get name to use for backup file and open file for output      */
    printf("Enter name for backup copy> ");
    scanf("%s", out_name);
    outp = fopen(out_name, "w");

    /*  Make backup copy one character at a time                      */
    for  (ch = getc(inp);  ch != EOF;  ch = getc(inp))
        putc(ch, outp);

    /*  Close files and notify user of backup completion              */
    fclose(inp);
    fclose(outp);
    printf("Copied %s to %s.\n", in_name, out_name);

    return(0);
}
```

(handwritten margin notes, partially legible):
could use
Sscanf(inp, "%c", &ch)
Sprintf(outp, "%c", &ch)

Figure 12.2   Input and Output Streams for File Backup Program

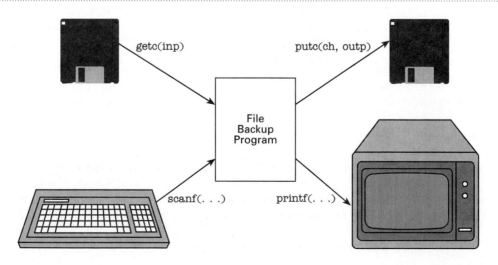

...

Self-Check

1. Assume these declarations for the problem that follows.

```
double x;
int    n;
char   ch, str[40];
```

Indicate the contents of these variables after each of the following input operations is performed. Assume that the file accessed by `indatap` consists of the data given and that each lettered group of operations occurs at the beginning of a program, immediately following a statement that opens the file.

123 3.145 xyz<newline>35 z<newline>

a. `fscanf(indatap, "%d%lf%s%c", &n, &x, str, &ch);`
b. `fscanf(indatap, "%d%lf", &n, &x);`
   `fscanf(indatap, "%s", str);`
   `ch = getc(indatap);`
c. `fscanf(indatap, "%lf%d%c%s", &x, &n, &ch, str);`
d. `fscanf(indatap, "%s%s%s%d%c%c", str, str, str, &n,
            &ch, &ch);`

2. List the library functions we have studied that require a file pointer argument.

Programming

1. Write a function that takes a file pointer input argument and returns a count of the number of alphabetic letters appearing on the current line of the file.
2. Rewrite the file backup program in Fig. 12.1 so it uses a function with file pointer parameters to do the actual file copy.

12.4 PROBLEM SOLVING ILLUSTRATED

In this section, we present a case study that demonstrates the use of files for input of data and for storage of results while using the standard I/O streams to obtain from the user the necessary file names at the time the program is running. The program also uses the screen to show the user the results and to provide messages when errors are detected. This case study reviews the use of array elements that are of a structured data type.

Case Study: Land Boundary Survey

PROBLEM

The surveying firm of Harris, Neilson, and Gallop has completed a land bound-ary survey. The result consists of the (x, y) coordinates of points defining the edges of a piece of property. These coordinates are stored in a data file, one pair per line. The firm needs to know the distance between adjacent points and the total length of the boundary. For error correction purposes, the firm would also like to know the percentage of the total length of each line and the cumulative percentage, starting with the first line. The output results will be written to an output file and also displayed on the screen in tabular form, as shown in Fig. 12.3.

ANALYSIS

First the program copies into an array of points the survey data from the input file named by the program user. Each point has an x component and a y component. The distance between adjacent points, whose (x, y) components are (x_i, y_i), and (x_j, y_j), is given by the formula

$$distance = \sqrt{(x_i - x_j)^2 + (y_i - y_j)^2}$$

The total length of the land boundary is the sum of the individual lengths. After we compute the total length, we can determine the percentage of the total boundary represented by each individual length, add it to the cumulative per-centage, and write the required output file and table.

**Figure 12.3
Land Survey
Table**

Harris, Neilson, and Gallop, Surveyors

The number of points processed was 6.
Total boundary length is 1365.685 feet.

Line Number	Start Point x	y	Line length (in feet)	% of Boundary	Cumulative %
1	100.000	100.000	141.421	10.355	10.355
2	200.000	200.000	141.421	10.355	20.711
3	300.000	300.000	141.421	10.355	31.066
4	400.000	400.000	400.000	29.289	60.355
5	0.000	400.000	400.000	29.289	89.645
6	0.000	0.000	141.421	10.355	100.000

Data Requirements

Input File
file of coordinates

Output File
file of line lengths and percentages

Structured Data Type
```
point_t
     components: double x, y  /*  (x, y) coordinates   */
```

Problem Constant
```
MAX   100            /*  size of the arrays              */
```

Problem Inputs
```
point_t pts[MAX]   /*  edge points                     */
```

Problem Outputs
coordinates of edge points
```
double length[MAX]   /*  distance between adjacent
                              points                      */
double pct[MAX]      /*  percentage of total boundary
                              length                      */
double cum_pct[MAX]  /*  cumulative percentage so far  */
int    n             /*  number of points on the
                              boundary                    */
double perim         /*  total boundary length         */
```

DESIGN

Initial Algorithm

1. Get all points from the data file and count how many there are.
2. Calculate the length of each line segment and the total boundary length.
3. Compute percentages of total boundary represented by each line segment and cumulative percentages.
4. Write the output file and table.

Algorithm Refinements

We will use functions to perform each step of the algorithm. Figure 12.4 shows the structure chart.

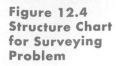

**Figure 12.4
Structure Chart
for Surveying
Problem**

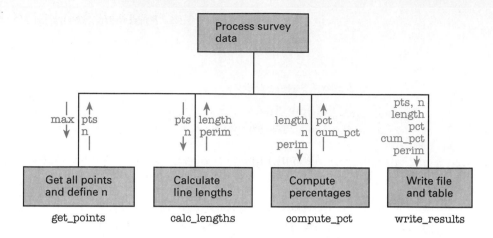

Figure 12.5   Function main for Land Boundary Survey Program

```
/*
 *  This program takes a collection of edge points around the boundary of
 *  a plot of land and computes the distances between adjacent points. The
 *  coordinates of the edge points, the lengths of the individual lines,
 *  and their percentages of the total perimeter are written along with
 *  the cumulative percentages to an output file. They are also displayed
 *  in a table.
 */
#include <stdio.h>

typedef struct point_s {
     double x, y;
} point_t;

/*  Include functions from Fig. 12.6-.9 here                              */

#define MAX 100

int
main(void)
{
     int     n;                /*  number of edge points                  */
     point_t pts[MAX];         /*  edge points                            */
     double  length[MAX],      /*  boundary line lengths                  */
             pct[MAX],         /*  percentages of perimeter               */
             cum_pct[MAX],     /*  cumulative percentages of perimeter    */
             perim;            /*  perimeter length                       */
```

(continued)

Figure 12.5 *(continued)*

```
    /*  Get edge points                                          */
    get_points(MAX, pts, &n);

    /*  Calculate the length of each line and the total perimeter */
    calc_lengths(pts, n, length, &perim);

    /*  Compute percentage each boundary line is of total perimeter */
    compute_pct(length, n, perim, pct, cum_pct);

    /*  Write output file and table                               */
    write_results(pts, length, pct, cum_pct, n, perim);

    return(0);
}
```

IMPLEMENTATION

Figure 12.5 shows the main function. It contains declarations for all arrays and simple variables listed in the data requirements section and includes calls to the four functions.

Function get_points

Function `get_points` begins by using the standard I/O stream to get from the user the name of the file containing the points (see Fig. 12.6). It then opens this file and uses `fscanf` in a loop with endfile/error-driven exit to fill the array of points. After loop exit, the output parameter accessed through `np` is defined.

Figure 12.6 **Function get_points for Land Boundary Survey Program**

```
#define STR_SIZ 80

/*
 *  Prompts user for name of text file containing survey data, loads
 *  points from this file, and sends back number of points loaded through
 *  output parameter np.
 */
```

(continued)

Figure 12.6 *(continued)*

```
void
get_points(int       max,    /* input - declared size of pts          */
           point_t  pts[], /* output - array of data                 */
           int      *np)    /* output - number of data values
                                        stored in pts                 */
{
     int      i, status;
     point_t point;
     char     file_name[STR_SIZ];
     FILE    *filep;

     /*  Get name of data file and open it                            */
     printf("Enter name of file containing points> ");
     scanf("%s", file_name);
     filep = fopen(file_name, "r");

     if (filep == NULL) { /* if file cannot be opened, give error
                              message and send back zero as number of points */
          printf("Cannot open file %s\n", file_name);
          *np = 0;
     } else { /* input loop exits on EOF, error, or when array filled */
          i = 0;
          for  (status = fscanf(filep, "%lf%lf", &point.x, &point.y);
                status == 2  &&  i < max;
                status = fscanf(filep, "%lf%lf", &point.x, &point.y)) {
             pts[i++] = point;
          }

          /* Issue error message on premature exit                    */
          if (status > EOF  &&  status < 2) {
               printf("*** Error in data format ***\n");
               printf("*** Using first %d points ***\n", i);
          } else if (status == 2) {
               printf("*** Error: more than %d points in file %s ",
                       max, file_name);
               printf("***\n*** Using first %d points only ***\n", i);
          }

          /* Send back size of used portion of array                  */
          *np = i;
     }
}
```

Function calc_lengths

Function `calc_lengths` computes the length of each line on the boundary. The first line connects the first two points, the second line connects the second and third points, and so on. The last line connects the last and first points. The function also tabulates the length of the perimeter. The algorithm follows.

Algorithm for calc_lengths

1. Initialize `perim` to zero.
2. For `i` from 0 through n − 2
>   3. Set `length[i]` to the length of the line from `pts[i]` to `pts[i+1]`.
>   4. Add new line length to `perim`.
5. Set `length[n-1]` to the length of the line from `pts[n-1]` to `pts[0]`.
6. Add the new line length to `perim`.

Figure 12.7 shows function `calc_lengths` along with function `distance`. Function `distance` calculates the length of the line whose end points are its input arguments.

Figure 12.7   Functions distance and calc_lengths for Land Boundary Survey Program

```
#include <math.h>

/*
 *  Computes the distance between points start and end
 */
double
distance(point_t start, point_t end) /* input - end points of a line */
{
     double xdiff, ydiff;

     xdiff = end.x - start.x;
     ydiff = end.y - start.y;

     return (sqrt(xdiff * xdiff + ydiff * ydiff));
}

/*
 *  Calculates the length of each line and the total boundary
 */
```

(continued)

Figure 12.7   *(continued)*

```
void
calc_lengths(const point_t pts[],     /*  input - list of points      */
             int           n,         /*  input - number of points    */
             double        length[],  /*  output - length of each line */
             double        *perim)    /*  output - total boundary length */
{
     int i;

     /*  Defines each individual line length and adds it to the total  */
     *perim = 0;
     for (i = 0;  i < n - 1;  ++i) {
         length[i] = distance(pts[i], pts[i + 1]);
         *perim += length[i];
     }

     length[n - 1] = distance(pts[n - 1], pts[0]);
     *perim += length[n - 1];
}
```

Function compute_pct

Function `compute_pct` performs the percentage calculations for each line, defining arrays `pct` and `cum_pct`. Figure 12.8 shows function `compute_pct`. In the `for` loop, the statements

```
pct[i] = length[i] / perim * 100.0;
tot_pct += pct[i];
cum_pct[i] = tot_pct;
```

define the percentage that the current line is of the full perimeter `pct[i]` and the cumulative percentage `cum_pct[i]`. The latter is obtained by adding `pct[i]` to the previous cumulative percentage `tot_pct`.

Figure 12.8   **Function compute_pct for Land Boundary Survey Program**

```
/*
 *  Calculates the percentage each line's length is of the full perimeter
 *  and the cumulative percentages.
 */
```

(continued)

Figure 12.8 *(continued)*

```
void
compute_pct(const double length[],  /*  input - length of each line      */
            int          n,          /*  input - number of points        */
            double       perim,      /*  input - length of full perimeter */
            double       pct[],      /*  output - percentages corresponding
                                                  to lengths              */
            double       cum_pct[])  /*  output - cumulative percentages  */
{
     int    i;
     double tot_pct = 0;

     for  (i = 0;  i < n;  ++i) {
          pct[i] = length[i] / perim * 100.0;
          tot_pct += pct[i];
          cum_pct[i] = tot_pct;
     }
}
```

Function `write_results` displays a table of results on the screen and saves the same table in the file named by the program user. The table contains one line for each segment of the land boundary. This line includes the coordinates of the segment's starting point, its length, the percentage of the total length, and the cumulative percentage so far. We display only the starting point of each line because of screen width limitations. In our heading, we need to print a percent sign (%), a character normally used in a format string to signal the beginning of a placeholder. In order to have *one* percent sign printed, we must put *two* percent signs in the format string. Figure 12.9 shows function `write_results`.

Figure 12.9   **Function write_results for Land Boundary Survey Program**

```
/*
 *  Displays survey results on the screen and also saves this table in a
 *  text file.
 */
void
write_results(const point_t pts[],    /*  input - edge points on boundary   */
              const double  length[], /*  input - lengths of boundary lines */
```

(continued)

Figure 12.9 *(continued)*

```
                  const double pct[],      /*  input - each line's % of total
                                                       boundary                  */
                  const double cum_pct[],  /*  input - cumulative % of total
                                                       so far                    */
                  int          n,          /*  input - number of edge points    */
                  double       perim)      /*  input - total boundary length    */
{
    char   file_name[STR_SIZ];  /*  name of output file                          */
    FILE *outp;                 /*  file pointer for text output file            */
    int    i;

    /*  Determine and open output file                                           */
    printf("Enter name of file in which to place results\n> ");
    scanf("%s", file_name);
    outp = fopen(file_name, "w");

    /*  Display and save table heading                                */
    printf("\n            Harris, Neilson, and Gallop, Surveyors\n\n");
    fprintf(outp,
            "            Harris, Neilson, and Gallop, Surveyors\n\n");
    printf("Land boundary has %d edge points.\n", n);
    fprintf(outp, "Land boundary has %d edge points.\n", n);
    printf("Boundary length = %.3f feet.\n\n", perim);
    fprintf(outp, "Boundary length = %.3f feet.\n\n", perim);
    printf
        ("Line          Start Point      Line Length      %% of Cumulative\n");
    fprintf
        (outp,
         "Line          Start Point      Line Length      %% of Cumulative\n");
    printf
        ("Number     x          y        (in feet)     Boundary      %%\n\n");
    fprintf
        (outp,
         "Number     x          y        (in feet)     Boundary      %%\n\n");

    /*  Display and save table of results                                        */
    for (i = 0;  i < n;  ++i) {
```

(continued)

Figure 12.9   *(continued)*

```
        printf("%3d%12.3f%12.3f%12.3f%12.3f%12.3f\n", i + 1, pts[i].x,
                pts[i].y, length[i], pct[i], cum_pct[i]);
        fprintf(outp, "%3d%12.3f%12.3f%12.3f%12.3f%12.3f\n", i + 1,
                pts[i].x, pts[i].y, length[i], pct[i], cum_pct[i]);
    }

    /*  Close output file                                              */
    fclose(outp);
}
```

TESTING

A sample run of the survey program will produce a table similar to the one shown
in the statement of the problem. Make sure that all values printed are positive and
that the final cumulative percentage is 100. To verify the correctness of the table,
try some adjacent points with the same *x* coordinates but with different *y* coordinates (or the same *y* coordinates but different *x* coordinates). In this case, the line
length should be the absolute value of the difference between the *y* coordinates.
See what happens to the display table when the first point is placed at the end of
the data file instead of at the beginning. All the table lines should move up one
position, and the last line displayed should be the same as the former first line.

  Also exercise your statements on test cases that give error messages. Try
an incorrect input file name. In addition, try an input file with a data format
error and one with too much data.

**EXERCISES FOR
SECTION 12.4**

Self-Check

1. The code for function `scan_unit` that we used in Chapter 11 to scan information regarding one unit of measurement is repeated with some blank lines
   added. Fill in the blank lines to create `fscan_unit`, a function that takes a
   file pointer argument in addition to the `unit_t` output argument. This function should get the conversion information for a unit from the file accessed
   by this pointer.

```
/*
 *  Gets data to fill output argument _____
 *  Returns standard error code:  1 => successful input,  0 => error,
 *                                negative EOF value => end of file
 *
 */
```

```
int
fscan_unit(_____
           unit_t *unitp)   /*  output - unit_t structure to fill */

{
     int status;

     status = ___scanf(_____,
                      "%s%s%s%lf", (*unitp).name,
                                   (*unitp).abbrev,
                                   (*unitp).class,
                                   &(*unitp).standard);

     if (status == 4)
          status = 1;
     else if (status != EOF)
          status = 0;

     return (status);
}
```

Programming

1. Modify the Universal Measurement Conversion Program from Chapter 11 so it uses an input data file for the database and interactive input for the conversion problems. Use `fscan_unit` that you wrote for the Self-Check Exercise just given.

12.5 BINARY FILES

When we use text files for storage of data, a program must expend a significant amount of effort to convert the stream of characters from an input file into the binary integers, type `double` mantissas and exponents, and character strings that are the representation in main memory of the same data (see Chapter 7). The program must again expend time in converting the internal data format back into a stream of characters for storage in an output file of text.

Many programs produce output files that are used as input files for other programs. If there is no need for a human to read the file, it is a waste of computer time for the first program to convert its internal data format to a stream of characters, and then for the second program to have to apply an inverse conversion to extract the intended data from the stream of characters. We can avoid this unnecessary translation by using a binary file rather than a text file.

A *binary file* is a file created by executing a program that stores directly in the file the computer's internal representation of each file component. For example, the code fragment in Fig. 12.10 creates a binary file named "nums.bin", which contains the even integers from 2 to 500.

You see in Fig. 12.10 that a binary file is declared in exactly the same way as a text file. The fopen and fclose functions are used just as they are for text files, except that the second argument to fopen is either "wb" (write binary) for output files or "rb" (read binary) for input files. However, a different stdio library function is used for copying values into the file. Function fwrite has four input parameters. The first parameter is the *address* of the first memory cell whose contents are to be copied to the file. In Fig. 12.10, we want the contents of the variable i copied to the file, so we provide fwrite with the address of i (&i) as the first argument.

The second parameter of function fwrite is the number of bytes to copy to the file for one component. In Chapter 1, we noted that a memory cell is a collection of smaller units called *bytes* and that a byte is the amount of storage needed to represent one character. A C operator sizeof can be applied to any data type name to find the number of bytes that the current implementation uses for storage of the data type. For example, these statements will print a sentence indicating how many bytes are being occupied by one integer.

```
printf("An integer requires %d bytes ", sizeof (int));
printf("in this implementation.\n");
```

The sizeof operator can be applied to both built-in and user-defined types.

The third parameter of fwrite is the number of values to write to the binary file. In our example, we are writing one integer at a time so we provide

Figure 12.10   Creating a Binary File of Integers

```
FILE *binaryp;
int   i;

binaryp = fopen("nums.bin", "wb");

for  (i = 2;   i <= 500;  i += 2)
    fwrite(&i, sizeof (int), 1, binaryp);

fclose(binaryp);
```

the constant 1 as this argument. However, it is possible to save the contents of an entire array using just one call to fwrite by providing the array's size as the third argument. The final argument to fwrite is a file pointer to the file being created, a file previously opened in mode "wb" using function fopen. For example, if array score is an array of 10 integers, the statement

```
fwrite(score, sizeof (int), 10, binaryp);
```

writes the entire array to the output file.

Writing the value of an integer variable i to a binary file using fwrite is faster than writing i to a text file. For example, if the value of i is 244, the statement from the for loop

```
fwrite(&i, sizeof (int), 1, binaryp);
```

copies the internal binary representation of i from memory to the file accessed by binaryp. If your computer uses two bytes to store an int value, the byte that stores the highest order bits would contain all zeros, and the byte that stores the lowest order bits would contain the binary string 11110100 (244 = 128 + 64 + 32 + 16 + 4). Both bytes would be written to disk as the next file component.

Assuming textp is a pointer to a text output file, the statement

```
fprintf(textp, "%d ", i);
```

writes the value of i to the file using four characters (four bytes). The computer must first convert the binary number in i to the character string "244 " and then write the binary codes for the characters 2, 4, 4, and blank to the file. Obviously, it takes more time to do the conversion and copy each character than it does to copy the internal binary representation to disk. Also, twice as much disk space is required to store four characters as to store the internal binary representation of the type int value (four bytes versus two).

Using a binary file has another advantage. Each time we write a type double value to a text file, the computer must convert this value to a character string whose precision is determined by the placeholder in the format string. A loss of accuracy may result.

The stdio library includes an input function fread that is comparable to fwrite. Function fread also requires four arguments:

1. Address of first memory cell to fill.
2. Size of one value.
3. Maximum number of elements to copy from the file into memory.
4. File pointer to a binary file opened in mode "rb" using function fopen.

Function `fread` returns as its value an integer indicating how many elements it successfully copied from the file. This number will be less than the value of the third argument of `fread` if EOF is encountered prematurely.

It is very important not to mix file types. A binary file created (written) using `fwrite` must be read using `fread`. A text file created using `fprintf` must be read using text file input functions such as `fscanf` or `getc`.

Table 12.2 compares the use of text and binary files for input and output of data of various types. The statements in both columns assume the following constant macros, type definition, and variable declarations.

```
#define STRSIZ   10
#define MAX      40

typedef struct planet_s {
     char name[STRSIZ];
     double diameter,        /* equatorial diameter in
                                km                    */
            dist_sun,        /* average distance from sun
                                in km                 */
            orbital_prd,     /* years to orbit sun once */
            axial_rot_prd;   /* hours to complete one
                                revolution on axis    */
} planet_t;
. . .
double   nums[MAX], data;
planet_t a_planet;
int i, n, status;
FILE *plan_bin_inp, *plan_bin_outp, *plan_txt_inp,
     *plan_txt_outp;
FILE *doub_bin_inp, *doub_bin_outp, *doub_txt_inp,
     *doub_txt_outp;
```

In Example 1 of Table 12.2, we use `fopen` to open our input files, and we store the file pointers returned by `fopen` in variables of type `FILE *`. Notice that the form of the call to `fopen` for opening a binary file differs from the call for opening a text file only in the value of the mode argument. In fact, even this difference is *optional*. Also notice that the type of the file pointer does not vary. We see a similar situation in the opening of output files in Example 2. One consequence of this similarity is that the ability of the C compiler and run-time support system to detect misuse of a file pointer is severely limited. It is the programmer's responsibility to keep track of which type of file each file pointer accesses and to use the right I/O function at the right time.

In Examples 3 and 4 of Table 12.2, we compare input/output of a user-defined structure type as it is done with text and binary files. In Examples 5 and 6,

Table 12.2   Data I/O Using Text and Binary Files

Example	Text File I/O	Binary File I/O	Purpose

1	`plan_txt_inp =`
	`    fopen("planets.txt", "r");`
	
	`doub_txt_inp =`
	`    fopen("nums.txt", "r");`
		`plan_bin_inp =`
		`    fopen("planets.bin", "rb");`
		
		`doub_bin_inp =`
		`    fopen("nums.bin", "rb");`
			Open for input a file of planets and a file of numbers, saving file pointers for use in calls to input functions.

2	`plan_txt_outp =`
	`    fopen("pl_out.txt", "w");`
	
	`doub_txt_outp =`
	`    fopen("nm_out.txt", "w");`
		`plan_bin_outp =`
		`    fopen("pl_out.bin", "wb");`
		
		`doub_bin_outp =`
		`    fopen("nm_out.bin", "wb");`
			Open for output a file of planets and a file of numbers, saving file pointers for use in calls to output functions.

3	`fscanf(plan_txt_inp,`
	`    "%s%lf%lf%lf%lf",`
	`    a_planet.name,`
	`    &a_planet.diameter,`
	`    &a_planet.dist_sun,`
	`    &a_planet.orbital_prd,`
	`    &a_planet.axial_rot_prd);`
		`fread(&a_planet,`
		`    sizeof (planet_t),`
		`    1, plan_bin_inp);`
			Copy one planet structure into memory from the data file.

4	`fprintf(plan_txt_outp,`
	`    "%s%e%e%e%e",`
	`    a_planet.name,`
	`    a_planet.diameter,`
	`    a_planet.dist_sun,`
	`    a_planet.orbital_prd,`
	`    a_planet.axial_rot_prd);`
		`fwrite(&a_planet,`
		`    sizeof (planet_t),`
		`    1, plan_bin_outp);`
			Write one planet structure to the output file.

(continued)

Table 12.2 *(continued)*

Example	Text File I/O	Binary File I/O	Purpose
| 5 | ```
for (i = 0; i < MAX; ++i)
    fscanf(doub_txt_inp,
        "%lf", &nums[i]);
``` | ```
fread(nums, sizeof (double),
    MAX, doub_bin_inp);
``` | Fill array nums with type double values from input file. |
| 6 | ```
for (i = 0; i < MAX; ++i)
    fprintf(doub_txt_outp,
        "%e\n", nums[i]);
``` | ```
fwrite(nums, sizeof (double),
    MAX, doub_bin_outp);
``` | Write contents of array nums to output file. |
| 7 | ```
n = 0;
for (status =
        fscanf(doub_txt_inp,
            "%lf", &data);
    status != EOF &&
        n < MAX;
    status =
        fscanf(doub_txt_inp,
            "%lf", &data))
    nums[n++] = data;
``` | ```
n = fread(nums,
        sizeof (double),
        MAX, doub_bin_inp);
``` | Fill nums with data until EOF encountered, setting n to the number of values stored. |
| 8 | ```
fclose(plan_txt_inp);
fclose(plan_txt_outp);
fclose(doub_txt_inp);
fclose(doub_txt_outp);
``` | ```
fclose(plan_bin_inp);
fclose(plan_bin_outp);
fclose(doub_bin_inp);
fclose(doub_bin_outp);
``` | Close all input and output files. |

we see input/output of an array of type `double` values. In the text file code, array elements are scanned or written one at a time in an indexed loop. When we use a binary file, we can fill the array from or copy it to the file using just one call to `fread` or `fwrite`. We see that the calls used to read/write array `nums` provide the size of one array element as the second argument to `fread` or `fwrite` and the number of array elements to process as the third argument. Example 7 demonstrates partially filling array `nums` and setting n to the number of elements filled. Example 8 shows that all files—binary or text, input or output—are closed in the same way.

EXERCISES FOR SECTION 12.5

Self-Check

Assume the environment shown, and complete the statements that follow so that they are valid.

```
#define NAME_LEN 50
#define SIZE      30

typedef struct person_s {
     char    name[NAME_LEN];
     int     age;
     double income;
} person_t;
. . .
int      num_err[SIZE];
person_t exec;
FILE     *nums_inp, *psn_inp, *psn_outp, *nums_outp;
         /* binary files */
FILE     *nums_txt_inp, *psn_txt_inp, *psn_txt_outp;
         /* text files   */

nums_inp = fopen("nums.bin", "rb");
nums_txt_inp = fopen("nums.txt", "r");
psn_inp = fopen("persons.bin", "rb");
psn_txt_inp = fopen("persons.txt", "r");
psn_outp = fopen("persout.bin", "wb");
psn_txt_outp = fopen("persout.txt", "w");
nums_outp = fopen("numsout.bin", "wb");
```

1. fread(_____, sizeof (person_t), 1,
   _____);
2. fscanf(psn_txt_____, "%s", _____);
3. fwrite(&exec, _____, 1, psn_____);

```
4. fwrite(num_err, _____, _____,
          nums_outp);
5. fread(&num_err[3], _____, _____,
         nums_inp);
6. fprintf(psn_txt_outp, "%s %d %f\n", _____,
          _____, _____);
```

Programming

1. Write a function `fread_units` that is similar to the `load_units` function from the Universal Measurement Conversion Program (see Fig. 11.12) except it assumes that the unit conversion data have been stored as a binary file. The function should ask the user for the name of a binary file, open the file, and get up to `unit_max unit_t` values to place in array `units`. Be sure to send back to the calling function the size of the used portion of the array.

12.6 SEARCHING A DATABASE

Computerized matching of data against a file of records is a common practice. For example, many real estate companies maintain a large file of property listings: A realtor can process the file to locate desirable properties for a client. Similarly, mail-order firms purchase large files of information on potential customers.

These large files of data are called *databases*. In this section, we will write a program that searches a database to find all records that match a proposed set of requirements.

Case Study: Database Inquiry

 **PROBLEM**

Periphs Plus is a mail-order computer supply company that maintains its inventory as a computer file in order to facilitate answering questions regarding that database. Some questions of interest might be

- What printer stands that cost less than $100 are available?
- What product has the code 5241?
- What types of data cartridges are available?

These questions and others can be answered if we know the correct way to ask them.

ANALYSIS

A database inquiry program has two phases: setting the search parameters and searching for records that satisfy the parameters. In our program, we will assume that all the structure components can be involved in the search. The program user must enter low and high bounds for each field of interest. Let's illustrate how we might set the search parameters to answer the question, What modems that cost less than $200 are available?

Assuming that the price of any Periphs Plus product does not exceed $1000, we can use the following menu-driven dialogue to set the search parameters.

```
Select by letter a search parameter to set, or enter q to accept
parameters shown.

Search Parameter                                    Current Value
  [a]   Low bound for stock number                     1111
  [b]   High bound for stock number                    9999
  [c]   Low bound for category                         aaaa
  [d]   High bound for category                        zzzz
  [e]   Low bound for technical description            aaaa
  [f]   High bound for technical description           zzzz
  [g]   Low bound for price                         $    0.00
  [h]   High bound for price                        $1000.00

Selection> c
New low bound for category> modem


Select by letter a search parameter to set, or enter q to
accept parameters shown.

Search Parameter                                    Current Value
  [a]   Low bound for stock number                     1111
  [b]   High bound for stock number                    9999
  [c]   Low bound for category                         modem
  [d]   High bound for category                        zzzz
  [e]   Low bound for technical description            aaaa
  [f]   High bound for technical description           zzzz
  [g]   Low bound for price                         $    0.00
  [h]   High bound for price                        $1000.00

Selection> d
New high bound for category> modem
```

```
Select by letter a search parameter to set, or enter q to
accept parameters shown.

Search Parameter                                       Current Value
[a]  Low bound for stock number                        1111
[b]  High bound for stock number                       9999
[c]  Low bound for category                            modem
[d]  High bound for category                           modem
[e]  Low bound for technical description               aaaa
[f]  High bound for technical description              zzzz
[g]  Low bound for price                               $   0.00
[h]  High bound for price                              $1000.00

Selection> h
New high bound for price> 199.99

Select by letter a search parameter to set, or enter q to
accept parameters shown.

Search Parameter                                       Current Value
[a]  Low bound for stock number                        1111
[b]  High bound for stock number                       9999
[c]  Low bound for category                            modem
[d]  High bound for category                           modem
[e]  Low bound for technical description               aaaa
[f]  High bound for technical description              zzzz
[g]  Low bound for price                               $   0.00
[h]  High bound for price                              $ 199.99

Selection> q
```

Data Requirements

Problem Inputs

```
search_params_t params;    /* search parameter
                              bounds              */
char inv_filename[STR_SIZ] /* name of inventory file */
```

Problem Outputs

all products that satisfy the search

**Figure 12.11
Structure Chart
for Database
Inquiry Problem**

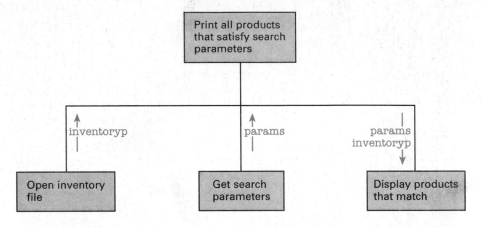

DESIGN

Initial Algorithm

1. Open inventory file.
2. Get search parameters.
3. Display all products that satisfy the search parameters.

The structure chart for the database inquiry problem is shown in Fig. 12.11. The refinement of this design is distributed through the development of functions `get_params` and `display_match`.

IMPLEMENTATION

In Fig. 12.12, we see an outline of the database program's implementation including the full code of function `main`. Our design and implementation of the functions called by `main` and most of their helper functions follow this outline.

Figure 12.12   Outline and Function main for Database Inquiry Program

```
/*
 *  Displays all products in the database that satisfy the search
 *  parameters specified by the program user.
 */
#include <stdio.h>
#include <string.h>

#define MIN_STOCK    1111    /* minimum stock number                      */
#define MAX_STOCK    9999    /* maximum stock number                      */
```

(continued)

Figure 12.12   *(continued)*

```
#define MAX_PRICE      1000.00 /* maximum product price              */
#define STR_SIZ        80      /* number of characters in a string   */

typedef struct product_s {    /* product structure type             */
      int    stock_num;               /* stock number               */
      char   category[STR_SIZ];
      char   tech_descript[STR_SIZ];
      double price;
} product_t;

typedef struct search_params_s {  /* search parameter bounds type   */
      int    low_stock, high_stock;
      char   low_category[STR_SIZ], high_category[STR_SIZ];
      char   low_tech_descript[STR_SIZ], high_tech_descript[STR_SIZ];
      double low_price, high_price;
} search_params_t;

/*  Insert functions needed by get_params and display_match          */

/*
 *  Prompts the user to enter the search parameters
 */
search_params_t
get_params(void)
{
   /* body of get_params to be inserted */
}

/*
 *  Displays records of all products in the inventory that satisfy search
 *  parameters.
 *  Pre:  databasep accesses a binary file of product_t records that has
 *        been opened as an input file, and params is defined
 */
void
display_match(FILE              *databasep, /* input - file pointer to binary
                                               database file           */
              search_params_t params)    /* input - search parameter
                                              bounds                   */
```

(continued)

Figure 12.12 *(continued)*

```
{
    /* body of display_match to be inserted */
}

int
main(void)
{
    char             inv_filename[STR_SIZ];  /* name of inventory file */
    FILE             *inventoryp;            /* inventory file pointer */
    search_params_t params;                  /* search parameter
                                                bounds                 */

    /*  Get name of inventory file and open it                        */
    printf("Enter name of inventory file> ");
    scanf("%s", inv_filename);
    inventoryp = fopen(inv_filename, "rb");

    /*  Get the search parameters                                      */
    params = get_params();

    /*  Display all products that satisfy the search parameters        */
    display_match(inventoryp, params);

    return(0);
}
```

Design of the Function Subprograms

Function `get_params` must first initialize the search parameters to allow the widest search possible and then let the user change some parameters to narrow the search. The local variables and algorithm for `get_params` follow; the structure chart is in Fig. 12.13.

Local Variables for get_params

```
search_params_t params;   /* structure whose components
                             must be defined          */
char choice;              /* user's response to menu  */
```

**Figure 12.13
Structure Chart
for get_params**

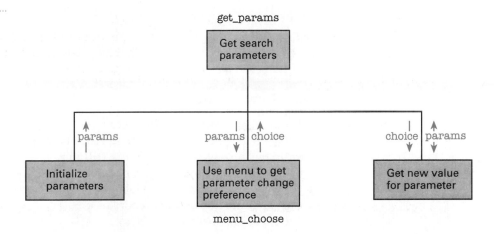

Algorithm for get_params

1. Initialize `params` to permit widest possible search.
2. Display menu and get response to store in `choice`.
3. Repeat while `choice` is not `'q'`
    4. Select appropriate prompt and get new parameter value.
    5. Display menu and get response to store in `choice`.
6. Return search parameters.

Function `display_match` must examine each file record with a stock number between the low and high bounds for stock numbers. If a record satisfies the search parameters, it is displayed. Function `display_match` will also print a message if no matches are found. The local variables, algorithm, and structure chart for the function follow (see Fig. 12.14).

**Figure 12.14
Structure Chart
for
display_match**

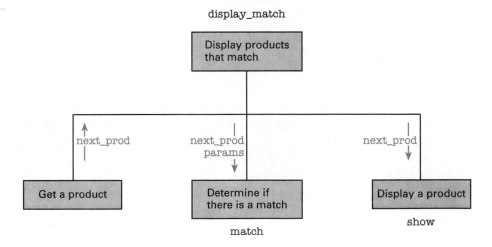

Local Variables for display_match

```
product_t next_prod   /*  the current product          */
int no_matches        /*  a flag indicating whether or
                          not there are any matches     */
```

Algorithm for display_match

1. Initialize no_matches to true(1).
2. Advance to the first record whose stock number is within range.
3. while the current stock number is still in range repeat
    4. if the search parameters match
        5. Display the product and set no_matches to false(0).
    6. Get the next product record.
7. if there are no matches
    8. Print a no products available message.

<u>**IMPLEMENTATION**</u>   of the function subprograms

Figure 12.15 shows the code of functions display_match, menu_choose, and match, along with a stub for function show.

Figure 12.15   Functions display_match, menu_choose, and match

```
/*
 *  Displays a lettered menu with the current values of search parameters.
 *  Returns the letter the user enters.  A letter in the range a..h selects
 *  a parameter to change; q quits, accepting search parameters shown.
 *  Post:  first non-whitespace character entered is returned
 */
char
menu_choose(search_params_t params) /* input - current search parameter
                                                 bounds                  */
{
    char choice;

    printf("Select by letter a search parameter to change or type q\n");
    printf("to quit, accepting search parameter bounds shown.\n\n");
    printf("     Search parameter                    ");
    printf("Current value\n\n");
    printf("[a]  Low bound for stock number                 %4d\n",
           params.low_stock);
```

(continued)

Figure 12.15 *(continued)*

```
        printf("[b]  High bound for stock number               %4d\n",
                params.high_stock);
        printf("[c]  Low bound for category                    %s\n",
                params.low_category);
        printf("[d]  High bound for category                   %s\n",
                params.high_category);
        printf("[e]  Low bound for technical description        %s\n",
                params.low_tech_descript);
        printf("[f]  High bound for technical description       %s\n",
                params.high_tech_descript);
        printf("[g]  Low bound for price                       %7.2f\n",
                params.low_price);
        printf("[h]  High bound for price                      %7.2f\n\n",
                params.high_price);

        printf("Selection> ");
        while (isspace(choice = getchar())) {}

        return (choice);
}


/*
 *  Determines whether record prod satisfies all search parameters
 */
int
match(product_t         prod,      /*  input - record to check          */
      search_params_t params)  /*  input - parameters to satisfy    */
{
        return (strcmp(params.low_category, prod.category) <= 0            &&
                strcmp(prod.category, params.high_category) <= 0          &&
                strcmp(params.low_tech_descript, prod.tech_descript) <= 0  &&
                strcmp(prod.tech_descript, params.high_tech_descript) <= 0 &&
                params.low_price <= prod.price                            &&
                prod.price <= params.high_price);
}
/*
 *  *** STUB ***
 *  Displays each field of prod.  Leaves a blank line after the product
 *  display.
 */
```

(continued)

Figure 12.15 *(continued)*

```
void
show(product_t prod)
{
     printf("Function show entered with product number %d\n",
          prod.stock_num);
}

/*
 *  Displays records of all products in the inventory that satisfy search
 *  parameters.
 *  Pre:  databasep accesses a binary file of product_t records that has
 *        been opened as an input file, and params is defined
 */
void
display_match(FILE           *databasep,  /*  file pointer to binary
                                               database file            */
          search_params_t params)     /*  input - search parameter
                                               bounds                   */
{
     product_t next_prod;       /* current product from database      */
     int       no_matches = 1;  /* flag indicating if no matches have
                                   been found                          */
     int       status;          /* input file status                  */

     /*  Advances to first record with a stock number greater than or
         equal to lower bound.                                         */
     for  (status = fread(&next_prod, sizeof (product_t), 1, databasep);
           status == 1 && params.low_stock > next_prod.stock_num;
           status = fread(&next_prod, sizeof (product_t), 1, databasep)) {}

     /*  Displays a list of the products which satisfy the search
         parameters                                                    */
     printf("\nProducts satisfying the search parameters:\n");
     while (next_prod.stock_num <= params.high_stock  &&
            status == 1) {
        if (match(next_prod, params)) {
             no_matches = 0;
             show(next_prod);
```

(continued)

Figure 12.15   *(continued)*

```
        }
        status = fread(&next_prod, sizeof (product_t), 1, databasep);
    }

    /*  Displays a message if no products found                         */
    if (no_matches)
        printf("Sorry, no products available\n");
}
```

EXERCISES FOR SECTION 12.6

Self-Check

1. What values would you use as search parameter bounds to answer the questions listed at the beginning of this section?
2. Which function in our database search program determines whether a particular record matches the search parameters? Which one displays each matching record?
3. Why does function `match` not need to check a product's `stock_num` field?

Programming

1. Write the functions `get_params` and `show` described in the database inquiry problem. Since `get_params` calls function `menu_choose`, your implementation of algorithm Step 4 for `get_params` must be sure to account for the fact that `menu_choose` does not validate the value the user enters.
2. Write a `void` function `make_product_file` that would convert a text file containing product information to a binary file of `product_t` structures. The function's parameters are file pointers to the text input and binary output files.

12.7 COMMON PROGRAMMING ERRORS

File processing in any programming language has many pitfalls; C is no exception. Remember to declare a file pointer variable (type `FILE *`) for each file you want to process. Because C makes no type distinction between file pointers accessing text files and those accessing binary files, it is easy to use the wrong library function with a file pointer. In a program that manipulates both file types, choose names for your file pointers that remind you of the type of file accessed. For example, you could choose names containing "_txt_" for text file pointers and names containing "_bin_" for binary file pointers.

It is also critical that you remember that library functions `fscanf`, `fprintf`, `getc`, and `putc` must be used for text I/O only; functions `fread` and `fwrite` are applied exclusively to binary files. You should have the summary table in this chapter handy for reference when you are using these functions to help you keep straight the order of their arguments. The fact that `fprintf`, `fscanf`, and `getc` take the file pointer as their first argument while `putc`, `fread`, and `fwrite` take it as the last argument is definitely confusing at first.

If you are permitting the program user to enter the name of a file to process, you will have two variables identifying the file—one to hold its name (a character string) and one to hold the pointer for file access. It is essential to remember that the only file operation in which the file *name* is used is the call to `fopen`. Keep in mind that opening a file for output by calling `fopen` with a second argument of `"w"` or `"wb"` typically results in a loss of any existing file whose name matches the first argument.

It is easy to forget that binary files cannot be created, viewed, or modified using an editor or word processor program. Rather, they must be created and interpreted by a program that reads values into or writes values from variables of the same type as the binary file's elements.

CHAPTER REVIEW

In this chapter, we reviewed the use of C's standard input/output files and explored the manipulation of additional I/O streams. We created a backup of a text file, processed a land boundary survey, and searched a database represented as a binary file of records.

First we focused on text files, continuous streams of character codes that can be viewed as broken into lines by the newline character. We saw that processing text files requires the transfer of sequences of characters between main memory and disk storage. In order to be processed as numbers, character strings taken as input from a text file must be converted to a different format such as `int` or `double` for storage in memory. We studied how output of numeric values to a text file requires conversion of the internal formats back to a sequence of characters.

We also studied binary files that permit storage of information using the computer's internal data format. Such files cannot be created using a word processor and are not meaningful when printed. However, the fact that their representation of data matches the format used in main memory means that neither time nor accuracy is lost through conversion of values transferred between main and secondary storage.

New C Constructs

Table 12.3 summarizes the new constructs and functions introduced in this chapter.

Table 12.3   Statements Used in File Processing

Statement	Effect
Declarations	
`char name_txt_in[50],` `    name_bin_out[50];`	Declares two string variables whose names imply that they may be used to hold names of a text file to be used for input and of a binary output file.
`FILE *text_inp, *text_outp,` `    *bin_inp, *bin_outp;`	Declares four file pointer variables.
Calls to stdio Library	

`text_inp = fopen(name_txt_in, "r");`
`text_outp = fopen("result.txt", "w");`
`bin_inp = fopen("data.bin", "rb");`
`bin_outp = fopen(name_bin_out, "wb");`
	Opens `"data.bin"` and the file whose name is the value of `name_txt_in` as input files; opens `"results.txt"` and the file whose name is the value of `name_bin_out` as output files. Pointers accessing the open files are stored in file pointer variables `text_inp`, `text_outp`, `bin_inp`, and `bin_outp`.

`fscanf(text_inp, "%s%d%lf", animal,` `        &age, &weight);`	Copies string, `int`, and `double` values from the *text* input file accessed by file pointer `text_inp`, storing the values in variables `animal`, `age`, and `weight`.
`fprintf(text_outp, "(%.2f, %.2f)",` `        x, y);`	Writes to the *text* output file accessed by file pointer `text_outp` a set of parentheses enclosing the values of `x` and `y` rounded to two decimal places.
`nextch = getc(text_inp);`	Stores in `nextch` the next character available in the *text* input file accessed by file pointer `text_inp`, or the integer `EOF` value if no characters remain.

(continued)

Table 12.3 *(continued)*

Statement	Effect
Calls to stdio Library	
`putc(ch, text_outp);`	Copies the value of `ch` into the *text* output file accessed by file pointer `text_outp`.
`fread(&var, sizeof (double), 1, bin_inp);`	Copies into type `double` variable `var` the next value from the *binary* input file accessed by file pointer `bin_inp`.
`fwrite(&insect, sizeof (insect_t), 1, bin_outp);`	Copies the value of type `insect_t` variable `insect` into the *binary* output file accessed by file pointer `bin_outp`.
`fclose(text_outp);` `fclose(bin_inp);`	Closes text file accessed by file pointer `text_outp` after writing the `<eof>` character. Closes binary file accessed by `bin_inp` so it is no longer available as an input source.

QUICK-CHECK EXERCISES

1. A _____ file consists of a stream of character codes; a _____ file is a sequence of values of any type represented exactly as they would be in main memory.
2. For each of these library functions, indicate whether it is used in processing binary or text files.

   ```
   fread       putc
   fscanf      fwrite
   getc        fprintf
   ```

3. What file pointer name(s) does a C program associate with the keyboard? With the screen?
4. A word processor can be used to create or view a _____ file but not a _____ file.
5. Write a prototype for a function `fprintf_blob` that writes to a text output file the value of a structure of type `blob_t`. The function does *not* open the output file; the function assumes the file is already open.
6. Write a prototype for a function `fwrite_blob` that writes to a binary output file the value of a structure of type `blob_t`. The function does *not* open the output file; the function assumes the file is already open.

7. The _____ character separates a _____ file into lines, and the _____ character appears at the end of a file.

8. Can a file be used for both input and output by the same program?

9. Comment on the correctness of this statement: It is more efficient to use a text file because the computer knows that each component is a single character that can be copied into a single byte of main memory; with a binary file, however, the size of the components may vary.

10. Consider the following code segment, and then choose the correct "next" statement from the two options given. Indicate how you know which is the right choice. If you can't determine which is right, explain what additional information you would need in order to decide.

```
FILE *inp;
int    n;

inp = fopen("data.in", "r");
```

"next" option 1
```
    fread(&n, sizeof (int), 1, inp);
```

"next" option 2
```
    fscanf(inp, "%d", &n);
```

ANSWERS TO QUICK-CHECK EXERCISES

1. text, binary
2. `fread`: binary; `fscanf`: text; `getc`: text; `putc`: text; `fwrite`: binary; `fprintf`: text
3. keyboard: `stdin`; screen: `stdout, stderr`
4. text, binary
5. `void`
   `fprintf_blob(FILE *filep, blob_t blob)`
6. `void`
   `fwrite_blob(FILE *filep, blob_t blob)`
7. newline (or `'\n'`), text, eof
8. Yes, it can be opened in one mode, closed, and then reopened in another mode.
9. The statement is not correct. Because no data conversions are necessary when you use binary files, binary files are more efficient than text files.

10. The code segment shown could be followed by either statement. In order to choose one option, it would be necessary to know whether `data.in` was a text file or a binary file of integers. If one were certain that the code's author always used the mode `"rb"` when opening a binary file, then option 2 would be the expected next statement.

REVIEW QUESTIONS

1. Where are files stored?
2. How would you modify the program in Fig. 12.1 so the data would be sent to the screen as well as written to the backup file?
3. Consider a file `empstat.txt` that contains employee records. The data for each employee consist of the employee's name (up to 20 characters), social security number (up to 11 characters), gross pay for the week (double), taxes deducted (double), and the net pay (double) for the week. Each record is a separate text line in file `empstat.txt`. Write a program that will create a text file `report.txt` with the heading line

   ```
   NAME                SOC.SEC.NUM    GROSS    TAXES    NET
   ```

   followed by two blank lines and the pertinent information under each column heading. The program should also produce a binary file version of `empstat.txt` named `empstat.bin`.
4. What are the characteristics of a binary file?
5. Write a program that takes as input the file `empstat.bin` created in Review Question 3 and produces a binary file `ssngross.bin` containing only social security numbers and gross pay for each employee.
6. Explain what a file pointer is.
7. A sparse matrix is one in which a large number of the elements are zero. Write a `void` function `store_sparse` that writes to a binary file a compressed representation of a 50×50 sparse matrix of type `int`. The function's parameters are the file pointer and the matrix. The function will store only the nonzero matrix values, writing for each of these a record containing three components: row subscript, column subscript, and value.
8. How would the prototype of function `store_sparse` be different if its purpose were to write the sparse matrix representation to a text file (see Review Question 7)? Discuss the implications of your answer.

PROGRAMMING PROJECTS

1. Write a `void` function that will merge the contents of two text files containing chemical elements sorted by atomic number and will produce a sort-

ed file of binary records. The function's parameters will be three file pointers. Each text file line will contain an integer atomic number followed by the element name, chemical symbol, and atomic weight. Here are two sample lines:

```
11   Sodium      Na   22.99
20   Calcium     Ca   40.08
```

The function can assume that one file does not have two copies of the same element and that the binary output file should have this same property. *Hint:* When one of the input files is exhausted, do not forget to copy the remaining elements of the other input file to the result file.

2. Develop a database inquiry program to search a binary file of aircraft data sorted in descending order by maximum cruise speed. Each aircraft record should include the name (up to 25 characters), maximum cruise speed (in km/h), wing span and length (in m), the character M (for military) or C (for civilian), and a descriptive phrase (up to 80 characters). Your system should implement a menu-driven interface that allows the user to search on all components except the descriptive phrase. Here are three planes to start your database:

```
SR-71 Blackbird                    (name)
3500                               (max cruise speed)
16.95   32.74   M                  (wing span, length, military/civilian)
high-speed strategic reconnaissance

EF-111A Raven
2280
19.21   23.16   M
electronic warfare

Concorde
2140
25.61   62.2   C
supersonic airliner
```

3. Each year the state legislature rates the productivity of the faculty of each of the state-supported colleges and universities. The rating is based on reports submitted by the faculty members indicating the average number of hours worked per week during the school year. Each faculty member is rated, and the university receives an overall rating based on the average of the reports from its faculty.

The faculty productivity ratings are computed as follows:

a. "Highly productive" means reported hours per week are over 55.

b. "Satisfactory" means reported hours per week are between 35 and 55.

c. "Overpaid" means reported hours per week are less than 35.
Take the following data from a text file:

Name	Hours
Herm	63
Flo	37
Jake	20
Maureen	55
Saul	72
Tony	40
Al	12

Your program should include functions corresponding to the prototypes shown.

```
/*  Displays table heading  */
void
print_header(void)

/*  Displays name, hours, and productivity rating  */
void
print_productivity(faculty_t fac) /* input */

/*  Gets one faculty member's data from text file returns 1
 *  for successful input, 0 for error, EOF for end of file
 */
int
scan_faculty(FILE      *text_inp, /* input - file pointer
                                     to data file         */
             faculty_t *fac)      /* output - structure of
                                     faculty data         */
```

4. Write a program that takes words from a text file and prints each one on a separate line of an output file followed by the number of letters (alphabetic characters) in the word. Any leading or trailing punctuation marks should be removed from the word before it is printed. When all the text has been processed, display on the screen a count of the words in the file. Assume that words are groups of nonwhitespace characters separated by one or more whitespace characters.

5. Compute the monthly payment and the total payment for a bank loan. You are given
   a. the amount of the loan
   b. the duration of the loan in months
   c. the interest rate for the loan

Your program should take from a data file the information for one loan at a time, perform the required computation, and display on the screen the data and the values of the monthly payment and the total payment.

Create a text file with at least the following data:

Loan	Months	Rate
16000	300	12.50
24000	360	8.50
30000	300	11.50
42000	360	10.50
22000	240	09.75

Hint: The formula for computing monthly payment is

$$monthpay = \frac{ratem \times expm^{months} \times loan}{expm^{months} - 1.0}$$

where

$$ratem = \frac{rate}{1200.00}$$

$$expm = (1.0 + ratem)$$

6. Use your solution to Project 5 as the basis for writing a program that will write a text file containing a table of the following form:

Loan Amount: $1000.00

Interest Rate	Duration (years)	Monthly Payment	Total Payment
10.00	20	_____	_____
10.00	25	_____	_____
10.00	30	_____	_____
10.25	20	_____	_____

.
.
.

The output file produced by your program should contain payment information on a particular loan amount for interest rates from 10% to 14% with increments of 0.25%. The loan durations should be 20, 25, and 30 years.

7. Cooking recipes can be stored on a computer and, with the use of files, can be quickly referenced.
   a. Write a function that will create a text file of recipes from information entered at the terminal. The format of the data to be stored is
      1) recipe type (dessert, meat, etc.)
      2) subtype (for dessert, use cake, pie, or cookies)
      3) name (e.g., German chocolate)
      4) number of lines in the recipe to follow
      5) the actual recipe
      Item 3 should be on a separate line.
   b. Write a function that will accept as parameters a file and a structured record of search parameter bounds. The function should display all recipes satisfying the search parameters.

8. College football teams need a service to keep track of records and vital statistics. Write a program that will maintain this information in a binary file. An update file will be posted weekly against the master file of all team statistics to date, and all the records will be updated. All the information in both files will be stored in order by ID number. Each master record will contain the team's ID number; the team's name; the number of games won, lost, and tied; total yards gained by the team's offense; total yards gained by the other teams against this one; total points scored by this team; and total points scored by the other teams against this one.

   For this program, use the master file `teams.bin` and update the master using file `weekly.bin`. Write the updated records to a new binary file called `newteams.bin`. In addition, each record of the weekly file should be echoed to the screen. At the completion of file processing, display a message indicating the number of weekly scores processed, the team that scored the most points, and the team with the most offensive yardage for this week.

9. Write a program that takes a master file of college football information (such as `teams.bin` from Project 8) and prints out teams that match a specified set of search parameters. The bounds on the search parameters could be set using a menu like the one used in our database inquiry case study. Some information you might want to print include all teams with a certain range of points scored or scored upon; all teams with a certain range of yardage gained or given up; all teams with a certain number of games won, tied, or lost.

CHAPTER 13

PROGRAMMING IN THE LARGE

13.1
Using Abstraction to Manage Complexity

13.2
Personal Libraries: Header Files

13.3
Personal Libraries: Implementation Files

13.4
Defining Macros with Parameters

13.5
Storage Classes

13.6
Modifying Functions for Inclusion in a Library
Case Study: Developing an Image
Enhancement Library

13.7
Conditional Compilation

13.8
Arguments to Function main

13.9
Common Programming Errors
Chapter Review

In this chapter, we examine the special difficulties associated with the development of large software systems. We explore how separating our expression of *what* we need to do from *how* we actually plan to accomplish it reduces the complexity of system development and maintenance (upkeep). This chapter introduces C's facilities for formalizing this separation of concerns.

We study how to define flexible macros that help to make a program more readable as well as easier to maintain. This chapter describes the storage classes of variables and functions we have been using along with some additional storage classes that may be useful in large program development. We also investigate how to build a library of reusable code from functions developed for specific contexts. We meet additional preprocessor directives that allow us to format libraries so they are easy to include in any combination.

13.1 USING ABSTRACTION TO MANAGE COMPLEXITY

Up to this point in your study of programming, you have been primarily concerned with writing relatively short programs that solve individual problems but otherwise have little general use. In this chapter, we focus on the design and maintenance of large-scale programs. We discuss how to modularize a large project so that individual pieces can be implemented by different programmers at different times. We also see how to write software modules in ways that simplify their reuse in other projects.

Procedural Abstraction

When a team of programmers is assigned the task of developing a large software system, they must have a rational approach to breaking down the overall problem into solvable chunks. Abstraction is a powerful technique that helps problem solvers deal with complex issues in a piecemeal fashion. The dictionary defines *abstraction* as the process of separating the inherent qualities or properties of something from the actual physical object to which they belong. One example of the use of abstraction is the representation of a program variable (for example, `velocity`) by a storage location in memory. We don't have to know anything about the physical structure of memory in order to use such a variable in programming.

In this text, we have applied aspects of two types of abstraction to program development. First, we practiced *procedural abstraction*, which is the philosophy that function development should separate the concern of *what* is to be achieved by a function from the details of *how* it is to be achieved. In other words, you can specify what you expect a function to do and then use that function in the design of a problem solution before you know how to implement the function.

For example, in Chapter 12, when we tackled our database inquiry problem, our initial algorithm was one that could lead directly to an outline of a program fragment that identifies three functions representing the major steps of a solution. The following outline defers the details of parameter lists and use of function values until after data flow information is added to the structure chart.

Initial Algorithm	**Program Outline**
1. Open inventory file.	`fopen(...)`
2. Get the search parameters.	`get_params(...)`
3. Display all products that satisfy the search parameters.	`display_match(...)`

In this example of procedural abstraction, we see that *what* one of the functions must accomplish (i.e., open a file) corresponds to the purpose of a library function we have studied. Reuse of this existing function means that we *never* have to concern ourselves with the details of *how* this task is accomplished. Clearly, the availability of powerful libraries of functions is of significant benefit in reducing the complexity of large systems. As we have already seen, the use of such libraries is a fundamental feature of the C programming language.

In the example shown, the other two functions identified in this first level of procedural abstraction are excellent candidates for assignment to separate members of a program development team. Once the purpose, preconditions, and parameter lists of each function are spelled out, neither developer will have any need to be concerned about the details of *how* the other member carries out the assigned task.

Data Abstraction

Data abstraction is another powerful tool we have seen for breaking down a large problem into manageable chunks. When we apply data abstraction to a complex problem, we initially specify the data objects involved and the operations to be performed on these data objects without being overly concerned with how the data objects will be represented and stored in memory. We can describe *what* information is stored in the data object without being specific as to *how* the information is organized and represented. This is the *logical view* of the data object as opposed to its *physical view*, the actual internal representation in memory. Once we understand the logical view, we can use the data object and its operators in our programs; however, we (or someone else) will eventually need to implement the data object and its operators before we can run any program that uses them.

One simple example of data abstraction is our use of the C data type `double`, which is an abstraction for the set of real numbers. The computer hardware limits the range of real numbers that can be represented, and not all real numbers within the specified range can be represented. Different computers use a variety of representation schemes for type `double`. However, we can generally use the data type `double` and its associated operators (+, −, *, /, =, ==, <, and so on) without being concerned with these details of its implementation. Another example of data abstraction is the definition of a data type and associated operators for complex numbers given in Chapter 11.

Information Hiding

One advantage of procedural abstraction and data abstraction is that they enable the designer to make implementation decisions in a piecemeal fashion. The designer can postpone making decisions regarding the actual internal representation of the data objects and the implementation of its operators. At the top levels of the design, the designer focuses on how to use a data object and its operators; at the lower levels of design, the designer works out the implementation details. In this way, the designer can methodically nibble at a large problem, controlling and reducing its overall complexity.

If the details of a data object's implementation are not known when a higher-level module is implemented, the higher-level module can access the data object only through its operators. This limitation is actually an advantage: It allows the designer to change his or her mind at a later date and possibly to choose a more efficient method of internal representation or implementation. If the higher-level modules reference a data object only through its operators, a change in the data object's representation will require no change in a higher-level module. The process of "hiding" the implementation details of a lower-level module from a higher-level module is called *information hiding*.

Reusable Code

One of the keys to productivity in software development is the writing of *reusable code*, code that can be reused in many different applications, preferably without having to be modified or recompiled. One way to facilitate reuse in C is to *encapsulate* a data object together with its operators in a personal library. Then we can use the `#include` preprocessor directive to give functions in a file access to this library.

Encapsulation is a powerful concept in everyday life that can be applied very profitably to software design. For example, one encapsulated object that we are all familiar with is an aspirin. Our familiarity is based strictly on *what* the object does (relieves pain and reduces fever) when activated through the standard interface (swallowing). Only its producers and prescribers care *how* an aspirin does what it does (the effect of acetylsalicylic acid on inflammation and blood flow to the skin surface). By applying the principles of procedural and data abstraction, we can package the "bitter" details of a complex problem's solution in equally neat, easy-to-use capsules.

EXERCISES FOR SECTION 13.1	Self-Check

1. Describe how each of the following encapsulated objects allows the user to focus on *what* the object does with little or no concern for *how* it does it.

       microwave oven   television set   calculator

2. Which of the following diagram types is used to model procedural abstraction?

       flowchart   structure chart

13.2 PERSONAL LIBRARIES: HEADER FILES

We have seen how the availability of C's standard libraries simplifies program development. However, the standard libraries are not extensive enough to handle every programming need. Often we write a function that would be useful in a context other than the one for which it was originally written. For example, after we developed our protected string functions `strassign`, `substr`, and `concat` in Chapter 9, we frequently used them in later programs. Copying the code of these functions into other programs to allow reuse is possible but cumbersome, especially when compared to the way we get access to standard libraries. In fact, one can use the C preprocessor directive `#include` to make available personal libraries as well. Since C permits source code files to be compiled separately and then linked prior to loading and execution, we can provide our personal libraries as object files; programs using our personal libraries need not first compile the functions in them. If we take another look at a diagram first presented in Chapter 1 and now repeated in Fig. 13.1, we are in a better position to understand the bubble that is marked with a colored arrow. Until now, the "other object files" that have been linked to our code have been the standard C libraries. When we learn to make our own library files, these files can also be provided to the linker as part of preparing our program for execution.

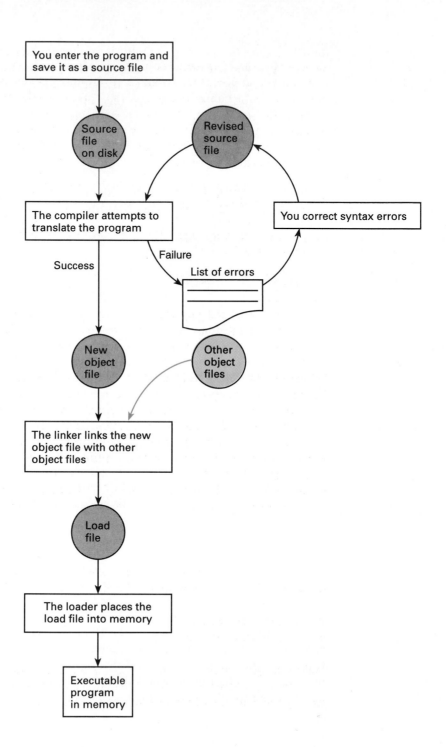

Figure 13.1
Preparing a
Program for
Execution

Header Files

In order to create a personal library, we must first make a *header file*. A header file is a text file containing all the information about a library needed by the compiler when compiling a program that uses the facilities defined in the library. Precisely this type of data is found in system header files such as `stdio.h`, `math.h`, and `string.h`. The form we recommend for a header file also provides all the information that a user of the library needs. Typical contents of a header file include

1. a block comment summarizing the library's purpose
2. `#define` directives naming constant macros
3. type definitions
4. block comments stating the purpose of each library function and declarations of the form

> extern *prototype*;

The use of the keyword `extern` in a function declaration notifies the compiler that the function's definition will be provided to the linker. Figures 13.2 and 13.3 show header files for libraries we might want to create using functions developed in earlier chapters. Figure 13.2 shows the contents of a header file for our protected string functions from Chapter 9, and Fig. 13.3 is a header file for our planet data type and operators from Chapter 11. In Fig. 13.4, we see the beginning of a source file that has need of facilities from these two libraries. We are assuming here that the header files are named `mystring.h` and `planet.h`, and that they are located in the directory in which the preprocessor first looks for files whose names appear in quotation marks after a `#include`. This issue is system dependent, but, in many cases, the directory first searched would be the one in which the current source file resides.

In our programming so far, we have used angular brackets (<>), as in

```
#include <stdio.h>
```

to indicate to the preprocessor that a header file is to be found in a system directory. Quotes around the header file name, as in

```
#include "mystring.h"
#include "planet.h"
```

mark it as information about a library belonging to the programmer.

When revising a source file, the C preprocessor replaces each `#include` line by the contents of the header file it references.

Figure 13.2   Header File mystring.h for Personal Library of Protected String Functions

```
/*
 *   mystring.h - header file
 *
 *   Library of protected string functions:  functions perform their
 *   operations without overflowing the target string variable; they also
 *   have no restrictions on overlap of string input arguments.
 *           strassign - string assignment
 *           substr    - substring extraction
 *           concat    - concatenation of two strings
 *           scanline  - input of one line of text
 */
#define MYSTRING_MAX_LEN 100

/*
 *   Copies into dest the string value of src, or as much as will fit given
 *   that dest has room for only dest_len characters, including \0.  Extra
 *   characters are truncated.
 */
extern char *
strassign(char        dest[],    /* output - destination string      */
          const char src[],      /* input  - source string           */
          int        dest_len);  /* input  - space available in dest  */

/*
 *   Extracts a substring from src and returns it in dest, truncating if
 *   the substring contains dest_len or more characters.  The substring
 *   extracted starts with src[st] and contains characters up to but not
 *   including src[end] unless src[end - 1] is beyond the end of src, in
 *   which case the substring returned is src[st] to the end of src.  The
 *   empty string is returned if st > end or if st >= strlen(src)
 */
extern char *
substr(char        dest[],    /* output - destination string          */
       const char src[],      /* input  - source string               */
       int        st,         /* input  - subscript of first character of
                                          src to include               */
       int        end,        /* input  - subscript of character following
                                          last character included      */
       int        dest_len);  /* input  - space available in dest      */
```

(continued)

Figure 13.2   *(continued)*

```
/*
 * Concatenates str1 and str2, copying as much of the result as will fit
 * into dest, which has space available for dest_len characters
 * Pre:  dest_len <= MYSTRING_MAX_LEN for correct results
 */
extern char *
concat(char        dest[],    /* output - destination string        */
       const char str1[],     /* input  - strings                   */
       const char str2[],     /*           to concatenate           */
       int         dest_len); /* input  - available space in dest   */


/*
 * Gets one line of data from standard input.  Returns an empty string on
 * end of file.
 */
extern char *
scanline(char dest[],         /* output - destination string        */
         int  dest_len);      /* input  - space available in dest   */
```

In Chapter 3 and Chapter 6 when we first met user-defined functions, we emphasized the importance of the block comment placed at the beginning of the function and the importance of the function prototype and the comments on its parameters. When taken together, this prototype and its associated commentary provide all the information needed by a programmer desiring to call the function: what the function does, what type of value it returns (if any), and what types of arguments it operates on. Notice that this is precisely the information placed in the header file.

Figure 13.3   Header File planet.h for Personal Library with Data Type and Associated Functions

```
/*  planet.h
 *
 *  abstract data type planet
 *
 *  Type planet_t has these components:
 *      name, diameter, dist_sun, orbital_prd, axial_rot_prd
```

(continued)

Figure 13.3   *(continued)*

```
 *
 *  Operators:
 *      print_planet, planet_equal, scan_planet
 */

#define PLANET_STRSIZ  10

typedef struct planet_s { /* planet structure */
      char name[PLANET_STRSIZ];
      double diameter,       /* equatorial diameter in km            */
             dist_sun,       /* average distance from sun in km      */
             orbital_prd,    /* years to orbit sun once              */
             axial_rot_prd;  /* hours to complete one revolution on
                                          axis                       */
} planet_t;

/*
 *  Prints with labels all components of a planet_t structure
 */
extern void
print_planet(planet_t pl);  /* input - one planet structure         */

/*
 *  Determines whether or not the components of planet_1 and planet_2
 *  match
 */
extern int
planet_equal(planet_t planet_1,  /* input - planets to              */
             planet_t planet_2); /*          compare                */

/*
 *  Fills a type planet_t structure with input data.  Integer returned as
 *  function result is success/failure/EOF indicator.
 *      1 => successful input of planet
 *      0 => error encountered
 *      EOF => insufficient data before end of file
 *  In case of error or EOF, value of type planet_t output argument is
 *  undefined.
 */
extern int
scan_planet(planet_t *plnp); /* output - address of planet_t structure to
                                          fill                       */
```

Figure 13.4   Portion of Program That Uses Functions from Personal Libraries

```
/*
 * Beginning of source file in which personal libraries and
 * system I/O library are used.
 */

#include <stdio.h>        /* system's standard I/O functions */

#include "mystring.h"  /* personal string library            */
#include "planet.h"    /* personal library with planet_t
                          data type and operators            */
. . .
```

An important aspect of dividing any problem into manageable chunks is defining the points at which the chunks of the solution come together to form the complete solution. The common boundary between two separate parts of a solution is called the *interface*. The header file's purpose is to define the interface between a library and any program that uses the library.

Cautionary Notes for Header File Design

You will notice that in both of our header file examples, the constant macros defined (MYSTRING_MAX_LEN and PLANET_STRSIZ) have long names that begin with the library name. This naming strategy reduces the likelihood that the name associated with a constant in the header file will conflict with other constant macro names in the program.

In Section 13.3, we will see how to create an implementation file for a personal library. The header (interface) file and the implementation file are the two essential source files in a personal library.

EXERCISES FOR SECTION 13.2

Self-Check

1. How can the C preprocessor determine if a header file name in an #include statement is the name of a system library or of a personal library?
2. A function's _____ and associated _____ are the collection of information that a programmer must know about the function in order to be able to use it.
3. A header (interface) file describes _____ the functions of a library do, not _____ they do it.

Programming

1. Look at the table of math library functions in Chapter 3 (Table 3.1). Define a header file `myops.h` that contains a full description of the interfaces of functions `fabs`, `sqrt`, and `pow`. Then add to this file information about the `factorial` function (see Chapter 6). Would anything about your interface information for `factorial` require your implementation of the function to be iterative? Would anything require the implementation to be recursive?

13.3 PERSONAL LIBRARIES: IMPLEMENTATION FILES

In Section 13.2, we saw how to create a library header file containing all the interface information needed by a program and programmer using the library. We created two header files and studied a program that uses the `#include` directive in order to make these headers a part of the program's code. In this section, we investigate how to create a library implementation file. The header file describes *what* the functions of the library do; the implementation file will show *how* the functions do it.

A library's implementation file must contain both the code of all the library functions and any other information needed for compilation of these functions. The elements of an implementation file are the same as the elements of any program and have many similarities with the elements of the library's header file. These elements are

1. a block comment summarizing the library's purpose
2. `#include` directives for this library's header file and for other libraries used by the functions in this library
3. `#define` directives naming constant macros used only inside this library
4. type definitions used only inside this library
5. function definitions including the usual comments

It may seem odd that we `#include` the header file for the library we are implementing since the prototypes found in it are redundant. We do this to make maintenance and modification of the library more straightforward. Alternatively, we could simply restate the constant macro and type definitions from the header file in the implementation file. However, then a modification of one of these definitions would require changes in *two* files. Using the header file `#include` as shown, we would simply modify the header file; when the implementation file is recompiled, the change will be taken into account. Figures 13.5 and 13.6 show implementation files that might be associated with the header files `mystring.h` and `planet.h`.

Figure 13.5 Implementation File mystring.c Containing Library of Protected String Functions

```
/*
 *  mystring.c - implementation file
 *
 *  Library of protected string functions:  functions perform their
 *  operations without overflowing the target string variable; they also
 *  have no restrictions on overlap of string input arguments.
 *          strassign - string assignment
 *          substr    - substring extraction
 *          concat    - concatenation of two strings
 *          scanline  - input of one line of text
 */

#include <stdio.h>
#include <string.h>
#include "mystring.h"

/*
 *  Copies into dest the string value of src, or as much as will fit
 *  given that dest has room for only dest_len characters, including \0.
 *  Extra characters are truncated.
 */
char *
strassign(char       dest[],     /* output - destination string     */
          const char src[],      /* input  - source string          */
          int        dest_len)   /* input  - space available in dest */
{
      int new_len,  /* number of characters to copy into dest        */
          i;

      if (strlen(src) < dest_len)
            new_len = strlen(src);
      else
            new_len = dest_len - 1;

      /*  Copy new_len chars from src to dest using function that gives
          correct results even if src and dest overlap                */
      memmove(dest, src, new_len);

      /*  Add null character at end of string                         */
      dest[new_len] = '\0';
```

(continued)

Figure 13.5 *(continued)*

```
        return (dest);
}

/*
 *  Extracts a substring from src and returns it in dest, truncating if
 *  the substring contains dest_len or more characters.  The substring
 *  extracted starts with src[st] and contains characters up to but not
 *  including src[end] unless src[end - 1] is beyond the end of src, in
 *  which case the substring returned is src[st] to the end of src.  The
 *  empty string is returned if st > end or if st >= strlen(src)
 */
char *
substr(char        dest[],   /* output - destination string            */
       const char src[],    /* input  - source string                 */
       int        st,        /* input  - subscript of first character of
                                         src to include                 */
       int        end,       /* input  - subscript of character following
                                         last character included        */
       int        dest_len)/* input  - space available in dest         */

{
    int sub_len;  /* length of substring returned                      */

    /*  Adjust st and end if they are beyond the ends of src           */
    if (end > strlen(src))
         end = strlen(src);
    if (st < 0)
         st = 0;
    if (st > end) { /* if starting point is past ending point          */
         dest[0] = '\0';
    } else {
         sub_len = end - st;
         if (sub_len >= dest_len)
              sub_len = dest_len - 1;
         memmove(dest, &src[st], sub_len);
         dest[sub_len] = '\0';
    }

    return (dest);
}
```

(continued)

Figure 13.5 *(continued)*

```
/*
 *  Concatenates str1 and str2, copying as much of the result as will fit
 *  into dest, which has space available for dest_len characters
 *  Pre:  dest_len <= MYSTRING_MAX_LEN for correct results
 */
char *
concat(char         dest[],     /* output - destination string             */
       const char str1[],       /* input  - strings                        */
       const char str2[],       /*           to concatenate                */
       int          dest_len)   /* input  - available space in dest        */
{
    char result[MYSTRING_MAX_LEN]; /* local string space for result  */

    /*  Check if result will be wrong due to lack of local space       */
    if (dest_len > MYSTRING_MAX_LEN  &&
        strlen(str1) + strlen(str2) >= MYSTRING_MAX_LEN)
          printf("\nInsufficient local storage causing loss of data\n");

    /*  Build result in local storage to properly handle overlap
        of dest and str1 or str2                                        */
    strassign(result, str1, MYSTRING_MAX_LEN);
    strncat(result, str2, MYSTRING_MAX_LEN - strlen(result) - 1);
    strassign(dest, result, dest_len);

    return (dest);
}

/*
 *  Gets one line of data from standard input.  Returns an empty string on
 *  end of file.
 */
char *
scanline(char dest[],        /* output - destination string             */
         int  dest_len)      /* input  - space available in dest        */
{
    /* Use library function fgets to get the next input line.  If
       fgets returns 0, signal end of file by returning an empty
       string.                                                         */
    if (fgets(dest, dest_len, stdin) == 0)
        dest[0] = '\0';
```

(continued)

Figure 13.5 *(continued)*

```
      /* Remove newline character if it is present                    */
      else if (dest[strlen(dest) - 1] == '\n')
            dest[strlen(dest) - 1] = '\0';

      return (dest);
}
```

Figure 13.6   Implementation File planet.c Containing Library with Planet Data Type and Operators

```
/*
 *
 *      planet.c
 */
#include <stdio.h>
#include <string.h>
#include "planet.h"
/*
 *  Prints with labels all components of a planet_t structure
 */
void
print_planet(planet_t pl)  /* input - one planet structure */
{
      printf("%s\n", pl.name);
      printf("  Equatorial diameter: %.0f km\n", pl.diameter);
      printf("  Average distance from the sun: %.4e km\n", pl.dist_sun);
      printf("  Time to complete one orbit of the sun: %.2f years\n",
            pl.orbital_prd);
      printf("  Time to complete one rotation on axis: %.4f hours\n",
            pl.axial_rot_prd);
}

/*
 *  Determines whether or not the components of planet_1 and planet_2 match
 */
```

(continued)

Figure 13.6   *(continued)*

```c
int
planet_equal(planet_t planet_1,  /* input - planets to                        */
             planet_t planet_2)  /*          compare                          */
{
      return (strcmp(planet_1.name, planet_2.name) == 0    &&
              planet_1.diameter == planet_2.diameter       &&
              planet_1.dist_sun == planet_2.dist_sun       &&
              planet_1.orbital_prd == planet_2.orbital_prd &&
              planet_1.axial_rot_prd == planet_2.axial_rot_prd);
}


/*
 *  Fills a type planet_t structure with input data.  Integer returned as
 *  function result is success/failure/EOF indicator.
 *      1 => successful input of planet
 *      0 => error encountered
 *      EOF => insufficient data before end of file
 *  In case of error or EOF, value of type planet_t output argument is
 *  undefined.
 */
int
scan_planet(planet_t *plnp) /* output - address of planet_t structure to
                                        fill                                   */
{
      int result;

      result = scanf("%s%lf%lf%lf%lf", (*plnp).name,
                                       &(*plnp).diameter,
                                       &(*plnp).dist_sun,
                                       &(*plnp).orbital_prd,
                                       &(*plnp).axial_rot_prd);
      if (result == 5)
            result = 1;
      else if (result != EOF)
            result = 0;

      return (result);
}
```

Using a Personal Library

To use a personal library, one must complete these steps:

Creation

C1 Create a header file containing the interface information for a program needing the library.

C2 Create an implementation file containing the code of the library functions and other details of the implementation that are hidden from the user program.

C3 Compile the implementation file. This step must be repeated any time either the header file or the implementation file is revised.

Use

U1 Include the library's header file in the user program through an `#include` directive.

U2 After compiling the user program, include both its object file and the object file created in C3 in the command that activates the linker.

EXERCISES FOR SECTION 13.3

Self-Check

1. Why are constant macros `PLANET_STRSIZ` and `MYSTRING_MAX_LEN` defined in the header files for libraries planet and mystring rather than having their definitions hidden in the implementation files?
2. If you see the following `#include` directives in a program, what do you assume about libraries red and blue?

   ```
   #include <red.h>
   #include "blue.h"
   ```

Programming

1. Create a library named complex that defines the complex arithmetic operators from Section 11.4.

13.4 DEFINING MACROS WITH PARAMETERS

We have consistently used the `#define` preprocessor directive we met in Chapter 2 for associating symbolic names with constant values. In Chapter 2, we discussed the fact that C's preprocessor actually revises the text of the source code, replacing each occurrence of a defined name by its meaning before turning the code over to the compiler. In this section we study how to define macros that have formal parameters. The form of such a macro definition is

#define *macro_name* (*parameter list*) *macro body*

Like functions, macros allow us to give a name to a commonly used statement or operation. Because macros are handled through textual substitution, however, macro calls execute without the overhead of space allocation and deallocation on the stack that is associated with functions. Of course, since the macro's meaning appears in the program at every call, the object file produced by the compiler typically requires more memory than the same program would require if it used a function rather than a macro.

Figure 13.7 shows a brief program that uses a macro named LABEL_PRINT_INT to print the value of an integer variable or expression with a label (a string). Notice that in the directive that defines LABEL_PRINT_INT, there is no space between the macro name and the left parenthesis of the parameter list. This detail is critical, for if there were a space, the preprocessor would misinterpret the macro definition.

Figure 13.7   Program Using a Macro with Formal Parameters

```
/*  Shows the definition and use of a macro                        */

#include <stdio.h>

#define LABEL_PRINT_INT(label, num) printf("%s = %d", (label), (num))

int
main(void)
{
      int r = 5, t = 12;

      LABEL_PRINT_INT("rabbit", r);
      printf("        ");
      LABEL_PRINT_INT("tiger", t + 2);
      printf("\n");

      return(0);
}
rabbit = 5      tiger = 14
```

Figure 13.8 Macro Expansion of Second Macro Call of Program in Fig. 13.7

```
LABEL_PRINT_INT("tiger", t + 2)
                  ↓         ↓
LABEL_PRINT_INT(label, num)
```
parameter matching →

```
                              "tiger"   t + 2
                                 ↓         ↓
          printf("%s = %d", (label), (num))
```
parameter replacement in body →

```
                    printf("%s = %d", ("tiger"), (t + 2))
```
result of macro expansion

The process of replacing a macro call like

```
LABEL_PRINT_INT("rabbit", r)
```

by its meaning,

```
printf("%s = %d", ("rabbit"), (r))
```

is called *macro expansion*. When doing this replacement, the C preprocessor matches each macro parameter name with the corresponding actual argument. Then, in a copy of the macro body, every occurrence of a formal parameter name is replaced by the actual argument. This modified macro body takes the place of the macro call in the text of the program. Figure 13.8 diagrams the process of macro expansion of the last macro call in our sample program. Notice that only the macro name and its argument list are involved in the macro expansion process. The semicolon at the end of the macro call line is unaffected. It would be a mistake to include a semicolon at the end of the `printf` call in the macro body. If a semicolon were placed there, the statements resulting from macro expansion of our two macro calls would both end in *two* semicolons.

Use of Parentheses in Macro Body

You will notice that in the body of `LABEL_PRINT_INT`, each occurrence of a formal parameter of the macro is enclosed in parentheses. The use of adequate parentheses in a macro's body is essential for correct evaluation. In Fig. 13.9, we see a program fragment that uses a macro to compute n^2. We show two versions of the macro definition and the different program outputs that result.

Figure 13.9   Macro Calls Showing Importance of Parentheses in Macro Body

Version 1   Version 2

```
#define SQUARE(n)  n * n        #define SQUARE(n)  ((n) * (n))

                    . . .
                    double x = 0.5, y = 2.0;
                    int    n = 4, m = 12;

                    printf("(%.2f + %.2f)squared = %.2f\n\n",
                           x, y, SQUARE(x + y));

                    printf("%d squared divided by\n", m);
                    printf("%d squared is %d\n", n,
                           SQUARE(m) / SQUARE(n));
```

```
(0.5 + 2.0)squared = 3.5      (0.5 + 2.0)squared = 6.25

12 squared divided by         12 squared divided by
4 squared is 152              4 squared is 9
```

Figure 13.10   Macro Expansions of Macro Calls from Fig. 13.9

Version 1   Version 2

```
SQUARE(x + y)                 SQUARE(x + y)
   becomes                       becomes
x + y * x + y                 ((x + y) * (x + y))
```

Problem: multiplication done
*   before addition.*

```
SQUARE(m) / SQUARE(n)         SQUARE(m) / SQUARE(n)
   becomes                       becomes
m * m / n * n                 ((m) * (m)) / ((n) * (n))
```

Problem: multiplication and
*   division are of equal precedence;*
*   they are performed left to right.*

Let's look at the different macro expansions that occur in Version 1 and Version 2. Examination of Fig. 13.10 reveals that the incorrect results of Version 1 are a simple consequence of the operator precedence rules.

To avoid the problems illustrated in Figs. 13.9 and 13.10, use parentheses liberally in macro bodies. Specifically, parenthesize each occurrence of a parameter in the macro body, and enclose the entire body in parentheses if it produces a result value. For instance, here is a macro for finding one real root of a quadratic equation:

```
#define ROOT1(a,b,c) ((-(b)+sqrt((b)*(b)-4*(a)*(c)))/(2*(a)))
```

The black parentheses are those normally required for proper evaluation of the expression. The parentheses in color are added in accordance with our guidelines for parenthesizing a macro definition.

One should avoid using operators with side effects in expressions passed as arguments in a macro call, since these expressions may be evaluated multiple times. For example, the statement

```
r = ROOT1(++n1, n2, n3);  /* error: applying ++ in a macro
                                argument */
```

would be expanded as

```
r = ((-(n2)+sqrt((n2)*(n2)-4*(++n1)*(n3)))/(2*(++n1)));
```

resulting in a statement that violates the principle that the object of an operator with a side effect should not be reused in the expression.

We urge you to use parentheses routinely in macro bodies as described earlier, even if you cannot conceive of any circumstance when a given set of parentheses could matter. One needs only to work with macros a short time to realize how limited is this ability of a programmer to foresee *all* possible situations!

We also encourage you to use all capital letters in your macro names. Remembering that you are calling a macro rather than a function is critical in helping you avoid the use of operators with side effects in your actual arguments.

Extending a Macro Over Two or More Lines

The preprocessor assumes that a macro definition fits on a single line unless the program indicates otherwise. To extend a macro over multiple lines, all but the last line of the definition must end with the backslash character \. For example, here is a macro that implements the header of a `for` statement to count from the value of `st` up to, but not including, the value of `end`:

```
#define INDEXED_FOR(ct, st, end)  \
        for  ((ct) = (st);   (ct) < (end);   ++(ct))
```

The following code fragment uses INDEXED_FOR to print the first X_MAX elements of array x.

```
INDEXED_FOR(i, 0, X_MAX)
        printf("x[%2d] = %6.2f\n", i, x[i]);
```

After macro expansion, the statement will be

```
for  ((i) = (0);   (i) < (X_MAX);   ++(i))
        printf("x[%2d] = %6.2f\n", i, x[i]);
```

**EXERCISES FOR
SECTION 13.4**

Self-Check

Given these macro definitions, write the macro expansion of each statement which follows. If the expansion seems not to be what the macro definer intended (you may assume the macro names are meaningful), indicate how you would correct the macro definition.

```
#define DOUBLE(x)  (x) + (x)
#define DISCRIMINANT (a,b,c)  ((b) * (b) - 4 * (a) * (c))
#define PRINT_PRODUCT(x, y)\
        printf("%.2f X %.2f = %.2f\n", (x), (y), (x) * (y));
```

```
1. y = DOUBLE(a - b);
2. y = y - DOUBLE(p);
3. if (DISCRIMINANT(a1, b1, c1) == 0)
        r1 = -b1 / (2 * a1);
4. PRINT_PRODUCT(a + b, a - b);
```

Programming

1. Define a macro named F_OF_X that would evaluate the following polynomial for the x value passed as its argument. You may assume that the math library has been included.

$$x^5 - 3x^3 + 4$$

2. Define a macro to print its argument preceded by a dollar sign and with two decimal places.

13.5 STORAGE CLASSES

C has five storage classes; so far we have seen three. Formal parameters and local variables of functions are variables that are *auto*matically allocated on the stack when a function is called and *auto*matically deallocated when the function returns; they are of storage class `auto`. In Chapter 6, we studied that the *scope* of these names, i.e., the program region in which the name is visible, extends from the point of declaration to the end of the function in which the declaration appears.

The names of the functions themselves are of storage class `extern`, meaning that they will be available to the linker. These functions may be called by any other function in a program, provided that necessary precautions are taken. From a function's definition to the end of the source file in which the definition appears, the scope rules we studied in Chapter 6 make the function directly visible. If there is a need to reference a function from a spot in its source file that precedes the function's definition or from anywhere in a different source file, the compiler must be assured that the linker will know where to find the function. The compiler also needs to know the following vital information about the function in order to translate a call to it: its return type, how many arguments it takes, and the data types of the arguments. Providing this information is the purpose of the

`extern` *prototype*`;`

statement of which we have seen numerous examples in library header files. This statement *does not create* a function of storage class `extern`; it merely *notifies* the compiler that such a function exists and that the linker will know where to find it. Figure 13.11 shows the two storage classes, `auto` and `extern`. Names in color are of storage class `auto`; those in boldface black are of storage class `extern`.

Figure 13.11 Storage Classes auto and extern as Previously Seen

```
void
fun_one(int arg_one, int arg_two)
 {
      int one_local;
      . . .
 }
```

(continued)

Figure 13.11 *(continued)*

```
int
fun_two (int a2_one, int a2_two)
{
     int local_var;
     . . .
}


int
main (void)
{
     int num;
     . . .
}
```

The shaded area of Fig. 13.11 marks the program's *top level*. Class `extern` is the default storage class for all names declared at this level.

Global Variables

We have seen only declarations of functions at the top level of a program. However, it is also possible (though usually inadvisable) to declare variables at the top level. The scope of such a variable name, like the scope of a function name, extends from the point of declaration to the end of the source file, except in functions where the same name is declared as a formal parameter or local variable. If we need to reference a top-level variable in the region of its source file that precedes its declaration or in another source file, the compiler can be alerted to the variable's existence by placing a declaration of the variable that begins with the keyword `extern` in the file prior to the first reference. Such a variable can be made accessible to *all* functions in a program and is, therefore, sometimes called a *global* variable. Figure 13.12 shows the declaration at the top level of `int` variable `global_var_x` of storage class `extern` in file `eg1.c` and an `extern` statement in `eg2.c` that makes the global variable accessible throughout this file as well. Only the *defining declaration*, the one in `eg1.c`, allocates space for `global_var_x`. A declaration beginning with the keyword `extern` allocates no memory; it simply provides information for the compiler.

Although there are applications in which global variables are unavoidable, such unrestricted access to a variable is generally regarded as detrimental to a program's readability and maintainability. Global access conflicts with the

**Figure 13.12
Declaration of a
Global Variable**

```
/* eg1.c */

int global_var_x;

void
afun(int n)
  . . .
```

```
/* eg2.c */

extern int global_var_x;

int
bfun(int p)
  . . .
```

"information-hiding" principle that data should be provided to functions on a need-to-know basis only, and then strictly through the documented interface as represented by the function prototype. However, one context in which a global variable can be used without reducing program readability is when the global represents a constant. We have been using globally visible macro constants throughout this text, and they have been a help, not a hindrance, in clarifying the meaning of a program. In Fig. 13.13, we see two global names that represent constant data structures. Because we plan to initialize these memory blocks

**Figure 13.13
Use of Variables
of Storage Class
extern**

```
/* fileone.c */

typedef struct complex_s{
        double real,
                    imag;
} complex_t;

/* Defining declarations of
   global structured constant
   complex_zero and of global
   constant array of month
   names */
const complex_t complex_zero
      = {0, 0};
const char *months[12] =
      {"January", "February",
       "March", "April", "May",
       "June", "July", "August",
       "September", "October",
       "November", "December"};

int
f1_fun1(int n)
{ . . . }

double
f1_fun2(double x)
{ . . . }

char
f1_fun3(char c1, char c2)
{  double months; . . . }
```

```
/* filetwo.c */

/* #define's and typedefs
   including  complex_t */


void
f2_fun1(int x)
{ . . . }

/* Compiler-notifying
   declarations -- no
   storage allocated */
extern const complex_t
      complex_zero;
extern const char
      *months[12];

void
f2_fun2(void)
{ . . . }

int
f2_fun3(int n)
{ . . . }
```

Table 13.1 Functions in Fig. 13.13 with Global Variable Access and Reasons

Function(s)	Can Access Variables of Class extern	Reason
f1_fun1 and f1_fun2	complex_zero and months	Their definitions follow in the same source file the top-level defining declarations of complex_zero and months. The functions have no parameters or local variables by these names.
f1_fun3	complex_zero only	Its definition follows in the same source file the top-level defining declaration of complex_zero, and it has no parameter or local variable by this name.
f2_fun1	none	Its definition precedes the declarations that notify the compiler of the existence of complex_zero and months.
f2_fun2 and f2_fun3	complex_zero and months	Their definitions follow in the same source file the declarations containing keyword extern that notify the compiler of the existence of global names complex_zero and months. The functions have no parameters or local variables by these names.

and never change their values, there is no harm in letting our whole program access them. We include the const type qualifier in our declarations that define the globals as well as in the extern declarations that give additional functions access to the globals. This qualifier notifies the compiler that the program can look at, but not modify, these locations.

Figure 13.13 also shows the third storage class that we have met before, namely, typedef. Including typedef in the set of storage classes is merely a notational convenience. As we saw in Chapter 11, a typedef statement does not allocate storage space!

Table 13.1 shows which functions are allowed to access globals complex_zero and months and why. We assume that any local variable declarations affecting access to the globals are shown.

Storage Classes static and register

C's remaining storage classes are static and register. Placing the static keyword at the beginning of a local variable declaration changes the way the variable is allocated. Let's compare variables once and many in the following function fragment.

```
int
fun_frag(int n)
{
      static int once = 0;
      int        many = 0;
      . . .
}
```

As a variable of storage class `auto`, `many` is allocated space on the stack each time `fun_frag` is called; for every call `many` is initialized to zero. Every time `fun_frag` returns, `many` is deallocated. In contrast, `static` variable `once` is allocated and initialized *one time*, prior to program execution. It remains allocated until the entire program terminates. If `fun_frag` changes the value of `once`, that value is retained between calls to `fun_frag`.

Using a `static` local variable to retain data from one call to a function to the next is usually a poor programming practice. If the function's behavior depends on these data, then the function is no longer performing a transformation based solely on its input arguments, and the complexity of its purpose from the program reader's perspective is vastly increased.

One situation in which the use of a `static` local variable does not degrade readability is in function `main`, since a return from this function terminates the program. On a system that allocates a relatively small run-time stack, one might wish to declare large arrays as `static` variables in function `main`. Then these arrays will not use up stack space.

The final storage class, `register`, is closely related to storage class `auto` and may be applied only to local variables and parameters. In fact, C implementations are not required to treat `register` variables differently from `auto` variables. Designating that a variable is of storage class `register` simply alerts the compiler to the fact that this memory cell will be referenced more often than most. By choosing storage class `register`, the programmer indicates an expectation that the program would run faster if a *register,* a special high-speed memory location *inside* the central processor, could be used for the variable. Variables serving as subscripts for large arrays are good candidates for this storage class. Here are declarations of variables in storage classes `static` and `register`.

```
static double matrix[50][40];
register int  i, j;
```

Self-Check

Reread the program in Fig. 9.16 that converts forms of date references.

1. Identify the storage classes of the following names used in the program.

   `date_string` (first parameter of `nums_to_string_date`)
   `found` (in function `search`)
   `search`
   `y` (in function `main`)

2. If the defining declaration of the `month_names` array of Fig. 9.16 were moved to the top level right after the `#define` statements, what would the array's storage class be?
3. Would it be reasonable to include a `const` qualifier in the declaration discussed in Exercise 2?
4. What other changes would be needed in the program if those suggested in Exercises 2 and 3 were made?
5. For which one of the variables in function `search` would it be a good idea to request storage class `register`?

13.6 MODIFYING FUNCTIONS FOR INCLUSION IN A LIBRARY

When building a personal library based on functions originally developed for use in a specific context, usually some modifications are advisable. A library function should be as general as possible, so all constants used should be examined to see if they could be replaced by input parameters. The library function's preconditions should be carefully defined.

In previous work, our functions have dealt with an error either by returning an error code or by printing an error message and returning a value that should permit continued execution. In some situations, however, it is better not to permit continued processing. For example, manipulation of a large two-dimensional array can be very time-consuming, and it might be pointless to expend this time on a matrix that violates a function's preconditions in a way that can be detected. Similarly, if our `factorial` function is called with a negative number, there is no way it can return a valid answer. Therefore, we might want to print a message and then terminate execution of a program in which this error occurs.

C's `exit` function from the standard library stdlib can be used in these types of situations to terminate execution prematurely. Calling `exit` with the argument 1 indicates that some failure led to the exit. Using the value 0 in an `exit` call implies no such failure, just as a 0 returned from function `main` indicates successful function completion. The `exit` function may also use one of the predefined constants `EXIT_SUCCESS` or `EXIT_FAILURE` as its return value. These constants are an option for use in the `return` statement as well,

Figure 13.14   Function factorial with Premature Exit on Negative Data

```
/*
 * Computes n!
 * Pre: n is greater than or equal to zero -- premature exit on
 * negative data
 */
int
factorial(int n)
{
      int i,              /* local variables */
          product = 1;

      if (n < 0) {
             printf("\n***ERROR: %d! is undefined***\n", n);
             exit(1);
      } else {
             /* Compute the product n x (n-1) x (n-2) x ... x
                 2 x 1 */
             for  (i = n;  i > 1;  --i) {
                 product = product * i;
             }

             /* Return function result */
             return (product);
      }
}
```

providing that the standard library stdlib is included. Figure 13.14 shows a library form of function `factorial` that terminates program execution prematurely on a negative input.

The following syntax display describes the `exit` function.

exit Function

SYNTAX: `exit(`*return_value*`);`

EXAMPLE: `/*`
`          *   Gets next positive number from input`
`          *   stream.  Returns EOF if end of file`

(continued)

```
             * is encountered. Exits program with error
             * message if erroneous input is encountered.
             */
            int
            get_positive(void)
            {
                  int n, status;

                  for  (status = scanf("%d", &n);
                        status == 1 && n <= 0;
                        status = scanf("%d", &n)) {}

                  if (status == 0) {
                        printf("\n***ERROR in data");
                        printf(" at >>%c<<***\n",
                                 getchar());
                        exit(1);
                  } else if (status == EOF) {
                        return (status);
                  } else {
                        return (n);
                  }
            }
```

INTERPRETATION: Execution of a call to `exit` causes program termination from any point in a program. The *return_value* is used to indicate whether termination was brought on by some type of failure. A *return_value* of 0 means normal exit. In general, the use of

```
exit(0);
```

should be avoided in functions other than `main` since placing "normal" termination of a program in one of its function subprograms tends to diminish the readability of function `main`. The use of

```
exit(1);
```

should be reserved for terminating execution in cases where error recovery is not possible or not useful.

Case Study: Developing an Image Enhancement Library

Many of today's technologies deal with images. These images range from photographs of manufactured parts used for quality control to ultrasound, X-ray, and magnetic resonance images used in medical diagnosis to images collected by satellite for intelligence gathering. Images often require sophisticated processing to bring out features useful in the particular application area. In this case study, we make a start on a C library of image enhancement functions.

We make the assumption that the analysis and design of the enhancement algorithms to be included has already been carried out and that in each case we are working from a program that is an implementation of an algorithm for a particular environment. Our focus will be on the types of changes we need to make in these programs in order to create functions appropriate for inclusion in our library. We will seek to generalize our functions to permit their application in a wide spectrum of image systems. We should note that images of the size we process in this problem are too large for use on some personal computers.

◀ PROBLEM ▶

Our initial library is to include three functions: one that removes noise, one that reduces the number of shades of gray in a black-and-white photo, and one that counts cells in a blob. Figure 13.15 shows successive application of these three functions to a noisy image of four mushrooms.

In our previous image study, we worked with a binary image, one in which the value of each pixel (picture element) was either 0 or 1. A different type of image is the subject of our noise-reduction function. A black-and-white photograph is actually composed of many shades of gray. Digitizing the photograph produces a grid of integers ranging from zero to a maximum value based on the number of shades of gray that are distinguished by the imaging system. This type of digitized picture is called a *gray-scale image*.

Noise Reduction

The quality of a gray-scale image can be degraded by the introduction of noise when the image is transmitted long distances or collected under less than ideal conditions. A pixel value that is very different from its neighboring pixels often represents noise. For example, in the image section

```
2 4 5 5 6
2 4 4 5 6
3 4 1 8 7
4 8 8 9 9
5 8 9 9 9
```

(a) **Noisy mushroom image**

(b) **Mushrooms with noise reduced**

(c) **Mushrooms sharpened by use of just three gray-scale shades**

(d) **Mushrooms with one uniformly shaded blob marked for sizing**

Figure 13.15   Reducing Noise, Reducing Shades of Gray, and Sizing a Blob in an Image

the pixel with the value 1 is likely to be noise because its value is so different from its neighbors. The program on which we will base our noise reduction library function assumes that if a pixel has a value that is different by 3 or more from its eight neighbors (the numbers in color in the section of pixels shown), it can be assumed to be noise. The program ignores the pixels on the edge of the picture and replaces a noisy value by the rounded average of all eight neighbors. In the example, the 1 would be replaced by a 6, the integer nearest to 6.25:

$$\frac{(4 + 4 + 4 + 5 + 8 + 9 + 8 + 8)}{8.0} = 6.25$$

Figure 13.16 shows the function clean on which we are to base our library function.

Figure 13.16   Function clean, Candidate for Image Enhancement Library

```
#include <stdlib.h>

#define NOISE_DIFF   3
#define MAXCOL       1024

/*
 * Finds each noisy pixel (a pixel whose value differs from all its neighbors
 * by NOISE_DIFF or more) and substitutes the average of its neighbors' values.
 * No change is made in boundary cells.
 */
void
clean(int image[][MAXCOL], /* input/output - numrow x MAXCOL gray-scale
                                              image to clean            */
      int numrow)             /* input - number of rows in image         */
{
      int pixel;   /* pixel currently being examined */
      int i, j;

      for  (i = 1;  i < numrow - 1;  ++i) {
          for  (j = 1;  j < MAXCOL - 1;  ++j) {
              pixel = image[i][j];
              if (abs(pixel - image[i - 1][j - 1]) >= NOISE_DIFF &&
                  abs(pixel - image[i - 1][j]) >= NOISE_DIFF &&
                  abs(pixel - image[i - 1][j + 1]) >= NOISE_DIFF &&
                  abs(pixel - image[i][j - 1]) >= NOISE_DIFF &&
                  abs(pixel - image[i][j + 1]) >= NOISE_DIFF &&
                  abs(pixel - image[i + 1][j - 1]) >= NOISE_DIFF &&
                  abs(pixel - image[i + 1][j]) >= NOISE_DIFF &&
                  abs(pixel - image[i + 1][j + 1]) >= NOISE_DIFF)
                      image[i][j] = (int)((image[i - 1][j - 1] + image[i - 1][j]
```

(continued)

Figure 13.16   (continued)

```
                            + image[i - 1][j + 1] + image[i][j - 1]
                            + image[i][j + 1] + image[i + 1][j - 1]
                            + image[i + 1][j] + image[i + 1][j + 1])
                            / 8.0 + 0.5);
        }
    }
}
```

This function requires very little revision for inclusion in our library. We will make just three changes. First, because the function name is a bit vague, we will name our library function `reduce_noise`. Second, we must recognize that a difference of 3 between a pixel and all its neighbors is less likely to indicate noise in an image with 256 shades of gray than in an image with 16 shades. To accommodate this difference in imaging systems, we will make `noise_diff` an input parameter rather than a constant. Third, we will include the library name in the name of our constant macro, so `MAXCOL` becomes `IMAGE_MAXCOL`. Our revised function is shown in Fig. 13.17.

Figure 13.17   Image Enhancement Library Function reduce_noise

```
#include <stdlib.h>

#define IMAGE_MAXCOL    1024

/*
 *  Finds each noisy pixel (a pixel whose value differs from all its neighbors
 *  by noise_diff or more) and substitutes the average of its neighbors' values.
 *  No change is made in boundary cells.
 */
void
reduce_noise(int image[][IMAGE_MAXCOL], /* input/output - numrow x IMAGE_
                                           MAXCOL gray-scale image to clean */
             int numrow,               /* input - number of rows in image    */
             int noise_diff)           /* input - minimum pixel difference
                                           meaning noise                      */
{
```

(continued)

Figure 13.17 *(continued)*

```
int pixel;    /* pixel currently being examined */
int i, j;

for  (i = 1;  i < numrow - 1;  ++i) {
    for  (j = 1;  j < IMAGE_MAXCOL - 1;  ++j) {
        pixel = image[i][j];
        if (abs(pixel - image[i - 1][j - 1]) >= noise_diff &&
            abs(pixel - image[i - 1][j]) >= noise_diff &&
            abs(pixel - image[i - 1][j + 1]) >= noise_diff &&
            abs(pixel - image[i][j - 1]) >= noise_diff &&
            abs(pixel - image[i][j + 1]) >= noise_diff &&
            abs(pixel - image[i + 1][j - 1]) >= noise_diff &&
            abs(pixel - image[i + 1][j]) >= noise_diff &&
            abs(pixel - image[i + 1][j + 1]) >= noise_diff))
            image[i][j] = (int)((image[i - 1][j - 1] + image[i - 1][j]
                            + image[i - 1][j + 1] + image[i][j - 1]
                            + image[i][j + 1] + image[i + 1][j - 1]
                            + image[i + 1][j] + image[i + 1][j + 1])
                            / 8.0 + 0.5);
    }
  }
}
```

Reducing Number of Shades of Gray

Our library function to reduce the number of shades of gray to just three shades will be based on a program that replaces all pixels with values 3 or less by a 0, larger pixels 6 or less by a 1, and all others by a 4. This original program was designed to produce an image distinguishable when its pixel values (ranging from 0 to 9) were simply printed rather than interpreted as gray-scale values (see Fig. 13.18). The function we will modify is shown in Fig. 13.19.

When we evaluate function `sharpen` for inclusion in our image library, its heavy reliance on constants (0, 1, 4, 3, and 6) is immediately a concern. Clearly, the cutoff values for dividing shades of gray into three groups would vary depending on the number of shades distinguished by the imaging system. The cutoff values should also be allowed to vary to accommodate very light or very dark images. Our library function will need the boundaries of the middle grouping to be input parameters. Similarly, the numeric values for white, medium gray, and black should not be rigidly prescribed but must also be allowed to vary. Thus, the three standard values should also be input parameters.

Figure 13.18   Digital Image Before (Top) and After (Bottom) Enhancement

```
21111112222121111112212122221121211121122211111113331111111111122112121111211111
12110001323322111003313032220132221232222102000212332000010122320020200032011
12880887002132211777899921988877997979999789891112889995877011323217778788220
10146144722121128455454916665540454616565654492024654645659122221366456445833
11456454582230094646046802455545544465166154071236651655449312022264165655821
23614041458222846045425822446460414654545554580006564615447123321355546649032
12645256515918666454645832650444545056644646470025454565458009212265245456922
13551446646496564565154832122201444556932119333115661464647013213156545544732
12655474564665156514664903222112565056823333333015666546548122622046424554910
10550481464566665214656920202110466464923233333311165516551547011236545645481233
10464670046545451116546732323110445065934933333313466664565911922565615447112
12540472125566402026414910182210554441822233332326651455149212126456565681122
11646480001122214014545813310802404465733233333300065466554471233256166146912
23664591221111111121540482328100045455592113333390914541551557013564655447222
21656570221111111016565812112381540455333333333326644646447031450525406100022
22665471021333331114406720382312656553333333333333316065141457111654464647123
22455571111333331114645922212111440646722233333211255066454471545604447212221
12446420011333331214654012283281444566232633333322131266645656456655666710190
62320010211111112020000210202220110003233333333333333333333003333302322123111312
12200201111111110101101122800808080828161333331001323231100023232232210119210
22233112133313232220100011342110101012122033333000220212110110113223211001111
```

```
00000000000000000000000000000000000000000000000000000000000000000000000000000000
00000000000000000000000000000000000000000000000000000000000000000000000000000000
00440444000000000444444400444444444444444444440004444414440000000044444444000
00011111400000000411111140111111111111141111111140001111111114000000001111111114000
00111111140000004111011400111111111111111111111140001111111114000000001111111114000
00111011114000411111101400111111111111111111111140001111111114000000001111111114000
00111011111404111111101400110111111111111140001111111114000000001101111114000
00110111111141111111111140000000001111114000000000011111111114000000001111111114000
00111141111111111011114000000001111114000000000011111111114000000001111011114000
00111140111111110011114000000001111114000000000011111111114000001111111140000
00111140011111110001111400000000011111140100000000111111111114000001111111140000
00111140001111100001111400000000011111114000000000011111111114000001111111140000
00111140000000001001111400000000011111140000000000111111111140000011111111140000
00111140000000000001111400000000011111140000000000001111111114000111111111400000
00111140000000000001111400000000011111100000000000011111111140001111011111100000
00111140000000000001111400000000011111100000000000101101111400011110111114000000
00111140000000000001111400000000011111140000000000011011111140111111111114000000
00111100000000000001110000000001111100000000000001111111111111114000000000
10000000000000000000000000000000000000000000000000000000000000000000000000000000
00000000000000000000000000000000000000000000000000000000000000000000000000000000
00000000000000000000000000000000000000000000000000000000000000000000000000000000
```

Our revised `sharpen` function is shown in Fig. 13.20. For those who find seven function arguments burdensome, there is another option. We could include the library of image functions and then write our own `MY_SHARPEN` macro, which takes only the parameters that are expected to vary and whose body provides the others as constants in a call to `sharpen`. For example, macro `MY_SHARPEN` would simulate the original sharpen function if defined as

```
#define MY_SHARPEN(img, nrow)\
    sharpen(img, nrow, 3, 6, STAND1, STAND2, STAND3)
```

Figure 13.19   Function sharpen on Which Library Function Will Be Based

```
#define MAXCOL 1024
#define STAND1 0
#define STAND2 1
#define STAND3 4

/*
 *  Replaces each digit in numrow x MAXCOL image by one of three
 *  standard values
 *
 *      digit      standard value
 *      0-3          STAND1
 *      4-6          STAND2
 *      7-9          STAND3
 */
void
sharpen(int image[][MAXCOL], /* input/output - image to sharpen   */
        int numrow)          /* input - number of rows in image   */
{
      int i, j;

      for  (i = 0;  i < numrow;  ++i) {
         for  (j = 0;  j < MAXCOL;  ++j) {
              if (image[i][j] <= 3)
                      image[i][j] = STAND1;
              else if (image[i][j] <= 6)
                      image[i][j] = STAND2;
              else
                      image[i][j] = STAND3;
         }
      }
}
```

Figure 13.20   Library Function sharpen

```
#define IMAGE_MAXCOL 1024  /* (appears just once in header file) */

/*
 *  Reduces to three the number of gray-scale values in the image.
 *  Assigns value low_val to pixels in the range 0..low_bd, value mid_val
 *  to pixels in the range low_bd + 1..high_bd, value high_val to others.
 */
void
sharpen(int image[][IMAGE_MAXCOL], /* input/output - image to sharpen   */
        int numrow,                /* input - number of rows in image   */
        int low_bd, int high_bd,   /* input - cutoffs for highest values
                                            in low and middle pixel groups */
        int low_val, int mid_val,  /* input - values to assign to pixels*/
        int high_val)              /*    in low, middle, and high
                                            groupings                   */
{
     int i, j;

     for  (i = 0; i < numrow;  ++i) {
         for  (j = 0; j < IMAGE_MAXCOL;  ++j) {
             if (image[i][j] <= low_bd)
                   image[i][j] = low_val;
             else if (image[i][j] <= high_bd)
                   image[i][j] = mid_val;
             else
                   image[i][j] = high_val;
         }
     }
}
```

Blob Sizes

Our third function is based on the case study in Section 10.7 in which we calculated the size of a blob containing a particular point. In our case study, we worked with a binary image in which one value meant "filled" and the other meant "empty." Only "filled" elements could contribute to a blob's size. The functions we developed are repeated here in Fig. 13.21.

Figure 13.21   Blob Count Functions to Revise for Library

```
#define N_ROWS   100
#define N_COLS   100

#define FILLED   1
#define EMPTY    0

/*
 *  Counts the number of filled array elements in the blob to which
 *  point (x, y) belongs.  If (x, y) itself is empty or point (x, y) is
 *  not within the N_ROWS x N_COLS grid, a zero is returned.
 *
 *  Side effect:  elements of blob to which (x, y) belongs are set to
 *  EMPTY
 */
int
blob_check(int grid[N_ROWS][N_COLS], /* input/output - grid containing blobs
                                                  left to process       */
           int x, int y)             /* input - coordinates of point in blob
                                                  of interest            */
{
      int ct;

      if (x < 0  ||  x >= N_COLS  ||  y < 0  ||  y >= N_ROWS) {
            ct = 0;
      } else if (grid[x][y] == EMPTY) {
            ct = 0;
      } else {
            grid[x][y] = EMPTY;
            ct = 1 + blob_check(grid, x-1, y+1) + blob_check(grid, x, y+1)
                   + blob_check(grid, x+1, y+1) + blob_check(grid, x+1, y)
                   + blob_check(grid, x+1, y-1) + blob_check(grid, x, y-1)
                   + blob_check(grid, x-1, y-1) + blob_check(grid, x-1, y);
      }

      return (ct);
}

/*
 *  Counts the number of filled cells in the blob containing point (x, y).
 *  Uses blob_check to perform the counting operation.  Since blob_check
 *  resets blob cells to EMPTY, passes blob_check a "disposable" copy of
 *  grid array.
 */
```

(continued)

Figure 13.21   *(continued)*

```
int
blob_size(const int grid[N_ROWS][N_COLS], /* input - grid of blobs         */
               int x, int y)               /* input - coordinates of point
                                               in blob of interest          */
{
     int i, j;
     int grid_copy[N_ROWS][N_COLS];

     for  (i = 0;  i < N_ROWS;  ++i)
          for  (j = 0;  j < N_COLS;  ++j)
               grid_copy[i][j] = grid[i][j];

     return (blob_check(grid_copy, x, y));
}
```

The purpose of our library function should be less restrictive, for we might wish to know the size of a blob of pixels composed of any particular gray-scale value. We will also represent the image parameter of the function in a manner consistent with the other functions in the library by fixing the number of columns at IMAGE_MAXCOL but allowing the number of rows to vary. Since our algorithm requires creation of a copy of the image, however, we will need to impose an upper bound on the number of rows (IMAGE_MAXROW) and provide for an error message if this limit is exceeded. We have elected to terminate the image processing if this condition arises. Other options for handling this situation include displaying an error message and proceeding with the processing using only the allowed number of rows or combining this second option with the addition of an output argument to carry back a success/failure return code. We will still need a value to fulfill the role of EMPTY in helper function blob_check in order to prevent repeated counting of one blob element. For this purpose, we have chosen to use a value 1 greater than the blob value. The library forms of function blob_size and its helper function blob_check are shown in Fig. 13.22.

In Fig. 13.23, we show the header file for our image library along with an outline of the implementation file. Notice especially that our header file contains neither a prototype for nor any reference to function blob_check because the library user is expected to call function blob_size. Only blob_size is to call blob_check, so the existence of the helper function is part of the "implementation details" that are hidden from the library user.

Figure 13.22   Image Library Function blob_size and Helper Function blob_check

```c
#define IMAGE_MAXCOL 1024
#define IMAGE_MAXROW 1024

/*
 *  Counts the number of array elements matching blob_value in the blob to
 *  which point (x, y) belongs.  If (x, y) itself does not match blob_value or
 *  point (x, y) is not within the numrow x IMAGE_MAXCOL grid, zero is
 *  returned.
 *
 *  Side effect:  elements of blob are set to blob_value + 1
 */
int
blob_check(int grid[][IMAGE_MAXCOL], /* input/output - grid containing blob
                                             elements left to process     */
           int numrow,               /* input - number of rows in image     */
           int x, int y,             /* input - coordinates of point in blob */
           int blob_value)           /* input - value in a targeted cell which
                                             is a member of current blob  */
{
      int ct;

      if (x < 0  ||  x >= numrow  ||  y < 0  ||  y >= IMAGE_MAXCOL) {
            ct = 0;
      } else if (grid[x][y] != blob_value) {
            ct = 0;
      } else {
            grid[x][y] = blob_value + 1;
            ct = 1 + blob_check(grid, numrow, x-1, y+1, blob_value)
                   + blob_check(grid, numrow, x, y+1, blob_value)
                   + blob_check(grid, numrow, x+1, y+1, blob_value)
                   + blob_check(grid, numrow, x+1, y, blob_value)
                   + blob_check(grid, numrow, x+1, y-1, blob_value)
                   + blob_check(grid, numrow, x, y-1, blob_value)
                   + blob_check(grid, numrow, x-1, y-1, blob_value)
                   + blob_check(grid, numrow, x-1, y, blob_value);
      }
      return(ct);
}
```

(continued)

Figure 13.22 *(continued)*

```
/*
 * Counts the number of cells in the blob containing point (x, y).  A blob is
 * a contiguous group of pixels of the same gray-scale value.
 * Pre:  numrow <= IMAGE_MAXROW
 */
int
blob_size(const int grid[][IMAGE_MAXCOL], /* input - gray-scale image       */
          int       numrow,               /* input - number of rows in image */
          int       x, int y)             /* input - coordinates of point in
                                                      blob of interest        */
{
     int i, j;
     int grid_copy[IMAGE_MAXROW][IMAGE_MAXCOL];

     if (numrow > IMAGE_MAXROW) {
          printf("\n***Error:  image length is %d.  Must not exceed %d.\n",
                 numrow, IMAGE_MAXROW);
          exit(1);
     } else {
          for  (i = 0;  i < numrow;  ++i)
               for  (j = 0;  j < IMAGE_MAXCOL;  ++j)
                    grid_copy[i][j] = grid[i][j];

          return(blob_check(grid_copy, numrow, x, y, grid[x][y]));
     }
}
```

Figure 13.23 **Image Library**

```
/*
 * image.h  -  header file
 *
 * Library of image processing functions designed for images of width
 * IMAGE_MAXCOL pixels;  length may vary.  Some functions impose a maximum
 * length of IMAGE_MAXROW pixels.
 *          reduce_noise
 *          sharpen        - uses only 3 gray-scale values
 *          blob_size      - counts pixels in a blob
 */
```

(continued)

Figure 13.23 *(continued)*

```
#define IMAGE_MAXCOL 1024
#define IMAGE_MAXROW 1024

/*
 *  Finds each noisy pixel (a pixel whose value differs from all its neighbors
 *  by noise_diff or more) and substitutes the average of its neighbors'
 *  values. No change is made in boundary cells.
 */
extern void
reduce_noise(int image[][IMAGE_MAXCOL], /* input/output - numrow x
                                           IMAGE_MAXCOL gray-scale image
                                           to clean                        */
             int numrow,                /* input - number of rows in image */
             int noise_diff);           /* input - minimum pixel difference
                                           meaning noise                   */
/*
 *  Reduces to three the number of gray-scale values in the image.  Assigns
 *  value low_val to pixels in the range 0..low_bd, value mid_val to pixels
 *  in the range low_bd + 1..high_bd, value high_val to others.
 */
extern void
sharpen(int image[][IMAGE_MAXCOL], /* input/output - image to sharpen      */
        int numrow,                /* input - number of rows in image      */
        int low_bd, int high_bd,   /* input - cutoffs for highest values
                                      in low and middle pixel groups       */
        int low_val, int mid_val,  /* input - values to assign to pixels   */
        int high_val);             /* in low, middle, and high groupings   */
/*
 *  Counts the number of cells in the blob containing point (x, y).  A blob is
 *  a contiguous group of pixels of the same gray-scale value.
 *  Pre:  numrow <= IMAGE_MAXROW
 */
extern int
blob_size(const int grid[][IMAGE_MAXCOL], /* input - gray-scale image      */
          int      numrow,                /* input - number of rows in image */
          int      x, int y);             /* input - coordinates of point in
                                             blob of interest               */


/*------------------------------------------------------------------------ */
```

(continued)

Figure 13.23   *(continued)*

```
/*
 * Outline of implementation file - image.c
 */

#include "image.h"

/*  Full definitions of reduce_noise, sharpen, blob_check, and blob_size    */
```

EXERCISES FOR SECTION 13.6

Self-Check

1. If the error check were omitted from function `blob_size`, what would happen when an image that was too long was passed to `blob_size` (refer to Fig. 13.22)?
2. Why would it not be better to include an `extern` declaration of function `blob_check` in the file `image.h`?

Programming

1. Write a library function `threshold` that takes a gray-scale image and a threshold value as parameters and sets all pixels over the threshold to one particular value and all other pixels to a different value.

13.7 CONDITIONAL COMPILATION

C's preprocessor recognizes commands that allow the user to select parts of a program to be compiled and parts to be omitted. This ability can be helpful in a variety of situations. For example, one can build in debugging `printf` calls when writing a function and then include these statements in the compiled program only when they are needed. Inclusion of header files is another activity that may need to be done conditionally. For example, we might have two libraries sp_one and sp_two, which both use a data type and operators of a third library, sp. The header files `sp_one.h` and `sp_two.h` would both have the directive `#include "sp.h"`. However, if we wanted a program to use the facilities of both sp_one and sp_two, including both of their header files would lead to inclusion of `sp.h` twice, resulting in duplicate declarations of the data type defined in `sp.h`. Because C prohibits such duplicate declarations, we must be able to prevent this situation. A third case in which conditional compilation is very helpful is the design of a system for use on a variety of computers. Conditional compilation allows one to compile only the code appropriate for the current computer.

Figure 13.24 shows a recursive function containing `printf` calls to create a trace of its execution. Compilation of these statements depends on the value of the condition

```
defined (TRACE)
```

The `defined` operator evaluates to 1 if the name that is its operand is defined in the preprocessor. Such definition is the result of using the name in a `#define` directive. Otherwise, the `defined` operator evaluates to 0.

Figure 13.24   Conditional Compilation of Tracing printf Calls

```c
/*
 *  Computes an integer quotient (m/n) using subtraction
 */
int
quotient(int m, int n)
{
        int ans;

#if defined (TRACE)
        printf("Entering quotient with m = %d, n = %d\n",
                m, n);
#endif

        if (n > m)
                ans = 0;
        else
                ans = 1 + quotient(m - n, n);

#if defined (TRACE)
        printf("Leaving quotient(%d, %d) with result = %d\n",
                m, n, ans);
#endif

        return (ans);
}
```

After creating functions like the one in Fig. 13.24, one need only include the directive

```
#define TRACE
```

somewhere in the source file prior to the function definition to "turn on" the compilation of the tracing `printf` calls. It is not necessary to explicitly associate a value with TRACE. Remember that, as for all preprocessor directives, the # of the conditional compilation directives *must* be the first nonblank character on the line. The `defined` operator exists exclusively for application in `#if` and `#elif` directives. The `#elif` means "else if" and is used when selecting among multiple alternatives as in Fig. 13.25.

Figure 13.25   Conditional Compilation of Tracing printf Calls

```
/*
 *  Computes an integer quotient (m/n) using subtraction
 */
int
quotient(int m, int n)
{
     int ans;

#if defined (TRACE_VERBOSE)
     printf("Entering quotient with m = %d, n = %d\n",
            m, n);
#elif defined (TRACE_BRIEF)
     printf(" => quotient(%d, %d)\n", m, n);
#endif

     if (n > m)
          ans = 0;
     else
          ans = 1 + quotient(m - n, n);

#if defined (TRACE_VERBOSE)
     printf("Leaving quotient(%d, %d) with result = %d\n",
            m, n, ans);
```

(continued)

Figure 13.25   *(continued)*

```
#elif defined (TRACE_BRIEF)
        printf("quotient(%d, %d) => %d\n", m, n, ans);
#endif

        return (ans);
}
```

One approach to the coordination of included files is illustrated in Fig. 13.26. Each header file is constructed so as to prevent duplicate compilation of its contents, regardless of the number of times the header file is included. The entire contents of a header file are enclosed in an #if that tests whether a name based on the header file name has been defined in a #define directive. Then the first time the header file is included, its entire contents are passed to the compiler. Since a #define of the critical name is in the file, additional #include directives for the same file will provide no code to the compiler.

C's #if and #elif directives are complemented by an #else directive to make possible a full range of selective compilation contructs. An #undef directive that cancels the preprocessor's definition of a particular name is also available.

Figure 13.26   **Header File That Protects Itself from Effects of Duplicate Inclusion**

```
/*  Header file planet.h  */
 *
 *   abstract data type planet
 *
 *   Type planet_t has these components:
 *        name, diameter, dist_sun, orbital_prd, axial_rot_prd
 *
 *   Operators:
 *        print_planet, planet_equal, scan_planet
 */

#if !defined (PLANET_H_INCL)
#define PLANET_H_INCL

#define PLANET_STRSIZ   10
```

(continued)

Figure 13.26 *(continued)*

```
typedef struct planet_s { /* planet structure */
      char name[PLANET_STRSIZ];
      double diameter,            /* equatorial diameter in km              */
             dist_sun,            /* average distance from sun in km        */
             orbital_prd,         /* years to orbit sun once                */
             axial_rot_prd;       /* hours to complete one revolution on
                                     axis                                   */
} planet_t;

/*
 *  Prints with labels all components of a planet_t structure
 */
extern void
print_planet(planet_t pl);   /* input - one planet structure             */

/*
 *  Determines whether or not the components of planet_1 and planet_2
 *  match
 */
extern int
planet_equal(planet_t planet_1,   /* input - planets to                 */
             planet_t planet_2); /*            compare                   */

/*
 *  Fills a type planet_t structure with input data.  Integer returned as
 *  function result is success/failure/EOF indicator.
 *      1 => successful input of planet
 *      0 => error encountered
 *      EOF => insufficient data before end of file
 *  In case of error or EOF, value of type planet_t output argument is
 *  undefined.
 */
extern int
scan_planet(planet_t *plnp); /* output- address of planet_t structure to
                                     fill                                   */

#endif
```

Self-Check

1. Use conditional compilation to select an appropriate call to `printf`. Assume that on a UNIX operating system the name `UNIX` will be defined in the C preprocessor; on the VMS operating system, the name `VMS` will be defined. The desired message on UNIX is

   ```
   Enter <ctrl-d> to quit.
   ```

   The desired message on VMS is

   ```
   Enter <ctrl-z> to quit.
   ```

2. Consider the header file shown in Fig. 13.26. Describe what happens (a) when the preprocessor first encounters a `#include "planet.h"` directive and (b) when the preprocessor encounters a second `#include "planet.h"` directive.

13.8 ARGUMENTS TO FUNCTION main

Up to this point, we have always defined function `main` with a `void` parameter list. However, as another possibility, we could use the following prototype that indicates that `main` has two formal parameters: an integer and an array of pointers to strings.

```
int
main(int    argc,    /* input - argument count (including
                                 program name)              */
      char *argv[]) /* input - argument vector               */
```

The way you cause your program to run varies from one operating system to another. However, most operating systems provide some way for you to specify values of options when you run a program. For example, on the Ultrix operating system, one would specify options `opt1`, `opt2`, and `opt3` when running a program named `prog` by typing the command line

```
prog opt1 opt2 opt3
```

The formal parameters `argc` and `argv` provide a mechanism for a C main function to access these command line options. If the program `prog` just mentioned were the machine code of a C program whose main function prototype had parameters `argc` and `argv`, then the command line

prog opt1 opt2 opt3

would result in these formal parameter values within `main`:

```
argc   4        argv[0]   "prog"
                    [1]   "opt1"
                    [2]   "opt2"
                    [3]   "opt3"
                    [4]   ""    (empty  string)
```

Figure 13.27 shows a revised version of our program from Chapter 12 to make a backup copy of a text file. Rather than prompting the user for the names of the file to copy and the file to be the backup, the new version expects the user to enter this information on the command line. For example, if the program is named `backup` and the user activates it by typing

backup old.txt new.txt

the formal parameters of `main` will have these values:

```
argc   3        argv[0]   "backup"
                    [1]   "old.txt"
                    [2]   "new.txt"
                    [3]   ""
```

If the program encounters any difficulty in opening either of the files named by the user, it exits with an appropriate error message. Otherwise, it proceeds with the copy operation.

Figure 13.27   File Backup Using Arguments to Function main

```c
/*
 * Makes a backup of the file whose name is the first command line argument.
 * The second command line argument is the name of the new file.
 */
#include <stdio.h>

int
main(int    argc,   /* input - argument count (including program name) */
     char *argv[]) /* input - argument vector                          */
```

(continued)

Figure 13.27 *(continued)*

```
{
      FILE *inp,    /* file pointers for input      */
           *outp;  /*     and backup files          */
      int   ch;     /* one character of input file */

      /* Open input and backup files if possible                         */
      inp = fopen(argv[1], "r");
      if (inp == NULL) {
            printf("\nCannot open file %s for input\n", argv[1]);
            exit(1);
      }

      outp = fopen(argv[2], "w");
      if (outp == NULL) {
            printf("\nCannot open file %s for output\n", argv[2]);
            exit(1);
      }

      /* Make backup copy one character at a time                        */
      for  (ch = getc(inp);  ch != EOF;  ch = getc(inp))
           putc(ch, outp);

      /*  Close files and notify user of backup completion               */
      fclose(inp);
      fclose(outp);
      printf("\nCopied %s to %s\n", argv[1], argv[2]);

      return(0);
}
```

EXERCISES FOR SECTION 13.8

Self-Check

1. How would you modify the program in Fig. 13.27 so that if a user typed a command line with fewer than two file names provided, an appropriate error message would be printed?
2. Write the prototype of an integer function `fun` that takes a single input parameter. Define the prototype so that `argv[1]` would be a legitimate actual argument to pass to `fun`.

Programming

1. Write a program that takes a single command line argument. The argument should be the name of a text file containing integers, and the program should sum the integers in the file. If any invalid data are encountered, the program should terminate with an error message that includes the file name and the invalid character.

13.9 COMMON PROGRAMMING ERRORS

The most common problem in the development of large systems by teams of programmers is a lack of agreement regarding the details of a system's design. If you apply the software development method presented in earlier chapters, you can achieve a rational, stepwise division of a large problem into smaller subproblems that correspond to individual functions. Then you can devise detailed descriptions of *what* each function is to do, *what type*(s) of data it is to manipulate, and *what preconditions* must be met for its proper execution. Only when representatives of all teams are in full agreement about this fundamental interface information is it wise to proceed with a system's implementation.

When developing personal libraries, it is easy to forget the long-range goal of having reusable functions in the rush of completing a current project. An unnecessarily restrictive assumption built into a library function can quickly negate the function's usefulness in another context.

Although macros provide a quick and often quite readable shorthand for the expressions they represent, they are also fertile ground for error growth. It is easy to slip and type a blank after the macro name in the definition of a macro with parameters, causing the preprocessor to misinterpret the definition. Operator precedence mistakes are sure to crop up unless the programmer is absolutely meticulous about parenthesizing every macro body that produces a result value as well as parenthesizing every occurrence of a macro parameter within the body. Following a consistent naming convention for macros can save hours of unnecessary debugging resulting from the programmer's erroneous assumption that a function, not a macro, is being called.

In the history of computing, the inappropriate use of global variables is notorious for corrupting a system's reliability. We cannot overemphasize the importance of maintaining visible interfaces among functions through their parameter lists. Companies whose programmers give in to the temptation to save a few keystrokes in function prototypes by replacing common parameters with global variables pay dearly in software maintenance and upgrade costs.

CHAPTER REVIEW

In this chapter, we ventured beyond the sheltered world of single problems solved by individual programs to grapple with the special difficulties associated with large systems. We have emphasized the importance of abstraction in dealing with complexity and have focused on C's provisions for personal libraries. We saw how dividing a library into a header file and an implementation file provides a natural separation of the description of *what* the library functions do from *how* they do it.

We met some additional features of C such as macros with parameters, the `exit` function, conditional compilation directives, and arguments to function `main`; and we studied how various declarations relate to the storage classes of the names declared. A library development case study gave us an opportunity to see specific ways in which library functions differ from typical special-purpose functions.

Table 13.2 summarizes the new constructs studied.

Table 13.2   Summary of New C Constructs in Chapter 13

C Construct	Meaning
Header File (with #if...#endif directives)	
```/* somelib.h */``` `#if !defined (SOMELIB_H_INCL)` `#define SOMELIB_H_INCL` `typedef struct some_s {` `int    comp;` `char   s[SOMELIB_MAX];` `} some_t;` `/*  Purpose of function make_some` ` *  Pre: ?? preconditions ??` ` */` `extern some_t` `make_some(int        n,` `const char str[]);` `/* other extern prototypes */` `#endif`	`somelib.h` is a header file to be included (`#include "somelib.h"`) in any program desiring to use its facilities. `somelib.h` uses conditional compilation (`#if...#endif`) to protect its contents from duplicate inclusion.

(continued)

Table 13.2 *(continued)*

C Construct	Meaning
Implementation File	

```
/* somelib.c */
#include "somelib.h"
#include <string.h>

/*  Purpose of function make_some
 *  Pre:  ?? preconditions ??
 */
some_t
make_some(int        n,
          const char str[])
{
     some_t result;

     result.comp = n;
     strcpy(result.s, str);

     return (result);
}

/*  other function definitions  */
```

somelib.c is the implementation file associated with somelib.h. Its object file must be linked to any other program that includes somelib.h.

Macro Definition and Call

```
#define AVG(x,y) (((x) + (y)) / 2.0)
. . .

ans = AVG(2*a, b);
```

Preprocessor will replace each call to AVG by its macro expansion. Statement shown becomes
```
    ans = (((2*a) + (b)) / 2.0);
```

exit Function

```
/*  Compute decimal equivalent of a
 *  common fraction
 *  Pre:  denom != 0
 */
double
dec_equiv(int num, int denom)
{
   if (denom == 0) {
     printf("Zero-divide: %d/%d\n",
            num, denom);
     exit(1);
   } else {
     return ((double)num /
             (double)denom);
   }
}
```

Function causes premature program termination if called with an invalid argument.

(continued)

Table 13.2 *(continued)*

C Construct	Meaning
Arguments to Function main	
| ```
int
main(int argc, char *argv[])
{
   if (argc == 3)
      process(argv[1], argv[2]);
   else
      printf
        ("Wrong number of options");

   return (0);
}
``` | Function `main` is expecting two command line arguments to pass to function `process`. |

QUICK-CHECK EXERCISES

1. A system designer who is breaking down a complex problem using _____ _____ will focus first on *what* a function is to do, leaving the details of *how* this is accomplished for later.
2. In order to use a library function, one must know the function's _____ , _____ , _____ , and _____ .
3. Functions that can be used in a variety of applications are examples of _____ code.
4. In C, a(n) _____ file contains information about *what* a library's functions do. The _____ file contains the details of *how* these actions are accomplished.
5. The keyword `extern` in a declaration notifies the _____ that the name declared will be known by the _____ .
6. When defining an implementation file `lib1.c`, why is it advantageous to `#include "lib1.h"`?
7. Given this definition of macro ABSDF,

   ```
   #define ABSDF(x, y)  (fabs((x) - (y)))
   ```
   ```

show what this statement will be after macro expansion:

```
if (ABSDF(a + b, c) > ABSDF(b + c, a))
      lgdiff = ABSDF(a + b, c);
```

8. Where are variables of storage class `auto` allocated and when? When are they deallocated?
9. When are variables of storage class `static` allocated? When are they deallocated?
10. Which of the following prototypes would be followed immediately by the code of function `mangle`?

```
double                          extern double
mangle(double x, double y)      mangle(double x, double y);
```

11. When generalizing a function for inclusion in a library, named constants are often replaced by _____ .
12. What directives could we add to header file `mylib.h` so that no matter how many `#include "mylib.h"` directives were processed, the contents of `mylib.h` would be compiled just once?

ANSWERS TO QUICK-CHECK EXERCISES

1. procedural abstraction
2. name, purpose, preconditions, parameter list
3. reusable
4. header, implementation
5. compiler, linker
6. Any necessary macros and data types are defined in just one file, the header file, so modification of a macro or of a data type does not require changes in more than one place.

7.
```
if ((fabs((a + b) - (c))) > (fabs((b + c) - (a))))
      lgdiff = (fabs((a + b) - (c)));
```

8. The variables are allocated on the stack at the time when a function is entered. They are deallocated when the function to which they belong returns.
9. The variables are allocated before program execution. They are deallocated at program termination.

10. the prototype on the left
11. function parameters
12. ```
#if !defined (MYLIB_H_INCL)
   #define MYLIB_H_INCL
      . . . rest of mylib.h . . .
   #endif
```

# REVIEW QUESTIONS

1. Define *procedural abstraction* and *data abstraction*.
2. What feature of C encourages the encapsulation of data objects and their operators?
3. Compare the typical contents of a library header file to the contents of an implementation file. Which of these files defines the interface between a library and a program?
4. How does the C compiler know whether to look for an included file in the system directory or in the program's directory?
5. Compare the execution of the macro call

    ```
    MAC(a, b)
    ```

    to the execution of an analogous function call

    ```
    mac(a, b)
    ```

    Which of the following two calls is sure to be valid and why?

    ```
    mac(++a, b)     or     MAC(++a, b)
    ```

6. When you write the body of a macro definition, where should you use parentheses?
7. What are C's five storage classes? What are the default storage classes for variables declared in each of the following environments?

    declared at the top level
    declared as function parameters
    declared as local variables of a function

8. What is the purpose of storage class `register`?
9. Discuss this statement: If a program has five functions that manipulate an array of data values, it makes more sense to declare this array at the program's top level so that each function does not need to have an array parameter.
    ```

10. Why is the argument value 1 used much more often than the argument value 0 in calls to the `exit` function?
11. Describe the purpose of the `defined` operator.
12. When function `main` of a C program has a `nonvoid` parameter list, why is the value of its first actual argument never less than 1?

PROGRAMMING PROJECTS

1. Create a library that defines a data type to represent a common fraction and provides functions for I/O, comparison (less than, equal to), and arithmetic operations (+, −, *, /) on these fractions. Use the library in a program that processes a list of fractions, finding the sum, the mean, the median, and the greatest absolute difference between consecutive elements. All results should be expressed as common fractions in reduced form.

2. Reuse the code from Fig. 10.22 as you develop a personal library of functions that perform the ∈ (is an element of), ⊆ (is a subset of), ∪ (union), ∩ (intersection), and − (set difference) operations on sets of letters and digits. Also include functions for interactive set I/O and functions to check for the empty set and to check that a certain set is valid. Be sure your library header file contains information about functions for only the operations listed. Any helper functions should appear only in the implementation file.

3. Develop a personal library that defines the `complex_t` data type and all the operators from Fig. 11.10 plus a `power` function that raises a complex number to an integer exponent. Then use this library in writing a program for applying Newton's method to the problem of approximating complex as well as real roots of a function (see Fig. 7.15).

   Try your program on a function with both real and complex roots such as

   $$f(x) = x^3 + 8x^2 - 16x - 128$$

   When looking for a complex root, use a complex guess.

4. You are developing a personal library of functions to assist in solving heat transfer problems. Your first step is to develop functions to solve simple conduction problems using various forms of the formula

   $$H = \frac{kA \, (t_2 - t_1)}{X}$$

   where H is the rate of heat transfer in calories/second, k is the coefficient of thermal conductivity for the particular substance, A is the cross-sectional area in cm^2, t_2 and t_1 are the temperatures in degrees Celsius on the two sides of the conductor, and X is the thickness of the conductor in cm.

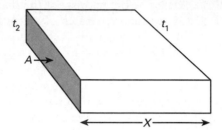

Your library will include not only a function to compute H given k, A, t_2, t_1, and X, but also functions to compute A given H, k, t_2, t_1, and X; t_2 given H, k, A, t_1, and X; and so on. Your library will define a data type `substance_t` with components `name` and `coef_cond` to be used in representing substance names and their coefficients of thermal conductivity. Your program should have available an array of common substances so the user can choose a substance by name rather than entering the actual constant.

Develop a program using your library that would interact with the user in a way such as

```
Respond to the prompts with the data known. For the
unknown quantity, enter a question mark (?)

Rate of heat transfer (cal/sec)>  180.0
Substance: (1) wood     (2) glass  (3) lead
           (4) steel    (5) other
> 2
Cross-sectional area of conductor (sq cm)> 1200
Temperature on one side (Celsius)> 25
Temperature on other side (Celsius)> ?
Thickness of conductor (cm)> .3
```

$$H = \frac{kA\,(t2 - t1)}{X}$$

```
H = 180.0 cal/sec
k = 0.0015 (glass)
A = 1200 sq cm
t2 = 25 degrees Celsius
t1 = -5 degrees Celsius
X = 0.3 cm

Temperature on the other side is -5 degrees Celsius.
```

If the user were to choose `other` for substance, the program would prompt for the substance's coefficient of thermal conductivity.

5. Write a program that takes a command line argument that is the name of a text file and creates a new text file with a heading line

```
***************** file name ********************
```

and the contents of the original file with line numbers added. If the file's name contains a period, use the part of the name before the period concatenated with `.lis` as the name of the new file. Otherwise, just concatenate `.lis` to the whole file name.

Character Sets

The charts in this appendix show the following character sets: ASCII (American Standard Code for Information Interchange), EBCDIC (Extended Binary Coded Decimal Interchange Code), and CDC[†] Scientific. Only printable characters are shown. The ordinal number for each character is shown in decimal. For example, in ASCII, the ordinal number for 'A' is 65, and the ordinal number for 'z' is 122. The blank character is denoted by □.

Left Digit(s) \ Right Digit	ASCII									
	0	**1**	**2**	**3**	**4**	**5**	**6**	**7**	**8**	**9**
3			□	!	"	#	$	%	&	'
4	(	)	*	+	,	−	.	/	0	1
5	2	3	4	5	6	7	8	9	:	;
6	<	=	>	?	@	A	B	C	D	E
7	F	G	H	I	J	K	L	M	N	O
8	P	Q	R	S	T	U	V	W	X	Y
9	Z	[	/	]	^	−	'	a	b	c
10	d	e	f	g	h	i	j	k	l	m
11	n	o	p	q	r	s	t	u	v	w
12	x	y	z	{	l	}				

Codes 00–31 and 127 are nonprintable control characters.

[†]CDC is a trademark of Control Data Corporation.

Left Digit(s) / Right Digit	**EBCDIC**									
	0	**1**	**2**	**3**	**4**	**5**	**6**	**7**	**8**	**9**
6					□					
7					¢	.	<	(	+	|
8	&									
9	!	$	*	)	;	¬	_	/		
10							^	,	%	—
11	>	?								
12			:	#	@	'	=	"		a
13	b	c	d	e	f	g	h	i		
14						j	k	l	m	n
15	o	p	q	r						
16			s	t	u	v	w	x	y	z
17								\	{	}
18	[	]								
19				A	B	C	D	E	F	G
20	H	I								J
21	K	L	M	N	O	P	Q	R		
22							S	T	U	V
23	W	X	Y	Z						
24	0	1	2	3	4	5	6	7	8	9

Codes 00–63 and 250–255 are nonprintable control characters.

Left Digit / Right Digit	**CDC**									
	0	**1**	**2**	**3**	**4**	**5**	**6**	**7**	**8**	**9**
0	:	A	B	C	D	E	F	G	H	I
1	J	K	L	M	N	O	P	Q	R	S
2	T	U	V	W	X	Y	Z	0	1	2
3	3	4	5	6	7	8	9	+	−	*
4	/	(	)	$	=	□	,	.	≡	[
5	]	%	≠	↱	∨	∧	↑	↓	<	>
6	≤	≥	¬	;						

Quick Reference Table: Selected Standard C Library Facilities

Function Name	Description	Number of Parameters	Type(s) of Parameters	Type of Function	Standard Header File
abs	integer absolute value	1	int	int	stdlib.h
acos	arc cosine	1	double	double	math.h
asin	arc sine	1	double	double	math.h
atan	arc tangent	1	double	double	math.h
atan2	arc tangent	2	double	double	math.h
calloc	dynamic array allocation	2	size_t[†]	void *	stdlib.h
ceil	smallest whole number not less than	1	double	double	math.h
cos	cosine	1	double	double	math.h
cosh	hyperbolic cosine	1	double	double	math.h
exit	program termination	1	int	void	stdlib.h
exp	exponential function (e^x)	1	double	double	math.h
fabs	double absolute value	1	double	double	math.h
fclose	file close	1	FILE *	int	stdio.h

(continued)

[†] unsigned integer type returned by sizeof operator

AP3

Appendix B   *(continued)*

Function Name	Description	Number of Parameters	Type(s) of Parameters	Type of Function	Standard Header File
fgets	string input from file	3	char * int FILE *	char *	stdio.h
floor	largest whole number not greater than	1	double	double	math.h
fopen	file open	2	char *	FILE *	stdio.h
fprintf	text file formatted output	varies	FILE * const char * types which match conversion specifications	int	stdio.h
fread	binary file input	4	void * size_t† size_t FILE *	size_t†	stdio.h
free	deallocates dynamically allocated memory	1	void *	void	stdlib.h
fscanf	text file input	varies	FILE * const char * types which match conversion specifications	int	stdio.h
fwrite	binary file output	4	void * size_t† size_t FILE *	size_t	stdio.h
getc	character input from text file	1	FILE *	int	stdio.h
getchar	character input from stdin	0		int	stdio.h

(continued)

Appendix B   *(continued)*

Function Name	Description	Number of Parameters	Type(s) of Parameters	Type of Function	Standard Header File
isalpha	checks for alphabetic character	1	int	int	ctype.h
isdigit	checks for base-10 digit character	1	int	int	ctype.h
islower	checks for lowercase letter	1	int	int	ctype.h
ispunct	checks for punctuation character	1	int	int	ctype.h
isspace	checks for whitespace character	1	int	int	ctype.h
isupper	checks for uppercase letter	1	int	int	ctype.h
log	natural logarithm	1	double	double	math.h
log10	base-10 logarithm	1	double	double	math.h
malloc	dynamic memory allocation	1	size_t†	void *	stdlib.h
memmove	copies given number of characters (bytes)	3	void * const void * size_t†	void *	string.h
pow	exponentiation	2	double	double	math.h
printf	formatted output to stdout	varies	const char * types which match conversion specifications	int	stdio.h
putc	character output to text file	2	int FILE *	int	stdio.h

(continued)

Appendix B *(continued)*

Function Name	Description	Number of Parameters	Type(s) of Parameters	Type of Function	Standard Header File
putchar	character output to stdout	1	int	int	stdio.h
rand	pseudorandom number	0		int	stdlib.h
scanf	input from stdin	varies	const char * types which match conversion specifications	int	stdio.h
sin	sine	1	double	double	math.h
sinh	hyperbolic sine	1	double	double	math.h
sprintf	formatted conversion to string	varies	char * const char * types which match conversion specifications	int	stdio.h
sqrt	square root	1	double	double	math.h
sscanf	formatted conversion from string	varies	const char * const char * types which match conversion specifications	int	stdio.h
strcat	string concatenation	2	char * const char *	char *	string.h
strcmp	lexical string comparison	2	const char *	int	string.h
strcpy	string copy	2	char * const char *	char *	string.h

(continued)

Appendix B   *(continued)*

Function Name	Description	Number of Parameters	Type(s) of Parameters	Type of Function	Standard Header File
strlen	string length (not counting \0)	1	const char *	size_t[†]	string.h
strncat	string concatenation up to maximum number of characters	3	char * const char * size_t[†]	char *	string.h
strncpy	string copy up to maximum number of characters	3	char * const char * size_t[†]	char *	string.h
system	calls operating system	1	const char *	int	stdlib.h
tan	tangent	1	double	double	math.h
tanh	hyperbolic tangent	1	double	double	math.h
tolower	converts uppercase letter to lowercase	1	int	int	ctype.h
toupper	converts lowercase letter to uppercase	1	int	int	ctype.h

APPENDIX C

C Operators

Table C.1 shows the precedence and associativity of the full range of C operators, including some operators not previously mentioned. In this table, an ellipsis (. . .) at the beginning of a group of operators indicates that these operators have equal precedence with those on the previous line. The precedence table is followed by a table listing each operator along with its name, the number of operands required, and the section of the text that explains the operator. New operators are marked by lowercase Roman numerals keyed to the descriptions following Table C.2.

Table C.1   Precedence and Associativity of Operations

Precedence	Operation	Associativity
highest (evaluated first)	`a[..]   f(..)     .     ->`	left
	postfix `++` postfix `--`	left
	prefix `++` prefix `--` `sizeof` `~` `!`	right
	`. . .` unary `+` unary `-` unary `&` unary `*`	
	casts	right
	`*` `/` `%`	left
	binary `+` binary `-`	left
	`<<` `>>`	left
	`<` `>` `<=` `>=`	left
	`==` `!=`	left
	binary `&`	left
	binary `^`	left
	binary `|`	left
	`&&`	left
	`||`	left
	`?  :`	right
	`=` `+=` `-=` `*=` `/=` `%=`	right
	`. . .` `<<=` `>>=` `&=` `^=` `|=`	
lowest (evaluated last)	`,`	left

AP8

Table C.2   Where To Find Operators in Text

Operator	Name	Number of Operands	Where Found
a[..]	subscript	1	8.1
f(..)	function call	varies	3.7
.	direct selection	2	11.1
->	indirect selection	2	11.2
++	increment	1	7.5
--	decrement	1	7.5
sizeof	size of memory block	1	12.5
~	bitwise negation	1	i
!	logical negation	1	7.3
&	address of	1	6.3
*	indirection	1	6.3
	or multiplication	2	2.6
(type name)	cast	1	7.1
/	division	2	2.6
%	remainder	2	2.6
+	unary plus	1	2.6
	or addition	2	2.6
-	unary minus	1	2.6
	or subtraction	2	2.6
<<	left shift	2	ii
>>	right shift	2	iii
<	less than	2	4.1
<=	less than or equal	2	4.1
>	greater than	2	4.1
>=	greater than or equal	2	4.1
==	equality	2	4.1
!=	inequality	2	4.1
&	bitwise and	2	iii
^	bitwise xor	2	iii
|	bitwise or	2	iii
&&	logical and	2	7.3
||	logical or	2	7.3
? :	conditional	3	iv
=	assignment	2	2.4
+= -= *=	compound assignment		
/= %=	(arithmetic)	2	7.5
<<= >>=	(shifts)	2	ii
&= ^= |=	(bitwise)	2	iii
,	sequential evaluation	2	v

Bitwise Operators

In Chapter 7, we studied that positive integers are represented in the computer by standard binary numbers. For example, on a machine where a type int value occupies 16 bits, the statement

n = 13;

would result in the following actual memory configuration:

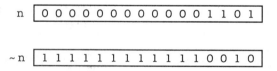

Ten of the operators given in Table C.1 take operands of any integer type but treat an operand as a collection of bits rather than as a single number. These operations are described below.

(i) Bitwise negation   Application of the ~ operator to an integer produces a value in which each bit of the operand has been replaced by its negation—that is, each 0 is replaced by a 1, and each 1 is replaced by a 0. Using our n value just shown, we compute ~n as follows:

n | 0 0 0 0 0 0 0 0 0 0 0 0 1 1 0 1 |

~n | 1 1 1 1 1 1 1 1 1 1 1 1 0 0 1 0 |

(ii) Shift operators   The shift operators << (left) and >> (right) take two integer operands. The value of the left operand is the number to be shifted and is viewed as a collection of bits that can be moved. To avoid problems with implementation variations, it is best to use left operands which are nonnegative when right shifting. The right operand is a nonnegative number telling how far to move the bits. The << operator shifts bits left, and the >> operator shifts them right. The bits that "fall off the end" are lost, and the "emptied" positions are filled with zeros. Here are some examples:

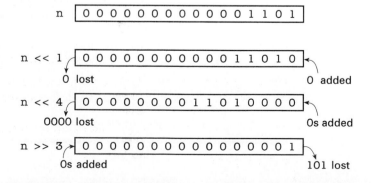

The compound assignment operators <<= and >>= cause the value resulting from the shift to be stored in the variable supplied as the left operand.

(iii) Bitwise and, xor, and or   The bitwise operators & (and), ^ (xor), and | (or) all take two integer operands that are viewed as strings of bits. The operators determine each bit of their result by considering corresponding bits of each operand. For example, if we denote the ith bit of operand n by n_i and the ith bit of operand m by m_i, then the ith bit of result r (r_i) is defined for each operator as shown in Table C.3.

Table C.3   Value of Each Bit of Result r for &, ^, and | with Operands n and m

Operator	Value of r_i	Explanation
&	n_i & m_i	r_i is 1 only if both corresponding operand bits are 1
^	n_i + m_i == 1	r_i is 1 only if the corresponding operand bits *do not* match
|	n_i | m_i	r_i is 1 if at least 1 of the corresponding operand bits is 1

The following is an example of applying each operator:

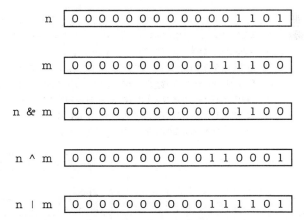

```
n     0 0 0 0 0 0 0 0 0 0 0 0 1 1 0 1

m     0 0 0 0 0 0 0 0 0 0 1 1 1 1 0 0

n & m 0 0 0 0 0 0 0 0 0 0 0 0 1 1 0 0

n ^ m 0 0 0 0 0 0 0 0 0 0 1 1 0 0 0 1

n | m 0 0 0 0 0 0 0 0 0 0 1 1 1 1 0 1
```

The compound assignment operators &=, ^=, and |= cause the result value to be stored in the variable supplied as the left operand.

(iv) Conditional   The conditional operator ? : takes three operands:

```
c ? r1 : r2
```

The value of an expression using the conditional is the value of either its second or third operand, depending on the value of the first operand. This evaluation could be pseudocoded as

```
if c
    result value is r1
else
    result value is r2
```

The conditional might be used in defining a macro to find the minimum of two values,

```
#define MIN(x,y)  (((x) <= (y)) ? (x) : (y))
```

(v) Sequential evaluation   The comma operator , evaluates its two operands in sequence, yielding the value of the second operand as the value of the expression. The value of the first operand is discarded. Following are two examples of the comma's use. In the first example, the value of the result of the comma's application is actually used: It is assigned to x. In the second example, the comma is merely a device to allow execution of two assignments in a context where only one expression is permitted.

EXAMPLE C.1   The effect of the assignment statement

```
x = (i += 2, a[i]);
```

is the same as the effect of these two statements:

```
i += 2;
x = a[i];
```

Notice that the parentheses around the comma expression in the first version are essential since the precedence of the assignment operator is higher than the precedence of the comma. Here are "before" and "after" snapshots of memory:

Before	After
a[0] 4.2	a[0] 4.2
[1] 12.1	[1] 12.1
[2] 6.8	[2] 6.8
[3] 10.5	[3] 10.5
i 1	i 3
x ?	x 10.5

 **EXAMPLE C.2**

In the code fragment that follows, the two loop control variables are initialized to 0. One of these variables is incremented by 2 at the end of each loop iteration while the second variable is incremented by the new value of the first.

```
for  (i = 0, j = 0;
     i < I_MAX  &&  j < J_MAX;
     i += 2, j += i)
  printf("i - %d,  j = %d\n", i, j);
```

The comma operator should be used sparingly, since frequent use greatly increases the code's complexity from the reader's point of view.

C Numeric Types

This text presents the numeric types int and double and points out that type char represents integer character codes. In fact, C provides quite a selection of numeric types for representing integers and for representing numbers that may have fractional parts (*floating-point numbers*).

Integer Types

Table D.1 summarizes the integer types (other than char) available in C. Types in the same row of the table require the same amount of memory. For example, signed int and unsigned int require the same size memory block. However, an unsigned type can represent a value of a magnitude larger than its companion signed type since the signed type must use one of its binary digits to represent the sign of its number.

Types in a column are arranged so that the size of one type is either the same as or larger than the types above it in the column. Of course, the larger the memory block, the larger the range of values that can be stored.

Table D.1   Integer Types in C (Other Than char)

Signed Type	Aliases	Unsigned Type	Aliases
short	short int signed short signed short int	unsigned short	unsigned short int
int	signed int signed	unsigned	unsigned int
long	long int signed long signed long int	unsigned long	unsigned long int

Integer Type char

Type char is also an integer type, but C implementations are free to treat type char as either signed or unsigned. The full ramifications of this variation are beyond the scope of this appendix. However, even the novice programmer may be affected by this variation when using library facilities such as getchar and getc, which return type int values. It is important to check the value returned to see if it is a negative integer representing EOF *before* any conversion of type int value to type char.

Floating-Point Types

Just as there are multiple integer types that differ in their memory requirements, ANSI C also provides for three floating-point types: float, double, and long double. Values of type float must have at least six decimal digits of precision; both type double and type long double values must have at least ten decimal digits. Throughout this text, we use type double, the type of constants such as 3.14159 and 2.1E10 and of floating-point parameters of library functions. To use constants of type float, we must append the suffix F, such as 3.14159F and 2.1E10F.

Enumerated Types

ANSI C provides for the definition of an enumerated type with a finite set of integer values represented by identifiers listed in the type definition. For example, a definition of an enumerated type `day_t` is

```
typedef enum day_e
       { sunday, monday, tuesday, wednesday, thursday,
         friday, saturday }
day_t;
```

This type definition has the effect of establishing the type name `day_t` as an equivalent of the keyword `enum` followed by the *enumeration tag* `day_e`. The identifiers `sunday`, `monday`, and so on, are the valid values of type `day_t`. They are automatically associated with the integers 0–6 (`sunday` is 0, `monday` is 1, and so on). An enumerated type serves to create a logical grouping of integer constants that are used to improve program readability.

For example, a declaration of a variable of type `day_t` and an instance of its use as the selector in a `switch` statement follow:

```
day_t current_day;

/* code that assigns current_day one of the day_t values   */
. . .

/*  selects a day to print */
switch (current_day) {
case sunday:
     printf("Sunday:   ");
     break;

case monday:
     printf("Monday:   ");
     break;

case tuesday:
     printf("Tuesday:   ");
     break;
```

```
case wednesday:
     printf("Wednesday:   ");
     break;

case thursday:
     printf("Thursday:   ");
     break;

case friday:
     printf("Friday:   ");
     break;

case saturday:
     printf("Saturday:   ");
     break;

default:
     printf("Invalid day");
}
```

Variables of an enumerated type may be manipulated just as one would handle any integer variable. The enumerated type values, called *enumeration constants*, may be used in any context where integer constants are valid.

Pointer Arithmetic

C permits application of the addition and subtraction operators to pointer operands if the pointers reference elements of an array. If p is a pointer to an array element, the value of the expression

p + 1

depends entirely on the size of the memory block occupied by one array element. C guarantees that if p is the address of an array's nth element, then p + 1 is the address of element $n + 1$.

An example to illustrate the role of context in the evaluation of a pointer expression follows. In Fig. F.1, our example uses two arrays: pl, which is an

Figure F.1   Pointer Arithmetic Example

```
typedef struct planet_s {
      char name[STRSIZ];
      double diameter,        /* equatorial diameter in km                  */
             dist_sun,        /* average distance from sun in km            */
             orbital_prd,     /* years to orbit sun once                    */
             axial_rot_prd;   /* hours to complete one revolution on axis   */
} planet_t;

. . .

planet_t pl[2] = {{"Earth", 12713.5, 1.5e+8, 1.0, 24.0},
                  {"Jupiter", 142800.0, 7.783e+8, 11.9, 9.925}};

int nm[5] = {4, 8, 10, 16, 22};
planet_t *p;
int *np;

p = pl + 1;
np = nm + 1;
```

(continued)

Figure F.1   *(continued)*

```
printf("sizeof (planet_t) = %d          sizeof (int) = %d\n",
       sizeof (planet_t), sizeof (int));
printf("pl = %d                  nm = %d\n", pl, nm);
printf(" p = %d (pl + %d)          \n", p, (int)p - (int)pl);
printf("np = %d (nm + %d)", np, (int)np - (int)nm);
printf(" p - pl = %d\n", p - pl);
```

array of planets, and nm, which is an array of integers. Figure F.2 shows the values of pointers p and np after they are assigned 1 more than pl and nm, respectively. In Fig. F.3, we see possible output produced when our example prints the contents of the four pointer variables as integers. We also see the effect of pointer subtraction on two pointers of the same type.

Figure F.2 Memory Snapshot at Completion of Pointer Arithmetic Example

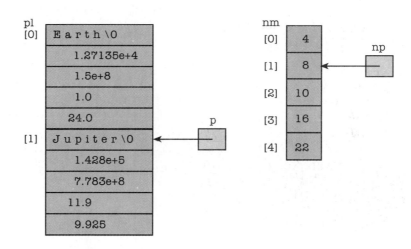

Figure F.3   Output from Pointer Arithmetic Example

```
sizeof (planet_t) = 52          sizeof (int) = 4
pl = 2145835092                 nm = 2145835316
 p = 2145835144 (pl + 52)       np = 2145835320 (nm + 4)
 p - pl = 1
```

ANSI C Reserved Words

auto	double	int	struct
break	else	long	switch
case	enum	register	typedef
char	extern	return	union
const	float	short	unsigned
continue	for	signed	void
default	goto	sizeof	volatile
do	if	static	while

Odd-Numbered Self-Check Exercises

CHAPTER 1

Section 1.2

1. −27.2 in cell 0, 75.62 in cell 999. Cell 998 contains the letter X, cell 2 contains 0.005.

Section 1.4

1. x = a + b + c; means "add the values represented by a, b, and c together and save the result in x."

x = y / z; means "divide the value represented by y by the value of z and save the result in x."

d = c − b + a; means "subtract the value represented by b from that in c, then add the value of a, and save the result in d."

x = x + 1; means "add 1 to the value in x."

kelvins = celsius + 273.15; means "add 273.15 to the value represented by celsius and save the result in kelvins."

Section 1.5

1. The *source file* contains the program written in a high-level language, which is then translated by a compiler into an *object file*. The linker combines the *object file* with necessary program units from other object files to create the *load file*. The *loader* then places the *load file* in main memory.

CHAPTER 2

Section 2.1

1. 1) State the problem clearly (requirements specification).
    2) Determine input/output requirements and relevant formulas (analysis).
    3) Design an algorithm (design).
    4) Implement the algorithm in C (implementation).
    5) Verify the algorithm and test the program (verification and testing).

Section 2.2

1. The preprocessor; #define and #include
3. Because it is a universal constant that will not be changed by the program. Furthermore, if the approximation used in a program needed to be changed, all occurrences would have to be changed. Using a constant macro makes this easier.

Section 2.3

1. Reserved words: `int, double`
    Conventional constant macros: `MAX_ENTRIES, G`
    Other valid identifiers: `time, this_is_a_long_one, xyz123`
    Invalid identifiers: `Sue's` (`'` is not allowed),
    `part#2` (`#` is not allowed), `"char"` (`"` is not allowed)

Section 2.4

1.  ```
    Enter two integers> 5 7
    m = 10
    n = 21
    ```
3.  ```
    My name is Jane Doe.
    I live in Ann Arbor, MI
    and I have 11 years of programming experience.
    ```

Section 2.5

1. First comment is terminated with incorrect comment delimiter (should be `*/`). Second comment includes a nested comment that is not allowed.
3.  ```c
    /*
     *   Compute and print the difference of two input values
     */

    #include <stdio.h>

    int
    main(void)
    {
          int   first,    /* first input value  */
                second,   /* second input value */
                sum;      /* sum of inputs      */

          /* Get input data. */
          scanf("%d%d", first, second);

          /* Compute the sum. */
          sum = first + second;

          /* Output the result. */
          printf("\n%d + %d = %d\n", first, second, sum);

          return(0);
    }
    ```

    The program prints the first number followed by ' + ' and the second number. Then ' = ' is printed, followed by the sum of the first and second numbers.
    ```

Section 2.6

1. type int constants: 15, -999
   type char constants: '*', 'x', '9'
   type double constants: 25.123, 15., .123, 32e-4
   Invalid constants: 'xyz', $, '-5'

3.
```
1.8            *          celsius            +                32.0
1.8        *          3               +        32.0
          5.4                          +        32.0
                      37.4
(salary    -    5000.0)        *    0.20        +        1425.0
(12400.0   -    5000.0)        *    0.20        +        1425.0
          7400.0              *    0.20        +        1425.0
                              1480.0            +     1425.0
                                      2905.0
```

5. PI = 3.14159   MAXI = 1000
   a = 5
   b = 2
   y = 2.0
   ----
   a. i = a % b;   1
   b. i = (989 - MAXI) / a;   -11/2 (??)
   c. i = b % a;   2
   d. x = PI * y;   6.28318
   e. i = a / -b;   5/-2 (??)
   f. x = a / b;   2.0
   g. x = a % (a / b);   1.0
   h. i = b / 0;   Divide by zero
   i. i = a % (990 - MAXI);   5/-10 (??)
   j. i = (MAXI - 990) / a;   2
   k. x = a / y;   2.5
   l. i = PI * a;   15
   m. x = PI / y;   1.570795
   n. x = b / a;   0.0
   o. i = (MAXI - 990) % a;   0
   p. i = a % 0;   Divide by zero
   q. i = a % (MAXI - 990);   5
   ?? means the result varies.

7. a. x = 4.0 * a * c;
   b. a = a * c;
   c. i = 5 * j * 3;
   d. k = 3 * (i + j);
   e. x = 5 * a + b * c;

Section 2.7

```
1.  printf("Salary is %10.2f", salary) ;
3.  x is #12.34   i is #100
    i is 100
    x is 12.3
```

Section 2.8

1. Calls to `printf` to display prompts precede calls to `scanf` to obtain data. Calls to `printf` follow calls to `scanf` when data are echoed. Prompts are used in interactive programs, but not in batch programs. Batch programs should echo input; interactive programs may also echo input.

CHAPTER 3

Section 3.1

1. Given three numbers, we must compute the average. The problem statement has not specified the type of these numbers so we will assume double.

    Analysis:
    ```
    Input : double num1, num2, num3 /* three numbers */
    Output: double avg             /* the average   */
    ```

    The average of three numbers is computed by dividing the sum of the three numbers by 3.

    Design:
    ```
    Get the three numbers num1, num2, and num3.
    sum = num1 + num2 + num3
    avg = sum / 3.0
    Output avg.
    ```

Section 3.2

1. The values of WASHER_DIAMETER and OUTER_DIAMETER must be changed.

    ```
    #define WASHER_DIAMETER (5.0/16.0)    /* diameter in inches of
                                           * a flat washer (diameter
                                           * of the hole)
                                           */
    #define OUTER_DIAMETER (5.0/8.0)      /* diameter of edge
                                           * of outer rim of
                                           * washer
                                           */
    ```

Section 3.3

1. Because you might want to perform steps on a variety of data

Section 3.4

1.

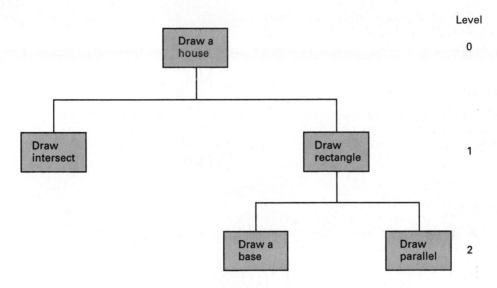

Level

0

1

2

3.

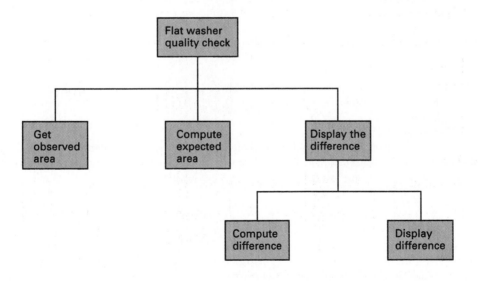

Section 3.5

1.
```
**    **
**    **
******
**    **
**    **

******
  **
  **
  **
******


    *        *
   ***      ***
  ** ** ** **
  **    ***    **
  **     *     **

******
**    **
**    **
**    **
******

    *        *
   ***      ***
  ** ** ** **
  **    ***    **
  **     *     **
```

Section 3.6

1. It simplifies the code of the main function, making it more readable. It isolates in one function all the statements that display instructions. Thus if the program usage changes, the programmer knows exactly where all the instructions are located, so the changes are localized.

Section 3.7

1. Arguments to `printf` hold information that is passed to function `printf` by the function that calls it. The arguments to `printf` include values to be printed and a format that specifies how they must be printed. Therefore, they are considered input arguments. Arguments to `scanf` (after the first) are output arguments, since they bring information back from the function (values obtained from the input device).

Section 3.8

1. a. `sqrt(u + v) * w * w   or sqrt(u + v) * pow(w, 2)`
   b. `log10(pow(x, y))`
   c. `sqrt(pow(x-y, 2))`
   d. `fabs(x * y - w / z)`

CHAPTER 4

Section 4.1

1. a. Always
   b. O.K.
3. ans is 2.

Section 4.2

```
1. if (x > y) {
        x = x + 10.0;
        printf("x Bigger");
   } else {
        printf("x Smaller");
        printf("y is %.2f", y);
   }
3. if (engine_type == 'J') {
        printf("Jet engine\n");
        speed_category = 1;
   } else {
        printf("Propellers\n");
        speed_category = 2;
   }
```

Section 4.3

1.

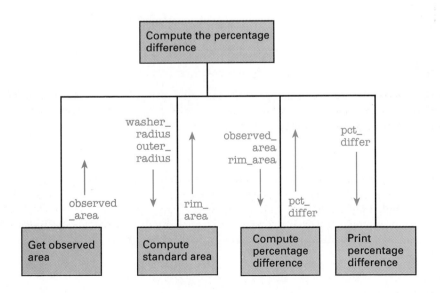

`pct_differ` is an output of subproblem "Compute percentage difference" and an input to subproblem "Print percentage difference."

Section 4.4

1. a. BCA

Algorithm Step	ch1	ch2	ch3	alpha_first	Effect
	?	?	?	?	
1. Get three letters	B	C	A		Gets the data
2.1.1 if ch1 precedes ch2					Is 'B' < 'C' ? value is true
2.1.2 alpha_first gets ch1				B	'B' is first so far
2.2.1 if ch3 precedes alpha_first					Is 'A' < 'B' ? value is true
2.2.2 alpha_first gets ch3				A	'A' is first
3. Display alpha_first					Prints A is the first letter...

b. ABC

Algorithm Step	ch1	ch2	ch3	alpha_first	Effect
	?	?	?	?	
1. Get three letters	A	B	C		Gets the data
2.1.1 if ch1 precedes ch2					Is 'A' < 'B' ? value is true
2.1.2 alpha_first gets ch2				A	'A' is first so far
2.2.1 if ch3 precedes alpha_first					Is 'C' < 'A' ? value is false
3. Display alpha_first					Prints A is the first letter...

c. BAC

Algorithm Step	ch1	ch2	ch3	alpha_first	Effect
	?	?	?	?	
1. Get three letters	B	A	C		Gets the data
2.1.1 if ch1 precedes ch2					Is 'B' < 'A' ? value is false
2.1.3 alpha_first gets ch2				A	'A' is first so far
2.2.1 if ch3 precedes alpha_first					Is 'C' < 'A' ? value is false
3. Display alpha_first					Prints A is the first letter...

3. a.

previous	current	unpaid	bill	used	use_chg	late
3222	3242	40	99	22	24.20	2.00

```
Output:
This program figures a water bill based on the demand charge
($35.00) and a $1.10 per 1000 gallons use charge.

A $2.00 surcharge is added to accounts with an unpaid balance.

Enter unpaid balance, previous and current meter readings
on separate lines after the prompts.
Press <return> or <enter> after typing each number.

Enter unpaid balance> $40.00
Enter previous meter reading> 3222
Enter current meter reading> 3242

Bill includes $2.00 late charge on unpaid balance of $40.00

Total due = $99.00
```

b.

previous	current	unpaid	bill	used	use_chg	late
4000	4030	0	68	30	3.30	0.0

(continued)

```
Output:
This program figures a water bill based on the demand charge
($35.00) and a $1.10 per 1000 gallons use charge.

A $2.00 surcharge is added to accounts with an unpaid balance.

Enter unpaid balance, previous and current meter readings
on separate lines after the prompts.
Press <return> or <enter> after typing each number.

Enter unpaid balance> $0.00
Enter previous meter reading> 4000
Enter current meter reading> 4030

Total due = $68.00
```

Section 4.5

1.

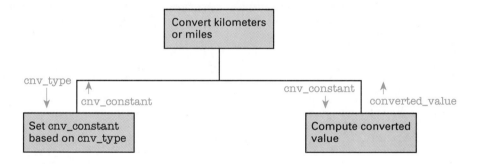

Section 4.6

1.

Statement Part	salary	tax	Effect
	23500.00	?	
if (salary < 0.0)			25300.0 < 0.0 is false
else if (salary < 15000.00)			23500.0 < 15000.0 is false
else if (salary < 30000.00)			23500.0 < 30000.0 is true
tax = (salary − 15000.00)			Evaluates to 8500.00
* 0.18			Evaluates to 1530.00
+ 2250.00			Evaluates to 3780.00

3.  ```
    if (ph > 7) {
          if (ph < 12)
                printf("Alkaline\n");
          else
                printf("Very alkaline\n");
    } else if (ph == 7) {
          printf("Neutral\n");
    } else if (ph > 2) {
          printf("Acidic\n");
    } else {
          printf("Very acidic\n");
    }                        Braces shown are optional.
    ```

Section 4.7

1.  ```
    red
    blue
    yellow
    ```

CHAPTER 5

Section 5.2

1. a.

Product	Count	x
5	0	5
25	1	
125	2	
625	3	
3125	4	

Output:

```
Enter an integer>
5
25
125
625
```

b.

Product	Count	x
6	0	6
36	1	
216	2	
1296	3	
7776	4	

Output:

```
Enter an integer>
6
36
216
1296
```

c.

Product	Count	x
7	0	7
49	1	
343	2	
2401	3	
16807	4	

Output:

```
Enter an integer>
7
49
343
2401
```

In general, this loop displays n, n^2, n^3, and n^4.

3.
```
count = 0;
while (count < 5) {
   count = count + 1;
   printf("Next number> ");
   scanf("%d", &next_num);
   sum = sum + next_num;
}
printf("%d numbers were added; ", count);
printf("their sum is %d.\n", sum);
```

Section 5.3

1.

sum	odd
0	1
1	3
4	5
9	7
16	9

Output:

```
Sum of positive odd numbers less than 8 is 16.
```

3. The answer for both questions is 0.

5. a.

j	i
10	1
8	2
6	3
4	4
2	5
0	6

Output:

```
1   10
2   8
3   6
4   4
5   2
```

b.
```
j = 10;
for (i = 0;  i < 5;  i = i + 1) {
    printf("%d  %d\n", i + 1, j);
    j = j - 2;
}
```

Section 5.4

1. Any initial supply less than 8000
3.
```
Number of barrels currently in tank>
8350.80 barrels are available.

Enter number of gallons removed>
After removal of 7581.00 gallons (180.50 barrels),
8170.30 barrels are available.
```

(continued)

```
Enter number of gallons removed>
After removal of 7984.20 gallons (190.10 barrels),
only 7980.20 barrels are left.

*** WARNING ***
Available supply is less than 10 percent of tank's 80000.00-barrel capacity.
```

Section 5.5

1. Step a: Initialization of the loop control variable
    Step c: The loop repetition condition (*n* is positive)
    Step e: The update of the loop control variable

Section 5.6

1. a. ```
        *
        **
        ***
        ****
        *****
        ```
1.  b.  ```
        ***
        ***
        ***
        ***
        ***
        ```

Section 5.7

1.
```c
/*
 * Calculate and print a chart showing the safety level of
 * a coffee room.
 */

#include <stdio.h>

#define SAFE_RAD     0.466  /* safe level of radiation     */
#define SAFETY_FACT 10.0   /* safety factor               */

int
main(void)
{
   int    day;            /* days elapsed since substance leak  */
   double init_radiation, /* radiation level right after leak    */
          radiation_lev,  /* current radiation level             */
          min_radiation;  /* safe level divided by safety factor */

   /* Initialize day and min_radiation                   */
   day = 0;
   min_radiation = SAFE_RAD / SAFETY_FACT;
```

```
    /* Prompt user to enter initial radiation level */
    printf("\nEnter the radiation level (in millirems)> ");
    scanf("%lf", &init_radiation);

    /* Display table                                    */
    printf("\n\n   Day   Radiation   Status\n        (millirems)");
    radiation_lev = init_radiation;
    while (radiation_lev > min_radiation) {
        if (radiation_lev > SAFE_RAD)
            printf("\n %3d  %9.4f  Unsafe", day, radiation_lev);
        else
            printf("\n %3d  %9.4f  Safe", day, radiation_lev);
        day = day + 3;
        radiation_lev = radiation_lev / 2.0;
    }
    printf("\n");

    return(0);
}
```

Section 5.8

```
1. for (count = 0;  count <= n;  count = count + 1) {
       printf("DEBUG*** count=%d\n", count);
       sum = sum + count;
       count = count + 1;
       printf("DEBUG*** sum=%d\n", sum);
   }
```

CHAPTER 6

Section 6.1

1. 86

Section 6.2

1. (User's responses are bolded.)
   ```
   Enter dimensions of rectangle within the limits shown.
   Length in the range 10 . . 100 characters> 16
   Width in lines (at least 2)> 3

   ****************
   **            **
   ****************

      16   X   3
   ```

Section 6.3

```
1. void
   sum_n_avg(double   n1,      /* input numbers */
             double   n2,
             double   n3,
             double *sump,  /* output - sum of the three numbers */
             double *avgp)  /* output - average of the numbers   */
```

3.

Reference	Where Legal	Data Type	Value
valp	sub	double *	pointer to shaded color cell
code	main	char	'g'
&code	main	char *	pointer to color cell
countp	sub	int *	pointer to shaded black cell
*countp	sub	int	14
*valp	sub	double	17.1
letp	sub	char *	pointer to color cell
&x	main	double *	pointer to shaded color cell

Section 6.4

```
1.                              num1     num2     num3
                                 8        12       10
   order(&num3, &num2);
   order(&num2, &num1);         12        8
   order(&num3, &num2);                   10       8
```

Code puts num1, num2, num3 in descending order (from largest to smallest).

Section 6.6

1. Prototype and first part of function body for onef:

```
void
onef(int dat, int *out1p, int *out2p)
{
   int tmp;
   twof(dat, &tmp, out2p);
   . . .
}
```

Prototype of twof:

```
void
twof(int indat, int *result1p, int *result2p)
```

Section 6.7

1. Because multiple values need to be returned and the only way to return them is by using output parameters

◄━━━ **CHAPTER 7** ━━━►

Section 7.1

1. Representation error occurs when the number of bits (binary digits) in the mantissa of a type `double` variable is insufficient to exactly represent a certain fraction. Cancellation error occurs when performing an operation on two numbers that have a very large difference in magnitude, and the smaller number's effect is lost.

3.
```
      x        y           m    n
    10.5     7.2           5    2
```

```
a. x / (double)m            2.1
b. x / m                    2.1
c. (double)(n * m)         10.0
d. (double)(n / m) + y      7.2
e. (double)(n / m)          0.0
```

Section 7.2

1. a. 3
    b. 'E'
    c. −1

Section 7.3

1.   x = 15.0   y = 25.0

```
a. x != y                1 (TRUE)
b. x < x                 0 (FALSE)
c. x >= y - x            1 (TRUE)
d. x == y + x - y        1 (TRUE)
```

3. x = 3.0   y = 4.0   z = 2.0   flag = 0

```
! flag          ||      y + z      >=     x - z
   0                    ‾‾‾‾‾‾‾‾‾‾‾‾‾‾‾‾‾‾‾‾‾‾‾
  ‾‾‾                        short circuited
   1
            ‾‾‾‾‾‾‾‾‾‾‾‾‾‾‾‾‾‾‾‾‾‾‾‾
                    1
```

```
! ( flag || y + z >= x - z)
     0
               ‾‾‾‾     ‾‾‾‾
                6.0      1.0
                   ‾‾‾‾‾‾
                     1
     ‾‾‾‾‾‾‾‾‾‾‾‾‾‾‾‾‾‾‾‾
              1
       ‾‾‾‾‾‾‾‾‾‾‾‾‾‾‾‾‾
              0
```

Section 7.4

1. !(n > 0   &&   n % 2   ==   0) or
    n <= 0 || n % 2 != 0

3. The `for` loop is better because the `do-while` tests the same condition twice on each iteration.

Section 7.5

1. `n = 32     m = 12     p = 11`
3. `r /= 10;`
   Not possible since `z = z * (x + 1);` is not equivalent to expression shown.
   `q += r * m;`
   `m -= n + p;`

Section 7.6

1. ```
   Initial guess for a root> 1.0
   The approximate root is 1.5000000000e+00
   The function value f(1.5000000000e+00) is 4.4408920985e-15
   6 guesses made.

   Initial guess for a root> -1.0
   The approximate root is -5.0000000001e-01
   The function value f(-5.0000000001e-01) is 5.2428728026e-11
   5 guesses made.

   Initial guess for a root> 10.0
   The approximate root is 1.5000000000e+00
   The function value f(1.5000000000e+00) is 1.4337864229e-11
   8 guesses made.

   Initial guess for a root> -10.0
   The approximate root is -5.0000000005e-01
   The function value f(-5.0000000005e-01) is 1.9159651643e-10
   8 guesses made.
   ```

   One can find the exact roots using the quadratic formula.

   ```
   x1 = (-b + sqrt(b ** 2 - 4 * a * c))/ (2 * a) and
   x2 = (-b - sqrt(b ** 2 - 4 * a * c))/ (2 * a)
   ```

   where `a * x ** 2 + b * x + c = 0`

<p align="center">◀ CHAPTER 8 ▶</p>

Section 8.1

1. `x3` is a valid variable name. `x[3]` is a reference to the fourth element of array `x`.
3. `double square[11];`
   `int cube[11];`
   ```

Section 8.2

1. Before:

x[0] x[1] x[2] x[3] x[4] x[5] x[6] x[7]

| 16.0 | 12.0 | 6.0 | 8.0 | 2.5 | 12.0 | 14.0 | -54.5 |

After:

x[0] x[1] x[2] x[3] x[4] x[5] x[6] x[7]

| 16.0 | 12.0 | 6.0 | 8.0 | 12.0 | 14.0 | 14.0 | -54.5 |

Section 8.3

```
1. #include <math.h>
   #define MAX_SIZE 11
   . . .
   double cube[MAX_SIZE];
   int sq_root[MAX_SIZE];
   int i;

   for (i = 0; i < MAX_SIZE; ++i) {
      sq_root[i] = sqrt((double)i);
      cube[i] = i * i * i;
   }
```

Section 8.4

```
1. seg_len = sqrt(pow(x[i+1] - x[i], 2) + pow(y[i+1]- y[i], 2));
```

Section 8.5

```
1. void
   convert_to_12hr(int time, int *hrsp, int *minp)
   {
      *hrsp = time / 100;
      if (*hrsp > 12)
         *hrsp -= 12;
      *minp = time % 100;
   }
```

Section 8.6

1. The value 1 is returned.

```
/*
 *  Searches for target item in first n elements of array arr
```

(continued)

```
    *   Returns how many times target appears
    *   Pre:  target and first n elements of array arr are
    *         defined and n≥0
    */
   int
   search(const int arr[],  /*  array to search          */
          int        target, /*  value searched for        */
          int        n)      /*  number of array elements
                                 to search               */
   {
      int i,
          cnt; /* Number of times the target is found. */

      /*  Compare each element to target.  */
      cnt = 0;
      for (i = 0; i < n; ++i)
         if (arr[i] == target)
            ++cnt;

      return (cnt);
   }
```

Section 8.7

```
1. /*
   * Gets data to place in dbl_arr until value of sentinel
   * is encountered in the input. Stops input prematurely
   * if there are more than dbl_max data values before the
   * sentinel or if invalid data is encountered.
   *    Pre:  sentinel and dbl_max are defined and dbl_max
   *          is the declared size of dbl_arr
   *
   *    int     dbl_max  input - declared size of dbl_arr
   *    double  sentinel input - end of data value in input list
   *    double  dbl_arr   output - array of data
   *    double *dbl_sizep output - number of data values stored in dbl_arr
   */
   int
   fill_to_sentinel(int dbl_max, double sentinel,
                    double  dbl_arr[], int *dbl_sizep)
   {
      double data;
      int     i, status, result = 1;

      /* Sentinel input loop */
      i = 0;
      for (status = scanf("%lf", &data);
```

```
              status == 1 && data != sentinel && i < dbl_max;
              status = scanf("%lf", &data)) {
        dbl_arr[i] = data;
        ++i;
    }

    /* Issue error message on premature exit */
    if (status != 1) {
        printf("***Error in data format ***\n");
        printf("***Using first %d data values ***\n", i);
        result = 0;
    } else if (data != sentinel) {
        printf("***Error: too much data before sentinel***\n");
        printf("***Using first %d data values ***\n", i);
        result = 0;
    }
    /* Send back size of used portion of array */
    *dbl_sizep = i;
    return (result);
}
3. void
   bubble(double list[], int n)
   {
       int i, pass, sorted;
       double temp;
   . . .
```

Section 8.9

```
1. a. int i, j, k;

      for (i = 0; i < MAXCRS; ++i) {
         printf("Processing course number %d: \n", i);
         for (j = 0; j < 5; ++j) {
            printf("  Campus %d\n", j);
            for (k = 0; k < 4; ++k)
               printf("    Enter number of ");
               switch (k) {
               case 0 :
                  printf("Freshmen > ");
                  break;

               case 1 :
                  printf("Sophomores > ");
                  break;
```

(continued)

```
          case 2 :
             printf("Juniors > ");
             break;

          case 3 :
             printf("Seniors > ");
             break;

          }
          scanf("%d", &enroll[i][j][k]);
       }
     }
   }
b. int i, j,
      jcnt;   /* Number of juniors. */
   jcnt = 0;
   for (i = 0; i < MAXCRS; ++i)
      for (j = 0; j < 5; ++j)
         jcnt += enroll[i][j][2];
c. /*
    *  Compute the number of students in a course who have a
    *  specific rank.
    *  returns -1 if rank or course is out of range.
    */
   int
   find_students (int enroll[][5][4], int rank, int course)
   {
      int i, cnt = 0;

      if ((rank >= 0 && rank <= 3)
             && (course >= 0 && course <= MAXCRS))
         for (i = 0; i < 5; ++i)
            cnt += enroll[course][i][rank];
      else
         cnt = -1;
      return (cnt);
   }

   To use,
      printf("Number of sophomores in course 2 is %d\n",
             find_students(enroll, 1, 2);
d. int i, j, total, upper;

   total = 0;
   upper = 0;
   for (j = 0; j < 5; ++j) {
      for (i = 0; i < MAXCRS; ++i)
```

```
              upper += enroll[i][j][2] + enroll[i][j][3];
           printf("Number of upperclass students on campus");
           printf("%d is %d.\n", j, upper);
           total += upper;
        }
        printf("Total upperclass students on all campuses is %d.\n",
               total);
```

<hr>

CHAPTER 9

Section 9.1

1. b
3.

```
                     /*            1           2          3 */
                     /* 123456789012345678901234567890 */
   char blanks[]    = "                             ";
      or
   char blanks[30] = "                             ";
```

Section 9.2

1. 12 John Quincy Join

Section 9.3

1. JOHN ADAMS

Section 9.4

```
1. if (strcmp(name1, name2) == 0)
       printf("Names match.\n");
   else
       printf("Names do not match.\n");

   if (strcmp(w1, w2) < 0)
       strassign(word, w1, STR_LEN);
   else
       strassign(word, w2, STR_LEN);

   int i, len;

   len = strlen(s1);
   i = strlen(s2);
   if (i < len)
       len = i;
   /*
       Since len will never be larger than STR_LEN, no need to
       check for overflow of strings.
```

(continued)

```
 */
 for (i = 0;  i < len  &&  s1[i] == s2[i];  ++i)
    mtch[i] = s1[i];
 mtch[i] = '\0';
```

Section 9.5

```
1. /*
    * Orders a list of strings according the string length --
    * shortest to longest
    */
   void
   order_by_len(char strings[][STRSIZ], /* input/output list of
                                           strings          */
             int num_str)        /* input - number of strings */
   void
   order_by_len(char *strings[],/* input/output list of
                                           strings          */
             int num_str)        /* input - number of strings */
```

Section 9.6

1. The problem is that isupper takes a character argument, not a string.

   Function substr returns a string (char *) not a char.

   ```
   if (isupper(str[0]))
      printf("%s begins with a capital letter\n", str);
   ```

Section 9.7

1. The & is not needed since dayp, mth_name and yearp are all addresses. Variables dayp and yearp are integer output arguments (type int *), and mth_name is a character array.

Section 9.8

1.

i	len	revstr	str
?	4	"??..."	"glob"
1		"b?..."	
2		"bo?..."	
3		"bol?..."	
4		"bolg..."	
5			
		"bolg"	

Section 9.9

3. Yes

5. No. In A, d5 becomes `"string functio"`; in B, d5 becomes `"string functions"` which overflows the 15-character array d5.

CHAPTER 10

Section 10.1

1. a. `multiply(5, 4) -> multiply(5, 3) -> multiply(5, 2) -> multiply(5, 1)`
              and add 5   and add 5   and add 5
   b. `count('d',"dad") -> count('d',"ad") -> count('d',"d") -> count('d',"")`
                  and add 1 if   and add 1 if   and add 1 if
                  'd' is a 'd'   'a' is a 'd'   'd' is a 'd'

Section 10.2

1. Stack trace of `multiply(6,3)`

```
n   m   ans
3   6   ?

2   6   ?
3   6   ?

1   6   6
2   6   ?
3   6   ?

2   6   12
3   6   ?

3   6   18
```

Section 10.3

1.
```
int
power_raiser(int base, int power)
{
  int ans;

  if (power == 0)
     ans = 1;
  else
     ans = base * power_raiser(base,power - 1);
  return (ans);
}
```

3. When `fibonacci`'s argument was 2, the `else` clause assignment statement would generate a call to
`fibonacci(fibonacci(2 - 2) or fibonacci(0))` whose argument value does not satisfy the
precondition.

Section 10.4

1.

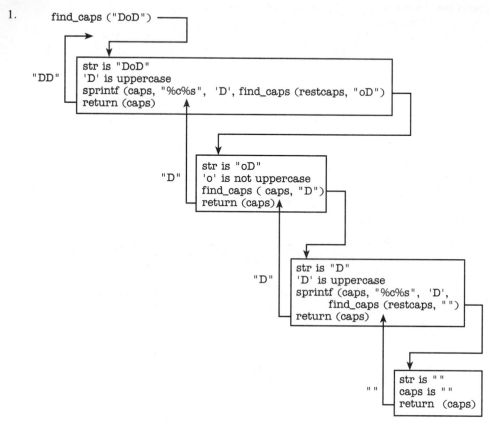

3. Replace the reference to `reststr` with `&str[1]`.

Section 10.5

1. Trace of is_element and is_subset on call to is_subset("bc","cebf")

```
Entering is_subset with sub = {b, c} and set = {c, e, b, f}
Entering is_element with ele = b and set = {c, e, b, f}
Entering is_element with ele = b and set = {e, b, f}
Entering is_element with ele = b and set = {b, f}
Exiting is_element with ele = b, set = {b, f}, and ans = 1
Exiting is_element with ele = b, set = {e, b, f}, and ans = 1
Exiting is_element with ele = b, set = {c, e, b, f}, and ans = 1
Entering is_subset with sub = {c} and set = {c, e, b, f}
Entering is_element with ele = c and set = {c, e, b, f}
```

(continued)

```
Exiting is_element with ele = c, set = {c, e, b, f}, and ans = 1
Entering is_subset with sub = {} and set = {c, e, b, f}
Exiting is_subset with sub = {}, set = {c, e, b, f}, and ans = 1
Exiting is_subset with sub = {c}, set = {c, e, b, f}, and ans = 1
Exiting is_subset with sub = {b, c}, set = {c, e, b, f}, and ans = 1
```

Section 10.6

1. By the formula, moves = $2^n - 1$. Thus a six-disk problem would require $2^6 - 1 = 63$ moves.

Section 10.7

1. (blob_check is abbreviated bc)
   a. bc(grid, 0, 0) = 0 (EMPTY)
   b. bc(grid, 0, 1):

         Mark (0, 1) EMPTY

         ct = 1 + $\underset{\text{0 (off grid)}}{\underline{\text{bc(grid, -1, 2)}}}$ + $\underset{\text{0 (EMPTY)}}{\underline{\text{bc(grid, 0, 2)}}}$ + $\underset{\text{0 (EMPTY)}}{\underline{\text{bc(grid, 1, 2)}}}$ +

              $\underset{\text{0 (EMPTY)}}{\underline{\text{bc(grid, 1, 1)}}}$ + $\underset{1}{\underline{\text{bc(grid, 1, 0)}}}$ + $\underset{\text{0 (EMPTY)}}{\underline{\text{bc(grid, 0, 0)}}}$ +

         Mark (1, 0) EMPTY

              $\underset{\text{0 (off grid)}}{\underline{\text{bc(grid, -1, 0)}}}$ + $\underset{\text{0 (off grid)}}{\underline{\text{bc(grid, -1, 1)}}}$
            = 2

CHAPTER 11

Section 11.1

1.
```
typedef struct long_lat_s {
    int     minutes,
            seconds;
    char    direction;
} long_lat_t;
```

3.
```
typedef struct catalog_entry_s {
    char    authors[50],
            title[50],
            publisher[50];
    int     year;
} catalog_entry_t;
```

(continued)

```
catalog_entry_t   book;

strassign(book.authors,"Hanly, Koffman, Friedman", 50);
strassign(book.title,"Problem Solving and Program Design in C",50);
strassign(book.publisher,"Addison-Wesley", 50);
book.year = 1993;
```

Section 11.2

```
1. /*
    *  Prints with labels all components of a long_lat_t structure
    */
   void
   print_long_lat(long_lat_t pos)  /* input - one long_lat structure */
   {
        printf("  Minutes:    %d deg\n", pos.minutes);
        printf("  Seconds:    %d deg\n", pos.seconds);
        printf("  Direction: %c\n", pos.direction);
   }

   /*
    *  Determines whether or not the components of pos_1 and post_2 match
    */
   int
   long_lat_equal(long_lat_t pos_1,  /* input - positions to         */
                  long_lat_t pos_2)  /*         compare              */
   {

        return (pos_1.minutes == pos_2.minutes      &&
                pos_1.seconds == pos_2.seconds      &&
                pos_1.direction == pos_2.direction);
   }

   /*
    *  Fills a type long_lat_t structure with input data.  Integer returned as
    *  function result is success/failure/EOF indicator.
    *       1 => successful input of pos
    *       0 => error encountered
    *       EOF => insufficient data before end of file
    *  In case of error or EOF, value of type long_lat_t output argument is
    *  undefined.
    */
   int
   scan_long_lat(long_lat_t *pos)  /* output - address of long_lat_t structure to
                                                fill                      */
   {
        int result;
```

```
        result = scanf("%d%d %c", &(*pos).minutes,
                                   &(*pos).seconds,
                                   &(*pos).direction);
        if (result == 3)
             result = 1;
        return (result);
  }
```

Section 11.3

1. When `time_now` is passed as an argument to function `new_time`, the values of its components are copied into `new_time`'s formal parameter `time_of_day`. Assignments to these components just change the function's local copy of the structure.

Section 11.4

1. `(6.50 + 5.00i) + (3.00 - 4.00i) = (9.50 + 1.00i)`
   `Second result = (1.50 + 5.00i)`

Section 11.5

1. The `&` is not applied to `units` because `units` is an array of type `unit_t`, and an array name with no subscript always represents the address of the array's initial element.

Section 11.6

1. 22 bytes are allocated for a variable of type `hair_info_t`, but only four are in use when `wear_wig` is valid.

CHAPTER 12

Section 12.1

1. (1) If the output is saved, it is possible to review the output later.
   (2) The output can be printed at a later time to provide hardcopy of the results.
   (3) The output of one program can be used as input into another.

Section 12.2

1. a. This loop scans in a line of characters and outputs only the uppercase characters.
   b. This loop scans in a file of characters and outputs only the uppercase characters.

Section 12.3

1. a. n = 123   x = 3.145   str = "xyz"   ch = \n
   b. n = 123   x = 3.145   str = "xyz"   ch = \n
   c. n = 3   x = 123.0   str = 145   ch = .
   d. n = 35   x = ??   str = xyz   ch = z

Section 12.4

```
1. /*
    *   Gets data to fill output argument unitp
    *   Returns standard error code:  1 => successful input,  0 => error,
    *                                  negative EOF value => end of file
    */
   int
   fscan_unit(FILE    *fpin,
              unit_t *unitp)  /*  output - unit_t structure to fill */
   {
         int status;

         status = fscanf(fpin,
              "%s%s%s%lf", (*unitp).name,
                                (*unitp).abbrev,
                                (*unitp).class,
                           &(*unitp).standard);

         if (status == 4)
                status = 1;

         return (status);
   }
```

Section 12.5

```
1. fread(&exec, sizeof (person_t), 1, psn_inp);
3. fwrite(&exec, sizeof (person_t), 1, psn_outp);
5. fread(&num_err[3], sizeof (int), 1, nums_inp);
```

Section 12.6

1. a. Low bound for category = `"printer stands"`
      High bound for category = `"printer stands"`
      High bound for price = `99.99`
   b. Low bound for stock number = `5241`
      High bound for stock number = `5241`
   c. Low bound for category = `"data cartridges"`
      High bound for category = `"data cartridges"`
3. `match` does not check stock number because it is called from within a `while` loop that calls it only for stock numbers that are in range.

CHAPTER 13

Section 13.1

1. a. A microwave oven quickly heats up the objects placed inside of it when the controls are correctly set. It is not necessary to know that the oven is actually emitting energy that is specifically designed to agitate the water molecules in a substance and thus heat up the food.
   b. A television allows one to see various programs simply by turning it on and turning the channels. The user is totally isolated from the electronics used to tune and display the signal the program is riding on.
   c. A calculator allows the user to compute a myriad of numerical calculations without any regard for the electronics and logic embedded in the calculator.

Section 13.2

1. A system header file name is surrounded by angular brackets(<>), whereas a personal header file name would be surrounded by quotes(" ").
3. what, how

Section 13.3

1. They are included in the header file so the user will know the string size for the planet structure, and so the user will be able to comply with function preconditions based on MYSTRING_MAX_LEN.

Section 13.4

1. `y = DOUBLE(a - b) -> y = (a - b) + (a - b)` OK,
   but the macro should have been written as `#define DOUBLE(x) ((x) + (x))`
3. `if (DISCRIMINANT(a1, b1, c1) == 0) ->`
   `if (((b1) * (b1) - 4 * (a1) * (c1)) == 0)`
   OK

Section 13.5

1. `date_string` is auto
   `found` is auto
   `search` is extern
   `y` is auto
3. Yes, since the month names should not be changed.
5. The variable `i` would be a good candidate for the register storage class, since it is frequently referenced.

Section 13.6

1. If the image were too large, the image copy would write over memory not actually allocated for `grid_copy`.

Section 13.7

```
1. #if defined (UNIX)
       printf("Enter <ctrl-d> to quit.")
   #elif defined (VMS)
       printf("Enter <ctrl-z> to quit.")
   #endif
```

Section 13.8

1. The following code would be added right after the line int ch;

```
/* See if arguments were included */
if (argc < 3) {
      printf("\nPlease include input and output file names.\n");
      exit(1);
}
```

A

Abacus, 2, 5
`abs`, 122, AP3
Absolute value functions, 122, AP3
Abstract data type, 586
Abstraction, 56, 670
    data, 586, 670
    procedural, 112, 670
Access
    random, 423
    sequential, 423
Accumulating sum, 196
`acos`, AP3
Activation frame, 521
Actual argument, *see* Argument
Addition, 43
Addition table, 229
Address, 8, 289, 406
Address-of operator (&), 47, 79, 292, 293, 414, 452
ADT, *see* Abstract data type
Algorithm, 15, 94
    refinement, 29, 91, 94
    tracing, 156
Alphabetizing a list, 472, 483
Analysis of a problem, 15, 91, 192
And operator
    bitwise (&), AP10
    logical (&&), 347
ANSI C, 6, 27
Apostrophe (single quote), 66
Approximations, iterative, 365
Area of polygon, 423

Argument, 116, 252
    actual, 257, 259, 324
    array as, 404, 414, 451
    conversion, 121
    correspondence to formal parameter, 261, 265
    expression as, 119
    input, 117
    input/output, 297, 412
    name independence, 256
    output, 117, 292
Arithmetic
    operators, 43
    overflow, 337
    underflow, 337
Arithmetic-logic unit (ALU), 10
Array, 384
    actual argument, 404, 412, 414
    declaration syntax, 387
    element as actual argument, 395, 400
    initialization, 387, 433
    input, 391, 415
    multidimensional, 430
    name as pointer, 406
    omitted dimension of, 387, 431
    output, 392
    parallel, 386, 593
    parameter
        input, 404, 409, 431
        input/output, 412, 431
        output, 412, 431, 451
    of pointers, 473
    reading from binary file, 647

    reference, 384
    search
        binary, 444
        linear, 410
    sort
        bubble, 418
        selection, 445, 539
    storage, 385
    of strings, 450, 478
    of structures, 594
    subscript, 384, 390, 395, 430
    two-dimensional, 430, 478
    writing to binary file, 647
ASCII, 343, 482, 494, AP1
`asin`, AP3
Assembly language, 16
Assignment
    compound operators (+=, −=, *=, /*, etc.), 364
    conversions during, 60, 340
    logical, 346
    mixed-type, 60, 340
    operator (=), 42
    pointer, 475
    statement, 42, 43
    string, 458
Associativity of operators, 62, AP8
Asterisk
    indirection operator, 293
    multiplication operator, 43, 65
    in pointer declaration, 289
`atan`, AP3
`atan2`, AP3
Atanasoff, Dr. John, 2, 5

`auto` storage class (automatic), 692
Average score, 341

B

Backslash (\), 48, 690
Bar graph, 380
Batch mode, 23, 74, 622
Bell Laboratories, 6, 27
Binary code, 343
Binary file, 643
Binary number, 17, 334
Binary operator, 61
Binary search, 444
Binary string, 57, 334
Bit, 9
Bitwise operators, AP10
Black box, 119
Blank
  leading, 69
  space, 53
Blob sizes, 557, 707
Block comment, 109
Body, 192
Boolean values as type `int`, 133
Booting a computer, 21
Bottom-up testing, 322
Boundary survey, 632
Boundary value, 238
Braces, 32, 36
`break`, 176
Breakpoint, 239
Bubble sort, 418
Bug, 75
Byte, 9

C

`%c` format string placeholder, 47
Call to function, 45, 108, 112, 119, 257
Call to macro, 687

`calloc`, AP3
Cancellation error, 337
Carriage return, 47, 78
`case` label, 175
Cast expression, 340
`ceil`, 122, AP3
Cell, memory, 8
Cells in a blob, 557, 707
Celsius to Fahrenheit, 205
Central processor unit, 8, 10
`char`, 65, 343
Character
  array, 450
  code, 343
  constant, 66, 176
  control, 344
  expression, 151, 343
  library functions, 479, 482
  null (\0), 450
  printable, 344
  representation of, 343, 467
  sets, AP1
  signed and unsigned, AP14
  string, *see* String
  variable, 65
Check, desk, 14
Close file function, 628
Collating sequence, 344
Column design, 329
Comma operator, AP12
Comment, 30, 53, 255
Comparing
  characters, 151, 343
  iteration and recursion, 530, 540, 557
  loop forms, 354, 362
  search algorithms, 445
  strings, 471, AP6
  structures, 577
Compass bearing, 167
Compilation, conditional, 713
Compiler, 17
  errors, 17, 76

listing, 76
Complement, 351
Complex number, 586
Component
  of a computer, 8
  selection operators, 573
  of a structure, 571
  of a `union`, 604
Compound statement, 102, 139
Computer
  categories, 7
  component, 8
  cost, 2
  definition, 2
  graphics, 11
  history of, 2
  personal, 3, 7
  timeshared, 20
Concatenating strings, 465, AP7
Condition, 133
  complement, 348, 351
  compound, 346
  `if` statement, 134
  loop repetition, 194, 202
  mutually exclusive, 164
  terminating, 523, 562
Conditional
  compilation, 713
  operator (`?:`), AP11
`const`, 405
Constant
  enumeration, AP17
  expression, 99
  macro, 35, 39, 149, 253
  named, 35
  string, 449
Continuation character (\), 690
Control
  character, 344

language, 21
structure, 102
transfer of, 112
unit, 10
Controlling expression of a `switch`, 178
Conversion
of arguments, 121
avoiding through binary file use, 642
Celsius to Fahrenheit, 205
character, 482
of dates, 487
of input, 484
miles to kilometers, 28
specification, 46
of units with structures, 595
using cast operation, 340
of values in mixed-type expressions, 61, 339
of values for output, 642
Copying
file, 628, 719
string, 458, 502, AP6
structure, 575
Correspondence of arguments to formal parameters, 253, 265, 292
`cos`, 122, AP3
`cosh`, AP3
Counter-controlled loop, 201
Counting cells in a blob, 557, 707
Counting down, 203
CPU, _see_ Central processor unit
Creating a file, 17, 22, 74, 626
Cryptogram, 491
`ctype.h` header file, 479
CU, _see_ Control unit

Cursor, 50

D

`%d` format string placeholder, 47, 69
Data
abstract type, 586
abstraction, 586
area of function, 112, 261, 307
file, 12
flow, 144, 150
input, 20
representation, 334, 343
requirements, 28
structure, 384
type, 38, 56
Database, 570, 649
Date conversion, 487
Debugger program, 238
Debugging, 75, 236, 322
Decimal places, 70
Decision, 145
double-alternative, 135, 138
multiple-alternative, 161
single-alternative, 136, 137
step, 104, 134, 145
table, 166
Declaration, 38, 40
array, 387
array parameter, 409, 413
defining, 693
external, 692
output parameter, 289, 413
pointer, 289
structure, 571
top level, 693
union, 604
Decrement operator (`--`), 363
`default` label, 175

`#define` preprocessor directive, 31, 37, 687, 714
`defined` preprocessor operator, 714
Defining declaration, 693
Degrees to radians, 337
DeMorgan's theorem, 353
Dependent statement, 139
Dereferencing, _see_ Indirection
Design, 15, 91, 214
Desk check, 14
Device
standard input, 45, 73
standard output, _see_ Keyboard
Diagnostic `printf` calls, 237
Dimension(s) of array, 430
Directive, preprocessor, 31, 34, 37
Directory, 12
Discarding input line characters, 79, 354
Discriminant, 123
Disk drive, 12
Display screen, _see_ Monitor
Displaying
instructions, 115
a table, 218
Distance, 632
Divide and conquer, 91
Division
integer, 58
operator (`/`), 43, 58
by zero, 78
Divisor, greatest common, 311, 320, 533
DNA mapping, 497
`do-while`, 354, 359
Documentation, 54
`double` data type, 56, 334
Driver program, 265

E

%e format string placeholder, 336

e approximation, 366

EBCDIC, 482, 494, AP2

Echo print, 74

Editor, 17, 22

Element
  of array of strings, 450, 473
  of one-dimensional array, 384
  of set, 544, 547

#elif preprocessor directive, 715

else, 134, 138, 141, 164, 173

#else preprocessor directive, 716

Empty set/empty string, 544

Encapsulation, 672

End
  of file, 221, 623
  of line (newline), 48, 354, 623

#endif preprocessor directive, 715

ENIAC, 3, 4, 6

enum, AP16

Enumerated type, AP16

EOF, 221, 624

Equality expressions, 133

Equation root, 369

Error
  cancellation, 337
  off-by-one iteration, 237
  relative, 92
  representational, 336
  in results, 78
  round-off, 334, 336
  run-time, 78
  syntax, 17, 76

Escape sequence, 48

Euclid's algorithm for GCD, 533

Evaluation
  of expressions, 62
  short-circuit, 348
  step-by-step, 63
  tree, 62

Execute
  to breakpoint, 239
  a program, 19, 22, 41
  single step, 238

Exit
  condition, 351
  function, 698, AP3

EXIT_SUCCESS, EXIT_FAILURE, 697

exp, 122, AP3

Expansion, macro, 688

Exponentiation function, *see* pow

Expression
  as actual argument, 119
  as constant macro, 99
  evaluation, 62, 349
  logical, 346
  mixed-type, 60, 340
  parenthesized, 62, 65
  tree, 62
  type of, 59

Extending
  a line, 690
  a solution, 96

Extent of declaration, 303, 692

extern, 692

F

%f format string placeholder, 48, 51, 70

fabs, 122, AP3

Factorial function
  with exit call, 698
  iterative, 254

recursive, 530

Factoring an integer, 276

False, representation of, 133

fclose, 628, AP3

fgets, 467, AP4

Fibonacci numbers, 246, 532

Field width, 69, 484

Field of a structure, *see* Component

File
  binary, 643
  close, 628
  copy, 628, 719
  creation, 17, 22, 74, 626
  data, 12, 73
  database, 649
  definition, 12
  header, 37
  implementation, 680
  inclusion, 31, 37
  input, 73
  load, 19
  object, 19, 673
  open, 626
  output, 12, 74
  pointer, 625
  source, 17
  of structures, 645
  text, 623

FILE * type, 626

First generation, 5

Flag, 359

float, AP15

Floating-point, *see* double

floor, 122, AP4

Floppy disk, 12

Flowchart, 135

fopen, 626, AP4

for
  indexed loop, 390
  statement, 201

Formal parameter, 253, 257
  array, 404, 409, 431

correspondence to arguments, 253, 265, 292
input, 262, 404, 409
output, 287, 431
Format
  conversion specification, 46
  placeholder, 46
  string, 46
  for strings, 451, 453
  for type `char`, 47
  for type `double`, 47, 48, 70, 336
  for type `int`, 47, 69
Formulas, 64
Fortran, 6, 16
Fourth generation, 5
`fprintf`, 627, AP4
Fractions
  arithmetic operations, 310
  reducing, 311
`fread`, 644
`free`, AP4
`fscanf`, 627, AP4
Function
  argument, *see* Argument
  call, 45, 108, 112, 119, 257
  data area, 112, 261, 307
  definition, 107, 109
  execution, 112
  `extern` declaration, 692
  interface, 255
  library (standard), 31, 122
  logical, 268
  `main`, 31, 718
  plot, 337, 455
  prototype, 109, 255
  recursive, 516
  reference, *see* Function call
  returning a result, 254

return, 34, 255, 562
table of library functions, 122
tracing, 521
type, 254
`void`, 109
`fwrite`, 643, AP4

G

Game of Life, 446
Generalizing functions for library, 700
Generations of computers, 5
`getc`, 627, AP4
`getchar`, 479, AP4
Global variable, 693
Graphics, 11
Graphing a function, 337
Gravitational constant, 216
Gray-scale image, 700
Greatest common divisor, 311, 320, 533

H

Hand trace, 156, 206
Hanoi, towers of, 552
Hard disk, 12
Hard-copy output, 11
Hardware, 8
Header files
  for personal library, 673, 716
  standard, 37
    `ctype.h`, 479
    `float.h`, 335
    `limits.h`, 335
    `math.h`, 37, 122
    `stdio.h`, 37
    `stdlib.h`, 122
    `string.h`, 458
Hierarchical structure, 572
High-level language, 15
History of computers, 2

I

IBM, 5, 6
Identifier, 36, 38
  local, 110, 253
  naming conventions, 38, 39, 289
  scope of, 303
  spelling rules, 38
`if` statement, 134, 141
`#if` preprocessor directive, 715
Image enhancement, 700
Imaginary part, 586
Implementation, 15, 91
  of C, 35
  file, 680
`#include` preprocessor directive, 31, 37, 675, 716
Increment operator (++), 363
Indentation, 141
Index of array, 390
Indexed loop, 390
Indirection operator (*), 293
Infinite loop, 195, 223
Information hiding, 672, 693, 709
Information loss, 60, 121, 340
Initialization
  of arrays, 387, 433
  in declaration, 220, 387, 450
  step of a loop, 195
  of strings, 450
  of structures, 571
Input
  data, 19
  device, 8, 11
  list, 47
  operation, 45
  parameter, 262, 404, 409
  prompt, 21, 23, 29, 209
  stream, 624

Input/output
  parameter, 295, 297, 412,
      431
  redirection, 73
  standard library, 31, 35, 37
Instruction register, 10
Instructions, displaying, 115
`int`, 57, 334
Integer
  division, 58
  placeholder in format
      string, 47, 69
  remainder, 58
  signed and unsigned,
      AP14
Integrated circuits, 6
Integration testing, 322
Interactive mode, 23
Interface of a function, 255,
      679
International Business
      Machines, *see* IBM
`isalpha`, 482, AP5
`isdigit`, 482, AP5
`islower`, 482, AP5
`ispunct`, 482, AP5
`isspace`, 482, AP5
`isupper`, 482, AP5
Iteration, 195
Iterative approximations, 365

K
Keyboard, 11, 624
Keyword, *see* Reserved word

L
Labels in a `switch`, 178
LAN, *see* Local area network
Language standard, 16, 27
Laptop, 7
Leading blanks, 72, 453
Left associativity, 62
Left-justified, 451

Length
  of memory block, *see*
      `sizeof`
  of string, *see* `strlen`
Library, 31, 35
  creation, 675, 680, 686
  personal, 672, 686
  standard functions, 122,
      AP3
  use, 121, 686
`limits.h` header file, 335
Line continuation in pre-
      processor directives,
      690
Line termination character,
      see Newline character
Linear search, 410
Linker, 19, 673
`lint` source code analyzer, 78
List, *see* Array
Listing, compiler, 76
Literal, string, 48
Load file, 19
Loader, 19
Local area network, 13
Local variable, 110, 253, 692
`log`, 122, AP5
Log on, 21
`log10`, 122, AP5
Logarithm, 122
Logical
  complement, 348, 351
  expressions, 133, 346
  functions, 268
  operators, 346
  values of type `int`, 133
`long`, AP14
Loop, 192
  body, 192
  boundaries, 238
  control variable, 194
  counter-controlled, 201
  `do-while`, 354, 359

  endfile-controlled, 221
  error, 237, 239
  flag-controlled, 359
  `for`, 201
  generalizing, 197
  infinite, 195, 223
  initialization step, 195,
      202, 209
  nested, 226
  repetition condition, 194,
      202
  sentinel-controlled, 219
  update step, 195, 202, 209
  `while`, 193
Lowercase, 39

M
Machine language, 17
Macros
  arguments (restrictions),
      690
  body, 687
  calls, 687
  constant, 35, 39, 99
  definition of, 687
  expansion, 688
  parameters, 687
  parenthesis use in, 99, 688
Mainframe, 8
`main` function, 31
  arguments to, 718
Main memory, 8
Maintenance, 102, 149
`malloc`, AP5
Manifest, *see* Constant macro
Manning's equation, 248
Mantissa, 334
`math.h` header file, 37, 122
Mathematical formula, 64
Mathematical library func-
      tions, 122
Matrix, 430
Maximum value, 404

Mean, 392
Measurement conversion, 595
memmove, 458, AP5
Memory buffer register, 10
Memory cell, 8
Menu-driven, 650
Merging lists, 444
Microcomputer, 7
Minicomputer, 7
Minimum value, AP12
Minus operator (−), 43
Mixed-type, 60
Monitor
    computer, 11
    storage tank, 210
Month conversion, 490
Mouse, 11
MS-DOS, 21
Multidimensional array, 430
Multiple-alternative decision, 161, 175
Multiple parameters, 262
Multiple results of a function, 287
Multiplication
    operator (*), 43, 65
    by recursive addition, 518
Mutually exclusive conditions, 164

N

Name independence, 261
Natural logarithm function, 122, AP5
Negation, 43, 348, 351, AP10
Nested if statements, 161, 225
Nested loops, 226
Network, 13
Newline character ('\n'), 48, 354, 623

Newton's method, 369
Noise reduction, 700
Nonterminating loop, *see* Infinite loop
Not operator (!), 348
Notebook, 7
Nucleotide sequence, 497
Null character ('\0'), 450
Null string, *see* Empty string
Null pointer, 627
Number-to-string conversion, 484
Numerical analysis, 365
Numerical inaccuracy, 334

O

Object file, 19
Off-by-one error, 237
One-dimensional array, 384
Open file function, 626
Operating system, 20, AP7
Operator precedence, 62, 348, 574, AP8
Operators, where to find, AP9
Options on command line, 718
Or operator
    bitwise (|), AP10
    logical (||), 347
Order of conditions, 164
Order of evaluation, 62, 348, AP8
Out-of-range error, 389, 430, 436
Output
    argument, 292, 412
    device, 8, 10
    file, 74, 622, 626
    format, 48
    operation, 45
    parameter, 287
    from program, 20

stream, 624
table, 218
Overflow, 337, 454
Overlapping structures, *see* union

P

Parallel arrays, 386
Parameter
    array, 404, 409, 412, 431
    correspondence, 253, 265, 292
    formal, 253
    input, 262, 404, 409
    input/output, 295, 297, 412, 431
    output, 287, 431
    storage class of, 692
    structure, 576
Parentheses
    in expressions, 62, 65
    in macros, 99, 688
Partial product, 198
Pass
    through an array, 419
    through a loop, 195
Password, 21
Perimeter, 606
Permanent file, 13, 22
Personal computer, 3, 5
Physics of falling body, 215
Pi approximation, 382
Picture processing, 700
Pixel, 557, 700
Placeholder, 46
Plotting function, 337, 455
Plus (+) operator, 43
Pointer, 289
    arithmetic, AP18
    array name, 406
    array of pointers, 473
    assignment, 475
    declaration, 289

Pointer *(continued)*
   file, 625
   output parameter, 289
Polygon, 423
Postcondition, 256
Postfix increment/decrement,
      363
`pow`, 122, AP5
Precedence of operators, *see*
      Operator precedence
Precondition, 255
Prefix increment/decrement,
      363
Preprocessor, 31
   directive, 31, 34, 37
   `#define`, 31, 37, 687, 714
   `defined`, 714
   `#elif`, 715
   `#else`, 716
   `#endif`, 715
   `#if`, 715
   `#include`, 31, 37, 675, 716
   `#undef`, 716
Prime number, 269
Printer, 11
`printf`, 31, 485, AP5
Printing
   formatted output, *see*
      Format
   set, 545, 549
   table, 218
Problem
   input, 93
   output, 93
   solving, 89, 214
   specification, 91
Procedural abstraction, 112,
      670
Product, computing in a loop,
      198
Program, 4, 13
   maintenance, 102, 149
   style, 27

Programming
   in the large, 669
   language, 15
   team, 671
Prompt, 21, 23, 49
Prototype, 35, 109, 255
Pseudocode, 145
Pseudorandom number, 381,
      AP6
`putc`, 627, AP5
`putchar`, 481

Q

Quadratic formula, 123
Qualifier, `const` type, 405
Query, 649

R

Radiation level, 232
`rand`, 381, AP6
Random access, 423
Random number, 381, AP6
Range violation, 389, 430,
      436
Read, *see* `scanf` *and* Format
Real number, *see* `double`
Record, *see* Structure
Recursion, 516
Recursive
   function, 516
   multiply, 518
   set functions, 543
Redirection, input/output, 73
Refinement of algorithm, 29,
      91, 94
Register
   definition, 10, 696
   storage class, 696
Relational operator, 133
Remainder (`%`) operator, 58
Repetition, 104. *See also*
      Loop.

Representation
   of `char`, 343
   of `double`, 334
   of `int`, 334
   of numeric data types, 334
   of string, 450, 466
Representational error, 336
Requirements specification,
      15, 91
Reserved word, 36, 40, AP20
Retrieve, 8
`return`, 34, 255, 562
Return, carriage, 47, 78
Returning deallocated space,
      504
Reuse, 121, 672
Right associativity, 62
Right-justified, 69
Ritchie, Dennis, 6
Root of equation, 369
Round-off error, 334, 336
Rounding, 265
Run, 22
Run-time error, 78

S

`%s` format string placeholder,
      451, 453
`scanf`, 32, 45, 47, 78, 221,
      223, 361, 451, 485,
      AP6
Scientific notation, 57, 336
Scope, 303, 692
Screen, 624
Search
   array, 410
   binary, 444
   database, 649
   linear, 410
   parameters, 650
Second generation, 5
Secondary memory (storage),
      5, 12

Selection
  direct component (.), 573
  indirect component (->),
    573
  sort, 445, 539
  step, 104, 134
Sentinel-controlled loop,
    219, 416, 472
Sequence, 102
Sequential access, 423
Series approximation, 366
Set operations, 543
Sharpening an image, 704
Shift operators, AP10
`short`, AP14
Short-circuit evaluation, 348
Side effect, 289, 362
`signed`, AP14
Simple case, 516
Simple variable, 384
`sin`, 122, AP6
Sine curve plot, 337
Single quote, 66
Single-step execution, 238
`sinh`, AP6
Size
  of array, 387
  of data type, 643
  of `union`, 605
`size_t`, AP3
`sizeof`, 643
Smallest number, AP12
Software engineering, 90
Software development
    method, 15, 91
Sort
  bubble, 418, 472, 475
  selection, 445
Sorting an array, 418, 445,
    472, 475
Source file, 17, 261
Specification, requirements,
    15

`sprintf`, 486, AP6
`sqrt`, 118, 122, AP6
`sscanf`, 486, AP6
Square root
  approximation, 329
  of sum, 118, 122
Stack, 525
Standard
  ANSI, 27
  deviation, 394
  input device, 45
  language, 16, 27
Statement
  assignment, 42
  `break`, 176
  compound, 102
  conditional, 134
  `do-while`, 354, 359
  empty, 137
  executable, 31, 41, 110
  extending over multiple
    lines, 52, 690
  `for`, 201
  function call, 45, 108, 112,
    119, 257
  `if`, 134
  `return`, 34, 255, 562
  `switch`, 175
  `while`, 193
`static` storage class, 695
Statistics, 391
`stderr`, 624
`stdin`, 469, 624
`stdio.h`, 35
`stdlib.h`, 122
`stdout`, 624
Stepwise refinement, 29, 91,
    94, 232
Stop execution, *see* Exit
Stored program, 4
Storage
  classes, 692
  of string, 450, 466

tank monitoring, 210
`strcat`, 502, AP6
`strcmp`, 471, AP6
`strcpy`, 502, AP6
Streams, 624
Stress on column, 329
String, 32, 449
  assignment, 458
  comparison, 470, AP6
  concatenation, 465, AP7
  constant, 449, 478
  conversion, 486
  end character, 450
  header file `string.h`,
    458, 502
  initialization, 450
  input, 451, 467
  length, 458, AP7
  library functions, 502
  literal, 48
  output, 451
  protected functions, 459,
    460, 462, 465, 467,
    480
  representation, 450, 466
  substring, 459
`strlen`, 458, AP7
`strncat`, AP7
`strncpy`, AP7
Structure(s)
  array of, 594
  assignment, 575
  binary file of, 645, 649
  chart, 104, 106, 150
  comparison, 577
  component selection, 573,
    579, 611
  copy, 575
  function returning, 583
  hierarchical, 572
  parameter, 576
  size, 572
  tag, 572

Structure(s) *(continued)*
  type definition, 572
  variable, 571
  with `union` component, 605
Structured programming, 101
Stub, 312, 316, 320
Subproblem, 91
Subprogram, *see* Function
Subscript, 384, 390, 395
Subscript-range error, 389,
    430, 436
Subset, 544, 548
Substring, 459
Sum of exam scores, 221
Summation notation, 366
Sun Sparcstation, 7
Supercomputer, 8
Survey, 632
`switch`, 175
Syntax, 16
  error, 17, 76
System
  function call to, AP7
  operating, 20, AP7

T
Table, 218
  heading, 283
Tag
  `enum`, AP16
  structure, 572
`tan`, 122, AP7
Tangent, 122, AP7
`tanh`, AP7
Target, 410
Team programming, 671
Telephone book, 568
Temperature conversion, 205
Temporary variable, 298
Tensile load, 281
Terminal, 11
Terminating condition, 523,
    562

Testing, 91, 239
  bottom-up, 322
  system integration, 322
  top-down, 320
  unit, 321
Text
  editor, 17, 22
  file, 623
Third generation, 5
Tic-tac-toe board, 430
Timeshared computer, 20
Top level, 693
Top-down
  design, 107, 232
  testing, 320
Towers of Hanoi, 552
Tracing
  algorithm, 156
  conditional, 714
  recursive function, 521
Transfer of control, 112
True, representation of, 133
Two-dimensional array, 430,
    478
Type
  automatic conversion, 61,
    121, 339
  cast, 340
  comparison of, 334
  declaration of variable, 38,
    40
  definition by user, 572
  enumerated, AP16
  explicit conversion, 340
  of expression, 59
  numeric, AP14
  standard data, 56
  structure, 572
  `union`, 604
`typedef`, 572

U
ULTRIX, 21

Unary
  minus and plus, 61
  operator, 61
Undeclared variable, 76
`#undef`, 716
Underflow, 337
Underscore, 38, 39
`union`, 604
Unit conversion, 595
UNIX, 6, 27
`unsigned`, AP14
Uppercase, 39
User-defined function, 107,
    109
User-defined type, 572

V
Validation, 167, 265, 355,
    360
Variable, 38
  declaration, 38, 384
  global, 693
  initialization, 387, 450
  local, 110, 253
Variable-length string, 450
VAX computer, 21
Vector, *see* Array
Verification, 15, 91
Visible, 304
`void` function, 109
Volatile, 13
Von Neumann, John, 4, 5

W
`while`, 193
Whitespace, 453
Word processor, 17, 22,
    449
Workstation, 6, 7

Z
Zero, division by, 78